Are you overwhelmed by the time it takes to find primary source documents, images, and maps for your research papers?

MyHistoryLab contains over **1,100 documents, images, maps, and video clips**— all in one place —to help make writing your research paper easier and more effective, and to help you better understand the course material.

Are you sometimes overwhelmed when you study for exams?

MyHistoryLab gives you a **quizzing and testing program** that shows what you've mastered, as well as where you need more work. Look for these icons on MyHistoryLab—

 PRE-TEST POST TEST EXAM

Did your professor assign other books to read?

50 FREE BOOKS!

MyHistoryLab allows you to read, download, or print fifty of the most commonly assigned works for this course —all at no additional cost!

History Bookshelf Partial Listing.

1. *Common Sense,* Thomas Paine (1776)
2. *The Federalist Papers;* Alexander Hamilton, John Jay, and James Madison (1787-1788)
3. *The Autobiography of Benjamin Franklin* (1788)
4. *The Last of the Mohicans,* James Fennimore Cooper (1826)
5. *Democracy in America* (Two Volumes), Alexis De Tocqueville (1835)
6. *The Narrative of the Life of Frederick Douglass, An American Slave* (1845)
7. *Civil Disobedience,* Henry David Thoreau (1849)
8. *Uncle Tom's Cabin,* Harriet Beecher Stowe (1852)
9. *Walden,* Henry David Thoreau (1854)
10. *Incidents in the Life of a Slave Girl,* Harriet Jacobs (1861)
11. *The Adventures of Huckleberry Finn,* Mark Twain (1885)
12. *Looking Backward, 2000-1887,* Edward Bellamy (1888)
13. *The Yellow Wallpaper,* Charlotte Perkins Gilman (1892)
14. *The Red Badge of Courage,* Stephen Crane (1895)
15. *The Awakening and Selected Short Stories,* Kate Chopin (1899)
16. *Up From Slavery,* Booker T. Washington (1901)
17. *The Jungle,* Upton Sinclair (1906)
18. *Rise of the New West,* Frederick Jackson Turner (1906)
19. *Anarchism and Other Essays,* Emma Goldman (1917)
20. *Babbitt,* Sinclair Lewis (1922)

Now, flip through this text. You will find the icons shown on the next page. Each icon will direct you to a place in MyHistoryLab to help you better understand the material. For example, when reading about the 1700's, you will find an icon that links you to a letter by an indentured servant; when reading about the 20th century, you will find an icon that links you to a video clip about the Cold War.

Example shown from Carnes, *The American Nation, 12/e*

DOCUMENT.
This icon will lead you to primary source documents, so you can see the original documents that pertain to the people and events you're studying.

IMAGE.
You'll find photos, cartoons, and art work that relate to the topic you're reading.

MAP.
Interactive maps will help you visualize the geography you are exploring in this course. You will also find printable map activities from one of Longman's workbooks, along with atlas maps.

AUDIO CLIP.
Hear the sounds of the past by listening to historical music in original recordings, or more contemporary performances of original works.

VIDEO CLIP.
Historical and political video clips from the last century bring history to life.

The American Nation,
Twelfth Edition, Primary Source Edition
It has everything students need to master the course!

A rich text with a clear, relevant, and balanced presentation of the social, economic, and cultural issues in the United States. A wealth of original primary source documents (at the end of this text) help make the material come alive by supporting the chapter content. Accompanying *Document Analysis* questions encourage students to delve deeper into the documents and explore how they relate to the events of the time. Documents are organized to correlate with chapter material.

How to Analyze Primary Source Documents

Would you like even more primary source documents?

myhistorylab™

Where it's a good time to connect to the past!

FREE when bundled with this book!

All of the primary source documents in this text plus hundreds more at no additional cost can be found on Longman's exclusive Web site—www.ablongman.com/myhistorylab

MyHistoryLab also contains a wealth of other resources including:

*   Images (photos, cartoons, and artwork), maps (including interactive maps), and audio and video clips (with historical music and historical and political video clips from the last century).

*   The electronic textbook (eBook) with multimedia icons that link to exciting resources, expanding upon the key topics students encounter as they read through the text.

*   An integrated quizzing and testing program—including pre-tests, post-tests, and chapter exams—to help students identify areas of strength and weakness.

*   "The History Bookshelf" where fifty of the most commonly assigned works like Thomas Paine's *Common Sense*, Upton Sinclair's *The Jungle*, or Booker T. Washington's *Up from Slavery* can be read, downloaded, or printed.

Professors get a wealth of instructor resources including a course management system, test bank, instructor's manual, PowerPoint® presentations, and more.

Go to www.myhistorylab.com, or read more about this exciting new Web site on the insert included in this textbook.

The American Nation

Volume One

The
American Nation

A History of the United States to 1877

TWELFTH EDITION

MARK C. CARNES

Ann Whitney Olin Professor of History
Barnard College, Columbia University

JOHN A. GARRATY

Gouverneur Morris Professor of History, Emeritus
Columbia University

PEARSON

Longman

New York San Francisco Boston
London Toronto Sydney Tokyo Singapore Madrid
Mexico City Munich Paris Cape Town Hong Kong Montreal

For Our Children:
Stephanie
and
Kathy, Jack, and Sarah

Executive Editor: Michael Boezi
Development Manager: Betty Slack
Executive Marketing Manager: Sue Westmoreland
Media and Supplements Editor: Kristi Olson
Senior Media Editor: Patrick McCarthy
Production Manager: Ellen MacElree
Project Coordination, Text Design, and Electronic Page Makeup: Nesbitt Graphics, Inc.
Cover Design Manager: Wendy Ann Fredericks
Cover Designer: Kay Petronio
Cover Photo: Wall clock, from the shop of Aaron Willard Sr., or Aaron William Jr., Boston, 1802–30 (gilded eastern pine, basewood, mahogany by Sydney Goodwin (fl. 1850–99). American School (19th century). Museum of Fine Arts, Houston, Texas, USA/Bridgeman Art Library. The Bayou Bend Collection, gift of Miss Ima Hogg.
Photo Researcher: Photosearch, Inc.
Senior Manufacturing Buyer: Dennis J. Para
Printer and Binder: Quebecor World/Versailles
Cover Printer: The Lehigh Press, Inc.

For permission to use copyrighted material, grateful acknowledgment is made to the copyright holders on pp. C1–C3, which are hereby made part of this copyright page.

Maps in the "Mapping the Past" features are adapted from Mark C. Carnes and John A. Garraty with Patrick Williams, *Mapping America's Past: A Historical Atlas,* © 1996 by Arcadia Editions Ltd.

Library of Congress Cataloging-in-Publication Data
Carnes, Mark (Mark Christopher)
     The American nation: a history of the United States/Mark C.
Carnes, John A. Garraty.—12th ed.
          p.   cm.
     Includes index.
     ISBN 0-321-31688-6 (complete ed.)
     1. United States—History—Textbooks. I.   Garraty, John Arthur   II. Title.
E178.1.C27   2006
973—dc22   2004063344

Copyright © 2006 by John A. Garraty. Maps, graphs, and all illustration captions and related text copyright © by Pearson Education, Inc.

Please visit our website at http://www.ablongman.com/carnes

ISBN: 0-321-42608-8 (Primary Source Edition, Complete Edition)
ISBN: 0-321-42607-X (Primary Source Edition, Volume I)
ISBN: 0-321-42606-1 (Primary Source Edition, Volume II)

1 2 3 4 5 6 7 8 9 10—QWD—08 07 06 05

Brief Contents

Detailed Contents

CHAPTER 3
America in the British Empire   78

CHAPTER 4
The American Revolution   110

CHAPTER 5
The Federalist Era:
Nationalism Triumphant   140

CHAPTER 6
Jeffersonian Democracy 168

CHAPTER 7
National Growing Pains 190

CHAPTER 8
Toward a National Economy 222

Maps and Graphs

MAPS

Additional maps, arranged by topic, appear in the "Mapping the Past" features.

Maps for every presidential election, 1889 to 2004, appear in the Appendix,
    pp. A19–A31.

GRAPHS

Features

Preface

From the Prologue ("Beginnings") tens of thousands of years ago to the war in Iraq and the 2004 election (Chapter 33), this edition of *The American Nation* includes many enhancements and new features. Yet the backbone remains the same. We focus on how the voices and actions of its many people have produced a particular political structure—the United States, a single nation—and how that nation has in turn influenced the lives of everyone.

FEATURES

New! Debating the Past

"Debating the Past" is a new feature in this edition of *The American Nation*. Historians argue about nearly every aspect of the nation's complex past, and each chapter now includes an essay on an important historiographical debate. Because such issues are hard to fix in memory, we have provided a photograph or picture to "trigger" the historiographical essay. For example, the question for Chapter 2—"Were puritan communities peaceful?"—is prefaced by a contemporary painting of a seventeenth-century puritan village, the question for Chapter 12—"Did the frontier change women's roles?"—commences with a photograph of a farm woman hauling buffalo chips in a wheelbarrow. Each essay concludes with a list of the major works cited. Our final debate—"Do historians ever get it right?" (Chapter 33)—poses a question that we hope will stimulate discussion.

In addition to "Debating the Past," each chapter of *The American Nation* contains one of three special features: an essay on a Hollywood movie's version of history ("Re-Viewing the Past"); a grouping of maps on a central topic in the chapter ("Mapping the Past"); or a biographical account of a major or representative person ("American Lives").

Re-Viewing the Past

The "Re-Viewing the Past" feature shows how particular movies shape our understanding of history. Directors often spend scores of millions of dollars to show what the past looked like. For example, *The Crucible* (discussed in Chapter 2), provides a vivid evocation of puritan Salem, and *Saving Private Ryan* (Chapter 28) of the Normandy invasion in World War II. Yet moviemakers often alter people and events for dramatic purposes; "reel history" should never be confused with "real history." These essays help our readers make sense of the bewildering array of historical facts and fictions presented in many historical movies. By offering guidance on which of Hollywood's reconstructions contain some measure of truthfulness, which do not, and how viewers can tell the difference, the "Re-Viewing the Past" essays help readers examine Hollywood's version of the past more critically. This edition of *The American Nation* includes two new "Re-Viewing the Past" essays: *Cold Mountain* (Chapter 15) and *Chicago* (Chapter 25).

Mapping the Past

Maps provide another visual way of representing the past. In addition to the standard maps depicting the routes of explorers, battles, or territorial acquisitions, more than half the chapters in *The American Nation* include separate map portfolios on social, economic, cultural, and political history. Topics examined in the "Mapping the Past" features range from "A Water Route to the Pacific?" (Chapter 6), which discusses the search for a water passage to the Pacific during the early 1800s; "Fertility and the Frontier," (Chapter 12), which considers whether frontier women had more children than women elsewhere; to "Planning Nuclear War" (Chapter 29), which describes the various strategies for winning a world war fought with thermonuclear weapons. *The American Nation*, even by its title, implies that we are one; yet this truism overlooks the persistence and significance of regional bonds and local variations. Many of the maps in the "Mapping the Past" features spotlight particular states, counties, cities, and towns. Such maps show how local factors influence national trends and vice versa. Because students often need help in determining how to read and understand a map, the "Mapping the Past" essay in Chapter 5, "Depicting History with Maps" includes a discussion of the various elements of a map and the information that each element conveys. Eight of the "Mapping the Past" essays are new to the twelfth edition of *The American Nation:*

- Depicting History with Maps (Chapter 5)
- Nature as a Civilizing Force (Chapter 11)
- Cholera: A New Disease Strikes the Nation (Chapter 19)
- Isolationism of the 1930s (Chapter 27)
- Planning Nuclear War (Chapter 29)
- School Segregation After the *Brown* Decision (Chapter 30)
- *Roe* v. *Wade* (1978) and the Abortion Controversy (Chapter 31)
- Twenty Years of Terrorism (Chapter 33)

American Lives

Biographies underscore the human dimension of historical complexity. The "American Lives" essays in the twelfth edition of *The American Nation* range from Tisquantum, the Indian who famously assisted the Pilgrims (Chapter 1), to Bill Gates, founder of Microsoft and the richest man in the world (Chapter 32). Two new "American Lives" essays have been added: Nat Love, a black cowboy who claimed to have been source of the "Deadeye Dick" legend (Chapter 17), and Emma Goldman, a radical leftist (Chapter 22).

MORE MAPS

In addition to the "Mapping the Past" feature, we have reconceptualized and redrawn many of the maps in the text and have added dozens more. Many of the latter offer visual representations and interpretations of uniquely specialized information: Loss of Indian Lands, 1850–2000 (Chapter 17), The Forging of U.S. Steel (Chapter 18), Prostitution in Nineteenth-Century New York (Chapter 19), The Advance of Woman Suffrage (Chapter 22), Japanese Expansion, 1920–1941, and German Expansion, 1938–1939 (both in Chapter 27), and Air Relief to Berlin (Chapter 29). The section on Presidential Elections in the Appendix for the twelfth edition includes a color map of the election results for every presidential election from 1789 to 2004.

PICTURES

In addition to its many maps, its evocation of Hollywood history, and its use of pictures to introduce the "Debating the Past" essays, *The American Nation* includes hundreds of pictures and artwork to accompany the text and enhance the narrative. Much as readers should examine Hollywood history critically and engage with historiographical debates, they should apply similar skills to paintings, photographs, and other visual representations of the past. Our captions are meant to stimulate thought, to provoke debate, and on occasion, to amuse. Each chapter opens with a work of art, ranging from an Aztec artist's depiction of a Spanish sailing ship (Chapter 1) to a famous photograph of the collapse of the World Trade Center (Chapter 33). We think that the pictures and photographs in themselves constitute a history of the nation's visual and material culture.

The text is as concise as we could make it. Yet the history of our nation is comprised of the words and actions of hundreds of millions of people over many decades. The story must be told in all its depth and complexity. It is not enough to know what happened; we also need to understand why.

INSTRUCTOR SUPPLEMENTS

For Qualified College Adopters

MyHistoryLab provides students with an online package complete with the entire textbook, numerous study aids, and course management. With over 1000 primary sources, images, audio clips, video clips, and over 150 map activities with gradable quizzes, geographic case studies, map workbook activities, and atlas maps, the site offers students a unique, interactive experience that brings history to life. The comprehensive site also includes a history bookshelf with twenty of the most commonly assigned books in history classes and a history toolkit with tutorials and helpful links.

LongmanAmericanHistory.com provides the same resources as MyHistoryLab, but without an e-book or course management.

History Digital Media Archive CD-ROM. The Digital Media Archive CD-ROM contains electronic images and interactive and static maps, along with media elements such as video. These media assets are fully customizable and ready for classroom presentation or easy downloading into your PowerPoint™ presentations or any other presentation software. ISBN: 0-321-14976-9.

Visual Archives of American History, **Updated Second Edition.** Now on two CD-ROMs and with added content, this encyclopedic collection contains dozens of narrated vignettes and videos as well as hundreds of photos and illustrations ready for use in your own PowerPoint™ presentations, course websites, or online courses. Free to qualified college adopters.

The American Nation Companion Website (www.ablongman.com/carnes). This Website, designed specifically for this book, is an invaluable tool for both students and instructors. It contains student resources such as self-testing, chapter outlines, and links to outside sources; instructor resources such as the instructor's manual, PowerPoint presentations, maps, graphs, and tables from the text, blank maps for quizzes, and helpful web links; and our unique syllabus manager that gives instructors and students access to the up-to-date syllabus at any time from any computer.

Instructor's Resource Manual. Written by Michael Mayer of the University of Montana, this tool is designed to aid both the novice and experienced instructor in teaching American history. Each chapter included a concise chapter overview, a list of points for student mastery, lecture supplements, and questions for class discussion. A special feature of each chapter is a set of excerpted documents with accompanying questions for student analysis.

Test Bank. Written by Larry Peterson of North Dakota State University, the test bank contains over 2000 test items, including multiple choice, true/false, and essay. The questions are keyed to topic, difficulty level, cognitive type, and relevant text page.

Computerized TestGen-EQ Computerized Testing System. This flexible, easy-to-use computerized test bank includes all the test items in the printed test bank. Available on a dual platform CD-ROM, the software allows you to edit existing questions and add your own items. Tests can be printed in several different formats and can include graphs and tables.

Text-specific Transparencies. A set of map transparencies from the text is available.

Comprehensive American History Transparency Set. This vast collection of American history transparencies is a necessary teaching aid. It includes over 200 maps covering social trends, wars, elections, immigration, and demographics. Included is a set of reproducible map exercises.

Discovering American History Through Maps and Views Transparency Set. Created by Gerald Danzer of the University of Illinois at Chicago, the recipient of the AHA's 1990 James Harvey Robinson Prize for his work in the development of map transparencies, this set of 140 four-color acetates is a unique instructional tool. It contains an introduction on teaching history through maps and a detailed commentary on each transparency. The collection includes cartographic and pictorial maps, views, and photos, urban plans, building diagrams, and works of art.

STUDENT SUPPLEMENTS

MyHistoryLab provides students with an online package complete with the entire textbook, numerous study aids, and course management. With over 1000 primary sources, images, audio clips, video clips, as well as 150+ map activities with gradable quizzes, geographic case studies, map workbook activities, and atlas maps, the site offers students a unique, interactive experience that brings history to life. The comprehensive site also includes a history bookshelf with twenty of the most commonly assigned books in history classes and a history toolkit with tutorials and helpful links.

LongmanAmericanHistory.com provides the same resources as MyHistoryLab, but without an e-book or course management.

SafariX Textbooks Online is an exciting new choice for students looking to save money. As an alternative to purchasing the print textbook, students can subscribe to the same content online and save up to 50 percent off the suggested list price of the print text. With a SafariX WebBook, students can search the text, make notes online, print out reading assignments that incorporate lecture notes, and bookmark important passages for later review. For more information, or to subscribe to the SafariX WebBook, visit www.safarix.com.

Study Cards for American History. Colorful, affordable, and packed with useful information, Allyn & Bacon/Longman's Study Cards make studying easier, more efficient, and more enjoyable. Course information is distilled down to the basics, helping you quickly master the fundamentals, review a subject for understanding, or prepare for an exam. Because they're laminated for durability, you can keep these Study Cards for years to come and pull them out whenever you need a quick review.

The American Nation Companion Website (www
.ablongman.com/carnes). This Website, designed
specifically for this book, is an invaluable tool for both
students and instructors. It contains student resources
such as self-testing, chapter outlines, and links to outside sources; instructor resources such as the instructor's manual; PowerPoint presentations, maps,
graphs, and tables from the text, blank maps for
quizzes, and helpful web links; and our unique syllabus manager that gives instructors and students
access to the up-to-date syllabus at any time from any
computer.

Study Guides. Written by Ken Weatherbie of Del Mar
College are designed to provide students with a comprehensive review of the text material and to encourage applications and critical analysis of the material.
Each chapter contains a chapter overview, learning
objectives, important glossary terms, identification,
map and critical thinking exercises, and multiple
choice and essay questions.

Research Navigator Guide. This guidebook includes
exercises and tips on how to use the Internet. It also
includes an access code for Research Navigator™—
the easiest way for students to start a research assignment or research paper. Research Navigator™ is
composed of three exclusive databases of credible
and reliable source material, including EBSCO's
ContentSelect™ Academic Journal Database, New
York Times Search by Subject Archive, and "Best of
the Web" Link Library. This comprehensive site also
includes a detailed help section by qualified college
adopters.

Longman American History Atlas. A four-color reference tool and visual guide to American history that
includes almost 100 maps and covers the full scope of
history. Atlas overhead transparencies available to
adopters. $3.00 when bundled by qualified college
adopters.

Mapping American History: Student Activities.
Written by Gerald Danzer of the University of Illinois
at Chicago, this free map workbook for students features exercises designed to teach how to interpret and
analyze cartographic materials as historical documents. Available free when bundled in advance with
the textbook.

Mapping America: A Guide to Historical Geography,
Second Edition. Written by Ken Weatherbie of Del
Mar College, this two-volume workbook contains 35
exercises correlated to the text that review basic
American historical geography and ask students to
interpret the role geography has played in American
history. *Mapping America* is available free to qualified college adopters when bundled with the text in
advance.

American History in a Box. Created by editors Julie
Roy Jeffrey and Peter Frederick, this unique "reader
in a box" is designed to give students an up-close and
personal view of history. The collection includes loose
facsimiles of written documents, visual materials and
artifacts, songs and sheet music, portraits, cartoons,
film posters, and more, so that students can learn
first-hand what history is and what historians do.
"Placing the Sources in Context" and "Questions to
Consider" accompanying each set of materials in the
collection help guide students through the practice of
historical analysis.

America Through the Eyes of Its People, **Second
Edition.** This single-volume collection of primary
documents reflects the rich and varied tapestry of
American life. The revised edition includes more social history and enhanced pedagogy. It is available
shrinkwrapped with *The American Nation* at no
charge to qualified college adopters when requested
by the instructor in advance.

Sources of the African American Past, **Second
Edition.** Edited by Roy Finkenbine of the University
of Detroit at Mercy, this collection of primary sources
covers key themes in the African American experience
from the West African background to the present.
Balanced between political and social history, it offers
a vivid snapshot of the lives of African Americans in
different historical periods, and includes documents
representing women and different regions of the
United States. Available at a minimum cost to qualified college adopters when bundled with the text.

Women and the National Experience, **Second
Edition.** Edited by Ellen Skinner of Pace University,
this primary source readers contains both classic and
unusual documents describing the history of women
in the United States. The documents provide dramatic evidence that outspoken women attained a
public voice and participated in the development of
national events and policies long before they could
vote. Chronologically organized and balanced between social and political history, this reader offers a
striking picture of the lives of women across American
history. Available at a minimum cost to qualified college adopters when bundled in advance with the text.

Reading the American West. Edited by Mitchel Roth
of Sam Houston State University, this primary source
reader uses letters, diary excerpts, speeches, interviews, and newspaper articles to let students experience how historians research and how history is written. Every document is accompanied by a contextual
headnote and study questions. The book is divided
into chapters with extensive introductions. Available
at a minimum cost to qualified college adopters when
bundled with the text.

A Short Guide to Writing About History, **Fourth Edition.** Written by Richard Marius (late) and Melvin E. Page, this practical text teaches students how to incorporate their own ideas into their papers and to tell a story about history that interests them and their peers. Focusing on more than just the conventions of good writing, this text shows students how first to think about history, and then how to organize their thoughts into coherent essays. The *Short Guide* covers both brief essays and the document resource paper as it explores the writing and researching processes, examines different modes of historical writing including argument, and concludes with guidelines for improving style.

Library of American Biography Series. Each of these interpretive biographies focuses on a figure whose actions and ideas significantly influenced the course of American history and national life. At the same time, each biography relates the life of its subjects to the broader theme and developments of the times. Brief and inexpensive, they are ideal for any U.S. history course. Editions include Edmund S. Morgan, *The Puritan Dilemma: The Story of John Winthrop;* Charles W. Akers, *Abigail Adams: An American Woman;* Harold C. Livesay, *Andrew Carnegie and the Rise of Big Business;* Randolph B. Campbell, *Sam Houston and the American Southwest;* Walter L. Hixson, *Charles Lindbergh: Lone Eagle;* Jack N. Rakove, *James Madison and the Creation of the American Republic;* Sam W. Haynes, *James K. Polk and the Expansionist Impulse;* and J. William T. Youngs, *Eleanor Roosevelt: A Personal and Public Life.*

Penguin Books. The partnership between Penguin-Putnam USA and Longman Publishers offers your students a discount on many titles when bundled with any Longman survey. Available titles include *Narrative of the Life of Frederick Douglass* by Frederick Douglass; *Why We Can't Wait* by Martin Luther King, Jr.; *Beloved* by Toni Morrison; and *Uncle Tom's Cabin* by Harriet Beecher Stowe.

ACKNOWLEDGMENTS

We wish to thank the many friends, colleagues, and students who, over the years, have given us the benefit of their advice and encouragement in keeping this book up to date. We are particularly grateful to Mary Elin Korchinsky for invaluable assistance, especially with the illustration program for this edition. We also thank the following reviewers for their comments and suggestions regarding this revision.

Larry Engelmann, San Jose State University
Howard Jablon, Purdue University, North Central
Juli Jones, St. Charles Community College
Timothy W. Kneeland, Nazareth College of Rochester
Suzanne Marshall, Jacksonville State University
David B. Parket, Kennesaw State University
Anne Paulet, Humboldt State University
Horacio Salinas Jr., Laredo Community College
John E. Sarles, University of the Incarnate Word
Robert M. Spector, Worcester State College
Amos St. Germain, Wentworth Institute of Technology
Ruth L. Suyanna, Los Angeles Mission College
Ken L. Weatherbie, Del Mar College

MARK C. CARNES
*Ann Whitney Olin Professor of History
Barnard College, Columbia University*

JOHN A. GARRATY
*Gouverneur Morris Professor of History, Emeritus
Columbia University*

About the Authors

Mark C. Carnes received his undergraduate degree from Harvard and his Ph.D. in history from Columbia University, where he studied and trained with Professor John A. Garraty. The Ann Whitney Olin Professor History at Barnard College, Columbia University, Professor Carnes has chaired both the departments of History and American Studies at Barnard. In addition to this textbook, Carnes and Garraty have co-authored *Mapping America's Past: A Historical Atlas* and are co-general editors of the 24-volume *American National Biography,* for which they were awarded the Waldo Leland Prize of the American Historical Association, the Darmouth Prize of the American Library Association, and the Hawkins Prize of the American Association of Publishers. In addition, Carnes has published numerous books in American social and cultural history, including *Past Imperfect: History According to the Movies* (1995), *Novel History: Historians and Novelists Confront America's Past (and Each Other)* (2001), and *Invisible Giants: 50 Americans That Shaped the Nation but Missed the History Books* (2002). Carnes also created "Reacting to the Past," which won the Theodore Hesburgh Award, sponsored by TIAA-CREF, as the outstanding pedagogical innovation of 2004.

"Garraty preaches a particular doctrine on historical writing, expounding on the details of a complex process whereby the murky abstractions of the past are distilled into clean, clear narrative. He insists that the writer's sole duty is to readers. This literary alchemy is all the more wondrous for being so devoid of artifice," Carnes observes.

▶ John A. Garraty *(left)* and Mark C. Carnes *(right)*

©1999 Joel Gordon

John A. Garraty. Holding a Ph.D. from Columbia University and an L.H.D. from Michigan State University, Professor Garraty is Gouverneur Morris Professor Emeritus of History at Columbia. He is the author, co-author, and editor of scores of books and articles, among them biographies of Silas Wright, Henry Cabot Lodge, Woodrow Wilson, George W. Perkins, and Theodore Roosevelt. Along with Mark Carnes, he is co-editor of the *American National Biography.* Garraty has also contributed a volume—*The New Commonwealth*—to the New American Nation series and edited *Quarrels That Shaped the Constitution.* He was a member of the Board of Directors of *American Heritage* magazine and served as both vice president and head of the teaching division of the American Historical Association. His areas of research interest include the Gilded Age, unemployment (in a historical sense), and the Great Depression of the 1930s. Of his collaboration with Carnes on *The American Nation,* Garraty says, "Although this volume is the work of two authors, it is as nearly the product of a single historical sensibility as is possible. Mark's scholarly specialization in cultural and social issues, especially gender, complements mine in politics and the economy. The book has benefited, too, from his special interest in postwar America. Over the many years of our collaborations, one of our favorite topics of discussion has been the craft of historical writing. We share a commitment to clarity and conciseness. We strive to avoid jargon and verbiage. We believe that while the political history of the nation provides a useful narrative framework, its people are what give the story meaning."

The
American Nation

Beginnings

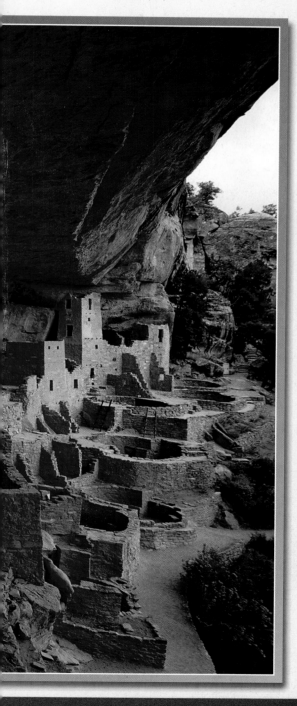

▼ Abstract geometric shapes such as rectangles and squares were common to the art of the early peoples of the Americas. The thousand-year-old ruins of the Anasazi cliff community at Mesa Verde, Colorado, reveal this tendency, with rectangular residential towers rising above circular pits, called *kivas,* used for ceremonial purposes.

lthough human beings emerged in Africa more than two million years ago, it was only about 50,000 years ago that the peoples who most resemble us in their aptitude for tools and facility with language appeared. Paleontologists—scientists who study fossils and prehistoric life—identify them as Cro-Magnon after a cave in France where their bones and tools were first found. At the same time humans were also making similar stone tools in east Africa and western Asia. These peoples developed stone-tipped spears and harpoons, bone fishhooks and needles, and other implements that made them adept at hunting, fighting, and protecting themselves from the elements. They also devised complex languages. Their ability to communicate strengthened emotional bonds and promoted cooperation. They spread through much of Africa and Europe, displacing those humans that had preceded them, and forcing others to adopt their innovations.

PASSAGE TO ALASKA

For tens of thousands of years the frozen wasteland of Siberia remained impenetrable to these tool-making humans. But as the supply of big mammals grew increasingly scarce elsewhere in Asia, hunters ventured farther north. What drew them especially were woolly mammoths. Weighing 16,000 pounds, about as much as a large elephant, a single mammoth provided enough meat to feed two dozen hunters nearly all winter. Its fur could be worn as clothing and its fat could be burned for heat. Its bones, when stretched with fur, functioned as simple tents. A woolly mammoth was a kind of movable mall, and hunters regarded it with the avidity of shoppers at a clearance sale. As mammoths moved deeper into the arctic tundra, so did their human predators.

About 12,000 years ago, perhaps far earlier, some of these hunters crossed what is now the Bering Strait to Alaska. This was during the last Ice Age, when so much ocean water had been captured as glacial ice

▲ Ancient Asian Migrations to North America

that ocean levels were 300–400 feet lower than nowadays. These hunters did not know that they had entered a new continent. Some trekked east, skirting the northern reaches of the Rocky Mountains. Beyond the foothills of the Rockies they encountered a shimmering plateau of ice that extended to the eastern horizon. Eventually they reached an ice-free corridor that funneled the mammoths and hunters southward.

In the vicinity of what is now Calgary, Canada, the hunters happened upon the Great Plains. The sight must have astonished them. On a limitless expanse of high, lush grass roamed vast herds of large animals. There were plenty of mammoths, but also equally enormous mastodons, with massive legs and stout feet; giant beavers the size of bears; 20-foot-long ground sloths weighing over 6000 pounds; strange monsters such as glyptodonts, which resembled armadillos but weighed over a ton, and also countless camels, horses, cheetahs, caribou, and deer.

THE DEMISE OF THE BIG MAMMALS

These animals had evolved over millions of years in the absence of human beings. If the big animals were unprepared to encounter humans, the hunters were ready for the big beasts. They had learned to divide spears into two 3-foot-long sections and connect them with a strip of leather. By swinging the lower shaft in a circular motion, the upper shaft, tipped with a sharp stone projectile, would whip forward with great force. The hunters also painstakingly chiseled long stone blades, which could more readily penetrate thick hides. Archaeologists have named these hunters after their ingenious blades, first found at Clovis, New Mexico.

Loosed upon herds of unwary animals, Clovis hunters seemingly slaughtered them almost at will, or stampeded them over cliffs. Archaeologists have found the blades of Clovis peoples in nearly every present-day American state and even at the southern tip of South America.

But the climate was warming; the Ice Age ended. Glacial ice melted and ocean levels rose, flooding the "land bridge" between Alaska and Asia. In the western region of what is now the United States, grasslands that had sustained the big mammals shrank.

And then the big mammals were gone. By about 9000 B.C.E.[1] most of the large mammals of North America had become extinct, including the mammoths, mastodons, saber-toothed cats, giant beavers, bears, horses, and camels. Whether the Clovis peoples killed off all the big mammals or the warming climate caused the blubbery, heavily furred animals to become extinct is a source of debate. (See Debating the Past, "Who—or what—killed the big mammals?" p. 6.) What is beyond dispute, however, is that the absence of large mammals had a profound effect on the subsequent course of human events.

THE ARCHAIC PERIOD: A WORLD WITHOUT BIG MAMMALS, 9000 B.C.E.–1000 B.C.E.

The loss of the big mammals marked the end of the Clovis culture. Descendants of the Clovis peoples had no choice but to find new sources of food, clothing, and shelter. For the next several thousand years, their lives were characterized by scarcity. A prolonged drought, or an especially severe winter, could lead to starvation. This period—known as the early Archaic—encompassed perhaps a hundred human generations.

The Archaic peoples learned to adapt to particular habitats. In woodland areas east of the Mississippi River, they hunted small animals, like rabbits and beaver, that had previously not been worth the bother; or they learned to find stealthy animals like bear and caribou or to sneak up on skittish ones like elk and deer. On the Great Plains, hunters for a time thrived on bison, which could be stampeded over cliffs. (The larger species of bison were among those that had disappeared around 10,000 B.C.E., but another species of bison still exists in North America.)

Most Archaic bands searched for game continuously. They migrated from one place to another according to a seasonal schedule, often returning to

---

[1] B.C.E. stands for "before the common era," and C.E. for "common era." These abbreviations are synonyms for B.C. and A.D., respectively. In this book dates not followed by B.C.E. refer to C.E.

▲ Ice Age art—or artifact: Carved into this shoulder bone of a large animal is a figure of a woolly mammoth, as suggested by the long curved tusk. This affirms the centrality of the animals to Ice Age peoples.

DEBATING THE PAST

Who—or what—killed the big mammals? Paul S. Martin (1984) estimated that Clovis peoples, numbering several hundred thousand at their peak, hunted to extinction some 93 billion pounds of animals throughout the western hemisphere. Critics of what has been dubbed the "overkill" hypothesis insisted that Martin's rendering of a swarm of human predators devouring entire species was far-fetched. Clovis "hunters" were mostly scavengers who rarely succeeded in killing woolly mammoths (see museum reconstruction above) and other huge beasts. The big mammals died off because the climate of North America grew far warmer and drier after 11,000 B.C.E.: this damaged the ecosystem on which the big, furry mammals depended. Proponents of the "overkill" hypothesis responded that the big mammals had previously endured millions of years of climate fluctuations, some far more severe than the waning of the last Ice Age. That all these species would vanish during a climate shift that coincided with the arrival of human predators seems an improbable coincidence. And if the climate change was so extreme, why did it not result in the demise of species of birds and fish? Alfred Crosby (1986) also showed that the disappearance of many species of large mammals in Australia coincided with the arrival of human beings to that continent. This debate has nevertheless raged for nearly a half century. It reminds us that history is not fixed; facts change, as does our way of looking at them.

Paul S. Martin and Richard G. Klein, eds., *Quaternary Extinctions* (1984), which includes Martin's essay and also those of supporters and critics; also Alfred Crosby, *Ecological Imperialism* (1986).

the same campsites year after year. In the spring, when fish spawn, Archaic peoples moved to rivers and streams. In the summer, they hunted small animals. In the fall, they shifted to upland woods to gather protein-rich nuts, some of which they hid in caves for

emergencies. In winter, they often migrated to forests in search of deer, bear, and caribou.

As Archaic peoples became more knowledgeable about local food sources, they traveled less frequently. They provided for special needs through a remarkably far-ranging trading system, as goods were passed from one band to another. Copper, used for tools and decorative objects, was acquired from the Lake Superior region; it was traded for chert, a crystalline stone that fractured into sharp, smooth surfaces, ideal for tool making.

Often perilously hungry, they discovered that sunflower seeds and sumpweed (a type of spinach) were edible. Around 2500 B.C.E., peoples in the Midwest planted some of the best seeds. They were the first inhabitants of what is now the United States to domesticate plants; plant cultivation gradually spread, though Archaic peoples remained primarily hunters and foragers.

THE FIRST SEDENTARY COMMUNITIES, 1000 B.C.E.

Some Archaic peoples happened on unusually rich habitats that could sustain them throughout the year. Peoples living along the coast and rivers of the Pacific Northwest and Alaska found fish so plentiful they could sometimes be scooped up in baskets. These people also learned to make nets and fishhooks and, in time, boats from bark and animal skins. Those living along the New England coast discovered a seemingly inexhaustible supply of shellfish. But for even these people, survival was a full-time job.

As tribes remained longer in one area, they began to regard it as their own. They built more substantial habitations, developed pottery to carry water and cook food, and buried the dead with distinctive rituals in special places, often marked with mounds.

One of the earliest sedentary communities was located at what is now Poverty Point, on the Mississippi River floodplains north of Delhi, Louisiana. It was founded around 1000 B.C.E. Poverty Point peoples, like those of the Pacific Northwest, became adept at fishing with nets. They also supplemented their diet with bottle gourd seeds and squash.

Poverty Point peoples filled countless grass baskets with earth and dumped them onto enormous mounds. One mound, shaped like an octagon, had six terraced levels on which were built some 400 to 600 houses. Another was more than 700 feet long and 70 feet high. Viewed from above, it resembled a hawk. In all, the mounds consisted of over a million cubic yards of dirt.

The enormity of their construction projects reveals much about the culture of Poverty Point peoples. They could not have diverted so much time and energy to construction if they were not proficient at acquiring food. Moreover, while most Archaic bands were egalitarian, with little differentiation in

▲ An infrared aerial photograph of Poverty Point, Louisiana. During the Archaic period, workers dumped a million cubic yards of earth in six layers—like a wedding cake—each layer nine feet high. These layers were in the shape of concentric circles (or, perhaps, octagons) and are still visible nearly three thousand years later.

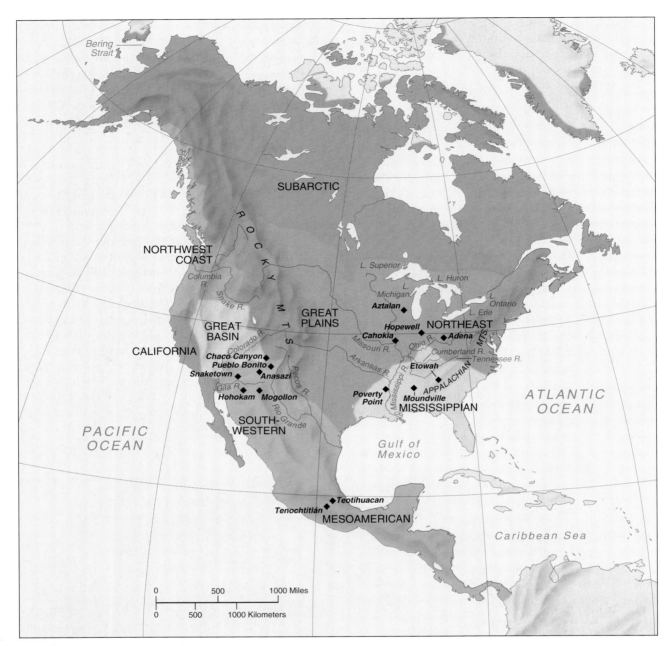

▲ **Ancient Native American Communities**

status, the social structure of Poverty Point was hier-archical. Leaders conceived the plans and directed the labor to build the earthworks.

After about five hundred years, Poverty Point was abandoned. No one knows why. Several hundred years later, scores of smaller mound communities, known as Adena, sprouted in the Ohio and Missis-sippi River valleys. The inhabitants of these communi-ties were also hunters and foragers who cultivated plants in their spare time. Analysis of burial artifacts indicates that they engaged in long-distance trade and were dominated by elites, distinguished by the exotic

goods found in their graves. The Adena communities lasted several hundred years.

From about 200 B.C.E. to 500 C.E., another clus-ter of mound builders, known as Hopewell, flour-ished in Ohio and Illinois. Hopewell mounds were of-ten shaped into squares, circles, and cones; but some, viewed from above, resembled birds or serpents. One Ohio burial mound contained 300 pounds of obsid-ian, found in Yellowstone, Wyoming; others included seashells from the Atlantic, silver from Canada, and bear teeth from the Rocky Mountains. Around 500 C.E. the Hopewell sites were abandoned.

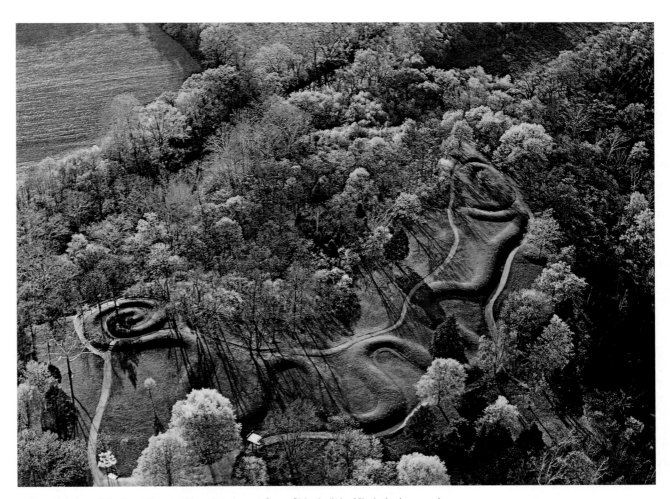

▲ An aerial view of the Great Serpent Mound, in Locust Grove Ohio, built by Mississippian peoples around 1100 C.E. Some Mississippian mounds were in the shape of squares, circles, or cones, but others resembled hawks or panthers, and still others, like this one, depicted a mythical creature or perhaps a snake devouring an egg. Scholars speculate that the shapes reflected religious beliefs or functioned as territorial markers for different clans.

The impermanence of these communities suggests the fragility of sedentary life and serves as a reminder that the transition from a hunting and gathering way of life to one based on settled agriculture was slow and uneven.

CORN TRANSFORMS THE SOUTHWEST

About two thousand years ago, when most of the peoples of North America lived in hunting bands, an urban civilization flourished in the central Mexican highlands; Teotihuacán, about forty miles north of what is now Mexico City, had a population approaching 100,000 and featured miles of paved streets and a pyramid as large as those of the Egyptians. Another civilization with impressive small cities and pyramids was emerging in the

Andes Mountains in Peru. The difference between the simpler peoples in what is now the United States and Canada and the classic civilizations of Mesoamerica and South America can be explained in a single word: corn. The people of the valley of Mexico and the high Andes of Peru had it; the peoples farther north did not.

Originally, corn was unimpressive. Its cobs were only an inch long. Mesoamericans domesticated corn by planting the seeds of the largest and hardiest plants. The improved corn made possible a Neolithic revolution, the transition from hunting and gathering to a predominantly farming way of life. By 2000 B.C.E. nearly every valley in central Mexico and mountainside above the central and South American rainforests bristled with cornstalks.

Eventually corn came to the attention of the people of the Southwest: the Hohokam and Mogollon of Arizona and New Mexico; and the Anasazi of the Colorado

▲ Anasazi earthenware jars, from about 1200 c.e. The development of pottery was part of the ascent of a farming life. Corn could be stored in such jars, warding off starvation in lean winter months. Note the juxtaposition of straight lines and circles, an artistic pattern common among early American peoples. (Compare these pottery designs with the photograph of Anasazi architecture, pp. 2–3.)

Plateau. Corn transformed the lives of these people. Communities abandoned hunting grounds and settled near rivers, built trenches and canals to channel water to the crops, dammed gullies to capture runoff from flash floods, and constructed homes near the cornfields.

Their culture revolved around corn. Sun and water became the focus of their religious beliefs, symbols of life and rebirth. Priest-astronomers carefully measured changes of the seasons. If corn was planted too early, it might shrivel before the late summer rains; if planted too late, it might be destroyed by frost. The centrality of corn to religious beliefs was underscored by the proximity of corn storage to sacred ceremonial pits, known as kivas. Corn Mother symbolism, suggesting a relationship between the fertility of the earth and of women, dominated religious practices. Moreover, control of the corn surplus was a key to political power.

Despite the aridity and blistering heat of the Southwest, the corn-cultivating peoples increased in number after 800 C.E. The Chaco Canyon, a 22-mile-long gorge in western New Mexico, witnessed the development of a most improbable human habitat. The Anasazi, who grew corn there, carved entire villages into the sandstone and shale cliffs. As population increased, the Anasazi built dozens of towns and villages linked by an elaborate system of roads. The largest of these cliff towns, Pueblo Bonito, had buildings more than five stories tall. The Hohokam constructed an irrigation canal system over hundreds of miles containing an intricate network of dams, sluices, and headgates. Snaketown, a Hohokam village 250 miles west of modern Phoenix, had a population of several thousand.

These communities were far smaller than those of their mightier neighbors to the south. But the triumph of the corn-growing Anasazi, Hohokam, and Mogollon is measured not by wealth and numbers but by the magnitude of the environmental challenges they overcame.

THE DIFFUSION OF CORN

Corn cultivation spread from the Southwestern deserts eastward. By about 200, cornfields dotted the southern Mississippi River valley. Thereafter, the advance of corn slowed. Farther north, early cold snaps killed existing varieties of the plant. Moreover, corn cultivation required unremitting labor, and few were eager to subject themselves to its incessant demands. Fields had to be cleared, usually by burning away the undergrowth. Then the soil was hoed using flat stones, clamshells, or the shoulder blades of large animals. After planting, the fields required constant weeding. When ripe, the corn had to be shucked and dried. In addition, hunters and foragers were accustomed to the thrill of the hunt, the taste of game, and the varied and often interesting tasks of foraging. They regarded farming as a subsidiary activity, a task best relegated to women.

But over time many hunting and gathering peoples learned that the alternative to agricultural work was starvation. Fields farther north and east were cleared and planted with corn, beans, and squash. Old skeletons provide a precise means of tracking corn's advance. When corn is chewed, enzymes in the mouth convert its carbohydrates to sugar, a major cause of dental cavities. Radiocarbon dating of skeletons from the vicinity of what is now St. Louis first shows cavities around 700 and those from southern Wisconsin, around 900. By 1000 cavities can be found in skeletons throughout the Midwest and the East. Corn had become king.

POPULATION GROWTH AFTER 800

Pre-Columbian Societies of the Americas

Corn stimulated population growth. An acre of woodlands fed two or three hunters or foragers; that same acre, planted in corn, provided for as many as two hundred people. Most hunting and foraging peoples found enough to eat in summer and fall, but in winter, the threat of starvation was acute, but dried corn, stored in glazed pots or sealed in underground pits, sustained large numbers of farming peoples over long periods. Corn cultivators may not have had a particularly nutritious diet, but they were less likely to starve.

Corn cultivators also had more children than hunting and gathering peoples. The high caloric corn diet caused women to menstruate at an earlier age, making it possible for them to have more children. Corn also promoted fertility by shortening the duration of breastfeeding. Even toothless infants could be fed a soft mush of boiled corn, they could be weaned earlier; and once mothers ceased breastfeeding, they were far more likely to become pregnant. Thus while hunter-gathering women would likely conceive no more frequently than once every four years, women in corn-consuming societies were likely to have children twice as often.

A sedentary lifestyle promoted population growth in other ways. Infants and toddlers were a nuisance on the trail; some hunting and foraging peoples practiced abortion or even infanticide to ensure mobility and reduce the number of mouths to feed. But farming peoples nearly always could make use of additional hands, even young ones, to help with plowing, hoeing, weeding, and harvesting. Because farmers rarely moved, they built more permanent homes and more successfully sheltered infants from inclement weather and physical dangers.

As in the Southwest, the corn-cultivating peoples of the Mississippi Valley responded to increasing population by clearing more woodland and planting more corn. At first, corn cultivators and hunting-foraging peoples successfully cohabited within the same ecosystem: hunters traded for corn, essential for survival during winter, and corn cultivators traded for game, a source of complex protein. A mutually advantageous trade system evolved. But over time the two groups often came into conflict, and when they did, the much more numerous corn cultivators prevailed.

The corn-cultivating societies expanded west into Dakota, east through the Carolinas, south into

Florida, and north into Wisconsin. Their villages consisted of clusters of homes, surrounded by cornfields. They shared a constellation of beliefs and ritual practices. Like the Hopewell, they built burial mounds, but those of the corn cultivators were much larger. Some villages became towns and even small cities. Large temples and granaries and the homes of the governing elite were located on top of the mounds.

The most important and populous of these communities was located in the vicinity of St. Louis. Archaeologists call it Cahokia.

CAHOKIA: THE HUB OF MISSISSIPPIAN CULTURE

By 1000, Cahokia was a major center of trade, shops and crafts, and religious and political activities. It was the first true urban center in what is now the United States. By 1150, at the height of its development, it covered 6 square miles and had about 15,000 inhabitants.

The earthworks at Cahokia included some 20 huge mounds around a downtown plaza, with another 100 large mounds in the outlying areas. The largest mound was 110 feet high, covered 14 acres, and contained 20 million cubic yards of earth. It was probably the largest earthen structure in the Americas. Atop the mound was a 50-foot-high wood-framed temple.

Cahokian society was characterized by sharp class divisions. The elite lived in larger homes and consumed a better and more varied diet (their garbage pits included bones from the best cuts of meat). The corpse of one chieftain was buried upon a bed of 20,000 beaded shells; nearby was a long piece of shaped copper from Lake Superior, several bushels of bird and animal sculptures made of mica, and over 1000 arrows, many with beautiful quartz or obsidian points. Near the chieftain's bones were the skeletons of 50 women ranging from 18 to 23 years old, likely sacrifices to the gods. Their bones were genetically different from the Cahokian skeletons, suggesting that the young women were captives in war or tribute sent by vassal states.

▲ An artist's rendering of downtown Cahokia, around 1150 C.E. The palisade, composed of enormous tree trunks, is the large oval surrounding the main mounds. The largest of these, in the center, was 100 feet high. Here the elite of Cahokia lived and performed some of the fundamental ceremonial tasks of Mississippian culture. The open space in the center was probably filled with the stalls of craftspeople.

▲ Adena, Hopewell, and Mississippian Mounds

Map legend:
◆ Major Adena or Hopewell Mounds
1000 B.C.E. to 1000 C.E.

● Major Mississippian Mounds
700 to 1700 C.E.

Map labels: Aztalan, Cahokia, Etowah, Moundville, Poverty Point

Scale: 0 — 300 Kilometers / 0 — 300 Miles

In a pit near these skeletons were those of four men whose heads and hands had been cut off; their necks and vertebrae bore multiple cuts indicating torture or mutilation. Another nearby burial pit included a mass grave. Some skeletons had been decapitated or their skulls smashed; a few of the fingers were in a vertical position, suggesting that the people were not dead at the time of burial and attempted to scratch their way out.

That the Cahokia had enemies is suggested by the existence of a 3-mile-long wooden palisade surrounding the central core of the city. It consisted of 20,000 enormous tree trunks, pounded deep into the ground, interspersed with several dozen watchtowers from which defenders could unloose arrows upon besiegers.

Despite its daunting fortifications, or perhaps because of them, the elite did not command a large army. Its power derived chiefly from its ability to create a compelling religious worldview and express it in tangible symbols. Cahokia was a cultural and religious center rather than a fortress. In the central plaza, skilled workers carved religious figurines from quartz, mica, and galena. Others painted similar symbols on pottery or etched them in copper goods. Lesser chieftains brought corn and other foodstuffs into Cahokia, perhaps as tribute, while the Cahokia rulers reciprocated with gifts of

figurines and copper or, in times of famine, grants of surplus corn. In Cahokia, too, priest-astronomers scrutinized the movements of the sun, moon, and stars.

Cahokia dominated a region of several hundred miles. Smaller mound-building communities emerged throughout the eastern woodlands and the Southeast. Two of the largest were Moundville, Alabama, and Etowah, Mississippi. Cahokia also established (or perhaps inspired) the creation of distant satellite communities. Around 800, Mississippian peoples moved into southern Wisconsin and built Aztalan (in what is now Jefferson County), with similar corn storage depots and large ceremonial mounds surrounding a central plaza.

Like Cahokia, Aztalan erected a massive tree-trunk palisade with watchtowers. Archaeologists have found burned and butchered body parts throughout the ruins, evidence of warfare. Some speculate that the corn-growing Mississippians encroached on the Oneota, a hunting and gathering people, and that the communities long remained hostile.

The Mississippian elites did more than supervise construction of their own massive earthen tombs. They also solved complicated problems of political and social organization.

THE COLLAPSE OF URBAN CENTERS

Cahokia and Aztalan soon declined. By 1200 Cahokia's population had been reduced to several thousand people; by 1350, it was deserted. Etowah and Moundville went into decline somewhat later.

The major towns and villages of the Southwest civilizations faded as well. By 1200, the inhabitants of Chaco Canyon had vanished and nearly all of the pueblos of the Anasazi had been abandoned. Snaketown and dozens of towns of the Hohokam had become empty ruins, their canals choked with weeds.

What caused the collapse of these communities has long been a source of debate. Some scholars cite protracted droughts during the 1200s and 1300s. Others note that population growth harmed the environment. Slash-and-burn wood clearance thinned the eastern forests, and corn cultivation exhausted the soil. Archaeologists have determined that each Cahokian house required 80 large wooden posts—a half million for the entire city. The palisade at Cahokia consisted of thousands of the trunks of fully grown trees, and it was repeatedly rebuilt. Denuded of big trees, the watershed around Cahokia became susceptible to erosion and flooding, further depleting exhausted topsoils.

The people of the Southwest also stripped their lands of trees for house and kiva construction, and for fuel. The wooden buildings at Chaco Canyon alone required nearly a quarter of a million trees. The irrigation system of the Hohokam harmed the environment in a different way. The canal networks distributed water from the Gila and (aptly named) Salt rivers, and in so doing deposited thousands of tons of mineral salts on cornfields. With little rainfall to leach the soils, the salt residues eventually reached toxic levels.

Crop yields declined as the demand for food in towns and villages was increasing. Studies of human skeletons in Mississippian burial mounds show higher incidences of disease and malnutrition after 1250. What happened next is unclear. Some archaeologists believe that many people left the cities and villages and quietly reverted to the hunting and foraging life of their Archaic forebears. Others argue that the end was calamitous. Late Mississippian skeletons were smaller and more likely to show signs of disease; they also had more broken bones; often arms, feet, and hands were dismembered. Recurrent famines and disease may have undermined the credibility of elites and the cultural system they supervised, weakening their control of poor urban people as well as chieftains in the hinterlands. The towering log palisades of the Mississippians and the impenetrable cliff dwellings of the Anasazi were manifestations of this collective insecurity.

Warfare became endemic among the corn-growing tribes of the Northeast. By 1300, the Iroquoian peoples of New York and Pennsylvania were building forts with defensive earthworks and palisades. Some tribes joined together to form military alliances. Soil exhaustion, perhaps aggravated by the droughts that had parched the cornfields of the Southwest, may have forced tribes to compete for land and resources.

▼ Anasazi paintings dating from 1350 C.E. on the walls of kivas, subterranean rooms used for religious ceremonies. Are the birds, as spiritual couriers, bringing gifts of corn seed? The human figure, with an animal mask and feathered headdress, represents a spirit. It stares directly at the viewer who, seven centuries ago, was likely a young man about to learn the religious mysteries of the tribe.

Some scholars propose that gender tensions may have exacerbated these conflicts. Men performed most of the hunting and foraging tasks, while women did most of the work in the cornfields. As corn supplanted game and fish as staples of the diet, women acquired more status and power. To reassert male dominance, men embarked on raids and warfare.

By 1500 nearly all of the large towns had been abandoned. Survivors puzzled over who had inhabited the ruins, or who had erected the massive earthen mounds. The Navajo Indians referred to their predecessors as the "Anasazi," the "Ancient Ones."

The collapse of the cities disrupted trade networks. Some goods continued to move many, many miles, being passed from one tribe to another; but the flow of trade goods slowed to a trickle. Tribes were becoming more self-sufficient. Moreover, if the rise of powerful urban communities had forced earlier groups to band together, the demise of the urban communities encouraged the breakup of large groups and tribes. Hundreds, perhaps thousands of small bands lived in relative isolation.

To them, the great Aztec city of Tenochtitlán, beyond the Mexican desert, was only a rumor. Of Europe, Africa, and Asia, they knew nothing. That was about to change.

AMERICAN BEGINNINGS IN EURASIA AND AFRICA

If the Neolithic revolution had made but fitful progress in North America by 1500, its advance through Africa and Eurasia was nearly complete. Wheat, first domesticated in Southwest Asia after 9000 B.C.E., spread through the Nile Valley and the Mediterranean and eastward to India and China. Rice, domesticated in China around the same time, diffused throughout Eurasia. These lead crops were followed by others—oats, peas, olives, grapes, almonds, barley, oranges, lentils, and millet. Several thousand years later, farmers in Africa domesticated sorghum, palm oil, and yams.

Location of Major Indian Groups and Culture Areas in the 1600s

The flow of people and crops between Eurasia and Africa was hindered after about 6000 B.C.E., when the climate of Africa shifted and the Sahara broadened into a nearly impenetrable desert the size of the United States. The animals of Eurasia were as diverse as its crops. In the Americas, few large mammals survived the era of the Clovis hunters. But the ancient peoples of Eurasia learned how to domesticate horses, pigs, cows, goats, sheep, and oxen. In addition to protein-rich meat, cows and goats provided milk and dairy products such as cheese that could be stored for winter; horses and oxen dragged trees and boulders from fields, pulled ploughs through tough sod, and contributed manure for fertilizer. Eurasians greatly increased the power of oxen and horses by harnessing them to wheeled vehicles. Because of the diversity and nutritional value of its food sources, the Eurasian population increased rapidly.

To accommodate the growing demand for food, Eurasian farmers cut down forests, filled in marshlands, and terraced hillsides. Monarchs joined with merchants and bankers to build port facilities, canals, and fleets of ships.

If cereal crops and animals dispersed throughout the vast Eurasian landmass, so did new diseases. The close physical proximity of people to their cows, pigs, goats, and sheep made them vulnerable to diseases borne by these animals. New strains of viruses and bacteria appeared in animal herds and spread to the humans that kept them. Diseases also spread readily, especially in large cities whose sanitation facilities were inadequate. Recurrent plagues swept across Eurasia. But those who survived acquired biological resistance.

West Africa evolved differently. The grassy savannah just south of the Sahara became the home for mostly herding peoples. Cities emerged in response to the growth of a trans-Sahara trade in gold, salt, kola—a caffeine rich nut—and slaves. Warlords leading horse-mounted cavalry vied for control of the trade routes across the Sahara. Conflict led to the great kingdoms of West Africa: Ghana, Mali, Songhay. Seldom did the kings of these empires penetrate far south into the tropical coastal region of west Africa. There the tsetse fly, carrier of sleeping sickness, decimated horse and cattle herds. Malaria, too, discouraged invaders. Relatively insulated from the imperial struggles farther north, peoples of the west African coast mostly kept to themselves, growing crops and harvesting the lush vegetation of the forest. By 1500, their lives, too, were about to change.

▲ Like most world-changing innovations, the printing press of fifteenth-century Europe took advantage of technological innovations, chiefly improvements in metallurgy (to cast letters and to carve the ridges of the pressing screw), and new concepts, such as increasingly standardized rules for writing. By facilitating the spread of ideas, the printing press generated further technological advances.

EUROPE IN FERMENT

During the 1400s Europe's population increased by nearly a third; by 1500, population pressure was acute. When harvests were poor or grain shipments failed to arrive, hunger riots destabilized the political order. From 1413 to 1453, for example, Genoa, in Italy, was convulsed by 14 revolutions. Overpopulation was one reason why Jews, a vulnerable minority, were expelled from Spain and Portugal in 1492, and from Sicily in 1493.

Scarcity shook many peasants from the land and drove the urban poor from one city to another. Christoforo Colombo—or Columbus, as we call him—was among the restless youths who left home and took to the sea in search of a better life.

New ideas further unsettled European society. Movable type, which made the printing of books profitable, was perfected during the 1440s. By 1500, over 100 cities in Europe had at least one printing press and as many as 20 million volumes had been published. Books advanced new ideas and weakened the hold of traditional ones. Within a few decades, the treatises of Martin Luther and John Calvin initiated the Protestant Reformation. Books also excited the imagination and gave tangible expression to all manner of dreams and longings. (Columbus's restless curiosity had been stimulated by books on geography and navigation.)

Incessant squabbles over land resulted in nearly constant warfare. The military arts advanced accordingly. Improvements in metallurgy made it possible to cast bronze and iron cannon capable of containing larger charges of gunpowder. By the early 1500s weapons weighing a ton or more were mounted in sailing ships or upon carriages pulled by teams of horses. Warfare of this nature was expensive; the cost of constructing fleets, equipping armies, and building massive fortifications required the collective resources of many thousands. No longer an activity of rival cities or contending noblemen, warfare demanded the resources of entire nations.

A restless hunger for land, a population made resistant to biological pathogens through recurrent exposure to them, an explosion in communication and knowledge, an avid acceptance of the new technology and organization of warfare, and the emergence of powerful and contentious monarchs all imparted a fateful dynamism to late fifteenth-century European society. Plainly, fifteenth-century Europeans had not solved their problems: population growth exceeded available food sources; poverty undermined political order; and war loomed larger and more ominous. Equally plainly, the people of North America had failed to solve basic social problems: those who practiced a hunting-gathering lifestyle were vulnerable to

starvation as well as to encroachments by the more numerous peoples of the corn-farming tribes. Farming peoples, on the other hand, despite new modes of social organization and cultural expression, found it difficult to sustain even small urban communities over a long period. In the absence of writing systems and larger "national" political organizations, few could join in broad enterprises; none possessed military technologies comparable to the Europeans. And the peoples of the Americas lacked the immunity from infectious diseases that so many Europeans had acquired.

Separating these two worlds was the impenetrable void of the Atlantic Ocean. Five hundred years earlier a Norseman, Leif Ericson, had sailed along the coast of Greenland to the shores of Labrador, but little came of his expeditions. But toward the close of the fifteenth century, European sailors of a different type, adept at navigating through the open sea and willing to sail far from land, were about to venture across the expanses of the Atlantic. In so doing they would transform it into a bridge that would join these worlds, and the west African coast as well, bringing all three into fateful collision.

MILESTONES

c. 12,000 B.C.E. (perhaps earlier)	Humans from Asia cross Beringia to Alaska	**c. 500 B.C.E.**	Corn cultivation begins in the Southwest
c. 12,000– 9000 B.C.E.	Humans diffuse throughout Americas Many species of large mammals become extinct in western hemisphere Clovis era ends Eurasians domesticate wheat and rice	**c. 200 C.E.**	Corn cultivation begins in the lower Mississippi Valley
		c. 700 C.E.	Cahokia is founded near today's St. Louis, Missouri
c. 3500 B.C.E.	Mesoamerican peoples cultivate corn and initiate Neolithic revolution	**c. 900 C.E.**	Corn cultivation begins in Wisconsin
		c. 1200s– 1300s	Protracted droughts in North America disrupt food supply; urban areas are abandoned
c. 2500 B.C.E.	Peoples of midwestern North America domesticate sunflowers and sumpweed		
c. 1000 B.C.E.	First sedentary North American community is founded at today's Poverty Point, Louisiana		

SUPPLEMENTARY READING

During the 1990s the prehistoric era in North America has witnessed an explosion of interest, especially among archaeologists. A global perspective, focusing on geography as a causal force, is outlined in Jared Diamond, *Guns, Germs, and Steel* (1997). David Hurst Thomas, *Exploring Native North America* (2000), provides detailed analyses of representative archaeological sites.

A good survey of the first peoples of North America is David J. Meltzer, *Search for the First Americans* (1993). The "overkill hypothesis" is developed in Paul Martin and Richard Klein, eds., *Quaternary Extinctions* (1984). The best survey on the southwestern peoples is Linda S. Cordell, *Prehistory of the Southwest* (1997). See also J. J. Brody, *The Anasazi* (1990), David Roberts, *In Search of the Old Ones:*

Exploring the Anasazi World of the Southwest (1995), R. Gwinn Vivian, *The Chacoan Prehistory of the San Juan Basin* (1990), John P. Andrews and Todd W. Bostwick, *Desert Farmers at the River's Edge: The Hohokam and Pueblo Grande* (1997), and, on early agriculture, R. G. Matson, *The Origins of Southwestern Agriculture* (1991). For a study of Hopewell peoples, see Bruce D. Smith, *Rivers of Change* (1992).

On the Mississippian societies, see Thomas E. Emerson, *Cahokia and the Archaeology of Power* (1997), Thomas E. Emerson and R. Barry Lewis, eds., *Cahokia and the Hinterlands: Middle Mississippian Cultures of the Midwest* (1991), Biloine W. Young and Robert Fowler, *Cahokia, The Great Native American Metropolis* (2000), Timothy Pauketat, *The Ascent of Chiefs: Cahokia and Mississippian Politics in Native North America* (1994), and Robert A. Birmingham and Leslie Eisenberg, *Indian Mounds of Wisconsin* (2000). For early peoples elsewhere, see Vance T. Holliday, *Paleoindian Geoarchaeology of the Southern High Plains* (1997) and Ruth Kirk and Richard D. Daugherty, *Hunters of the Whale* (1974), for the Makah of the Northwest.

For an overview of political structures, see Robert D. Drennan, *Chiefdoms in the Americas* (1987). That warfare was a product of gender tensions is explored in Bruce G. Trigger, *Natives and Newcomers* (1985). The contention that the early peoples of North America lived in perfect harmony with nature is rebutted in Shepard Krech, *The Ecological Indian* (1999). Another common assumption, based on Native American folklore, of the essentially peaceful character of Southwestern peoples has been challenged by recent studies such as Glen E. Rice and Steven A. Leblanc, eds., *Deadly Landscapes: Case Studies in Prehistoric Southwestern Warfare* (2001), and Tim D. White, *Prehistoric Cannibalism at Mancos* (1992). In *Eve's Seed: Biology, the Sexes and the Course of History* (2001), Robert S. McElvaine argues that men enshrined raids and warfare in response to women's increasingly important economic role in farming activities.

SUGGESTED WEBSITES

Pre-Contact and Colonial Maps

http://www.lib.utexas.edu/maps/americas/

This University of Texas site contains numerous maps from the pre-contact and colonial periods.

Ancient Mesoamerican Civilization

http://www.angelfire.com/ca/humanorigins/index.html

Kevin L. Callahan of the University of Minnesota Department of Anthropology maintains this page that supplies information regarding Mesoamerican civilizations with well-organized essays and photos.

National Museum of the American Indian

http://www.si.edu/nmai

The Smithsonian Institution museum is dedicated to the Native American experience.

Cahokia Mounds

http://medicine.wustel/edu/~mckinney/cahokia/cahokia.html

The Cahokia Mounds State Historical site gives information about this fascinating pre-Columbian North American culture.

Alien Encounters: Europe in the Americas

▼ An Aztec artist's depiction of the arrival of the Spaniards, whose blank faces scarcely appear human. Compare them to the detailed, grim expression of the Aztec scout, hidden at the top of the palm tree *(upper right)*. Historical interpretation always depends on one's point of view.

CHAPTER CONTENTS

At about two o'clock on the morning of October 12, 1492, a sailor named Roderigo de Triana, clinging in a gale to the mast of the *Pinta*, saw a gleam of white on the moonlit horizon and shouted: *"Tierra! Tierra!"* The land he had spied was an island in the West Indies called Guanahani by its inhabitants, a place distinguished neither for beauty nor size. Nevertheless, when Triana's master, Christopher Columbus, went ashore bearing the flag of Spain, he named it San Salvador, or Holy Savior. Columbus selected this imposing name for the island out of gratitude and wonder at having found it—he had sailed with three frail vessels more than 3000 miles for 33 days without sighting land.

San Salvador was the gateway to two continents. Columbus did not know it, and he refused to accept the truth, but his voyage threw open to exploitation by the peoples of western Europe more than a quarter of all the land in the world, a region of more than 16 million square miles, an area lushly endowed with every imaginable resource. He made possible a mass movement into the New World from Europe—and later from Africa and other regions. By 1600, about 240,000 Spaniards had made their way to the Americas. Gathering force rapidly, this movement brought over 100 million persons from throughout the world to the western hemisphere.

Columbus

Columbus was an intelligent as well as a dedicated and skillful mariner. He failed to grasp the significance of his accomplishment because he had no idea that he was on the edge of two huge continents previously unknown to Europeans. He was seeking a way to China and Japan and the Indies, the amazing countries described by the Venetian Marco Polo in the late thirteenth century.

Having read carefully Marco Polo's account of his adventures in the service of Kublai Khan, Columbus had decided that these rich lands could be reached by sailing directly west from Europe. The idea was not original, but while others merely talked about it, Columbus pursued it with brilliant persistence.

If one could sail to Asia directly, the trading possibilities and the resulting profits would be limitless. Asian products were highly valued all over Europe. Spices such as pepper, cinnamon, ginger, nutmeg, and cloves were of primary importance, their role being not so much to titillate the palate as to disguise the taste of spoiled meats in regions that had little ice. Europeans also prized such tropical foods as rice, figs, and oranges, as well as perfumes (often used as a substitute for soap), silk and cotton, rugs, textiles such as muslin and damask, dyestuffs, fine steel products, precious stones, and various drugs.

But the cost of Asian products remained high. To transport spices from the Indies, silk from China, or rugs, cloth, and steel from the Middle East was extremely costly. The combined routes through central Asia were long and complicated—across strange seas, through deserts, over high mountain passes—with pirates or highwaymen a constant threat. Every petty tyrant through whose domain the caravans passed levied taxes, a quasi-legal form of robbery. Few merchants operated on a continental scale; typically, goods passed from hand to hand and were loaded and unloaded many times between Eastern producer and Western consumer, with each middleman exacting as large a profit as he could. In the end the western European consumer had to pay for all this.

If the produce of eastern Asia could be carried to Europe by sea, the trip would be both cheaper and more comfortable. The goods would have to be loaded and unloaded only once. A small number of sailors could provide all the necessary labor, and the free wind would supply the power to move the cargo to its destination. By the fifteenth century, this idea was beginning to be transformed into action.

The great figure in the transformation was Prince Henry the Navigator, third son of John I, king of Portugal. After distinguishing himself in 1415 in the capture of Ceuta, on the African side of the Strait of Gibraltar, he became interested in navigation and exploration. Sailing a vessel out of sight of land was still, in Henry's day, more an art than a science and was extremely hazardous. Ships were small and clumsy. Primitive compasses and instruments for reckoning latitude existed, but under shipboard conditions they were very inaccurate. Navigators could determine longitude only by keeping track of direction and estimating speed; even the most skilled could place little faith in their estimates.

Henry attempted to improve and codify navigational knowledge. At his court at Sagres, hard by Cape St. Vincent, the extreme southwestern point of Europe, he built an observatory and supervised the preparation of tables measuring the declination of the sun and other navigational data. But most improvements in navigation were the result of practical experience. Searching for a new route to Asia, Henry's captains sailed westward to the Madeiras and the Canaries and south along the coast of Africa, seeking a way around that continent. In 1445 Dinis Dias reached Cape Verde, site of present-day Dakar.

For 20 years after Henry's death in 1460, the Portuguese concentrated on exploiting his discoveries. In the 1480s King John II undertook systematic new explorations focused on reaching India. Gradually his caravels probed southward along the sweltering coast—to the equator, to the region of Angola, and beyond.

Into this bustling, prosperous, expectant little country in the corner of Europe came Christopher Columbus in 1476. Columbus was a weaver's son from Genoa, born in 1451. He had taken to the sea early, ranging widely in the Mediterranean. His arrival in Portugal was unplanned, since it resulted from the loss of his ship in a battle off the coast. For a time he worked as a chartmaker in Lisbon. He married a local woman. Then he was again at sea. He cruised northward, perhaps as far as Iceland, south to the equator, westward in the Atlantic to the Azores. Had his interest lain in that direction, he might well have been the first person to reach Asia by way of Africa, for in 1488 in Lisbon he met and talked with Bartholomeu Dias, just returned from his voyage around the southern tip of Africa, which had demonstrated that the way lay clear for a voyage eastward to the Indies.

But by this time Columbus had committed himself to the westward route. When King John II refused to finance him, he turned to the Spanish court, where, after many disappointments, he persuaded Queen Isabella to equip his expedition. In August 1492 he set out from the port of Palos with his tiny fleet, the *Santa Maria*, the *Pinta*, and the *Niña*. A little more than two months later, after a stopover in the Canary Islands to repair the *Pinta*'s rudder, his lookout sighted land.

▲ **European Voyages of Discovery**

Columbus's success was due in large part to his single-minded conviction that the Indies could be reached by sailing westward for a relatively short distance and that a profitable trade would develop over this route. He had persuaded Isabella to grant him, in addition to the title Admiral of the Ocean Sea, political control over all the lands he might discover and 10 percent of the profits of the trade that would follow in the wake of his expedition. Now the combination of zeal and tenacity that had gotten him across the

Atlantic cost him dearly. He refused to accept the plain evidence, which everywhere confronted him, that this was an entirely new world. All about were strange plants, known neither to Europe nor to Asia. The copper-colored people who paddled out to inspect his fleet could no more follow the Arabic widely understood in the East than they could Spanish. Yet Columbus, consulting his charts, convinced himself that he had reached the Indies. That is why he called the natives Indians, a misnomer that became nearly universal, and was increasingly used even by the native peoples themselves.

From *The Journal of Christopher Columbus*

Searching for treasure, Columbus pushed on to Cuba. When he heard the native word *Cubanocan,* meaning "middle of Cuba," he mistook it for *El Gran Can* (Marco Polo's "Grand Khan") and sent emissaries on a fruitless search through the tropical jungle for the khan's palace. He finally returned to Spain relatively empty-handed but certain that he had explored the edge of Asia. Three later voyages failed to shake his conviction.

SPAIN'S AMERICAN EMPIRE

Columbus died in 1506. By that time other captains had taken up the work, most of them more willing than he to accept what Europeans called the New World on its own terms. As early as 1493, Pope Alexander VI had divided the non-Christian world between Spain and Portugal. The next year, in the Treaty of Tordesillas, these powers negotiated an agreement about exploiting the new discoveries. In effect, Portugal continued to concentrate on Africa, leaving the New World, except for what eventually became Brazil, to the Spanish. Thereafter, from their base on Hispaniola (Santo Domingo), founded by Columbus, the Spaniards quickly fanned out through the Caribbean and then over large parts of the two continents that bordered it.

In 1513 Vasco Nuñez de Balboa crossed the Isthmus of Panama and discovered the Pacific Ocean. In 1519 Hernán Cortés landed an army in Mexico and overran the empire of the Aztecs, rich in gold and silver. That same year Ferdinand Magellan set out on his epic three-year voyage around the world. By discovering the strait at the southern tip of South America that bears his name, he gave the Spanish a clear idea of the size of the continent. In the 1530s Francisco Pizarro subdued the Inca empire in Peru, providing the Spaniards with still more treasure, drawn chiefly from the silver mines of Potosí.

Cabeza de Vaca, "Indians of the Rio Grande"

Meanwhile other Spanish explorers had surveyed vast regions of what is now the United States. Juan Ponce de Léon, a shipmate of Columbus on the Admiral's second voyage, made the first Spanish landing on the mainland of North America, exploring the east coast of Florida in 1513. In the 1520s Pánfilo de Narváez explored the Gulf Coast of North America westward from Florida, and after his death his lieutenant, Alvar Núñez Cabeza de Vaca, wandered for years in the region north of the Gulf. Finally, along with three

▲ Horses (blindfolded) being loaded onto Spanish warships for shipment to the Americas. Native peoples had never seen horses (which had been extinct in the Americas for over ten thousand years). Nor had they seen enormous wooden warships, powered by sails and carrying heavy cannons, nor warriors, seated on horses and encased in armor.

companions, one a black slave named Esteban, Cabeza de Vaca made his way across what is now New Mexico and Arizona and then south to Mexico City. Between 1539 and 1543 Hernando de Soto traveled north from Florida to the Carolinas, then westward to the Mississippi River. During the same period Francisco Vásquez de Coronado ventured as far north as Kansas and west to the Grand Canyon. Fifty years after Columbus's first landfall, Spain was master of a huge American empire covering all of South America except Brazil, and also the southern fringe of North America, extending from California east to Florida. By the early 1600s Spanish explorers had reached Virginia, and there were small Spanish settlements at Saint Augustine in Florida and at Santa Fe in New Mexico.

The Spanish developed a distinct civilization in this enormous region. By the 1570s they had founded about 200 cities and towns, set up printing presses and published pamphlets and books, and established universities in Mexico City and Lima. With the help of Indian artisans, they had constructed and decorated lavishly a large number of impressive cathedrals.

What explains this mighty surge of exploration, conquest, and development? Greed for gold and power certainly, but also a sense of adventure, the wish of ordinary Spaniards to make better lives for themselves, and the desire to Christianize the Indians—mixed motives propelled the *conquistadores* and their followers onward. Some saw the New World as a reincarnation of the Garden of Eden, a land of infinite promise. Ponce de Léon and many others actually expected to find the Fountain of Youth in America. Their visions, at once so selfish and so exalted, reveal the central paradox of New World history. This immense land brought out both the best and the worst in human beings. The "New" World, "Virgin" America inspired conflicting feelings in their hearts. They worshiped it for its purity and promise, yet they could not resist the opportunity to take advantage of its seeming innocence.

INDIANS AND EUROPEANS

The *conquistadores* were brave and imaginative men. It must not, however, be forgotten that they wrenched their empire from innocent hands; in an important sense, the settlement of the New World ranks among the most flagrant examples of unprovoked aggression in human history. When Columbus landed on San Salvador he planted a cross, "as a sign," he explained to Ferdinand and Isabella, "that your Highnesses held this land as your own." Of the Lucayans, the native inhabitants of San Salvador, Columbus wrote: "The people of this island . . . are artless and generous with what they have, to such a degree as no one would believe. . . . If it be asked for, they never say no, but rather invite the person to accept it, and show as much lovingness as though they would give their hearts."

The Indians of San Salvador behaved this way because to them the Spaniards seemed the very gods. "All believe that power and goodness dwell in the sky," Columbus reported, "and they are firmly convinced that I have come from the sky."

The products of Europe fascinated the Indians. The early observer Thomas Harriot noticed that such everyday things as compasses, magnets, and clocks seemed to them "rather the works of gods than of men."

Columbus also remarked of the Lucayans: "These people are very unskilled in arms . . . with fifty men they could all be subjected and made to do all that

one wished." He and his compatriots tricked and cheated the Indians at every turn. Before entering a new area, Spanish generals customarily read a *Requerimiento* (requirement) to the inhabitants. This long-winded document recited a Spanish version of the history of the human race from the Creation to the division of the non-Christian world by Pope Alexander VI and then called on the Indians to recognize the sovereignty of the reigning Spanish monarch. ("If you do so . . . we shall receive you in all love and charity.") If this demand was rejected, the Spanish promised: "We shall powerfully enter into your country, and . . . shall take you, your wives, and your children, and shall make slaves of them. . . . The death and losses which shall accrue from this are your fault." This arrogant harangue was read in Spanish and often out of earshot of the Indians. When they responded by fighting, the Spaniards decimated them, drove them from their lands, and held the broken survivors in contempt.

Wherever they went, Europeans mistreated and sometimes slaughtered the people they encountered. The French philosopher Montaigne wrote that in the East Indies (now Indonesia), cities were ransacked and "the best part of the world topsiturvied" by Spain merely to profit from "the traffic of Pearls and pepper." When the Portuguese reached Africa, they carried off thousands into slavery. The Dutch behaved shamefully in the East Indies, as did the French in their colonial possessions.

Conquistadores Torturing Native Amerindians

English settlers described the Indians as being "of a tractable, free, and loving nature, without guile or treachery," yet in most instances they exploited and all but exterminated them. "Why should you take by force from us that which you can obtain by love?" one puzzled chief asked an early Virginia colonist, according to the latter's own account.

The first settlers of New England dealt fairly with the local inhabitants. They made honest, if somewhat misguided, efforts to Christianize and educate them and to respect their rights. But within a few years their relations with the Indians deteriorated. The settelers seized more land and their livestock ruined Indian crops and hunting grounds. In King Philip's War (1675–1676), a protracted slaughter on both sides, culminated in the massacre of perhaps 4000 Indians at the Great Swamp in Rhode Island.

RELATIVITY OF CULTURAL VALUES

If some of the natives were naive in thinking that the invaders, with their potent fire sticks and huge ships, which seemed to be "moving islands," were

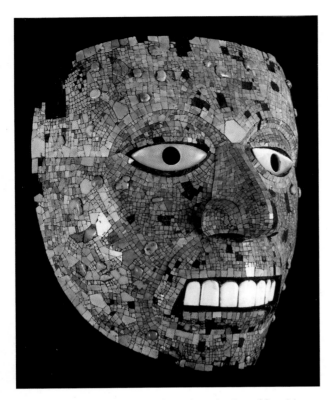

▲ A turquoise Aztec burial mask from about the time of Spanish contact. Such masks conveyed the Aztec sense of social hierarchy—only the most prominent were adorned with masks like this one—and its notion of an afterlife. The beautiful turquoise "face" would resist, as mortal flesh did not, the ravages of time.

gods, these "gods" were equally naive in their thinking. Since the Indians did not worship the Christian God and indeed worshiped a large number of other gods, the Europeans dismissed them as contemptible heathens. Some insisted that the Indians were servants of Satan. "Probably the devil decoyed these miserable savages hither," one English colonist explained.

In fact, many Indians were deeply religious people. But their religious values were so different from those of the Europeans that many of the latter believed that even if the Indians were not minions of Satan, they were unworthy of becoming Christians. Others, such as the Spanish friars, did try to convert the Indians, and with considerable success; but as late as 1569, when Spain introduced the Inquisition into its colonies, the natives were exempted from its control on the ground that they were incapable of rational judgment and thus not responsible for their "heretical" religious beliefs.

That the Indians allowed their environment to remain pristine is a myth. Long before contact with the Europeans, they had cleared fields, burned the underbrush of forests, diverted rivers and streams, built roads and settlements, and deposited immense quantities of earth upon mounds. The Europeans, nevertheless, left a deeper imprint on the American landscape. Their iron-tipped ploughs dug into the earth and made more of it accessible to cultivation, and their iron axes and saws enabled them to clear vast forests and use the lumber for construction.

Indians who depended on hunting and fishing had small use for personal property that was not easily portable. They had little interest in amassing wealth, as individuals or as tribes. Even the Aztecs, with their treasures of gold and silver, valued the metals for their durability and the beautiful things that could be made with them rather than as objects of commerce. The Narragansett Indians had a ritual in which they collected "almost all the riches they have to their gods"—kettles, hatchets, beads, knives—and burned them in a great fire.

This lack of concern for material things led Europeans to conclude that the native people of America were childlike creatures, not to be treated as equals. "[Indians] do but run over the grass, as do also foxes and wild beasts," an Englishman wrote in 1622, "so it is lawful now to take a land, which none useth, and make use of it." In the sense that the Indians lived in close harmony with nature, the first part of this statement contained a grain of truth, although of course the second did not follow from it logically.

Other troubles grew out of similar misunderstandings. English colonists assumed that Indian chiefs ruled with the same authority as their own kings. For example, the Wampanoag called their leader Metacom; the English referred to him as "King Philip," likely a term of derision. When Indians, whose loyalties were shaped by complex kinship relations more than by identification with any one leader, sometimes failed to honor commitments made by their chiefs, the English accused them of treachery.

For their part, Indians found many aspects of European society incomprehensible. When a group of Indians were presented to the 12-year-old king of Spain, Charles IX, they could not understand why his Swiss guards, "so many grown men, bearded, strong, and armed . . . should submit to obey a child" instead of putting one of their members in command.

The Europeans' inability to grasp the communal nature of land tenure among Indians also led to innumerable quarrels. Traditional tribal boundaries were neither spelled out in deeds or treaties nor

▲ European soldiers, clad in armor and wielding iron weapons, were nearly invincible in close fighting—all the more so when their foes were unarmed, as in this drawing. Here Cortés and his men slash through Montezuma's Aztec court.

marked by fences or any other sign of occupation. Often corn grown by a number of families was stored in a common bin and drawn on by all as needed. Such practices were utterly alien to the European mind. Indians resented, too, the intensity of English cultivation. Algonquians taunted English captives while burying them alive: "You English have grown exceedingly above the Ground. Let us now see how you will grow when planted into the ground." Nowhere was the cultural chasm between Indians and Europeans more evident than in warfare. Indians did not seek to possess land, so they sought not so much to destroy the enemy as to display their valor, to avenge an insult or perceived wrong, or to acquire captives who could take the place of missing family members. The Indians preferred to ambush an opponent and seize the stragglers; when confronted by a superior force, they usually melted into the woods. The Europeans preferred to fight in heavily armed masses in order to obliterate the enemy. Colonists denounced Indian perfidy for burning houses and towns; but they saw no inconsistency in burning Indian "nests," "wigwams," and "camps." Conversely, the Indians thought it within their rights to slaughter the cattle that devoured their crops and spoiled their hunting grounds. But when the Indians tortured the beasts in fury, the colonists regarded them as savages.

DISEASE AND POPULATION LOSSES

Scholars agree on only one fact concerning the population history of the North American Indians following the arrival of Columbus: the number of Indians declined. (See the feature essay Debating the Past: "How many Indians perished with European settlement?" on p. 26.) Historian David Stannard's book on the subject, *American Holocaust,* was pointedly published in 1992, the five hundredth anniversary of Columbus's famous excursion. He contended that Columbus's actions constituted "genocide" against the native peoples of the Americas.

Native American Population Loss, 1500–1700

The terms *holocaust* and *genocide* usually refer to the systematic destruction of entire peoples, such as the Nazi attempt to exterminate the European Jews. But the objectives of the Europeans who came to the Americas were as different as the people themselves: soldiers, farmers, missionaries, women as well as men, Protestants, Catholics, and Jews. Many colonists depended on the Indians: The Spanish needed them to work the mines, till the soil, and build roads and buildings; French traders needed them to provide furs and other items for export; English settlers depended on them for additional food and knowledge. For most Europeans, a live Indian was better than a dead one.

Yet millions did die; and from the outset of the Europeans' invasion of the New World, sensitive observers had been appalled by their barbarity. The first to come under sharp scrutiny were the Spaniards. Bartolomé de Las Casas, a Dominican missionary who arrived in Hispaniola nearly a decade after Columbus, compiled a passionate and grisly indictment:

> It was the general rule among Spaniards to be cruel; not just cruel, but extraordinarily cruel so that harsh and bitter treatment would prevent Indians from daring to think of themselves as human beings or having a minute to think at all. So they would cut an Indian's hands and leave them dangling by a shred of skin and they would send him on saying "Go now, spread the news to your chiefs." They would test their swords and their manly strength on captured Indians and place bets on the slicing off of heads or the cutting of bodies in half with one blow.

These and countless similar stories gave rise to the "Black Legend" of Spanish tyranny and oppression, a standard so low that English and French

DEBATING THE PAST

How many Indians perished with European settlement? In 1518 smallpox, long a scourge in Europe, ravaged the native peoples of the New World. This picture shows Aztec victims being attended by a medicine man. "Those who did survive," reported Cortes's secretary, "having scratched themselves, were left in such a condition that they frightened the others with the many deep pits on their faces, hands, and bodies."

To calculate the magnitude of Indian losses, scholars had to determine the population at first contact with Europeans, a difficult task in the absence of Indian records. Early in the twentieth century, scholars gathered fragmentary population statistics as compiled by Catholic priests, Spanish officials, travelers, and soldiers. By aggregating this information for all tribes, including guesses where no data was available, the scholars estimated an Indian population in the United States and Canada in the early sixteenth century of a little more than 1 million.

By the 1960s and 1970s, some thought this estimate far too low. They complained that it minimized both the achievements of Indian civilizations as well as the extent of the destruction wrought by European diseases and guns. Anthropologist Henry Dobyns (1983) found that when smallpox, measles, or tuberculosis struck an Indian village, 19 out of 20 Indians would die. He thought this ratio characteristic of populations that lacked immunity to such diseases. He therefore multiplied the earlier population figures by twenty. After a few adjustments, he calculated the Indian population of the United States and Canada at 10 to 12 million, and of the entire western hemisphere, at over 100 million.

Dobyns's methodology came under fire, but Thornton (1987) and others devised pre-contact estimates ranging from 4 to 8 million. Since then, mathematicians have concluded that the data are so riddled with guesswork that no numerical estimates are reliable. But it is probably safe to conclude that Indian losses north of the Rio Grande numbered in the millions, and in the remainder of the western hemisphere, tens of millions.

Henry Dobyns, *Their Number Became Thinned: Native American Population Dynamics in Eastern North America* (1983), Russell Thornton, *American Indian Holocaust and Survival: A Population History Since 1492* (1987).

colonists believed they could not sink beneath it. In fact, English barbarities rivaled those of the Spaniards.

In Virginia in 1610, for example, George Percy, an English officer, when ordered to punish a Powhatan chief for insolence, proudly described how his men marched into an Indian town, seized some of the natives, "putt some fiftene or sixtene to the Sworde" and cut off their heads. Then he ordered his men to burn the houses and crops. When the expedition returned to its boats, his men complained that Percy had spared an Indian "quene and her Children." Percy relented, and threw the children overboard "shoteinge owtt their Braynes in the water." His men insisted that he burn the queen alive, but Percy, less cruel, stabbed her to death.

Of all the weapons the Europeans brought to the New World, the most potent was one they could not see and of which they were unaware: microorganisms that carried diseases such as smallpox, measles, bubonic plague, diphtheria, influenza, malaria, yellow fever, and typhoid. Most Europeans had been exposed to these diseases and thus carried antibodies for them in their blood; but the Indians initially lacked these antibodies. When these diseases first struck, many Indian villages were nearly wiped out.

In 1585, for example, Sir Francis Drake, preparing for a raid against the Spanish, stopped at the Cape Verde Islands. There some of his men contracted a fever—probably typhus—but sailed for Florida undaunted by their discomfort. When they landed at St. Augustine, the disease spread to the Indians who, according to Drake, "died verie fast and said amongst themselves, it was the Englisshe God that made them die so faste." Some 30 years later an outbreak of smallpox almost wiped out the Indians of Plymouth Bay, prompting the puritan divine, Cotton Mather, to offer thanks to God for having cleared the lands "of those pernicious creatures, to make room for better growth." Over the next three centuries, the Indian losses from such diseases were incalculable, though the lowest estimates begin in the millions.

SPAIN'S EUROPEAN RIVALS

DOCUMENT

Letters of Patent Granted to John Cabot

While Spain waxed fat on the wealth of the Americas, the other nations of western Europe did little. In 1497 and 1498 King Henry VII of England sent Captain John Cabot to explore the New World. Cabot visited Newfoundland and the northeastern coast of the continent. His explorations formed the basis for later British claims in North America, but they were not followed up for many decades. In 1524 Giovanni da Verrazano made a similar voyage for France, coasting the continent from Carolina to Nova Scotia. Some ten years later the Frenchman Jacques Cartier explored the St. Lawrence River as far inland as present-day Montréal. During the sixteenth century, fishermen from France, Spain, Portugal, and England began exploiting the limitless supplies of cod and other fish they found in the cold waters off Newfoundland. They landed at many points along the mainland coast from Nova Scotia to Labrador to collect water and wood and to dry their catches, but they made no permanent settlements until the next century.

There were many reasons for this delay, the most important probably being the fact that Spain had achieved a large measure of internal tranquility by the sixteenth century, while France and England were still torn by serious religious and political conflicts. The Spanish also profited from having seized on those areas in America best suited to producing quick returns. Furthermore, in the first half of the sixteenth century, Spain, under Charles V, dominated Europe as well as America. Charles controlled the Low Countries, most of central Europe, and part of Italy. Reinforced by the treasure of the Aztecs and the Incas, Spain seemed too mighty to be challenged in either the New World or the Old World.

Under Philip II, who succeeded Charles in 1556, Spanish strength seemed at its peak, especially after Philip added Portugal to his domain in 1580. But beneath the pomp and splendor (so well captured by such painters as Velázquez and El Greco) the great empire was in trouble. The corruption of the Spanish court had much to do with this. So did the ever-increasing dependence of Spain on the gold and silver of its colonies, which tended to undermine the local Spanish economy. Even more important was the disruption of the Catholic Church throughout Europe by the Protestant Reformation.

THE PROTESTANT REFORMATION

The spiritual lethargy and bureaucratic corruption besetting the Roman Catholic Church in the early sixteenth century made it a fit target for reform. The thriving business in the sale of indulgences, payments that were supposed to win for departed loved ones forgiveness for their earthly sins and thus release from purgatory, was a public scandal. The luxurious lifestyle of the popes and the papal court in Rome was another. Yet there had been countless earlier religious reform movements that had led to little or no change. The fact that the movement launched by Martin Luther in 1517 and carried

▲ St. Peter's Basilica in the Vatican was built between 1506 and 1626. Catholic popes defended the magnificent church as a suitable expression of man's love for a God who had redeemed mankind. Protestant critics denounced St. Peter's as a form of idolatry that celebrated man's attainments rather than those of God. Puritans insisted that their houses of worship be simple and their altars plain.

forward by men like John Calvin addressed genuine shortcomings in the Roman Catholic Church does not entirely explain why it led so directly to the rupture of Christendom.

The charismatic leadership of Luther and the compelling brilliance of Calvin made their protests more effective than earlier efforts at reform. Probably more important, so did the political possibilities let loose by their challenge to Rome's spiritual authority. German princes seized on Luther's campaign against the sale of indulgences to stop all payments to Rome and to confiscate church property within their domains. Swiss cities like Geneva, where Calvin took up residence in 1536, and Zurich joined the Protestant revolt for spiritual reasons, but also to establish their political independence from Catholic kings. Francis I of France remained a Catholic, but he took advantage of Rome's troubles to secure control over the clergy of his kingdom. The efforts of Spain to suppress Protestantism in the Low Countries only further stimulated nationalist movements there, especially among the Dutch.

The decision of Henry VIII of England in 1534 to break with Rome was at bottom a political one. The refusal of Pope Clement VII to agree to an annulment of Henry's marriage of 20 years to Catherine of Aragon, the daughter of Ferdinand and Isabella, provided the occasion. Catherine had given birth to six children, but only a daughter, Mary, survived childhood; Henry was without a male heir. By repudiating the pope's spiritual authority and declaring himself head of the English (Anglican) church, Henry freed himself to divorce Catherine and to marry whomever—and however often—he saw fit. By the time of his death five wives and 13 years later, England had become a Protestant nation. More important for our story, the dominant character of the future English colonies in America had also been determined.

The growing political and religious conflict had economic overtones. Modern students have exploded the theory that the merchant classes were attracted to Protestantism because the Catholic Church, preaching outdated concepts like "just price" and frowning on the accumulation of wealth as an end in itself, stifled their acquisitiveness. Few merchants were more devoted to the quests for riches than the Italians, yet they remained loyal Catholics. So did the wool merchants of Flanders, among the most important in all Europe. Nonetheless, in some lands the business classes tended to support Protestant leaders, in part because the new sects, stressing simplicity, made fewer financial demands on the faithful than the Catholics did.

As the commercial classes rose to positions of influence, England, France, and the United Provinces of the Netherlands experienced a flowering of trade and industry. The Dutch built the largest merchant fleet in the world. Dutch traders captured most of the Far Eastern business once monopolized by the Portuguese, and they infiltrated Spain's Caribbean stronghold. A number of English merchant companies, soon to play a vital role as colonizers, sprang up in the last half of the sixteenth century. These joint-stock companies, ancestors of the modern corporation, enabled groups of investors to pool their capital and limit their individual responsibilities to the sums actually invested—a very important protection in such risky enterprises. The Muscovy Company, the Levant Company, and the East India Company were the most important of these ventures.

ENGLISH BEGINNINGS IN AMERICA

English merchants took part in many kinds of international activity. The Muscovy Company spent large sums searching for a passage to China around Scandinavia and dispatched six overland expeditions in an effort to reach East Asia by way of Russia and Persia. In the 1570s Martin Frobisher made three voyages across the Atlantic, hoping to discover a northwest passage to East Asia or new gold-bearing lands.

Such projects, particularly in the area of North America, received strong but concealed support from the Crown. Queen Elizabeth I (1558–1603) invested heavily in Frobisher's expeditions. England was still too weak to challenge Spain openly, but Elizabeth hoped to break the Spanish overseas monopoly just the same. She encouraged her boldest sea dogs to plunder Spanish merchant ships on the high seas. When Captain Francis Drake was about to set sail on his fabulous round-the-world voyage in 1577, the queen said to him: "Drake . . . I would gladly be revenged on the King of Spain for divers injuries that I have received." Drake took her at her word. He sailed through the Strait of Magellan and terrorized the west coast of South America, capturing the Spanish treasure ship *Cacafuego,* heavily laden with Peruvian silver. After exploring the coast of California, which he claimed for England, Drake crossed the Pacific and went on to circumnavigate the globe, returning home in triumph in 1580. Although Elizabeth took pains to deny it to the Spanish ambassador, Drake's voyage was officially sponsored. Elizabeth being the principal shareholder in the venture, most of the ill-gotten Spanish bullion went into the Royal Treasury rather than Drake's pocket.

When schemes to place settlers in the New World began to mature at about this time, the queen again became involved. The first English effort was led by Sir Humphrey Gilbert, an Oxford educated soldier and courtier. The queen authorized him to explore and colonize "heathen lands not actually possessed by any Christian prince."

We know almost nothing about Gilbert's first attempt except that it occurred in 1578 and 1579; in 1583 he set sail again with five ships and over 200 settlers. He landed them on Newfoundland, then evidently decided to seek a more congenial site farther south. However, no colony was established, and on his way back to England his ship went down in a storm off the Azores.

Gilbert's half-brother, Sir Walter Raleigh, took up the work. Handsome, ambitious, and impulsive, Raleigh was a great favorite of Elizabeth. He sent a number of expeditions to explore the east coast of North America, a land he named Virginia in honor of his unmarried sovereign. In 1585 he settled about a hundred men on Roanoke Island, off the North Carolina coast, but these settlers returned home the next year. In 1587 Raleigh sent another group to Roanoke, including a number of women and children. Unfortunately, the supply ships sent to the colony in 1588 failed to arrive; when help did get there in 1590, not a soul could be found. The fate of the settlers has never been determined.

▲ Elizabeth I, standing upon a map of England. This contemporary miniature (1592) might have struck viewers as ludicrous were it not for the fact that Queen Elizabeth was a consummate political strategist and formidable military foe. She built the fleet that destroyed the Spanish Armada in 1588.

One reason for the delay in getting aid to the Roanoke colonists was the attack of the Spanish Armada on England in 1588. Angered by English raids on his shipping and by the assistance Elizabeth was giving to the rebels in the Netherlands, King Philip II decided to invade England. His motives were religious as well as political and economic, for England now seemed committed to Protestantism. His great fleet of some 130 ships bore huge crosses on the sails as if on another crusade. The Armada carried 30,000 men and 2400 guns, the largest naval force ever assembled up to that time. However, the English fleet of 197 ships shattered this armada, and a series of storms completed its destruction. Thereafter, although the war continued and Spanish sea power remained formidable, Spain could no longer block English penetration of the New World.

Experience had shown that the cost of planting settlements in a wilderness 3000 miles from England was more than any individual purse could bear. (Raleigh lost about £40,000 in his overseas ventures; early in the game he began to advocate government support of colonization.) As early as 1584 Richard Hakluyt, England's foremost authority on the Americas and a talented propagandist for colonization, made a convincing case for royal aid. In his *Discourse on Western Planting,* Hakluyt stressed the military advantages of building "two or three strong fortes" along the Atlantic coast of North America. Ships operating from such bases would make life uncomfortable for "King Phillipe" by intercepting his treasure fleets—a matter, Hakluyt added coolly, "that toucheth him indeede to the quicke." Colonies in America would also spread the Protestant religion and enrich the parent country by expanding the market for English woolens, bringing in valuable tax revenues, and providing employment for the swarms of "lustie youthes that be turned to no provitable use" at home. From the great American forests would come the timber and naval stores needed to build a bigger navy and merchant marine.

Queen Elizabeth read Hakluyt's essay, but she was too cautious and too devious to act boldly on his suggestions. Only after her death in 1603 did full-scale efforts to found English colonies in America begin, and even then the organizing force came from merchant capitalists, not from the Crown.

THE SETTLEMENT OF VIRGINIA

In September 1605 two groups of English merchants petitioned the new king, James I, for a license to colonize Virginia, as the whole area claimed by England was then named. This was granted the following April, and two joint-stock companies were organized, one controlled by London merchants, the other by a group from the area around Plymouth and Bristol.[1] Both were under the control of a Royal Council for Virginia, but James appointed prominent stockholders to the council, which meant that the companies had considerable independence.

This first charter revealed the commercial motivation of both king and company in the plainest terms. Although it spoke of spreading Christianity and bringing "the Infidels and Savages, living in those Parts, to human Civility," it stressed the right "to dig, mine, and search for all Manner of Mines of Gold, Silver, and Copper." On December 20, 1606, the London Company dispatched about a hundred settlers aboard the *Susan Constant, Discovery,* and *Godspeed.* This little band reached the Chesapeake Bay area in May 1607 and founded Jamestown, the first permanent English colony in the New World.

From the start everything seemed to go wrong. The immigrants established themselves in what was a mosquito-infested swamp simply because it appeared easily defensible against Indian attack. They failed to get a crop in the ground because of the lateness of the season and were soon almost without food. Their leaders, mere deputies of the London merchants, did not respond to the challenges of the wilderness. The settlers lacked the skills pioneers need. More than a third of them were "gentlemen" unused to manual labor, and many of the rest were the gentlemen's servants, almost equally unequipped for the task of colony building. During the first winter more than half of the settlers died.

All the land belonged to the company, and aside from the gentlemen and their retainers, most of the settlers were only hired laborers who had contracted to work for it for seven years. This was unfortunate. The situation demanded people skilled in agriculture, and such a labor force was available. In England times were bad. The growth of the textile industry had led to an increased demand for wool, and great landowners were dismissing laborers and tenant farmers and shifting from labor-intensive agriculture to sheep-raising. Inflation, caused by a shortage of goods to supply the needs of a growing population and by the influx of large amounts of American silver into Europe, worsened the plight of the dispossessed. Many landless farmers were eager to migrate if offered a decent opportunity to obtain land and make new lives for themselves.

---

[1]The London Company was to colonize southern Virginia, while the Plymouth Company, the Plymouth-Bristol group of merchants, was granted northern Virginia.

The merchant directors of the London Company, knowing little or nothing about Virginia, failed to provide the colony with effective guidance. They set up a council of settlers, but they kept all real power in their own hands. Instead of stressing farming and public improvements, they directed the energies of the colonists into such futile labors as searching for gold (the first supply ship devoted precious space to two goldsmiths and two "refiners"), glassblowing, silk raising, winemaking, and exploring the local rivers in hopes of finding a water route to the Pacific and the riches of China.

One colonist, Captain John Smith, tried to stop some of this foolishness. Smith had come to Virginia after a fantastic career as a soldier of fortune in eastern Europe, where he had fought many battles, been enslaved by a Turkish pasha, and triumphed in a variety of adventures, military and amorous. He quickly realized that building houses and raising food were essential to survival, and he soon became an expert forager and Indian trader. Smith was as eager as any seventeenth-century European to take advantage of the Indians and he had few compunctions about the methods employed in doing so. But he recognized both the limits of the colonists' power and the vast differences between Indian customs and values and his own. It was necessary, he insisted, to dominate the "proud Savages" yet to avoid bloodshed.

DOCUMENT

John Smith, "The Starving Time"

Smith pleaded with company officials in London to send over more people accustomed to working with their hands, such as farmers, fishermen, carpenters, masons, "diggers up of trees," and fewer gentlemen and "Tuftaffety humorists."[2] "A plaine soldier who can use a pickaxe and a spade is better than five knights," he said.

Whether Smith was actually rescued from death at the hands of the Indians by the princess Pocahontas is not certain, but there is little doubt that without his direction, the colony would have perished in the early days. However, he stayed in Virginia only two years.

Lacking intelligent leaders and faced with appalling hardships, the Jamestown colonists failed to develop a sufficient sense of common purpose. Each year they died in wholesale lots from disease, starvation (there was even a case of cannibalism among the desperate survivors), Indian attack, and, above all, ignorance and folly. Between 1606 and 1622 the London Company invested more than £160,000 in Virginia and sent over about 6000 settlers. Yet no dividends were ever earned, and of the 6000, fewer

---

[2]Smith was referring to the gold tassels worn by titled students at Oxford and Cambridge at that time.

▲ This 1616 portrait depicts Pocahontas, daughter of Powhatan, the foremost chief of coastal Virginia. The colonists, in a dispute with Powhatan, took her hostage in 1613 and kept her in Jamestown. The next year she converted to Anglicanism, took the name "Lady Rebecca," and married John Rolfe, an alliance that helped defuse tensions between colonists and Indians. In 1616 the couple came to England with their infant son, where "Lady Rebecca" was received by King James I. She became celebrated as the "belle sauvage." She was the most prominent exemplar of those "intermediaries" who readily crossed the porous boundaries between colonist and Indian cultures.

than 2000 were still alive in 1622. In 1625 the population was down to about 1300. The only profits were those taken by certain shrewd investors who had organized a joint-stock company to transport women to Virginia "to be made wives" by the colonists.

One major problem, the mishandling of the local Indians, was largely the colonists' doing. It is quite likely that the settlement would not have survived if the Powhatan Indians had not given the colonists food in the first hard winters, taught them the ways of the forest, introduced them to valuable new crops such as corn and yams, and showed them how to clear dense timber by girdling the trees and burning them down after they were dead. The settlers accepted Indian aid, then took whatever else they wanted by force.

The Indians did not submit meekly to such treatment. They proved brave, skillful, and ferocious fighters once they understood that their very existence was at stake. The burden of Indian fighting might easily have been more than the frail settlement could bear.

What saved the white Virginians was not the brushing aside of the Indians but the gradual realization that they must produce their own food—cattle raising was especially important—and the cultivation of tobacco, which flourished there and could be sold profitably in England. Once the settlers discovered tobacco, no amount of company pressure could keep them at wasteful tasks like looking for gold. The "restraint of plantinge Tobacco," one company official commented, "is a thinge so distastefull to them that they will with no patience indure to heare of it."

John Rolfe, who is also famous for marrying Pocahontas, introduced West Indian tobacco—much milder than the local "weed" and thus more valuable—in 1612. With money earned from the sale of tobacco, the colonists could buy the manufactured articles they could not produce in a raw new country; this freed them from dependence on outside subsidies. It did not mean profit for the London Company, however, for by the time tobacco caught on, the surviving original colonists had served their seven years and were no longer hired hands. To attract more settlers, the company had permitted first tenancy and then outright ownership of farms. Thus the profits of tobacco went largely to the planters, not to the "adventurers" who had organized the colony.

Important administrative reforms helped Virginia to forge ahead. A revised charter in 1612 extended the London Company's control over its own affairs in Virginia. Despite serious intracompany rivalry between groups headed by Sir Thomas Smythe and Sir Edwin Sandys, a somewhat more intelligent direction of Virginia's affairs resulted. First, the merchants appointed a single resident governor and gave him sufficient authority to control the settlers. Then they made it much easier for settlers to obtain land of their own. In 1619 a rudimentary form of self-government was instituted: A House of Burgesses, consisting of delegates chosen in each district, met at Jamestown to advise the governor on local problems. The company was not bound by the actions of the burgesses, but from this seed sprang the system of representative government that became the American pattern.

These reforms, however, came too late to save the fortunes of the London Company. In 1619 the Sandys faction won control and started an extensive development program, but in 1622 a bloody Indian attack took the lives of 347 colonists. Morale sank, and James I, who disliked Sandys, decided that the colony was being badly managed. In 1624 the charter was revoked and Virginia became a royal colony, subject to direct control by the royal bureaucracy in London. As a financial proposition the company was a fiasco; the shareholders lost every penny they had invested. Nonetheless, by 1624 Virginia was firmly established and beginning to prosper.

"PURIFYING" THE CHURCH OF ENGLAND

Through all the social and political reshuffling that occurred in Virginia in its opening decades, the people, by and large, kept their eyes fixed on the main change. But although the prospect of a better material life brought most English settlers to America, for some, economic opportunity was not the only reason they abandoned what their contemporary William Shakespeare called "dear mother England." A profound unease with England's spiritual state—and therefore with their own while they remained there—explains why many colonists embarked on their "errand into the wilderness."

Despite the attempt of Henry VIII's older daughter, Queen Mary, to reinstate Catholicism during her brief reign (1553–1558), the Anglican Church became once and for all the official Church of England during the long reign of Elizabeth I (1558–1603). Like her father, Elizabeth took more interest in politics than in religion. So long as England had its own church, with her at its head, and with English rather than Latin as its official language, she was content. Aside from these changes, the Anglican Church under Elizabeth closely resembled the Catholic Church it had replaced.

This middle way satisfied most, but not all, of Elizabeth's subjects. Steadfast Catholics could not accept it. Some left England; the rest practiced their faith in private. At the other extreme, more radical Protestants, including a large percentage of England's university-trained clergy, insisted that Elizabeth had not gone far enough. The Anglican Church was still too much like the Church of Rome, they claimed. They objected to the richly decorated vestments worn by the clergy and to the use of candles, incense, and music in church services. They insisted that emphasis should be put on reading the Bible and analyzing the meaning of the Scriptures in order to encourage ordinary worshipers to truly understand their faith. Since they wanted to "purify" Anglicanism, these critics were called puritans. At first the name was a pejorative assigned to them by their opponents, but later it became a badge of honor.

Puritans objected to the way Elizabeth's bishops interpreted the Protestant doctrine of predestination. Their reading of the Book of Genesis convinced them that all human beings were properly damned by Adam's original sin and that what one did on earth had no effect on a person's fate after death. To believe otherwise was to limit God's power, which was precisely what the Catholic Church did in stressing its ability to forgive sins by granting indulgences. The Anglicans implied that while God had already decided whether or not a person was saved, an individual's efforts to lead a good life could somehow cause God to change His mind. The Anglican clergy did not come right out and say that good works could win a person admission to Heaven—that heresy was called Arminianism. But they encouraged people to hope that good works were something more than ends in themselves. Puritans differed as to whether or not the ideal church should have any structure beyond the local congregation. Some—later called Congregationalists—favored a completely decentralized arrangement, with the members of each church and their chosen minister beholden only to one another. Others, called Presbyterians, favored some organization above the local level, but one controlled by elected laymen, not by the clergy.

Puritans were also of two minds as to whether reform could be accomplished within the Anglican Church. During Elizabeth's reign most hoped that it could. Whatever they did in their local churches, the puritans remained professed Anglicans. After James I succeeded Elizabeth I in 1603, however, their fears that the royal court might be backsliding into its old "popish" ways mounted. James was married to a Catholic, and the fact that he favored toleration for Catholics gave further substance to the rumor that he was himself a secret member of that church. This rumor proved to be false, but in his 22-year reign (1603–1625) James did little to advance the Protestant cause. His one contribution—which had a significance far beyond what he or anyone else anticipated—was to authorize a new translation of the Bible. The King James Version (1611) was both a monumental scholarly achievement and a literary masterpiece of the first order.

BRADFORD AND PLYMOUTH COLONY

Plymouth Colony

In 1606, worried about the future of their faith, members of the church in Scrooby, Nottinghamshire, "separated" from the Anglican Church, declaring it corrupt beyond salvage. In seventeenth-century England, Separatists had to go either underground or into exile. Since only the latter would permit them to practice

▲ The story of the first 30 years of pilgrim life in Plymouth, Massachusetts, is preserved in Governor William Bradford's *Of Plymouth Plantation.* A glimpse of the first colony is shown in this reconstruction.

their religious faith openly, exile it was. In 1608 some 125 of the group departed England for the Low Countries. They were led by their pastor, John Robinson; church elder William Brewster; and a 16-year-old youth, William Bradford. After a brief stay in Amsterdam, the group settled in the town of Leyden. In 1619, however, disheartened by the difficulties they had encountered in making a living, disappointed by the failure of others in England to join them, and distressed because their children were being "subjected to the great licentiousness of the youth" in Holland, these "Pilgrims" decided to move again—to seek "a place where they might have liberty and live comfortably."

Negotiations between the Pilgrims in Leyden and Sir Edwin Sandys of the Virginia Company raised the possibility of America. Although unsympathetic to their religious views, Sandys appreciated the Pilgrims' inherent worth and supported their request to establish a settlement near the mouth of the Hudson River, on the northern boundary of the Virginia Company's grant. Since the Pilgrims were short of money, they formed a joint-stock company with other prospective emigrants and some optimistic investors who agreed to pay the expenses of the group in return for half the profits of the venture. In September 1620, about 100 strong—only 35 of them Pilgrims from Leyden—they set out from Plymouth, England, on the *Mayflower.*

▶ *text continues on page 36*

American Lives

Tisquantum

In March 1621 Samoset, an Algonquian Indian who spoke broken English, introduced the Pilgrims to a friend named Tisquantum, a member of the Patuxet tribe, which inhabited the area around Plymouth. He explained that Tisquantum "had been in England and could speak better English than himself." For this reason, the Pilgrims were delighted to make his acquaintance.

Tisquantum, whose name the Pilgrims soon shortened to Squanto, had up to this point lived a life that had been unusual to say the least. In 1605 George Waymouth, an English captain in the employ of Sir Ferdinando Gorges, an official of the Plymouth Company, brought Tisquantum and four other Indians from a region now part of Maine to Bristol, England, where he "delivered" Tisquantum and two of the others to Gorges. Gorges, who was eager to learn all he could about the New World, took Tisquantum "into his own house." In time all three of the Indians "acquired a sufficient command of the English tongue to communicate to him a knowledge of their country."

▲ Tisquantum

How long Tisquantum remained in Sir Ferdinando's household is unclear, but in 1614 when Gorges sent two ships commanded by Captain John Smith to New England to prepare to found a colony, Tisquantum went along as interpreter. However, after Smith returned to England, his second in command, Captain Thomas Hunt, kidnapped Tisquantum and a number of other Indians, took them to Malaga, Spain, and sold them as slaves.

Nothing is known of Tisquantum's life in Malaga except that after several years he escaped aboard a vessel sailing, perhaps by way of Newfoundland, for England. (It seems likely that because he could speak English, Tisquantum attracted the sympathy of one or more English sailors, who agreed to take him aboard when they left Malaga.) In London he was befriended by John Slany, the treasurer of the Newfoundland Company. Thereafter he made two trips to New England as a pilot, one in 1618 to an English settlement in Newfoundland, the other in 1619 to New England as a pilot on a vessel commanded by Captain Thomas Dermer. He left Dermer's ship somewhere on Cape Cod and made his way to Patuxet, only to discover that the Patuxet had been wiped out by a plague.

Tisquantum's first service to the Pilgrims was to act as interpreter at a dramatic meeting of the Pilgrim leaders with the most powerful chief of the region, the Wampanoag sachem, Massasoit. At this conference, after an elaborate exchange of gifts and speeches, a treaty of peace and mutual defense was negotiated. Tisquantum's services as interpreter were of inestimable value in reaching this agreement.

Thereafter, as Governor William Bradford explained in a famous passage in his history *Of Plymouth Plantation,* his value to the Pilgrims increased enormously. "Squanto," Bradford wrote, "was a special instrument sent of God for their good beyond their expectation. He directed them how to set their corn [and] where to take fish" to be used to fertilize the crop, a practice he almost certainly learned from English settlers in Newfoundland, since the Wampanoag were unfamiliar with the practice. "Squanto," Bradford added, "was also their pilot to bring them to unknown places for their profit, and never left them till he died."

That event occurred in November 1622, when Tisquantum contracted a fever while on a trading expedition with the Pilgrims on Cape Cod. According to Governor Bradford, his dying words were a request that Bradford "pray for him that he might go to the Englishmen's God in Heaven."

▲ The "deer" on the left side of the stream carry bows and arrows: the English engraver was impressed by the Indians' ability to disguise themselves as their prey. The acquisition of such skills helped the English survive in an unfamiliar environment. Europeans and colonists learned about the "new world" by reading pamphlets and books—such as the one in which this engraving appeared. Indians learned about the newcomers only from what they saw or heard by word of mouth. This left the Indians at a disadvantage.

Tisquantum's life in the brief months between his meeting the Pilgrims and his death was not, however, the idyll this passage suggests. Rather it illustrates an ambivalence common when the two cultures, European and Indian, coexist in the same person. As the historian James Phinney Baxter put it, Tisquantum's "mind has been enlarged beyond his fellows by contact with European civilization and a knowledge of the great world." This, in effect, made him an alien in both camps. At times he exaggerated his influence on the Pilgrims in an effort to "aggrandize himself in the estimation of the Indians." Bradford admitted that "Squanto . . . played his own game by putting the Indians in fear and drawing gifts from them to enrich himself."

Such behavior naturally caused the Indians to resent him. At one point Massasoit, citing terms of the treaty, demanded that the Pilgrims turn Tisquantum over to him for "punishment," clearly a euphemism for execution. Bradford

was able to avoid doing so, but the incident compelled Tisquantum "to stick close to the English," and goes a long way to explain why, in Bradford's above-quoted words, he "never left them till he died."

For their part the Pilgrims were sincerely thankful for the many services their "Squanto" provided. When the powerful Narragansett chief Corbitant was reported to have killed him, the Pilgrims sent 15 armed men to "cut off Corbitant's head," if the rumor proved true. (Fortunately it did not.) But the Pilgrims treated neither Tisquantum nor any other Indian as an equal. Despite their generally harmonious relations with the Wampanoag, they routinely referred to them as "savages." After his moving description of Squanto's death in his history, Bradford continued his account of the trading expedition with a routine summary of the goods collected—"about 26 or 28 hogs-heads of corn and beans. . . ."

Had the *Mayflower* reached the passengers' intended destination, the Pilgrims might have been soon forgotten. Instead their ship touched America slightly to the north, on Cape Cod Bay. Unwilling to remain longer at the mercy of storm-tossed December seas, they decided to settle where they were. Since they were outside the jurisdiction of the London Company, some members of the group claimed to be free of all governmental control. Therefore, before going ashore, the Pilgrims drew up the Mayflower Compact. "We whose names are underwritten," the Compact ran, "do by these Presents, solemnly and mutually in the presence of God and one another covenant and combine ourselves under into a civil Body Politick . . . and by Virtue hereof do enact . . . such just and equal laws . . . as shall be thought most meet and convenient for the general Good of the Colony."

Thus early in American history the idea was advanced that a society should be based on a set of rules chosen by its members, an idea carried further in the Declaration of Independence. The Pilgrims chose William Bradford as their first governor. In this simple manner, ordinary people created a government that they hoped would enable them to cope with the unknown wilderness confronting them.

DOCUMENT
Bradford, from
*History of
Plymouth
Plantation*

The story of the first 30 years of the Pilgrims' colony has been preserved in *Of Plymouth Plantation*, written by Bradford. Having landed on the bleak Massachusetts shore in December 1620 at a place they called Plymouth, the Pilgrims had to endure a winter of desperate hunger. About half of them died. But by great good luck there was an Indian in the area, named Squanto, who spoke English! In addition to serving as an interpreter, he showed them the best places to fish and what to plant and how to cultivate it. They, in turn, worked hard, got their crops in the ground in good time, and after a bountiful harvest the following November, they treated themselves and their Indian neighbors to the first Thanksgiving feast.

But if the Pilgrims had quickly secured themselves a safe place in the wilderness, what followed was hardly all cranberries and drumsticks. Bradford's flock grew neither rich nor numerous on the thin New England soil. In 1650 there were still fewer than a thousand settlers, most of them living beyond the reach of the original church. Among these were a few who tried to take advantage of the freedom from social control afforded by the wilderness. In 1628 a group led by one Thomas Morton, "Lord of Misrule" of the outlying community of Mount Wollaston, which he renamed Merrymount, declared their liberation from all restraints by setting up a maypole. They then invited neighboring

Indian women to join them, provided drinks all round, and began (as the disapproving Bradford described the doings) "dancing and frisking together like so many fairies." Troops were dispatched to break up the carousing and take Morton into custody, after which he was packed off to England.

Morton was not a Pilgrim, and his antics do not jeopardize the Pilgrims' place in American history. That place is one of honor. Theirs were victories won not with sword and gunpowder like those of Cortés or with bulldozer and dynamite like those of modern pioneers, but with simple courage and practical piety.

WINTHROP AND MASSACHUSETTS BAY COLONY

The Pilgrims were not the first English colonists to inhabit the northern regions. The Plymouth Company had settled a group on the Kennebec River in 1607. These colonists gave up after a few months, but fishermen and traders continued to visit the area, which was christened New England by Captain John Smith after an expedition there in 1614.

In 1620 the Plymouth Company was reorganized as the Council for New England, which had among its principal stockholders Sir Ferdinando Gorges and his friend John Mason, former governor of an English settlement on Newfoundland. Their particular domain included a considerable part of what is now Maine and New Hampshire. More interested in real estate deals than in colonizing, the council disposed of a number of tracts in the area north of Cape Cod. The most significant of these grants was a small one made to a group of puritans from Dorchester, who established a settlement at Salem in 1629.

Later that year these Dorchester puritans organized the Massachusetts Bay Company and obtained a royal grant to the area between the Charles and Merrimack rivers. The Massachusetts Bay Company was organized like any other commercial venture, but the puritans, acting with single-minded determination, made it a way of obtaining religious refuge in America.

Unlike the Separatists in Plymouth, most puritans had managed to satisfy both Crown and conscience while James I was king. The England of his son Charles I, who succeeded to the throne in 1625, posed a more serious challenge. Whereas James had been content to keep puritans at bay, Charles and his favorite Anglican cleric, William Laud, intended to bring them to heel. With the king's support, Laud proceeded to embellish the already elaborate Anglican ritual and to tighten the central control that the

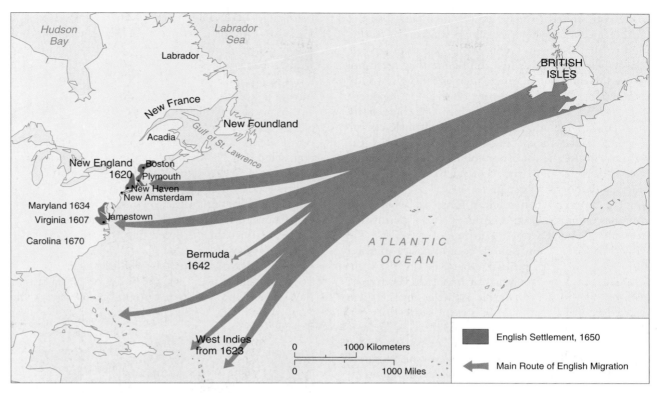

Labrador Sea

Hudson Bay

Labrador

New France

New Foundland

Acadia

Gulf of St. Lawrence

BRITISH ISLES

New England 1620

Boston

Plymouth

New Haven

New Amsterdam

Maryland 1634

Virginia 1607

Jamestown

Carolina 1670

Bermuda 1642

ATLANTIC OCEAN

West Indies from 1623

	English Settlement, 1650
	Main Route of English Migration

0   1000 Kilometers
0   1000 Miles

▲ **The Great English Migration**

puritans found so distasteful. He removed ministers with puritan leanings from their pulpits and threatened church elders who harbored such ministers with imprisonment.

No longer able to remain within the Anglican fold in good conscience and now facing prison if they tried to worship in the way they believed right, many puritans decided to migrate to America. In the summer of 1630 nearly a thousand of them set out from England, carrying the charter of the Massachusetts Bay Company with them. By fall, they had founded Boston and several other towns. The puritan commonwealth was under way.

Massachusetts settlers suffered fewer hardships in the early years than had the early Jamestown and Plymouth colonists. Luck played a part in this, but so did the careful planning that went into the transplantation. They also benefited from a constant influx of new recruits, who came with families and worldly possessions in tow. Continuing bad times and the persecution of puritans at home led to the Great Migration of the 1630s. Only a minority came to Massachusetts (many thousands more poured into new English colonies in the West Indies), but by 1640 well over 10,000 had arrived. This concentrated group of industrious, well-educated, and fairly prosperous colonists swiftly created a complex and distinct culture on the edge of what one of the pessimists among them called "a hideous and desolate wilderness, full of wild beasts and wild men."

The directors of the Massachusetts Bay Company believed their enterprise to be divinely inspired. Before leaving England, they elected John Winthrop, a 29-year-old Oxford-trained attorney, as governor of the colony. Throughout his 20 years of almost continuous service as governor, Winthrop spoke for the solid and sensible core of the puritans and their high-minded experiment. His lay sermon, "A Modelle of Christian Charity," delivered in mid-Atlantic on the deck of the *Arbella* in 1630, made clear his sense of the momentousness of that experiment:

DOCUMENT

Winthrop, "A Model of Christian Charity"

> Wee must Consider that wee shall be as a Citty upon a Hill, the eies of all people are upon us; soe that if wee shall deale falsely with our god in this worke wee have undertaken and soe cause him to withdrawe his present help from us, wee shall be made a story and a by-word through the world, wee shall open the mouthes of enemies to speake evill of the wayes of god and all professours for Gods sake.

The colonists created an elected legislature, the General Court. Their system was not democratic in the modern sense because the right to vote and hold office was limited to male church members, but this did not mean that the government was run by clergymen or that it was not sensitive to the popular will. Clergymen were influential, but since they were not allowed to hold public office, their authority was indirect and based on the respect of their parishioners, not on law or force. At least until the mid-1640s, most families included at least one adult male church member. Since these "freemen" soon secured the right to choose the governor and elect the representatives ("deputies") to the General Court, a kind of practical democracy existed.

The puritans had a clear sense of what their churches should be like. After getting permission from the General Court, a group of colonists who wished to form a new church could select a minister and conduct their spiritual affairs as they saw fit. Membership, however, was not open to everyone or even to all who led outwardly blameless lives. It was restricted to those who could present satisfactory evidence of their having experienced "saving grace," such as by a compelling recounting of some extraordinary emotional experience, some mystical sign of intimate contact with God. This meant that full membership in the churches of early Massachusetts was reserved for "visible saints." During the 1630s, however, few applicants were denied membership. Having removed oneself from England was considered in most cases sufficient proof of spiritual purity.

TROUBLEMAKERS: ROGER WILLIAMS AND ANNE HUTCHINSON

As Winthrop had on more than one occasion to lament, most of the colony's early troublemakers came not from those of doubtful spiritual condition but from its certified saints. The "godly and zealous" Roger Williams was a prime example. The Pilgrim leader William Bradford described Williams as possessed of "many precious parts, but very unsettled in judgment." Even by Plymouth's standards Williams was an extreme separatist. He was ready to bring down the wrath of Charles I on New England rather than accept the charters signed by him or his father, even if these documents provided the only legal basis for the governments of Plymouth and Massachusetts Bay.

Williams had arrived in Massachusetts in 1631. Following a short stay in Plymouth, he joined the church in Salem, which elected him minister in 1635. Well before then, however, his opposition to the alliance of church and civil government turned both ministers and magistrates against him. Part of his contrariness stemmed from his religious libertarianism. Magistrates should have no voice in spiritual matters,

he insisted—"forced religion stinks in God's nostrils." He also offended property owners (which meant nearly everyone) by advancing the radical idea that it was "a Nationale sinne" for anyone, including the king, to take possession of any American land without buying it from the Indians.

As long as Williams enjoyed the support of his Salem church, there was little the magistrates could do to silence him. But his refusal to heed those who counseled moderation—"all truths are not seasonable at all times," Governor Winthrop reminded him—swiftly eroded that support. In the fall of 1635, economic pressure put on the town of Salem by the General Court turned his congregation against him. The General Court then ordered him to leave the colony within six weeks.

Williams departed Massachusetts in January 1636, traveling south to the head of Narragansett Bay. There he worked out mutually acceptable

▲ On this headstone in a puritan graveyard in Salem, Massachusetts, two images preach a sermon. On top is an hourglass lying on its side: for the deceased, the "clock" of mortal existence has stopped. Below is a "death's head" atop wings to carry the soul to heaven. But every puritan who walked past this gravestone doubtless wondered whether God had indeed selected the deceased to be among His Saints.

arrangements with the local Indians and founded the town of Providence. In 1644, after obtaining a charter in England from Parliament, he established the colony of Rhode Island and Providence Plantations. The government was relatively democratic, all religions were tolerated, and church and state were rigidly separated. Whatever Williams's temperamental excesses, he was more than ready to practice what he preached when given the opportunity.

Anne Hutchinson, who arrived in Boston in 1631, was another "visible saint" who, in the judgment of the puritan establishment, went too far. Hutchinson was not to be taken lightly. According to Governor Winthrop, her husband William was "a man of mild temper and weak parts, wholly guided by his wife." (He was not so weak as to be unable to father Anne's 15 children.) Duties as a midwife brought her into the homes of other Boston women, with whom she discussed and more than occasionally criticized the sermons of their minister, John Wilson.

The issue in dispute was whether God's saints could be confident of having truly received His gift of eternal life. Wilson and most of the ministers of the colony thought not. God's saints should ceaselessly monitor their thoughts and behavior. But Hutchinson thought this emphasis on behavior was similar to the Catholic belief that an individual's good deeds and penitence could bring God's salvation. Ministers should not demean God, Hutchinson declared, by suggesting that He would be impressed by human actions. She insisted that God's saints knew who they were; those presumed "saints" who had doubts on the matter were likely destined for eternal hell instead.

Hutchinson suggested that those possessed of God's grace were exempt from the rules of good behavior and even from the laws of the commonwealth. As her detractors pointed out, this was the conclusion some of the earliest German Protestants had reached, for which they were judged guilty of the heresy of antinomianism ("against the law") and burned at the stake.

In 1636 the General Court charged Hutchinson with defaming the clergy and brought her to trial. When her accusers quoted the Bible ("Honor thy father and thy mother") to make their case, she coolly announced that even the Ten Commandments must yield to one's own insights if these were directly inspired by God. When pressed for details, she acknowledged that she was a regular recipient of divine insights, communicated, as they were to Abraham, "by the voice of His own spirit in my soul." The General Court, on hearing this claim, banished her.

Hutchinson, together with her large family and a group of supporters, left Massachusetts in the spring of 1637 for Rhode Island, thereby adding to the reputation of that colony as the "sink" of New England.

After her husband died in 1642, she and six of her children moved to the Dutch colony of New Netherland, where, the following year, she and all but her youngest daughter were killed by Indians.

The banishment of dissenters like Roger Williams and Anne Hutchinson did not endear the Massachusetts puritans to posterity. In both cases outspoken individualists seem to have been done in by frightened politicians and self-serving ministers. Yet Williams and Hutchinson posed genuine threats to the puritan community. Massachusetts was truly a social experiment. Could it accommodate such uncooperative spirits and remain intact? When forced to choose between the peace of the commonwealth and sending dissenters packing, Winthrop, the magistrates, and the ministers did not hesitate.

OTHER NEW ENGLAND COLONIES

From the successful Massachusetts Bay Colony, settlement radiated outward to other areas of New England, propelled by an expanding population and puritan intolerance. In 1629 Sir Ferdinando Gorges and John Mason divided their holdings, Gorges taking the Maine section (enlarged in 1639) and Mason, New Hampshire, but neither succeeded in making much of his claim. Massachusetts gradually took over these areas. The heirs of Gorges and Mason managed to regain legal possession briefly in the 1670s, but Massachusetts bought title to Maine for a pittance (£1250) in 1677. New Hampshire became a royal colony in 1680.

Meanwhile, beginning in 1635, a number of Massachusetts congregations had pushed southwestward into the fertile valley of the Connecticut River. A group headed by the Reverend Thomas Hooker founded Hartford in 1636. Hooker was influential in the drafting of the Fundamental Orders, a sort of constitution creating a government for the valley towns, in 1639. The Fundamental Orders resembled the Massachusetts system, except that they did not limit voting to church members. Other groups of puritans came directly from England to settle towns in and around New Haven in the 1630s. These were incorporated into Connecticut shortly after the Hooker colony obtained a royal charter in 1662.

FRENCH AND DUTCH SETTLEMENTS

While the English were settling Virginia and New England, other Europeans were challenging Spain's monopoly in the New World. French explorers had pushed up the St. Lawrence as far as the site of Montréal in the 1530s, and beginning in 1603, Samuel de

Champlain made several voyages to the region. In 1608 he founded Québec, and he had penetrated as far inland as Lake Huron before the Pilgrims left Leyden. The French also planted colonies in St. Christopher, Guadeloupe, Martinique, and other islands in the West Indies after 1625.

Through their West India Company, the Dutch also established themselves in the West Indies. On the mainland they founded New Netherland in the Hudson Valley, basing their claim to the region on the explorations of Henry Hudson in 1609. As early as 1624 they established an outpost, Fort Orange, on the site of present-day Albany. Two years later they founded New Amsterdam at the mouth of the Hudson River, and Peter Minuit, the director general of the West India Company, purchased Manhattan Island from the Indians for trading goods worth about 60 guilders.

The Dutch traded with the Indians for furs and plundered Spanish colonial commerce enthusiastically. Through the Charter of Privileges of Patroons, which authorized large grants of land to individuals who would bring over 50 settlers, they tried to encourage large-scale agriculture. Only one such estate—Rensselaerswyck, on the Hudson south of Fort Orange, owned by the rich Amsterdam merchant Kiliaen Van Rensselaer—was successful. Peter Minuit was removed from his post in New Amsterdam in 1631, but he organized a group of Swedish settlers several years later and founded the colony of New Sweden on the lower reaches of the Delaware River. New Sweden was in constant conflict with the Dutch, who finally overran it in 1655.

MARYLAND AND THE CAROLINAS

The Virginia and New England colonies were essentially corporate ventures. Most of the other English colonies in America were founded by individuals or by a handful of partners who obtained charters from the ruling sovereign. It was becoming easier to establish settlements in America, for experience had taught the English a great deal about the colonization process. Settlers knew better what to bring with them and what to do after they arrived. Moreover, the psychological barrier was much less formidable. Like a modern athlete seeking to run a mile in less than four minutes, colonizers knew after about 1630 that what they were attempting could be accomplished. And conditions in Europe in the mid-seventeenth century encouraged thousands to migrate. Both in England and on the Continent the economic future seemed unpromising, while political and religious persecution erupted in one country after another, each time supplying America with new waves of refugees.

▲ In this 1670 illustration by the court painter for King Charles II, young Cecilius Calvert receives a map of Maryland from his grandfather, the second Lord Baltimore. The king's charter for Maryland provided that Cecilius's father and his heirs (first, Cecilius) were to hold the province as "true and absolute lords." The notion was as preposterous as Cecilius's aristocratic clothing. Cecilius died in 1682, before he could even attempt to rule Maryland like a feudal lord.

Numbers of influential Englishmen were eager to try their luck as colonizers. The grants they received made them "proprietors" of great estates, which were, at least in theory, their personal property. By granting land to settlers in return for a small annual rent, they hoped to obtain a steadily increasing income while holding a valuable speculative interest in all undeveloped land. At the same time, their political power, guaranteed by charter, would become increasingly important as their colonies expanded. In practice, however, the realities of life in America limited their freedom of action and their profits.

One of the first proprietary colonies was Maryland, granted by Charles I to George Calvert, Lord Baltimore. Calvert had a deep interest in America, being a member both of the London Company and of the Council for New England. He hoped to profit financially from Maryland, but, since he was a Catholic, he also intended the colony to be a haven for his co-religionists.

Calvert died shortly before Charles approved his charter, so the grant went to his son Cecilius. The first settlers arrived in 1634, founding St. Mary's, just north of the Potomac. The presence of the now well-established Virginia colony nearby greatly aided the Marylanders; they had little difficulty in getting started and in developing an economy based, like Virginia's, on tobacco. According to the Maryland charter, Lord Baltimore had the right to establish feudal manors, hold people in serfdom, make laws, and set up his own courts. He soon discovered, however, that to attract settlers he had to allow them to own their farms and that to maintain any political influence at all he had to give the settlers considerable say in local affairs. Other wise concessions marked his handling of the religious question. He would have preferred an exclusively Catholic colony, but while Catholics did go to Maryland, there existed from the beginning a large Protestant majority. Baltimore dealt with this problem by agreeing to a Toleration Act (1649) that guaranteed freedom of religion to anyone "professing to believe in Jesus Christ." Though religious disputes persisted, the Calvert's compromise enabled them to make a fortune and maintain an influence in Maryland until the Revolution.

The Carolina charter, like that of Maryland, accorded the proprietors wide authority. With the help of the political philosopher John Locke, they drafted a grandiose plan of government called the Fundamental Constitutions, which created a hereditary nobility and provided for huge paper land grants to a hierarchy headed by the proprietors and lesser "landgraves" and "caciques." The human effort to support the feudal society was to be supplied by peasants (what the Fundamental Constitutions called "leet-men").

This complicated system proved unworkable. The landgraves and caciques got grants, but they could not find leet-men willing to toil on their domains. Probably the purpose of all this elaborate feudal nonsense was promotional; the proprietor hoped to convince investors that they could make fortunes in Carolina rivaling those of English lords. Life followed a more mundane pattern similar to what was going on in Virginia and Maryland, with property relatively easy to obtain.

The first settlers arrived in 1670, most of them from the sugar plantations of Barbados, where slave labor was driving out small independent farmers. Charles Town (now Charleston) was founded in 1680. Another center of population sprang up in the Albemarle district, just south of Virginia, settled largely by individuals from that colony. Two quite different societies grew up in these areas. The Charleston

▲ This 1651 engraving, the first known view of Manhattan Island, shows the fort of New Amsterdam in the 1620s. Indians bring beaver pelts in their canoes to trade with the Dutch.

▲ Historian James Merrell notes several errors in Benjamin West's famous 1771 painting, *William Penn's Treaty with the Indians.* In 1682, when the treaty was negotiated, Penn was not yet so fat; the colonists' clothing and brick buildings resemble a scene in Philadelphia in the 1750s, not the 1680s; and the Indians are implausibly posed like Greek and Roman statues. Most important, the painting includes no translator, the one indispensable figure in the proceedings. All Indian and settler exchanges required "go-betweens" or "negotiators" to help each group explain itself to the other.

colony, with an economy based on a thriving trade in furs and on the export of foodstuffs to the West Indies, was prosperous and cosmopolitan. The Albemarle settlement, where the soil was less fertile, was poorer and more primitive. Eventually, in 1712, the two were formally separated, becoming North and South Carolina.

THE MIDDLE COLONIES

Gradually it became clear that the English would dominate the entire coast between the St. Lawrence Valley and Florida. After 1660 only the Dutch challenged their monopoly. The two nations, once allies against Spain, had fallen out because of the fierce competition of their textile manufacturers and merchants.

England's efforts to bar Dutch merchant vessels from its colonial trade also brought the two countries into conflict in America. Charles II precipitated a showdown by granting his brother James, Duke of York, the entire area between Connecticut and Maryland. This was tantamount to declaring war. In 1664 English forces captured New Amsterdam without a fight—there were only 1500 people in the town—and soon the rest of the Dutch settlements capitulated. New Amsterdam became New York. The duke did not interfere much with the way of life of the Dutch settlers, and they were quickly reconciled to English rule. New York had no local assembly until the 1680s, but there had been no such body under the Dutch either.

In 1664, even before the capture of New Amsterdam, the Duke of York gave New Jersey, the region between the Hudson and the Delaware, to John,

Lord Berkeley, and Sir George Carteret. To attract settlers, these proprietors offered land on easy terms and established freedom of religion and a democratic system of local government. A considerable number of puritans from New England and Long Island moved to the new province.

In 1674 Berkeley sold his interest in New Jersey to two Quakers. Quakers believed that they could communicate directly with their Maker; their religion required neither ritual nor ministers. Originally a sect emotional to the point of fanaticism, by the 1670s the Quakers had come to stress the doctrine of the Inner Light—the direct, mystical experience of religious truth—which they believed possible for all persons. They were at once humble and fiercely proud, pacifistic yet unwilling to bow before any person or to surrender their right to worship as they pleased. They distrusted the intellect in religious matters and, while ardent proselytizers of their own beliefs, they tolerated those of others cheerfully. When faced with opposition, they resorted to passive resistance, a tactic that embroiled them in grave difficulties in England and in most of the American colonies. In Massachusetts Bay, for example, four Quakers were executed when they refused either to conform to puritan ideas or to leave the colony.

The acquisition of New Jersey gave the Quakers a place where they could practice their religion in peace. The proprietors, in keeping with their principles, drafted an extremely liberal constitution for the colony, the Concessions and Agreements of 1677, which created an autonomous legislature and guaranteed settlers freedom of conscience, the right of trial by jury, and other civil rights.

The main Quaker effort at colonization came in the region immediately west of New Jersey, a fertile area belonging to William Penn, the son of a wealthy English admiral. Penn had early rejected a life of ease and had become a Quaker missionary. As a result, he was twice jailed. Yet he possessed qualities that enabled him to hold the respect and friendship of people who found his religious ideas abhorrent. From his father, Penn had inherited a claim to £16,000 that the admiral had lent Charles II. The king, reluctant to part with that much cash, paid off the debt in 1681 by giving Penn the region north of Maryland and west of the Delaware River, insisting only that it be named Pennsylvania, in honor of the admiral. In 1682 Penn founded Philadelphia. The Duke of York then added Delaware, the region between Maryland and the Delaware Bay, to Penn's holdings.

William Penn considered his colony a "Holy Experiment." He treated the Indians fairly, buying title to their lands and trying to protect them in their dealings with settlers and traders. Anyone who believed in "one Almighty and Eternal God" was entitled to freedom of worship. Penn's political ideas were paternalistic rather than democratic; the assembly he established could only approve or reject laws proposed by the governor and council. But individual rights were as well protected in Pennsylvania as in New Jersey.

Penn's altruism, however, did not prevent him from taking excellent care of his own interests. He sold both large and small tracts of land to settlers on easy terms but reserved huge tracts for himself. He promoted Pennsylvania tirelessly, writing glowing, although perfectly honest, descriptions of the colony, which were circulated widely in England and, in translation, in Europe. These attracted many settlers, including large numbers of Germans—the Pennsylvania "Dutch" (a corruption of *Deutsch,* meaning "German").

William Penn was neither a doctrinaire nor an ivory tower philosopher. He came to Pennsylvania himself when trouble developed between settlers and his representatives and agreed to adjustments in his first Frame of Government when he realized that local conditions demonstrated the need for change. His combination of toughness, liberality, and good salesmanship helped the colony to prosper and grow rapidly. Of course the presence of well-settled colonies on all sides and the richness of the soil had much to do with this happy state of affairs. By 1685 there were almost 9000 settlers in Pennsylvania, and by 1700 twice that number, a heartening contrast to the early history of Virginia and Plymouth. Pennsylvania produced wheat, corn, rye, and other crops in abundance and found a ready market for its surpluses on the sugar plantations of the West Indies.

INDIANS AND EUROPEANS AS "AMERICANIZERS"

Increase Mather, a puritan leader, worried that "Christians in this Land have become too like unto the Indians." Little wonder, he observed, that God had "afflicted us by them" through disease and other trials. Yet Mather's comments suggested that interaction between European settlers and the native peoples was characteristic of life in all the colonies. *Interaction* is the key word in this sentence. The so-called Columbian Exchange between Indian and European was a two-way street. The colonists learned a great deal about how to live in the American forest from the Indians: the names of plants and animals (hickory, pecan, raccoon, skunk, moose); what to eat in their new home and how to catch or grow it; what to wear (leather leggings and especially moccasins);

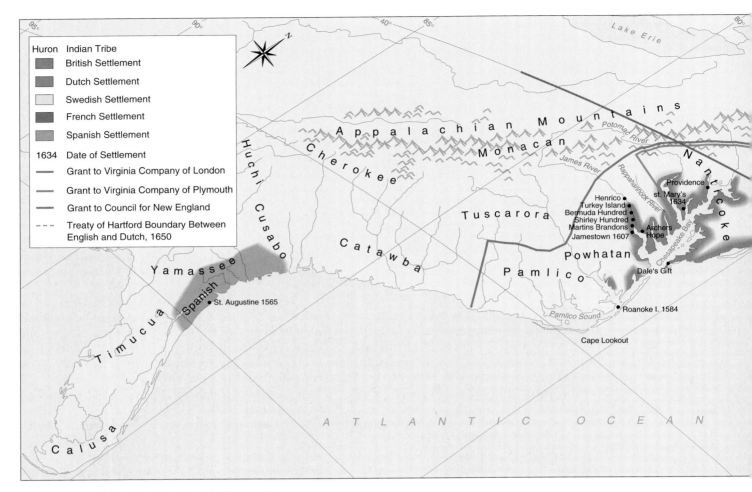

▲ European Footholds Along the Atlantic, 1584–1650

how best to get from one place to another; how to fight; and in some respects how to think.

The colonists learned from the Indians how best to use many plants and animals for food and clothing, but they would probably have discovered most of these if the continent had been devoid of human life when they arrived. Corn, however, the staple of the diet of agricultural tribes, was something the Indians had domesticated. Its contribution to the success of English colonization was enormous.

The colonists also took advantage of that marvel of Indian technology, the birchbark canoe. An early explorer, Martin Pring, brought one back to England in 1603; it was 17 feet long and 4 feet wide and capable, according to Pring, of carrying nine full-grown men. Yet it weighed "not at the most above sixtie pounds," a thing, Pring added, "almost incredible in regard to the largenesse and capacitie thereof."

For their part, the Indians adopted European technology eagerly. All metal objects were indeed of great usefulness to them, although the products and

tools that metals replaced were neither crude nor inefficient in most cases. (A bowman could get off six times as many shots in a given time as a seventeenth-century soldier armed with a firelock, and would probably hit the target more frequently.)

Indians took on many of the Europeans' attitudes along with their tools, clothing, weapons, alcohol, and ornaments. Some tribes used the products of European technology to tyrannize tribes in more remote areas. During wars, Indians fought almost as often with European settlers against other Indians as with other Indians against settlers.

The fur trade illustrates the pervasiveness of Indian-European interaction. It was in some ways a perfect business arrangement. Both groups profited greatly. The colonists got "valuable" furs for "cheap" European products, while the Indians got "priceless" tools, knives, and other trade goods in exchange for "cheap" beaver pelts and deerskins. The demand for furs caused the Indians to become more efficient hunters and trappers and even to

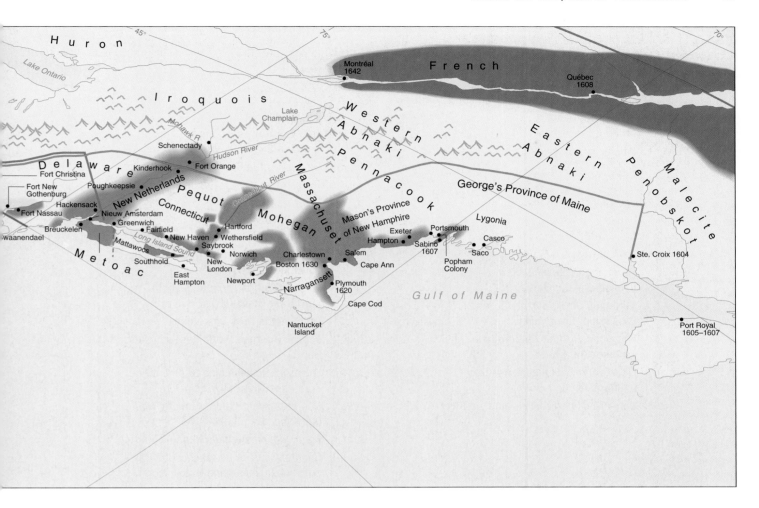

absorb some of the settlers' ideas about private property and capitalist accumulation. Hunting parties became larger. Farming tribes shifted their villages in order to be nearer trade routes and waterways. In some cases tribal organization was altered: small groups combined into confederations in order to control more territory when their hunting reduced the supplies of furs nearer home. Early in the seventeenth century, Huron Indians in the Great Lakes region, who had probably never seen a Frenchman, owned French products obtained from eastern tribes in exchange for Huron corn.

Although the colonists learned much from the Indians and adopted certain elements of Indian culture and technology eagerly, their objective was not to be like the Indians, whom they considered the epitome of savagery and barbarism. That they feared they might become "Indianized" is clear from the adage "It is very easy to make an Indian out of a white man, but you cannot make a white man out of an Indian." Yet this repudiation of the Indians was part of the collective identity of the settlers, part of what made them Americans rather than transplanted Europeans. The constant conflicts with Indians forced the colonists to band together and in time gave them a sense of having shared a common history. And later, when they broke away from Great Britain, they used the image of the Indian to symbolize the freedom and independence they sought for themselves.

In sum, during the first 200-odd years that followed Columbus's first landfall in the Caribbean, a complex development had taken place in the Americas. Sometimes these alien encounters were amiable, as Indians and colonists exchanged ideas, skills, and goods; sometimes the encounters were hostile and bloody, with unimaginable cruelties inflicted by and on both sides. But mostly the coming together of Indians and European settlers was characterized by ambiguity and confusion, as markedly different peoples drew from their own traditions to make sense of a new world that little resembled what they knew. In time, their world would become our own.

MILESTONES

EXPLORATION

c. 1000	Leif Eriksson reaches Newfoundland
1445–1488	Portuguese sailors explore west coast of Africa
1492	First voyage of Christopher Columbus
1497	John Cabot explores east coast of North America
1498	Vasco da Gama sails around Africa to India
1513	Ponce de Leon explores Florida
1519–1521	Hernán Cortes conquers Mexico
1519–1522	Ferdinand Magellan's crew circumnavigates globe
1539–1542	Hernando de Soto explores lower Mississippi River Valley
1540–1542	Francisco Vasquez de Coronado explores Southwest
1579	Francis Drake explores coast of California
1609	Henry Hudson discovers Hudson River

SETTLEMENT

1493	Columbus founds La Navidad, Hispaniola
1494	Treaty of Tordesillas divides New World between Spain and Portugal
1576	Spanish settle St. Augustine
1587	English found "Lost Colony" of Roanoke Island
1607	English settle Jamestown
1608	French found Québec
1612	John Rolfe introduces tobacco cultivation in Virginia
1620	Pilgrims settle Plymouth, sign Mayflower Compact
1624	Dutch settle New Amsterdam
1630	English puritans settle Massachusetts Bay
1630–1640	Waves of English come to America during the Great Migration
1634	George Calvert, Lord Baltimore, founds Maryland as Catholic haven
1636	Roger Williams founds Rhode Island
	General Court of Massachusetts Bay Colony banishes Anne Hutchinson
1639	Thomas Hooker founds Connecticut
1642	French found Montréal
1664	English conquer Dutch New Amsterdam
1670	First settlers arrive in Carolina
1680	Charles Town (now Charleston) is settled
1682	William Penn founds Philadelphia

SUPPLEMENTARY READING

On the explorers and the world they opened up, see Samuel E. Morison, *The European Discovery of America* (1971–1974). Morison's biography of Columbus, *Admiral of the Ocean Sea* (1942), is a classic; for a recent study see Miles Davidson, *Columbus Then and Now* (1997). David Stannard, *American Holocaust* (1992), and Kirkpatrick Sale, *The Conquest of Paradise* (1990), are highly critical of Columbus. The history of Spanish colonization in the Southwest is treated in David J. Weber, *The Spanish Frontier in North America* (1992) and, in the Southeast, in Paul E. Hoffman, *A New Andalucia and a Way to the Orient* (1991) and *Florida's Frontiers* (2002). The classic study is Charles Gibson, *Spain in America* (1966). For an imaginative attempt to reconstruct the Native American response,

see Ramon Guitierrez, *When Jesus Came, The Corn Mothers Went Away* (1991).

Accounts of the English background of colonization can be found in Nicholas Canny, ed., *The Oxford History of the British Empire: The Origins of Empire* (1998). On French colonization, see William J. Eccles, *The French in North America, 1500–1765* (1998), Carl J. Ekberg, *French Roots in the Illinois Country* (1998), and Carole Blackburn, *Harvest of Souls* (2000), which focuses on the Jesuit Missionaries.

Contemporary scholarship on Indian-colonist relations focuses on their interactions. Important studies in that vein include Richard White, *Indians, Empires and Republics in the Great Lakes Region, 1650–1815* (1991), James Merrell, *Into the American Woods: Negotiators on the Pennsylvania*

Frontier (1999), Jill Lepore, *Name of War: King Philip's War and the Origins of American Identity* (1999), and Karen Kupperman, *Indians and English: Facing Off in Early America* (2000).

The impact of the Europeans is discussed in the Debating the Past (p. 26). See also Alfred W. Crosby, *Ecological Imperialism: The Biological Expansion of Europe, 900–1900* (1993) and, though it deals with a later period, Robert Boyd, *The Coming of the Spirit of Pestilence: Introduced Infectious Diseases and Population Decline among Northwest Coast Indians* (1999). Joyce E. Chaplin, *Subject Matter: Technology, the Body, and Science on the Anglo-American Frontier, 1500–1676* (2001) argues that Europeans did not assume that they were racially superior until they saw how readily native peoples died of diseases.

For a general study of American slave trade, see David Eltis, *The Rise of African Slavery in the Americas* (2000). General surveys of slavery include Ira Berlin, *Many Thousands Gone* (1998), and Peter Kolchin, *American Slavery, 1619–1877* (1993).

On Virginia, see David H. Fischer and James C. Kelly, *Bound Away: Virginia and the Westward Movement* (2000), and Edmund S. Morgan, *American Slavery, American Freedom* (1975). Jack P. Greene, *Pursuits of Happiness* (1988), argues for the centrality of the Chesapeake in the formation of American identity. On Roanoke, see Ivor

Noel Hume, *The Virginia Adventure* (1994). See also Everett Emerson, *Captain John Smith* (1993). For Maryland, consult Gloria T. Main, *Tobacco Colony* (1982), and A. C. Land, *Colonial Maryland* (1981); for Carolina, see Roger Ekirch, *Poor Carolina* (1981).

For the middle colonies, see Michael Kammen, *Colonial New York* (1975) and Donna Merwick, *Possessing Albany, 1630–1710: The Dutch and English Experiences* (1990). In addition to Merrell, see Mary Geiter, *William Penn* (2000);

On New England, Edmund Morgan's *The Puritan Dilemma: The Story of John Winthrop* (1958), long a classic, has been superseded by Francis J. Bremer, *John Winthrop: America's Forgotten Founding Father* (2003). The dispute over Anne Hutchinson has been enlivened by Michael P. Winship, *Making Heretics: Militant Protestantism and Free Grace in Massachusetts, 1636–1641* (2002), who notes that few at the time accused Hutchinson of antinomianism; see also his *Anne Hutchinson* (2005). Louise A. Breen, *Transgressing the Bounds: Subversive Enterprises among the Puritan Elite in Massachusetts, 1630–1692* (2001) draws a connection between religious dissenters such as Hutchinson and economic entrepreneurship. For Rhode Island, see Edwin S. Gaustad, *Liberty of Conscience: Roger Williams in America* (1991). William Bradford's classic, *Of Plymouth Plantation,* is also well worth sampling.

SUGGESTED WEBSITES

Vikings in the New World

http://www.anthro.mankato.msus.edu/prehistory/vikings/vikhome.html

This site explores the history of some of the earliest European visitors to the Americas.

The Columbus Doors

http://xroads.virginia.edu/~cap/columbus/col1.html

On this University of Virginia Website, historians discuss the Columbus myth and how it has changed over time.

1492: An Ongoing Voyage

http://www.ibiblio.org/expo/1492.exhibit/Intro.html

An exhibit of the Library of Congress, Washington, D.C., that includes brief essays and images about early civilizations and contact in the Americas.

The Computerized Information Retrieval System on Columbus and the Age of Discovery

http://www.millersv.edu/~columbus/

The History Department and Academic Computing Services of Millersville University, Pennsylvania, provide this text retrieval system containing more than 1000 articles from various magazines, journals, newspapers, speeches, official calendars, and other sources relating to various encounter themes.

Interacting with Native Americans in New Hampshire

http://seacoastnh.com/history/contact/index.html

This brief history of contact era New Hampshire has interesting links and gives a good picture of the earliest contacts.

The Discoverers' Web

http://www.win.tue.nl/cs/fm/engels/discovery/

Andre Engels offers information on the various exploration efforts.

The Plymouth Colony Archives Project at the University of Virginia

http://www.people.virginia.edu/~jfd3a/

This site contains extensive information about late seventeenth-century Plymouth colony.

Jamestown Rediscovery

http://www.apva.org/

This site, mounted by the Association for the Preservation of Virginia Antiquity, has excellent material on archaeological excavations at Jamestown.

Jamestown

http://www.nps.gov/colo/

This National Park Service site has information on Jamestown and other important colonial historical sites.

Williamsburg

http://www.history.org/

This commercial site explores colonial Williamsburg, Virginia.

William Penn, Visionary Proprietor

http://xroads.virginia.edu/~CAP/PENN/pnhome.html

William Penn had an interesting life, and this University site is a good introduction to the man and some of his achievements.

CHAPTER 7

American Society in the Making

CHAPTER CONTENTS

▼ *The Fishing Lady,* a needlepoint depicting the "genteel culture" of the colonial elite. Gentility entailed good posture, delicate detail, and refined conversation. Nature was tamed, as evidenced by the ordered landscape, the frolicking animals, and the accommodating fish.

The colonies were settled chiefly by English people at first, with a leavening of Germans, Scots, Scots-Irish, Dutch, French, Swedes, Finns, a scattering of other nationalities, a handful of Sephardic Jews, and a gradually increasing number of black African slaves. The cultures these people brought with them varied according to the nationality, social status, and taste of the individual. The newcomers never lost this heritage entirely, but they—and certainly their descendants—became something quite different from their relatives who remained in the Old World. They became what we call Americans.

But not right away.

WHAT IS AN AMERICAN?

Why did America become something different from Europe? Why was New England not merely a new England, the struggling Spanish outpost at Santa Fe not a miniature Cadíz or Córdoba? If not just another "poor European immigrant" away from home, a French settler, Hector St. John de Crèvecoeur, wondered in 1762, "what then is the American, this new man?" And how did he—and she—come to be?

The fact of physical separation provides an important part of the answer. America was isolated from Europe by 3000 miles of ocean, or, as a poet put it, by "nine hundred leagues of roaring seas." The crossing took anywhere from a few weeks to several months, depending on wind and weather. No one undertook an ocean voyage lightly, and few who made the westward crossing ever thought seriously of returning. The modern mind can scarcely grasp the awful isolation that enveloped all the settlers. Each had to construct a new life or perish—if not of hunger, then of loneliness.

More than physical separation went into the process by which the colonists fashioned for themselves a new national identity and the outlines of a distinctive civilization. Varying conditions affected some settlers differently than others. Factors as material as the landscape encountered, as quantifiable as population patterns, as elusive as chance and calculation all shaped colonial social arrangements. Their cumulative impact did not at first produce anything like a uniform society. The "Americans" who evolved in what is now the United States were in many ways as different from each other as all were from their foreign cousins. The process by which these identities merged into an American nation remained incomplete. It was—and is—ongoing.

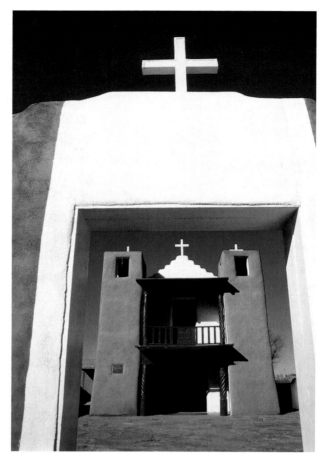

▲ In building mission churches, Spanish Franciscan friars exploited Indian materials to achieve precise symmetry, like the cross at the apex of their faith. The towers resembled those of the great churches of Spain.

SPANISH SETTLEMENT

Life in Spanish North America was shaped principally by Franciscan friars who, backed by soldiers and the financial support of kings Philip IV and Charles II, established strings of mission settlements among the Pueblo Indians of the upper reaches of the Rio Grande and among the tribes of northern Florida and the coastal regions of present-day Georgia and South Carolina. The actual construction of the missions was the work of local Indians, whom the friars intended to convert to Christianity in order to free them, as one priest put it, "from the obscure darkness of their idolatry."

The friars were for the most part dedicated men. Thousands of mission Indians were baptized and instructed in the rudiments of the Catholic faith. They were also taught to use European tools, to grow wheat and other European crops, and to raise chickens and pigs and other barnyard animals. But being

dedicated to their holy task, the friars paid little heed to how their activities undermined the Indians' traditional way of life.

The friars also exacted a heavy price in labor from the people they presumed to enlighten and civilize. The Indians built and maintained the missions, tilled the surrounding fields, and served the every need of the friars and other Spanish colonists. For this they were paid and fed little or nothing.

During the seventeenth century this kind of treatment led to rebellions in many of the missions in New Mexico and Florida, rebellions that, being isolated during most of the period, were easily repressed. In 1680, however, the Pueblo Indians came together under a religious leader named Popé. They caught the Spaniards entirely by surprise, killing some 400 of them. They then razed the town of Santa Fe and drove the surviving mission Spaniards all the way back to El Paso.

DOCUMENT

Legal statement by Pedro Hidalgo, soldier, Santa Fe 1680

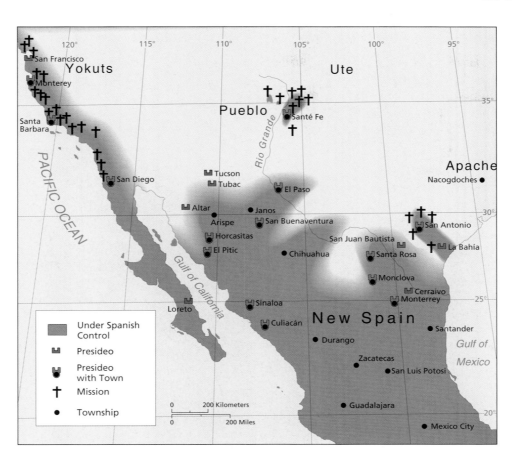

◀ **Spain's North American Frontier, c. 1800**

In the mid-1690s the Spaniards regained control of most of the upper Rio Grande and thereafter maintained control without difficulty. There were no more rebellions, partly because the Spaniards had learned to deal less harshly with the Pueblo people and partly because of their common need to repel attacks by the Ute, the Apache, and other Indian tribes.

The mission settlements in Florida were also badly battered in the last decades of the century, partly by mistreated Indians, partly by English colonists from Carolina. Many of the mission converts were enslaved by the Carolinians and shipped off to Barbados and other English colonies.

THE CHESAPEAKE COLONIES

The southern parts of English North America comprised three regions: the Chesapeake Bay, consisting of "tidewater" Virginia and Maryland; the "low country" of the Carolinas (and eventually Georgia); and the "back country," a vast territory that extended from the "fall line" in the foothills of the Appalachians, where falls and rapids put an end to navigation on the tidal rivers, to the farthest point of western settlement. Not until well into the eighteenth century

would the emergence of common features—export-oriented agricultural economies, a labor force in which black slaves figured prominently, the absence of towns of any size—prompt people to think of the "South" as a single region. When the English philosopher Thomas Hobbes wrote in 1651 that human life tended to be "nasty, brutish, and short," he might well have had in mind the royal colony of Virginia. Although the colony grew from about 1300 to nearly 5000 in the decade after the Crown took it over in 1624, the death rate remained appalling. Since more than 9000 immigrants had entered the colony, nearly half the population died during that decade.

The climate helped make the Chesapeake area a death trap. "Hot and moist" is how Robert Beverly described the weather in *The History and Present State of Virginia* (1705), the dampness "occasioned by the abundance of low grounds, marshes, creeks, and rivers." Almost without exception newcomers underwent "seasoning," a period of illness that in its mildest form consisted of "two or three fits of a feaver and ague." Actually the relatively dry summers were the chief cause of the high death rate. During the summer the slower flow of the James River allowed relatively dense salt water to penetrate inland. This blocked the flow of polluted river water, which the colonists drank.

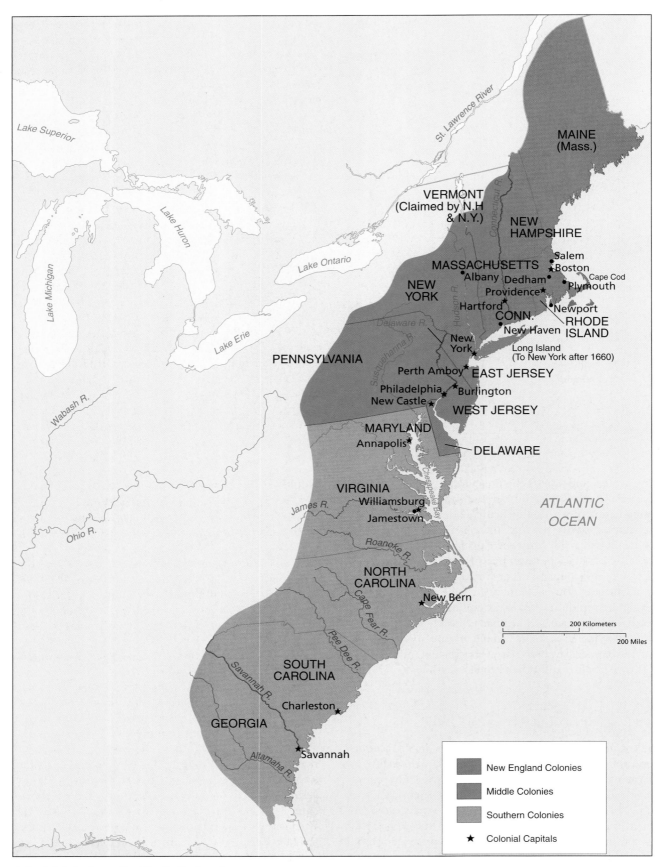

▲ **English Colonies on the Atlantic Seaboard**

The result was dysentery, the "bloody flux." If they survived the flux, and a great many did not, settlers still ran the seasonal risk of contracting a particularly virulent strain of malaria, which, though seldom fatal in itself, could so debilitate its victims that they often died of typhoid fever and other ailments.

Long after food shortages and Indian warfare had ceased to be serious problems, life in the Chesapeake remained precarious. Well into the 1700s a white male of 20 in Middlesex County, Virginia, could look forward only to about 25 more years of life. Across Chesapeake Bay, in Charles County, Maryland, life expectancy was even lower. The high death rate had important effects on family structure. Because relatively few people lived beyond their forties, more often than not children lost at least one of their parents before they reached maturity and in many instances both. Remarriage was a way of life. Apparently this situation did not cause drastic emotional problems for most people of the region. Men provided generously for their families in their wills, despite knowing that their wives would probably remarry quickly. The effects on children of the deaths of their parents are hard to gauge but apparently were not often psychologically damaging, no doubt because they were so common and because, with the acute shortage of labor, someone could always be found to take in and care for an orphan. Being brought up entirely by stepparents was so common that children tended to accept it almost as a matter of course.

Because of the persistent shortage of women in the Chesapeake region (men outnumbered women by three to two even in the early 1700s), widows easily found new husbands. Many men spent their entire lives alone or in the company of other men. Others married Indian women and became part of Indian society.

All Chesapeake settlers felt the psychological effects of their precarious and frustrating existence. Random mayhem and calculated violence posed a continuous threat to life and limb. Life was coarse at best and often as "brutish" as Hobbes had claimed, even allowing for the difficulties involved in carving out a community in the wilderness.

THE LURE OF LAND

Agriculture was the bulwark of life for the Chesapeake settlers and the rest of the colonial South; the tragic experiences of the Jamestown settlement revealed this quickly enough. Jamestown also suggested that a colony could not succeed unless its inhabitants were allowed to own their own land. The first colonists, it will be recalled, had agreed to work for seven years in return for a share of the profits. When their contracts expired there were few profits. To satisfy these settlers and to attract new capital, the London Company declared a "dividend" of land, its only asset. The surviving colonists each received 100 acres. Thereafter, as prospects continued poor, the company relied more and more on grants of land to attract both capital and labor. A number of wealthy Englishmen were given immense tracts, some running to several hundred thousand acres. Lesser persons willing to settle in Virginia received more modest grants. Whether dangled before a great tycoon, a country squire, or a poor farmer, the offer of land had the effect of encouraging immigration to the colony. This was a much-desired end, for without the labor to develop it the land was worthless.

Soon what was known as the headright system became entrenched in both Virginia and Maryland. Behind the system lay the eminently sound principle that land should be parceled out according to the availability of labor to cultivate it. For each "head" entering the colony authorities issued a "right" to take any 50 acres of unoccupied land. To "seat" a claim and receive title to the property, the holder of the headright had to mark out its boundaries, plant a crop, and construct some sort of habitation. This system was adopted in all the southern colonies and in Pennsylvania and New Jersey.

The first headrights were issued with no strings attached, but generally the grantor demanded a small annual payment called a quitrent. A quitrent was actually a tax, perhaps a shilling for 50 acres, which provided a way for the proprietors to derive incomes from their colonies. Quitrents were usually resented and difficult to collect.

The headright system encouraged landless Europeans to migrate to America. More often than not, however, those most eager to come could not afford passage across the Atlantic. To bring such people to America, the indentured servant system was developed. Indenture resembled apprenticeship. In return for transportation indentured servants agreed to work for a stated period, usually about five years. During that time they were subject to strict control by the master and received no compensation beyond their keep. Indentured women were forbidden to marry and if they became pregnant (as many did in a land where men outnumbered women by seven to one) the time lost from work that resulted was added to their terms of service.

DOCUMENT

Wessell Webling, His Indenture, 1622

Servants lacked any incentive to work hard, whereas masters tended to "abuse their servantes . . . with intollerable oppression." In this clash of wills the advantage lay with the master; servants lacked full political and civil rights, and masters could administer physical punishment and otherwise abuse them. An indenture, however, was a contract; servants could and did sue when planters failed to fulfill their parts of the bargain, and surviving court records suggest that they fared reasonably well when they did so.

Servants who completed their years of labor became free. Usually the former servant was entitled to an "outfit" (a suit of clothes, some farm tools, seed, and perhaps a gun). Custom varied from colony to colony. In the Carolinas and in Pennsylvania, for example, servants also received small grants of land from the colony when their service was completed.

The headrights issued when indentured servants entered the colonies went to whoever paid their passage, not to the servants. Thus the system gave a double reward to capital—land and labor for the price of the labor alone. Since well over half of the white settlers of the southern colonies came as indentured servants, the effect on the structure of southern society was enormous.

Most servants eventually became landowners, but with the passage of time their lot became harder. The best land belonged to the large planters, and low tobacco prices and high local taxes combined to keep many former servants in dire poverty. Some were forced to become "squatters" on land along the fringes of settlement that no one had yet claimed. Squatting often led to trouble; eventually, when someone turned up with a legal title to the land, the squatters demanded "squatters' rights," the privilege of buying the land from the legal owner without paying for the improvements they had made upon it. This led to lawsuits and sometimes to violence.

In the 1670s conflicts between Virginians who owned choice land and former servants on the outer edge of settlement brought the colony to the brink of class warfare. The costs of meeting the region's ever-growing need for labor with indentured servants were becoming prohibitive. Some other solution was needed.

"Solving" the Labor Shortage: Slavery

Probably the first African blacks brought to English North America arrived on a Dutch ship and were sold at Jamestown in 1619. Early records are vague and incomplete, so it is not possible to say whether these Africans were treated as slaves or freed after a period of years like indentured servants. What is certain is that by about 1640 *some* blacks were slaves (a few, with equal certainty, were free) and that by the 1660s local statutes had firmly established the institution in Virginia and Maryland.

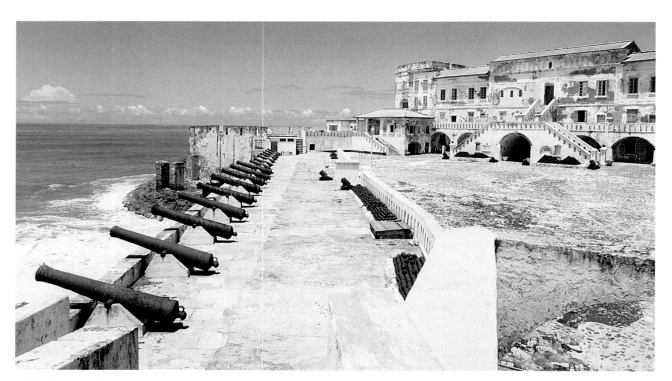

▲ The Cape Coast Castle, on the slave coast of West Africa, looking out on the Atlantic Ocean. One of a dozen such forts operated by Britain, Spain, or the Netherlands, this castle held hundreds of African captives. Captains of slaving ships paid about 6 ounces of gold or 200 gallons of rum for each slave. The price was lower if the captains wanted to deal directly with African chieftains, but this required long, dangerous trips inland.

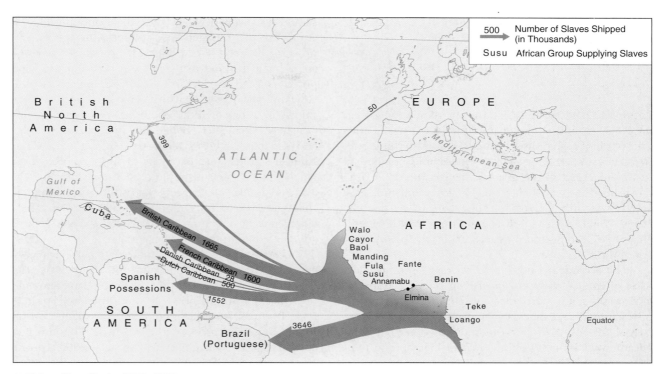

▲ **African Slave Trade, 1451–1870**

Whether slavery produced race prejudice in America or prejudice led to slavery is a hotly debated, important, and difficult-to-answer question. Most seventeenth-century Europeans were prejudiced against Africans; the usual reasons that led them to look down on "heathens" with customs other than their own were in the case of Africans greatly reinforced by the latter's blackness, which the English equated with dirt, the Devil, danger, and death. "Black is the Colour of Night, Frightful, Dark and Horrid," a popular disquisition of 1704 proclaimed. Yet the English knew that the Portuguese and Spaniards had enslaved blacks—*negro* is Spanish for black. Since the English adopted the word as a name for Africans, their treatment of Africans in the New World may also have derived from the Spanish, which suggests that they treated the first blacks in their colonies as slaves from the start. Prejudice and existing enslavement interacted with each other as both cause and effect. Slavery soon spread throughout the colonies. As early as 1626 there were 11 slaves in New Netherland, and when the English conquered that colony in 1664 there were 700 slaves in a population of about 8000. The Massachusetts Body of Liberties of 1641—strange title—provided that "there shall never be any bond-slavery . . . amongst us; unlesse it be lawful captives taken in just warrs [*i.e.*, Indians] and such strangers as willingly sell themselves, or *are solde* to us." However, relatively few blacks were imported until late in the seventeenth century, even in the southern colonies. In 1650 there were only 300 blacks in Virginia and as late as 1670 no more than 2000.

White servants were much more highly prized. The African, after all, was almost entirely alien to both the European and the American ways of life. In a country starved for capital, the cost of slaves—roughly five times that of indentured servants—was another disadvantage. In 1664 the governor of Maryland informed Lord Baltimore that local planters would use more "neigros" "if our purses would endure it." For these reasons, so long as white servants could be had in sufficient numbers, there were few slaves in the Chesapeake, and those that were generally worked alongside white servants and shared roughly the same food, clothing, and quarters.

In the 1670s the flow of indentured servants slackened, the result of improving economic conditions in England and the competition of other colonies for servants. At the same time, the formation of the Royal African Company (1672) made slaves more readily available. Then in 1689 a war in Europe cut off a principal market for tobacco, causing the price to fall and thus making migration to the colonies less attractive. The indenture system began to give way to slavery as the "permanent" solution to the southern colonies' chronic need for labor. An additional inducement causing planters and politicians to switch was the recognition that, unlike white servants, black slaves (and their offspring) would be forever barred from competing with whites for land or political power. By 1700, nearly 30,000 slaves lived in the English colonies.

PROSPERITY IN A PIPE: TOBACCO

Labor and land made agriculture possible, but it was necessary to find a market for American crops in the Old World if the colonists were to enjoy anything but the crudest sort of existence. They could not begin to manufacture all the articles they required; to obtain from England such items as plows and muskets and books and chinaware, they had to have cash crops, what their English creditors called "merchantable commodities." Here, at least, fortune favored the Chesapeake.

The founders of Virginia tried to produce all sorts of things that were needed in the old country: grapes and silk in particular, indigo, cotton, oranges, olives, sugar, and many other plants. But it was tobacco, unwanted, even strongly opposed at first, that became for farmers on both sides of Chesapeake Bay "their darling."

Tobacco was unknown in Europe until Spanish explorers brought it back from the West Indies. It was not common in England until the time of Sir Walter Raleigh. Then it quickly proved irresistible to

thousands of devotees. At first the London Company discouraged its colonists from growing tobacco. Since it clearly contained some habit-forming drug, many people opposed its use. King James I wrote a pamphlet attacking the weed, in which, among other things, he anticipated the findings of modern cancer researchers by saying that smoking was a "vile and stinking" habit "dangerous to the Lungs." But English smokers and partakers of snuff ignored their king, and the Virginians ignored their company. By 1617 a pound of tobacco was worth more than 5 shillings in London. Company and Crown then changed their tune, granting the colonists a monopoly and encouraging them in every way.

DOCUMENT

James I, "A Counterblaste to Tobacco"

Unlike wheat, which required expensive plows and oxen to clear the land and prepare the soil, tobacco plants could be set on semicleared land and cultivated with a simple hoe. Although tobacco required lots of human labor, a single laborer working two or three acres could produce as much as 1200 pounds of cured tobacco, which, in a good year, yielded a profit of more than 200 percent. This being the case, production in America leaped from 2500 pounds in 1616 to nearly 30 million pounds in the late seventeenth century, or roughly 400 pounds of tobacco for every man, woman, and child in the Chesapeake colonies.

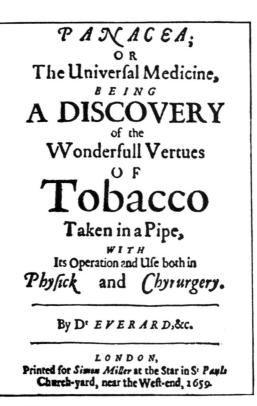

▲ Tobacco companies advertised their product as far back as the seventeenth century. This 1659 advertisement lauds tobacco as a medical "panacea."

The tidewater region was blessed with many navigable rivers and the planters spread along their banks, giving the Chesapeake a shabby, helter-skelter character of rough habitations and growing tobacco, mostly planted in stump-littered fields, surrounded by fallow land and thickets interspersed with dense forest. There were no towns and almost no roads. English ships made their way up the rivers from farm to farm, gathering the tobacco at each planter's wharf. The vessels also served as general stores of a sort where planters could exchange tobacco for everything from cloth, shoes, tools, salt, and nails to such exotic items as tea, coffee, chocolate, and spices.

However, the tremendous increase in the production of tobacco caused the price to plummet in the late seventeenth century. This did not stop the expansion of the colonies, but it did alter the structure of their society. Small farmers found it more difficult to make a decent living. At the same time men with capital and individuals with political influence were amassing large tracts of land. If well managed, a big plantation gave its owner important competitive advantages over the small farmer. Tobacco was notorious for the speed with which it exhausted the fertility of the soil. Growers with a lot of land could shift frequently to new fields within their holdings, allowing the old fields to lie fallow and thus maintain high yields, but the only option that small farmers had when their land gave out was to move to unsettled land on the frontier. To do that in the 1670s was to risk trouble with properly indignant Indians. It might also violate colonial laws designed to slow westward migration and limit tobacco production. Neither was about to stop settlement.

Bacon's Rebellion

Chesapeake settlers showed little respect for constituted authority, partly because most people lived on isolated plantations and partly because the London authorities were usually ignorant of their needs. The first Virginians often ignored directives of the London Company, while early Marylanders regularly disputed the right of the Calverts' agents to direct the affairs of the proprietorship. The most serious challenge took place in Virginia in 1676. Planters in the outlying counties heartily disliked the officials in Jamestown who ran the colony. The royal governor, Sir William Berkeley, and his "Green Spring" faction (the organization took its name from the governor's plantation) had ruled Virginia for more than 30 years. Outsiders resented the way Berkeley and his henchmen used their offices to line their pockets. They also resented their social pretensions, for Green Springers made no effort to conceal their opinion, which had considerable basis in fact, that western planters were a crude and vulgar lot.

▲ Sir William Berkeley looks every inch the autocrat in this portrait, a copy of one painted by Sir Peter Lely. After Bacon's death, Berkeley took his revenge and had 23 rebels hanged. Said King Charles II: "The old fool has killed more people in that naked country than I have done for the murder of my father."

Early in 1676 planters on the western edge of settlement, always looking for excuses to grab land by doing away with the Indians who owned it, asked Berkeley to authorize an expedition against Indians who had been attacking nearby plantations. Berkeley refused. The planters then took matters into their own hands. Their leader, Nathaniel Bacon, was (and remains today) a controversial figure. His foes described him as extremely ambitious and possessed "of a most imperious and dangerous hidden Pride of heart." But even his sharpest critics conceded that he was "of an inviting aspect and powerful elocution" and well qualified "to lead a giddy and unthinking multitude."

When Berkeley refused to authorize him to attack the Indians, Bacon promptly showed himself only too willing to lead that multitude not only against Indians but against the governor. Without permission he raised an army of 500 men, described by the Berkeley faction as "rabble of the basest sort." Berkeley then declared him a traitor.

Several months of confusion followed. Bacon murdered some peaceful Indians, marched on Jamestown and forced Berkeley to legitimize his authority, then headed west again to kill more Indians. In September he returned to Jamestown and burned it to the ground. Berkeley fled across Chesapeake Bay to the Eastern Shore. The Baconites plundered the estates of some of the Green Spring faction. But a few weeks later, Bacon came down with a "violent flux"—probably it was a bad case of dysentery—and he died. Soon thereafter an English naval squadron arrived with enough soldiers to restore order. Bacon's Rebellion came to an end.

On the surface, the uprising changed nothing. No sudden shift in political power occurred. Indeed, Bacon had not sought to change either the political system or the social and economic structure of the colony. But if the *rebellion* did not change anything, nothing was ever again quite the same after it ended. With seeming impartiality, the Baconites had warred against Indians and against other planters. But which was the real enemy? Surely the Baconite and Green Springer factions had no differences that could not be compromised. And their common interest extended beyond the question of how to deal with Indians. Both wanted cheap labor.

In the quarter-century following Bacon's Rebellion the Chesapeake region thus became committed to black slavery. And slave ownership resulted in large differences in the wealth and lifestyles of growers of tobacco. The few who succeeded in accumulating 20 or more slaves and enough land to keep them occupied grew richer. The majority either grew poorer or at best had to struggle to hold their own.

More important, however, Bacon's Rebellion sealed an implicit contract between the inhabitants of the "great houses" and those who lived in more modest lodgings: Southern whites might differ greatly in wealth and influence, but they stood as one and forever behind the principle that Africans must have neither. This was the basis—the price—of the harmony and prosperity achieved by those who survived "seasoning" in the Chesapeake colonies.

The Carolinas

The English and, after 1700, the Scots-Irish settlers of the tidewater parts of the Carolinas turned to agriculture as enthusiastically as had their Chesapeake neighbors. In substantial sections of what became North Carolina, tobacco flourished. In South Carolina, after two decades in which furs and cereals were the chief products, Madagascar rice was introduced in the low-lying coastal areas in 1696. It quickly proved its worth as a cash crop. By 1700 almost 100,000 pounds were being exported annually; by the eve of the Revolution rice exports from South Carolina and Georgia exceeded 65 million pounds a year.

Rice culture required water for flooding the fields. At first freshwater swamps were adapted to the crop, but by the middle of the eighteenth century the chief rice fields lay along the tidal rivers and inlets. Dikes and floodgates allowed fresh water to flow across the fields with the rising tide; when the tide fell, the gates closed automatically to keep the water in. The process was reversed when it was necessary to drain the land. Then the water ran out as the tide ebbed, and the pressure of the next flood pushed the gates shut.

In the 1740s another cash crop, indigo, was introduced in South Carolina by Eliza Lucas. Indigo did not compete with rice either for land or labor. It prospered on high ground and needed care in seasons when the slaves were not busy in the rice paddies. The British were delighted to have a new source of indigo because the blue dye was important in their woolens industry. Parliament quickly placed a bounty—a bonus—on it to stimulate production.

Their tobacco, rice, and indigo, along with furs and forest products such as lumber, tar, and resin, meant that the southern colonies had no difficulty in obtaining manufactured articles from abroad. Planters dealt with agents in England and Scotland, called factors, who managed the sale of their crops, filled their orders for manufactures, and supplied them with credit. This was a great convenience but not necessarily an advantage, for it prevented the development of a diversified economy. Throughout the colonial era, while small-scale manufacturing developed rapidly in the North, it was stillborn in the South.

Reliance on European middlemen also retarded the development of urban life. Until the rise of Baltimore in the 1750s, Charleston was the only city of importance in the entire South. But despite its rich export trade, its fine harbor, and the easy availability of excellent lumber, Charleston's shipbuilding industry never remotely rivaled that of Boston, New York, or Philadelphia.

On the South Carolina rice plantations, slave labor predominated from the beginning, for free workers would not submit to its backbreaking and unhealthy regimen. The first quarter of the eighteenth century saw an enormous influx of Africans into all the southern colonies. By 1730 roughly three out of every ten people south of Pennsylvania were black, and in South Carolina the blacks outnumbered the whites by two to one. "Carolina," remarked a newcomer in 1737, "looks more like a negro country than like a country settled by white people."

Given the existing race prejudice and the degrading impact of slavery, this demographic change had an enormous impact on life wherever African Americans were concentrated. In each colony regulations governing the behavior of blacks, both free and slave, increased in severity as the density of the black population increased. The South Carolina Negro Act of 1740 denied slaves "freedom of movement, freedom of assembly, freedom to raise [their own] food, to earn money, to learn to read English." The blacks had no civil rights under any of these codes, and punishments

▲ Slaves on a South Carolina plantation, around 1790. Likely of Yoruba descent, they play west African instruments, such as the banjo, and also wear elaborate headgear, another Yoruba trait. But unlike their Yoruban contemporaries, who adorned faces and limbs with elaborate tattoos or scars, these slaves bear no evident body decorations. These people are African, indisputably, but also American.

were sickeningly severe. For minor offenses, whipping was common, for serious crimes, death by hanging or by being burned alive. Slaves were sometimes castrated for sexual offenses—even for lewd talk about white women—or for repeated attempts to escape.

The "master" race sought to acculturate the slaves in order to make them more efficient workers. A slave who could understand English was easier to order about; one who could handle farm tools or wait on tables was more useful than one who could not; a carpenter or a mason was more valuable still. But acculturation increased the slave's independence and mobility, and this posed problems. Most field hands seldom tried to escape; they expressed their dissatisfactions by pilferage and petty sabotage, by laziness, or by feigning stupidity. Most runaways were artisans who hoped to "pass" as free in a nearby town. It was one of the many paradoxes of slavery that the more valuable a slave became, the harder that slave was to control.

Few runaway slaves became rebels, however. Indeed, organized slave rebellions were rare, and while individual assaults by blacks on whites were common enough, personal violence was also common among whites, then and throughout American history. But the masters had sound reasons for fearing their slaves; the particular viciousness of the system lay in the fact that oppression bred resentment, which in turn produced still greater oppression.

What is superficially astonishing is that the whites grossly exaggerated the danger of slave revolts. They pictured the black as a kind of malevolent ogre, powerful, bestial, and lascivious, a caldron of animal emotions that had to be restrained at any cost. Probably the characteristics they attributed to the blacks were really projections of their own passions. The most striking illustration was white fear that if blacks were free, they would breed with whites. Yet in practice, the interbreeding, which indeed took place, was almost exclusively the result of white men using their power as masters to have sexual relations with female slaves.

Thus the "peculiar institution" was fastened on America with economic, social, and psychic barbs. Ignorance and self-interest, lust for gold and for the flesh, primitive prejudices and complex social and legal ties, all combined to convince the whites that black slavery was not so much good as a fact of life. A few Quakers attacked the institution on the religious ground that all human beings are equal before God:

"Christ dyed for all, both *Turks, Barbarians, Tartarians*, and *Ethyopians*." Yet some Quakers owned slaves, and even the majority who did not usually succumbed to color prejudice. Blackness was a defect, but it was no justification for enslavement, they argued. But the Quaker view attracted little attention anywhere—none in areas where slavery was important.

HOME AND FAMILY IN THE SOUTH

Life for all but the most affluent planters was by modern standards uncomfortable. Houses were mostly one- and two-room affairs, small, dark, and crowded. Furniture and utensils were sparse and crudely made. Chairs were rare; if a family possessed one it was reserved for the head of the house. People sat, slept, and ate on benches and planks. The typical dining table (the term itself was not in use) was made of two boards covered, if by anything, with a "board cloth." Toilets and plumbing of any kind were unknown; even chamber pots, which eliminated the nighttime trek to the privy, were beyond the reach of poorer families.

Clothes were equally crude and, since soap was expensive, rarely washed and therefore foul-smelling and often infested with vermin. Food was plentiful. Corn, served as bread, hominy, pancakes, and in various other forms, was the chief staple. But there was plenty of beef, pork, and game, usually boiled with various vegetables over an open fire.

White women (even indentured ones) rarely worked in the fields. Household maintenance, including tending to farm animals, making butter and cheese, pickling and preserving, spinning and sewing, and, of course, caring for children, which often involved orphans and stepchildren because of the fragility of life in the region, was their responsibility. For exceptional women, the labor shortage created opportunities. Some managed large plantations; Eliza Lucas ran three in South Carolina for her absent father while still in her teens, and after the death of her husband, Charles Pinckney, she managed his extensive property holdings.

Southern children were not usually subjected to as strict discipline as children in New England were, but the difference was relative. Formal schooling for all but the rich was nonexistent; the rural character of society made the maintenance of schools prohibitively expensive. Whatever most children learned, they got from their parents or other relatives. A large percentage of Southerners were illiterate. As in other regions, children were put to some kind of useful work at an early age.

More well-to-do, "middling" planters had more comfortable lifestyles, but they still lived in relatively crowded quarters, having perhaps three rooms to house a family of four or five and a couple of servants.

To sleep between sheets in a soft bed under blankets and quilts was luxury indeed in that world. Food in greater variety and abundance was another indication of a higher standard of living.

Until the early eighteenth century only a handful achieved real affluence. (The richest by far was Robert "King" Carter of Lancaster County, Virginia, who at the time of his death in 1732 owned 1000 slaves and 300,000 acres.) Those fortunate few, masters of several plantations and many slaves, lived in solid, two-story houses of six or more rooms, furnished with English and other imported carpets, chairs, tables, wardrobes, chests, china, and silver. When the occasion warranted, the men wore fine broadcloth, the women the latest (or more likely the next-to-latest) fashions. Some even sent their children abroad for schooling. The founding of the College of William and Mary in Williamsburg, Virginia, in 1693 was an effort to provide the region with its own institution of higher learning, mainly in order to train clergymen. For decades, however, the College of William and Mary was not much more than a grammar school. Lawyers were relatively numerous, though rarely learned in the law. Doctors were so scarce that one sick planter wrote a letter to his brother in England describing his symptoms and asking him to consult a physician and let him know the diagnosis.

These large planters also held the commissions in the militia, the county judgeships, and the seats in the colonial legislatures. The control that these "leading families" exercised over their neighbors was not entirely unearned. They were, in general, responsible leaders. And they recognized the necessity of throwing open their houses and serving copious amounts of punch and rum to ordinary voters when election time rolled around. Such gatherings served to acknowledge the representative character of the system.

No matter what their station, southern families led relatively isolated lives. Churches, which might be expected to serve as centers of community life, were few and far between. By the middle of the eighteenth century the Anglican Church was the "established" religion, its ministers supported by public funds. The Virginia assembly had made attendance at Anglican services compulsory in 1619. In Maryland, Lord Baltimore's Toleration Act did not survive the settlement in the colony of large numbers of militant puritans. It was repealed in 1654, reenacted in 1657, then repealed again in 1692 when the Anglican Church was established.

For all its legal standing, the Anglican Church was not a powerful force in the South. Most of the ministers the Bishop of London sent to America were second-rate men who had been unable to obtain decent livings at home. If they had intellectual or spiritual ambitions when they arrived, their rural circumstances

▲ The harbor of Charleston, South Carolina, as depicted in the 1730s. Nearly a half dozen church steeples can be seen behind the commercial buildings along the bustling waterfront. Americans usually think of the 1600s as the great age of religion, but most colonial churches were founded after the 1740s.

provided little opportunity to develop them. Most people had few opportunities to attend formal services. One result was that marriages tended to become civil rather than religious ceremonies.

Social events of any kind were great occasions. Births, marriages, and especially funerals called for much feasting; if there were neither heirs nor debts to satisfy, it was possible to "consume" the entire contents of a modest estate in celebrating the deceased's passing. (At one Maryland funeral the guests were provided with 55 gallons of an alcoholic concoction composed of brandy, cider, and sugar.)

Other forms of entertainment and relaxation included hunting and fishing, cockfighting, and horse racing. Horses were widely owned, but used for getting from place to place rather than as draft animals, since tobacco was transported by water and cultivated with hoes, not plows.

Even the most successful planters were conserving types, not idle grandees chiefly concerned with conspicuous display. The vast, undeveloped country encouraged them to produce and then invest their savings in more production. William Byrd II (1674–1744), one of the richest men in Virginia, habitually rose before dawn. Besides his tobacco fields, he operated a sawmill and a grist mill, prospected for iron and coal, and engaged in the Indian trade.

GEORGIA AND THE BACK COUNTRY

West of the fall line of the many rivers that irrigated tidewater Chesapeake and Carolina lay the back country. This region included the Great Valley of Virginia, the Piedmont, and what became the final English colony, Georgia, founded by a group of London philanthropists in 1733. These men were concerned over the plight of honest persons imprisoned for debt, whom they intended to settle in the New World. (Many Europeans were still beguiled by the prospect of regenerating their society in the colonies. All told, about 50,000 British convicts were "transported" to America in the colonial period, partly to get rid of "undesirables," but partly for humane reasons.) The government, eager to create a buffer between South Carolina and the hostile Spanish in Florida, readily granted a charter (1732) to the group, whose members agreed to manage the colony without profit to themselves for a period of 21 years.

In 1733 their leader, James Oglethorpe, founded Savannah. Oglethorpe was a complicated person, vain, high-handed, and straitlaced, yet idealistic. He hoped to people the colony with sober and industrious yeoman farmers. Land grants were limited to 50 acres and made nontransferable. To ensure sobriety, rum and other "Spirits and Strong Waters" were banned. To guarantee that the colonists would have to work hard, the entry of "any Black . . . Negroe" was prohibited. The Indian trade was to be strictly regulated in the interest of fair dealing.

Oglethorpe intended that silk, wine, and olive oil would be the main products—none of which, unfortunately, could be profitably produced in Georgia. His noble intentions came to naught. The settlers swiftly found ways to circumvent all restrictions. Rum flowed, slaves were imported, large land holdings amassed. Georgia developed an economy much like South Carolina's. In 1752 the founders, disillusioned, abandoned their responsibilities. Georgia then became a royal colony.

Now settlers penetrated the rest of the southern back country. So long as cheap land remained available closer to the coast and Indians along the frontier remained a threat, only the most daring and footloose hunters or fur traders lived far inland. But once settlement began, it came with a rush. Chief among those making the trek were Scots-Irish and German immigrants. By 1770 the back country contained about 250,000 settlers, 10 percent of the population of the colonies.

This internal migration did not proceed altogether peacefully. In 1771 frontiersmen in North Carolina calling themselves Regulators fought a pitched battle with 1200 troops dispatched by the Carolina assembly, which was dominated by low-country interests. The Regulators were protesting their lack of representation in the assembly. They were crushed and their leaders executed. This was neither the last nor the bloodiest sectional conflict in American history.

Puritan New England

If survival in the Chesapeake required junking many European notions about social arrangements and submitting to the dictates of the wilderness, was this also true in Massachusetts and Connecticut? Ultimately it probably was, but at first puritan ideas certainly fought the New England reality to a draw.

Boston is located slightly more than 5° latitude north of Jamestown and almost 10° north of Charleston. Like other early New England towns and unlike these southern ones, Boston had a dependable water supply. The surrounding patchwork of forest, pond, dunes, and tide marsh was much more open than the malaria-infected terrain of the tidewater and low-country South. As a consequence New Englanders escaped "the agues and fevers" that beset settlers to the south, leaving them free to attend to their spiritual, economic, and social well-being. These differences alone made New England a much healthier habitat for settlers.

The Puritan Family

New England's puritans were set apart from other English settlers by how much—and how long—they lived out of their baggage. The supplies the first arrivals brought with them eased their adjustment, as did the wherewithal of later, equally heavily laden arrivals. The puritans' baggage, however, included besides pots and pans, and saws and shovels, a plan for the proper ordering of society.

At the center of the plan was a covenant, or agreement, to ensure the upright behavior of all who took up residence. They sought to provide what John Winthrop described to the passengers on the *Arbella*

as the imperative of human existence: "that every man might have need of other, and from hence they might be all knitt more nearly together in the Bond of brotherly affection."

The first and most important covenant governing puritan behavior was that binding family members. The family's authority was backed by the Fifth Commandment: "Honor thy father and thy mother, that thy days may be long upon the land." In a properly ordered puritan family, as elsewhere in the colonies, authority flowed downward. Sociologists describe such a family as nuclear and patriarchal; each household contained one family, and in it, the father was boss. His principal responsibilities consisted of providing for the physical welfare of the household, including any servants, and making sure they behaved properly. All economic dealings between the family and other parties were also transacted by him, even when the property involved had been owned by his wife prior to their marriage.

The Reverend John Cotton's outline of a woman's responsibilities clearly establishes her subordinate position: she should keep house, educate the children, and improve "what is got by the industry of the man." The poet Anne Bradstreet reduced the functions of a puritan woman to two: "loving Mother and obedient Wife." Colonial New England, and the southern colonies as well, did have their female blacksmiths, silversmiths, shipwrights, gunsmiths, and butchers as well as shopkeepers and teachers. Such early examples of domestic "liberation," however, were mostly widows and the wives of incapacitated husbands. Even so, most widows, especially young ones, quickly remarried.

Puritan Women and Children

Dealings with neighbors and relatives and involvement in church activities marked the outer limits of the social range of most puritan women. Care of the children was a full-time occupation when broods of 12 or 14 were more common than those of 1 or 2. Fewer children died in New England than in the Chesapeake or in Europe, though few families escaped a miscarriage or a child's death along the way. Childbearing and motherhood, therefore, commonly extended over three decades of a woman's life. Meanwhile, she also functioned as the chief operating officer of the household. Cooking, baking, sewing, and supervising servants, as well as mastering such arcane knowledge as the chemistry needed to make cheese from milk, bacon from pork, bread from grain, and beer from malt, all fell to her. These jobs were physically demanding, though not so debilitating as to prevent large numbers of New England wives from seeing one or more husbands off to the hereafter.

REat and manifold were the bleſſings (moſt dread Soueraigne) which Almighty G O D, the Father of all Mercies, beſtowed vpon vs the people of E N G L A N D, when firſt he ſent your Maieſties Royall perſon to rule and raigne ouer vs. For whereas it was the expectation of many, who wiſhed not well vnto our S I O N, that vpon the ſetting of that bright *Occidentall Starre* Queene E L I Z A B E T H of moſt happy memory, ſome thicke and palpable cloudes of darkeneſſe would ſo haue ouerſhadowed this land, that men ſhould haue bene in doubt which way they were to walke, and that it ſhould hardly be knowen, who was to direct the vnſetled State: the appearance of your M A I E S T I E, as of the *Sunne* in his ſtrength, inſtantly diſpelled thoſe ſuppoſed and ſurmiſed miſts, and gaue vnto all that were well affected, exceeding cauſe of comfort; eſpecially when we beheld the gouernment eſtabliſhed in your H I G H N E S S E, and your hopefull Seed, by an vndoubted Title, and this alſo accompanied with Peace and tranquillitie, at home and abroad.

But amongſt all our Ioyes, there was no one that more filled our hearts, then the bleſſed continuance of the Preaching of G O D s ſacred word amongſt vs, which is that ineſtimable treaſure, which excelleth all the riches of the earth, becauſe the fruit thereof extendeth it ſelfe, not onely to the time ſpent in this tranſitory world, but directeth and diſpoſeth men vr to that Eternall happineſſe which is aboue in Heauen.

Then, not to ſuffer this to fall to the ground, but rather to take it vp, and to continue it in that ſtate, wherein the famous predeceſſour of your H I G H N E S S E did leaue it; Nay, to goe forward with the confidence and reſo-

A 2   lution

▲ This 1611 Bible is dedicated "To the most high and mightie Prince, James." King James maintained that kings were "God's lieutenant's on earth," a martial analogy well-suited to the bloody religious disputes of the age. It took 47 ministers and 7 years to prepare the King James Bible.

As puritan social standards required husbands to rule over wives, so parents ruled over children. The virtue most insistently impressed on New England children was obedience; refusal to submit to parental direction was disturbing in itself and for what it implied about the child's eternal condition. Cotton Mather's advice, "better whipt, than damned," graced many a New England rod taken up by a parent in anger, from there to be rapidly transferred to the afterparts of misbehaving offspring. But household chores kept children out of mischief. By age six or

seven girls did sewing and helped with housework and boys were put to work outdoors. Older children might be sent to live with another family to work as servants or apprentices.

Such practices, particularly when set beside portraits of early New England families that depict toddlers as somber-faced miniature adults wearing clothes indistinguishable from those of their parents, may convey the impression that puritans hustled their young through childhood with as little love as possible. New Englanders harbored no illusions. "Innocent vipers" is how one minister described children, having 14 of his own to submit as evidence. Anne Bradstreet, mother of eight, characterized one as harboring "a perverse will, a love of what's forbid / a serpent's sting in pleasing face lay hid." Yet for all their acceptance of the doctrine of infant damnation, puritan parents were not indifferent to the fate of their children. "I do hope," Cotton Mather confessed at the burial of one of the eight children he lost before the age of two, "that when my children are gone they are not lost; but carried unto the Heavenly Feast with Abraham." Another minister assigned children who died in infancy "the easiest room in hell."

Population growth reinforced puritan ideas about the family. When the outbreak of the English Civil War put an end to the Great Migration in the early 1640s, immigration declined sharply. Thereafter growth was chiefly due to the region's extraordinarily high birthrate (50 births for every 1000 population, which is more than three times the rate today) and strikingly low mortality rate (about 20 per 1000). This resulted in a population much more evenly distributed by age and sex than that in the South. The fact that most New England women married in their early twenties rather than their late teens suggests that the demand for women matched the supply. Demographic realities joined with puritan expectations to create a society of nuclear families distinct to the region.

VISIBLE PURITAN SAINTS AND OTHERS

When it came to religion, puritans believed that church membership ought to be the joint decision of a would-be member and those already in the church. Those seeking admission would tell the congregation why they believed that they had received God's grace. Obvious sinners and those ignorant of Christian doctrine were rejected out of hand. But what of pious and God-fearing applicants who lacked compelling evidence of salvation? In the late 1630s, with the Great Migration in full swing and new arrivals clamoring for admission to the churches, such "merit-mongers"

▲ New England children like David, Joanna, and Abigail Mason (painted by an unknown artist around 1670) were expected to emulate adults in their chores and their appearance. Nevertheless, diaries and letters indicate that children were cherished by their parents in a way closer to modern family love than what their European contemporaries experienced.

were excluded, thereby limiting church membership to the community's "visible saints." A decade later, the Great Migration over and applications down, some of the saints began to have second thoughts.

By the early 1650s fewer than half of all New England adults were church members, and so exacting had the examination for membership become, particularly in churches where the minister and elders outdid each other in the ferocity of their questioning, that most young people refused to submit themselves to it. How these growing numbers of nonmembers could be compelled to attend church services was a problem ministers could not long defer. Meanwhile, the magistrates found it harder to defend the policy of not letting taxpayers vote because they were not church members. But what really forced reconsideration of the membership policy were the concerns of nonmember parents about the souls of their children, who could not be baptized.

At first the churches permitted baptism of the children of church members. Later, some biblical purists came out against infant baptism altogether, but most puritans approved this practice, which allowed them the hope that a child who died after receiving baptism might at least be spared Hell's hottest precincts. Since most of the first generation were church members, nearly all the second-generation New Englanders were baptized, whether they became church members or not. The problem began with the third generation, the offspring of parents who had been baptized but who did not become church members. By the mid-1650s it was clear that if nothing were done, soon a majority of the people would be living in a state of original sin. If that happened, how could the churches remain the dominant force in New England life?

Fortunately, a way out was at hand. In 1657 an assembly of Massachusetts and Connecticut ministers recommended a form of intermediate church membership that would permit the baptism of people who were not visible saints. Five years later, some 80 ministers and laymen met at Boston's First Church to hammer out what came to be called the Half-Way Covenant. It provided limited (halfway) membership for any applicant not known to be a sinner who was willing to accept the provisions of the church covenant. They and their children could be baptized, but the sacrament of communion and a voice in church decision making were reserved for full members.

The General Court of Massachusetts endorsed the recommendations of the Half-Way Synod and urged all the churches of the Commonwealth to adopt them. Two years later it quietly extended the right to vote to halfway church members.

Opponents of the Half-Way Covenant argued that it reflected a slackening of religious fervor. Michael Wigglesworth gave poetic voice to these views in "God's Controversy with New England" and "The Day of Doom," both written in 1662. Perry Miller, an authority on puritan New England, argued that the early 1660s marked the beginning of the decline, or "declension," of the puritan experiment. Some loss of religious intensity there may have been, but the rise in church memberships, the continuing prestige accorded ministers, and the lessening of the intrachurch squabbling after the 1660s suggest that the secularization of New England society had a long way to go.

DEMOCRACIES WITHOUT DEMOCRATS

Like the southern colonies, the New England colonies derived their authority from charters granted by the Crown or Parliament. Except for rare fits of meddling by London bureaucrats, they were largely left to their own devices where matters of purely local interest were concerned. This typically involved maintaining order by regulating how people behaved.

According to puritan theory, government was both a civil covenant, entered into by all who came within its jurisdiction, and the principal mechanism for policing the institutions on which the maintenance of the social order depended. When Massachusetts and Connecticut passed laws requiring church attendance, levying taxes for the support of the clergy, and banning Quakers from practicing their faith, they were acting as "shield of the churches." When they provided the death penalty both for adultery and for blaspheming a parent, they were defending the integrity of families. When they set the price a laborer might charge for his services or even the amount of gold braid that servants might wear on their jackets, they believed they were enforcing the puritan principle that people must accept their assigned stations in life. Puritan communities were, for a time, close-knit: murder, assault, and theft were rare. Disputes were adjudicated through an active court system.

But puritan civil authorities and ministers of the puritan (Congregational) church came under sharp attack from English Anglicans, Presbyterians, and Quakers. When the Massachusetts General Court hanged four stubborn Quakers who returned after being expelled from the colony, a royal order of 1662 forbade further executions.

Laws like these have prompted historians and Americans generally to characterize New England colonial legislation as socially repressive and personally invasive. Yet many of the laws remained in force through the colonial period without rousing much local opposition. Others, particularly those upholding religious discrimination or restricting economic activity, were repealed at the insistence of Parliament.

A healthy respect for the backsliding ways of humanity obliged New Englanders not to depend too much on provincial governments, whose jurisdiction extended over several thousand square miles. Almost of necessity, the primary responsibility for maintaining "Good Order and Peace" fell to the more than 500 towns of the region. These differed greatly in size and development. By the early eighteenth century the largest, Boston, Newport, and Portsmouth, were on their way toward becoming urban centers. This was before "frontier" towns like Amherst, Kent, and Hanover had even been founded. Nonetheless, town life gave New England the distinctiveness it has still not wholly lost.

THE DOMINION OF NEW ENGLAND

The most serious threat to these arrangements occurred in the 1680s. Following the execution of Charles I in 1649, England was ruled by one man, the Lord Protector, Oliver Cromwell, a puritan. Cromwell's death in 1658 led to the restoration of the Stuart monarchy in the person of Charles II (1660–1685). During his reign and the abbreviated one of his brother, James II (1685–1688), the government sought to bring the colonies under effective royal control.

Massachusetts seemed in particular need of supervision. Accordingly, in 1684 its charter was annulled and the colony, along with all those north of Pennsylvania, became part of the Dominion of New England, governed by Edmund Andros.

Andros arrived in Boston in late 1686 with orders to make the northern colonies behave like colonies, not like sovereign powers. He set out to abolish popular assemblies, to change the land-grant system so as to provide the king with quitrents, and to enforce religious toleration, particularly of Anglicans. Andros, being a professional soldier and administrator, scoffed at those who resisted his authority. "Knoweing no other government than their owne," he said, they "think it best, and are wedded to . . . it."

Fortunately for New Englanders so wedded, the Dominion fell victim two years later to yet another political turnabout in England, the Glorious Revolution. In 1688 Parliament decided it had had enough of the Catholic-leaning Stuarts and sent James II packing. In his place it installed James's daughter Mary and her resolutely Protestant Dutch husband, William of Orange. When news of these events reached Boston in the spring of 1689, a force of more than a thousand colonists led by a contingent of ministers seized Andros and lodged him in jail. Two years later Massachusetts was made a royal colony that also included Plymouth and Maine. As in all such colonies the governor was appointed by the king. The new General Court was elected by property owners; church membership was no longer a requirement for voting.

SALEM BEWITCHED

In 1666, families living in the rural outback of the thriving town of Salem petitioned the General Court for the right to establish their own church. For political and economic reasons this was a questionable move, but in 1672 the General Court authorized the establishment of a separate parish. In so doing the Court put the 600-odd inhabitants of the village on their own politically as well.

Over the next 15 years three preachers came and went before, in 1689, one Samuel Parris became minister. Parris had spent 20 years in the Caribbean as a merchant and had taken up preaching only three years before coming to Salem. Accompanying him were his wife; a daughter, Betty; a niece, Abigail; and the family's West Indian slave, Tituba, who told fortunes and practiced magic on the side.

Parris proved as incapable of bringing peace to the feuding factions of Salem Village as had his predecessors. In January 1692 the church voted to dismiss him. At this point Betty and Abigail, now 9 and 11,

DOCUMENT
Ann Putnam's Deposition (1692)

along with Ann Putnam, a 12-year-old, started "uttering foolish, ridiculous speeches which neither they themselves nor any others could make sense of." A doctor diagnosed the girls' ravings as the work of the "Evil Hand" and declared them bewitched.

But who had done the bewitching? The first persons accused were three women whose unsavory reputations and frightening appearances made them likely candidates. Sarah Good, a pauper with a nasty tongue; Sarah Osborne, a bedridden widow; and the slave Tituba, who had brought suspicion on herself by volunteering to bake a "witch cake," made of rye meal and the girls' urine. The cake should be fed to a dog, Tituba said. If the girls were truly afflicted, the dog would show signs of bewitchment!

"Lookie There!"

The three women were brought before the local deputies to the General Court. As each was questioned, the girls went into contortions: "their arms, necks and backs turned this way and that way . . . their mouths stopped, their throats choaked, their limbs wracked and tormented." Tituba, likely impressed by the powers ascribed to her, promptly confessed to being a witch. Sarah Good and Sarah Osborne each claimed to be innocent, although Sarah Good expressed doubts about Sarah Osborne. All three were sent to jail on suspicion of practicing witchcraft.

These proceedings triggered new accusations. By the end of April 1692, 24 more people had been charged with practicing witchcraft. Officials in neighboring Andover, lacking their own "bewitched," called in the girls to help with their investigations. By May the hunt had extended to Maine and Boston and up the social ladder to some of the colony's most prominent citizens, including Lady Mary Phips, whose husband, William, had just been appointed governor.

By June, when Governor Phips convened a special court consisting of members of his council, more than 150 persons (Lady Phips no longer among them) stood formally charged with practicing witchcraft. In the next four months the court convicted 28 of them, most of them women. Five "confessed" and were spared; the rest were condemned to death. Several others escaped. But 19 persons were hanged. The husband of a convicted witch refused to enter a plea when charged with being a "wizard." He was executed by having stones piled on him until he suffocated.

Anyone who spoke in defense of the accused was in danger of being charged with witchcraft, but some brave souls challenged both the procedures and the findings of the court. Finally, at the urging of the leading ministers of the Commonwealth, Governor Phips adjourned the court and forbade any further executions.

No one involved in these gruesome proceedings escaped with reputation intact, but those whose reputations suffered most were the ministers. Among the clergy only Increase Mather deserves any credit. He persuaded Phips to halt the executions, arguing that "it were better that ten witches should escape, than that one innocent person should be condemned." The behavior of his son Cotton defies apology. It was not that Cotton Mather accepted the existence of witches—at the time everyone did, which incidentally suggests that Tituba was not the only person in Salem who practiced witchcraft—or even that Mather took such pride in being the resident expert on demonology. It was rather his vindictiveness. He even stood at the foot of the gallows bullying hesitant hangmen into doing "their duty."

The episode also highlights the anxieties puritan men felt toward women. Many puritans believed that Satan worked his will especially through the allure of female sexuality. Moreover, many of the accused witches were widows of high status or older women who owned property; some of the women, like Tituba, had mastered herbal medicine and other suspiciously potent healing arts. Such women, especially those who lived apart from the daily guidance of men, potentially subverted the patriarchal authorities of church and state. (For more on this topic, see the feature essay, Re-Viewing the Past "*The Crucible,*" pp. 68–69.)

HIGHER EDUCATION IN NEW ENGLAND

Along with the farmers and artisans who settled in New England with their families during the Great Migration came nearly 150 university-trained colonists. Nearly all had studied divinity. These men became the first ministers in Massachusetts and Connecticut, and a brisk "seller's market" existed for them. Larger churches began stockpiling candidates by hiring newly arrived Cambridge and Oxford graduates as assistants or teachers in anticipation of the retirement of their senior ministers. But New England puritans could not forever remain dependent on the graduates of English universities.

In 1636 the Massachusetts General Court appropriated £400 to found "a schoole or colledge." Two years later, just as the first freshmen gathered in Cambridge, John Harvard, a recent arrival who had died of tuberculosis, left the college £800 and his library. After a shaky start, during which students conducted a hunger strike against a sadistic and larcenous headmaster, Harvard settled into an annual pattern of admitting a dozen or so 14-year-old boys, stuffing their heads with four years of theology, logic, and mathematics, and then sending them out into

▲ *Examination of a Witch.* A stern puritan patriarch adjusts his glasses to better examine a beautiful—and partially disrobed—young woman. Ostensibly, he's looking for the "witch's teats" with which she suckled "black dogs" and other creatures of the Devil. Completed in 1853 by T. H. Matteson, this painting subtly indicts puritan men as lecherous hypocrites. In fact, most accused witches were in their forties or fifties. The painting thus reveals more about the nineteenth-century reaction against puritanism than about the puritans themselves.

the wider world of New England. In 1650 Harvard received from the General Court the charter under which it is still governed.

Immediately below Harvard on the educational ladder came the grammar schools, where boys spent seven years learning Latin and Greek "so far as they may be fitted for the Universitie." Boston founded the first—the Boston Latin School—in 1636. Massachusetts and Connecticut soon passed education acts, which required all towns of any size to establish such schools. New Englanders hoped, as the preamble to the Massachusetts law of 1647 stated, to thwart "that old deluder, Satan," whose "chief object was to keep men from the knowledge of the Scriptures," by ensuring "that Learning may not be buried in the graves of our forefathers." Not every New England town required to maintain a school actually did so. Those that did often paid their teachers poorly. Only the most dedicated Harvard graduates took up teaching as a career. Some parents kept their children at their chores rather than at school.

Yet the cumulative effect of the puritan community's educational institutions, the family and the church as well as the school, was impressive. A majority of men in mid-seventeenth-century New England could read and a somewhat smaller percentage could also write. By the middle of the eighteenth century, male literacy was almost universal. In Europe only Scotland and Sweden had achieved this happy state so early. Literacy among women also improved steadily, despite the almost total neglect of formal education for girls.

Spreading literacy created a thriving market for the printed word. Many of the first settlers brought impressive libraries with them, and large numbers of English books were imported throughout the colonial period. The first printing press in the English colonies was founded in Cambridge in 1638, and by 1700 Boston was producing an avalanche of printed matter. Most of these publications were reprints of sermons; ministers required only the smallest encouragement

► *text continues on page 70*

Re-Viewing the Past

The Crucible

Winona Ryder stars in the 1996 movie based on Arthur Miller's 1953 play, *The Crucible,* an interpretation of the Salem witch trials of 1692. Ryder plays Abigail Williams, consumed with desire for John Proctor (Daniel Day-Lewis), a married man. Proctor has broken off their affair and reconciled with his wife, Elizabeth (Joan Allen). As the movie begins, Abigail and some other girls have sneaked into the woods with Tituba, a slave who practices black magic. They ask about their future husbands, and some beg her to cast a spell on their favorites. Abigail whispers something to Tituba, who recoils in horror. Abigail's dark eyes, glowing with fury, inform the movie audience of her message: she wants Elizabeth Proctor dead. Tituba slips into a trance and begins conjuring. Exhilarated by their illicit flouting of puritan convention, and quivering with sexual energy, the girls dance wildly around a fire, some throwing off all their clothes.

Then the minister happens onto the scene. The girls flee in terror. Some become hysterical. When confronted by church elders Abigail, glancing furtively at the other girls, blurts out that Tituba was a witch who was trying to steal their souls. Tituba initially denies the charges, but after being whipped she confesses. Pressed further, she names two other women as accomplices. At the mention of their names, Abigail's face contorts with pain and she moans; taking the cue, the other girls scream and writhe upon the floor. They supply the names of more witches. Alarmed by the enormity of Satan's plot, Massachusetts authorities initiate a thorough investigation.

After one court session, Abigail saunters over to John, standing by the side of the church. When he asks what "mischief" she has been up to, Abigail averts her eyes demurely and then gives him a wicked grin. John smiles at this prodigy in the seductive arts. She responds with a kiss, her hand groping for his groin. He hesitates, but then roughly pushes her away. Her eyes blaze with hatred.

The girls' hysterics intensify. Eventually over 100 suspected witches, most of them women, are arrested. The Proctors themselves come under suspicion. Asked to recite the Ten Commandments, John omits the injunction against adultery; the magistrate looks at him searchingly. When Abigail accuses Elizabeth of being a witch, John lashes out at the girl.

"She is a whore," he declares in court. "I have known her, sir."

"He is lying," she hisses. Suddenly her eyes widen, horror-stricken, and she screams that he, too, is in league with Satan. Her flawless histrionics again prevail: he is arrested.

During the trials, the magistrates look for physical evidence of satanic possession: unnatural flaps of skin or unusual warts—witch's teats—with which Satan's minions sap human souls. Family and neighbors, too, furnish evidence. Some cite occasions when the accused lost their tempers or stole livestock. But the main evidence is the behavior of the girls themselves, who squirm and howl, claiming that the spirits of the accused torment them. This "spectral" evidence unsettles the magistrates. Seeking stronger proof, they urge prisoners to confess. Those who do will be spared, for the act of confession signifies their break with Satan. Those who refuse must be hanged.

▼ Few portraits of single puritan women exist; their invisibility may help explain why some sought attention, perhaps by making witchcraft accusations. The young woman in this portrait became "visible" by becoming a mother.

The Proctors are among those convicted and sentenced to death. (Because Elizabeth is pregnant, her execution is postponed.) When given the opportunity to save himself, John signs a confession. But inspired by his wife's quiet courage, he repudiates it, choosing to die with honor rather than live in shame. His noble death at the scaffold, and the deaths of others like him, cause the people of Massachusetts to end the witch hunt.

The movie warrants consideration apart from Ryder's remarkable performance. For one, the movie vividly recreates a puritan world inhabited by palpable spirits. Contemporary viewers may snicker at scenes of adults scanning the night sky for flying witches and evil birds, but the puritans believed in such things. They regarded comets, meteors, and lightning as signals from God. When Cotton Mather lost the pages of some lectures, he concluded that "Spectres, or Agents in the invisible World, were the Robbers."

Episodes and language taken directly from trial records, though sometimes altered, infuse the movie with verisimilitude. For example, the Proctors were in fact interrogated on their biblical knowledge. Whereas in the movie John falters by omitting the commandment against adultery, in history, the fatal mistake was Elizabeth's. Asked to recite the Lord's Prayer, she substituted "hollowed be thy name" for "hallowed be thy name." The magistrates declared this to be a "depraving" act, for she had transformed the prayer into a curse—proof of satanic possession.

The movie's rendering of the girls' hysteria mostly corresponds with what we know from the historical record. A bewildered John Hale, a minister from Beverly, recorded that Abigail and her cousin were

> bitten and pinched by invisible agents. Their arms, necks and backs turned this way and that way, and returned back again, so as it was impossible for them to do of themselves. . . . Sometimes they were taken dumb, their mouths stopped, their throats choked, their limbs wracked and tormented so as might move an heart of stone . . . with bowels of compassion for them.

Historians still puzzle over the girls' behavior. Probably they were seeking attention, or venting anxiety over their fate as women in a patriarchal society; certainly their choice of victims suggests that they were voicing parental enmity toward neighbors. The movie alludes to such issues, but mostly attributes the girls' hysteria to sexual frustration, a consequence of puritan repression.

Ryder's Abigail symbolizes adolescent sexuality: her lust for John (and corresponding hatred of Elizabeth) precipitates the witch hunt. In point of fact, the real Abigail did accuse Elizabeth of witchcraft. The trial record reports that when Elizabeth denied the charge, Abigail raised her hand as if to strike her, but instead touched Elizabeth's hood "very lightly" and cried out, "My fingers! My fingers—burned!" Then Abigail swooned to the floor. But if these few details provide some basis for Abigail's conjectured affair with Elizabeth's husband, others call it into question, the most awkward being the gap in their ages: The real Abigail was 11 and Proctor, 60.

▶ Winona Ryder as a young puritan who accuses others of witchcraft.

Whatever the merits of playwright Arthur Miller's speculation about Abigail and John, his larger questions have long intrigued historians: Were the puritans sexually repressive? If so, did young people assent to puritan strictures or rebel against them?

Such questions cannot be answered with certainty. Few puritans left written accounts of their illicit thoughts and sexual behavior. Social historians have approached the matter from a different angle. Nearly all marriages and births in colonial New England (and most other places) were recorded. Scholars have scoured such records to determine how many brides gave birth to babies within six months of marriage; such women almost certainly had engaged in premarital intercourse.

This data for about a dozen communities in puritan New England indicate an extraordinarily low rate of premarital intercourse, far below England's at the same time or New England's a century later. This confirms that young puritan couples were watched closely. Governor William Bradford of Plymouth Colony, commenting on the relative absence of premarital pregnancy, concluded that sinners there were "more discovered and seen and made public by due search, inquisition and due punishment; for the churches look narrowly to their members, and the magistrates over all, more strictly than in other places." On the other hand, the low rate of premarital pregnancy might not signify puritan repression so much as young people's acceptance of puritan values.

When critics confronted Arthur Miller on his deviations from the historical record, and especially when they expressed skepticism over whether young Abigail Williams and the elderly John Proctor had an affair, Miller was unrepentant. "What's real?" he retorted. "We don't know what these people were like." Perhaps so, but one suspects that Winona Ryder's Abigail would have had a hard time of it in Salem in 1692. Could a bloom of such pungent and venomous precocity have emerged through the stony soil of New England Puritanism, and if so, could it have survived the assiduous weeding of the puritans themselves?

from their congregations to send off last Sunday's re-marks to the local printer. But if ministers exercised a near monopoly of the printed word, they did not limit their output to religious topics. They also produced modest amounts of history, poetry, reports of scientific investigations, and treatises on political theory.

Colonial Families: Adult and Child Reading

By the early eighteenth century the intellectual life of New England had taken on a character potentially at odds with the ideas of the first puritans. In the 1690s Harvard acquired a reputation for encouraging religious toleration. According to orthodox puritans, its graduates were unfit for the ministry and its professors were no longer interested in training young men for the clergy. In 1701 several Connecticut ministers, most of them Harvard graduates, founded a new "Collegiate School" designed to uphold the puritan values that Harvard seemed ready to abandon. The new college was named after its first English benefactor, Elihu Yale. It fulfilled its founders' hopes by sending more than half of its early graduates into the ministry. Nonetheless, as became all too clear at commencement ceremonies in 1722 when its president and six tutors announced themselves Anglicans, Yale quickly acquired purposes well beyond those assigned it by its creators.

The assumption that the clergy had the last word on learned matters, still operative at the time of the witchcraft episode, came under direct challenge in 1721. When a smallpox epidemic swept through Boston that summer, Cotton Mather, at the time the most prestigious clergyman in New England, recommended that the citizenry be inoculated. Instead of accepting Mather's authority, his heretofore silent critics seized on his support of the then-radical idea of inoculation to challenge both his motives and his professional credentials. They filled the unsigned contributor columns of New England's first newspaper, the *Boston Gazette,* and the *New England Courant,* which started in the midst of the inoculation controversy, with their views.

The *Courant* was published by James Franklin and his 16-year-old brother, Benjamin. The younger Franklin's "Silence Dogood" essays were particularly infuriating to members of the Boston intellectual establishment. Franklin described Harvard as an institution where rich and lazy "blockheads . . . learn little more than how to carry themselves handsomely . . . and from whence they return, after Abundance of Trouble, as Blockheads as ever, only more proud and conceited."

James Franklin was jailed in 1722 for criticizing the General Court, and shortly thereafter the *New England Courant* went out of business. Meanwhile, Ben had departed Boston for Philadelphia, where fame and fortune awaited him.

PROSPERITY UNDERMINES PURITANISM

Prior experience (and the need to eat) turned the first New Englanders to farming. They grew barley (used to make beer), rye, oats, green vegetables, and also native crops such as potatoes, pumpkins, and, most important, Indian corn, or maize. Corn was easily cultivated, and its yield per acre under rough frontier conditions exceeded that of other grains. It proved versatile and tasty when prepared in a variety of ways and also made excellent fodder for livestock. In the form of corn liquor, it was easy to store, to transport, and, in a pinch, to imbibe.

The colonists also had plenty of meat. They grazed cattle, sheep, and hogs on the common pastures or in the surrounding woodlands. Deer, along with turkey and other game birds, abounded. The Atlantic provided fish, especially cod, which was easily preserved by salting. In short, New Englanders ate an extremely nutritious diet. Abundant surpluses of fire-wood kept the winter cold from their doors. The combination contributed significantly to their good health and longevity.

The trouble was that virtually everything that New England farmers grew could be grown in Europe. The shortness of the growing season, the rocky and often hilly terrain, and careless methods of cultivation, which exhausted the soil, meant that farmers did not produce large surpluses. Thus, while New Englanders could feed themselves without difficulty, they had relatively little to spare and no place to sell it.

The earliest puritans accepted this economic marginality. The more pious positively welcomed it as insurance against "the serpent prosperity," which might otherwise deflect their spiritual mission into commercial opportunism. No prominent English merchants joined the Great Migration, though many were devoted puritans and some had invested in the Massachusetts Bay Company. Settlers who turned to business on arrival attracted suspicion, if not open hostility. Laws against usury (lending money at excessive rates) and profiteering in scarce commodities were in effect from the first days of settlement. Robert Keayne, a prosperous Boston merchant, was twice fined £200 by the General Court and admonished by his church for "taking above six-pence in the shilling profit; in some above eight-pence; and in some small things, above two for one." Keayne paid the fines and made "penitential acknowledgment" to his church, all the while convinced that "my goods and prices were cheap pennyworths."

Early puritan leaders resisted the argument of people like Keayne that business was a calling no less socially useful than the ministry or public office.

DEBATING THE PAST

Were puritan communities peaceable? A smooth, quiet river flows past this eighteenth-century puritan town. A church spire rises, treelike, from its center. The painting is a composition in harmony. In *The Scarlet Letter* (1850), however, Nathaniel Hawthorne shattered this placid image: Puritan towns were plagued with envy, intolerance, and hypocrisy. Hawthorne's harsh assessment, which many historians shared, persisted into the twentieth century. This view changed with Perry Miller (1933), whose elegant analysis of puritan sermons and writings amply demonstrated "the majesty and coherence of Puritan thinking." The rise of atheistic communism in the Soviet Union after World War II further contributed to an appreciation of the nation's puritan roots. Daniel Boorstin (1958) wrote approvingly of the strong families, religious faith, and democratic governance of puritan towns. During the 1960s a new generation of historians examined the issue. They had been influenced by Fernand Braudel, a French scholar. Braudel encouraged historians to reconstruct the "total history" of particular communities, rather like anthropologists. The publication of four such studies in 1970 reinvigorated colonial social history. John Demos discovered that families in Plymouth, Massachusetts, were beset with psychological conflicts; Philip Greven and Kenneth Lockridge found that Dedham and Andover, Massachusetts lost cohesion rapidly; Paul Zuckerman, on the other hand, concluded that his puritan towns most nearly resembled "peaceable kingdoms." Other studies complicated the picture further: Paul Boyer and Stephen Nissenbaum (1974) contended that Salem was wracked with class and religious tensions, while other scholars found communities that became increasingly cohesive. Which towns reflected the characteristic puritan pattern? The focus in recent decades has shifted from individual towns. David Hackett Fischer (1989) and Alan Taylor (2001) insisted that the puritans should be examined not in towns such as this one, but in relation to a much larger, even trans-Atlantic, context.

Perry Miller, *Orthodoxy in Massachusetts* (1933) and *The New England Mind* (1939), Daniel Boorstin, *The Colonial Experience* (1958), John Demos, *A Little Commonwealth* (1970), Philip J. Greven, *Four Generations* (1970), Kenneth Lockridge, *A New England Town* (1970), Michael Zuckerman, *Peaceable Kingdoms* (1970), Paul Boyer and Stephen Nissenbaum, *Salem Possessed* (1974), David Hackett Fischer, *Albion's Seed* (1989), Alan Taylor, *American Colonies* (2001).

Differences in wealth should be modest and should favor those to whom the community looked for leadership. In the puritan scheme of things, since Governor Winthrop was a far more valuable member of the community than Robert Keayne, he should stand higher than Keayne in all rankings, wealth included.

But Winthrop died in 1649 broke and in debt, whereas Keayne died three years later in sufficient prosperity (despite those stiff fines) to leave the town of Boston and Harvard College impressive benefactions. The gap between the puritan ideal and the emerging reality was becoming embarrassingly clear.

A Merchant's World

Winthrop's generation had tried to minimize dependence on European-manufactured goods such as iron tools, glass, and cloth by producing their own. When their efforts failed, they next pinned their hopes on establishing direct trade links with European suppliers by offering the skins of beaver and such other fur-bearing animals as otter, muskrat, and mink. Unfortunately, the beavers soon caught wind of what was going on and took off for points west and north. By the end of the late 1650s the New Englanders were back where they started. As one English merchant wrote, as trading partners New Englanders "have noe returns."

The colonists then turned to indirect trading schemes, in which merchants like Robert Keayne played a central role and from which they ultimately derived stature as well as wealth. The anticommercial bias of the early puritans did not, however, vanish as quickly as the elusive beaver had. At the beginning of the eighteenth century a Boston minister could still tell his congregation this story with every confidence that they shared his belief that his colleague got the better of the Maine fisherman: Once, some years after Keayne's death, a minister in Maine was reminding his flock that "the main end of planting this wilderness" was religion. A prominent member of the congregation could not contain his disagreement. "Sir," he cried out, "you are mistaken. You think you are preaching to the people of the Bay; our main end was to catch fish."

Colonial Products

Fish, caught offshore on grounds that extended from Cape Cod to Newfoundland, provided merchants with their opening into the world of transatlantic commerce. In 1643 five New England vessels set out with their holds packed with fish that they sold in Spain and the Canary Islands; they took payment in sherry and madeira, for which a market existed in England. One of these ships also had the dubious distinction of initiating New England into the business of trafficking in human beings when its captain took payment in African slaves, whom he subsequently sold in the West Indies. This was the start of the famous "triangular trade." Only occasionally was the pattern truly triangular; more often, intermediate legs gave it a polygonal character. So long as their ships ended up with something that could be exchanged for English goods needed at home, it did not matter what they started out with or how many things they bought and sold along the way.

So maritime trade and those who engaged in it became the driving force of the New England economy, important all out of proportion to the number of persons directly involved. Because those engaged

congregated in Portsmouth, Salem, Boston, Newport, and New Haven, these towns soon differed greatly from towns in the interior. They were larger and faster growing, and a smaller percentage of their inhabitants was engaged in farming.

The largest and most thriving town was Boston, which by 1720 had become the commercial hub of the region. It had a population of more than 10,000; in the entire British Empire, only London and Bristol were larger. More than one-quarter of Boston's male adults had either invested in shipbuilding or were directly employed in maritime commerce. Ship captains and merchants held most of the public offices.

Beneath this emergent mercantile elite lived a stratum of artisans and small shopkeepers, and beneath these a substantial population of mariners, laborers, and "unattached" people with little or no property and still less political voice. In the 1670s, at least a dozen prostitutes plied their trade in Boston. By 1720 crime and poverty had become serious problems; public relief rolls frequently exceeded 200 souls, and dozens of criminals languished in the town jail. Boston bore little resemblance to what the first puritans had in mind when they planted their "City upon a Hill." But neither was it like any eighteenth-century European city. It stood there on Massachusetts Bay, midway between its Puritan origins and its American future.

The Middle Colonies: Economic Basis

New York, New Jersey, Pennsylvania, and Delaware owe their collective name, the Middle Colonies, to geography. Sandwiched between New England and the Chesapeake region, they often receive only passing notice in accounts of colonial America. The lack of a distinctive institution, such as slavery or the town meeting, explains part of this neglect.

The Colonies to 1740

Actually, both institutions existed there. Black slaves made up about 10 percent of the population; indeed, one New York county in the 1740s had proportionally more blacks than large sections of Virginia. And eastern Long Island was settled by people from Connecticut who brought the town meeting system with them.

This quality of "in-betweenness" extended to other economic and social arrangements. Like colonists elsewhere, most Middle Colonists became farmers. But where northern farmers concentrated on producing crops for local consumption and southerners for export, Middle Colony farmers did both. In addition to raising foodstuffs and keeping livestock, they grew wheat, which the thin soil and shorter growing season of New England did not permit but for which there existed an expanding market in the densely settled Caribbean sugar islands.

Social arrangements differed more in degree than in kind from those in other colonies. Unlike New England settlers, who clustered together in agricultural villages, families in the Hudson Valley of New York and in southeastern Pennsylvania lived on the land they cultivated, often as spatially dispersed as the tobacco planters of the Chesapeake. In contrast with Virginia and Maryland, however, substantial numbers congregated in the seaport centers of New York City and Philadelphia. They also settled interior towns like Albany, an important center of the fur trade on the upper Hudson, and Germantown, an "urban village" northwest of Philadelphia where many people were engaged in trades like weaving and tailoring and flour milling.

THE MIDDLE COLONIES: AN INTERMINGLING OF PEOPLES

The Middle Colonists also possessed traits that later would be seen as distinctly "American." Their ethnic and religious heterogeneity is a case in point. In the 1640s, when New Amsterdam was only a village, one visitor claimed to have heard 18 languages spoken there. Traveling through Pennsylvania a century later, the Swedish botanist Peter Kalm encountered "a very mixed company of different nations and religions." In addition to "Scots, English, Dutch, Germans, and Irish," he reported, "there were Roman Catholics, Presbyterians, Quakers, Methodists, Seventh day men, Moravians, Anabaptists, and one Jew." In New York City one embattled English resident complained: "Our chiefest unhappiness here is too great a mixture of nations, & English the least part."

Scandinavian and Dutch settlers outnumbered the English in New Jersey and Delaware even after the English took over these colonies. William Penn's first success in attracting colonists was with German Quakers and other persecuted religious sects, among them Mennonites and Moravians from the Rhine Valley. The first substantial influx of immigrants into New York after it became a royal colony consisted of French Huguenots.

Early in the eighteenth century, hordes of Scots-Irish settlers from northern Ireland and Scotland descended on Pennsylvania. These colonists spoke English but felt little loyalty to the English government,

▲ This painting is presumably of Lord Cornbury, the royal governor of New York and New Jersey in the early 1700s, in a dress. Why it was painted and by whom is unknown. Some regard the painting as proof that the eighteenth century tolerated a wide range of sexual behaviors. In *The Lord Cornbury Scandal* (1998), however, Patricia Bonomi views the painting as part of a plot to unseat a brusque and high-handed governor. Some of his enemies in the colonies dispatched letters to officials in London complaining of Cornbury's penchant for wearing women's clothing in public. Bonomi doubts that the charges were true.

which had treated them badly back home, and less to the Anglican Church, since most of them were Presbyterians. Large numbers of them followed the valleys of the Appalachians south into the back country of Virginia and the Carolinas.

Why so few English in the Middle Colonies? Here, again, timing provides the best answer. The English economy was booming. There seemed to be work for all. Migration to North America, while never drying up, slowed to a trickle. The result was colonies in which English settlers were a minority.

The intermingling of ethnic groups gave rise to many prejudices. Benjamin Franklin, though generally complimentary toward Pennsylvania's hard-working Germans, thought them clannish to a fault.

▲ **Ethnic Groups in Eastern North America, 1750**

Distribution of Predominant Immigrant Group
- English
- Germans and Swiss
- Scots-Irish
- Blacks
- Dutch
- Scottish Highlanders
- French

"THE BEST POOR MAN'S COUNTRY"

Ethnic differences seldom caused conflict in the Middle Colonies because they seldom limited opportunity. The promise of prosperity (promotional pamphlets proclaimed Pennsylvania "the best poor man's country in the world") had attracted all in the first place, and achieving prosperity was relatively easy, even for those who came with only a willingness to work. From its founding, Pennsylvania granted upward of 500 acres of land to families on arrival, provided they would pay the proprietor an annual quitrent. Similar arrangements existed in New Jersey and Delaware. Soon travelers in the Middle Colonies were being struck by "a pleasing uniformity of decent competence."

New York was something of an exception to this favorable economic situation. When the English took over New York, they extended the Dutch patroon system by creating 30 manorial estates covering about 2 million acres. But ordinary New Yorkers never lacked ways of becoming landowners. A hundred acres along the Hudson River could be bought in 1730 for what an unskilled laborer could earn in three months. Even tenants on the manorial estates could obtain long-term leases that had most of the advantages of ownership but did not require the investment of any capital. "One may think oneself to be a great lord," one frustrated "lord" of a New York manor wrote a colleague, "but it does not amount to much, as you well know."

Mixed farming offered the most commonly trod path to prosperity in the Middle Colonies, but not the only one. Inland communities offered comfortable livelihoods for artisans. Farmers always needed barrels, candles, rope, horseshoes and nails, and dozens of other articles in everyday use. Countless opportunities awaited the ambitious settler in the shops, yards, and offices of New York and Philadelphia. Unlike Boston, New York and Philadelphia profited from navigable rivers that penetrated deep

The already cited French traveler Hector St. John de Crèvecoeur, while marveling at the adaptive qualities of "this promiscuous breed," complained that "the Irish . . . love to drink and to quarrel; they are litigious, and soon take to the gun, which is the ruin of everything." Yet by and large the various types managed to get along with each other successfully enough. Crèvecoeur attended a wedding in Pennsylvania where the groom's grandparents were English and Dutch and one of his uncles had married a Frenchwoman. The groom and his three brothers, Crèvecoeur added with some amazement, "now have four wives of different nations."

into the back country. Although founded half a century after New York and Boston, Philadelphia grew more rapidly than either. In the 1750s, when its population reached 15,000, it passed Boston to become the largest city in English America.

Most Philadelphians who stuck to their business, particularly if it happened to be maritime commerce, did well for themselves. John Bringhurst, a merchant, began his career as a clerk. At his death in 1751 he left an estate of several thousand pounds. The city's "leather-apron" artisans often accumulated estates of more than £400, a substantial sum at the time. By way of contrast, in Boston after 1710, economic stagnation made it much more difficult for a skilled artisan to rise in the world.

THE POLITICS OF DIVERSITY

"Cannot more friendly and private courses be taken to set matters right in an infant province?" an exasperated William Penn asked the people of Pennsylvania in 1704. "For the love of God, me, and the poor country, be not so governmentish." However well-intentioned Penn's advice, however justified his annoyance, the Pennsylvanians ignored him. Instead, they and their fellows throughout the region constructed a political culture that diverged sharply from the patterns of New England and the South both in contentiousness and in the sophistication required of local politicians.

Superficially the governments of the Middle Colonies closely resembled those of earlier settlements. All had popularly elected representative assemblies, and most white male adults could vote. In Pennsylvania, where Penn had insisted that there be no religious test and where 50 acres constituted a freehold, something close to white universal manhood suffrage existed. In New York even non-property-holding white male residents voted in local elections, and rural tenants with lifetime leases enjoyed full voting rights.

In Pennsylvania and most of New York, representatives were elected by counties. In this they resembled Virginia and Maryland. But unlike the Southerners, voters did not tend to defer in politics to the landed gentry. In New York, in 1689, during the political vacuum following the abdication of King James II, Jacob Leisler, a disgruntled merchant and militia captain, seized control of the government. "Leisler's Rebellion" did not amount to much. He held power for less than two years before he was overthrown and sent to the gallows. Yet for two decades New York politics continued to be a struggle between the Leislerians, and other self-conscious "outs" who shared Leisler's dislike of English rule, and anti-Leislerians, who had in common only that they had opposed his takeover. Each group sought the support of a succession of ineffective governors,

and the one that failed to get it invariably proceeded to make that poor man's tenure as miserable as possible.

New York lapsed into political tranquility during the governorship of Robert Hunter (1710–1719), but in the early 1730s conflict broke out over a claim for back salary by Governor William Cosby. When Lewis Morris, the chief justice of the supreme court, opposed Cosby's claim, the governor replaced him. Morris and his assembly allies responded by establishing the *New York Weekly Journal*. To edit the paper they hired an itinerant German printer, John Peter Zenger.

Governor Cosby might have tolerated the *Weekly Journal*'s front-page lectures on the right of the people to criticize their rulers had the back pages not contained advertisements referring to his supporters as spaniels and to him as a monkey. After submitting to two months of "open and implacable malice against me," he shut down the paper, arrested Zenger, and charged him with seditious libel.

What began as a squalid salary dispute became one of the most celebrated tests of freedom of the press in the history of journalism. At the trial Zenger's attorney, James Hamilton, argued that the truth of his client's criticisms of Cosby constituted a proper defense against seditious libel. This reasoning (though contrary to English law at the time) persuaded the jury to acquit Zenger.

Politics in Pennsylvania turned on conflict between two interest groups, one clustered around the proprietor, the other around the assembly, which was controlled by a coalition of Quaker representatives from Philadelphia and the German-speaking Pennsylvania Dutch.

Neither the proprietary party nor the Quaker party qualifies as a political party in the modern sense of being organized and maintained for the purpose of winning elections. Nor can they be categorized as standing for "democratic" or "aristocratic" interests. But their existence guaranteed that the political leaders had to take popular opinion into account. Moreover, having once appealed to public opinion, they had to be prepared to defer to it. Success turned as much on knowing how to follow as on knowing how to lead.

The 1763 uprising of the "Paxton Boys" of western Pennsylvania put this policy to a full test. The uprising was triggered by eastern indifference to Indian attacks on the frontier—an indifference made possible by the fact that the east outnumbered the west in the assembly, 26 to 10. Fuming because they could obtain no help from Philadelphia against the Indians, a group of Scots-Irish from Lancaster county fell on a village of peaceful Conestoga Indians and murdered them in cold blood. Then these Paxton Boys marched on Philadelphia, several hundred strong.

Fortunately a delegation of burghers, headed by Benjamin Franklin, talked the Paxton Boys out of attacking the town by acknowledging the legitimacy of their grievances about representation and by promising to vote a bounty on Indian scalps! It was just such fancy footwork that established Franklin, the leader of the assembly party, as Pennsylvania's consummate politician. "Tell me, Mr. Franklin," a testy member of the proprietary party asked, "how is it that you are always with the majority?" Soon thereafter, the assembly sent Franklin to London to defend local interests against the British authorities, a situation in which he would definitely not be "with the majority."

REBELLIOUS WOMEN

Overlaying the political disputes and contentions of the era was a general anxiety over the role of women. Anne Hutchinson had drawn the wrath of Massachusetts puritan authorities by criticizing their teachings and humiliating them in public debate; puritan anxieties toward unattached or independent women surfaced later in the Salem witch trials. This concern was not confined to New England. In 1661 Governor Berkeley of Virginia issued a proclamation threatening Quaker women, but not men, with imprisonment if they persisted in disseminating "schismaticall and hereticall doctrines." These and other attempts to suppress women's activity in church and political meetings backfired. Many women endorsed Bacon's Rebellion; some were imprisoned when it was crushed. The governor's inability to control refractory women was symptomatic of widespread uneasiness toward women among the seemingly omnipotent planter elite. If men could not control their wives, how could they claim to be gentlemen at all?

The authority of husbands, and indeed of male political leaders and elites, differed over time and place. But the general trend was away from a model of social and political power derived from the hierarchical example of a family, where the authority of the husband was analogous to that of the monarch. Although this shift was toward political egalitarianism, it did not empower women. Before the eighteenth century, women who headed a family could assume authority in public matters. But by the mid-eighteenth century, white women were expected to confine themselves to private matters within the home.

MILESTONES

1619	First Africans are sold in Virginia	1692	Salem village holds witchcraft trials
1636	Puritans found Boston Latin School and Harvard College	1696	Virginia colonists found College of William and Mary
1657	Half-Way Covenant leads to rise in puritan church memberships		Rice cultivation is introduced in South Carolina
1676	Western planters launch Bacon's Rebellion in Virginia	1701	Connecticut ministers found Yale College
1684–1688	Edmund Andros rules Dominion of New England	1733	George Oglethorpe leads settlement of Georgia
1689	Leisler's Rebellion in New York seizes control of government		

SUPPLEMENTARY READING

Among general interpretations, D. J. Boorstin's *The Americans: The Colonial Experience* (1958), emphasizes the modern aspects of colonial society; Jon Butler's *Becoming America: The Revolution before 1776* (2000) similarly and more broadly emphasizes the rapid evolution of colonial society. Alan Kulikoff, *From British Peasants to Colonial American Farmers* (2000) underscores the importance of land in defining American life. Alan Taylor, *American Colonies* (2001) emphasizes the links between European and American societies.

On economic conditions, see John J. McCusker and Russell R. Menard, eds., *The Economy of British America, 1607–1789* (1991). For the economic growth of colonial New England, see Margaret Ellen Newell, *From Dependency to Independence* (1998). On the chronologically and geographically uneven development of slavery in America, consult Ira Berlin, *Generations of Captivity: A History of African-American Slaves* (2003) and *Many Thousands Gone* (1998). See also Philip D. Morgan, *Slave Counterpoint* (1998) and P. D. Curtin, *The Rise and Fall of the Plantation Complex* (1990). Alan Gallay, *The Indian Slave Trade* (2002) uncovers an issue that has long been overlooked.

On life in the colonial South, see T. W. Tate and David Ammerman, eds., *The Chesapeake in the Seventeenth Century* (1979), Allan Kulikoff, *Tobacco and Slaves* (1986),

D. B. and A. H. Rutman, *A Place in Time* (1984), and Timothy H. Breen and Stephen Innes, *"Myne Owne Ground": Race and Freedom on Virginia's Eastern Shore* (1980).

Family and community life are surveyed in D. F. Hawke, *Everyday Life in Early America* (1988), and Edmund S. Morgan, *The Puritan Family* (1966). The places of women and children are effectively presented in Laurel T. Ulrich, *Good Wives: Image and Reality in the Lives of Women in Northern New England* (1982), and Philip Greven, *The Protestant Temperament: Patterns of Child-Rearing, Religious Experience, and the Self in Early America* (1980). Richard Godbeer, *Sexual Revolution in Early America* (2002) corrects the stereotype of the puritans as sexually repressive.

The works of Perry Miller remain the starting point for any serious study of the cultural life of colonial New England. Among them, *Errand into the Wilderness* (1956) provides a good introduction. More recent studies, most of which modify Miller's judgments, include D. D. Hall, *Worlds of Wonder, Days of Judgment* (1989), and Patricia U. Bonomi, *Under the Cope of Heaven* (1986). Some recent scholarship contends that Puritan practices complemented economic development: for example, John Frederick Martin, *Profits in the Wilderness* (1991), Stephen Innes, *Creating the Commonwealth* (1995), and Mark A. Peterson, *The Price of Redemption* (1997).

Larry D. Gragg, *The Salem Witch Crisis* (1992) provides a narrative account. Paul Boyer and Stephen Nissenbaum, *Salem Possessed* (1974), argue that the episode grew out of tensions between different factions within the community. Mary Beth Norton, *In the Devil's Snare: The Salem Witchcraft Crisis of 1692* (2002), views the crisis as a response to fear of Indians. The subject is considered more generally in John Demos, *Entertaining Satan: Witchcraft and the Culture of Early New England* (1982). On women and witchcraft, see Elizabeth Reis, *Damned Women* (1997), Elaine G. Breslaw, *Tituba, Reluctant Witch of Salem* (1996), and Carol F. Karlsen, *The Devil in the Shape of a Woman* (1987).

For an engaging overview of the ideology of gender authority in the seventeenth century, see Mary Beth Norton, *Founding Mothers and Fathers* (1996). On women and religion in New England, see also Susan Juster, *Disorderly Women* (1994). Karin Wolf, *Not All Wives* (2000), describes the range of women's activities in Philadelphia. For the role of women in Virginia, see Kathleen M. Brown, *Good Wives, Nasty Wenches and Anxious Patriarchs* (1996).

Educational and intellectual developments are treated in Bernard Bailyn, *Education in the Forming of American Society* (1960), and L. A. Cremin, *American Education: The Colonial Experience* (1970).

In the past decade there has been a profusion of studies on the interrelationship between settlers and Indians: Jane T. Merritt, *At the Crossroads: Indians and Empire on a Mid-Atlantic Frontier* (2003), Richard White, *The Middle Ground* (1991), Daniel K. Richter, *Ordeal of the Longhouse* (1992), Daniel H. Usner, *Indians, Settlers, and Slaves in a Frontier Exchange Economy* (1992), Colin G. Calloway, *New Worlds for All: Indians, Europeans, and the Remaking of Early America* (1997), Karen O. Kupperman, *Indians and English* (2001), and James F. Brooks, *Captives and Cousins* (2002).

SUGGESTED WEBSITES

LVA Colonial Records Project—Index of Digital Facsimiles of Documents on Early Virginia
http://ajax.lva.lib.va.us/F/?func=file&file_name=find-b-clas27&local_base=CLAS27
This site contains reproductions of numerous documents.

DSL Archives: Slave Movement During the Eighteenth and Nineteenth Centuries (Wisconsin)
http://dpls.dacc.wisc.edu/slavedata/index.html
This site explores the slave ships and the slave trade that carried thousands of Africans to the New World.

Witchcraft in Salem Village
http://etext.virginia.edu/salem/witchcraft/
This University of Virginia site offers an extensive archive of the 1692 trials as well as life in late seventeenth-century Massachusetts.

Salem Witchcraft Trials (1692)
http://www.law.umkc.edu/faculty/projects/ftrials/salem/salem.htm
Images, chronology, court and officials documents by Dr. Doug Linder of the University of Missouri–Kansas City Law School.

Benjamin Franklin
http://sln.fi.edu/franklin/rotten.html
This Benjamin Franklin Institute site contains information and sources treating one of early-America's most well-known figures.

Religion and the Founding of the American Republic
http://lcweb.loc.gov/exhibits/religion/religion.html
This Library of Congress site is an online exhibit about religion and the formation of the United States.

DoHistory, Harvard University Film Center
http://www.dohistory.org/
Focusing on the life of Martha Ballard, a late eighteenth-century New England woman, this site employs selections from her diary, excerpts from a book and film about her life, and other primary documents that enable students to conduct their own historical investigation.

Anglicans, Puritans, and Quakers in Colonial America
http://www.mun.ca/rels/ang/texts/
This site provides information on the major religious movements in colonial America.

America in the British Empire

▼ British warships at anchor off New York harbor. The British Empire offered protection to its colonies, and the colonies provided advantageous terms of trade to the mother country. The fleet doubtless reassured the people of New York, yet it also reminded them of their subordination.

Since the colonies were founded piecemeal by persons with varying motives and backgrounds, common traditions and loyalties developed slowly. For the same reason, the British government was slow to think of its American possessions as a unit or to deal with them in any centralized way. They were the king's possessions. As a good sovereign he was obligated to use them in a manner consonant with the public interest, but it was left to him and his advisers to decide what that interest was. No authority challenged the monarch's right to dispose of one section of the American domain to this group of merchants under such-and-such terms and another to that personal friend or creditor under a different arrangement. The specific form of each colony's government and the degree of local independence similarly depended on the nature of those particular arrangements.

THE BRITISH COLONIAL SYSTEM

There was a pattern basic to all colonial governments and a general framework of imperial control for all the king's overseas plantations. English political and legal institutions took hold everywhere in British America. While the colonists and the home authorities often had different motives in establishing new settlements, their motives seldom conflicted. Ruler and ruled alike sought prosperity, political and economic expansion, and the reproduction of Old World civilization.

In the earliest days of any settlement, the need to rely on home authorities was so obvious that few questioned England's sovereignty. Thereafter, as the fledglings grew strong enough to think of using their own wings, distance and British political inefficiency combined to allow them a great deal of freedom. External affairs were controlled entirely by London, and royal representatives in America tried to direct colonial policy. But in practice the Crown generally yielded the initiative in local matters to the colonies while reserving the right to veto actions it deemed to be against the national interest.

▲ Lewis Morris, a wealthy landowner, had extensive holdings in the Middle Colonies. He was named New Jersey's first governor when the colony became politically independent from New York in 1738. Honest but overbearing, Morris quarreled constantly with the state assembly over taxation, the militia, and land titles.

Each colony had a governor. By the eighteenth century he was an appointed official, except in Rhode Island and Connecticut. Governors were chosen by the king in the case of the royal colonies and by the proprietors of Maryland, Delaware, and Pennsylvania. The governors' powers were much like those of the king in Great Britain. They executed the local laws, appointed many minor officials, summoned and dismissed the colonial assemblies, and proposed legislation to them. They possessed the right to veto colonial laws, but in most colonies, again like the king, they were financially dependent on their "subjects."

Each colony also had a legislature. Except in Pennsylvania, these assemblies consisted of two houses. The lower house, chosen by qualified voters, had general legislative powers, including control of the purse. In all the royal colonies members of the upper house, or council, were appointed by the king, except in Massachusetts, where they were elected by the General Court. The councils served primarily as advisors to the governors, but they also had some judicial and legislative powers. Judges were appointed by the king and served at his pleasure. Yet both councilors and judges were normally selected from among the leaders of the local communities; London had neither the time nor the will to investigate their political beliefs. The system therefore tended to strengthen the influence of the entrenched colonials.

Although the power of the lower houses was severely restricted in theory, they dominated the government in nearly every colony. Financial power (including the right to set the governor's salary) gave them some importance, and as did the fact that they usually had the backing of public opinion.

Most colonial legislators were practical men. Knowing their own interests, they pursued them steadily, without much regard for political theories or the desires of the royal authorities. They extended their influence by slow accretion. They saw themselves as miniature Houses of Commons, steadily "nibbling" at the authority of the Crown. The king appointed their governors, but governors came and went. The lawmakers remained, accumulating experience, building on precedent, widening decade by decade their control over colonial affairs.

The official representatives of the Crown, whatever their powers, whatever their intentions, were prisoners of their surroundings. A royal governor lived thousands of miles from London, alone in a colonial world. Governors had no security of tenure; they served at the whim of the government in London. In their dealings with the assemblies they were often bound by rigid and impractical royal instructions. They had few jobs and favors to offer in their efforts to influence the legislators. Judges might interpret the law according to English precedents, but in local matters colonial juries had the final say. And juries were seldom awed by precedents that clashed with their own conceptions of justice.

Within the British government the king's Privy Council had the responsibility for formulating colonial policy. It could and did disallow (annul) specific colonial laws, but it did not proclaim constitutional principles to which all colonial legislatures must conform. It acted as a court of last appeal in colonial disputes and handled each case individually. One day the council might issue a set of instructions to the governor of Virginia, the next a different set to the governor of South Carolina. No one person or committee thought broadly about the administration of the overseas empire.

At times British authorities, uneasy about their lack of control over the colonies, attempted to create a more effective system. Whenever possible the original, broadly worded charters were revoked. In the 1680s James II brought New York, New Jersey, and all of New England under one administration, the Dominion of New England; he apparently planned to unify the southern colonies in a similar manner. But James's actions were deeply resented by the colonists, and after the Glorious Revolution and the collapse of the Dominion of New England, no further important efforts at unification were attempted. Instead, the tendency was in the other direction. Delaware partially separated from Pennsylvania in 1704, and the two Carolinas formally split in 1712.

In 1696 colonial policy was effectively determined by a new Board of Trade, which nominated colonial governors and other high officials. It reviewed all the laws passed by the colonial legislatures, recommending the disallowance of those that seemed to conflict with imperial policy. The efficiency, assiduousness, and wisdom of the Board of Trade fluctuated over the years, but the Privy Council and the Crown nearly always accepted its recommendations.

Colonists naturally disliked having their laws disallowed, but London exercised this power with considerable restraint; only about 5 percent of the laws reviewed were rejected. Furthermore, the board served as an important intermediary for colonists seeking to influence king and Parliament. All the colonies in the eighteenth century maintained agents in London to present the colonial point of view before board members. The most famous colonial agent was Benjamin Franklin, who represented Pennsylvania, Georgia, New Jersey, and Massachusetts at various times during his long career. In general, however, colonial agents were seldom able to exert much influence on British policy.

The British never developed an effective, centralized government for the American colonies. By and large, their American "subjects" ran their own affairs. This fact more than any other explains our present federal system and the wide areas in which the state governments are sovereign and independent.

MERCANTILISM

The Board of Trade was concerned with commerce as well as colonial administration. According to prevailing European opinion, colonies were important for economic reasons, chiefly as a source of raw materials. To obtain these, British officials developed a number of loosely related policies that later economists called mercantilism. The most important raw materials in the eyes of mercantilists were gold and silver, since these metals, being universally valued and relatively rare, could be exchanged at any time for anything the owner desired or, being durable and compact, stored indefinitely for future use. For these reasons, how much gold and silver ("treasure" according to mercantilists) a nation possessed was considered the best barometer of its prosperity and power.

DOCUMENT

Mun, "England's Treasure by Foreign Trade"

Since gold and silver could not be mined in significant amounts in western Europe, every early colonist dreamed of finding "El Dorado." The Spanish were the winners in this search; from the mines of Mexico and South America a treasure in gold and silver poured into the Iberian peninsula. Failing to control the precious metals at the source, the other powers tried to obtain them by guile and warfare (witness the exploits of Francis Drake).

In the mid-seventeenth century another method, less hazardous and in the long run far more profitable, called itself to the attention of the statesmen of western Europe. If a country could make itself as self-sufficient as possible and also keep its citizens busy producing items sought in other lands, it could sell more goods abroad than it imported. This was known as having "a favorable balance of trade." A country with an unfavorable balance was obliged to make up the difference by "exporting" gold and silver. Mercantilists regarded colonies as a means of acquiring precious metals by helping the mother country generate a favorable trade balance. Colonists thus were to supply raw materials that would otherwise have to be purchased from foreign sources or colonists were to buy substantial amounts of manufactured goods produced in the mother country.

Of the English colonies in the New World, those in tropical and subtropical climes were valued for their raw materials. The more northerly ones were important as markets, but because they were small in the seventeenth century, in English eyes they took second place. In

▲ *Sea Captains Carousing in Surinam* by John Greenwood, a late eighteenth-century oil painting that describes the effects of alcohol—one man guzzles his rum punch straight from the bowl, another vomits onto the floor, while a third pours his punch onto an insensate colleague. Greenwood implicitly denounces as well the trade in sugar (rum) and slaves in which these captains were engaged.

1680 the sugar imported from the single West Indian island of Barbados was worth more than the goods sent to England by all the mainland colonies.

If the possession of gold and silver signified wealth, trade was the route that led to riches, and merchants were the captains who would pilot the ship of state to prosperity. "Trade is the Wealth of the World," Daniel Defoe wrote in 1728. One must, of course, have something to sell, so internal production must be stimulated. Parliament encouraged the British people to concentrate on manufacturing by placing tariffs on foreign manufactured goods and subsidizing British-made textiles, iron, and other products.

THE NAVIGATION ACTS

The nurture of commerce was fundamental. Toward this end Parliament enacted the Navigation Acts. These laws, put into effect over a period of half a century and more, were designed to bring gold and silver into the Royal Treasury, to develop the imperial merchant fleet, to channel the flow of colonial raw materials into England, and to keep foreign goods and vessels out of colonial ports.

The system originated in the 1650s in response to stiff commercial competition by the Dutch, whose sailors roamed the world's oceans in search of business. Before 1650 a large share of the produce of the English colonies in America reached Europe in Dutch vessels; the first slaves in Virginia, it will be recalled, arrived on a Dutch ship and were doubtless paid for in tobacco that was later burned in the clay pipes of the burghers of Amsterdam and Rotterdam.

The Navigation Act of 1660 reserved the entire trade of the colonies to English ships and required that the captain and three-quarters of his crew be English. (Colonists, of course, were English, and their ships were treated on the same terms as those sailing out of London or Liverpool.) The act also provided that certain colonial "enumerated articles"—sugar, tobacco, cotton, ginger, and dyes like indigo (purple) and fustic (yellow)—could not be "shipped, carried, conveyed or transported" outside the empire. Three years later Parliament required that with trifling exceptions all European products destined for the colonies be brought to England before being shipped across the Atlantic. Since trade between England and the colonies was reserved to English vessels, this meant that the goods would have to be unloaded and reloaded in England.

Early in the eighteenth century the list of enumerated articles was expanded to include rice, molasses, naval stores, furs, and copper.

The English looked on the empire broadly; they envisioned the colonies as part of an economic unit, not as servile dependencies to be exploited for England's selfish benefit. The growing of tobacco in England was prohibited, and valuable bounties were paid to colonial producers of indigo and naval stores. A planned economy, England specializing in manufacturing and the colonies in the production of raw materials, was the grand design. By and large the system suited the realities of life in an underdeveloped country rich in raw materials and suffering from a chronic labor shortage.

Much has been made by some historians of the restrictions that the British placed on colonial manufacturing. The Wool Act of 1699 prohibited the export (but not the manufacture for local sale) of colonial woolen cloth. A similar law regarding hats was passed in 1732, and in 1750 an Iron Act outlawed the construction of new rolling and slitting mills in America. No other restrictions on manufacturing were imposed.

At most the Wool Act stifled a potential American industry; the law was directed chiefly at Irish woolens rather than American ones. The hat industry cannot be considered a major one. Iron, however, was important; by 1775 the industry was thriving in Virginia, Maryland, New Jersey, and Pennsylvania, and America was turning out one-seventh of the world supply. Yet the Iron Act was designed to steer the American iron industry in a certain direction, not to destroy it. Eager for iron to feed English mills, Parliament eliminated all duties on colonial pig and bar iron entering England, a great stimulus to the basic industry.

THE EFFECTS OF MERCANTILISM

AUDIO

"The Connecticut Peddler"

Colonists increasingly complained about mercantilism, but did it harm them? The chronic colonial shortage of hard money was superficially caused by the flow of specie—gold and silver—to England to meet the "unfavorable" balance of trade. The rapidly growing colonial economy consumed far more manufactured products than it could pay for out of current production. To be "in debt" to England really meant that the English were investing capital in America, a state of affairs that benefited lender and borrower alike.

Important colonial products for which no market existed in England (such as fish, wheat, and corn) were never enumerated and moved freely and directly to foreign ports. Most colonial manufacturing was untouched by English law. Shipbuilding benefited from the Navigation Acts, since many English merchants bought vessels built in the colonies. Between 1769 and 1771, Massachusetts, New Hampshire, and Rhode Island yards constructed perhaps 250 ships of

100 to 400 tons for transatlantic commerce and twice that many sloops and schooners for fishermen and coastal traders.

Two forces that worked in opposite directions must be considered before arriving at any judgment about English mercantilism. While the theory presupposed a general imperial interest above that of both colony and mother country, when conflicts of interest arose the latter nearly always predominated. Whenever Parliament or the Board of Trade resolved an Anglo-American disagreement, the colonists tended to lose.

Complementary interests conspired to keep conflicts at a minimum, but in the long run, as the American economy became more complex, the colonies would have been seriously hampered and much more trouble would have occurred had the system continued to operate.

On the other hand, the restrictions of English mercantilism were greatly lessened by inefficiency. The king and his ministers handed out government posts to win political favor or to repay political debts, regardless of the recipient's ability to perform the duties of the office.

Transported to remote America, this bumbling and cynical system scarcely functioned at all when local opinion resisted it. Smuggling became a respected profession, bribery of English officials standard practice. Despite a supposedly prohibitive duty of sixpence a gallon imposed by the Molasses Act of 1733, molasses from the French West Indies continued to be imported. The duty was seldom collected. A customs officer in Salem offered to pass French molasses for 10 percent of the legal tax, and in New Jersey the collectors "entered into a composition with the Merchants and took a Dollar a Hogshead or some such small matter."

Mercantilist policies hurt some colonists such as the tobacco planters, who grew far more tobacco than British consumers could smoke. Tobacco planters wanted to ship directly to Dutch or French ports. But the policies helped others, and most people proved adept at getting around those aspects of the system that threatened them. In any case, the colonies enjoyed almost continuous prosperity, as even so dedicated a foe of mercantilist restrictions as Adam Smith admitted.

By the same token, England profited greatly from its overseas possessions. With all its inefficiencies, mercantilism worked. Prime Minister Sir Robert Walpole's famous policy of "salutary neglect," which involved looking the other way when Americans violated the Navigation Acts, was partly a bowing to the inevitable, partly the result of complacency. English manufactures were better and cheaper than those of other nations. This fact, together with ties of language and a common heritage, predisposed Americans toward doing business in England. All else followed naturally; the mercantilist laws merely steered the American economy in a direction it had already taken.

▶ **Colonial Trade with England,**
   1700–1774

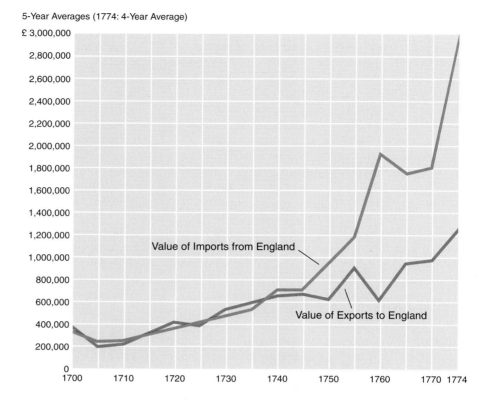

5-Year Averages (1774: 4-Year Average)

Value of Imports from England

Value of Exports to England

£ 3,000,000 / 2,800,000 / 2,600,000 / 2,400,000 / 2,200,000 / 2,000,000 / 1,800,000 / 1,600,000 / 1,400,000 / 1,200,000 / 1,000,000 / 800,000 / 600,000 / 400,000 / 200,000 / 0

1700 1710 1720 1730 1740 1750 1760 1770 1774

THE GREAT AWAKENING

Although a majority of the settlers were of English, Scotch, or Scotch-Irish descent, and their interests generally coincided with those of their cousins in the mother country, people in the colonies were beginning to recognize their common interests and character. Their loyalties were still predominantly local, but by 1750 the word American, used to describe something characteristic of all the British possessions in North America, had entered the language. Events in one part of America were beginning to have direct effects on other regions. One of the first of these developments was the so-called Great Awakening.

By the early eighteenth century, religious fervor had slackened in all the colonies. Prosperity turned many colonists away from their forebears' preoccupation with the rewards of the next world to the more tangible ones of this one. John Winthrop invested his faith in God and his own efforts in the task of creating a spiritual community; his grandsons invested in Connecticut real estate.

The proliferation of religious denominations made it impracticable to enforce laws requiring regular religious observances. Even in South Carolina, the colony that came closest to having an "Anglican Establishment," only a minority were churchgoers. Settlers in frontier districts lived beyond the reach of church or clergy. The result was a large and growing number of "persons careless of all religion."

This state of affairs came to an abrupt end with the Great Awakening of the 1740s. The Awakening began in the Middle Colonies as the result of religious developments that originated in Europe. In the late 1720s two newly arrived ministers, Theodore Frelinghuysen, a Calvinist from Westphalia, and William Tennent, an Irish-born Presbyterian, sought to instill in their sleepy Pennsylvania and New Jersey congregations the evangelical zeal and spiritual enthusiasm they had witnessed among the Pietists in Germany and the Methodist followers of John Wesley in England. Their example inspired other clergymen, including Tennent's two sons.

A more significant surge of religious enthusiasm followed the arrival in 1738 in Georgia of the Reverend George Whitefield, a young Oxford-trained Anglican minister. Whitefield was a marvelous pulpit orator and no mean actor. He played on the feelings of his audience the way a conductor directs a symphony. Whitefield undertook a series of fund-raising tours throughout the colonies. The most successful began in Philadelphia in 1739. Benjamin Franklin, not a very religious person and not easily moved by emotional appeals, heard one of these sermons. "I silently resolved he should get nothing from me," he later recalled.

DOCUMENT

Franklin on George Whitefield (1771)

I had in my Pocket a Handful of Copper Money, three or four silver Dollars, and five Pistoles in Gold. As he proceeded I began to soften and concluded to give the Coppers. Another Stroke of his Oratory . . . determin'd me to give the Silver; and he finish'd so admirably that I empty'd my Pocket wholly into the Collector's Dish.

Whitefield's visit changed the "manners of our inhabitants," Franklin added.

Wherever Whitefield went he filled the churches. If no local clergyman offered his pulpit, he attracted thousands to meetings out of doors. During a three-day visit to Boston, 19,000 people (more than the population of the town) thronged to hear him. His oratorical brilliance aside, Whitefield succeeded in releasing an epidemic of religious emotionalism because his message was so well suited to American ears. By preaching a theology that one critic said was "scaled down to the comprehension of twelve-year-olds," he spared his audiences the rigors of hard thought. Though he usually began by chastising his listeners as sinners, "half animals and half devils," he invariably took care to leave them with the hope that eternal salvation could be theirs. While not denying the doctrine of predestination, he preached a God responsive to good intentions. He disregarded sectarian differences and encouraged his listeners to do the same. "God help us to forget party names and become Christians in deed and truth," he prayed.

Whitefield attracted some supporters among ministers with established congregations, but many more from among younger "itinerants," as preachers who lacked permanent pulpits were called. A visit from him or one of his followers inevitably prompted comparisons between this new, emotionally charged style and the more restrained "plaine style" favored by the typical settled minister. Parishioners who had heard a revivalist preacher listened the next Sunday to the droning of their regular minister with what one of Whitefield's imitators claimed was the fear that their souls were at risk because they had been "living under the ministry of dead men."

Of course not everyone found the Whitefield style edifying. When those who did not spoke up, churches sometimes split into factions. Those who supported the incumbent minister were called, among Congregationalists, "Old Lights," and among Presbyterians, "Old Sides," while those who favored revivalism were known as "New Lights" and "New Sides." These splits often ran along class lines. The richer, better-educated, and more influential members of the church tended to stay with the traditional arrangements.

But many were deeply moved by the new ideas. Persons chafing under the restraints of puritan authoritarianism, or feeling guilty over their preoccupation with material goods, now found release in religious ferment. For some the release was more than spiritual; Timothy Cutler, a conservative Anglican clergyman, complained that as a result of the Awakening "our presses are forever teeming with books and our women with bastards." Whether or not Cutler was correct, the Great Awakening helped some people to rid themselves of the idea that disobedience to authority entailed damnation. Anything that God justified, human law could not condemn.

Other institutions besides the churches were affected by the Great Awakening. In 1741 the president of Yale College criticized the theology of itinerant ministers. One of these promptly retorted that a Yale faculty member had no more divine grace than a chair! Other revivalists called on the New Light churches of Connecticut to withdraw their support from Yale and endow a college of their own. The result was the

▲ In this painting evangelist George Whitefield appears to be cross-eyed. This is no fault of John Wollaston, the painter. Whitefield had eye problems; his detractors called him "Dr. Squintum." The woman's rapturous gaze is unaffected by Whitefield's own curious visage.

College of New Jersey (now Princeton), founded in 1746 by New Side Presbyterians. Three other educational by-products of the Great Awakening followed: the College of Rhode Island (Brown), founded by Baptists in 1765; Queen's College (Rutgers), founded by Dutch Reformers in 1766; and Dartmouth, founded by New Light Congregationalists in 1769.

These institutions promptly set about to refute the charge that the evangelical temperament was hostile to learning.

THE RISE AND FALL OF JONATHAN EDWARDS

Jonathan Edwards, the most famous native-born revivalist of the Great Awakening, was living proof that the evangelical temperament need not be hostile to learning. Edwards, though deeply pious, was passionately devoted to intellectual pursuits. But in 1725, four years after graduating from Yale, he was offered the position of assistant at his grandfather Solomon Stoddard's church in Northampton, Massachusetts. He accepted, and when Stoddard died two years later, Edwards became pastor.

During his six decades in Northampton, Stoddard had so dominated the ministers of the Connecticut Valley that some referred to him as "pope." His prominence came in part from the "open enrollment" admission policy he adopted for his own church. Evidence of saving grace was neither required nor expected of members: mere good behavior sufficed. As a result, the grandson inherited a congregation whose members were possessed of an "inordinate engagedness after this world." How ready they were to meet their Maker in the next was another question.

DOCUMENT

Edwards, "Sinners in the Hands of an Angry God"

For all his learning and intellectual brilliance, Edwards did not stick at dramatizing what unconverted listeners had to look forward to. The heat of Hell's consuming fires and the stench of brimstone became palpable at his rendering. In his most famous sermon, "Sinners in the Hands of an Angry God," delivered at Enfield, Connecticut, in 1741, he pulled out all the stops, depicting a "dreadfully provoked" God holding the unconverted over the pit of Hell, "much as one holds a spider, or some loathsome insect." Later, on the off-chance that his listeners did not recognize themselves among the "insects" in God's hand, he declared that "this is the dismal case of every soul in this congregation that has not been born again, however moral and strict, sober and religious, they may otherwise be." A great moaning reverberated through the church. People cried out, "What must I do to be saved?"

Unfortunately for some church members, Edwards's warnings about the state of their souls caused much anxiety. One disconsolate member, Joseph Hawley, slit his throat. Edwards took the suicide calmly. "Satan seems to be in a great rage," he declared. But for some of Edwards's most prominent parishioners, Hawley's death roused doubts. They began to miss the forgiving God of Solomon Stoddard.

Rather than soften his message, Edwards persisted, and in 1749 his parishioners voted unanimously to dismiss him. He became a missionary to some Indians in Stockbridge, Massachusetts. In 1759 he was appointed president of Princeton, but he died of smallpox before he could take office.

By the early 1750s a reaction had set in against religious "enthusiasm" in all its forms. Except in the religion-starved South, where traveling New Side Presbyterians and Baptists continued their evangelizing efforts, the Great Awakening had run its course. Whitefield's tour of the colonies in 1754 attracted little notice.

Although it caused divisions, the Great Awakening also fostered religious toleration. If one group claimed the right to worship in its own way, how could it deny to other Protestant churches equal freedom? The Awakening was also the first truly national event in American history. It marks the time when the previously distinct histories of New England, the Middle Colonies, and the South began to intersect. Powerful links were being forged. As early as 1691 there was a rudimentary intercolonial postal system. In 1754, not long after the Awakening, the farsighted Benjamin Franklin advanced his Albany Plan for a colonial union to deal with common problems, such as defense against Indian attacks on the frontier. Thirteen once-isolated colonies, expanding to the north and south as well as westward, were merging.

THE ENLIGHTENMENT IN AMERICA

The Great Awakening pointed ahead to an America marked by religious pluralism; by the 1740s many colonists were rejecting not only the stern Calvinism of Edwards but even the easy Arminianism of Solomon Stoddard in favor of a far less forbidding theology, one more in keeping with the ideas of the European Enlightenment.

The Enlightenment had an enormous impact in America. The founders of the colonies were contemporaries of the astronomer Galileo Galilei (1564–1642), the philosopher-mathematician René Descartes (1596–1650), and Sir Isaac Newton (1642–1727), the genius who revealed to the world the workings of gravity and other laws of motion. American society developed amid the excitement generated by these

DEBATING THE PAST

Was economic gain the colonists' main motivation? This bustling New York farm scene was painted in 1732 on a wood plank. Were those who first placed it above their mantelpiece enshrining their prosperity or their family? Perhaps the first important account of the eighteenth century was by James Truslow Adams (1927), a Wall Street broker who amassed a fortune, retired at age 34, and turned to history. The colonists, he believed, were likewise consumed with acquiring better and more abundant food, clothing, furnishings, housing, and the status such goods signified. He doubted that they cared much about anything else. In the 1950s many scholars, flush with post–World War II patriotism, insisted that the colonists cared deeply about religious, political, and family values. Edmund Morgan (1958) best exemplified this viewpoint. But Adams's position resurfaced several decades later. James Lemon (1972) claimed that Pennsylvania attracted middle-class immigrants who quickly became profit-maximizing farmers. Jack Greene (1988) and Alan Kulikoff (1992) showed that farmers in the Chesapeake and the South had almost from the start been preoccupied with money and land. The studies of colonial towns during the 1970s transformed the debate. Philip Greven (1970) and others discovered that while nearly everyone craved land, they did so chiefly for their families. Parents sought enough land to give or bequeath to their many children, who otherwise, on attaining adulthood, would be forced to scatter. This focus on parents and family life also spotlighted the central role of women in colonial society, a theme that was developed by Linda Kerber (1980), Mary Beth Norton (1980), and many others.

James Truslow Adams, *Provincial Society* (1927), Edmund Morgan, *A Puritan Dilemma* (1958), James Lemon, *Best Poor Man's Country* (1972), Jack Greene, *Pursuits of Happiness* (1988), Alan Kulikoff, *Agrarian Origins of American Capitalism* (1992), Philip Greven, *Four Generations* (1970), Linda Kerber, *Women of the Republic* (1980), Mary Beth Norton, *Liberty's Daughters* (1980).

great discoverers, who provided both a new understanding of the natural world and a mode of thought that implied that impersonal, scientific laws governed the behavior of all matter, animate and inanimate. Earth and the heavens, human beings and the lower animals—all seemed parts of an immense, intricate machine. God had set it all in motion and remained the master technician (the divine watchmaker) overseeing it, but He took fewer and fewer occasions to interfere with its immutable operation. If human reasoning powers and direct observation of natural phenomena rather than God's revelations provided the key to knowledge, it followed that knowledge of the laws of nature, by enabling people to understand the workings of the universe, would enable them to control their earthly destinies and to have at least a voice in their eternal destinies.

Most creative thinkers of the European Enlightenment realized that human beings were not entirely rational and that a complete understanding of the physical world was beyond their grasp. They did, however, believe that human beings were becoming more rational and would be able, by using their rational

powers, to discover the laws governing the physical world. Their faith in these ideas produced the so-called Age of Reason. And while their confidence in human rationality now seems naive and the "laws" they formulated no longer appear so mechanically perfect (the universe is far less orderly than they imagined) they added immensely to knowledge.

Many churchgoing colonists, especially better educated ones, accepted the assumptions of the Age of Reason wholeheartedly. Some repudiated the doctrine of original sin and asserted the benevolence of God. Others came to doubt the divinity of Christ and eventually declared themselves Unitarians. Still others, among them Benjamin Franklin, embraced Deism, a faith that revered God for the marvels of His universe rather than for His power over humankind.

The impact of Enlightenment ideas went far beyond religion. The writings of John Locke and other political theorists found a receptive audience. So did the work of the Scottish philosophers Francis Hutcheson and David Hume and the French *philosophes*, particularly Montesquieu and Voltaire. Ideas generated in Europe often reached America with startling speed.

No colonial political controversy really heated up in America until all involved had published pamphlets citing half a dozen European authorities. Radical ideas that in Europe were discussed only by an intellectual elite became almost commonplace in the colonies.

As the topics of learned discourse expanded, ministers lost their monopoly on intellectual life. By the 1750s, only a minority of Harvard and Yale graduates were becoming ministers. The College of Philadelphia (later the University of Pennsylvania), founded in 1751, and King's College (later Columbia), founded in New York in 1754, added two institutions to the growing ranks of American colleges, which were never primarily training grounds for clergymen.

Lawyers, who first appeared in any number in colonial towns in the 1740s, swiftly asserted their intellectual authority in public affairs. Physicians and the handful of professors of natural history declared themselves better able to make sense of the new scientific discoveries than clergymen. Yet because fields of knowledge were far less specialized than in modern times, self-educated amateurs could also make useful contributions.

The most famous instances of popular participation occurred in Philadelphia. It was there, in 1727, that 21-year-old Benjamin Franklin founded the Junto, a club at which he and other young artisans gathered on Friday evenings to discuss "any point of morals, politics, or natural philosophy." In 1743 Franklin established an expanded version of the Junto, the American Philosophical Society, which he hoped would "cultivate the finer arts and improve the common stock of knowledge."

COLONIAL SCIENTIFIC ACHIEVEMENTS

America produced no Galileo or Newton, but colonists contributed significantly to the collection of scientific knowledge. The unexplored continent provided a laboratory for the study of natural phenomena. The Philadelphia Quaker John Bartram, a "down right plain Country Man," ranged from Florida to the Great Lakes during the middle years of the eighteenth century, gathering and classifying hundreds of plants. Bartram also studied Indians closely, speculating about their origins and collecting information about their culture.

Benjamin Franklin's far-ranging curiosity extended to science. "No one of the present age has made more important discoveries," Thomas Jefferson declared. One of Franklin's biographers has similarly called him a "harmonious human multitude." His studies of electricity, which he capped in 1752 with his famous kite experiment, established him as a scientist of international stature. He also invented the

▲ Benjamin Franklin is most often depicted as he looked in later life, with his own thinning hair rather than the wig that was de rigueur for an eighteenth-century man of good family. In this 1767 portrait, a younger Franklin follows the fashion.

lightning rod, the iron Franklin stove (a far more efficient way to heat a room than an open fireplace), bifocal spectacles, and several other ingenious devices. In addition he served 14 years (1751–1764) in the Pennsylvania assembly. He founded a circulating library and helped to get the first hospital in Philadelphia built. He came up with the idea of a lottery to raise money for public purposes. In his spare time he taught himself Latin, French, Spanish, and Italian.

Franklin wrote so much about the virtues of hard work and thrift that some historians have described him as stuffy and straitlaced. Nothing could be further from the truth. He recognized the social value of conventional behavior, but he was no slave to convention. He wrote satirical essays on such subjects as the advantage of having affairs with older and plain-looking women (who were, he claimed, more likely to appreciate the attention). And he had the perfect temperament, being open-minded and imaginative as well as shrewd and judicious—an unbeatable combination.

Franklin's international fame notwithstanding, the theoretical contributions of American thinkers and scientists were modest. No colony produced a Voltaire, or Gibbon, or Rousseau. Most were practical rather than speculative types, tinkerers rather than constructors of grand designs. As one observer noted, they were easily diverted "by Business or Inclination from profound Study, and prying into the Depth of Things." Thomas Jefferson, for example, made no theoretical discovery of importance, but his range was almost without limit: linguist, bibliophile, political scientist, architect, inventor, scientific farmer, and—above all—apostle of reason. "Fix reason firmly in her seat," he wrote, "and call to her tribunal every fact, every opinion."

Involvement at even the most marginal level in the intellectual affairs of Europe gave influential New Englanders, Middle Colonists, and Southerners a chance to get to know one another. Although their role in what Jefferson called "the Republic of Letters" was still minor, by mid-century their influence on the intellectual climate of the colonies was growing. That climate was one of eager curiosity, flexibility of outlook, and confidence.

REPERCUSSIONS OF DISTANT WARS

The British colonies were part of a great empire that was part of a still larger world. Seemingly isolated in their remote communities, scattered like a broken string of beads between the wide Atlantic and the trackless Appalachian forests, Americans were constantly affected by outside events both in the Old World and in the New. Under the spell of mercantilist logic, the western European nations competed fiercely for markets and colonial raw materials. War—hot and cold, declared and undeclared—was almost a permanent condition of seventeenth- and eighteenth-century life, and when the powers clashed they fought wherever they could get at one another, in America, in Europe, and elsewhere.

Although the American colonies were minor pieces in the game and were sometimes casually exchanged or sacrificed by the masterminds in London, Paris, and Madrid in pursuit of some supposedly more important objective, the colonists quickly generated their own international animosities. Frenchmen and Spaniards clashed savagely in Florida as early as the sixteenth century. Before the landing of the Pilgrims, Samuel Argall of Virginia was sacking French settlements in Maine and carrying off Jesuit priests into captivity at Jamestown. Instead of fostering tranquility and generosity, the abundance of America seemed to make the settlers belligerent and greedy.

The North Atlantic fisheries quickly became a source of trouble between Canadian and New England colonists, despite the fact that the waters of the Grand Banks teemed with cod and other fish. To dry and salt their catch the fishermen needed land bases, and French and English Americans struggled constantly over the harbors of Maine, Nova Scotia, and Newfoundland.

Even more troublesome was the fur trade. The yield of the forest was easily exhausted by indiscriminate slaughter, and traders contended bitterly to control valuable hunting grounds. The French in Canada conducted their fur trading through tribes such as the Algonquin and the Huron. This brought them into conflict with the Five Nations, the powerful Iroquois confederation of central New York. As early as 1609 the Five Nations were at war with the French and their Indian allies. For decades this struggle flared sporadically, the Iroquois more than holding their own both as fighters and as traders. The Iroquois brought quantities of beaver pelts to the Dutch at Albany, some obtained by their own trappers, others taken by ambushing the fur-laden canoes of their enemies. They preyed on and ultimately destroyed the Huron in the land north of Lake Ontario and dickered with Indian trappers in far-off Michigan. When the English took over the New Amsterdam colony they eagerly adopted the Iroquois as allies, buying their furs and supplying them with trading goods and guns.

By the last decade of the seventeenth century it had become clear that the Dutch lacked the strength to maintain a big empire and that Spain was fast declining. The future, especially in North America, belonged to England and France. In the wars of the next 125 years European alliances shifted dramatically, yet the English and what the Boston lawyer John Adams called "the turbulent Gallicks" were always on opposite sides.

In the first three of these conflicts colonists played only minor parts. The fighting in America consisted chiefly of sneak attacks on isolated outposts. In King William's War (1689–1697), the American phase of the War of the League of Augsburg, French forces raided Schenectady in New York and frontier settlements in New England. English colonists retaliated by capturing Port Royal, Nova Scotia, only to lose that outpost in a counterattack in 1691. The Peace of Ryswick in 1697 restored all captured territory in America to the original owners.

The next struggle was the War of the Spanish Succession (1702–1713), fought to prevent the union of Spain and France under the Bourbons. The Americans named this conflict Queen Anne's War. French-inspired Indians razed Deerfield, Massachusetts (see the feature essay, American Lives, "Eunice Williams/Gannenstenhawi," pp. 90–91). A party of Carolinians burned St. Augustine in Spanish Florida. The New Englanders retook Port Royal. In the Treaty of Utrecht in 1713, France yielded Nova Scotia, Newfoundland, and the Hudson Bay region to Great Britain.

► *text continues on page 92*

American Lives

Eunice Williams/Gannenstenhawi

The sound of glass shattering and wood splintering woke seven-year-old Eunice Williams. Indians were ransacking the house. Her father shouted for help. Then footsteps pounded up the stairs and strangers rushed into her room. Strong hands yanked her out of bed and pushed her toward the stairs and down. John, only six, clung to her. The barn was ablaze. Her father, arms tied, was in his nightshirt. Indians taunted him with strange words and waved their hatchets before his face. After a time several grabbed John and the baby and took them outside; another Indian followed with a club. Eunice's mother screamed but they held her back. After a few moments the Indians came back in and seized Parthena, a slave. They dragged her outside and her screams stopped.

Soon, morning light filtered through the broken window. The Indians untied one of Eunice's father's arms, gave him his pants and gestured for him to dress. They also thrust clothes toward her, and she put them on. Then she and her family were herded outside, where Parthena and Little John lay dead in the snow, and the baby in a heap near a boulder. The Indians rushed them into the meeting house. Inside, many of Eunice's neighbors were huddled against a wall. The Indians gave them all moccasins, and forced them to run toward the woods. Gunshots clattered at the far edge of the village, and the Indians made them run faster, deep into the forest. Those who lingered were dispatched with clubs or hatchets.

Throughout the day the captives scrambled onward. When Eunice stumbled and fell, exhausted, an Indian carried her on his shoulders, mile after mile. At night he covered her with a blanket. Sunrise brought the same frantic rush to the north. Eunice's mother, weakened from the new baby, fell behind. Her father tried to help her but could not. He paused with her to pray, but the Indians pushed him forward. Eunice never saw her mother again.

The Indians broke into smaller groups, and Eunice was separated from her father and brothers. The same Indian as before carried her. When they rested, he gave her the best pieces of meat. He smiled, saying something she didn't understand.

During the weeks that followed she was taken several hundred miles to a large Mohawk settlement near Montréal. There, the captive men were stripped naked and forced to run past the villagers, who beat and poked them with clubs and burning sticks. The women and children were treated more leniently. Their hair was cut; some had their ears pierced. Amidst great ceremony, they were immersed in water and their bodies were painted. Then they were given Mohawk clothing. Women wore loose sleeveless tunics, skirts that hung to their knees, leggings ornamented with moosehair, and leather moccasins. Their hair was greased and pulled back, fastened with a ribbon of eelskin.

Eunice was settled among a Mohawk family, and she came to understand that she had been adopted by them. But the family was unlike the one she had known. Mohawk husbands and wives lived apart from each other, with their own parents; children stayed with their mother and her large group of relatives.

In 1706, two years after Eunice had been taken from Deerfield, her father, a puritan minister, was ransomed and returned home. Her brothers were similarly "redeemed" soon afterward. But the Mohawk made no offer to redeem Eunice. In response to written pleas from her father, the Mohawk stated that they "would as soon part with their hearts" as with Eunice; besides, they added, the girl was "unwilling to return" to Massachusetts. In 1713 her father received word that his daughter had married a Mohawk.

Shortly afterward, English and French officials prevailed on the Mohawk to allow Eunice to speak with a trader sent by her father. By then, she had forgotten English, so the trader was obliged to speak to her through an interpreter. He pleaded for her to return home. She sat in stony silence. Finally, she uttered two Mohawk words: "Jaghte Oghte"—"maybe not." She would remain with her people: the Mohawk.

Decades later, she agreed to visit her English brothers. The women of Deerfield gave her a dress and invited her to stay in their homes, but she wrapped herself in an Indian blanket and slept in an orchard with her husband. She returned to Canada and died there in 1785, where she was known by the name, Gannenstenhawi, "she who brings in corn."

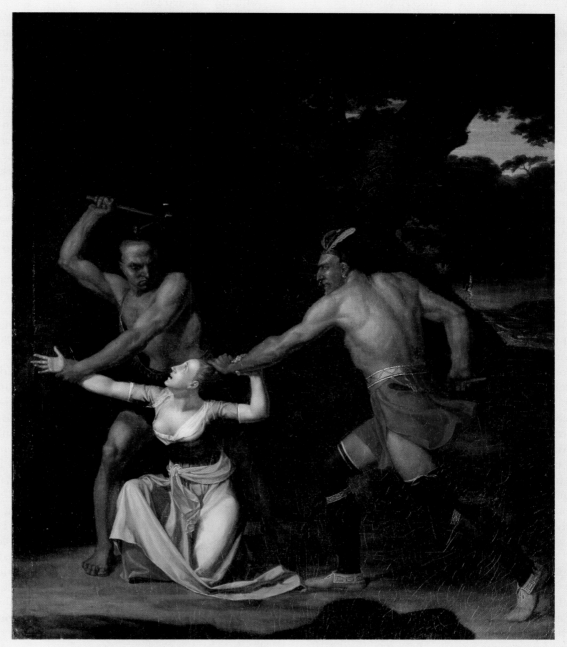

▲ In *The Death of Jane McCrae* (1803–1804), the young painter John Vanderlyn, who had been studying in Europe, poses the Indians and their victim in the manner of ancient Greek sculpture. Although little is known about the real McCrae, she was captured and killed, at age 25, while sneaking off to marry a British soldier. She became one of the American nation's first heroines. Such scenes, though, were unusual. Indians such as the Mohawks fought "mourning wars" specifically to acquire captives to replace population losses from disease and war. Abenaki Indians, who also participated in the raid on Deerfield, preferred to sell their captives or hold them for ransom.

If the colonies were mere pawns in these wars, battle casualties were proportionately high and the civilian population of New England (and of Canada) paid heavily because of the fighting. Many frontier settlers were killed in the raids. Hundreds of townspeople died during the campaigns in Nova Scotia. Massachusetts taxes went up sharply and the colony issued large amounts of paper currency to pay its bills, causing an inflation that ate into the living standards of wage earners.

The American phase of the third Anglo-French conflict, the War of the Austrian Succession (1740–1748), was called King George's War. The usual Indian raids were launched in both directions across the lonely forests that separated the St. Lawrence settlements from the New York and New England frontier. A New England force captured the strategic fortress of Louisbourg on Cape Breton Island, guarding the entrance to the Gulf of St. Lawrence. The Treaty of Aix-la-Chapelle in 1748, however, required the return of Louisbourg, much to the chagrin of the New Englanders.

As this incident suggests, the colonial wars generated a certain amount of trouble between England and the colonies; matters that seemed unimportant in London might loom large in American eyes, and vice versa. But the conflicts were seldom serious. The wars did, however, increase the bad feelings between settlers north and south of the St. Lawrence. Every Indian raid was attributed to French provocateurs, although more often than not the English colonists themselves were responsible for the Indian troubles. Conflicting land claims further aggravated the situation. Massachusetts, Connecticut, and Virginia possessed overlapping claims to the Ohio Valley, and Pennsylvania and New York also had pretensions in the region. Yet the French, ranging broadly across the mid-continent, insisted that the Ohio country was exclusively theirs.

THE GREAT WAR FOR THE EMPIRE

In this beautiful, almost untouched land, a handful of individuals determined the future of the continent. Over the years the French had established a chain of forts and trading posts running from Mackinac Island in northern Michigan to Kaskaskia on the Mississippi and Vincennes on the Wabash, and from Niagara in the east to the Bourbon River, near Lake Winnipeg, in the west. By the 1740s, however, Pennsylvania fur traders, led by George Croghan, a rugged Irishman, were setting up posts north of the Ohio River and bargaining with Miami and Huron Indians, who ordinarily sold their furs to the French. In 1748 Croghan built a fort at Pickawillany, deep in the Miami country, in what is now western Ohio. That same year agents of a group of Virginia land speculators who had recently organized what they called the Ohio Company reached this area.

With trifling exceptions, an insulating band of wilderness had always separated the French and English in America. Now the two powers came into contact. The immediate result was a showdown battle for control of North America, the "great war for the empire." Thoroughly alarmed by the presence of the English on land they had long considered their own, the French struck hard. Attacking suddenly in 1752, they wiped out Croghan's post at Pickawillany and drove his traders back into Pennsylvania. Then they built a string of barrier forts south from Lake Erie along the Pennsylvania line: Fort Presque Isle, Fort Le Boeuf, Fort Venango.

The Pennsylvania authorities chose to ignore this action, but Lieutenant Governor Robert Dinwiddie of Virginia (who was an investor in the Ohio Company) dispatched a 21-year-old surveyor named George Washington to warn the French that they were trespassing on Virginia territory.

Washington, a gangling, inarticulate, and intensely ambitious young planter, made his way northwest in the fall of 1753 and delivered Dinwiddie's message to the commandant at Fort Le Boeuf. It made no impression. "[The French] told me," Washington reported, "that it was their absolute Design to take Possession of the Ohio, and by G— they would do it." Governor Dinwiddie thereupon promoted Washington to lieutenant colonel and sent him back in the spring of 1754 with 150 men to seize a strategic junction south of the new French forts, where the Allegheny and Monongahela rivers join to form the Ohio.

Eager but inexperienced in battle, young Washington botched his assignment. As his force labored painfully through the tangled mountain country southeast of the fork of the Ohio, he received word that the French had already occupied the position and were constructing a powerful post, Fort Duquesne. Outnumbered by perhaps four to one, Washington foolishly pushed on. He surprised and routed a French reconnaissance party, but this brought on him the main body of enemy troops.

Hastily he threw up a defensive position, aptly named Fort Necessity, but the ground was ill chosen; the French easily surrounded the fort and Washington had to surrender. After tricking the young officer, who could not read French, into signing an admission that he had "assassinated" the leader of the reconnaissance party, his captors, with the gateway to the Ohio country firmly in their hands, permitted him and his men to march off. Nevertheless, Washington returned to Virginia a hero, for although still undeclared, this was war, and he had struck the first blow against the hated French.

In the resulting conflict, which historians call the French and Indian War (to the colonists it was simply "the French War"), the English outnumbered the French by about 1.5 million to 90,000. But the English were divided and disorganized, the French disciplined and united. The French controlled the disputed territory, and most of the Indians took their side. As a colonial official wrote, together they made formidable forest fighters, "sometimes in our Front, sometimes in our Rear, and often on all sides of us, Hussar Fashion, taking the Advantage of every Tree and Bush." With an ignorance and arrogance typical of eighteenth-century colonial administration, the British mismanaged the war and failed to make effective use of local resources. For several years they stumbled from one defeat to another.

General Edward Braddock, a competent but uninspired soldier, was dispatched to Virginia to take command. In June 1755 he marched against Fort Duquesne with 1400 Redcoats and a smaller number of colonials, only to be decisively defeated by a much smaller force of French and Indians. Braddock died bravely in battle, and only 500 of his men, led by Colonel Washington, who was serving as his aide-de-camp, made their way back to Virginia.

Elsewhere Anglo-American arms fared little better in the early years of the war. Expeditions against Fort Niagara, key to all French defenses in the west, and Crown Point, gateway to Montréal, bogged down. Meanwhile Indians, armed by the French, bathed the frontier in blood. Venting the frustration caused by 150 years of white advance, they attacked defenseless outposts with unrestrained brutality.

The most feared of the "French" Indians were the Delaware, a once-peaceful Pennsylvania tribe that had been harried from their homelands by English and Iroquois. General Braddock paid his Indian allies only £5 each for French scalps but offered £200 for the hair of Shinngass, the Delaware chieftain.

The Seven Years' War

In 1756 the conflict spread to Europe to become the Seven Years' War. Prussia sided with Great Britain, Austria with the French. On the world stage, too, things went badly for the British. Finally, in 1758, as defeat succeeded defeat, King George II was forced to allow William Pitt, whom he detested, to take over leadership of the war effort. Pitt, grandson of "Diamond" Pitt, a nouveau riche East India merchant, was an unstable man who spent much of his life on the verge of madness, but he was a brilliant strategist and capable of inspiring the nation in its hour of trial.

▲ This, the first portrait of George Washington, was done by Charles Willson Peale in 1772. Washington's right hand is inside his vest, a convention later associated with Napoleon; his left hand is behind his back. Perhaps this was to spare the painter of the trouble of rendering hands and fingers, always a challenge.

Pitt recognized, as few contemporaries did, the potential value of North America. Instead of relying on the tightfisted and shortsighted colonial assemblies for men and money, he poured regiment after regiment of British regulars and the full resources of the British treasury into the contest, mortgaging the future recklessly to secure the prize. Grasping the importance of sea power in fighting a war on the other side of the Atlantic, he used the British navy to bottle up the enemy fleet and hamper French communications with Canada. He possessed a keen eye for military genius, and when he discovered it, he ignored seniority and the outraged feelings of mediocre generals and promoted talented young officers to top commands. (His greatest find was James Wolfe, whom he made a brigadier at age 31.)

In the winter of 1758, as Pitt's grand strategy matured, Fort Duquesne fell. It was appropriately

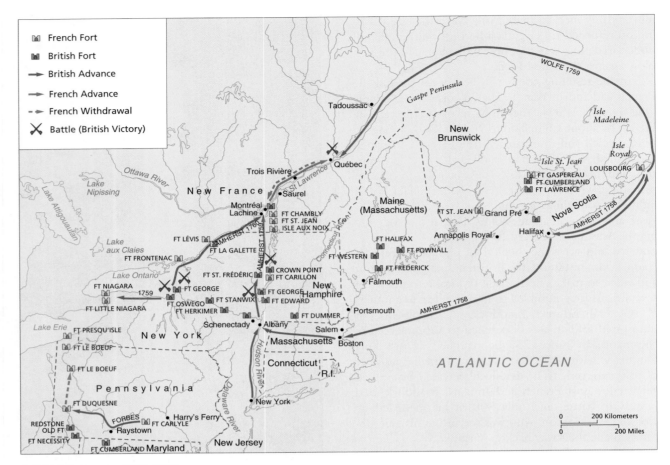

▲ **British Successes, 1758–1763**

renamed Fort Pitt, the present Pittsburgh. The following summer Fort Niagara was overrun. General Jeffrey Amherst took Crown Point, and Wolfe sailed up the St. Lawrence to Québec. There General Louis Joseph de Montcalm had prepared formidable defenses, but after months of probing and planning, Wolfe found and exploited a chink in the city's armor and captured it. Both he and Montcalm died in the battle. In 1760 Montréal fell and the French abandoned all Canada to the British. The British also won major victories against Spanish forces in Cuba and Manila, and against the French in the West Indies and India.

THE PEACE OF PARIS

Peace was restored in 1763 by the Treaty of Paris. Its terms were moderate considering the extent of the British triumph. France abandoned all claim to North America except for two small islands near Newfoundland; Great Britain took over Canada and the eastern half of the Mississippi Valley. Spain got back both the Philippine Islands and Cuba, but in exchange ceded East and West Florida to Great Britain. In a separate treaty, Spain also got New Orleans and the huge area of North America west of the Mississippi River.

"Half the continent," the historian Francis Parkman wrote, "had changed hands at the scratch of a pen." From the point of view of the English colonists in America, the victory was overwhelming. All threat to their frontiers seemed to have been swept away. Surely, they believed in the first happy moments of victory, their peaceful and prosperous expansion was ensured for countless generations.

No honest American could deny that the victory had been won chiefly by British troops and with British gold. Colonial militiamen fought well in defense of their homes or when some highly prized objective seemed ripe for the plucking; they lacked discipline and determination when required to fight far from home and under commanders they did not know. As one American official admitted, it was difficult to get New Englanders to enlist "unless assurances can be given that they shall not march to the southward of certain limits."

Colonials were delighted that scarlet-clad British regulars had borne the brunt of the fighting and hap-

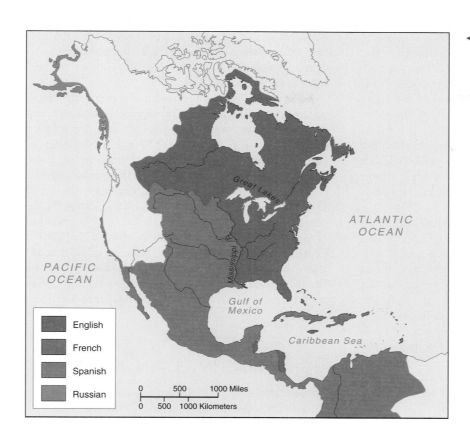

◀ **European Claims in All of North America, 1763**

pier still that the Crown had shouldered most of the financial burden of the long struggle. The local assemblies contributed to the cost, but except for Massachusetts and Virginia their outlays were trivial compared with the £82 million poured into the worldwide conflict by the British.

Little wonder that the great victory produced a burst of praise for king and mother country throughout America. Parades, cannonading, fireworks, banquets, the pealing of church bells—these were the order of the day in every colonial town. "Nothing," said Thomas Pownall, wartime governor of Massachusetts and a student of colonial administration, "can eradicate from [the colonists'] hearts their natural, almost mechanical affection to Great Britain." A young South Carolinian who had been educated in England claimed that the colonists were "more wrapped up in a king" than any people he had ever heard of.

PUTTING THE EMPIRE RIGHT

In London peace proved a time for reassessment; that the empire of 1763 was not the same as the empire of 1754 was obvious. The new, far larger dominion would be much more expensive to maintain. Pitt had spent a huge sum winning and securing it,

much of it borrowed money. Great Britain's national debt had doubled between 1754 and 1763. Now this debt must be serviced and repaid, and the strain that this would place on the economy was clear to all. Furthermore, the day-to-day cost of administering an empire that extended from the Hudson Bay to India was far larger than that which the already burdened British taxpayer could be expected to bear. Before the great war for the empire, Britain's North American possessions were administered for about £70,000 a year; after 1763 the cost was five times as much.

The American empire had also become far more complex. A system of administration that treated it as a string of separate plantations struggling to exist on the edge of the forest would no longer suffice. The war had been fought for control of the Ohio Valley. Now that the prize had been secured, ten thousand hands were eager to make off with it. The urge to expand was, despite the continent's enormous empty spaces, an old American drive. As early as the 1670s eastern stay-at-homes were lamenting the "insatiable desire after Land" that made people willing to "live like Heathen, only that so they might have Elbow-room enough in the world." Frontier warfare had frustrated this urge for seven long years. How best could it be satisfied now that peace had come?

Conflicting colonial claims, based on charters drafted by men who thought the Pacific lay over the next hill, threatened to make the Ohio valley a battleground once more. The Indians remained "unpacified." Rival land companies contested for charters, while fur traders strove to hold back the wave of settlement that must inevitably destroy the world of the beaver and the deer. One Englishman who traveled through America at this time predicted that if the colonists were left to their own devices, "there would soon be civil war from one end of the continent to the other."

Apparently only Great Britain could deal with these problems and rivalries, for when Franklin had proposed a rudimentary form of colonial union—the Albany Plan of 1754—it was rejected by almost everyone. Unfortunately, the British government did not rise to the challenge. Perhaps this was to be expected. A handful of aristocrats (fewer than 150 peers were active in government affairs) dominated British politics, and they were more concerned with local offices and personal advantage than with large questions of policy. An American who spent some time in London in 1764 trying to obtain approval for a plan for the development of the West reported: "The people hear Spend thire time in Nothing but abuseing one Another and Strieveing who shall be in power with a view to Serve themselves and Thire friends." King George III was not a tyrant, as once was commonly believed, but he was an inept politician and the victim of frequent bouts of illness.

Serene in their ignorance, most English leaders insisted that colonials were uncouth and generally inferior beings. During the French and Indian War, British commanders repeatedly expressed contempt for colonial militiamen, whom they considered fit only for "fatigue" duties such as digging trenches, chopping wood, and other noncombat tasks. General Wolfe characterized colonial troops as the "most contemptible cowardly dogs you can conceive," and another English officer, annoyed by their unsanitary habits, complained that they "infect the air with a disagreeable stink." The British officers failed to understand that colonial soldiers were volunteers who had formally contracted to serve under specific conditions. Lord Loudoun, the British commander-in-chief during the French and Indian War, was flabbergasted to discover that New England troops refused to obey one of his direct orders on the ground that it violated their contracts. Little wonder that any officer with a royal commission outranked all officers of the colonial militia, regardless of title. Young Colonel Washington, for example, had to travel all the way from Virginia to the headquarters of the commander-in-chief in Boston to establish his precedence over one Captain John Dagworthy, a Maryland officer who had formerly held a royal commission and who did not propose to let a mere colonial colonel outrank him.

Many English people resented Americans simply because the colonies were rapidly becoming rich and powerful. They were growing at an extraordinary rate. Between 1750 and 1770 the population of British America increased from 1 million to more than 2 million. As early as 1751, Benjamin Franklin predicted that in a century "the greatest number of Englishmen will be on this Side of the Water." (His guess was nearly on the mark: in 1850 the population of Great Britain was 20.8 million, that of the United States 23.1 million, including some 4 million slaves and others who were not of British descent.) If the English did not say much about this possibility, they too considered it from time to time—without Franklin's complacency.

TIGHTENING IMPERIAL CONTROLS

The attempt of the inefficient, ignorant, and indignant British government to deal with the intricate colonial problems that resulted from the great war for the empire led to the American Revolution. Trouble began when the British decided after the French and Indian War to intervene more actively in American affairs. Theoretically the colonies were entirely subordinate to Crown and Parliament, yet except for the disastrous attempt to centralize control of the colonies in the 1680s, they had been allowed a remarkable degree of freedom to manage their own affairs. Of course they had come to expect this as their right.

Parliament had never attempted to tax American colonists. "Compelling the colonies to pay money without their consent would be rather like raising contributions in an enemy's country than taxing Englishmen for their own benefit," Benjamin Franklin wrote. Sir Robert Walpole, initiator of the policy of salutary neglect, recognized the colonial viewpoint. He responded to a suggestion that Parliament tax the colonies by saying: "I will leave that for some of my successors, who may have more courage than I have." Nevertheless, the *legality* of parliamentary taxation, or of other parliamentary intervention in colonial affairs, had not been seriously contested. During King George's War and again during the French and Indian War many British officials in America suggested that Parliament tax the colonies.

Despite the peace treaty of 1763, the American colonies continued to be a drain on the British treasury. Mostly this was due to the cost of fighting Indians. Freed of the restraint posed by French competition,

▲ This engraving depicts Pontiac confronting Colonel Henry Bouquet. Pontiac had good reason to be angry. In a letter dated July 16, 1763 Sir Jeffrey Amherst, commander of British forces in North America, advised Bouquet to infect Pontiac's Indians with smallpox: "You will do well to try to Innoculate the Indians by means of Blancketts, as well as to try Every other method that can serve to Extirpate this Execrable Race." Bouquet responded a week later: "all your directions will be observed."

This Proclamation of 1763 excited much indignation in America. The frustration of dozens of schemes for land development in the Ohio Valley angered many influential colonists. Colonel Washington referred to the proclamation contemptuously as "a temporary expedient to quiet the minds of Indians," and he continued to stake out claims to western lands.

Originally the British had intended the proclamation to be temporary. With the passage of time, however, checking westward expansion seemed a good way to save money, prevent trouble with the Indians, and keep the colonies tied closely to the mother country. The proclamation line, the Board of Trade declared, was "necessary for the preservation of the colonies in due subordination."[1] Naturally this attitude caused resentment in America. To close off the West temporarily in order to pacify the Indians made some sense; to keep it closed was like trying to contain a tidal wave.

Englishmen and colonists increased their pressure on the Indians. Fur traders cheated them outrageously, while callous military men hoped to exterminate them like vermin. One British officer expressed the wish that they could be hunted down with dogs.

Led by an Ottawa chief named Pontiac, the tribes made one last effort to drive the whites back across the mountains. What the whites called Pontiac's "Rebellion" caused much havoc, but it failed. By 1764 most of the western tribes had accepted the peace terms offered by a royal commissioner, Sir William Johnson, one of the few whites who understood and sympathized with them. The British government then placed 15 regiments, some 6000 soldiers, in posts along the entire arc of the frontier, as much to protect the Indians from the settlers as the settlers from the Indians. It proclaimed a new western policy: no settlers were to cross the Appalachian divide. Only licensed traders might do business with the Indians beyond that line. The purchase of Indian land was forbidden. In compensation, three new colonies—Québec, East Florida, and West Florida—were created, but they were not permitted to set up local assemblies.

THE SUGAR ACT

Americans disliked the new western policy but realized that the problems were knotty and that no simple solution existed. Their protests were somewhat muted. Great Britain's effort to raise money in America to help support the increased cost of colonial administration caused far more vehement complaints. George Grenville, who became prime minister in 1763, was a fairly able man, although long-winded and rather narrow in outlook. His reputation as a financial expert was based chiefly on his eagerness to reduce government spending. Under his leadership Parliament passed, in April 1764, the so-called Sugar Act. This law placed tariffs on sugar, coffee, wines, and other things imported into America in substantial amounts. At the same time, measures aimed at en-

---

[1]The British were particularly concerned about preserving the colonies as markets for their manufactures. They feared that the spread of population beyond the mountains would stimulate local manufacturing because the high cost of land transportation would make British goods prohibitively expensive.

▶ **Proclamation of 1763**
 George III's Proclamation of 1763 in effect reserved for the Indians the vast area across the Appalachians (except for the new royal colonies of Québec, East Florida, and West Florida) as far west as Spanish Louisiana and as far north as the Hudson Bay Company preserve.

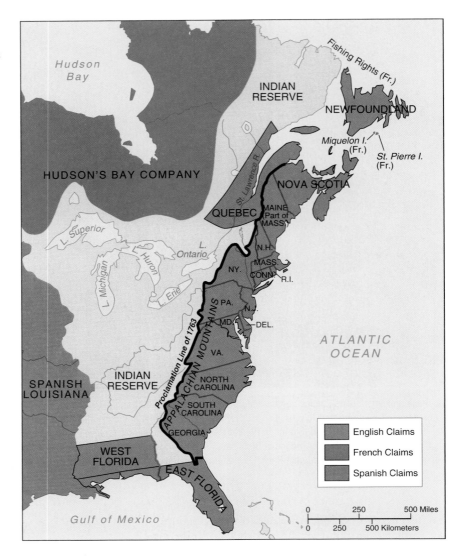

forcing all the trade laws were put into effect. Those accused of violating the Sugar Act were to be tried before British naval officers in vice admiralty courts. Grenville was determined to end smuggling, corruption, and inefficiency. Soon the customs service was collecting each year 15 times as much in duties as it had before the war.

Otis, The Rights of the British Colonies Asserted and Proved

More alarming was the nature of the Sugar Act and the manner of its passage. The Navigation Act duties had been intended to regulate commerce, and the sums collected had not cut deeply into profits. Indeed, the Navigation Acts might well be considered an instrument of imperial foreign policy, an area of government that everyone willingly conceded to London. Yet few Americans were willing to concede that Parliament had the right to tax them. As *Englishmen* they believed that no one should be deprived arbitrarily of property and that, as James Otis put it in his stirring pamphlet *The Rights of the British Colonies Asserted and Proved* (1764), written during the controversy over writs of assistance, everyone should be "free from all taxes but what he consents to in person, or by his representative." John Locke had made clear in his *Second Treatise on Government* (1690) that property ought never be taken from people without their consent, not because material values transcend all others but because human liberty can never be secure when arbitrary power of any kind exists. "If our Trade may be taxed why not our Lands?" the Boston town meeting asked when news of the Sugar Act reached America. "Why not the produce of our Lands and every Thing we possess or make use of?"

AMERICAN COLONISTS DEMAND RIGHTS

To most people in Great Britain the colonial protest against taxation without representation seemed a hypocritical quibble, and it is probably true that in 1764 many of the protesters had not thought the argument through. The distinction between tax laws and other types of legislation was artificial, the British reasoned. Either Parliament was sovereign in America or it was not, and only a fool or a traitor would argue that it was not. If the colonists were loyal subjects of George III, as they claimed, they should bear cheerfully their fair share of the cost of governing his widespread dominions. As to representation, the colonies *were* represented in Parliament; every member of that body stood for the interests of the entire empire. If Americans had no say in the election of members of Commons, neither did most English subjects.

This concept of "virtual" representation accurately described the British system. But it made no sense in America, where from the time of the first settlements members of the colonial assemblies had represented the people of the districts in which they stood for office. The confusion between virtual and actual (geographically based) representation revealed the extent to which colonial and British political practices had diverged over the years.

The British were correct in concluding that selfish motives influenced colonial objections to the Sugar Act. The colonists denounced taxation without representation, but an offer of a reasonable number of seats in Parliament would not have satisfied them. They would probably have complained about paying taxes to support imperial administration even if imposed by their own assemblies. American abundance and the simplicity of colonial life had enabled them to prosper without assuming any considerable tax burden. Now their maturing society was beginning to require communal rather than individual solutions to the problems of existence. Not many of them were prepared to face up to this hard truth.

Over the course of colonial history Americans had taken a narrow view of imperial concerns. They had avoided complying with the Navigation Acts whenever they could profit by doing so. Colonial militiamen had compiled a sorry record when asked to fight for Britain or even for the inhabitants of colonies other than their own. True, most Americans professed loyalty to the Crown, but not many would voluntarily open their purses except to benefit themselves. In short they were provincials, in attitude and in fact.

Although the colonists were opposed in principle to taxation without representation, they failed to agree on a common plan of resistance. Many of the assemblies drafted protests, but these varied in force as well as in form. Merchant groups that tried to organize boycotts of products subject to the new taxes met with indifferent success. Then in 1765 Parliament provided the flux necessary for welding colonial opinion by passing the Stamp Act.

THE STAMP ACT: THE POT SET TO BOILING

The Stamp Act placed stiff excise taxes on all kinds of printed matter. No one could sell newspapers or pamphlets, or convey licenses, diplomas, or legal papers without first buying special stamps and affixing them to the printed matter. Stamp duties were intended to be relatively painless to pay and cheap to

Stamp Act Stamps

▲ Outraged at the Stamp Act of 1765, which implemented a direct tax on printed matter, an angry mob burned the stamps in protest. Note the enthusiastic participation of women and a young black; that they are not wearing shoes indicates that they were of working-class background.

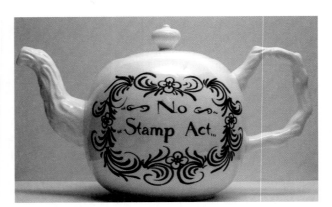

▲ By the mid-eighteenth century, tea had become a staple of the colonists' diet. (In 1766, for example, the residents of the Philadelphia poor house demanded that they be served Bohea tea rather than cheaper substitutes.) But colonial ceramics could not withstand boiling water. Thus tea cups and tea pots were manufactured in Staffordshire, England, which had perfected high-temperature ceramics. This "No Stamp Tax" teapot—ironically—was manufactured in England.

collect; in England similar taxes brought in about £100,000 annually. Grenville hoped the Stamp Act would produce £60,000 a year in America, and the law provided that all revenue should be applied to "defraying the necessary expenses of defending, protecting, and securing, the . . . colonies."

Hardly a farthing was collected. As the Boston clergyman Jonathan Mayhew explained, "Almost every British American . . . considered it as an infraction of their rights, or their dearly purchased privileges." The Sugar Act had been related to Parliament's uncontested power to control colonial trade, but the Stamp Act was a direct tax. When Parliament ignored the politely phrased petitions of the colonial assemblies, more vigorous protests quickly followed.

Virginia took the lead. In late May 1765 Patrick Henry introduced resolutions asserting redundantly that the Burgesses possessed "the only and sole and exclusive right and power to lay taxes" on Virginians and suggesting that Parliament had no legal authority to tax the colonies at all. Henry spoke for what the royal governor called the "Young, hot and Giddy Members" of the legislature (most of whom, incidentally, had absented themselves from the meeting). The more extreme of Henry's resolutions were defeated, but the debate they occasioned attracted wide and favorable attention. On June 6 the Massachusetts assembly proposed an intercolonial Stamp Act Congress, which, when it met in New York City in October, passed another series of resolutions of protest. The Stamp Act and other recent acts of Parliament were "burthensome and grievous," the delegates declared.

"It is unquestionably essential to the freedom of a people . . . that no taxes be imposed on them but with their own consent."

During the summer irregular organizations known as Sons of Liberty began to agitate against the act. Far more than anyone realized, this marked the start of the revolution. For the first time extralegal organized resistance was taking place, distinct from protest and argument conducted by constituted organs of government like the House of Burgesses and the Massachusetts General Court.

Although led by men of character and position, the "Liberty Boys" frequently resorted to violence to achieve their aims. In Boston they staged vicious riots, looting and vandalizing the houses of the stamp master and his brother-in-law, Lieutenant Governor Thomas Hutchinson. In Connecticut stamp master Jared Ingersoll, a man of great courage and dignity, faced an angry mob demanding his resignation. When threatened with death if he refused, he coolly replied that he was prepared to die "perhaps as well now as another Time." Probably his life was not really in danger, but the size and determination of the crowd convinced him that resistance was useless, and he capitulated.

The stamps were printed in England and shipped to stamp masters (all Americans) in the colonies well in advance of November 1, 1765, the date the law was to go into effect. The New York stamp master had resigned, but the stamps were stored in the city under military guard. Radicals distributed placards reading: "The first Man that either distributes or makes use of Stampt Paper let him take care of his House, Person, and Effects. We dare." When Major Thomas James, the British officer who had charge of the stamps, promised that "the stamps would be crammed down New Yorkers' throats," a mob responded by breaking into his house, drinking all his wine, and smashing his furniture and china.

In some colonies the stamps were snatched by mobs and put to the torch amid rejoicing. Elsewhere they were locked up in secret by British officials or held on shipboard. For a time no business requiring stamped paper was transacted; then, gradually, people began to defy the law by issuing and accepting unstamped documents. Threatened by mob action should they resist, British officials stood by helplessly. The law was a dead letter.

The looting associated with this crisis alarmed many colonists, including some prominent opponents of the Stamp Act. "When the pot is set to boil," the lawyer John Adams remarked sadly, "the scum rises to the top." Another Bostonian called the vandalizing of Thomas Hutchinson's house a "flagrant instance of to what a pitch of infatuation an

DOCUMENT

Franklin, Testimony Against the Stamp Act

incensed populace can rise." Such people worried that the protests might be aimed at the wealthy and powerful in America as well as at British tyranny. This does not mean that they disapproved of crowd protests, or even the destruction of property during such protests, as distinct from stealing. Many such people took part in the rioting. "State-quakes," John Adams also said, this time complacently, were comparable to "earthquakes" and other kinds of natural violence.

RIOTERS OR REBELS?

That many of the poor resented the colonial elite goes without saying, as does the fact that in many instances the rioting got out of hand and took on a social as well as a political character. Times were hard, and the colonial elite, including most of the leading critics of British policy, had little compassion for the poor, whom they feared could be corrupted by anyone who offered them a square meal or a glass of rum. Once roused, laborers and artisans may well have directed their energies toward righting what they considered local wrongs.

Yet the mass of the people, being owners of property and capable of influencing political decisions, were not social revolutionaries. They might envy and resent the wealth and power of the great landowners and merchants, but there is little evidence that they wished to overthrow the established order.

The British were not surprised that Americans disliked the Stamp Act. They had not anticipated, however, that Americans would react so violently and so unanimously. Americans did so for many reasons. Business continued to be poor in 1765, and at a time when 3 shillings was a day's wage for an urban laborer, the stamp tax was 2 shillings for an advertisement in a newspaper, 5 shillings for a will, and 20 shillings for a license to sell liquor. The taxes would hurt the business of lawyers, merchants, newspaper editors, and tavernkeepers. Even clergymen dealt with papers requiring stamps. The protests of such influential and articulate people had a powerful impact on public opinion.

The greatest cause of concern to the colonists was Great Britain's flat rejection of the principle of no taxation without representation. This alarmed them for two closely related reasons. First of all, *as Americans* they objected to being taxed by a legislative body they had not been involved in choosing. To buy a stamp was to surrender all claim to self-government. Secondly, as *British subjects* they valued what they called "the rights of Englishmen." They saw the Stamp Act as only the worst in a series of arbitrary invasions of these rights.

Already Parliament had passed still another measure, the Quartering Act, requiring local legislatures to house and feed new British troops sent to the colonies. Besides being a form of indirect taxation, a standing army was universally deemed to be a threat to liberty. Why were Redcoats necessary in Boston and New York where there was no foreign enemy for thousands of miles in any direction? In hard times, soldiers were particularly unwelcome because, being miserably underpaid, they took any odd jobs they could get in their off hours, thus competing with unemployed colonists.

Reluctantly, many Americans were beginning to fear that the London authorities had organized a conspiracy to subvert the liberties of all British subjects.

TAXATION OR TYRANNY?

In the eighteenth century the English were universally recognized to be the freest people in the world. In Mozart's opera, *The Abduction from the Seraglio* (1782), when the Turk Osmin tells the kidnapped Blonda that she is his slave, a "gift" from his master, she replies contemptuously: "A slave! I am an Englishwoman, born to freedom." Americans, like their English cousins, attributed their freedom to what they called their balanced government. In Britain power appeared to be shared by the Crown, the House of Lords (representing the aristocracy), and the House of Commons (representing the rest of the realm). The governors, councils, and assemblies seemed to play analogous roles in the colonies.

In reality this balance of separate forces never existed, either in Britain or in America. The apparent harmony of society was in both instances the product of a lack of seriously divisive issues, not of dynamic tension between rival forces. But the new laws seemed to Americans to threaten the balance, and this idea was reinforced by their observations of the corruption of English elections. Benjamin Franklin, being a colonial agent in London, knew British politics well. He complained that the entire country was "at market" and "might be bought . . . by the Devil himself" for about £12 million. A clique seeking unlimited power was trying to destroy balanced government in Britain and in America, or so many colonists thought.

There was no such conspiracy, yet no certain answer can be made to the question, Were American rights actually in danger? Grenville and his successors were English politicians, not tyrants. They looked down on bumptious colonials but surely had no wish to destroy them or their prosperity. The British attitude was like that of a parent making a recalcitrant youngster swallow a bitter medicine: protests were understandable, but in the patient's own interest they must be ignored. Franklin reported one high official in London as saying: "His Majesty's Instructions . . . are the LAW OF THE LAND; *they are*, the Law of the Land, and as such *ought to be* OBEYED."

At the same time, British leaders believed that the time had come to assert royal authority and centralize imperial power at the expense of colonial autonomy. The need to maintain a substantial British army in America to control the western Indians tempted the government to use some of the troops to "control" white Americans as well. This attitude probably had as much to do with the coming of the revolution as any specific act of Parliament because it flew in the face of the reality that the colonies had progressed beyond the "childhood" stage. They were no longer entirely dependent on "the mother country." Indeed, an increasing number of important colonists believed that America would soon become what Franklin called "a great country, populous and mighty . . . able to shake off any shackles that may be imposed on her."

This view of America's future place in the world did not necessarily mean breaking away from the British Empire. However, it surely meant dealing with Great Britain on terms approaching equality. But psychologically British leaders were not ready to deal with Americans as equals or to consider American interests on a par with their own. In the long run, American liberty would be destroyed if this attitude was not changed.

Besides refusing to use stamps, Americans responded to the Stamp Act by boycotting British goods. Nearly a thousand merchants signed nonimportation agreements. These struck British merchants hard in their pocketbooks, and they began to pressure Parliament for repeal. After a hot debate—Grenville, whose ministry had fallen over another issue, advocated using the army to enforce the act—the hated law was repealed in March 1766. In America there was jubilation at the news. The ban on British goods was lifted and the colonists congratulated themselves on having stood fast in defense of principle.

THE DECLARATORY ACT

The great controversy over the constitutional relationship of colony to mother country was only beginning. The same day that it repealed the Stamp Act, Parliament passed a Declaratory Act stating that the colonies were "subordinate" and that Parliament could enact any law it wished "to bind the colonies and people of America."

To most Americans this bald statement of parliamentary authority seemed unconstitutional—a flagrant violation of their understanding of how the British imperial system was supposed to work. Actually the Declaratory Act highlighted the degree to which British and American views of the system had drifted apart. The English and the colonials were using the same words but giving them different meanings. Their conflicting definitions of the word *representation* was a case in point. Another involved the word *constitution,* the term that James Otis had used in his attack on writs of assistance. To the British the Constitution meant the totality of laws, customs, and institutions that had developed over time and under which the nation functioned. In America, partly because governments were based on specific charters, the word meant a written document or contract spelling out, and thus limiting, the powers of government. If in England Parliament passed an "unconstitutional" law, the result might be rebellion, but that the law existed none would deny. "If the parliament will positively enact a thing to be done which is unreasonable," the great eighteenth-century English legal authority Sir William Blackstone wrote, "I know of no power that can control it." In America people were beginning to think that an unconstitutional law simply had no force.

Even more basic were the differing meanings that English and Americans were giving to the word *sovereignty.* Eighteenth-century English political thinkers believed that sovereignty (ultimate political power) could not be divided. Government and law being based ultimately on force, some "final, unqualified, indivisible" authority had to exist if social order was to be preserved. The Glorious Revolution in England had settled the question of where sovereignty resided—in Parliament. The Declaratory Act, so obnoxious to Americans, seemed to the English the mere explication of the obvious. That colonial governments had passed local laws the English did not deny, but they had done so at the sufferance of the sovereign legislative power, Parliament.

Given these ideas and the long tradition out of which they had sprung, one can sympathize with the British failure to follow the colonists' reasoning (which had not yet evolved into a specific proposal for constitutional reform). But most responsible British officials refused even to listen to the American argument.

THE TOWNSHEND DUTIES

Despite the repeal of the Stamp Act, the British did not abandon the policy of taxing the colonies. If direct taxes were inexpedient, indirect ones like the Sugar Act certainly were not. To persuade Parliament to repeal the Stamp Act, some Americans (most notably Benjamin Franklin) had claimed that the colonists objected only to direct taxes. To draw such a distinction as a matter of principle was absurd, and in fact few colonists had done so. British leaders saw the absurdity but easily convinced themselves that Americans were making the distinction.

Therefore, in June 1767, the chancellor of the exchequer, Charles Townshend, introduced a series of levies on glass, lead, paints, paper, and tea imported into the colonies. Townshend was a charming man experienced in colonial administration, but he was something of a playboy (his nickname was Champagne Charlie), and he lacked both integrity and common sense. He liked to think of Americans as ungrateful children; he once said he would rather see the colonies turned into "Primitive Desarts" than treat them as equals. Townshend thought it "perfect nonsense" to draw a distinction between direct and indirect taxation, yet in his arrogance he believed the colonists were stupid enough to do so.

By this time the colonists were thoroughly on guard, and they responded quickly to the Townshend levies with a new boycott of British goods. In addition they made elaborate efforts to stimulate colonial manufacturing. By the end of 1769 imports from the mother country had been almost halved. Meanwhile, administrative measures enacted along with the Townshend duties were creating more ill will. A Board of Customs Commissioners, with headquarters in Boston, took charge of enforcing the trade laws, and new vice admiralty courts were set up at Halifax, Boston, Philadelphia, and Charleston to handle violations. These courts operated without juries, and many colonists considered the new commissioners rapacious racketeers who systematically attempted to obtain judgments against honest merchants in order to collect the huge forfeitures—one-third of the value of ship and cargo—that were their share of all seizures.

The struggle forced Americans to do some deep thinking about both American and imperial political affairs. The colonies' common interests and growing economic and social interrelationships probably made some kind of union inevitable. Trouble with England speeded the process. In 1765 the Stamp Act Congress (another extralegal organization and thus a further step in the direction of revolution) had brought the delegates of nine colonies to New York. Now, in 1768, the Massachusetts General Court took the next step. It sent the legislatures of the other colonies a "Circular Letter" expressing the "humble opinion" that the Townshend Acts were "Infringements of their natural & constitutional Rights."

The question of the limits of British power in America was much debated, and this too was no doubt inevitable, again because of change and growth. Even in the late seventeenth century the assumptions that led Parliament to pass the Declaratory Act would have been unrealistic. By 1766 they were absurd.

After the passage of the Townshend Acts, John Dickinson, a Philadelphia lawyer, published "Letters from a Farmer in Pennsylvania to the Inhabitants of the British Colonies." Dickinson considered himself a loyal British subject trying to find a solution to colonial troubles. "Let us behave like dutiful children, who have received unmerited blows from a beloved parent," he wrote. Nevertheless, he stated plainly that Parliament had no right to tax the colonies. Another moderate Philadelphian, John Raynell, put it this way: "If the Americans are to be taxed by a Parliament where they are not . . . Represented, they are no longer Englishmen but Slaves."

Some Americans were much more radical than Dickinson. Samuel Adams of Boston, a genuine revolutionary agitator, believed by 1768 that Parliament had no right at all to legislate for the colonies. If few were ready to go that far, fewer still accepted the reasoning behind the Declaratory Act.

The British ignored American thinking. The Massachusetts Circular Letter had been framed in moderate language and clearly reflected the convictions of most of the people in the Bay Colony, yet when news of it reached England, the secretary of state for the colonies, Lord Hillsborough, ordered the governor to dissolve the legislature. Two regiments of British troops were transferred from the frontier to Boston, part of the aforementioned policy of bringing the army closer to the centers of colonial unrest.

THE BOSTON MASSACRE

These acts convinced more Americans that the British were conspiring to destroy their liberties. Resentment was particularly strong in Boston, where the postwar depression had come on top of two decades of economic stagnation. Crowding 4000 tough British soldiers into a town of 16,000 people, many of them as capable of taking care of themselves when challenged as any Redcoat, was a formula for disorder.

How many brawls and minor riots took place in the waterfront taverns and darkened alleys of the colonial ports that winter is lost to history. In January 1770 scuffles between Liberty Boys and Redcoats in the Golden Hill section of New York City resulted in a number of injuries. Then, in Boston on March 5, 1770, real trouble erupted. Late that afternoon a crowd of idlers began tossing snowballs at a company of Redcoats guarding the Custom House. Some of these missiles had been carefully wrapped around suitably sized rocks. Gradually the crowd increased in size and its mood grew meaner. The

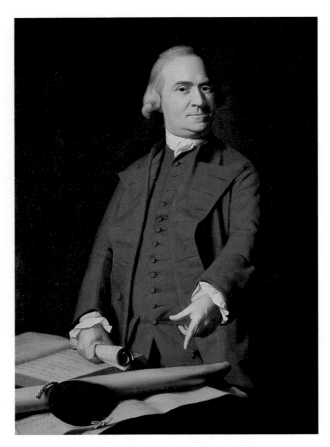

▲ This portrait is from 1772, when Samuel Adams was furious over the Boston massacre. The painter was John Singleton Copley. Although his parents were impoverished Irish immigrants, Copley had recently married the daughter of a rich Tory merchant. Did Copley side with his father-in-law, who detested Adams as a tribune of the "mob," or with Adams?

soldiers panicked and began firing their muskets. When the smoke cleared, five Bostonians lay dead and dying on the bloody ground.

This so-called Boston Massacre infuriated the populace. The violence played into the hands of radicals like Samuel Adams. But just as at the time of the Stamp Act riots, cooler heads prevailed. Announcing that he was "defending the rights of man and unconquerable truth," John Adams volunteered his services to make sure the soldiers got a fair trial. Most were acquitted; the rest were treated leniently by the standards of the day. In Great Britain, confrontation also gave way to adjustment. In April 1770 all the Townshend duties except a threepenny tax on tea were repealed. The tea tax was maintained as a matter of principle. "A peppercorn in acknowledgment of the right was of more value than millions without it," one British peer declared smugly—a glib fallacy.

At this point the nonimportation movement collapsed; although the boycott on tea was continued, many merchants imported British tea and paid the tax too. "Drank green tea," one patriot wrote in describing an afternoon at the merchant John Hancock's. "From Holland, I hope, but don't know."

A kind of postmassacre truce settled over Boston and the rest of British America. During the next two years no serious crisis erupted. Imports of British goods were nearly 50 percent higher than before the nonimportation agreement. So long as the British continued to be conciliatory, the colonists seemed satisfied with their place in the empire.

THE POT SPILLS OVER

In 1772 this informal truce ended and new troubles broke out. The first was plainly the fault of the colonists involved. Early in June the British patrol boat *Gaspee* ran aground in Narragansett Bay, south of Providence, while pursuing a suspected smuggler. The *Gaspee*'s commander, Lieutenant Dudingston, had antagonized everyone in the area by his officiousness and zeal; that night a gang of local people boarded the helpless *Gaspee* and put it to the torch. This action was clearly criminal, but when the British attempted to bring the culprits to justice no one would testify against them. The British, frustrated and angry, were strengthened in their conviction that the colonists were utterly lawless.

Then Thomas Hutchinson, now governor of Massachusetts, announced that henceforth the Crown rather than the local legislature would pay his salary. Since control over the salaries of royal officials gave the legislature a powerful hold on them, this development was disturbing. Groups of radicals formed "committees of correspondence" and stepped up communications with one another, planning joint action in case of trouble. This was another monumental step along the road to revolution; an organized colony-wide resistance movement, lacking in any "legitimate" authority but ready to consult and act in the name of the public interest, was taking shape.

THE TEA ACT CRISIS

In the spring of 1773 an entirely unrelated event precipitated the final crisis. The British East India Company held a monopoly of all trade between India and the rest of the empire. This monopoly had yielded fabulous returns, but decades of corruption and inefficiency together with heavy military expenses in recent years had weakened the company until it was almost bankrupt.

The BLOODY MASSACRE perpetrated in King Street BOSTON on March 5th 1770 by a party of the 29th REG.

Unhappy Boston! see thy Sons deplore,
Thy hallow'd Walks besmear'd with guiltless Gore.
While faithless P——n and his savage Bands,
With murd'rous Rancour stretch their bloody Hands;
Like fierce Barbarians grinning o'er their Prey,
Approve the Carnage and enjoy the Day.

If scalding drops from Rage from Anguish Wrung,
If speechless Sorrows lab'ring for a Tongue,
Or if a weeping World can ought appease
The plaintive Ghosts of Victims such as these;
The Patriot's copious Tears for each are shed,
A glorious Tribute which embalms the Dead.

But know, Fate summons to that awful Goal,
Where Justice strips the Murd'rer of his Soul:
Should venal C——ts the scandal of the Land,
Snatch the relentless Villain from her Hand,
Keen Execrations on this Plate inscrib'd,
Shall reach a Judge who never can be brib'd.

Engrav'd Printed & Sold by Paul Revere Boston

▲ This engraving of the Boston Massacre (1770) became the most reprinted depiction of the event, and probably the most inaccurate. It was done by Paul Revere, engraver, silversmith, and eventual patriot. The British soldiers did not form ranks and fire on command at the crowd. The judge at the subsequent trial of the British soldiers warned jurors not to be influenced by "the prints exhibited in our houses" that added "wings to fancy"—prints, specifically, such as this one. The jury of colonists acquitted all the British soldiers but two, who received mild punishments.

however, to preserve (as Lord North said when the East India Company directors suggested its repeal) the principle of Parliament's right to tax the colonies.

The company then shipped 1700 chests of tea to colonial ports. Though the idea of high-quality tea offered at bargain prices was tempting, after a little thought nearly everyone in America appreciated the dangers involved in buying it. If Parliament could grant the East India Company a monopoly of the tea trade, it could parcel out all or any part of American commerce to whomever it pleased. More important, the act appeared utterly diabolical, a dastardly trick to trap them into paying the tea tax. The plot seemed obvious: the real price of Lord North's tea was American submission to parliamentary taxation.

Public indignation was so great in New York and Philadelphia that when the tea ships arrived, the authorities ordered them back to England without attempting to unload. The tea could be landed only "under the Protection of the Point of the Bayonet and Muzzle of the Cannon," the governor of New York reported. "Even then," he added, "I do not see how the Sales or Consumption could be effected."

The situation in Boston was different. The tea ship *Dartmouth* arrived on November 27. The radicals, marshaled by Sam Adams, were determined to prevent it from landing its cargo; Governor Hutchinson (who had managed to have two of his sons appointed to receive and sell the tea) was equally determined to collect the tax and enforce the law. For days the town seethed. Crowds milled in the streets, harangued by Adams and his friends, while the *Dartmouth* and two later arrivals swung with the tides on their moorings. Then, on the night of December 16, as Hutchinson was preparing to seize the tea for nonpayment of the duty, a band of colonists disguised as Indians rowed out to the ships and dumped the hated tea chests into the harbor.

The destruction of the tea was a serious crime and it was obvious that a solid majority of the people of Boston approved of it. The painted "Patriots" who

Among the assets of this venerable institution were some 17 million pounds of tea stored in English warehouses. The decline of the American market, a result first of the boycott and then of the smuggling of cheaper Dutch tea, partly accounted for the glut. Normally, East India Company tea was sold to English wholesalers. They in turn sold it to American wholesalers, who distributed it to local merchants for sale to the consumer. A substantial British tax was levied on the tea as well as the threepenny Townshend duty. Now Lord North, the new prime minister, decided to remit the British tax and to allow the company to sell directly in America through its own agents. The savings would permit a sharp reduction of the retail price and at the same time yield a nice profit to the company. The Townshend tax was retained,

◄ A noose hanging from a "Liberty Tree" reveals this artist's bias: the "tar-and-feathering" of a British official would doubtless culminate in greater violence. As historian Gordon Wood points out, however, the mob actions of the colonists often "grew out of folk festivals and traditional popular rites." A "tar-and-feathering," though painful and occasionally dangerous, was mostly a humiliation. By the early 1770s, though, the mockery was becoming tinged with violence.

jettisoned the chests were a veritable cross-section of society, and a huge crowd gathered at wharfside and cheered them on. The British burned with indignation when news of the "Tea Party" reached London. People talked (fortunately it was only talk) of flattening Boston with heavy artillery. Nearly everyone, even such a self-described British friend of the colonists as Edmund Burke, agreed that the colonists must be taught a lesson. George III himself said, "We must master them or totally leave them to themselves."

What particularly infuriated the British was the certain knowledge that no American jury would render a judgment against the criminals. The memory of the *Gaspee* affair was fresh in everyone's mind in England, as undoubtedly it was in the minds of those Bostonians who, wearing the thinnest of disguises, brazenly destroyed the tea.

▲ This British caricature of 1775 mocks the protest of the "Patriotic Ladies at Edenton in North Carolina." While women in the background empty their tea canisters, others (amidst some distractions) sign a pledge "not to Conform to the Pernicious Custom of Drinking Tea."

FROM RESISTANCE TO REVOLUTION

Parliament responded in the spring of 1774 by passing the Coercive Acts. The Boston Port Act closed the harbor of Boston to all commerce until its citizens paid for the tea. The Administration of Justice Act provided for the transfer of cases to courts outside Massachusetts when the governor felt that an impartial trial could not be had within the colony. The Massachusetts Government Act revised the colony's charter drastically, strengthening the power of the governor, weakening that of the local town meetings, making the council appointive rather than elective, and changing the method by which juries were selected. These were unwise laws—they cost Great Britain an empire. All of them, and especially the Port Act, were unjust laws as well. Parliament was punishing the entire community for the crimes of individuals. Even more significant, they marked a drastic change in British policy—from legislation and strict administration to treating colonial protesters as criminals, from attempts to persuade and conciliate to coercion and punishment.

The Americans named the Coercive Acts the Intolerable Acts. That the British answer to the crisis was coercion the Americans found unendurable. Although neither the British nor the colonists yet realized it, the American Revolution had begun.

▲ A Philadelphia street scene such as might have been viewed by delegates to the First Continental Congress in 1774. Public space in the colonial city often brought together many different peoples—artisans and gentlemen, black servants (or slaves), and fashionable ladies.

Step by step, in the course of a single decade, a group of separate political bodies, inhabited by people who (if we put aside the slaves who were outside the political system) were loyal subjects of Great Britain, had been forced by the logic of events—by new British policies and by a growing awareness of their common interests—to take political power into their own hands and to unite with one another to exercise that power effectively. Ordinary working people, not just merchants, lawyers, and other well-to-do people, played increasingly more prominent roles in public life as crisis after crisis roused their indignation. This did not yet mean that most Americans wanted to be free from British rule. Nearly every colonist was willing to see Great Britain continue to control, or at least regulate, such things as foreign relations, commercial policy, and other matters of general American interest. Parliament, however—and in the last analysis George III and most Britishers—insisted that their

authority over the colonies was unlimited. Behind their stubbornness lay the arrogant psychology of the European: "*Colonists are inferior. . . . We own you.*"

Lord North directed the Coercive Acts at Massachusetts alone because he assumed that the other colonies, profiting from the discomfiture of Massachusetts, would not intervene, and because of the British tendency to think of the colonies as separate units connected only through London. His strategy failed because his assumption was incorrect: the colonies began at once to act in concert.

Extralegal political acts now became a matter of course. In June 1774 Massachusetts called for a meeting of delegates from all the colonies to consider common action. This First Continental Congress met at Philadelphia in September; only Georgia failed to send delegates. Many points of view were represented, but even the so-called conservative proposal, introduced by Joseph Galloway of Pennsylvania, called for a thorough overhaul of the empire. Galloway suggested an *American* government, consisting of a president general appointed by the king and a grand council chosen by the colonial assemblies, that would manage intercolonial affairs and possess a veto over parliamentary acts affecting the colonies.

This was not what the majority wanted. If taxation without representation was tyranny, so was all legislation. Therefore Parliament had no right to legislate in any way for the colonies. John Adams, while prepared to *allow* Parliament to regulate colonial trade, now believed that Parliament had no inherent right to control it. "The foundation . . . of all free government," he declared, "is a right in the people to participate in their legislative council." Americans "are entitled to a free and exclusive power of legislation in their several provincial legislatures."

Propelled by the reasoning of Adams and others, the Congress passed a declaration of grievances and resolves that amounted to a complete condemnation of Britain's actions since 1763. A Massachusetts proposal

that the people take up arms to defend their rights was endorsed. The delegates also organized a "Continental Association" to boycott British goods and to stop all exports to the empire. To enforce this boycott, committees were appointed locally "to observe the conduct of all persons touching this association" and to expose violators to public scorn.

If the Continental Congress reflected the views of the majority—there is no reason to suspect that it did not—it is clear that the Americans had decided that drastic changes must be made. It was not merely a question of mutual defense against the threat of British power, not only (in Franklin's aphorism) a matter of hanging together lest they hang separately. A nation was being born.

Looking back many years later, one of the delegates to the First Continental Congress made just these points. He was John Adams of Massachusetts, and he said: "The revolution was complete, in the minds of the people, and the Union of the colonies, before the war commenced."

MILESTONES

1650–1696	Parliament enacts Navigation Acts	**1760**	George III becomes king of England
1689–1697	King William's War (War of the League of Augsburg)	**1763**	George III's Proclamation forbids settlement beyond Appalachians
1699–1750	Parliament enacts laws regulating colonial manufacturing	**1764**	Sugar Act places tariffs on sugar, coffee, wines, and other imports
1702–1713	Queen Anne's War (War of the Spanish Succession): France loses Nova Scotia, Newfoundland, and Hudson Bay to Britain	**1765**	Stamp Act places excise taxes on all printed matter, leads to Stamp Tax Congress
1733	Molasses Act's duty leads to smuggling	**1766**	Stamp Act is repealed; Declaratory Act asserts parliamentary authority over colonies
1738–1742	Religious enthusiasm surges during Great Awakening	**1767**	Townshend Duties lead to Massachusetts Circular Letter
1740–1748	King George's War (War of the Austrian Succession)	**1770**	Five American colonists die in Boston Massacre
1743	Benjamin Franklin founds American Philosophical Society	**1772**	Colonists burn *Gaspee*
1752	Franklin discovers nature of lightning	**1773**	Tea Act leads to Boston Tea Party
1754	Albany Congress paves way for Stamp Act Congress and Continental Congress	**1774**	Coercive Acts lead to First Continental Congress
1754–1763	British and American Colonists fight French and Indians in French and Indian War (Seven Years' War)		

SUPPLEMENTARY READING

A full analysis of the British imperial system can be found in the early volumes of L. H. Gipson's *British Empire Before the American Revolution* (1936–1968). See also James A. Henretta, *The Evolution of American Society* (1973), and Michael Kammen, *Empire and Interest* (1974). Jack P. Greene, *Peripheries and Center* (1989), describes how the colonists extended their control of political affairs. On colonial trade and the mercantilist system, see J. J. McCusker and R. R. Menard, *The Economy of British America* (1985), and P. J. Marshall, ed., *The Oxford History of the British Empire: The Eighteenth Century* (1998).

On the Great Awakening, Richard Bushman, *From Puritan to Yankee* (1967) emphasizes psycho-social factors while Frank Lambert, *Inventing the "Great Awakening"* (1999) focuses on the intersection of religion and economics. Catherine A. Brekus, *Strangers and Pilgrims: Female Preaching in America* (1998) addresses a long-neglected subject. See also P. U. Bonami, *Under the Cope of Heaven: Religion, Society, and Politics in Colonial America* (1986). For the Enlightenment, see H. F. May, *The Enlightenment in America* (1976). Fred Anderson, *The Crucible of War* (2000) is a readable and thorough narrative of the Great War for the Empire; see also his *A People's Army: Massachusetts Soldiers and Society in the Seven Years' War* (1984).

On the causes of the Revolution, see Pauline Maier, *From Resistance to Revolution* (1972), Edmund S. Morgan, *The Birth of the Republic* (1977), and Edward Countryman, *The American Revolution* (1985). Valuable local studies include T. H. Breen, *Tobacco Culture* (1985), on Virginia; Countryman's *A People in Revolution* (1989), on New York; and T. M. Doerflinger, *A Vigorous Spirit of Enterprise* (1986), on Philadelphia. Specific issues during the period are treated in E. S. and H. M. Morgan, *The Stamp Act Crisis* (1953), John Shy, *Toward Lexington* (1965), and Alfred F. Young, *The Shoemaker and the Tea Party* (1999).

Bernard Bailyn's *The Ideological Origins of the American Revolution* (1967) and *The Origins of American Politics* (1968) are brilliant analyses of the political thinking and political structure of eighteenth-century America. Other seminal works include Gordon S. Wood, *The Radicalism of the American Revolution* (1992), and Edmund S. Morgan, *Inventing the People: The Rise of Popular Sovereignty in England and America* (1988). See also Pauline Maier, *The Old Revolutionaries* (1980). On Benjamin Franklin, see two good recent biographies, by Edmund Morgan (2002) and Walter Isaacson (2003).

The full story of Eunice Williams/Gannenstenhawi is brilliantly told in John Demos, *The Unredeemed Captive* (1994); for the Indian perspective of the same event, see *Evan Haefeli* and *Kevin Sweeney, Captors and Captives: The 1704 French and Indian Raid on Deerfield* (2003).

SUGGESTED WEBSITES

Colonial Era Timeline
www.historyplace.com/unitedstates/revolution/rev-col.htm
This site provides information about colonial-era issues.

Colonial Documents
http://www.yale.edu/lawweb/avalon/18th.htm
The key documents are reproduced on this Yale University site, as are some important documents from other periods of U.S. history.

Jonathan Edwards
http://www.jonathanedwards.com/
This site includes the text of speeches delivered by Preacher Jonathan Edwards.

The French and Indian War
http://web.syr.edu/~laroux/
This site, treating the French and Indian War, includes chronologies and documents, as well as materials dealing with the French soldiers who fought in the conflict.

The Early America Review
http://earlyamerica.com/
This site explores the colonies through the colonial media.

White Oak Fur Post
http://www.whiteoak.org/
This site documents an eighteenth-century fur trading post among the Indians in the region that would become Minnesota.

The American Revolution

BOSTON

CHARLES TOWN

▼ On June 17, 1775, the British tried to dislodge Continentals from fortified (and concealed) positions atop Breed's Hill. The misnamed Battle of Bunker Hill resulted in the loss of 1000 Redcoats, and only 400 colonists.

CHAPTER CONTENTS

The actions of the First Continental Congress led the British authorities to force a showdown with their bumptious colonial offspring. "The New England governments are in a state of rebellion," George III announced. "Blows must decide whether they are to be subject to this country or independent." General Thomas Gage, veteran of Braddock's ill-fated expedition against Fort Duquesne and now commander-in-chief of all British forces in North America, had already been appointed governor of Massachusetts. Some 4000 Redcoats were concentrated in Boston, camped on the town common once peacefully reserved for the citizens' cows.

Parliament echoed with demands for a show of strength in America. After the Tea Party the general impression was that resistance to British rule was concentrated in Massachusetts. Based on the behavior of colonial militia in the French and Indian War, most Britishers did not think people in the other colonies would be inclined to fight outside their own region. General James Grant announced that with 1000 men he "would undertake to go from one end of America to the other, and geld all the males, partly by force and partly by a little coaxing."

Some opposed the idea of crushing the colonists, and others believed that it could not be easily managed, but they were a small minority. The House of Commons listened to Edmund Burke's magnificent speech on conciliating the colonies and then voted 270 to 78 against him.

"THE SHOT HEARD ROUND THE WORLD"

The London government decided to use troops against Massachusetts in January 1775, but the order did not reach General Gage until April. In the interim both sides were active. Parliament voted new troop levies and declared Massachusetts to be in a state of rebellion. The Massachusetts Patriots, as they were now calling themselves, formed an extralegal provincial assembly, reorganized the militia, and began training "Minute Men" and other fighters. Soon companies armed with anything that would shoot were drilling on town commons throughout Massachusetts and in other colonies too.

When Gage received his orders on April 14, he acted swiftly. The Patriots had been accumulating

▲ Two weeks after the battle of Lexington and Concord, Ralph Earl, a colonial militiaman from Connecticut, was ordered to make sketches and paintings of what had transpired. Earl revisited the battlefield and interviewed those who had fought. He was an accurate painter, but not a very good one. Note that each of the British formations, facing officers, contains exactly 25 men.

arms at Concord, some 20 miles west of Boston. On the night of April 18, Gage dispatched 700 crack troops to seize these supplies. The Patriots were prepared. Paul Revere and other horsemen rode off to alert the countryside and warn John Hancock and Sam Adams, leaders of the provincial assembly, whose arrests had been ordered.

DOCUMENT

Warren, "Account of the Battle of Lexington"

When the Redcoats reached Lexington early the next morning, they found the common occupied by about 70 Minute Men. After an argument, the Americans began to withdraw. Then someone fired a shot. There was a flurry of gunfire and the Minute Men fled, leaving eight of their number dead. The British then marched on to Concord, where they destroyed whatever supplies the Patriots had been unable to carry off.

But militiamen were pouring into the area from all sides. A hot skirmish at Concord's North Bridge forced the Redcoats to yield that position. Becoming alarmed, they began to march back to Boston. Soon they were being subjected to a withering fire from American irregulars along their line of march. A strange battle developed on a "field" 16 miles long and only a few hundred yards wide. Gage was obliged to send out an additional 1500 soldiers, and total disaster was avoided only by deploying skirmishers to root out snipers hiding in barns and farmhouses along the road to Boston. When the first day of the Revolutionary War ended, the British had sustained 273 casualties, the Americans fewer than 100. "The Rebels are not the despicable rabble too many have supposed them to be," General Gage admitted.

For a brief moment of history tiny Massachusetts stood alone at arms against an empire that had humbled France and Spain. Yet Massachusetts assumed the offensive! The provincial government organized an expedition that captured Fort Ticonderoga and Crown Point, on Lake Champlain. The other colonies rallied quickly to the cause, sending reinforcements to Cambridge. When news of the battle reached Virginia, George Washington wrote sadly, "A brother's sword has been sheathed in a brother's breast and the once happy and peaceful plains of America are either to be drenched in blood or inhabited by a race of slaves." And then he added: "Can a virtuous man hesitate in his choice?"

THE SECOND CONTINENTAL CONGRESS

On May 10, 1775, the day Ticonderoga fell, the Second Continental Congress met in Philadelphia. It was a distinguished group, more radical than the First

Congress. Besides John and Sam Adams, Patrick Henry and Richard Henry Lee of Virginia, and Christopher Gadsden of South Carolina, all holdovers from the First Congress, there was Thomas Jefferson, a lanky, sandy-haired young planter from Virginia. Jefferson had recently published "A Summary View of the Rights of British America," an essay criticizing the institution of monarchy and warning George III that "kings are the servants, not the proprietors of the people." The Virginia convention had also sent George Washington, who knew more than any other colonist about commanding men and who wore his buff-and-blue colonel's uniform, a not-too-subtle in-dication of his willingness to place this knowledge at the disposal of the Congress. The renowned Ben-jamin Franklin was a delegate, moving rapidly to the radical position.

The Boston merchant John Hancock was chosen president of the Congress, which, like the first, had no legal authority. Yet the delegates had to make ago-nizing decisions under the pressure of rapidly unfold-ing military events, with the future of every American depending on their actions. Delicate negotiations and honeyed words might yet persuade king and Parlia-ment to change their ways, but precipitate, bold ef-fort was essential to save Massachusetts.

In this predicament the Congress naturally dealt first with the military crisis. It organized the forces gathering around Boston into the so-called Conti-nental Army and appointed George Washington com-mander-in-chief. After Washington and his staff left for Massachusetts on June 23, the Congress turned to the task of requisitioning men and supplies.

THE BATTLE OF BUNKER HILL

Meanwhile, in Massachusetts, the first major battle of the war had been fought. The British position on the peninsula of Boston was impregnable to direct assault, but high ground north and south, at Charlestown and Dorchester Heights, could be used to pound the city with artillery. When the Continentals seized Bunker Hill and Breed's Hill at Charlestown and set up de-fenses on the latter, Gage determined at once to drive them off. This was accomplished on June 17. Twice the Redcoats marched in close ranks, bayonets fixed, up Breed's Hill, each time being driven back after suf-fering heavy losses. Stubbornly they came again, and this time they carried the redoubt, for the defenders had run out of ammunition.

The British then cleared the Charlestown penin-sula, but the victory was really the Americans', for they had proved themselves against professional sol-diers and had exacted a terrible toll. More than 1000 Redcoats had fallen in a couple of hours, out of a

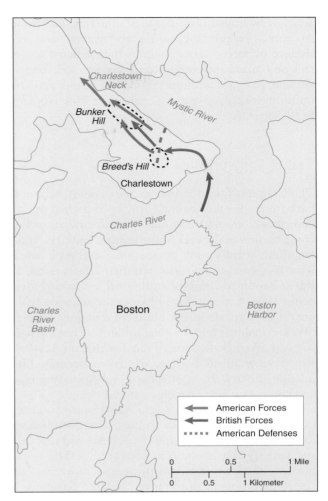

▲ **The Battle of Bunker Hill**
Most of the so-called Battle of Bunker Hill actually took place on Breed's Hill nearby. This area today is all part of the city of Boston.

force of some 2500, while the Continentals lost only 400 men, most of them cut down by British bayonets after the hill was taken. "The day ended in glory," a British officer wrote, "but the loss was uncommon in officers for the number engaged."

The Battle of Bunker Hill, as it was called for no good reason, greatly reduced whatever hope remained for a negotiated settlement. The spilling of so much blood left each side determined to force the other's submission. The British recalled General Gage, replac-ing him with General William Howe, a respected vet-eran of the French and Indian War, and George III formally proclaimed the colonies to be "in open rebel-lion." The Continental Congress dispatched one last plea to the king (the Olive Branch Petition), but this was a sop to the moderates. Immediately thereafter it adopted the Declaration of the Causes and Necessity of Taking Up Arms, which condemned everything the British had done since 1763. Americans were "a people attacked by unprovoked enemies"; the time had come to choose between "submission" to "tyranny" and "resistance by force." The Congress then ordered an attack on Canada and created committees to seek foreign aid and to buy munitions abroad. It authorized the outfitting of a navy under Commodore Esek Hopkins of Rhode Island.

THE GREAT DECLARATION

The Congress (and the bulk of the people) still hung back from a break with the Crown. To declare for independence would be to burn the last bridge, to become traitors in the eyes of the mother country. Aside from the word's ugly associations, everyone knew what happened to traitors when their efforts failed. It was sobering to think of casting off everything that being English meant: love of king, the traditions of a great nation, pride in the power of a mighty empire. "Where shall we find another Britain?" John Dickinson had asked at the time of the Townshend Acts crisis. "Torn from the body to which we are united by religion, liberty, laws, affections, relation, language and commerce, we must bleed at every vein."

Then, too, rebellion might end in horrors worse than submission to British tyranny. The disturbances following the Stamp Act and the Tea Act had revealed an alarming fact about American society. The organizers of those protests, mostly persons of wealth and status, had thought in terms of "ordered resistance." They countenanced violence only as a means of forcing the British authorities to pay attention to their complaints. But protest meetings and mob actions had brought thousands of ordinary citizens into the struggle for local self-government. Some of the upper-class leaders among the Patriots, while eager to have their support, were concerned about what they would make of actual independence. In addition, not all the property that had been destroyed belonged to Loyalists and British officials. Too much exalted talk about "rights" and "liberties" might well give the poor (to say nothing of the slaves) an exaggerated impression of their importance.

Finally, in a world where every country had some kind of monarch, could common people *really* govern themselves? The most ardent defender of American rights might well hesitate after considering all the implications of independence.

Yet independence was probably inevitable by the end of 1775. The belief that George III had been misled by evil or stupid advisers on both sides of the Atlantic became progressively more difficult to sustain. Mistrust of Parliament—indeed, of the whole of British society—grew apace.

Two events in January 1776 pushed the colonies a long step toward a final break. First came the news that the British were sending hired Hessian soldiers to fight against them. Colonists associated mercenaries with looting and rape and feared that the German-speaking Hessians would run amok among them. Such callousness on the part of Britain made reconciliation seem out of the question.

The second decisive event was the publication of *Common Sense*. This tract was written by Thomas Paine, a one-time English corsetmaker and civil servant turned pamphleteer, a man who had been in America scarcely a year. *Common Sense* called boldly for complete independence. It attacked not only George III but the idea of monarchy itself. Paine applied the uncomplicated logic of the zealot to the recent history of America. Where the colonists had been humbly petitioning George III and swallowing their resentment when he ignored them, Paine called George a "Royal Brute" and "the hardened sullen-tempered Pharaoh of England." Many Americans had wanted to control their own affairs but feared the instability of untried republican government. To them Paine said: "We have it in our power to begin the world again." "A government of our own is our natural right," he insisted. "O! ye that love mankind! Ye that dare oppose not only tyranny but the tyrant, stand forth!"

Virtually everyone in the colonies must have read *Common Sense* or heard it explained and discussed. About 150,000 copies were sold in the critical period between January and July. Not every Patriot was impressed by Paine's arguments. John Adams dismissed *Common Sense* as "a tolerable summary of arguments which I had been repeating again and again in Congress for nine months." But no one disputed the impact of Paine's pamphlet on public opinion.

The tone of the debate changed sharply as Paine's slashing attack took effect. In March 1776 the Congress unleashed privateers against British commerce; in April it opened American ports to foreign shipping; in May it urged the Patriots who had set up extralegal provincial conventions to frame constitutions and establish state governments.

On June 7 Richard Henry Lee of Virginia introduced a resolution of the Virginia Convention:

> RESOLVED: That these United Colonies are, and of right ought to be, free and independent States, that they are absolved from all allegiance to the British Crown, and that all political connection between them and the State of Great Britain is, and ought to be, totally dissolved.

This momentous resolution was not passed until July 2; the Congress first appointed a committee

▲ This 1857 painting depicts the destruction of a statue of King George III during the Revolution. This rendering purges the "mob" action of its menacing violence: the arm gestures are celebratory rather than threatening, and the women and children are well-to-do. This is a middle-class view of the American Revolution, bloodless, public-spirited, and consensual.

consisting of Thomas Jefferson, Benjamin Franklin, John Adams, Roger Sherman, and Robert Livingston to frame a suitable justification of independence. Livingston, a member of one of the great New York landowning families, was put on the committee in an effort to push New York toward independence. Sherman, a self-educated Connecticut lawyer and merchant, was a conservative who opposed parliamentary control over colonial affairs. Franklin, the best known of all Americans and an experienced writer, was a natural choice; so was John Adams, whose devotion to the cause of independence combined with his solid conservative qualities made him perhaps the typical man of the Revolution.

Thomas Jefferson was probably placed on the committee because politics required that a Virginian be included and because of his literary skill and general intelligence. Aside from writing *A Summary View of the Rights of British America*, he had done little to attract notice. At age 33 he was the youngest member of the Continental Congress and was only marginally interested in its deliberations. He had been slow to take his seat in the fall of 1775, and he had gone home to Virginia before Christmas. He put off returning several times and arrived in Philadelphia only on May 14. Had he delayed another month, someone else would have written the Declaration of Independence.

The committee asked Jefferson to prepare a draft. The result, with a few amendments made by Franklin and Adams and somewhat toned down by the whole Congress, was officially adopted by the delegates on July 4, 1776, two days after the delegates had voted for the decisive break with Great Britain.

Jefferson's Declaration of Independence (see the text of the document in the Appendix, pp. A3–A4) consisted of two parts. The first, introductory part justified the abstract

DOCUMENT

Jefferson, "Rough Draft" of the Declaration of Independence

right of any people to revolt and described the theory on which the Americans based their creation of a new, republican government. The second, much longer section was a list of the "injuries and usurpations" of George III, a bill of indictment explaining why the colonists felt driven to exercise the rights outlined in the first part of the document. Here Jefferson stressed the monarch's interference with the functioning of representative government in America, his harsh administration of colonial affairs, his restrictions on civil rights, and his maintenance of troops in the colonies without their consent.

Jefferson sought to marshal every possible evidence of British perfidy, and he made George III, rather than Parliament, the villain because the king was the personification of the nation against which America was rebelling. He held the monarch responsible for Parliament's efforts to tax the colonies and restrict their trade, for many actions by subordinates that George III had never deliberately authorized, and for some things that never happened. He even blamed the king for the existence of slavery in the colonies, a charge the Congress cut from the document not entirely because of its concern for accuracy. The long bill of particulars reads more like a lawyer's brief than a careful analysis, but it was intended to convince the world that the Americans had good reasons for exercising their right to form a government of their own.

Jefferson's general statement of the right of revolution has inspired oppressed peoples all over the world for more than 200 years:

> We hold these truths to be self-evident, that all men are created equal, that they are endowed by their Creator with certain unalienable Rights, that among these are Life, Liberty and the pursuit of Happiness. That to secure these rights, Governments are instituted among Men, deriving their just powers from the consent of the governed, That whenever any Form of Government becomes destructive of these ends, it is the Right of the People to alter or to abolish it, and to institute new Government. . . .

The Declaration was intended to influence foreign opinion, but its proclamation had little immediate effect outside Great Britain, and there it only made people angry and determined to subdue the rebels. A substantial number of European military men offered their services to the new nation, and a few of these might be called idealists, but most were adventurers and soldiers of fortune, thinking mostly of their own advantage. Why, then, has the Declaration had so much influence on modern history? Not because the thought was original with Jefferson. As John Adams later pointed out— Adams viewed his great contemporary with a mixture of affection, respect, and jealousy—the basic idea was commonplace among eighteenth-century liberals. "I did not consider it any part of my charge to invent new ideas," Jefferson explained, "but to place before mankind the common sense of the subject, in terms so plain and firm as to command their assent. . . . It was intended to be an expression of the American mind."

Revolution was not new, but the spectacle of a people solemnly explaining and justifying their right, in an orderly manner, to throw off their oppressors and establish a new system on their own authority was almost without precedent. Soon the French would be drawing on this example in their revolution, and rebels everywhere have since done likewise. And if Jefferson did not create the concept, he gave it a nearly perfect form.

1776: THE BALANCE OF FORCES

A formal declaration of independence merely cleared the way for tackling the problems of founding a new nation. Lacking both traditions and authority based in law, the Congress had to create political institutions and a new national spirit, all in the midst of war.

Always the military situation took precedence, for a single disastrous setback might make everything else meaningless. At the start the Americans already possessed their lands (except for the few square miles occupied by British troops). Although thousands of colonists fought for George III, the British soon learned that to put down the American rebellion they would have to bring in men and supplies from bases on the other side of the Atlantic. This was a most formidable task.

Certain long-run factors operated in America's favor. Although His Majesty's soldiers were brave and well disciplined, the army was as inefficient and ill directed as the rest of the British government. Whereas nearly everyone in Great Britain wanted to crack down on Boston after the Tea Party, many boggled at engaging in a full-scale war against all the colonies. Aside from a reluctance to spill so much blood, there was the question of expense. Finally, the idea of dispatching the cream of the British army to America while powerful enemies on the Continent still smarted from past defeats seemed risky. For all these reasons the British approached gingerly the task of subduing the rebellion. When Washington fortified Dorchester Heights overlooking Boston, General Howe withdrew his troops to Halifax rather than risk another Bunker Hill.

The American Revolution

For a time, the initiative remained with the Americans. An expedition under General Richard Montgomery captured Montréal in November 1775,

▲ Forts were crucial in eighteenth-century warfare. They provided a repository for gunpowder and munitions, and a platform for heavy cannon. Fort Stanwix *(above)* was located at a crucial site on the Mohawk River. In 1777, a British army under Barry St. Leger surrounded the fort and nearly forced it to surrender when an audacious Patriot general arrived and forced St. Leger to retreat. His name was Benedict Arnold.

and another small force under Benedict Arnold advanced to the gates of Québec after a grueling march across the wilderness from Maine. Montgomery and Arnold attempted to storm the Québec defenses on December 31, 1775, but were repulsed with heavy losses. Even so, the British troops in Canada could not drive the remnants of the American army—perhaps 500 men in all—out of the province until reinforcements arrived in the spring.

Awareness of Britain's problems undoubtedly spurred the Continental Congress to the bold actions of the spring of 1776. However, on July 2, 1776, the same day that Congress voted for independence, General Howe was back on American soil, landing in force on Staten Island in New York harbor in preparation for an assault on the city. Soon Howe had at hand 32,000 well-equipped troops and a powerful fleet commanded by his brother, Richard, Lord Howe. If the British controlled New York City and the Hudson River, they could, as Washington realized, "stop intercourse between the northern and southern Colonies, upon which depends the Safety of America."

Suddenly the full strength of the empire seemed to have descended on the Americans. Superior British resources (a population of 9 million to the colonies' 2.5 million, large stocks of war materials and the industrial capacity to boost them further, mastery of the seas, a well-trained and experienced army, a highly centralized and, when necessary, ruthless government) were now all too evident.

The demonstration of British might in New York harbor accentuated American military and economic weaknesses: Both money and the tools of war were continually in short supply in a predominantly agricultural country. Many of Washington's soldiers were armed with weapons no more lethal than spears and tomahawks. Few had proper uniforms. Even the most patriotic resisted conforming to the conventions of military discipline; the men hated drilling and all parade-ground formality. And all these problems were complicated by the fact that Washington had to create an army organization out of whole cloth at the same time that he was fighting a war.

Supply problems were handled inefficiently and often corruptly. Few officers knew much about such mundane but vital matters as how to construct and maintain proper sanitary facilities when large numbers of soldiers were camped at one place for extended periods of time. What was inelegantly known as "the itch" afflicted soldiers throughout the war.

LOYALISTS

Behind the lines, the country was far from united. Whereas nearly all colonists had objected to British policies, many still hesitated to take up arms against the mother country. Even Massachusetts harbored many Loyalists, or Tories, as they were called; about a thousand Americans left Boston with General Howe, abandoning their homes rather than submit to the rebel army.

No one knows exactly how the colonists divided on the question of independence. John Adams's off-the-cuff estimate was that a third of the people were ardent Patriots, another third loyal to Great Britain, and the rest neutral or tending to favor whichever side seemed to be winning. This guess is probably as useful as any, although in keeping with Adams's character he may have understated the number who agreed with him and overstated those opposed to his position. Most historians think that about a fifth of the people were Loyalists and about two-fifths Patriots, but there are few hard figures to go by. What is certain is that large elements, perhaps a majority of the people, were more or less indifferent to the conflict or, in Tom Paine's famous phrase, were summer soldiers and sunshine patriots—they supported the Revolution when all was going well and lost their enthusiasm in difficult hours.

The divisions cut across geographical, social, and economic lines. A high proportion of those holding royal appointments and many Anglican clergymen remained loyal to King George, as did numbers of merchants with close connections in Britain. There were important pockets of Tory strength in rural sections of New York, in the North Carolina backcountry, and among persons of non-English origin and other minority groups who tended to count on London for protection against the local majority.

Many became Tories simply out of distaste for change or because they were pessimistic about the condition of society and the possibility of improving it. "What is the whole history of human life," wrote the Tory clergyman and schoolmaster Jonathan Boucher of Virginia, "but a series of disappointments?" Still others believed that the actions of the British, however unfair and misguided, did not justify rebellion. Knowing that they possessed a remarkably free and equitable system of government, they could not stomach shedding blood merely to avoid paying more taxes or to escape from what they considered minor restrictions on their activities. "The Annals of no Country can produce an Instance of so virulent a Rebellion . . . originating from such trivial Causes," one Loyalist complained.

The Tories lacked organization. While Patriot leaders worked closely together, many of the Tory "leaders" did not even know one another. They had no central committee to lay plans or coordinate their efforts. When the revolutionaries took over a colony, some Tories fled; others sought the protection of the British army; others took up arms; and still others accommodated themselves silently to the new regime.

If the differences separating Patriot from Loyalist are unclear, feelings were nonetheless bitter. Individual Loyalists were often set upon by mobs, tarred and feathered, and otherwise abused. Some were thrown into jail for no legitimate reason; others were exiled and their property confiscated. Battles between Tory units and the Continental Army were often exceptionally bloody. "Neighbor was against neighbor, father against son and son against father," one Connecticut Tory reported. "He that would not thrust his own blade through his brother's heart was called an infamous villain."

EARLY BRITISH VICTORIES

General Howe's campaign against New York brought to light another American weakness—the lack of military experience. Washington, expecting Howe to attack New York, had moved south to meet the threat immediately after Howe had abandoned Boston. But both he and his men failed badly in this first major test. Late in August Howe crossed from Staten Island to Brooklyn. In the Battle of Long Island he easily outflanked and defeated Washington's army. Had he acted decisively, he could probably have ended the war on the spot, but Howe could not make up his mind whether to be a peacemaker or a conqueror. This hesitation in consolidating his gains permitted Washington to withdraw his troops to Manhattan Island.

Howe could still have trapped Washington simply by using his fleet to land troops on the northern end of Manhattan; instead he attacked New York City directly, leaving the Americans an escape route to the north. Again Patriot troops proved no match for British regulars. Although Washington threw his hat to the ground in a rage and threatened to shoot cowardly Connecticut soldiers as they fled the battlefield, he could not stop the rout and had to fall back on Harlem Heights in upper Manhattan. Yet once more Howe failed to pursue his advantage promptly.

Still, Washington refused to see the peril in remaining on an island while the enemy commanded the surrounding waters. Only when Howe shifted a powerful force to Westchester, directly threatening his rear, did Washington move north to the mainland. Finally, after several narrow escapes, he crossed the Hudson River and marched south to New Jersey, where the British could not use their naval superiority against him.

◄ **New York and New Jersey Campaigns, 1776–1777**

The battles in and around New York City seemed to presage an easy British triumph. Yet somehow Washington salvaged a moral victory from these ignominious defeats. He learned rapidly; seldom thereafter did he place his troops in such vulnerable positions. And his men, in spite of repeated failure, had become an army. In November and December 1776 they retreated across New Jersey and into Pennsylvania. General Howe then abandoned the campaign, going into winter quarters in New York but posting garrisons at Trenton, Princeton, and other strategic points.

The troops at Trenton were hated Hessian mercenaries, and Washington decided to attack them. He crossed the ice-clogged Delaware River with 2400 men on Christmas night during a wild storm. The little army then marched nine miles to Trenton, arriving at daybreak in the midst of a sleet storm. The Hessians were taken completely by surprise. Those who could fled in disorder; the rest—900 of them—surrendered.

The Hessians were first-class professional soldiers, probably the most competent troops in Europe at that time. The victory gave a boost to American morale. A few days later Washington outmaneuvered General Cornwallis, who had rushed to Trenton with reinforcements, and won another battle at Princeton. These engagements had little strategic importance, since both armies then went into winter quarters. Without them, however, there might not have been an army to resume the war in the spring.

SARATOGA AND THE FRENCH ALLIANCE

When spring reached New Jersey in April 1777, Washington had fewer than 5000 men under arms. Great plans—far too many and too complicated, as it turned out—were afoot in the British camp. The strategy called for General John Burgoyne to lead a large army from Canada down Lake Champlain toward Albany while a smaller force under Lieutenant Colonel Barry St. Leger pushed eastward toward Albany from Fort Oswego on

▲ The British generals were criticized at home for their losses during the Revolutionary War. This 1779 cartoon shows a British commander in America relaxing in his command tent while his defeated colleagues surrender at Saratoga.

Lake Ontario. General Howe was to lead a third force north up the Hudson. The Patriots would be trapped and the New England states isolated from the rest.

As a venture in coordinated military tactics, the British campaign of 1777 was a fiasco. General Howe had spent the winter in New York wining and dining his officers and prominent local Loyalists and having a torrid affair with the wife of the officer in charge of prisoners of war. He was less attentive to his responsibilities for the British army advancing south from Canada.

General "Gentleman Johnny" Burgoyne, a charming if somewhat bombastic character, part politician, part poet, part gambler, part ladies' man, yet also a brave soldier, had begun his march from Canada in mid June. By early July his army, which consisted of 500 Indians, 650 Loyalists, and 6000 regulars, had captured Fort Ticonderoga at the southern end of Lake Champlain. He quickly pushed beyond Lake George but then bogged down. Burdened by a huge baggage train that included 138 pieces of generally useless artillery, more than 30 carts laden with his personal wardrobe and supply of champagne, and his mistress, he could advance at but a snail's pace through the dense woods north of Saratoga.[1] Patriot militia impeded his way by felling trees across the forest trails.

---

[1] Many soldiers, enlisted men as well as officers, were accompanied by their wives or other women on campaigns. More than 2000 accompanied the Burgoyne expedition. At one point Washington complained of "the multitude of women . . . especially those who are pregnant, or have children [that] clog upon every movement." Actually, women in eighteenth-century armies worked hard, doing most of the cooking, washing, and other "housekeeping" tasks.

St. Leger was also slow in carrying out his part of the grand design. He did not leave Fort Oswego until July 26, and when he stopped to besiege a Patriot force at Fort Stanwix, General Benedict Arnold had time to march west with 1000 men from the army resisting Burgoyne and drive him back to Oswego.

Meanwhile, with magnificent disregard for the agreed-on plan, Howe wasted time trying to trap Washington into exposing his army in New Jersey. This enabled Washington to send some of his best troops to buttress the militia units opposing Burgoyne. Then, just when St. Leger was setting out for Albany, Howe took the bulk of his army off by sea to attack Philadelphia, leaving only a small force commanded by General Sir Henry Clinton to aid Burgoyne.

When Washington moved south to oppose Howe, the Britisher taught him a series of lessons in tactics, defeating him at the Battle of Brandywine, then feinting him out of position and moving unopposed into Philadelphia. But by that time it was late September, and disaster was about to befall General Burgoyne.

The American forces under Philip Schuyler and later under Horatio Gates and Benedict Arnold had erected formidable defenses immediately south of Saratoga near the town of Stillwater. Burgoyne struck at this position twice and was thrown back both times with heavy losses. Each day more local militia swelled the American forces. Soon Burgoyne was under siege, his troops pinned down by withering fire from every direction, unable even to bury their dead. The only hope was General Clinton, who had finally started up the Hudson from New York. Clinton got as far as

Map labels:
British Advance
American Advance
British Withdrawal
Battle (American Victory)

Ottawa River
Montréal
FORT ST. JOHN
St Lawrence River
ST. LEGER
C A N A D A
Richelieu River
Lake Champlain
BURGOYNE
Lake Ontario
New York
Vermont
FORT TICONDEROGA
July 6, 1777
Lake George
FORT OSWEGO
July 25, 1777
Lake Oneida
FORT ANNE
FORT EDWARD
Manchester
FORT STANWIX
Saratoga
July–August 1777
STARK
August 3, 1777:
Beginning of Siege by St. Leger
Mohawk River
October 17, 1777:
Surrounded by an Overwhelming American Force Burgoyne Surrenders
August 16, 1777
August 6, 1777:
Battle of Oriskany
ARNOLD
GATES
Hudson R.
Bennington
August 22, 1777:
St. Leger Retreats to Fort Oswego
Albany
Massachusetts
0   20 Kilometers
0   20 Miles

Kingston, about 80 miles below Saratoga, but on October 16 he decided to return to New York for reinforcements. The next day, at Saratoga, Burgoyne surrendered. Some 5700 British prisoners were marched off to Virginia.

This overwhelming triumph changed the course and character of the war. France would probably have entered the war in any case; the country had never reconciled itself to its losses in the Seven Years' War and for years had been building a navy capable of taking on the British. Helping the Americans was simply another way of weakening their British enemy. As early as May 1776 the Comte de Vergennes, France's foreign minister, had persuaded Louis XVI to authorize the expenditure of 1 million livres for munitions for America, and more was added the next year. Spain also contributed, not out of sympathy for the Revolution but because of its desire to injure Great Britain. Soon vital supplies were being funneled secretly to the rebels through a dummy company, Roderigue Hortalez et Cie. When news of the victory at Saratoga reached Paris, the time seemed ripe and Louis XVI recognized the United States. Then Vergennes and three American commissioners in Paris,

Benjamin Franklin, Arthur Lee, and Silas Deane, drafted a commercial treaty and a formal treaty of alliance. The two nations agreed to make "common cause and aid each other mutually" should war "break out" between France and Great Britain. Meanwhile, France guaranteed "the sovereignty and independence absolute and unlimited" of the United States. The help of Spain and France, Washington declared, "will not fail of establishing the Independence of America in a short time."

When the news of Saratoga reached England, Lord North realized that a Franco-American alliance was almost inevitable. To forestall it, he was ready to give in on all the issues that had agitated the colonies before 1775. Both the Coercive Acts and the Tea Act would be repealed; Parliament would pledge never to tax the colonies.

Instead of implementing this proposal promptly, Parliament delayed until March 1778. Royal peace commissioners did not reach Philadelphia until June, a month after Congress had ratified the French treaty. The British proposals were icily rejected, and while the peace commissioners were still in Philadelphia, war broke out between France and Great Britain.

▶ **Campaign in the South, 1779–1781**

	British Army Assembly Area, Jan. 1781
	American Army Assembly Area, Jan. 1781
→	British Advance
■	British Outpost, 1781
	American Clearing Operation, Late 1781
☾•	Town Still Held by British, End 1781
✳	British Victory
✳	American Victory

The American Revolution, however, had yet to be won. After the loss of Philadelphia, Washington had settled his army for the winter at Valley Forge, 20 miles to the northwest. The army's supply system collapsed. Often the men had nothing to eat but "fire cake," a mixture of ground grain and water molded on a stick or in a pan and baked in a campfire. According to the Marquis de Lafayette, one of many Europeans who volunteered to fight on the American side, "the unfortunate soldiers . . . had neither coats, nor hats, nor shirts, nor shoes; their feet and legs froze till they grew black, and it was often necessary to amputate them."

To make matters worse, there was grumbling in Congress over Washington's failure to win victories and talk of replacing him as commander-in-chief with Horatio Gates, the "hero" of Saratoga. (In fact, Gates was an indifferent soldier, lacking in decisiveness and unable to instill confidence in his subordinates.)

As the winter dragged on, the Continental Army melted away. So many officers resigned that Washington was heard to say that he was afraid of "being left Alone with the Soldiers only." Since enlisted men could not legally resign, they deserted by the hundreds. Yet the army survived. Gradually the soldiers who remained became a tough, professional fighting force.

THE WAR MOVES SOUTH

Spring brought a revival of American hopes in the form of more supplies, new recruits, and, above all, word of the French alliance. In May 1778 the British replaced General Howe as commander with General Clinton, who decided to transfer his base back to New York. While Clinton was moving across New Jersey, Washington attacked him at Monmouth Court

House. The fight was inconclusive, but the Americans held the field when the day ended and were able to claim a victory.

Thereafter British strategy changed. Fighting in the northern states degenerated into skirmishes and other small-unit clashes. Instead, relying on sea power, the supposed presence of many Tories in the South, and the possibility of obtaining the help of slaves, the British concentrated their efforts in South Carolina and Georgia. Savannah fell to them late in 1778, and most of the settled parts of Georgia were overrun during 1779. In 1780 Clinton led a massive expedition against Charleston. When the city surrendered in May, more than 3000 soldiers were captured, the most overwhelming American defeat of the war. Leaving General Cornwallis and some 8000 men to carry on the campaign, Clinton then sailed back to New York.

The Tories in South Carolina and Georgia came closer to meeting British expectations than in any other region, but the callous behavior of the British troops persuaded large numbers of hesitating citizens to join the Patriot cause. Guerrilla bands led by Francis Marion, the "Swamp Fox," Thomas Sumter, after whom Fort Sumter, famous in the Civil War, was named, and others like them provided a nucleus of resistance in areas that had supposedly been subdued.

But the tide soon turned. In 1779 the Spanish governor of Louisiana, José de Gálvez, administered a stinging defeat to British troops in Florida, and in 1780 and 1781 he captured the British-held Gulf ports of Pensacola and Mobile. More important, in June 1780 Congress placed Horatio Gates in charge of a southern army consisting of the irregular militia units and a hard core of Continentals transferred from Washington's command. Gates encountered Cornwallis at Camden, South Carolina. Foolishly, he entrusted a key sector of his line to untrained militiamen, who panicked when the British charged with fixed bayonets. Gates suffered heavy losses and had to fall back. Congress then recalled him, sensibly permitting Washington to replace him with General Nathanael Greene, a first-rate officer.

A band of militiamen had trapped a contingent of Tories at King's Mountain and forced its surrender. Greene, avoiding a major engagement with Cornwallis's superior numbers, divided his troops and staged a series of raids on scattered points. In January 1781, at the Battle of Cowpens in northwestern South Carolina, General Daniel Morgan inflicted a costly defeat on Colonel Banastre Tarleton, one of Cornwallis's most effective officers. Cornwallis pursued Morgan hotly, but the American rejoined Greene, and at Guilford Court House they again inflicted heavy losses on the British. Then Cornwallis withdrew to Wilmington, North Carolina, where he could rely on the fleet for support and reinforcements. Greene's Patriots quickly regained control of the Carolina backcountry.

VICTORY AT YORKTOWN

Seeing no future in the Carolinas and unwilling to vegetate at Wilmington, Cornwallis marched north into Virginia, where he joined forces with troops under Benedict Arnold. (Disaffected by what he considered unjust criticism of his generalship, Arnold had sold out to the British in 1780. He intended to betray the bastion of West Point on the Hudson River. The scheme was foiled when incriminating papers were found on the person of a British spy, Major John André. Arnold fled to the British and André was hanged.) As in the Carolina campaign, the British had numerical superiority at first but lost it rapidly when local militia and Continental forces concentrated against them. Cornwallis soon discovered that Virginia Tories were of little help in such a situation. "When a Storm threatens, our friends disappear," he grumbled.

General Clinton ordered Cornwallis to establish a base at Yorktown, where he could be supplied by sea. It was a terrible mistake. The British navy in American waters far outnumbered American and French vessels, but the Atlantic is wide, and in those days communication was slow. The French had a fleet in the West Indies under Admiral François de Grasse and another squadron at Newport, Rhode Island, where a French army was stationed. In the summer of 1781 Washington, de Grasse, and the Comte de Rochambeau, commander of French land forces, designed and carried out with an efficiency unparalleled in eighteenth-century warfare a complex plan to bottle up Cornwallis.

The British navy in the West Indies and at New York might have forestalled this scheme had it moved promptly and in force. But Admiral Sir George Rodney sent only part of his Indies fleet. As a result, de Grasse, after a battle with a British fleet commanded by Admiral Thomas Graves, won control of the Chesapeake and cut Cornwallis off from the sea.

The next move was up to Washington, and this was his finest hour as a commander. He desperately wanted to attack the British base at New York, but at the urging of Rochambeau he agreed instead to strike

▶ *text continues on page 126*

Re-Viewing the Past

The Patriot

As the opening credits roll, Benjamin Martin (played by Mel Gibson) pries open a wooden box. It contains yellowing papers, a few medals and a tomahawk. He lifts the tomahawk, fingers its handle gingerly, and stares at the blade. "I had long feared that my sins would revisit me," a voice intones, "and the cost is more than I can bear." The viewer suspects—rightly, it turns out—that Martin's sins were violent, and that they had something to do with hacking people apart. But at the outset of *The Patriot,* Hollywood's $100-million blockbuster on the American Revolution, Martin is more pacifist than patriot. When the South Carolina legislature votes to go to war with Great Britain, he publicly declares that his chief obligation is to his family: "I will not fight." He soon changes his mind.

The British capture of Charleston (1780) brings onto the scene a villainous British cavalry officer, Colonel Tavington. Ordered by General Cornwallis to subdue the insurrection in the countryside, Tavington ransacks plantations, forces slaves into the King's service, and hounds the rebel militia. He also arrests Gabriel (Heath Ledger), Martin's oldest son, and orders the boy's execution as a spy. When Gabriel's younger brother tries to intervene, Tavington shoots the boy dead. Overcome with rage, Martin races to his room, grabs the hatchet, and proceeds to bury it—repeatedly—in the chests and skulls of countless British soldiers. He takes command of the militia, recruits more Patriots, and harries the British at every turn.

Tavington responds by intensifying his campaign against the rebels. His culminating barbarity is to round up the villagers of Wakefield (including Gabriel's fiancé), corral them in a church, and set it ablaze. All perish in unimaginable (and mercifully unfilmed) agony. Martin checks his rage long enough to plot the defeat of Cornwallis's army. This occurs at the Battle of Cowpens, where the militia holds its position despite being blasted by British artillery and decimated by repeated fusillades. When Tavington leads a cavalry charge, Martin's eyes widen and he reaches for the tomahawk. Tavington dies at Martin's hands, and Cornwallis is routed, too; the latter's subsequent surrender at Yorktown is now a foregone conclusion.

Historians have found much to criticize in the movie's retelling of the war in the South. There was no such person as Benjamin Martin, though elements of his story can be

▲ Francis Marion, a Patriot whose guerrilla warfare helped drive the British from South Carolina.

found in the exploits of guerrilla leaders such as Francis Marion ("the Swamp Fox"), Thomas Sumter, Andrew Pickens, and General Daniel Morgan, who commanded the Continentals at Cowpens. Although the British cavalry wear red uniforms in the movie, they were known as the Green Dragoons for a reason that seemingly eluded the filmmakers. The movie's version of the Battle of Cowpens featured a glorious display of fireworks, though neither army's artillery in South Carolina was capable of firing explosive shells. Cornwallis was not humiliated at Cowpens because he was not there. In the movie the British are caricatured as either evil geniuses or bungling twits; and the Patriots, as large-hearted rogues or pious patriarchs. The real combatants doubtless adhered less predictably to type. The most serious deviation from the historical record was the incineration of the occupied church: there is no record of any such event. "*The Patriot* is to history what Godzilla was to biology," declared historian David Hackett Fischer.

However, *The Patriot* raises and thoughtfully addresses an important historical issue: How can any society reconcile peaceable virtues—love for family, neighborliness, cooperation—with the violence of war? In *The Patriot,* the dilemma is symbolized by Martin's tomahawk. This weapon helps free his captured son and vanquish the evil Tavington; and yet it is also a manifestation of Martin's savage, even pathological, rage. Martin's secret shame, alluded to in the opening scene, was his dismembering corpses after a particularly brutal battle during the French and Indian War.

Eighteenth-century Europeans were in fact preoccupied with reconciling the violence of war with the need for social order. Their particular refinement in the military arts was the ordered massing of musket fire. Because muskets were highly inaccurate, a troop of soldiers, dispersed and firing on their own, were unlikely to drive an enemy from the field. But when the soldiers were brought together in concentrated formations and ordered to fire at the same moment, the enemy would be decimated. The technology of warfare required intense military discipline; and the new penchant for military order imposed seeming coherence upon the chaos of the battlefield.

The Patriot provides a vivid rendering of this juxtaposition. Soldiers in beautifully colored uniforms march in straight, regular columns to the steady cadence of drums while officers bark precise commands: "Circle right. Face forward. Lift weapons . . . " These stately preliminaries, depicted on ripening fields beneath a summer sun, provide an unsettling backdrop for the ensuing violence: volleys of musket fire shatter the formations; low-velocity cannon balls decapitate individual soldiers; soldiers thrust bayonets into the chests of enemies.

Martin, once he has again taken up his tomahawk, concludes that the British cannot be defeated in this type of battle. And, in fact, they seldom were. Martin advocates guerrilla warfare, as did many southern Patriot militiamen. The British had good reason to doubt the legitimacy of this type of warfare. When men went wild on the battlefield, or fired shots and then hid among civilians, they were criminals, not soldiers. If such behavior were condoned, warfare would become barbarity.

▼ Mel Gibson as Patriot leader with Jason Isaacs as Colonel Tavington, a barbarous British officer.

► Colonel Banastre Tarleton, on whom Tavington was based.

The movie develops this point at considerable length. During a truce, Martin confers with Cornwallis, who complains that the Patriot militia aimed at officers at the beginning of battles. Such behavior was inconsistent with "civilized warfare." Officers, as gentlemen, were bound by codes of honor. If they were killed, who would "restrain" the regular soldiers— keep them from reverting, as did Martin, to a frenzy of terror and rage?

The movie's debate over the nature of "civilized" warfare parallels an ongoing debate at the time. At the outset of the conflict, British officers took an oath affirming the British Articles of War, which protected citizens and soldiers who had surrendered. The American Congress also adopted the British Articles of War as the basis for discipline and military justice. But with the outbreak of guerrilla warfare in the South, both sides frequently ignored these rules.

"Colonel Tavington" was obviously based on Banastre Tarleton, the actual commander of the Green Dragoons. Tarleton became notorious after his soldiers raped three plantation women and killed several militiamen who had surrendered. This behavior worried Cornwallis, who sent a dispatch commending his subordinate's courage and zeal but also warning: "Use your utmost endeavors to prevent the troops under your command from committing irregularities." In a subsequent engagement at Waxhaws, however, Tarleton again lost control of his men, who stabbed and slashed vanquished foes. An American officer discovered that the American corpses at Waxhaws had each received, on the average, 16 wounds.

British and American officers sought to affirm that the war could be civilized. But such high-minded notions were repeatedly subverted during tomahawk-wielding guerrilla warfare and by excessively zealous commanders. The question then remained, as it does today, whether unchecked aggression is, among soldiers, a virtue or a vice. *The Patriot* raises these issues but does not resolve them. Martin, surely, should have kept his tomahawk in its locked box; but if he had, would the Patriots have won?

125

▶ **The Yorktown Campaign, April–September 1781**

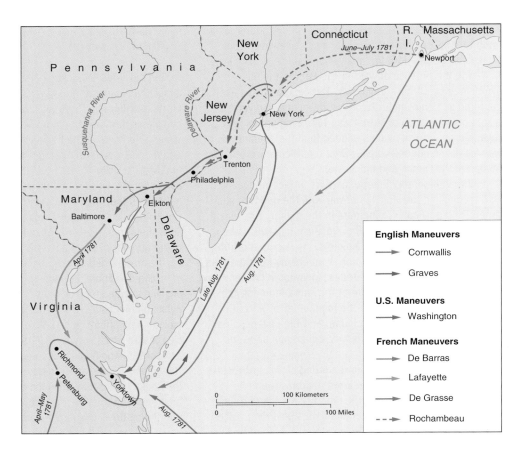

at Yorktown. After tricking Clinton into thinking he was heading for New York, he pushed boldly south. In early September he reached Yorktown and joined up with an army commanded by Lafayette and troops from de Grasse's fleet. He soon had nearly 17,000 French and American veterans in position.

"The Liberty Song"

Cornwallis was helpless. He held out until October 17 and then asked for terms. Two days later more than 7000 British soldiers marched out of their lines and laid down their arms. Then the jubilant Lafayette ordered his military band to play "Yankee Doodle."

THE PEACE OF PARIS

The British gave up trying to suppress the rebellion after Yorktown, but the event that confirmed the existence of the United States as an independent nation was the signing of a peace treaty with Great Britain. Yorktown had been only one of a string of defeats suffered by British arms in the Mediterranean, the West Indies, Africa, and Asia. The national debt had doubled again since 1775. In March 1782 Lord North resigned after Parliament renounced all further efforts to coerce the colonies. At once the new ministry of

Lord Rockingham prepared to negotiate a peace settlement with America.

The problem of peacemaking was complicated. The United States and France had pledged not to make a separate peace. Spain, at war with Great Britain since 1779, was allied with France but not with America. Although eager to profit at British expense, the Spanish hoped to limit American expansion beyond the Appalachians, for they had ambitions of their own in the eastern half of the Mississippi Valley. France, while ready enough to see America independent, did not want the new country to become *too* powerful; in a conflict of interest between America and Spain, France tended to support Spain.

The Continental Congress appointed John Adams, Benjamin Franklin, John Jay, Thomas Jefferson, and Henry Laurens as a commission to conduct peace talks. Franklin and Jay did most of the actual negotiating. Congress, grateful for French aid during the Revolution, had instructed the commissioners to rely on the advice of the Comte de Vergennes. In Paris, however, the commissioners soon discovered that Vergennes was not the perfect friend of America that Congress believed him to be. He was, after all, a French official, and France had other interests far more important than concern for its American ally. Vergennes "means to keep his hand under our chin to

▲ The surrender of Cornwallis at Yorktown on October 19, 1781, by John Trumbull in 1820. In 1789 Trumbull, who had served as an aide to Washington, wrote to Thomas Jefferson that he wanted to make paintings "to preserve and diffuse the memory of the noblest series of actions which have e'er presented themselves to the history of man"—the American revolution. The next year he went to London to study painting with Benjamin West; he was promptly arrested as an American spy. Fortunately, West had made connections with King George III and managed to spare Trumbull from the gallows.

prevent us from drowning," Adams complained, "but not to lift our head out of the water."

Franklin, whose fame as a scientist and sage had spread to Europe, was wined and dined by the cream of Paris and petted and fussed over by some of the city's most beautiful women. He did not press the American point of view as forcefully as he might have. But this was because he took the long view, which was to achieve a true reconciliation with the British, not simply to drive the hardest bargain possible. John Jay was somewhat more tough-minded. But on basic issues all the Americans were in agreement. They hinted to the British representative, Richard Oswald, that they would consider a separate peace if it were a generous one and suggested that Great Britain would be far better off with America, a nation that favored free trade, in control of the trans-Appalachian region than with a mercantilist power like Spain.

The British government reacted favorably, authorizing Oswald "to treat with the Commissioners appointed by the Colonys, under the title of Thirteen United States." Soon the Americans were deep in negotiations with Oswald. They told Vergennes what they were doing but did not discuss details.

Oswald was cooperative, and the Americans drove a hard bargain. One scrap of conversation reveals the tenor of the talks.

OSWALD: We can never be such damned sots as to disturb you.

ADAMS: Thank you. . . . But nations don't feel as you and I do, and your nation, when it gets a little refreshed from the fatigues of the war, and when men and money become plentiful, and allies at hand, will not feel as it does now.

OSWALD: We can never be such damned sots as to think of differing again with you.

ADAMS: Why, in truth I have never been able to comprehend the reason why you ever thought of differing with us.

By the end of November 1782 a preliminary treaty had been signed. "His Britannic Majesty," Article 1

DEBATING THE PAST

Was the American Revolution rooted in class struggle? This 1795 engraving of a Stamp Act protest delineates a class division. The three British Tories—one suspended, two sprawled below—are wealthy. The Patriots surrounding them are not. The progressive historian Carl Becker declared that the Revolution was fought "not only about home rule but also about who should rule at home." The leaders of the Revolution sought not only to defeat the Crown in England but also the rabble in Boston and New York—the Patriots as depicted here. Another progressive historian, Arthur Schlesinger, Sr. (1918) wrote that commercial elites "instigated" popular opposition to British policies, grew alarmed at the "engulfing tide of radicalism" that led to war, and then turned against the farmers and workers who did most of the fighting. Edmund Morgan rejected the notion that the Revolution grew out of class divisions. It did not constitute a victory of the rich over the poor, but "a union of three million cantankerous colonists into a new nation." Historians during the tumultuous 1960s underscored the divisions in American society. Gary B. Nash showed how declining opportunities had radicalized urban workers. Other social historians found yet other cleavages: Mary Beth Norton between men and women; Sylvia R. Frey between masters and slaves; Colin Calloway between colonists and Indians.

Carl Becker, *History of Political Parties in New York* (1909), Arthur M. Schlesinger, Sr., *The Colonial Merchants and the American Revolution* (1918), Edmund Morgan, *The Birth of the Republic* (1956), Gary B. Nash, *The Urban Crucible* (1989), Mary Beth Norton, *Founding Mothers and Fathers* (1996), Sylvia R. Frey, *Water from the Rock* (1991), Colin Calloway, *American Revolution in Indian Country* (1995).

began, "acknowledges the said United States . . . to be free, sovereign and independent States." Other terms were equally in line with American hopes and objectives. The boundaries of the nation were set at the Great Lakes, the Mississippi River, and 31° north latitude (roughly the northern boundary of Florida, which the British turned over to Spain).[2] Britain recognized the right of Americans to take fish on the Grand Banks off Newfoundland and, far more important, to dry and cure their catch on unsettled beaches in Labrador and Nova Scotia. The British agreed to withdraw their troops from American soil "with all convenient speed." Where the touchy problem of Tory property seized during the Revolution was concerned, the Americans agreed only that Congress would "earnestly recommend" that the states "provide for the restitution of all estates, rights and properties which have been confiscated." They promised to prevent further property confiscation and prosecutions of Tories—certainly a wise as well as a humane policy—and they agreed not to impede the collection of debts owed British subjects. Vergennes was flabbergasted by the success of the Americans. "The English buy the peace more than they make it," he wrote. "Their concessions . . . exceed all that I should have thought possible."

The American commissioners obtained these favorable terms because they were shrewd diplomats and because of the rivalries that existed among the great European powers. In the last analysis, Britain preferred to have a weak nation of English-speaking people in command of the Mississippi Valley rather than France or Spain.

From their experience at the peace talks, the American leaders learned the importance of playing one power against another without committing themselves completely to any. This policy demanded constant contact with European affairs and skill at adjusting policies to changes in the European balance of power. It enabled the United States, a young and relatively feeble country, to grow and prosper.

FORMING A NATIONAL GOVERNMENT

Independence was won on the battlefield and at the Paris Peace Conference, but it could not have been achieved without the work of the Continental Congress and the new state governments. The delegates recognized that the Congress was essentially a legislative body rather than a complete government and

DOCUMENT

The Articles of Confederation

---

[2]Much of this vast region, of course, was controlled not by the British but by various Indian tribes.

from the start they struggled to create a workable central authority. But their effort was handicapped by much confusion and bickering, and early military defeats sapped their energy and morale. In July 1776 John Dickinson prepared a draft national constitution, but it could not command much support. The larger states objected to equal representation of all the states, and the states with large western land claims refused to cede them to the central government. It was not until November 1777 that the Articles of Confederation were submitted to the states for ratification.

It was necessary to obtain the approval of all the states before the Articles could go into effect. All acted fairly promptly but Maryland, which did not ratify the document until 1781. Maryland held out in order to force a change that would authorize Congress to determine the western limits of states with land claims beyond the Appalachians. There were many good reasons why this should be done. The state claims to the West were overlapping, vaguely defined, and in some instances preposterous. To have permitted a few states to monopolize the West would have unbalanced the Union from the start.

Many people in the "landed" states recognized the justice of Maryland's suggestion, yet Maryland had a more selfish motive. Land speculators in the state had obtained from the Indians rights to large tracts in the Ohio Valley claimed by Virginia. Under Virginia, the Maryland titles would be worthless, but under a national administration they might be made to stand up.

Virginia resented its neighbor's efforts to grasp these valuable lands by indirection, but with the British about to advance into the state, Virginia agreed to surrender its claim to all land west and north of the Ohio River. It thwarted the Maryland speculators by insisting that all titles based on Indian purchases be declared void. Maryland then had no recourse but to ratify the Articles.

The Articles merely provided a legal basis for authority that the Continental Congress had already been exercising. Each state, regardless of size, was to have but one vote; the union it created was only a "league of friendship." Article 2 defined the limit of national power: "Each state retains its sovereignty, freedom, and independence, and every Power, jurisdiction, and right, which is not by this confederation expressly delegated to the United States, in Congress assembled."

Time proved this an inadequate arrangement, chiefly because the central government lacked the authority to impose taxes and had no way of enforcing the powers it did have.

FINANCING THE WAR

In practice, Congress and the states carried on the war cooperatively. General officers were appointed by Congress, lesser ones locally. The Continental Army, the backbone of Washington's force, was supported by Congress. The states raised militia chiefly for short-term service. Militiamen fought well at times but often proved unreliable, especially when asked to fight at any great distance from their homes. Washington continually fretted about their "dirty mercenary spirit" and their "intractable" nature, yet he could not have won the war without them.

The fact that Congress's requisitions of money often went unhonored by the states does not mean that the states failed to contribute heavily to the war effort. Altogether they spent about $5.8 million in hard money, and they met Congress's demands for beef, corn, rum, fodder, and other military supplies. In addition, Congress raised large sums by borrowing. Americans bought bonds worth between $7 and $8 million during the war. Foreign governments lent another $8 million, most of this furnished by France. Congress also issued more than $240 million in paper money, the states over $200 million more. This currency fell rapidly in value, resulting in an inflation that caused hardship and grumbling. The people, in

▲ The Continental Army brought together men from all over the colonies and from a wide range of backgrounds. Their variety is suggested in this watercolor by a French officer who served in America during the Revolution. From left to right are a black infantryman with a light rifle, a musketman, a soldier carrying a heavy rifle, and an artilleryman.

effect, paid much of the cost of the war through the depreciation of their savings, but it is hard to see how else the war could have been financed, given the prejudice of the populace against paying taxes to fight a war against British taxation.

At about the time the Articles of Confederation were ratified, Congress established Departments of Foreign Affairs, War, and Finance, with individual heads responsible to it. The most important of the new department heads was the superintendent of finance, Robert Morris, a Philadelphia merchant. When Morris took office, the Continental dollar was worthless, the system of supplying the army chaotic, the credit of the government exhausted. He set up an efficient method of obtaining food and uniforms for the army, persuaded Congress to charter a national Bank of North America, and aided by the slackening of military activity after Yorktown, got the country back on a hard money basis. New foreign loans were obtained, partly because Morris's efficiency and industry inspired confidence.

State Republican Governments

However crucial the role of Congress, in an important sense the real revolution occurred when the individual colonies broke their ties with Great Britain. Using their colonial charters as a basis, the states began framing new constitutions even before the Declaration of Independence. By early 1777 all but Connecticut and Rhode Island, which continued under their colonial charters well into the nineteenth century, had taken this decisive step.

On the surface the new governments were not drastically different from those they replaced. The most significant change was the removal of outside control, which had the effect of making the governments more responsive to public opinion. Gone were the times when a governor could be appointed and maintained in office by orders from London. The new constitutions varied in detail, but all provided for an elected legislature, an executive, and a system of courts. In general the powers of the governor and of judges were limited, the theory being that elected rulers no less than those appointed by kings were subject to the temptations of authority, that, as one Patriot put it, all men are "tyrants enough at heart." The typical governor had no voice in legislation and little in appointments. Pennsylvania went so far as to eliminate the office of governor, replacing it with an elected council of 12.

Power was concentrated in the legislature, which the people had come to count on to defend their interests. In addition to the lawmaking authority exercised by the colonial assemblies, the state constitutions gave the legislatures the power to declare war, conduct foreign relations, control the courts, and perform many other essentially executive functions. While continuing to require that voters be property owners or taxpayers, the constitution makers remained suspicious even of the legislature.

They rejected the British concept of virtual representation. They saw legislators as representatives, that is, agents reflecting the interests of the voters of a particular district rather than superior persons chosen to decide public issues according to their own best judgment. Where political power was involved, the common American principle was every man for himself, but also everyone for the nation, the republic. People were no longer subjects, but citizens, *parts* of government, obedient to its laws, but not blindly subordinate to governmental authority epitomized in the monarch.

A majority of the constitutions contained bills of rights (such as the one George Mason wrote for Virginia) protecting the people's civil liberties against all branches of the government. In Britain such guarantees checked only the Crown; the Americans invoked them against their elected representatives as well.

The state governments combined the best of the British system, including its respect for status, fairness, and due process, with the uniquely American stress on individualism and a healthy dislike of too much authority. The idea of drafting written frames of government—contracts between the people and their representatives that carefully spelled out the powers and duties of the latter—grew out of the experience of the colonists after 1763, when the vagueness of the unwritten British constitution had caused so much controversy, and from the compact principle, the heart of republican government as described so eloquently in the Declaration of Independence. This constitutionalism represented one of the most important innovations of the Revolutionary era: a peaceful method for altering the political system. In the midst of violence, the states changed their frames of government in an orderly, legal manner—a truly remarkable achievement that became a beacon of hope to reformers all over the world. The states' example, the Reverend Simeon Howard of Massachusetts predicted, "will encourage the friends and rouse a spirit of liberty through other nations."

Social Reform

Many states seized the occasion of constitution making to introduce important political and social reforms. In Pennsylvania, Virginia, North Carolina, and other states the seats in the legislature were reapportioned in order to give the western districts their fair share. Primogeniture, entail (the right of an owner of property to prevent heirs from ever disposing of it), and quitrents were abolished wherever they had existed. Steps toward greater freedom of religion were taken, especially in states where the Anglican Church had enjoyed a privileged position. In Virginia the movement to separate church and state was given the force of law by Jefferson's Statute of Religious Liberty, enacted in 1786. "Our civil rights have no dependence on our religious opinions, any more than our opinions in physics or geometry," the statute declared. "Truth is great and will prevail if left to herself." Therefore, "no man shall be compelled to frequent or support any religious worship, place, or ministry . . . nor shall otherwise suffer on account of his religious opinions or belief."

Many states continued to support religion; Massachusetts did not end public support of Congregational churches until the 1830s. But after the Revolution the states usually distributed the money roughly in accordance with the numerical strength of the various Protestant denominations.

A number of states moved tentatively against slavery. In attacking British policy after 1763, colonists had frequently claimed that Parliament was trying to make slaves of them. No less a personage than George Washington wrote in 1774: "We must assert our rights, or submit to every imposition, that can be heaped upon us, till custom and use shall make us tame and abject slaves." However exaggerated the language, such reasoning led to denunciations of slavery, often vague but significant in their effects on public opinion. The fact that practically every important thinker of the European Enlightenment (Montesquieu, Voltaire, Diderot, and Rousseau in France, David Hume, Samuel Johnson, and Adam Smith in England, to name the most important) had criticized slavery on moral and economic grounds also had an impact on educated opinion. Then, too, the forthright statements in the Declaration of Independence about liberty and equality seemed impossible to reconcile with slaveholding. "How is it," asked Dr. Johnson, who opposed independence vehemently, "that we hear the loudest yelps for liberty among the drivers of negroes?"

The war opened direct paths to freedom for some slaves. In November 1775 Lord Dunmore, the royal governor of Virginia, proclaimed that all slaves "able and willing to bear arms" for the British would be liberated. In fact, the British treated slaves as captured property, seizing them by the thousands in their campaigns in the south. The fate of these blacks is obscure. Some ended up in the West Indies, still slaves. Others were evacuated to Canada and liberated, and

some of them settled the British colony of Sierra Leone in West Africa, founded in 1787. Probably many more escaped from bondage by running away during the confusion accompanying the British campaigns in the South.

About 5000 blacks served in the Patriot army and navy. Most black soldiers were assigned noncombat duties, but there were some black soldiers in every major battle from Lexington to Yorktown.

Beginning with Pennsylvania in 1780, the northern states all did away with slavery. In most cases slaves born after a certain date were to become free on reaching maturity. Since New York did not pass a gradual emancipation law until 1799 and New Jersey not until 1804, there were numbers of slaves in the so-called free states well into the nineteenth century—more than 3500 as late as 1830. But the institution was on its way toward extinction. All the states prohibited the importation of slaves from abroad, and except for Georgia and South Carolina, the southern states passed laws removing restrictions on the right of individual owners to free their slaves. The greatest success of voluntary emancipation came in Virginia, where, between 1782 and 1790, as many as 10,000 blacks were freed.

These advances encouraged foes of slavery to hope that the institution would soon disappear. But slavery died only where it was not economically important. Except for owners whose slaves were "carried off" by the British, only in Massachusetts, where the state supreme court ruled slavery unconstitutional in 1783, were owners deprived of existing slaves against their will.

Despite the continuing subordination of blacks, there is no question that the Revolution permanently changed the tone of American society. In the way they dressed, in their manner of speech, and in the way they dealt with one another in public places, Americans paid at least lip service to the idea of equality.

After the publication of *Common Sense* and the Declaration of Independence, with their excoriations of that "Royal Brute," King George III, it became fashionable to denounce the granting of titles of nobility, all "aristocrats," and any privilege based on birth. In 1783 a group of army officers founded a fraternal organization, the Society of Cincinnati. Although the revered George Washington was its president, many citizens found the mere existence of a club restricted to officers alarming; the fact that membership was to be hereditary, passing on the death of a member to his oldest son, caused a furor.

Nevertheless, little of the social and economic upheaval usually associated with revolutions occurred, before, during, or after 1776. At least part of the urban violence of the period (just how large a part is difficult to determine at this distance) had no social objective. America had its share of criminals, mischievous youths eager to flex their muscles, and other people unable to resist the temptation to break the law when it could be done without much risk of punishment. Certainly there was no wholesale proscription of any class, faith, or profession.

The property of Tories was frequently seized by the state governments, but almost never with the idea of redistributing wealth or providing the poor with land. While some large Tory estates were broken up and sold to small farmers, others passed intact to wealthy individuals or to groups of speculators. The war disrupted many traditional business relationships. Some merchants were unable to cope with the changes; others adapted well and grew rich. But the changes occurred without regard for the political beliefs or social values of either those who profited or those who lost.

During the war, conflicts erupted over economic issues involving land and taxation, yet no single class or interest triumphed in all the states or in the national government. In Pennsylvania, where the western radical element was strong, the constitution was extremely democratic; in Maryland and South Carolina the conservatives maintained control handily. Throughout the country, many great landowners were ardent Patriots, but others became Tories—and so did many small farmers.

In some instances the state legislatures wrote the new constitutions. In others the legislatures ordered special elections to choose delegates to conventions empowered to draft the charters. The convention method was a further important product of the Revolutionary era, an additional illustration of the idea that constitutions are contracts between the people and their leaders. Massachusetts even required that its new constitution be ratified by the people after it was drafted.

Finally, the new governments became more responsive to public opinion, no matter what the particular shape of their political institutions. This was true principally because *Common Sense*, the Declaration of Independence, and the experience of participating in a revolution had made people conscious of their rights in a republic and of their power to enforce those rights. Conservatives swiftly discovered that state constitutions designed to insulate legislators and officials from popular pressures were ineffective when the populace felt strongly about any issue.

EFFECTS OF THE REVOLUTION ON WOMEN

In the late eighteenth century there was a trend in the Western world, barely perceptible at the time, toward increasing the legal rights of women. This movement was strengthened in America by the events leading up to the break with Great Britain and still more by the Declaration of Independence. When Americans began to think and talk about the rights of the individual and the evils of arbitrary rule, subtle effects on relations between the sexes followed. For example, it became somewhat easier for women to obtain divorces. In colonial times divorces were relatively rare, but easier for men to obtain than for women. After the Revolution the difference did not disappear, but it became considerably smaller. In Massachusetts, before the 1770s no woman is known to have obtained a divorce on the ground of her husband's adultery. Thereafter, successful suits by wives against errant husbands were not unusual. In 1791 a South Carolina judge went so far as to say that the law protecting "the absolute dominion" of husbands was "the

▲ A 1797 engraving of Deborah Sampson, the first woman to serve as a soldier in the Revolution. Born in 1760, Sampson in 1782 put on men's clothes and enlisted in the Massachusetts Militia under the name of Timothy Thayer. Her imposture was discovered and she was expelled. She then enlisted as Robert Shurtlieff in the Continental army. At a battle against Loyalists at Tarrytown, New York she was wounded in the thigh. Rather than let a doctor treat her—and discover her gender—she extracted the musket ball herself. After the war, she continued to wear men's clothing until she married and had children.

▲ Abigail Adams, in asking her husband John to "remember the ladies" when reforming society, was not advocating political rights for women. Rather, she wanted fairer treatment for women within the family. "Do not put such unlimited power into the hands of the husbands," she wrote him. "Remember all men would be tyrants if they could."

However, the war effort increased the influence of women in several ways. With so many men in uniform, women took over the management of countless farms, shops, and businesses, and they became involved in the handling of other day-to-day matters that men had normally conducted. Their experiences made both them and in many cases their fathers and husbands more aware of their ability to take on all sorts of chores previously considered exclusively masculine in character. At the same time, women wanted to contribute to the winning of independence, and their efforts to do so made them conscious of their importance. Furthermore, the rhetoric of the Revolution, with its stress on liberty and equality, affected women in the same way that it caused many whites of both sexes to question the morality of slavery.

Attitudes toward the education of women also changed because of the Revolution. According to the best estimates, at least half the white women in America could not read or write as late as the 1780s. In a land of opportunity like the United States, women seemed particularly important, not only because they themselves were citizens, but because of their role in training the next generation. "You distribute 'mental nourishment' along with physical," one orator told the women of America in 1795. "The reformation of the world is in your power. . . . The solidity and stability of your country rest with you." The idea of female education began to catch on. Schools for girls were founded, and the level of female literacy gradually rose.

offspring of a rude and barbarous age." The "progress of civilization," he continued, "has tended to ameliorate the condition of women, and to allow even to wives, something like personal identity."

As the tone of this "liberal" opinion indicates, the change in male attitudes that took place in America because of the Revolution was small. Courts in New York and Massachusetts refused to take action against Tory women whose husbands were Tories on the ground that it was the duty of women to obey their husbands, and when John Adams's wife Abigail warned him in 1776 that if he and his fellow rebels did not "remember the ladies" when reforming society, the women would "foment a Rebellion" of their own, he treated her remarks as a joke. Adams believed that voting (and as he wrote on another occasion, writing history) was "not the Province of the Ladies."[3]

---

[3]Adams's distaste for women historians may have been based on the fact that in his friend Mercy Otis Warren's *History of the Rise, Progress, and Termination of the American Revolution* (1805) Warren claimed that Adams sometimes allowed his "prejudices" to distort his judgment.

GROWTH OF A NATIONAL SPIRIT

American independence and control of a wide and rich domain were the most obvious results of the Revolution. Changes in the structure of society, as we have seen, were relatively minor. Economic developments, such as the growth of new trade connections and the expansion of manufacturing in an effort to replace British goods, were of only modest significance. By far the most important social and economic changes involved the Tories and were thus by-products of the political revolution rather than a determined reorganization of a people's way of life.

There was another important result of the Revolution: the growth of American nationalism. Most modern revolutions have been *caused* by nationalism and have *resulted* in independence. In the case of the American Revolution, the desire to be free antedated any intense national feeling. The colonies entered into a political union not because they felt an overwhelming desire to bring all Americans under one rule but because unity offered the only hope of winning a war against Great Britain. That they remained united after throwing off British rule reflects the degree to which nationalism had developed during the conflict.

By the middle of the eighteenth century the colonists had begun to think of themselves as a separate society distinct from Europe and even from Britain. Benjamin Franklin described himself not as a British subject but as "an American subject of the King," and in 1750 a Boston newspaper could urge its readers to drink "American" beer in order to free themselves from being "beholden to Foreigners" for their alcoholic beverages. Little political nationalism existed before the Revolution, however, in part because most people knew little about life outside their own colony. When a delegate to the first Continental Congress mentioned "Colonel Washington" to John Adams soon after the Congress met, Adams had to ask him who this "Colonel Washington" was. He had never heard the name before.

Local ties remained predominant. A few might say, with Patrick Henry in 1774, "The distinctions between Virginians, Pennsylvanians, New Yorkers, and New Englanders are no more. I am not a Virginian, but an American." But Henry was being carried away by his own oratory; he was actually of two minds on the subject of national versus local loyalty. People who really put America first were rare indeed before the final break with Great Britain.

The new nationalism arose from a number of sources and expressed itself in different ways. Common sacrifices in war certainly played a part; the soldiers of the Continental Army fought in the summer heat of the Carolinas for the same cause that had led them to brave the ice floes of the Delaware in order to surprise the Hessians. Such men lost interest in state boundary lines; they became Americans.

John Marshall of Fauquier County, Virginia, for example, was a 20-year-old militiaman in 1775. The next year he joined the Continental Army. He served in Pennsylvania, New Jersey, and New York and endured the winter of 1777–1778 at Valley Forge. "I found myself associated with brave men from different states who were risking life and everything valuable in a common cause," he later wrote. "I was confirmed in the habit of considering America as my country and Congress as my government."

Andrew Jackson, child of the Carolina frontier, was only nine years old when the Revolution broke out. One brother was killed in battle; another died as a result of untreated wounds. Young Andrew took up arms and was captured by the Redcoats. A British officer ordered Jackson to black his boots and, when the boy refused, struck him across the face with the flat of his sword. Jackson bore the scar to his grave—and became an ardent nationalist on the spot. He and Marshall had very different ideas and came to be bitter enemies in later life. Nevertheless, they were both American nationalists—and for the same reason.

Civilians as well as soldiers reacted in this way. A Carolina farmer whose home and barn were protected against British looters by men who spoke with the harsh nasal twang of New England adopted a broader outlook toward politics. When the news came that thousands of Redcoats had stacked their arms in defeat after Yorktown, few people cared what state or section had made the victory possible—it was an American triumph.

The war caused many people to move from place to place. Soldiers traveled as the tide of war fluctuated; so too—far more than in earlier times—did prominent leaders. Members of Congress from every state had to travel to Philadelphia; in the process they saw much of the country and the people who inhabited it. Listening to their fellows and serving with them on committees almost inevitably broadened these men, most of them highly influential in their local communities.

With its 13 stars and 13 stripes representing the states, the American flag symbolized national unity and reflected the common feeling that such a symbol was necessary. Yet the flag had separate stars and stripes; local interests and local loyalties remained extremely strong, and these could be divisive when conflicts of interest arose.

Certain practical problems that demanded common solutions also drew the states together. No one seriously considered having 13 postal systems or 13 sets of diplomatic representatives abroad. Every new diplomatic appointment, every treaty of friendship or commerce signed, committed all to a common policy and thus bound them more closely together. And economic developments had a unifying effect. Cutting off English goods encouraged manufacturing, making America more self-sufficient and stimulating both interstate trade and national pride.

THE GREAT LAND ORDINANCES

The western lands, which had divided the states in the beginning, became a force for unity once they had been ceded to the national government. Everyone realized what a priceless national asset they were, and all now understood that no one state could determine the future of the West.

Western Land Claims Ceded by the States

The politicians argued hotly about how these lands should be developed. Some advocated selling the land in township units in the traditional New England manner to groups or companies; others favored

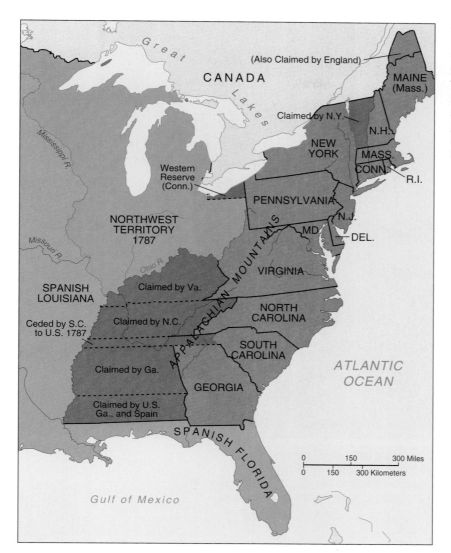

letting individual pioneers stake out farms in the helter-skelter manner common in the colonial South. The decision was a compromise. The Land Ordinance of 1785 provided for surveying western territories into 6-mile-square townships before sale. Every other township was to be further subdivided into 36 sections of 640 acres (1 square mile) each. The land was sold at auction at a minimum price of $1 an acre. The law favored speculative land-development companies, for even the 640-acre units were far too large and expensive for the typical frontier family. But the fact that the land was to be surveyed and sold by the central government was a nationalizing force. It ensured orderly development of the West and simplified the task of defending the frontier in the event of Indian attack. Congress set aside the sixteenth section of every township for the maintenance of schools, another farsighted decision.

Still more significant was the Northwest Ordinance of 1787, which established governments for the West. As early as 1775 settlers in frontier districts were petitioning Congress to allow them to enter the Union as independent states, and in 1780 Congress had resolved that all lands ceded to the nation by the existing states should be "formed into distinct republican States" with "the same rights of sovereignty, freedom and independence" as the original 13. In 1784 a committee headed by Thomas Jefferson worked out a plan for doing this, and in 1787 it was enacted into law. The area bounded by the Ohio, the Mississippi, and the Great Lakes was to be carved into not fewer than three or more than five territories. Until the adult male population of the entire area reached 5000, it was to be ruled by a governor and three judges, all

DOCUMENT

Northwest Ordinance, 1787

▲ The Land Ordinance of 1785 called for surveying and dividing the Western Territories into one-mile square mile subdivisions—640 acres. These were further subdivided and sold as 40 acre tracts. Few pieces of legislation have left a more visible imprint upon the landscape. Nowadays the Midwest, as seen from an airplane, resembles a patchwork quilt of 40-acre squares, like the section of Kansas above.

appointed by Congress. When 5000 men of voting age had settled in the territory, the Ordinance authorized them to elect a legislature, which could send a nonvoting delegate to Congress. Finally, when 60,000 persons had settled in any one of the political subdivisions, it was to become a state. It could draft a constitution and operate in any way it wished, save that the government had to be "republican" and that slavery was prohibited.

Seldom has a legislative body acted more wisely. That the western districts must become states everyone conceded from the start. The people had had their fill of colonialism under British rule, and the rebellious temper of frontier settlers made it impossible even to consider maintaining the West in a dependent status. (When North Carolina ceded its trans-Appalachian lands to the United States in 1784, the settlers there, uncertain how they would fare under federal rule, hastily organized an extralegal state of Franklin, and it was not until 1789 that

the national government obtained control.) But it would have been unfair to turn the territories over to the firstcomers, who would have been unable to manage such large domains and would surely have taken advantage of their priority to dictate to later arrivals. A period of tutelage was necessary, a period when the "mother country" must guide and nourish its growing offspring.

Thus the intermediate territorial governments corresponded almost exactly to the governments of British royal colonies. The appointed governors could veto acts of the assemblies and could "convene, prorogue, and dissolve" them at their discretion. The territorial delegates to Congress were not unlike colonial agents. Yet it was vital that this intermediate stage end and that its end be determined in advance so that no argument could develop over when the territory was ready for statehood.

The system worked well and was applied to nearly all the regions absorbed by the nation as it advanced westward. Together with the Ordinance of 1785, which branded its checkerboard pattern on the physical shape of the West, this law gave the growing country a unity essential to the growth of a national spirit.

NATIONAL HEROES

Benjamin Franklin, c. 1794–1802

The Revolution further fostered nationalism by giving the people their first commonly revered heroes. Benjamin Franklin was widely known before the break with Great Britain through his experiments with electricity, his immensely successful *Poor Richard's Almanack,* and his invention of the Franklin stove. His staunch support of the Patriot cause, his work in the Continental Congress, and his diplomatic successes in France, where he was extravagantly admired, added to his fame. Franklin demonstrated, to Europeans and to Americans themselves, that not all Americans need be ignorant rustics.

Washington, however, was "the chief human symbol of a common Americanism." Stern, cold, a man of few words, the great Virginian did not seem a likely candidate for hero worship. "My countenance never yet revealed my feelings," he himself admitted. Yet he had qualities that made people name babies after him and call him "the Father of His Country" long before the war was won: his personal sacrifices in the cause of independence, his integrity, and above all, perhaps, his obvious desire to retire to his Mount Vernon estate (for many Americans feared any powerful leader and worried lest Washington seek to become a dictator).

As a general, Washington was not a brilliant strategist like Napoleon. Neither was he a tactician of the quality of Caesar or Robert E. Lee. But he was a remarkable organizer and administrator—patient, thoughtful, conciliatory. In a way, his lack of genius made his achievements all the more impressive. He held his forces together in adversity, avoiding both useless slaughter and catastrophic defeat. People of all sections, from every walk of life, looked on Washington as the embodiment of American virtues: a man of deeds rather than words; a man of substance accustomed to luxury yet capable of enduring great hardships stoically and as much at home in the wilderness as an Indian; a bold Patriot, quick to take arms against British tyranny, yet eminently respectable. The Revolution might have been won without Washington, but it is unlikely that the free United States would have become so easily a true nation had he not been at its call.

A NATIONAL CULTURE

Breaking away from Great Britain accentuated certain trends toward social and intellectual independence and strengthened the national desire to create an American culture. The Anglican Church in America had to form a new organization once the connection with the Crown was severed. It painfully weaned itself from government support, and in 1786 it became the Protestant Episcopal Church. The Dutch and German Reformed churches also became independent of their European connections. Roman Catholics in America had been under the administration of the vicar apostolic of England; after the Revolution, Father John Carroll of Baltimore assumed these duties, and in 1789 he became the first American Roman Catholic bishop.

The impact of post-Revolutionary nationalism on American education was best reflected in the immense success of the textbooks of Noah Webster, later famous for his American dictionary. Webster was an ardent patriot. "We ought not to consider ourselves as inhabitants of a particular state only," he wrote in 1785, "but as *Americans.*" Webster's famous *Spelling Book* appeared in 1783 when he was a young schoolteacher in Goshen, New York. It emphasized American forms and usage and contained a patriotic preface urging Americans to pay proper respect to their own literature. Webster's *Reader,* published shortly thereafter, included selections from the speeches of Revolutionary leaders, who, according to the compiler, were the equals of Cicero and Demosthenes as orators. Some 15 million copies of the *Speller* were sold in the next five decades, several times that number by 1900. The *Reader* was also a continuing best-seller.

Webster's work was not the only sign of nationalism in education. In 1787 John M'Culloch published the first American history textbook. The colleges saw a great outburst of patriotic spirit. King's College (founded in 1754) received a new name, Columbia, in 1784. Everywhere it was recognized that the republic required educated and cultivated leaders.

Nationalism affected the arts and sciences in the years after the Revolution. Jedidiah Morse's popular *American Geography* (1789) was a paean in praise of the "astonishing" progress of the country, all the result of the "natural genius of Americans." The American Academy of Arts and Sciences, founded at Boston during the Revolution, was created "to advance the interest, honor, dignity and happiness of a free, independent and virtuous people."

American painters and writers of the period usually chose extremely patriotic themes. Mercy Otis Warren, a sister of James Otis, published an impressive *History of the Rise, Progress and Termination of the American Revolution* in 1805. The artist John Trumbull helped capture Dorchester Heights and force the evacuation of Boston, took part in the defense of northern New York against Burgoyne, and fought in Pennsylvania and Rhode Island. When he took up painting, he went to London to study, but he produced such pictures as *The Battle of Bunker's Hill, The Surrender of Lord Cornwallis at Yorktown,* and *The Declaration of Independence.* Trumbull referred to these and similar efforts as his "national work." Joel Barlow intended his *Vision of Columbus,* written between 1779 and 1787, to prove that America was "the noblest and most elevated part of the earth." Royall Tyler's play *The Contrast,* which was produced in New York in 1787, compared American virtue (the hero was called Colonel Manly) with British vice and contained such chauvinistic lines as these:

Why should our thoughts to distant countries roam When each refinement may be found at home?

In a more subtle way, American nationalism revealed itself in the fondness of the Revolutionary generation for ancient Greek and Roman architecture, which it saw as expressing democratic and republican values. Jefferson, for example, built his home at Monticello in a classical style and modeled the Virginia Capitol on the Roman *Maison Carré* in Nimes, France.

The United States in the 1780s was far from the powerful centralized nation it has since become. Probably most citizens still gave their first loyalty to their own states. In certain important respects the confederation was pitifully ineffectual. However, people were increasingly aware of their common interests and increasingly proud of their common heritage. The motto of the new nation, *E pluribus unum*—"from many, one"—describes a process that was gradually gathering force in the years after Yorktown.

MILESTONES

1774	Thomas Jefferson writes *A Summary View of the Rights of British America*
	General Thomas Gage, commander-in-chief of British army in North America, is named governor of Massachusetts
1775	Colonists fight British in Battles of Lexington and Concord
	Second Continental Congress names George Washington commander-in-chief (of Continental Army)
	Gage is replaced as British commander by General Sir William Howe after Battle of Bunker Hill
1776	Thomas Paine publishes *Common Sense*
	Washington's troops occupy Boston
	Second Continental Congress issues Declaration of Independence
	Washington's troops are defeated in Battle of Long Island
	Washington evacuates New York City
	Washington's victory at Battle of Trenton boosts morale

1777	Washington's troops win Battle of Princeton
	American victory at Saratoga turns the tide and leads to alliance with France
	British occupy Philadelphia after Battle of Germantown
1777–1778	Continental Army winters at Valley Forge
1778	British capture Savannah
1780	British capture Charleston
1781	States ratify Articles of Confederation
	General Cornwallis surrenders at Yorktown
1783	Great Britain recognizes independence of United States by signing Peace of Paris
1785	Congress passes Land Ordinance of 1785
1787	Northwest Ordinance establishes governments for the West

SUPPLEMENTARY READING

Good brief surveys of the Revolutionary years are Edward Countryman, *The American Revolution* (1985) and E. S. Morgan, *The Birth of the Republic* (1977). The best one-volume account of the war is Piers Mackesey, *The War for America, 1775–1783* (1964). See also Jack Greene, *Understanding the American Revolution* (1995). David Hackett Fischer's account of the battle of Lexington and Concord in *Paul Revere's Ride* (1994) shows why the colonists won the war; his *Washington's Crossing* (2004) outlines the importance of the New Jersey campaign. See also John W. Shy, *A People Numerous and Armed* (1990).

For a short biography of Washington, see James MacGregor Burns and Susan Dunn, *George Washington* (2004). Longer biographies include Richard Norton Smith, *Patriarch: George Washington and the New American Nation* (1993), and Henry Wiencek, *Imperfect God: George Washington, His Slaves, and the Creator of America* (2003). John E. Ferling, *Setting the World Ablaze* (2000) and his *A Leap in the Dark* (2003) provide a good overview of how Washington, Jefferson, and John Adams interacted. See also Joseph Ellis, *Founding Brothers: The Revolutionary Generation* (2000), and David McCullough *John Adams* (2001).

On the broader context of the Revolution, see Lester Langley, *The Americas in the Age of Revolution, 1750–1850* (1996); Eliga Gould emphasizes the continuity in America of British political culture, *The Persistence of Empire* (2000).

On the Continental Congress and the Articles of Confederation, see Jackson T. Main, *The Sovereign States* (1973) and Jack N. Rakove, *The Beginnings of National Politics* (1979). P. S. Onuf, *Statehood and Union* (1987), deals with the Northwest Ordinance. Eric Foner, *Tom Paine and Revolutionary America* (1976), is an excellent brief biography. James K. Martin makes a case for his subject in *Benedict Arnold, Revolutionary Hero* (1997).

The classic study of the Declaration of Independence is C. L. Becker, *The Declaration of Independence* (1922); for contemporary analysis see Pauline Maier, *American Scripture* (1997), and Jay Fliegelman, *Declaring Independence* (1993).

The early history of the state governments is covered in W. P. Adams, *The First American Constitutions* (1980). Edward Countryman, *A People in Revolution* (1982), deals with conditions in New York; for Maryland, see Jean B. Lee, *The Price of Nationhood* (1994). The development of political and social ideas, before, during, and after the Revolution, is admirably described and analyzed in G. S. Wood, *The Creation of the American Republic* (1969) and *The Radicalism of the American Revolution* (1992).

The effects of the Revolution on slavery are treated in W. D. Jordan, *White over Black* (1968), and on the Indians, in Colin G. Calloway, *The American Revolution in Indian Country* (1995). For an account of Indians, debtors, and slaves in Virginia, see Woody Holton, *Forced Founders* (1999). L. K. Kerber, *Women of the Republic* (1980), M. B. Norton, *Liberty's Daughters* (1980), and Joy Day Buel and Richard Buel, *The Way of Duty* (1984) discuss the effects of the Revolution on women and the family.

SUGGESTED WEBSITES

Revolutionary War Songs
http://www.mcneilmusic.com/rev.html
This site contains colonial and revolutionary era songs.

Maryland Loyalists and the American Revolution
http://users.erols.com/candidus/index.htm
This examination of Maryland's Loyalists promotes the author's book on that subject. Nonetheless, the site has good information about an underappreciated phenomenon, including Loyalist songs and poems.

The American Revolution
http://revolution.h-net.msu.edu/
This site accompanies the PBS series *Revolution* with essays and resource links.

Georgia's Rare Map Collection
http://scarlett.libs.uga.edu/darchive/hargrett/maps/colamer.html
http://scarlett.libs.uga.edu/darchive/hargrett/maps/revamer.html
These two University of Georgia sites contain maps of colonial and revolutionary America.

Canada History
http://www.civilization.ca
Canada and the United States shared a colonial past, but developed along different lines. This site is part of the virtual museum of the Canadian Museum of Civilization Corporation.

The Federalist Era: Nationalism Triumphant

▼ George Washington, "father of the nation," also designed his home, Mount Vernon: a broad, solid edifice which, though it evolved over decades, retained a rigid symmetry. "Everything," he instructed the builders, was to be "exactly answerable and uniform." He held a similar view about the structure of government.

CHAPTER CONTENTS

At first, only a relative handful of Americans resented the constraints imposed by the confederation on the power of the central government. Once the war was over, the need for unity seemed less pressing and interstate conflicts reasserted themselves. Modern research has modified but not contradicted the thesis, advanced by John Fiske in *The Critical Period of American History* (1888), that the national government was demoralized and inadequate. If, as Washington said, it moved "on crutches . . . tottering at every step," it did move. The negotiation of a successful peace treaty ending the Revolutionary War, the humane and farsighted federal land policies, and even the establishment of a rudimentary federal bureaucracy to manage routine affairs were remarkable achievements, all carried out under the Articles. Yet the country's evolution placed demands on the national government that its creators had not anticipated.

BORDER PROBLEMS

The government had to struggle to win actual control over the territory granted the United States in the treaty ending the Revolution. Both Great Britain and Spain stood in the way of this objective. The British had promised to withdraw all their troops from American soil promptly, and so they did—within the settled portions of the 13 states. Beyond the frontier, however, they had established a string of seven military posts, running from the northern end of Lake Champlain through Niagara and Detroit to the tip of the Michigan peninsula. These, despite the Treaty of Paris, they refused to surrender. Pressing against America's exposed frontier like hot coals, the posts seared national pride. They threatened to set off another Indian war, for the British intrigued constantly to stir up the tribes. The great prize was the rich fur trade of the region, which the British still controlled.

The British justified holding on to these positions by citing the failure of the Americans to live up to some terms of the peace treaty. The United States had agreed not to impede British creditors seeking to collect prewar debts and to "earnestly recommend" that the states restore confiscated Tory property. The national government complied with both requirements (which called only for words on Congress's part), but the states did not cooperate. Many passed laws making it impossible for British creditors to collect debts, and the property of Tory émigrés was not returned.

Yet those violations of the peace terms had little to do with the continued presence of the British. They would probably not have evacuated the posts at this time even if every farthing of the debt had been paid and every acre of confiscated land restored. Americans found the presence of British troops galling. When the French had pushed a line of forts into the Ohio country in the 1750s, it had seemed to most colonists a matter of local concern, to be dealt with by Virginia or Pennsylvania. Three decades later the inability to eject the British seemed a national disgrace.

Then there was the question of the Spanish in the Southwest. Spain had been a co-belligerent, not an ally, in the war with Great Britain. In the peace negotiations it had won back Florida and the Gulf Coast region east of New Orleans. Spanish troops had captured Natchez during the war, and although the post lay far north of the boundary, Spain refused to turn it over to the United States. Far more serious, in 1784 the Spaniards had closed the lower Mississippi River to American commerce. Because of the prohibitive cost of moving bulky farm produce over the mountains, settlers beyond the Appalachians depended on the Mississippi and its network of tributaries to get their corn, tobacco, and other products to eastern and European markets. The Spanish governor of Louisiana, Esteban Miró, soon opened the river to American produce, subject only to a modest tariff, but if Spain ever denied them the right to "deposit" goods at New Orleans while awaiting oceangoing transportation, Westerners could not sell their surpluses. A stronger central government might have dealt with these foreign problems more effectively, but it could not have eliminated them. United or decentralized, until the country grew more powerful, or until the Europeans began to fight among themselves, the United States was bound to suffer at their hands.

▲ New Orleans, by linking flatboats on the Mississippi River with seagoing vessels, became a major commercial port. Like most ports, it sustained a profitable business in prostitution. These tidy white cottages with shuttered windows were likely homes of the city's mulatto mistresses and prostitutes. Neighborhood children, crouching behind a wall, keenly watch the proceedings.

FOREIGN TRADE

The fact that the Revolution freed American trade from the restrictions of British mercantilism proved a mixed blessing in the short run. The commercial benefits that Tom Paine had described in *Common Sense* did not materialize. Americans could now trade directly with Europe, and commercial treaties were negotiated with a number of European nations. Beginning in 1784, when the 360-ton *Empress of China* reached Canton with a cargo of furs and cotton to be exchanged for silks, tea, and spices, a valuable East Asian trade sprang up where none had existed before. But exclusion from Britain's imperial trade union brought losses of a much larger magnitude.

Immediately after the Revolution a controversy broke out in Great Britain over fitting the former colonies into the mercantilist system. Some people, influenced by Adam Smith's *The Wealth of Nations,* published in 1776, argued that any restriction on the buying and selling of goods was wasteful; if people could trade freely, all parties would benefit. Others, while remaining mercantilists, realized how important the American trade was for British prosperity and argued that special treatment should be afforded the former colonists. Unfortunately, a proud empire recently humbled in war could hardly be expected to exercise such forbearance. Persuaded in part by the reasoning of Lord Sheffield's pamphlet *Observations on the Commerce of the American States* that Britain could get all the American commerce it wished without making concessions, Parliament voted to try building up exports to America while holding imports to a minimum, all according to the best tenets of mercantilism.

At the same time British merchants, eager to regain markets closed to them during the Revolution, poured low-priced manufactured goods of all kinds into the United States. Americans, long deprived of British products, rushed to take advantage of the bargains. Soon imports of British goods were approaching the levels of the early 1770s, while exports to the empire reached no more than half their earlier volume.

The influx of British goods aggravated the situation just when the economy was suffering a certain dislocation as a result of the ending of the war. From 1784 to 1786 the country went through a period of bad times. The inability of Congress to find money to pay the nation's debts undermined public confidence. Veterans who had still not been paid, and private individuals and foreign governments that had lent the government money during the Revolution, were clamoring for their due. In some regions crop failures compounded the difficulties.

The depression made the states stingier than ever about supplying the requisitions of Congress; at the same time many of them levied heavy property taxes in order to pay off their own war debts. Everywhere people were hard-pressed for cash. "As Money has ever been considered the root of all evils," one Massachusetts man commented sourly, "may we not presage happy times, as this source is almost done away?"

An obvious way of dealing with these problems would have been to place tariffs on British goods in order to limit imports or force the British to open the West Indies to all American goods, but the Confederation lacked the authority to do this. When individual states erected tariff barriers, British merchants easily got around them by bringing their goods in through states that did not. That the central government lacked the power to control commerce disturbed merchants, other businessmen, and the ever-increasing number of national-minded citizens in every walk of life.

Thus a movement developed to give the Confederation the power to tax imports, and in 1781 Congress sought authority to levy a 5 percent tariff duty. This would enable Congress to pay off some of its obligations and also put pressure on the British to relax their restrictions on American trade with the West Indies. Every state but Rhode Island agreed, but the measure required the unanimous consent of the states and therefore failed.

Defeat of the tariff pointed up the need for revising the Articles of Confederation, for here was a case where a large percentage of the states were ready to increase the power of the national government yet were unable to do so. Although many individuals in every region were worried about creating a centralized monster that might gobble up the sovereignty of the states, the practical needs of the times convinced many others that this risk must be taken.

THE SPECTER OF INFLATION

The depression and the unfavorable balance of trade led to increased pressures in the states for the printing of paper money and the passage of laws designed to make life easier for debtors. Before the Revolution the colonists had grappled with the chronic shortage of hard money resulting from their unfavorable balance of trade in many ways—declaring various staple products such as furs, tobacco, and even Indian wampum to be legal tender; deliberately overvaluing foreign coins to discourage their export; making it illegal to ship coins abroad; and printing paper currency. In response to wartime needs, both the Continental Congress and the states issued large amounts of paper money during the Revolution, with inflationary results (the Continental dollar became utterly worthless by 1781, and Virginia's paper money nearly so).

After the war some states set out to restore their credit by imposing heavy taxes and severely restricting new issues of money. Combined with the postwar depression and the increase in imports, this sharply lowered prices and wages. Soon debtors, especially farmers, were crying for relief, both in the form of laws that would make it difficult to collect debts and through the printing of more paper money. If more money were put in circulation, wages and prices would rise and debts would be easier to pay.

More than half the states yielded to this pressure in 1785 and 1786. Issues in South Carolina, New York, and Pennsylvania were conservatively handled and succeeded, but some states printed up so much money it depreciated rapidly. The most disastrous experience was that of Rhode Island, where the government attempted to legislate public confidence in £100,000 of paper. Any landowner could borrow a share of this money from the state for 14 years, using real estate as security. Creditors feared that the loans would never be repaid, but the legislature passed a law fining persons who refused to accept it £100. When creditors fled the state to avoid being confronted, the legislature authorized debtors to discharge their obligations by turning the necessary currency over to a judge. A conservative poet described Rhode Island as a "realm of rogues, renown'd for fraud and guile" where "Bankrupts their creditors with rage pursue."

Daniel Shays's "Little Rebellion"

Although the Rhode Island case was atypical, it alarmed conservatives. Then, close on its heels, came a disturbing outbreak of violence in Massachusetts. The Massachusetts legislature was determined to pay off the state debt and maintain a sound currency. Taxes amounting to almost £1.9 million were levied between 1780 and 1786, the burden falling most heavily on those of moderate income. The average Massachusetts farmer paid about a third of every year's income in taxes. Bad times and deflation led to many foreclosures, and the prisons were crowded with honest debtors. "Our Property is torn from us," one town complained, "our Gaols filled & still our Debts are not discharged."

In the summer of 1786 mobs in the western communities began to stop foreclosures by forcibly preventing the courts from holding their sessions. Under the leadership of Daniel Shays, a veteran of Bunker Hill, Ticonderoga, and Saratoga, the "rebels" marched on Springfield and prevented the state

▲ This broadside lauds Daniel Shays *(left),* who headed the armed rebellion against Massachusetts, which was cracking down on debtors. Shays is pictured in his Continental uniform. For his efforts at the battle of Saratoga in 1777, Marquis de Lafayette had presented Shays with a ceremonial sword, pictured here. Shays sold the sword to pay off his debts.

supreme court from meeting. When the state government sent troops against them, the rebels attacked the Springfield arsenal. They were routed, and the uprising then collapsed. Shays fled to Vermont.

As Thomas Jefferson observed at safe remove from the trouble in Paris, where he was serving as minister to France, Shays's uprising was only "a *little* rebellion" and as such "a medicine necessary for the sound health of government." But Shays and his followers were genuinely exasperated by the refusal of the government even to try to provide relief for their troubles. By taking up arms they forced the authorities to heed them: At its next session the legislature made some concessions to their demands.

But unlike Jefferson, most well-to-do Americans considered the uprising "Liberty run mad." "What, gracious God, is man! that there should be such inconsistency and perfidiousness in his conduct?" the usually unexcitable George Washington asked when news of the riots reached Virginia. "We are fast verging to anarchy and confusion!" During the crisis private persons had had to subscribe funds to put the rebels down, and when Massachusetts had appealed to Congress for help there was little Congress could legally do. The lessons seemed plain: Liberty must not become an excuse for license; greater authority must be vested in the central government.

DOCUMENT

Military Reports on Shays's Rebellion

The Rhode Island excesses and the uprising in Massachusetts illustrated the clash between local and national interests. Newspapers in all the states followed the bizarre spectacle of debtors in Rhode Island pursuing their creditors with fistfuls of worthless paper money. The revolt of Daniel Shays worried planters in far-off Virginia and the Carolinas almost as much as it did the merchants of Boston. Bacon's Rebellion, a far more serious affair, had evoked no such reaction in the seventeenth century, nor had the Regulator War in North Carolina as late as 1771.

To Philadelphia, and the Constitution

If most people wanted to increase the power of Congress, they were also afraid to shift the balance too far lest they destroy the sovereignty of the states and the rights of individuals. The machinery for change established in the Articles of Confederation, which required the unanimous consent of the states for all amendments, posed a particularly delicate problem. Experience had shown it unworkable, yet to bypass it would be revolutionary and therefore dangerous.

The first fumbling step toward reform was taken in March 1785 when representatives of Virginia and Maryland, meeting at the home of George Washington to settle a dispute over the improvement of navigation on the Potomac River, suggested a conference of all the states to discuss common problems of commerce. In January 1786 the Virginia legislature sent out a formal call for such a gathering to be held in September at Annapolis. However, the Annapolis Convention disappointed advocates of reform; delegates from only five states appeared; even Maryland, supposedly the host state, did not send a representative. Being so few the group did not feel it worthwhile to propose changes.

Alexander Hamilton—Portrait

Among the delegates was a young New York lawyer named Alexander Hamilton, a brilliant, imaginative, and daring man who was convinced that only drastic centralization would save the nation from disintegration. Hamilton described himself as a "nationalist." While the war still raged he contrasted the virtues of "a great Federal Republic" with the existing system of "petty states with the appearance only of union, jarring, jealous, and perverse." Instead of giving up, he proposed calling another convention to meet at Philadelphia to deal generally with constitutional reform. Delegates should be empowered to work out a broad plan for correcting "such defects as may be discovered to exist" in the Articles of Confederation.

The Annapolis group approved Hamilton's suggestion, and Congress reluctantly endorsed it. This time all the states but Rhode Island sent delegates. On May 25, 1787, the convention opened its proceedings at the State House in Philadelphia and unanimously elected George Washington its president. When it adjourned four months later, it had drafted the Constitution.

The Great Convention

As the decades have passed and the Constitution has grown more and more tradition-encrusted without losing any of its flexibility, each generation has tried to explain how a people so young and inexperienced, so free-swinging and unruly, could have produced it. At the time of the hundredth anniversary of its signing, the British statesman William E. Gladstone called it "the most wonderful work ever struck off at a given time by the brain of man." One reason for its durability was the ability of those who drafted it. The Founders were remarkable men. Although he later had reason to quarrel with certain aspects of their handiwork, Jefferson, who was on a foreign assignment and did not attend the convention, called them "demigods." A presumably more impartial French diplomat said that "even in Europe," he had never seen "an assembly more respectable for the talents, knowledge, disinterestedness, and patriotism."

Collectively the delegates possessed a rare combination of talents. Most of them had had considerable experience in politics, and the many lawyers among them were skilled in logic and debate. Furthermore, the times made them acutely aware of their opportunities. It was "a time when the greatest lawgivers of antiquity would have wished to live," an opportunity to "establish the wisest and happiest government that human wisdom can contrive," John Adams wrote. "We . . . decide for ever the fate of republican government," James Madison said during the deliberations.

If these remarks overstated the importance of their deliberations, they nonetheless represented the opinion of most of those present. They were boldly optimistic about their country. "We are laying the foundation of a great empire," Madison predicted. At the same time the delegates recognized the difficulties they faced. The ancient Roman republic was one model, and all knew that it had been overthrown by tyrants and eventually overrun by barbarians. The framers were also familiar with Enlightenment thinkers such as John Locke, Thomas Hobbes, and Montesquieu, and also with the ideas that swirled around the great disputes between Parliament and the Stuart monarchs during the seventeenth century.

▲ James Madison was a key figure at the Great Convention of 1787. He not only influenced the shaping of the Constitution but also kept the most complete record of the proceedings. "Every person," wrote one delegate, "seems to acknowledge his greatness."

Fortunately, they were nearly all of one mind on basic questions. That there should be a federal system, with both independent state governments and a national government with limited powers to handle matters of common interest, was accepted by all but one or two of them. Republican government, drawing its authority from the people and remaining responsible to them, was a universal assumption. A measure of democracy followed inevitably from this principle, for even the most aristocratic delegates agreed that ordinary citizens should share in the process of selecting those who were to make and execute the laws.

All agreed that no group within society, no matter how numerous, should have unrestricted authority. They looked on political power much as we today view nuclear energy: a force with tremendous potential value for humankind, but one easily misused and therefore dangerous to unleash. People meant well and had limitless possibilities, the constitution makers believed, but they were selfish by nature and could not be counted on to respect the interests of others. The ordinary people—small farmers, artisans, any taxpayer—should have a say in government in order to be able to protect themselves against those who would exploit their weakness, and the majority must

somehow be prevented from plundering the rich, for property must be secure or no government could be stable. No single state or section must be allowed to predominate, nor should the legislature be supreme over the executive or the courts. Power, in short, must be divided, and the segments must be balanced one against the other.

At the outset the delegates decided to keep the proceedings secret. That way no one was tempted to play to the gallery or seek some personal political advantage at the expense of the common good. Next they agreed to go beyond their instructions to revise the Articles of Confederation and draft an entirely new form of government. This was a bold, perhaps illegal act, but it was in no way irresponsible because nothing the convention might recommend was binding on anyone, and it was absolutely essential because under the Articles a single state could have prevented the adoption of any change. Alexander Hamilton captured the mood of the gathering when he said: "We can only propose and recommend—the power of ratifying or rejecting is still in the States. . . . We ought not to sacrifice the public Good to narrow Scruples."

THE COMPROMISES THAT PRODUCED THE CONSTITUTION

The delegates voted on May 30, 1787 that "a national Government ought to be established." They then set to work hammering out a specific plan. Furthermore, the delegates believed that the national government should have separate executive and judicial branches as well as a legislature. But two big questions had to be answered. The first—*What powers should this national government be granted?*—occasioned relatively little discussion. The right to levy taxes and to regulate interstate and foreign commerce was assigned to the central government almost without debate. So was the power to raise and maintain an army and navy and to summon the militia of the states to enforce national laws and suppress insurrections. With equal absence of argument, the states were deprived of their rights to issue money, to make treaties, and to tax either imports or exports without the permission of Congress. Thus, in summary fashion, was brought about a massive shift of power, a shift made necessary by the problems that had brought the delegates to Philadelphia and made practicable by the new nationalism of the 1780s.

The second major question—*Who shall control the national government?*—proved more difficult to answer in a manner satisfactory to all. Led by Virginia, the larger states pushed for representation in the national legislature based on population. The smaller states wished to maintain the existing system of equal representation for each state regardless of population. The large states rallied behind the Virginia Plan, drafted by James Madison and presented to the convention by Edmund Randolph, governor of the state. The small states supported the New Jersey Plan, prepared by William Paterson, a former attorney general of that state. The question was important; equal state representation would have been undemocratic, whereas a proportional system would have effectively destroyed the influence of all the states as states. But the delegates saw it in terms of combinations of large or small states, and this old-fashioned view was unrealistic: When the states combined, they did so on geographic, economic, or social grounds that seldom had anything to do with size. Nevertheless, the debate was long and heated, and for a time it threatened to disrupt the convention.

Day after day in the stifling heat of high summer, the weary delegates struggled to find a suitable compromise. Madison and a few others had to use every weapon in their arsenal of argument to hold the group together. (All told, during the 88 sessions of the convention, a total of 569 votes were taken.) July 2 was perhaps the most fateful day of the whole proceedings. "We are at full stop," said Roger Sherman of Connecticut, who had been one of the drafters of the Declaration of Independence. "If we do not concede on both sides," a North Carolina delegate warned, "our business must soon be at an end."

But the delegates did "concede on both sides," and the debates went on. Again on July 17 collapse threatened as the representatives of the larger states caucused to consider walking out of the convention. Fortunately they did not walk out, and finally the delegates adopted what is known as the Great Compromise. In the lower branch of the new legislature—the House of Representatives—places were to be assigned according to population and filled by popular vote. In the upper house—the Senate—each state was to have two members, elected by its legislature.

Then a complicated struggle took place between northern and southern delegates, occasioned by the institution of slavery and the differing economic interests of the regions. About one American in seven in the 1780s was a slave. Northerners contended that slaves should be counted in deciding each state's share of direct federal taxes. Southerners, of course, wanted to exclude slaves from the count. Yet Southerners wished to include slaves in determining each district's representation in the House of Representatives, although they had no intention of permitting the slaves to vote. In the Three-fifths Compromise it was agreed that "three-fifths of all other Persons"

should be counted for both purposes. (As it turned out, the compromise was a victory for the Southerners, for direct taxes were only rarely levied by Congress before the Civil War.) Settlement of the knotty issue of the African slave trade was postponed by a clause making it illegal for Congress to outlaw the trade before 1808.

Questions involving the regulation of less controversial commerce also caused sectional disagreement. Southerners disliked export taxes because their staple products were largely sold abroad. In return for a clause prohibiting such taxes, they dropped their demand that all laws regulating foreign commerce be approved by two-thirds of both houses of Congress. Many other differences of opinion were resolved by the give-and-take of practical compromise.

The final document (see the text of the Constitution in the Appendix, pp. A9–A18), signed on September 17, established a legislature of two houses; an executive branch, consisting of a president with wide powers and a vice president whose only function was to preside over the Senate; and a national judiciary consisting of a Supreme Court and such "inferior courts" as Congress might decide to create. The lower, popularly elected branch of the Congress was supposed to represent especially the mass of ordinary citizens. It was given the sole right to introduce bills for raising revenue. The 26-member Senate was looked on by many as a sort of advisory council similar to the upper houses of the colonial legislatures. Its consent was required before any treaty could go into effect and for major presidential appointments. The Founders also intended the Senate to represent in Congress the interests not only of the separate states but of what Hamilton called "the rich and the well-born" as contrasted with "the great mass of the people."

The creation of a powerful president was the most drastic departure from past experience, and it is doubtful that the Founders would have gone so far had everyone not counted on Washington, a man universally esteemed for character, wisdom, and impartiality, to be the first to occupy the office. Besides giving him general responsibility for executing the laws, the Constitution made the president commander-in-chief of the armed forces of the nation and general supervisor of its foreign relations. He was to appoint federal judges and other officials, and he might veto any law of Congress, although his veto could be overridden by a two-thirds majority of both houses. While not specifically ordered to submit a program of legislation to Congress, he was to deliver periodic reports on the "State of the Union" and recommend "such Measures as he shall judge necessary and expedient." Most modern presidents have interpreted this requirement as authorizing

DEBATING THE PAST

What ideas shaped the Constitution? In this 1788 cartoon, the angel "Concord" presents the Constitution to "Columbia"—an embodiment of the United States; a Greek temple sits in the background, upheld by thirteen pillars representing the colonies. Were the authors of the Constitution inspired by classical antiquity? No, declared Charles A. Beard. Their chief concerns were to protect their property and business interests.

Few historians found much confirmation of Beard's thesis; but what, then, *were* they thinking? Daniel Boorstin regarded the Founders as practical men who "found a refuge from the diversity of ideas in the satisfying concreteness of experience." Bernard Bailyn rejected this argument. His research revealed that the revolutionary leaders learned to cherish republican virtue and citizenship from ancient Roman philosophers such as Plutarch and Tacitus, from thinkers of the European Enlightenment, and from critics of eighteenth-century British monarchs. Joyce Appleby countered that if ideas were at the heart of the Constitution, they came from John Locke, a seventeenth-century philosopher who enshrined property rights. The Constitution was a blueprint for capitalist development. Jack Rakove searched in vain to find the "original intent" of the Founders. They favored a government strong enough to protect people and promote their interests; they also favored individual rights and freedom. Which mattered more, they could not agree.

Charles A. Beard, *An Economic Interpretation of the Constitution of the United States* (1913), Daniel Boorstin, *The Lost World of Thomas Jefferson* (1948), Bernard Bailyn, *The Ideological Origins of the American Revolution* (1967), Joyce Appleby, *Capitalism and a New Social Order* (1984), Jack Rakove, *Original Meanings* (1996).

them to submit detailed legislative proposals and to use the full power and prestige of the office to get Congress to enact them.

Looking beyond Washington, whose choice was sure to come about under any system, the Constitution established a cumbersome method of electing presidents. Each state was to choose "electors" equal in number to its representation in Congress. The electors, meeting separately in their own states, were to vote for two persons for president. Supposedly the procedure would prevent anyone less universally admired than Washington from getting a majority in the "electoral college," in which case the House of Representatives would choose the president from among the leading candidates, each state having but one vote. However, the swift rise of national political parties prevented the expected fragmentation of the electors' votes, and only two elections have ever gone to the House for settlement.

The national court system was set up to adjudicate disputes under the laws and treaties of the United States. No such system had existed under the Articles, a major weakness. Although the Constitution did not specifically authorize the courts to declare laws void when they conflicted with the Constitution, the courts soon exercised this right of "judicial review" in cases involving both state and federal laws.

That the Constitution reflected the commonly held beliefs of its framers is everywhere evident in the document. It greatly expanded the powers of the central government yet did not seriously threaten the independence of the states. Foes of centralization, at the time and ever since, have predicted the imminent disappearance of the states as sovereign bodies. But despite a steady trend toward centralization, probably inevitable as American society has grown ever more complex, the states remain powerful political organizations that are sovereign in many areas of government.

The Founders believed that since the new powers of government might easily be misused, each should be held within safe limits by some countervailing force. The Constitution is full of ingenious devices ("checks and balances") whereby one power controls and limits another without reducing it to impotence. "Let Congress Legislate, let others execute, let others judge," John Jay suggested. This separation of legislative, executive, and judicial functions is the fundamental example of the principle. Other examples are the president's veto; Congress's power of impeachment, cleverly divided between House and Senate; the Senate's power over treaties and appointments; and the balance between Congress's right to declare war and the president's control of the armed forces.

RATIFYING THE CONSTITUTION

Influenced by the widespread approval of the decision of Massachusetts to submit its state constitution of 1780 to the voters for ratification, the framers of the Constitution provided (Article VII) that their handiwork be ratified by special state conventions. This procedure gave the Constitution what Madison called "the highest source of authority"—the endorsement of the people, expressed through representatives chosen specifically to vote on it. The framers may also have been motivated by a desire to bypass the state legislatures, where many members might resent the reductions being made in state authority. This was not of central importance because the legislatures could have blocked ratification by refusing to call conventions. Only Rhode Island did so, and since the Constitution was to go into operation when nine states had approved it, Rhode Island's stubbornness did no vital harm.

Such a complex and controversial document as the Constitution naturally excited argument throughout the country. Those who favored it called themselves Federalists, thereby avoiding the more accurate but politically unattractive label of Centralizers. Their opponents thus became the Anti-Federalists.

It is difficult to generalize about the members of these groups. The Federalists tended to be substantial individuals, members of the professions, well-to-do, active in commercial affairs, and somewhat alarmed by the changes wrought by the Revolution. They were more interested, perhaps, in orderly and efficient government than in safeguarding the maximum freedom of individual choice.

The Anti-Federalists were more often small farmers, debtors, and persons to whom free choice was more important than power and who resented those who sought and held power. "Lawyers and men of learning and money men . . . expect to be the managers of the Const[itution], and get all the power and all the money into their own hands," a Massachusetts Anti-Federalist complained. "Then they will swallow up all us little folks . . . just as the whale swallowed up *Jonah*." But many rich and worldly citizens opposed the Constitution, and many poor and obscure persons were for it. It seems likely that most did not support or oppose the new system for narrowly selfish reasons. The historian David Ramsay, who lived at the time when these groups were forming, was probably correct when he wrote that "the great body of independent men who saw the necessity of an energetic government" swung the balance in favor of the Constitution.

Whether the Anti-Federalists were more democratic than the Federalists is an interesting question. Those who are loud for local autonomy do not necessarily believe in equal rights for all the locals. Many Anti-Federalist leaders, including Richard Henry Lee, the man who had introduced the resolution that resulted in the Declaration of Independence, had reservations about democracy. On the other hand, even Hamilton, no admirer of democracy, believed that ordinary citizens should have some say about their government. In general, practice still stood well ahead of theory when it came to popular participation in politics.

It is important to keep in mind that the country was large and sparsely settled, that communication was primitive, and that the central government did not influence the lives of most people to any great degree. Many persons, including some who had been in the forefront of the struggle for independence, believed that a centralized republican system would not work in a country so large and with so many varied interests as the United States. Patrick Henry considered the Constitution "horribly frightful." It "squints toward monarchy," he added. That Congress could pass all laws "necessary and proper" to carry out the functions assigned it and legislate for the "general welfare" of the country

DOCUMENT

Henry Against Ratification of the Constitution

▲ Patrick Henry, an ardent revolutionary, was perhaps the main opponent to ratification of the Constitution. Such a "consolidated government," he declared in 1788, would be "extremely pernicious, impolitic, and dangerous." This painting by Thomas Sully dates from the mid-nineteenth century.

▲ New Yorkers honor Hamilton during a parade marking ratification of the Constitution. That Hamilton stood on a ship was fitting, not only because he sought to strengthen the federal "ship of state" but also because New York merchants were among his staunchest backers.

seemed alarmingly all-inclusive. The first sentence of the Constitution, beginning "We the people of the United States" rather than "We the states," convinced many that the document represented centralization run wild. Another old revolutionary who expressed doubts was Samuel Adams, who remarked: "As I enter the Building I stumble at the Threshold."

Very little of the opposition to the Constitution grew out of economic issues. Most people wanted the national debt paid off; nearly everyone opposed an unstable currency; most favored uniform trade policies; most were ready to give the new government a chance if they could be convinced that it would not destroy the states. When backers agreed to add amendments guaranteeing the civil liberties of the people against challenge by the national government and reserving all unmentioned power to the states, much of the opposition disappeared. Sam Adams ended up voting for the Constitution in the Massachusetts convention after the additions had been promised.

No one knows exactly how public opinion divided on the question of ratification. The Federalists were usually able to create an impression of strength far beyond their numbers and to overwhelm doubters with the mass of their arguments. They excelled in political organization and in persuasiveness. James Madison, for example, demolished the thesis that a centralized republican government could not function efficiently in a large country. In rule by the majority lay protection against the "cabals" of special interest groups. "Extend the sphere," Madison argued, "and you take in a greater variety of parties and interests; you make it less probable that a majority of the whole will have a common motive to invade the rights of other citizens." Moreover, the management of national affairs would surely attract leaders of greater ability and sounder character to public service than the handling of petty local concerns ever could in a decentralized system.

DOCUMENT

Madison Defends the Constitution

The Constitution met with remarkably little opposition in most of the state ratifying conventions, considering the importance of the changes it instituted. Delaware acted first, ratifying unanimously on December 7, 1787. Pennsylvania followed a few days later, voting for the document by a 2 to 1 majority. New Jersey approved unanimously on December 18; so did Georgia on January 2, 1788. A week later Connecticut fell in line, 128 to 40.

The Massachusetts convention provided the first close contest. Early in February, after an extensive debate, the delegates ratified by a vote of 187 to 168. In April, Maryland accepted the Constitution by nearly 6 to 1, and in May, South Carolina approved, 149 to 73. New Hampshire came along on June 21, voting 57 to 47 for the Constitution. This was the ninth state, making the Constitution legally operative.

Before the news from New Hampshire had spread throughout the country, the Virginia convention debated the issue. Virginia, the largest state and the home of so many prestigious figures, was absolutely essential if the Constitution was to succeed. With unquestioned patriots like Richard Henry Lee and Patrick Henry opposed, the result was not easy to predict. But when the vote came on June 25, Virginia ratified, 89 to 79. Aside from Rhode Island, this left only New York and North Carolina outside the Union.

New York politics presented a complex and baffling picture. Resistance to independence had been strong there in 1776 and remained a problem all through the war. Although New York was the third largest state, with a population rapidly approaching 340,000, it sided with the small states at Philadelphia, and two of its three delegates (Hamilton was the exception) walked out of the convention and took the lead in opposing ratification. A handful of great landowning and mercantile families dominated politics, but they were divided into shifting factions. In general, New York City, including most ordinary working people as well as the merchants, favored ratification and the rural areas were against it.

The Anti-Federalists, well organized and competently led in New York by Governor George Clinton, won 46 of the 65 seats at the ratifying convention. The New York Federalists had one great asset in the fact that so many states had already ratified and another in the person of Alexander Hamilton. Although contemptuous of the *weakness* of the Constitution, Hamilton supported it with all his energies as being incomparably stronger than the old government. Working with Madison and John Jay, he produced the *Federalist Papers,* a series of brilliant essays explaining and defending the new system. In his articles, Hamilton stressed the need for a strong federal executive, while Madison sought to allay fears that the new

national government would have too much power by emphasizing the many checks and balances in the Constitution. The essays were published in the local press and later in book form. Although generations of judges and lawyers have treated them almost as parts of the Constitution, their impact on contemporary public opinion was probably slight. Open-minded members of the convention were undoubtedly influenced, but few delegates were open-minded.

Hamilton became a kind of one-man army in defense of the Constitution, plying hesitating delegates with dinners and drinks, facing obstinate ones with the threat that New York City would secede from the state if the Constitution were rejected. Once New Hampshire and Virginia had ratified, opposition in New York became a good deal less intransigent. In the end, by promising to support a call for a second national convention to consider amendments, the Federalists carried the day, 30 to 27. With New York in the fold, the new government was free to get under way. North Carolina finally ratified in November 1789, Rhode Island the following year, in May 1790.

WASHINGTON AS PRESIDENT

Elections took place in the states during January and February 1789, and by early April enough congressmen had gathered in New York, the temporary national capital, to commence operation. The ballots of the presidential electors were officially counted in the Senate on April 6, Washington being the unanimous choice. John Adams, with 34 electoral votes, won the vice-presidency.

When he left Mount Vernon for the eight-day trip to New York for his inauguration, Washington's progress was a series of celebrations. In every town he was met by bands, honor guards, local dignitaries, and crowds of cheering citizens. The people were informally ratifying the decision to create a new and more powerful United States. On April 30 Washington took the oath of office at New York's Federal Hall.

Washington's Arrival in New York City, 1789

Washington made a firm, dignified, conscientious, but cautious president. His acute sense of responsibility led him to face the task "with feelings not unlike those of a culprit who is going to the place of his execution." Each presidential action must of necessity establish a precedent. "The eyes of Argus are upon me," he complained, "and no slip will pass unnoticed." Hoping to make the presidency appear respectable in the eyes of the world, he saw to it that his

► *text continues on page 154*

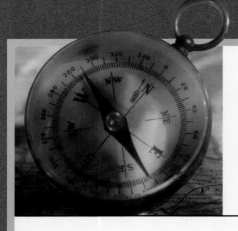

Mapping
the Past

Depicting History with Maps

History consists of the stories people tell about the past. Because historians work mostly with written sources, they use words to describe the past. Pictures help too, which is why this book has so many of them. But maps effectively show movement over time and through space.

An Indian Map

Maps come in many different forms. Consider the map below by Lean Wolf, a Hidatsa warrior. It depicts his raid on a Sioux village to steal horses. In the map, Lean Wolf represents himself as a wolf—four legs, with dark black snout. The lodges of the Hidatsa village are shown as circles, with the dots representing support poles: a lodge with five poles contains a large extended family, a lodge with two, a small one. His route to the Sioux village is indicated by a dashed line. Crosses identify Sioux lodges; squares mark whites' houses. A cross with a square denotes a Hidatsa–Sioux intermarriage; a cross within a square indicates where a white man lives with a Sioux woman. Lean Wolf used forward-facing hoofprints to show the route back home. Thus, the map indicates that his venture succeeded; he did manage to steal horses from the Sioux.

Lean Wolf's map displays complicated information that doubtless was informative to him and other Hidatsa warriors. The rest of us may not find it so easy to decipher.

▲ Lean Wolf's Map

For one thing, the map lacks a title to convey the main idea. What was the relationship between the horse raid and the information on Sioux dwellings and marriage patterns? Did he refrain from taking horses from Sioux habitations occupied by mixed Hidatsa-Sioux couples? We don't know.

Second, the map lacks a key—a list of the various pictographic symbols and an explanation of what they represent. Third, it lacks geographical reference points and distance markers. How far did Lean Wolf travel and in what direction? From the map, we do not know that the villages were located near Fort Buford, North Dakota. Fourth, the base map lacks labels. Did the nearly straight line between the villages represent a stream, a trail, or something else?

Examples of Modern Maps: Ratification of the Constitution

All the maps in this book tell stories about the past, but they include titles, keys, geographical and chronological references, and other labels. Consider the map on the right that represents one of the key events discussed in this chapter.

The map's title—Ratification of the Federal Constitution, 1787–1790—explains its theme. The key provides information necessary to understand the map: teal green represents areas where a majority voted for the Constitution, and red where a majority voted against the Constitution, and so on. Latitude and longitude lines on the map show precisely where the votes occurred. The compass point indicates north. (In maps of North America, north is customarily toward the top of the page; but sometimes it makes more sense to reorient the page. For example, the map of the long Atlantic seaboard in the seventeenth century stretches across two pages in Chapter 1 of this book (see pp. 44–45); the compass therefore points not to the top of the page, but to the upper right-hand corner.

Beneath the compass is a scale of miles and kilometers. Labels on the map indicate the relevant dates and identify relevant geographic and political features. (Many historical maps, but not this one, convey movement; Lean Wolf used hoofprints to indicate movement; most mapmakers use an Indian implement—an arrow—for this purpose.)

Ratification of the Federal Constitution, 1787–1790

- majority for constitution
- majority against ratification
- even
- not voting

Historians use maps to formulate and illustrate interpretations. Jackson Turner Main regarded this map on ratification as visual confirmation of his thesis: those favoring the Constitution (the green areas) generally lived in the more settled and economically prosperous regions along the coast; those opposed (red areas) were concentrated in "backwoods" New England and the western frontiers of Pennsylvania, Virginia, and the Carolinas.

But why, if Main's thesis is true, were there some red areas (opposing the Constitution) in coastal North Carolina and Maryland, and a few townships in coastal New England? And why

were there some green areas (favoring the Constitution) in backcountry New England, Pennsylvania, and the South?

Maps alone cannot answer these questions. It is also necessary to learn what people thought, said, and did. The search for answers leads historians to written sources—diaries, letters, newspaper accounts—and also to paintings, cartoons, and other visual sources. From information gleaned from all these sources, a more complete picture gradually emerges, although readers must decide for themselves the persuasiveness of any historical argument.

carriage was drawn by six cream-colored horses, and when he rode (he was a magnificent horseman), it was on a great white charger, with the saddle of leopard skin and the cloth edged in gold. Twenty-one servants (seven of them slaves) attended his needs at the presidential mansion on Broadway.

Washington meticulously avoided treading on the toes of Congress, for he took seriously the principle of the separation of powers. Never would he speak for or against a candidate for Congress, nor did he think that the president should push or even propose legislation. When he knew a controversial question was to be discussed in Congress, he avoided the subject in his annual message. The veto, he believed, should be employed only when the president considered a bill unconstitutional.

Although the Constitution said nothing about a presidential Cabinet, Washington established the system of calling his department heads together for general advice, a practice that was followed by his successors. In selecting these department heads and other important administrators, he favored no particular faction. He insisted only that appointees be competent and "of known attachment to the Government we have chosen." He picked Hamilton for secretary of the treasury, Jefferson for secretary of state, General Henry Knox of Massachusetts for secretary of war, and Edmund Randolph for attorney general. He called on them for advice according to the logic of his particular needs and frequently without regard for their own specialties. Thus he sometimes consulted Jefferson about financial matters and Hamilton about foreign affairs. This system caused resentment and confusion, especially when rival factions began to coalesce around Hamilton and Jefferson.

Despite his respect for the opinions of others, Washington was a strong chief executive. As Hamilton put it, he "consulted much, pondered much, resolved slowly, resolved surely." His stress on the dignity of his office suited the needs of a new country whose people tended to be perhaps too informal. It was indeed important that the first president be particularly concerned about establishing precedents. His scrupulous care lest he overstep the bounds of presidential power helped erase the prejudices of those who feared that republican government must inevitably succumb to dictatorship and tyranny. When each step is an experiment, when foreign dangers loom at the end of every errant path, it is surely wise to go slowly. And no one should forget that Washington's devotion to duty did not always come easily. Occasionally he exploded. Thomas Jefferson has left us a graphic description of the president at a Cabinet meeting, in a rage because of some unfair criticism, swearing that "by god he had rather be on his farm than to be made emperor of the world."

CONGRESS UNDER WAY

By September 1789 Congress had created the State, Treasury, and War departments and passed a Judiciary Act establishing 13 federal district courts and 3 circuit courts of appeal. The number of Supreme Court justices was set at six, and Washington named John Jay the chief justice.

True to Federalist promises—for a large majority of both houses were friendly to the Constitution—Congress prepared a list of a dozen amendments (ten were ratified) guaranteeing what Congressman James Madison, who drafted the amendments, called the "great rights of mankind." These amendments, known as the Bill of Rights (See Amendments to the Constitution in the Appendix, pp. A14–A18), provided that Congress should make no law infringing freedom of speech, the press, or religion. The right of trial by jury was reaffirmed, the right to bear arms guaranteed. No one was to be subject to "unreasonable" searches or seizures or compelled to testify against himself or herself in a criminal case. No one was to "be deprived of life, liberty, or property, without due process of law."

Despite Washington's reluctance to interfere with the activities of Congress, he urged acceptance of these amendments so that the "rights of freemen" would be "impregnably fortified." The Bill of Rights was unique; the English Bill of Rights of 1689 was much less broad-gauged and, being an act of Parliament, was subject to repeal by Parliament at any time. The Tenth Amendment—not, strictly speaking, a part of the Bill of Rights—was designed to mollify those who feared that the states would be destroyed by the new government. It provided that powers not delegated to the United States or denied specifically to the states by the Constitution were to reside either in the states or in the people.

As experts pointed out, the amendments were not logically necessary because the federal government had no authority to act in such matters to begin with. But many had wanted to be reassured. Experience has proved repeatedly that whatever the logic of the situation, the protection afforded individuals by the Bill of Rights has been anything but unnecessary.

The Bill of Rights did much to convince doubters that the new government would not become too powerful. More complex was the task of proving that it was powerful enough to deal with those national problems that the Confederation had not been able to solve: the threat to the West posed by the British, Spaniards, and Indians; the disruption of the pattern of American foreign commerce resulting from independence; and the collapse of the financial structure of the country.

HAMILTON AND FINANCIAL REFORM

One of the first acts of Congress in 1789 was to employ its new power to tax. The simplest means of raising money seemed to be that first attempted by the British after 1763, a tariff on foreign imports. Congress levied a 5 percent duty on all foreign products entering the United States, applying higher rates to certain products, such as hemp, glass, and nails, as a measure of protection for American producers. The Tariff Act of 1789 also placed heavy tonnage duties on all foreign shipping, a mercantilist measure designed to stimulate the American merchant marine.

Raising money for current expenses was a small and relatively simple aspect of the financial problem faced by Washington's administration. The nation's debt was large, its credit shaky, its economic future uncertain. In October 1789 Congress deposited on the slender shoulders of Secretary of the Treasury Hamilton the task of straightening out the fiscal mess and stimulating the country's economic development.

Hamilton at age 34 had already proved himself a remarkable man. Born in the British West Indies, the illegitimate son of a shiftless Scot who was little better than a beachcomber, and raised by his mother's family, he came to New York in 1773 to attend King's College. When the Revolution broke out, he joined the Continentals. At 22 he was a staff colonel, aide-de-camp to Washington. Later, at Yorktown, he led a line regiment, displaying a bravery approaching foolhardiness. He married the daughter of Philip Schuyler, a wealthy and influential New Yorker, and after the Revolution he practiced law in that state.

Hamilton was a bundle of contradictions. Witty, charming, possessed of a mind like a sharp knife, he was sometimes the soul of practicality, sometimes an incurable romantic. No more hard-headed realist ever lived, yet he was quick to resent any slight to his honor, even—tragically—ready to fight a duel though he abhorred the custom of dueling. A self-made man, he admired aristocracy and disparaged the abilities of the common run of mankind who, he said, "seldom judge or determine right." Although granting that Americans must be allowed to govern themselves, he was as apprehensive of the "turbulence" of the masses as a small boy passing a graveyard in the dark. "No popular government was ever without its Catilines and its Caesars," he warned—a typical example of that generation's concern about the fate of the Roman republic.

The country, Hamilton insisted, needed a strong national government. "I acknowledge," he wrote in one of the *Federalist Papers*, "my aversion to every project that is calculated to disarm the government of a single weapon, which in any possible contingency

▲ "To confess my weakness," Hamilton wrote when he was only 14, "my ambition is prevalent." This pastel drawing by James Sharples was made about 1796.

might be usefully employed for the general defense and security." He avowed that government should be "a great Federal Republic," not "a number of petty states, with the appearance only of union, jarring, jealous, perverse, without any determined direction." He wished to reduce the states to mere administrative units, like English counties.

As secretary of the treasury, Hamilton proved to be a farsighted economic planner. The United States, a "Hercules in the cradle," needed capital to develop its untapped material and human resources. To persuade investors to commit their funds in America, the country would have to convince them that it would meet every obligation in full. His *Report on the Public Credit* outlined a plan for the federal government to borrow money to pay all of its debts as well as those of the states.

While most members of Congress agreed, albeit somewhat grudgingly, that the debt should be paid in full, they had misgivings as to who should get those payments. Many of the soldiers, farmers, and merchants who had been forced to accept government securities in lieu of cash for goods and services, had sold their securities for a fraction of their face value to speculators; under Hamilton's proposal, the speculators—now paid for the full value of the securities—would make a killing. To the argument for divided payment, Hamilton answered coldly: "[The speculator] paid what the commodity was worth in the market, and took the risks. . . . He . . . ought to reap the benefit of his hazard."

Hamilton was essentially correct, and in the end Congress had to go along. After all, the speculators had not caused the securities to fall in value; indeed, as a group they had favored sound money and a strong government. The best way to restore the nation's credit was to convince investors that the government would honor all obligations in full. What infuriated his contemporaries and still attracts the scorn of many historians was Hamilton's motive. He deliberately intended his plan to give a special advantage to the rich. The government would be strong, he thought, only if well-to-do Americans enthusiastically supported it. What better way to win them over than to make it worth their while financially to do so?

In part, opposition to the funding plan was sectional, for citizens of the northern states held more than four-fifths of the national debt. The scheme for assuming the state debts aggravated the controversy, since most of the southern states had already paid off much of their Revolutionary War obligations. For months Congress was deadlocked. Finally, in July 1790, Hamilton worked out a compromise with Representative James Madison and Secretary of State Jefferson. The two Virginians swung a few southern votes, and Hamilton induced some of his followers to support the southern plan for locating the permanent capital of the Union on the Potomac River.

Jefferson later claimed that Hamilton had hoodwinked him. Having only recently returned from Europe, he said, "I was really a stranger to the whole subject." Hamilton had persuaded him to "rally around" by the false tale that "our Union" was threatened with dissolution. This was nonsense; Jefferson agreed to the compromise because he expected that Virginia and the rest of the South would profit from having the capital so near at hand.

The assumption bill passed, and the entire funding plan was a great success. Soon the United States had the highest possible credit rating in the world's financial centers. Foreign capital poured into the country.

Alexander
Hamilton, "Bank"

Hamilton next proposed that Congress charter a national bank. Such an institution would provide safe storage for government funds and serve as an agent for the government in the collection, movement, and expenditure of tax money. Most important, because of its substantial resources a bank could finance new and expanding business enterprises, greatly speeding the economic growth of the nation. It would also be able to issue bank notes, thereby providing a vitally needed medium of exchange for the specie-starved economy. This Bank of the United States was to be partly owned by the government, but 80 percent of the $10 million stock issue was to be sold to private individuals.

The country had much to gain from such a bank, but again—Hamilton's cleverness was never more in evidence—the well-to-do commercial classes would gain still more. Government balances in the bank belonging to all the people would earn dividends for a handful of rich investors. Manufacturers and other capitalists would profit from the bank's credit facilities. Public funds would be invested in the bank, but control would remain in private hands, since the government would appoint only 5 of the 25 directors. Nevertheless, the bill creating the bank passed both houses of Congress with relative ease in February 1791.

President Washington, however, hesitated to sign it, for the bill's constitutionality had been questioned during the debate in Congress. Nowhere did the Constitution specifically authorize Congress to charter corporations or engage in the banking business. As was his wont when in doubt, Washington called on Jefferson and Hamilton for advice.

Hamilton defended the legality of the bank by enunciating the doctrine of "implied powers." If a logical connection existed between the purpose of the bill and powers clearly stated in the Constitution, he wrote, the bill was constitutional.

> If the *end* be clearly comprehended within any of the specified powers, and if the measure have an obvious relation to that *end* . . . it may safely be deemed to come within the compass of the national authority.
> . . . A bank has a natural relation to the power of collecting taxes—to that of regulating trade—to that of providing for the common defence.

Jefferson disagreed. Congress could only do what the Constitution specifically authorized, he said. The "elastic clause" granting it the right to pass "all Laws which shall be necessary and proper" to carry out the specified powers must be interpreted literally or Congress would "take possession of a boundless field of power, no longer susceptible to any definition." Because a bank was obviously not necessary, it was not authorized.

Although not entirely convinced, Washington accepted Hamilton's reasoning and signed the bill. He could just as easily have followed Jefferson, for the Constitution is not clear. If one stresses *proper* in the "necessary and proper" clause in Article I, Section 8 of the Constitution, one ends up a Hamiltonian; if one stresses *necessary,* then Jefferson's view is correct. Historically (and this is the important point) politicians have nearly always adopted the "loose" Hamiltonian "implied powers" interpretation when they favored a measure and the "strict" Jeffersonian one when they do not. Jefferson disliked the bank; therefore, he claimed it was unconstitutional. Had he approved, he doubtless would have taken a different tack.

In 1819 the Supreme Court officially sanctioned Hamilton's construction of the "necessary and proper" clause, and in general that interpretation has prevailed. Because the majority tends naturally toward an argument that increases its freedom of action, the pressure for this view has been continual and formidable. The Bank of the United States succeeded from the start. When its stock went on sale, investors snapped up every share in a matter of hours. People eagerly accepted its bank notes at face value. Business ventures of all kinds found it easier to raise new capital. Soon state-chartered banks entered the field. There were only 3 state banks in 1791; by 1801, there were 32.

Hamilton had not finished. In December 1791 he submitted his *Report on Manufactures,* a bold call for economic planning. The pre-Revolutionary nonimportation agreements and wartime shortages had stimulated interest in manufacturing. Already a number of joint-stock companies had been founded to manufacture textiles, and an elaborate argument for economic diversification had been worked out by American economists such as Tench Coxe and Mathew Carey. Hamilton was familiar with these developments. In his *Report* he called for government tariffs, subsidies, and awards to encourage American manufacturing. He hoped to change an essentially agricultural nation into one with a complex, self-sufficient economy. Once again business and commercial interests in particular would benefit. They would be protected against foreign competition and otherwise subsidized, whereas the general taxpayer, particularly the farmer, would pay the bill in the form of higher taxes and higher prices on manufactured goods. Hamilton argued that in the long run every interest would profit, and he was undoubtedly sincere, being too much the nationalist to favor one section at the expense of another. A majority of the Congress, however, balked at so broad-gauged a scheme. Hamilton's *Report* was set aside, although many of the specific tariffs he recommended were enacted into law in 1792.

Nevertheless, the secretary of the treasury had managed to transform the financial structure of the country and to prepare the ground for an economic revolution. The constitutional reforms of 1787 had made this possible, and Hamilton turned possibility into reality.

THE OHIO COUNTRY: A DARK AND BLOODY GROUND

The western issues and those related to international trade proved more difficult because other nations were involved. The British showed no disposition to evacuate their posts on American soil simply because the American people had decided to strengthen their central government, nor did the western Indians suddenly agree to abandon their hunting grounds to the white invaders.

Trouble came swiftly when white settlers moved onto the land north of the Ohio River in large numbers. The Indians, determined to hold this country at all costs, struck hard at the invaders. In 1790 the Miami chief Little Turtle, a gifted strategist, inflicted a double defeat on militia units commanded by General Josiah Harmar. The next year Little Turtle and his men defeated the forces of General Arthur St. Clair still more convincingly. Both Harmar and St. Clair resigned from the army, their careers ruined, but the defeats led Congress to authorize raising a regular army of 5000 men.

By early 1792 the Indians had driven the whites into "beachheads" at Marietta and Cincinnati on the Ohio. Resentment of the federal government in the western counties of every state from New York to the Carolinas mounted, the people feeling that it was ignoring their interests. They were convinced that the British were inciting the Indians to attack them, yet the supposedly powerful national government seemed unable to force Great Britain to surrender its forts in the West.

Still worse, the Westerners believed, was the way the government was taxing them. In 1791, as part of his plan to take over the debts of the states, Hamilton had persuaded Congress to adopt an excise tax of 8 cents a gallon on American-made whiskey. Excise taxes were particularly disliked by most Americans. A duty on imported products was collected from merchants and passed on to consumers as part of the price, and it was by its nature imposed only on foreign-made products. People who did not want to pay it usually could find a domestic alternative. But the collection of excise taxes on American goods required hordes of tax collectors, armed with the power to snoop into one's affairs. Westerners, who were heavy drinkers and who turned much of their grain into whiskey in order to cope with the high cost of transportation, were especially angered by the tax on whiskey.

Knowing that the tax would be unpopular, Hamilton promised that the distillers would "be secured from every species of injury by the misconduct of the officers to be employed" in collecting it. But he was determined to enforce the law. To western complaints, he coolly suggested that farmers drank too much to begin with. If they found the tax oppressive, they should cut down on their consumption. Of course this did nothing to reduce western opposition to the tax. Resistance was especially intense in western Pennsylvania. When treasury agents tried to collect it there, they were forcibly prevented from doing so.

REVOLUTION IN FRANCE

Momentous events in Europe were also affecting the situation. In 1789 the French Revolution erupted, and four years later war broke out between France and Great Britain and most of the rest of Europe. With France fighting Great Britain and Spain, there arose the question of America's obligations under the Alliance of 1778. That treaty required the United States to defend the French West Indies "forever against all other powers." Suppose the British attacked Martinique; must America then go to war? Morally the United States was so obligated, but no

▲ King Louis XVI of France, beheaded in Paris, January 21, 1793. Alexander Hamilton recommended termination of the nation's alliance with France. Thomas Jefferson argued that the treaty should be preserved because it had been made with the French people and not the monarch. As the French Revolution became still bloodier, American enthusiasm for the French radicals, and for radicalism in general, began to wane.

responsible American statesman urged such a policy. With the British in Canada and Spanish forces to the west and south, the nation would be in serious danger if it entered the war. Instead, in April 1793, Washington issued a proclamation of neutrality committing the United States to be "friendly and impartial" toward both sides in the war.

Meanwhile the French had sent a special representative, Edmond Charles Genet, to the United States to seek support. During its early stages, especially when France declared itself a republic in 1792, the revolution had excited much enthusiasm in the United States, for it seemed to indicate that American democratic ideas were already engulfing the world. The increasing radicalism in France tended to dampen some of the enthusiasm, yet when "Citizen" Genet landed at Charleston, South Carolina, in April 1793, the majority of Americans probably wished the revolutionaries well. As Genet, a charming, ebullient young man, made his way northward to present his credentials, cheering crowds welcomed him in every town. Quickly concluding that the proclamation of neutrality was "a harmless little pleasantry designed to throw dust in the eyes of the British," he began, in plain violation of American law, to license American vessels to operate as privateers against British shipping and to grant French military commissions to a number of Americans in order to mount expeditions against Spanish and British possessions in North America.

Washington received Genet coolly, and soon thereafter demanded that he stop his illegal activities. Genet, whose capacity for self-deception was monumental, appealed to public opinion over the president's head and continued to commission privateers. Even Jefferson was soon exasperated by Genet, whom he described as "hot headed, all imagination, no judgment and even indecent toward the P[resident]." Washington then requested his recall. The incident ended on a ludicrous note. When Genet left France, he had been in the forefront of the Revolution. But events there had marched swiftly leftward, and the new leaders in Paris considered him a dangerous reactionary. His replacement arrived in America with an order for his arrest. To return might well mean the guillotine, so Genet asked the government that was expelling him for political asylum! Washington agreed, for he was not a vindictive man. A few months later the bold revolutionary married the daughter of the governor of New York and settled down as a farmer on Long Island, where he raised a large family and "moved agreeably in society."

The Genet affair was incidental to a far graver problem. Although the European war increased the foreign demand for American products, it also led to attacks on American shipping by both France and Great Britain. Each power captured American vessels headed for the other's ports whenever it could. In 1793 and 1794 about 600 United States ships were seized.

The British attacks caused far more damage, both physically and psychologically, because the British fleet was much larger than France's, and France at least professed to be America's friend and to favor freedom of trade for neutrals. In addition the British issued secret orders late in 1793 turning their navy loose on neutral ships headed for the French West Indies. Pouncing without warning, British warships captured about 250 American vessels and sent them off as prizes to British ports. The merchant marine, one American diplomat declared angrily, was being "kicked, cuffed, and plundered all over the Ocean."

The attacks roused a storm in America, reviving hatreds that had been smoldering since the Revolution. The continuing presence of British troops in the Northwest (in 1794 the British began to build a new fort in the Ohio country) and the restrictions imposed on American trade with the British West Indies raised tempers still further. To try to avoid a war, for he wisely believed that the United States should not become embroiled in the Anglo-French conflict, Washington sent Chief Justice John Jay to London to seek a settlement with the British.

FEDERALISTS AND REPUBLICANS: THE RISE OF POLITICAL PARTIES

The furor over the violations of neutral rights focused attention on a new development, the formation of political parties. Why national political parties emerged after the ratification of a Constitution that made no provision for such organizations is a question that has long intrigued historians. Probably the main reason was the obvious one: By creating a strong central government the Constitution produced national issues and a focus for national discussion and settlement of these issues. Furthermore, by failing to create machinery for nominating candidates for federal offices, the Constitution left a vacuum, which informal party organizations filled. That the universally admired Washington headed the government was a force limiting partisanship, but his principal advisers, Hamilton and Jefferson, were in sharp disagreement, and they soon became the leaders around which parties coalesced.

In the spring of 1791 Jefferson and James Madison began to sound out other politicians about forming an informal political organization. Jefferson also appointed the poet Philip Freneau to a minor state department post and Freneau then began publishing a newspaper, the *National Gazette,* to disseminate the views of what became known as the Republican party. The *Gazette* was soon describing Jefferson as a "Colossus of Liberty" and flailing away editorially at Hamilton's policies. Hamilton hit back promptly, organizing his own followers in the Federalist party, the organ of which was John Fenno's *Gazette of the United States.*

The personal nature of early American political controversies goes far toward explaining why the party battles of the era were so bitter. So does the continuing anxiety that plagued partisans of both persuasions about the supposed frailty of a republican government. The United States was still very much an experiment; leaders who sincerely proclaimed their own devotion to its welfare suspected that their opponents wanted to undermine its institutions. Federalists feared that the Jeffersonians sought a dictatorship based on "mob rule," Republicans that the Hamiltonians hid "under the mask of Federalism hearts devoted to monarchy."

At the start Hamilton had the ear of the president, and his allies controlled a majority in Congress. Jefferson, who disliked controversy, avoided a direct confrontation as long as he could. He went along with Hamilton's funding plan and traded the assumption of state debts for a capital on the Potomac. However, when Hamilton proposed the Bank of the United States, he dug in his heels. It seemed designed to benefit the northeastern commercial classes at the expense of southern and western farmers. He sensed a dastardly plot to milk the producing masses for the benefit of a few capitalists.

The growing controversy over the French Revolution and the resulting war between France and Great Britain widened the split between the parties. After the radicals in France executed Louis XVI and instituted the Reign of Terror, American conservatives were horrified. The Jeffersonians were also deeply shocked. However, they continued to defend the Revolution. Great southern landlords whose French counterparts were losing their estates—some their heads—extolled "the glorious successes of our Gallic brethren." In the same way the Federalists began to idealize the British, whom they considered the embodiment of the forces that were resisting French radicalism.

This created an explosive situation. Enthusiasm for a foreign country might tempt Americans, all unwittingly, to betray their own. Hamilton came to believe that Jefferson was so prejudiced in favor of

France as to be unable to conduct foreign affairs rationally, and Jefferson could say contemptuously: "Hamilton is panick struck, if we refuse our breech to every kick which Great Britain may choose to give it." This, of course, was an exaggeration, but Hamilton was certainly predisposed toward England. As he put it to an English official, *"we think in English."*

In fact, Jefferson never lost his sense of perspective. When the Anglo-French war erupted, he recommended neutrality. In the Genet affair, although originally sympathetic to the young envoy, Jefferson cordially approved Washington's decision to send Genet packing. Hamilton perhaps went a little too far in his friendliness to Great Britain, but the real danger was that some of Hamilton's and Jefferson's excitable followers might become so committed as to forget the true interests of the United States.

1794: CRISIS AND RESOLUTION

During the summer of 1794 several superficially unrelated events brought the partisan conflicts of the period to a peak. For the better part of two years the government had been unable to collect Hamilton's whiskey tax in the West. In Pennsylvania, mobs had burned the homes of revenue agents, and several men had been killed. Late in July, 7000 "rebels" converged on Pittsburgh, threatening to set fire to the town. They were turned away by the sight of federal artillery and the liberal dispensation of whiskey by the frightened inhabitants.

Early in August President Washington determined "to go to every length that the Constitution and laws would permit" to enforce the law. He mustered an enormous army of nearly 13,000 militiamen. This had the desired effect; when the troops arrived in western Pennsylvania, rebels were nowhere to be seen. The expected Whiskey Rebellion simply did not happen. Good sense had triumphed. Moderates in the region (not everyone, after all, was a distiller) agreed that even unpopular laws should be obeyed.

More important, perhaps, than the militia in pacifying the Pennsylvania frontier was another event that occurred while that army was being mobilized. This was the Battle of Fallen Timbers in Ohio near present-day Toledo, where the regular army troops of Major General "Mad Anthony" Wayne won a decisive victory over the Indians. Wayne's victory opened the way for the settlement of the region. Some 2000 of the whiskey tax rebels simply pulled up stakes and headed for Ohio after the effort to avoid the excise collapsed.

JAY'S TREATY

Still more significant was the outcome of President Washington's decision to send John Jay to England to seek a treaty settling the conflicts that vexed the relations of the two nations. The British genuinely wanted to reach an accommodation with the United States—as one minister quipped, the Americans "are so much in debt to this country that we scarcely dare to quarrel with them." Jay was received by both the King and Queen and wined and dined by the foreign secretary, the prime minister, and other officials. The British also feared that the two new republics, France and the United States, would draw together in a battle against Europe's monarchies. On the other hand, the British were riding the crest of a wave of important victories in the war in Europe and were not disposed to make concessions to the Americans simply to avoid trouble.

The treaty that Jay brought home did contain a number of concessions. The British agreed to evacuate the posts in the West. They also promised to compensate American

▲ In 1792 farmers in western Pennsylvania, outraged over Hamilton's tax on liquor, rose up in rebellion against tax collectors. Their banners included the slogan of the French revolutionaries: "Liberty, Equality, and Fraternity!" Washington crushed the rebellion.

shipowners for seizures in the West Indies and to open up their colonies in Asia to American ships. They conceded nothing, however, to American demands that the rights of neutrals on the high seas be respected; no one really expected them to do so in wartime. A provision opening the British West Indies to American commerce was so hedged with qualifications limiting the size of American vessels and the type of goods allowed that the United States refused to accept it.

Jay also committed the United States to paying pre-Revolutionary debts still owed British merchants, a slap in the face to many states whose courts had been impeding their collection. Yet nothing was said about the British paying for the slaves they had "abducted" during the fighting in the South.

Although Jay might have driven a harder bargain, this was a valuable treaty for the United States. But it was also a humiliating one. Most of what the United States gained already legally belonged to it, and the treaty sacrificed principles of importance to a nation dependent on foreign trade. When the terms became known, they raised a storm of popular protest. It seemed possible that President Washington would repudiate the treaty or that if he did not, the Senate would refuse to ratify it.

1795: ALL'S WELL THAT ENDS WELL

Washington did not repudiate the Jay Treaty and after long debate the Senate ratified it in June 1795. After a bitter debate, with most Republicans opposing the

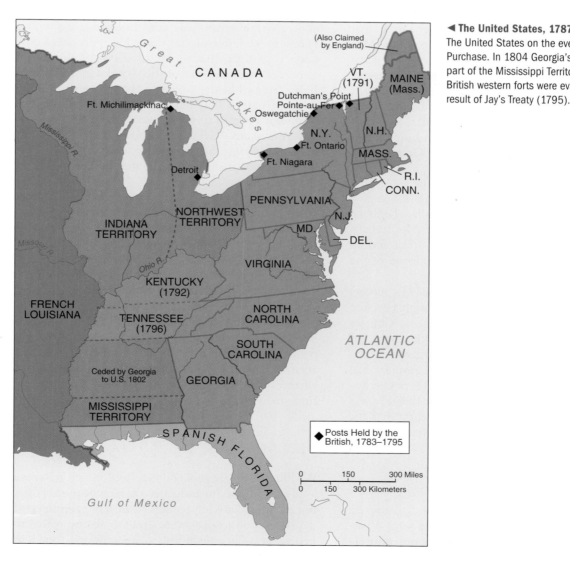

◀ **The United States, 1787–1802**
The United States on the eve of the Louisiana Purchase. In 1804 Georgia's cession became part of the Mississippi Territory. The seven British western forts were evacuated as a result of Jay's Treaty (1795).

measure, the House passed the requisite funding resolution. The treaty marked an important step toward the regularization of Anglo-American relations, which in the long run was essential for both the economic and political security of the nation. And the evacuation of the British forts in the Northwest was of enormous immediate benefit.

Still another benefit was totally unplanned. Unexpectedly, the Jay Treaty enabled the United States to solve its problems on its southeastern frontier. During the early 1790s Spain had entered into alliances with the Cherokee, Creek, and other Indian tribes hostile to the Americans and built forts on territory ceded to the United States by Great Britain in the Treaty of Paris. In 1795, however, Spain intended to withdraw from the European war against France. Fearing a joint Anglo-American attack on Louisiana and its other American possessions, it decided to improve relations with the United States. Therefore the king's chief minister, Manuel de Godoy, known as "the Prince of Peace," offered the American envoy Thomas Pinckney a treaty that granted the United States the free navigation of the Mississippi River and the right of deposit at New Orleans that western Americans so urgently needed. This Treaty of San Lorenzo, popularly known as Pinckney's Treaty, also accepted the American version of the boundary between Spanish Florida and the United States.

The Senate ratified the Jay Treaty in June. Pinckney signed the Treaty of San Lorenzo in October that same year. These agreements put an end, at least temporarily, to European pressures in the trans-Appalachian region. Between the signings, in August 1795, as an aftermath of the Battle of Fallen Timbers, 12 tribes signed the Treaty of Greenville. The Indians surrendered huge sections of their lands, thus ending a struggle that had consumed a major portion of the government's revenues for years.

After the events of 1794 and 1795, settlers poured into the West as water bursts through a broken dike. "I believe scarcely anything short of a Chinese Wall or a line of Troops will restrain . . . the Incroachment of Settlers, upon the Indian Territory," President Washington explained in 1796. Kentucky had become a state in 1792; now, in 1796, Tennessee was admitted. Two years later the Mississippi Territory was organized, and at the end of the century, the Indiana Territory. The great westward flood reached full tide.

WASHINGTON'S FAREWELL

Settlement of western problems did not, however, put an end to partisan strife. Even the sainted Washington was neither immune to attack nor entirely

George Washington, Farewell Address

above the battle. On questions of finance and foreign policy he usually sided with Hamilton and thus increasingly incurred the anger of the Jeffersonians. But he was, after all, a Virginian. Only the most rabid partisan could think him a tool of northern commercial interests. He remained as he intended himself to be, a symbol of national unity. But he was determined to put away the cares of office at the end of his second term. In September 1796 he announced his retirement in a "Farewell Address" to the nation.

Washington found the acrimonious rivalry between Federalists and Republicans most disturbing. Hamilton advocated national unity, yet he seemed prepared to smash any individual or faction that disagreed with his vision of the country's future. Jefferson had risked his neck for independence, but he opposed the economic development needed to make America strong enough to defend that independence. Washington was less brilliant than either Hamilton or Jefferson but wiser. He appreciated how important it was that the new nation should remain at peace—with the rest of the world and with itself. In his farewell he deplored the "baneful effects of the spirit of party" that led honest people to use unscrupulous means to win a mean advantage over fellow Americans. He tried to show how the North benefited from the prosperity of the South, the South from that of the North, and the East and West also, in reciprocal fashion.

Washington urged the people to avoid both "inveterate antipathies" and "passionate attachments" to any foreign nation. Nothing had alarmed him more than the sight of Americans dividing into "French" and "English" factions. Furthermore, France had repeatedly interfered in American domestic affairs. "Against the insidious wiles of foreign influence," Washington now warned, "the jealousy of a free people ought to be constantly awake." America should develop its foreign trade but steer clear of foreign political connections as far as possible. "Permanent alliances" should be avoided, although "temporary alliances for extraordinary emergencies" might sometimes be useful.

THE ELECTION OF 1796

Washington's Farewell Address was destined to have a long and important influence on American thinking, but its immediate impact was small. He had intended it to cool political passions. Instead, in the words of Federalist congressman Fisher Ames, people took it as "a signal, like dropping a hat, for the party racers to start." By the time the 1796 presidential campaign had ended, many Federalists and Republicans were refusing to speak to one another.

Jefferson was the only Republican candidate seriously considered in 1796. The logical Federalist was Hamilton, but, as was to happen so often in American history with powerful leaders, he was not considered "available" because his controversial policies had made him many enemies. Gathering in caucus, the Federalists in Congress nominated Vice President John Adams for the top office and Thomas Pinckney of South Carolina, negotiator of the popular Spanish treaty, for vice president. In the election the Federalists were victorious.

Hamilton, hoping to run the new administration from the wings, preferred Pinckney to Adams. He arranged for some of the Federalist electors from South Carolina to vote only for Pinckney. (Pinckney, who was on the high seas at the time, did not even know he was running for vice president!) Catching wind of this, a number of New England electors retaliated by cutting Pinckney. As a result, Adams won in the electoral college, 71 to 68, over *Jefferson*, who thus became vice president. Pinckney got only 59 electoral votes.

That Adams would now be obliged to work with a vice president who led the opposition seemed to presage a decline in partisanship. Adams actually preferred the Virginian to Pinckney for the vice presidency, while Jefferson said that if Adams would "relinquish his bias to an English constitution," he might make a fine chief executive. The two had in common a distaste for Hamilton—a powerful bond.

However, the closeness of the election indicated a trend toward the Republicans, who were making constant and effective use of the charge that the Federalists were "monocrats" (monarchists) determined to destroy American liberty. Without Washington to lead them, the Federalist politicians were already quarreling among themselves; honest, able, hardworking John Adams was too caustic and too scathingly frank to unite them. Everything seemed to indicate a Republican victory at the next election.

THE XYZ AFFAIR

At this point occurred one of the most remarkable reversals of public feeling in American history. French attacks on American shipping, begun out of irritation at the Jay Treaty and in order to influence

▲ This flattering portrait of John Adams by John Trumbull was done in 1793. Jeffersonian newspapers referred to Adams derisively as "His Rotundity." Benjamin Bache, editor of the Philadelphia *Aurora*, described him as "blind, bald, toothless, querulous," which was three-quarters true but irrelevant.

the election, continued after Adams took office. Hoping to stop them, Adams appointed three commissioners (Charles Pinckney, United States minister to France, and elder brother of Thomas[1]; John Marshall, a Virginia Federalist lawyer; and Elbridge Gerry of Massachusetts, who was not closely identified with either party) to try to negotiate a settlement. They were instructed to seek a moderate settlement, to "terminate our differences . . . without referring to the merits."

Their mission was a fiasco. Talleyrand, the French foreign minister, sent an agent later spoken of as X to demand "something for the pocket," a "gratification,"—read a bribe—as the price of making a deal. Later two other Tallyrand agents, Y and Z, made the same demand. The Americans refused, more because they suspected Talleyrand's good faith than because of any particular distaste for bribery. "No, no, not a sixpence," Pinckney later told X. The talks broke up, and in April 1798 President Adams released the commissioners' reports.

---

[1]The Pinckney brothers were children of Eliza Pinckney, the woman responsible for the introduction of indigo cultivation to America.

▲ The 1797 cartoon refers to the infamous XYZ affair. Here the five-headed monster (France) demands "Money, Money, Money!!" while the three American representatives answer, "We will not give you six pence."

They caused a sensation. Americans' sense of national honor, perhaps overly tender because the country was so young and insecure, was outraged. Pinckney's laconic refusal to pay a bribe was translated into the grandiose phrase "Millions for defense, but not one cent for tribute!" and broadcast throughout the land. John Adams, never a man with mass appeal, suddenly found himself a national hero. Federalist hotheads burned for a fight. Congress unilaterally abrogated the French Alliance, created a Navy Department, and appropriated enough money to build 40-odd warships and triple the size of the army. Washington came out of retirement to lead the forces, with Hamilton, now a general, as second in command. On the seas American privateers began to attack French shipping.

Adams did not much like the French and he could be extremely stubborn. A declaration of war would have been immensely popular. But perhaps—it is not an entirely illogical surmise about John Adams, who later in life described himself with some relish as "obnoxious, suspected, and unpopular"—the president did not want to be popular. Instead of calling for war, he contented himself with approving the buildup of the armed forces.

The Republicans, however, committed to friendship with France, did not appreciate Adams's moderation. Although angered by the XYZ Affair, they tried, one Federalist complained, "to clog the wheels of government" by opposing the military appropriations. John Daly Burk of the New York *Time Piece* called Adams a "mock Monarch" surrounded by a "court composed of tories and speculators," which of course was a flat lie.

Many Federalists expected the Republicans to side with France if war broke out. Hysterical and near panic, they easily persuaded themselves that the danger of subversion was acute. The French Revolution and the resulting war were churning European society to the depths, stirring the hopes of liberals and striking fear in the hearts of conservatives. Refugees of both persuasions were flocking to the United States. Suddenly the presence of these foreigners seemed threatening to "native" Americans.

THE ALIEN AND SEDITION ACTS

Conservative Federalists saw in this situation a chance to smash the opposition. In June and July 1798 they pushed through Congress a series of repressive measures known as the Alien and Sedition Acts. The least offensive of these laws, the Naturalization Act, increased the period a foreigner had to reside in the United States before being eligible for citizenship from 5 to 14 years. The Alien Enemies Act gave the president the power to arrest or expel aliens in time of "declared war," but since the quasi-war with France was never declared, this measure had no practical importance. The Alien Act authorized the president to expel all aliens whom he thought "dangerous to the peace and safety of the United States." (Adams never invoked this law, but a number of aliens left the country out of fear that he might.)

DOCUMENT

The Alien and Sedition Acts

Finally, there was the Sedition Act. Its first section, making it a crime "to impede the operation of any law" or to attempt to instigate a riot or insurrection, was reasonable enough; but the act also made it illegal to publish, or even to utter, any "false, scandalous and malicious" criticism of high government officials. Although milder than British sedition laws, this proviso rested, as James Madison said, on "the exploded doctrine" that government officials "are the masters and not the servants of the people."

As the election of 1800 approached, the Federalists made a systematic attempt to silence the leading Republican newspapers. Twenty-five persons were prosecuted and ten convicted, all in patently unfair trials. In typical cases, the editor Thomas Cooper, an English-born radical, later president of the University of South Carolina, was sentenced to six months in jail and fined $400; the editor Charles Holt got three months and a $200 fine; and the editor James Callender got nine months and a $200 fine.

THE KENTUCKY AND VIRGINIA RESOLVES

While Thomas Jefferson did not object to state sedition laws, he believed that the Alien and Sedition Acts violated the First Amendment's guarantees of freedom of speech and the press and were an invasion of the rights of the states. In 1798 he and Madison decided to draw up resolutions arguing that the laws were unconstitutional. Madison's draft was presented to the Virginia legislature and Jefferson's to the legislature of Kentucky.

Jefferson argued that since the Constitution was a compact made by sovereign states, each state had "an equal right to judge for itself" when the compact had been violated. Thus a state could declare a law of Congress unconstitutional. Madison's Virginia Resolves took an only slightly less forthright position.

DOCUMENT

The Virginia and Kentucky Resolutions

Neither Kentucky nor Virginia tried to implement these resolves or to prevent the enforcement of the Alien and Sedition Acts. Jefferson and Madison were protesting Federalist high-handedness and firing the opening salvo of Jefferson's campaign for the presidency, not advancing a new constitutional theory of extreme states' rights. "Keep away all show of force," Jefferson advised his supporters.

This was sound advice, for events were again playing into the hands of the Republicans. Talleyrand had never wanted war with the United States. When he discovered how vehemently the Americans had reacted to his little attempt to replenish his personal fortune, he let Adams know that new negotiators would be properly received.

President Adams quickly grasped the importance of the French change of heart. Other leading Federalists, however, had lost their heads. By shouting about the French danger, they had roused the country against radicalism, and they did not intend to surrender this advantage tamely. Hamilton in particular wanted war at almost any price—if not against France, then against Spain. He saw himself at the head of the new American army sweeping first across Louisiana and the Floridas, then on to the South. "We ought to squint at South America," he suggested. "Tempting objects will be without our grasp."

But the Puritan John Adams was a specialist at resisting temptation. At this critical point his intelligence, his moderate political philosophy, and his stubborn integrity stood him in good stead. He would neither go to war merely to destroy the political opposition in America nor follow "the fools who were intriguing to plunge us into an alliance with England . . . and wild expeditions to South America." Instead he submitted to the Senate the name of a new minister plenipotentiary to France, and when the Federalists tried to block the appointment, he threatened to resign. That would have made Jefferson president! So the furious Federalists had to give in, although they forced Adams to send three men instead of one.

Napoleon had taken over France by the time the Americans arrived, and he drove a harder bargain than Talleyrand would have. But in the end he signed an agreement (the Convention of 1800) abrogating the Franco-American treaties of 1778. Nothing was said about the damage done to American shipping by the French, but the war scare was over.

MILESTONES

1781	States fail to approve Congress's tariff
1786	Rhode Island Supreme Court upholds state legal tender act (*Trevett* v. *Weeden*)
	Shays's Rebellion collapses in Springfield, Massachusetts
	Only five states send delegates to Annapolis Convention
1787	Delegates meet at Philadelphia Constitutional Convention
1787–1788	All states but North Carolina and Rhode Island ratify Constitution
1789	President Washington is inaugurated
	Storming of Paris Bastille begins French Revolution
1790	Hamilton issues his *Report on Public Credit*
1791	Hamilton issues his *Report on Manufactures*
	First Ten Amendments (Bill of Rights) to the Constitution are ratified
	Republican and Federalist political parties are organized
	Philip Freneau's *National Gazette* and John Fenno's *Gazette of the United States* are founded

1793	French revolutionaries execute King Louis XVI
	Washington issues Declaration of Neutrality
1794	"Mad Anthony" Wayne's troops defeat Indians at Battle of Fallen Timbers
	Washington's militiamen thwart Whiskey Rebellion in Pennsylvania
1795	Senate ratifies humiliating Jay Treaty
1796	Washington announces his retirement in Farewell Address
	John Adams is elected president
1798	French demand bribe during XYZ Affair
	Congress passes Alien and Sedition Acts
1798–1799	Jefferson presents Kentucky Resolutions
	Madison presents Virginia Resolutions

SUPPLEMENTARY READING

On the Constitution, in addition to the works cited in the Debating the Past (p. 148), see Reginald Horsman, *The New Republic* (2000), a good brief survey. Bernard Bailyn, *To Begin the World Anew* (2003) shows how the founders embraced ambiguity. For Madison's role, see Lance Banning, *The Sacred Fire of Liberty* (1995), Drew R. McCoy, *The Last of the Fathers* (1989), and Gary Rosen, *American Compact* (1999). On Hamilton, Ronald Chernow, *Alexander Hamilton* (2004) offers a balanced account while Richard Brookhiser's brief *Alexander Hamilton, American* (1999) is more partisan. See also Karl-Friedrich Walling, *Republican Empire: Alexander Hamilton on War and Free Government* (1999). The *Federalist Papers* of Hamilton, Madison, and Jay, available in many editions, are essential for the arguments of the supporters of the new government. For the Bill of Rights, consult Bernard Schwartz, *The Great Rights of Mankind* (1977).

For Washington, in addition to the works cited in the previous chapter, see Alexander De Conde, *Entangling Alliance: Politics and Diplomacy Under George Washington* (1958), Harry Ammon, *The Genet Mission* (1973), two volumes by S. F. Bemis, *Jay's Treaty* (1923) and *Pinckney's Treaty* (1926), Alexander De Conde, *The Quasi-War* (1966), and William Stinchcombe, *The XYZ Affair* (1980). On economic development, see E. J. Ferguson, *The Power of the Purse* (1968), and C. P. Nettels, *The Emergence of a National Economy* (1962), which puts this subject in the broader perspective of the period 1775–1815. On the radical western movements, see D. P. Szatmary, *Shays' Rebellion* (1980) and Thomas P. Slaughter, *The Whiskey Rebellion* (1986).

John Patrick Diggins, *John Adams* (2003) is a useful brief biography. Excellent full-length biographies include Joseph J. Ellis, *Passionate Sage* (1993), and David McCullough, *John*

Adams (2001). Stanley Elkins and Eric McKitrick, *The Age of Federalism* (1993), and James Roger Sharp, *American Politics in the Early Republic* (1993), provide detailed accounts of the politics of this period. For the Alien and Sedition Acts, see J. M. Smith, *Freedom's Fetters* (1956), and L. W. Levy, *Freedom of Speech and Press in Early American History* (1963). Paul Nagel's collective biography, *The Adams Women* (1987), provides a superb account of a remarkable family.

On the role of maps generally, see Susan Schulten, *The Geographical Imagination in America, 1880–1950 (2001)*.

SUGGESTED WEBSITES

George Washington at Home
http://www.mountvernon.org/
Pictures and documents from Mount Vernon, the home of the first president, George Washington.

George Washington
http://memory.loc.gov/ammem/gwhtml/gwhome.html
This Library of Congress site contains information on Washington and his papers.

Biographies of the Founders
http://www.colonialhall.com/
This site provides interesting information about the men who signed the Declaration of Independence and includes a trivia section.

The *Federalist Papers*
http://www.law.emory.edu/FEDERAL/federalist/
This Emory University site is a collection of the most important *Federalist Papers*, a series of documents designed to convince people to support the new Constitution and the Federalist Party.

The Continental Congress and the Constitutional Convention, 1774–1798
http://memory.loc.gov/ammem/bdsds/bdsdhome.html
The Continental Congress Broadside Collection (253 titles) and the Constitutional Convention Broadside Collection (21 titles) contain 274 documents relating to the work of Congress and the drafting and ratification of the Constitution.

The Constitution and the Amendments
http://www.law.emory.edu/FEDERAL/usconst.html
A searchable Constitution site, especially useful for its information on the Bill of Rights and other constitutional amendments.

The George Washington Papers
http://www.virginia.edu/gwpapers/
This site provides information on the University of Virginia publishing project, with selected documents, essays, and an index to the published volumes.

Archiving Early America
http://earlyamerica.com
Old newspapers provide a window into issues of the past. This site includes the Keigwin and Matthews collection of historic newspapers.

Alexander Hamilton
http://odur.let.rug.nl/~usa/B/hamilton/hamilxx.htm
This site from *A Hypertext of American History* examines Hamilton's life and influence in the United States during the early national period.

The XYZ Affair
http://ap.grolier.com/article?assetid=0425920-00&templatename=/article/article.html
This site examines the XYZ affair, the first major crisis of U.S. foreign policy.

Jeffersonian Democracy

▼ Jefferson envisioned an American democracy consisting of sturdy, yeoman farmers such as these, painted by 22-year-old Francis Alexander (1822). Notwithstanding this charming rendering of farm life, Alexander took up painting to escape farm chores.

CHAPTER CONTENTS

Once the furor over war and subversion subsided, public attention focused on the presidential contest between Adams and Jefferson. Because of his stand for peace, Adams personally escaped the brunt of popular indignation against the Federalist party. His solid qualities had a strong appeal to conservatives, and fear that the Republicans would introduce radical "French" social reforms did not disappear when the danger of war with France ended. Many nationalist-minded voters worried that the Republicans, waving the banner of states' rights, would weaken the strong government established by the Federalists. The economic progress stimulated by Hamilton's financial reforms also seemed threatened. But when the electors' votes were counted in February 1801, the Republicans were discovered to have won narrowly, 73 to 65.

But which Republican was to be president? The Constitution did not distinguish between presidential and vice presidential candidates; it provided only that each elector vote for two candidates, the one with the most votes becoming president and the runner-up vice president. The development of national political parties made this system impractical. The vice presidential candidate of the Republicans was Aaron Burr of New York, a former senator and a rival of Hamilton in law and politics. But Republican party solidarity had been perfect; Jefferson and Burr received 73 votes each. Because of the tie, the Constitution required that the House of Representatives (voting by states) choose between them.

In the House the Republicans could control only 8 of the 16 state delegations. On the first ballot Jefferson got these 8 votes, 1 short of election, while 6 states voted for Burr. Two state delegations, being evenly split, lost their votes. Through 35 ballots the deadlock persisted; the Federalist congressmen, fearful of Jefferson's supposed radicalism, voted solidly for Burr.

Pressures were exerted on both candidates to make deals to win additional support. Officially at least, both refused. Burr put on a great show of remaining above the battle. (Had he been an honorable man, he would have withdrawn, since the voters had clearly intended him for the second spot.) Whether Jefferson made any promises is uncertain; there is some evidence that to break the deadlock he assured the Federalists that he would preserve Hamilton's financial system and continue the Washington-Adams foreign policy.

In the end, Alexander Hamilton decided who would be the next president. Although he considered Jefferson "too much in earnest in his democracy" and "not very mindful of truth," he detested Burr. He exerted his considerable influence on Federalist congressmen on Jefferson's behalf. Finally, on February 17, 1801, Jefferson was elected. Burr became vice president.

To make sure that this deadlock would never be repeated, the Twelfth Amendment was drafted, providing for separate balloting in the Electoral College for president and vice president. This change was ratified in 1804, shortly before the next election.

The Federalist Contribution

On March 4, 1801, in the raw new national capital on the Potomac River named in honor of George Washington, the Father of his Country, Thomas Jefferson took the presidential oath and delivered his inaugural address. His goal was to recapture the simplicity and austerity—the "pure republicanism"—that had characterized "the spirit of '76." The new president believed that a revolution as important as that heralded by his immortal Declaration of Independence had occurred, and for once most of his political enemies agreed with him.

Certainly an era had ended. In the years between the Peace of Paris and Jay's Treaty, the Federalists had practically monopolized the political good sense of the nation. In the perspective of history they were "right" in strengthening the federal government, in establishing a sound fiscal system, in trying to diversify the economy, in seeking an accommodation with Great Britain, and in refusing to be carried away with enthusiasm for France despite the bright dreams inspired by the French Revolution.

The Federalists had displayed remarkable self-control and moderation at least until 1798. They were nationalists who did not try to destroy local patriotism, aristocrats willing to live with the spirit of democracy. The Constitution—with its wise compromises, its

balance of forces, its restraints, and its practical concessions to local prejudices—is their monument.

But the Federalists were unable to face up to defeat. When they saw the Republicans gathering strength by developing clever new techniques of party organization and propaganda, mouthing slogans about liberty, attacking "monocrats," glorifying both the past with its satisfying simplicity and the future with its promise of a glorious day when all men would be free, equal, and brothers, they panicked. Abandoning the sober wisdom of their great period, they fought to save themselves at any cost. The effort turned defeat into rout. The Republican victory, close in the Electoral College, approached landslide proportions in the congressional elections, where popular feeling expressed itself directly.

Jefferson erred, however, in calling this triumph a revolution. The real upheaval had been attempted in 1798; it was Federalist-inspired, and it failed. In 1800 the voters expressed a preference for the old over the new; that is, for individual freedom and limited national power. And Jefferson, despite Federalist fears that he would destroy the Constitution and establish a radical social order, presided instead over a regime that confirmed the great achievements of the Federalist era.

What was most significant about the election of 1800 was that it was *not* a revolution. After a bitter contest, the Jeffersonians took power and proceeded to change the policy of the government. They did so peacefully. Thus American republican government passed a crucial test: Control of its machinery had changed hands in a democratic and orderly way. And only slightly less significant, the informal party system had demonstrated its usefulness. The Jeffersonians had organized popular dissatisfaction with Federalist policies, formulated a platform of reform, chosen leaders to put their plans into effect, and elected those leaders to office.

Thomas Jefferson: Political Theorist

Jefferson hardly seemed cut out for politics. Although in some ways a typical, pleasure-loving southern planter, he had in him something of the Spartan. He grew tobacco but did not smoke, and he partook only sparingly of meat and alcohol. Unlike most planters he never hunted or gambled, though he was a fine horseman and enjoyed dancing, music, and other social diversions. His practical interests ranged enormously—from architecture and geology to natural history and scientific farming—yet he displayed little interest in managing men. Controversy dismayed him, and he tended to avoid it by assigning to some

DEBATING THE PAST

Did Thomas Jefferson father a child by his slave? The photo *(left)* shows Thomas Jefferson's bedroom at Monticello. He designed the alcove to ensure privacy. A page from his farm accounts *(right)* in his own writing lists as slaves Sally Hemings and several of her children, including Madison, born in 1805, and Eston, born in 1808. In 1787, Sally Hemings, a young slave from the Jefferson plantation, was sent to Paris to serve Thomas Jefferson, U.S. minister to France, and his two daughters. Jefferson's wife had died five years earlier. When Jefferson was elected president in 1800, a newspaper published several articles claiming that he had fathered all of Hemings's children. Jefferson ignored the charges and his political allies denounced them as lies. In 1873 Madison Hemings told an Ohio reporter that his mother, Sally Hemings, had said that his father was Thomas Jefferson. Few took the story seriously. Jefferson scholar Merrill Peterson (1960) was the first to mention Madison Hemings's story, which he attributed to Federalists seeking to embarrass Jefferson and abolitionists seeking to discredit slavery. Dumas Malone (1948–1981), the preeminent Jefferson biographer, flatly rejected the possibility of a Jefferson-Hemings liaison. Among scholars, Malone's views went mostly unchallenged for decades. But Gordon-Reed (1997), a lawyer, accumulated considerable evidence in support of Madison Hemings's story, though she did not think it proven. The next year a forensic pathologist compared a DNA sample of a descendant of Field Jefferson, Thomas Jefferson's uncle, to that of a descendant of Eston Hemings. A genetic sequence matched. Eston had been fathered by a Jefferson. Some pointed to Jefferson's younger brother, Randolph, as the father, but most Jefferson scholars concluded that Thomas Jefferson was the more likely father. No such revelations could diminish Jefferson's significance as statesman, but they further complicate our understanding of one of the nation's foremost apostles of freedom.

Merrill Peterson, *The Jefferson Image in the American Mind* (1960), Dumas Malone, *Jefferson and His Time*, 6 volumes (1948–1981), Anette Gordon-Reed, *Thomas Jefferson and Sally Hemings* (1997). See also Joseph Ellis, *American Sphynx* (1998).

thicker-skinned associate the task of attacking his enemies. Nevertheless, he wanted to have a say in shaping the future of the country, and once engaged, he fought stubbornly and at times deviously to get and hold power.

DOCUMENT
"Memoirs of a Monticello Slave"

Like Hamilton, Jefferson thought human beings basically selfish. "Lions and tigers are mere lambs compared with men," he once said. Although he claimed to have some doubts about the subject, he suspected that blacks were "inferior to whites in the endowments both of body and mind." (Hamilton, who also owned slaves, stated flatly of blacks: "Their natural faculties are as good as ours.") Jefferson's pronouncements on race are yet more troubling in light of recent research, including DNA studies, that point to the likelihood that he fathered one or more children by Sally Hemings, one of his slaves.

Yet like a good child of the Enlightenment, Jefferson believed that "no definite limits can be assigned to the improvability of the human race" and that unless people were free to follow the dictates of reason, the march of civilization would grind quickly to a halt. "To preserve the freedom of the human mind," he wrote, "every spirit should be ready to devote itself to martyrdom." Democracy seemed to him not so much an ideal as a practical necessity. If people could not govern themselves, how could they be expected to govern their fellows? He had no patience with Hamilton's fondness for magnifying the virtues of the rich and the well-born. He believed that "genius" was a rare quality but one "which nature has shown as liberally among poor as rich." When a very old man he wrote: "The mass of mankind has not been born with saddles on their backs, nor a favored few booted and spurred, ready to ride them legitimately, by the grace of God."

Jefferson believed *all* government a necessary evil at best, for by its nature it restricted the freedom of the individual. For this reason, he wanted the United States to remain a society of small independent farmers. Such a nation did not need much political organization.

Jefferson's main objection to Hamilton was that Hamilton wanted to commercialize and centralize the country. This Jefferson feared, for it would mean the growth of cities, which would complicate society and hence require more regulation. "The mobs of great cities add just as much to the support of pure government," he said, "as sores do to the strength of the human body." Later in life he warned a nephew to avoid "populous cities" because, he said, in such places young men acquire "habits and partialities which do not contribute to the happiness of their afterlife." Like Hamilton, he believed that city workers were easy prey for demagogues. "I consider the class of artificers as the panders of vice, and the instruments by which the liberties of a country are usually overturned," he said. "Those who labor in the earth," he also said, "are the chosen people of God, if ever He had a chosen people."

Jefferson objected to what he considered Hamilton's pro-British orientation. Despite his support of the Revolution, Hamilton admired English society and the orderliness of the British government, and he modeled much of his financial program on the British example. To the author of the Declaration of Independence, these attitudes passed all understanding. Jefferson thought English society immoral and decadent, the British system of government fundamentally corrupt. Toward France, the two took opposite positions. Jefferson was in Paris when the French Revolution broke out; he was delighted to see another blow struck at tyranny. Leading French liberals consulted him at every turn. Later, as secretary of state, he excused the excesses of the French upheaval far more than most Americans. To Hamilton, the violence and social disruption caused by the French Revolution were anathema.

JEFFERSON AS PRESIDENT

The novelty of the new administration lay in its style and its moderation. Both were apparent in Jefferson's inaugural address. The new president's opening remarks showed that he was neither a demagogue nor a firebrand. "The task is above my talents," he said modestly, "and . . . I approach it with . . . anxious and awful presentiments." The people had spoken, and their voice must be heeded, but the rights of dissenters must be respected. "All . . . will bear in mind this sacred principle," he said, "that though the will of the majority is in all cases to prevail, that will to be rightful must be reasonable; that the minority possess their equal rights, which equal law must protect, and to violate would be oppression."

DOCUMENT

Thomas Jefferson, First Inaugural Address

Jefferson spoke at some length about specific policies. He declared himself against "entangling alliances" and for economy in government, and he promised to pay off the national debt, preserve the government's credit, and stimulate both agriculture and its "handmaid," commerce. His main stress was on the cooling of partisan passions. "Every difference of opinion is not a difference of principle. We have called by different names brethren of the same principle. We are all Republicans—we are all Federalists." And he promised the country "a wise and frugal Government, which shall restrain men from injuring one another" and "leave them otherwise free to regulate their own pursuits."

Jefferson quickly demonstrated the sincerity of his remarks. He saw to it that the whiskey tax and other Federalist excises were repealed, and he made sharp cuts in military and naval expenditures to keep the budget in balance. The national debt was reduced from $83 million to $57 million during his eight years in office. The Naturalization Act of 1798 was repealed, and the old five-year residence requirement for citizenship restored. The Sedition Act and the Alien Act expired of their own accord in 1801 and 1802.

The changes were not drastic. Jefferson made no effort to tear down the fiscal structure that Hamilton had erected. "We can pay off his debt," the new president confessed, "but we cannot get rid of his financial system." Nor did the author of the Kentucky Resolves try to alter the balance of federal-state power.

Yet there was a different tone to the new regime. Jefferson had no desire to surround himself with pomp and ceremony; the excessive formality of the Washington and Adams administrations had been distasteful to him. From the moment of his election, he played down the ceremonial aspects of the presidency. He asked that he be notified of his election by mail rather than by a committee, and he would have preferred to have taken the oath at Charlottesville, near Monticello, his home, rather than at Washington. After the inauguration, he returned to his boardinghouse on foot and took dinner in his usual seat at the common table.

DOCUMENT

Reflections Upon Meeting Jefferson

In the White House he often wore a frayed coat and carpet slippers, even to receive the representatives of foreign powers when they arrived, resplendent with silk ribbons and a sense of their own importance, to present their credentials. At social affairs he paid little heed to the status and seniority of his guests. When dinner was announced, he offered his arm to whichever lady he was talking to at the moment and placed her at his right; other guests were free to sit wherever they found an empty chair. During business hours congressmen, friends, foreign officials, and plain citizens coming to call took their turn in the order of their arrival. "The principle of society with us," Jefferson explained, "is the equal rights of all. . . . Nobody shall be above you, nor you above anybody, *pell-mell* is our law."

"Pell-mell" was also good politics, and Jefferson turned out to be a superb politician. He gave dozens of small stag dinner parties for congressmen, serving the food personally from a dumbwaiter connected with the White House kitchen. The guests, carefully chosen to make congenial groups, were seated at a round table to encourage general conversation, and the food and wine were first-class. These were ostensibly social occasions—shoptalk was avoided—yet they paid large political dividends. Jefferson learned to know every congressman personally, Democratic Republican and Federalist alike, and not only their political views but their strengths, their quirks, and their flaws as well. And he worked his personal magic on them, displaying the breadth of his knowledge, his charm and wit, his lack of pomposity. "You see, we are alone, and *our walls have no ears*," he would say, and while the wine flowed and the guests sampled delicacies prepared by Jefferson's French chef, the president manufactured political capital. "You drink as you please and converse at your ease," one guest reported.

Jefferson made effective use of his close supporters in Congress and of Cabinet members as well, in persuading Congress to go along with his proposals. His state papers were models of reason, minimizing conflicts, stressing areas where all honest people must agree. After all, as he indicated in his inaugural address, nearly all Americans believed in having both a federal government and a republican system. No great principle divided them into irreconcilable camps. Jefferson set out to bring them all into *his* camp, and he succeeded so well in four years that when he ran for reelection against Charles Pinckney, he got 162 of the 176 electoral votes cast. Eventually

▲ This 1800 painting of Thomas Jefferson was by Rembrandt Peale (1800). Rembrandt's father—the painter Charles Willson Peale—named his other sons after painters, too: Rubens, Titian, and Raphaelle, and Titian II. Rembrandt Peale did this painting, adjudged to be extremely accurate, when he was twenty.

even John Quincy Adams, son of the second president, became a Jeffersonian.

At the same time, Jefferson was anything but nonpartisan in the sense that Washington had been. His Cabinet consisted exclusively of men of his own party. He exerted almost continuous pressure on Congress to make sure that his legislative program was enacted into law. He did not remove many Federalist officeholders, and at one point he remarked ruefully that government officials seldom died and never resigned. But when he could, he used his power of appointment to reward his friends and punish his enemies.

JEFFERSON'S ATTACK ON THE JUDICIARY

Although notably open-minded and tolerant, Jefferson had a few stubborn prejudices. One was against kings, another against the British system of government. A third was against judges, or rather, against entrenched judicial power. While recognizing that judges must have a degree of independence, he feared what he called their "habit of going out of the question before them, to throw an anchor ahead, and grapple further hold for future advances of power." The biased behavior of Federalist judges during the trials under the Sedition Act had enormously increased this distrust, and it burst all bounds when the Federalist majority of the dying Congress rammed through the Judiciary Act of 1801.

The Judiciary Act created six new circuit courts, presided over by 16 new federal judges and a small army of attorneys, marshals, and clerks. The expanding country needed the judges, but with the enthusiastic cooperation of President Adams, the Federalists made shameless use of the opportunity to fill all the new positions with conservative members of their own party. The new appointees were dubbed "midnight justices" because Adams had stayed up until midnight on March 3, his last day as president, feverishly signing their commissions.

The Republicans retaliated as soon as the new Congress met by repealing the Judiciary Act of 1801, but on taking office Jefferson had discovered that in the confusion of Adams's last hours, the commissions of a number of justices of the peace for the new District of Columbia had not been distributed. While these were small fry indeed, Jefferson was so angry that he ordered the commissions held up even though they had been signed by Adams.

One of the appointees, William Marbury, then petitioned the Supreme Court for a writ of mandamus (Latin for "we order") directing the new secretary of state, James Madison, to give him his commission.

DOCUMENT

Opinion of the Supreme Court for *Marbury* v. *Madison*

The case of *Marbury* v. *Madison* (1803) placed Chief Justice John Marshall, one of Adams's "midnight" appointments, in an embarrassing position. Marbury had a strong claim; if Marshall refused to issue a mandamus, everyone would say he dared not stand up to Jefferson, and the prestige of the Court would suffer. If he issued the writ, however, he would place the Court in direct conflict with the executive. Jefferson particularly disliked Marshall. He would probably tell Madison to ignore the order, and in the prevailing state of public opinion nothing could be done about it. This would be a still more staggering blow to the judiciary. What should the chief justice do?

Marshall had studied law only briefly and had no previous judicial experience, but in this crisis he first displayed the genius that was to mark him as a great judge. By right Marbury should have his commission, he announced. However, the Court could not require Madison to give it to him. Marbury's request for a mandamus had been based on an ambiguous clause in the Judiciary Act of 1789. That clause was unconstitu-

tional, Marshall declared, and therefore void. Congress could not legally give the Supreme Court the right to issue writs of mandamus in such circumstances.

With the skill and foresight of a chess grand master, Marshall turned what had looked like a trap into a triumph. By sacrificing the pawn, Marbury, he established the power of the Supreme Court to invalidate federal laws that conflicted with the Constitution. Jefferson could not check him because Marshall had *refused* power instead of throwing an anchor ahead, as Jefferson had feared. Yet he had certainly grappled a "further hold for future advances of power," and the president could do nothing to stop him.

The Marbury case made Jefferson more determined to strike at the Federalist-dominated courts. He decided to press for the impeachment of some of the more partisan judges. First he had the House of Representatives bring charges against District Judge John Pickering. Pickering was clearly deranged—he had frequently delivered profane and drunken harangues from the bench—and the Senate quickly voted to remove him. Then Jefferson went after a much larger fish, Samuel Chase, associate justice of the Supreme Court.

Chase had been prominent for decades, an early leader of the Sons of Liberty, a signer of the Declaration of Independence, active in the affairs of the Continental Congress. Washington had named him to the Supreme Court in 1796, and he had delivered a number of important opinions. But his handling of cases under the Sedition Act had been outrageously high-handed. Defense lawyers had become so exasperated as to throw down their briefs in disgust at some of his prejudiced rulings. However, the trial demonstrated that Chase's actions had not constituted the "high crimes and misdemeanors" required by the Constitution to remove a judge. Even Jefferson became disenchanted with the efforts of some of his more extreme followers and accepted Chase's acquittal with equanimity.

THE BARBARY PIRATES

Aside from these perhaps salutary setbacks, Jefferson's first term was a parade of triumphs. Although he cut back the army and navy sharply in order to save money, he temporarily escaped the consequences of leaving the country undefended because of the lull in the European war signalized by the Treaty of Amiens between Great Britain and France in March 1802. Despite the fact that he had only seven frigates, he even managed to fight a small naval war with the Barbary pirates without damage to American interests or prestige.

The North African Arab states of Morocco, Algiers, Tunis, and Tripoli had for decades made a business of piracy, seizing vessels all over the Mediterranean and holding crews and passengers for ransom. The European powers found it simpler to pay them annual protection money than to crush them. Under Washington and Adams, the United States joined in the payment of this tribute; while large, the sums were less than the increased costs of insurance for shippers when the protection was not purchased.

Such spinelessness ran against Jefferson's grain. "When this idea comes across my mind, my faculties are absolutely suspended between indignation and impatience," he said. When the pasha of Tripoli tried to raise the charges, he balked. Tripoli then declared war in May 1801, and Jefferson dispatched a squadron to the Mediterranean.

In the words of one historian, the action was "halfhearted and ill-starred." The pirates were not overwhelmed, and a major American warship, the frigate *Philadelphia*, had to be destroyed after running aground off the Tripolitan coast. The payment of tribute continued until 1815. Just the same, America, though far removed from the pirate bases, was the only maritime nation that tried to resist the blackmail. Although the war failed to achieve Jefferson's purpose of ending the payments, the pasha agreed to a new treaty more favorable to the United States, and American sailors, led by Commodore Edward Preble, won valuable experience and a large portion of fame. The greatest hero was Lieutenant Stephen Decatur, who captured two pirate ships, led ten men in a daring raid on another in which he took on a gigantic sailor in a wild battle of cutlass against boarding pike,[1] and snatched the stricken *Philadelphia* from the pirates by sneaking aboard and setting it afire.

THE LOUISIANA PURCHASE

The Louisiana Purchase

The major achievements of Jefferson's first term had to do with the American West, and the greatest by far was the acquisition of the huge area between the Mississippi River and the Rocky Mountains. In a sense the purchase of this region, called Louisiana, was fortuitous, an accidental by-product of European political adjustments and the whim of Napoleon Bonaparte. Certainly Jefferson had not planned it, for in his inaugural address he had expressed the opinion that the country already had all the land it would need "for a thousand generations." It was nonetheless the perfectly logical—one might almost say inevitable—result of a long series of events in the history of the Mississippi Valley.

Along with every other American who had even a superficial interest in the West, Jefferson understood that the United States must have access to the mouth of the Mississippi and the city of New Orleans or eventually lose everything beyond the Appalachians. "There is on the globe one single spot, the possessor of which is our natural and habitual enemy," he was soon to write. "It is New Orleans." Thus when he learned shortly after his inauguration that Spain had given Louisiana back to France, he was immediately on his guard. Control of Louisiana by Spain, a "feeble" country with "pacific dispositions," could be tolerated; control by a resurgent France dominated by Napoleon, the greatest military genius of the age, was entirely different. Did Napoleon have designs on Canada? Did he perhaps mean to resume the old Spanish and British game of encouraging the Indians to harry the American frontier? And what now would be the status of Pinckney's precious treaty?

Deeply worried, the president instructed his minister to France, Robert R. Livingston, to seek assurances that American rights in New Orleans would be respected and to negotiate the purchase of West Florida in case that region had also been turned over to France.

Jefferson's concern was well founded; France was indeed planning new imperial ventures in North America. Immediately after settling its difficulties with the United States through the Convention of 1800, France signed the secret Treaty of San Ildefonso with Spain, which returned Louisiana to France. Napoleon hoped to use this region as a breadbasket for the French West Indian sugar plantations, just as colonies like Pennsylvania and Massachusetts had fed the British sugar islands before the Revolution.

However, the most important French island, Saint Domingue (Hispaniola), at the time occupied entirely by the nation of Haiti, had slipped from French control. During the French Revolution, the slaves of the island had revolted. In 1793 they were granted personal freedom, but they fought on under the leadership of the "Black Napoleon," a self-taught genius named Toussaint Louverture, and by 1801 the island was entirely in their hands. The original Napoleon, taking advantage of the slackening of war in Europe, dispatched an army of 20,000 men under General Charles Leclerc to reconquer it.

When Jefferson learned of the Leclerc expedition, he had no trouble divining its relationship to Louisiana. His uneasiness became outright alarm. In April 1802 he again urged Minister Livingston to attempt the purchase of New Orleans and Florida or, as an alternative, to buy a tract of land near the mouth of the Mississippi where a new port could be constructed. Of necessity, the mild-mannered, idealistic president now became an aggressive realist. If the

[1]Decatur killed the pirate by drawing a small pistol from his pocket as his opponent was about to skewer him.

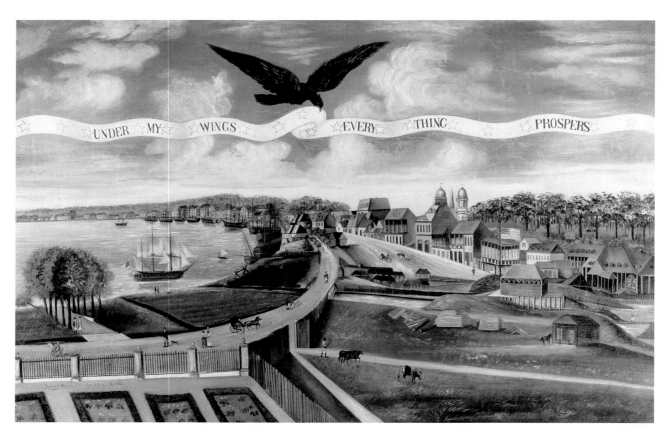

▲ New Orleans in 1803, when the city was acquired—along with much of the modern United States—in the Louisiana Purchase. It was known as the Crescent City because of the way it hugged a curved section of the Mississippi River. In 1803, its population was about 8000, including 4000 whites, 2700 slaves, and about 1300 free "persons of color."

right of deposit could not be preserved through negotiation, it must be purchased with gunpowder, even if that meant acting in conjunction with the despised British. "The day that France takes possession of New Orleans," he warned, "we must marry ourselves to the British fleet and nation."

In October 1802 the Spanish, who had not yet actually turned Louisiana over to France, heightened the tension by suddenly revoking the right of deposit at New Orleans. We now know that the French had no hand in this action, but it was beyond reason to expect Jefferson or the American people to believe it at the time. With the West clamoring for relief, Jefferson appointed his friend and disciple James Monroe minister plenipotentiary and sent him to Paris with instructions to offer up to $10 million for New Orleans and Florida. If France refused, he and Livingston should open negotiations for a "closer connection" with the British.

The tension broke before Monroe even reached France. General Leclerc's Saint Domingue expedition ended in disaster. Although Toussaint surrendered, Haitian resistance continued. Yellow fever raged through the French army; Leclerc himself fell to the fever, which wiped out practically his entire force.

When news of this calamity reached Napoleon early in 1803, he began to have second thoughts about reviving French imperialism in the New World. Without Saint Domingue, the wilderness of Louisiana seemed of little value. Napoleon was preparing a new campaign in Europe. He could no longer spare troops to recapture a rebellious West Indian island or to hold Louisiana against a possible British attack, and he needed money.

For some weeks the commander of the most powerful army in the world mulled the question without consulting anyone. Then, with characteristic suddenness, he made up his mind. On April 10 he ordered Foreign Minister Talleyrand to offer not merely New Orleans but all of Louisiana to the Americans. The next day Talleyrand summoned Livingston to his office on the rue du Bac and dropped this bombshell. Livingston was almost struck speechless but quickly recovered his composure. When Talleyrand asked what the United States would give for the province, he suggested the French equivalent of about $5 million. Talleyrand pronounced the sum "too low" and urged Livingston to think about the subject for a day or two.

DOCUMENT
The Louisiana Purchase

Livingston faced a situation that no modern diplomat would ever have to confront. His instructions said nothing about buying an area almost as large as the entire United States, and there was no time to write home for new instructions. The offer staggered the imagination. Luckily, Monroe arrived the next day to share the responsibility. The two Americans consulted, dickered with the French, and finally agreed—they could scarcely have done otherwise—to accept the proposal. Early in May they signed a treaty. For 60 million francs—about $15 million—the United States was to have all of Louisiana.

No one knew exactly how large the region was or what it contained. When Livingston asked Talleyrand about the boundaries of the purchase, he replied: "I can give you no direction. You have made a noble bargain for yourselves, and I suppose you will make the most of it." Never, as the historian Henry Adams wrote, "did the United States government get so much for so little."

Napoleon's unexpected concession caused consternation in America, though there was never real doubt that the treaty would be ratified. Jefferson did not believe that the government had the power under the Constitution to add new territory or to grant American citizenship to the 50,000 residents of Louisiana by executive act, as the treaty required. He even drafted a constitutional amendment: "The province of Louisiana is incorporated with the United States and made part thereof," but his advisers convinced him that it would be dangerous to delay approval of the treaty until an amendment could be acted on by three-fourths of the states. Jefferson then suggested that the Senate ratify the treaty and submit an amendment afterward "confirming an act which the nation had not previously authorized." This idea was so obviously illogical that he quickly dropped it. Finally, he came to believe "that the less we say about constitutional difficulties the better." Since what he called "the good sense of our country" clearly wanted Louisiana, he decided to "acquiesce with satisfaction" while Congress overlooked the "metaphysical subtleties" of the problem and ratified the treaty.

DOCUMENT
Fisher Ames on the Louisiana Purchase

Some of the more partisan Federalists, who had been eager to fight Spain for New Orleans, attacked Jefferson for undermining the Constitution. One such critic described Louisiana contemptuously as a "Gallo-Hispano-Indian" collection of "savages and adventurers." Even Hamilton expressed hesitation about absorbing "this new, immense, unbounded world," though he had dreamed of seizing still larger domains himself. In the end Hamilton's nationalism reasserted itself, and he urged ratification of the treaty, as did such other important Federalists as John Adams and John Marshall. And in a way the Louisiana Purchase was as much Hamilton's doing as Jefferson's. Napoleon accepted payment in United States bonds, which he promptly sold to European investors. If Hamilton had not established the nation's credit so soundly, such a large issue could never have been so easily disposed of.

It was ironic—and a man as perceptive as Hamilton must surely have recognized the irony—that the acquisition of Louisiana ensured Jefferson's reelection and further contributed to the downfall of the Federalists. The purchase was popular even in the New England bastions of that party. While the negotiations were progressing in Paris, Jefferson had written of partisan political affairs: "If we can settle happily the difficulties of the Mississippi, I think we may promise ourselves smooth seas during our time." These words turned out to be no more accurate than most political predictions, but the Louisiana Purchase drove another spike into the Federalists' coffin.

THE FEDERALISTS DISCREDITED

The West and South were solidly for Jefferson, and the North was rapidly succumbing to his charm. The addition of new western states would soon further

▲ The 1790 slave rebellion in Haiti, led by Toussaint Louverture, caused thousands of French to flee the island; many settled in South Carolina. Their stories fueled fears of a slave uprising in the South.

reduce New England's power in national affairs. So complete did the Republican triumph seem that a handful of diehard Federalists in New England began to think of secession. Led by former secretary of state Timothy Pickering, a sour, implacable conservative, a group known as the Essex Junto organized in 1804 a scheme to break away from the Union and establish a "northern confederacy."

Even within the dwindling Federalist ranks the junto had little support. Nevertheless, Pickering and his friends pushed ahead, drafting a plan whereby, having captured political control of New York, they would take the entire Northeast out of the Union. Since they could not begin to win New York for anyone in their own ranks, they hit on the idea of supporting Vice President Aaron Burr, who was running against the "regular" Republican candidate for governor of New York. Although Burr did not promise to bring New York into their confederacy if elected, he encouraged them enough to win their backing. The foolishness of the plot was revealed in the April elections: Burr was overwhelmed by the regular Republican. The junto's scheme collapsed.

The incident, however, had a tragic aftermath. Hamilton had campaigned against Burr, whom he considered "an embryo Caesar." When he continued after the election to cast aspersions on Burr's character (not a very difficult assignment, since Burr, despite being a grandson of the preacher Jonathan Edwards, frequently violated both the political and sexual mores of the day), Burr challenged him to a duel. It was well known that Hamilton opposed dueling in principle, his own son having been slain in such an encounter, and he certainly had no need to prove his courage. But he believed that his honor was at stake. The two met with pistols on July 11, 1804, at Weehawken, New Jersey, across the Hudson from New York City. Hamilton made no effort to hit the challenger, but Burr took careful aim. Hamilton fell, wounded; he died the next day. Thus a great, if enigmatic, man was cut off in his prime. His work, in a sense, had been completed, and his philosophy of government was being everywhere rejected, yet the nation's loss was large.

LEWIS AND CLARK

While the disgruntled Federalists dreamed of secession, Jefferson was planning the exploration of Louisiana and the region beyond. He especially hoped to find a water route to connect the upper Mississippi or its tributaries with the Pacific Ocean. Early in 1803 he got $2500 from Congress and obtained the permission of the French to send his exploring party across Louisiana. To command the expedition he appointed his private secretary, Meriwether Lewis, a young Virginian who had seen considerable service with the army in the West and who possessed, according to Jefferson, "a great mass of accurate information on all the subjects of nature." Lewis chose as his companion officer William Clark, another soldier (he had served with General Anthony Wayne at the Battle of Fallen Timbers) who had much experience in negotiating with Indians.

Jefferson, whose interest in the West was scientific as well as political, issued precise instructions to Lewis:

DOCUMENT

Thomas Jefferson to Meriwether Lewis

Other objects worthy of notice will be, the soil and face of the country . . . the remains and accounts of any animals which may be deemed, or are extinct; the mineral productions of every kind . . . climate, as characterized by the thermometer, by the proportion of rainy, cloudy, and clear days, by lightning, hail, snow, ice, by the access and recess of frost, by the winds prevailing at different seasons, the dates at which particular plants put forth or lose their

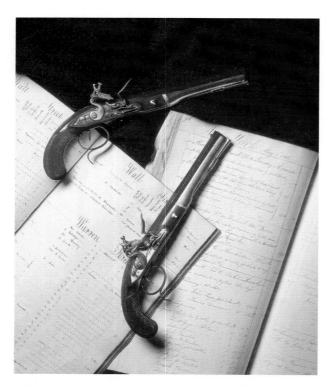

▲ Pistols used in the duel between Aaron Burr and Alexander Hamilton. Before the duel Hamilton's lawyer drew up a contract specifying the terms: the duelists were to shoot from 10 paces, and the barrels of the guns were to be no longer than eleven inches. Hamilton seems never to have discharged his pistol, but Burr took deadly aim, firing a .54-calibre ball that hit Hamilton in the chest. It ricocheted off his rib, punctured his liver, and lodged in his backbone. He died the next day.

flower or leaf, times of appearance of particular birds, reptiles or insects . . .

Scientific matters were inextricably intertwined with practical ones, such as the fur trade, for in his nature studies Jefferson concentrated on "useful" plants and animals. He was haunted by imperialistic visions of an expanding America that were not unlike those of Hamilton. After the consummation of the Louisiana Purchase, he instructed Lewis to try to establish official relations with the Indians in the Spanish territories beyond. Lewis should assure the tribes that "they will find in us faithful friends and protectors," Jefferson said. That the expedition would be moving across Spanish territory need not concern the travelers because of "the expiring state of Spain's interests there."

▲ The "Flat Head" (Chinook Indians) acquired their name through shaping in infancy, as shown in a diagram from the Lewis and Clark journals. More remarkable to the explorers than the shape of the Indian heads was the tribeswomen's open sexuality. "The young females are fond of the attention of our men and appear to meet the sincere approbation of their friends and connections for thus obtaining their favors," Captain Clark confided in his diary.

Lewis and Clark gathered a group of 48 experienced men near St. Louis during the winter of 1803–1804. In the spring they made their way slowly up the Missouri River in a 55-foot keelboat and two dugout canoes, called pirogues. By late fall they had reached what is now North Dakota, where they built a small station, Fort Mandan, and spent the winter there. In April 1805, having shipped back to the president more than 30 boxes of plants, minerals, animal skins and bones, and Indian artifacts, they struck out again toward the mountains, accompanied by a Shoshone woman, Sacajawea, and her French-Canadian husband, Toussaint Charbonneau, who acted as interpreters and guides. They passed the Great Falls of the Missouri and then clambered over the Continental Divide at Lemhi Pass in southwestern Montana. Soon thereafter the going became easier, and they descended to the Pacific by way of the Clearwater and Columbia Rivers, reaching their destination in November. They had hoped to return by ship, but during the long, damp winter not a single vessel appeared. In the spring of 1806 they headed back by land, reaching St. Louis on September 23.

DOCUMENT

Lewis and Clark Meet the Shoshone

The country greeted the news of their return with delight. Besides locating several passes across the Rockies, Lewis and Clark had established friendly relations with a great many Indian tribes to whom they presented gifts, medals, American flags, and a sales talk designed to promote peace and the fur trade. They brought back a wealth of data about the country and its resources. The journals kept by members of the group were published and, along with their accurate maps, became major sources for scientists, students, and future explorers. To Jefferson's great personal satisfaction, Lewis provided him with many specimens of the local wildlife, including two grizzly bear cubs, which he kept for a time in a stone pit in the White House lawn.

The success of Lewis and Clark did not open the gates of Louisiana very wide. Other explorers sent out by Jefferson accomplished far less. Thomas Freeman, an Irish-born surveyor, led a small party up the Red River but ran into a powerful Spanish force near the present junction of Arkansas, Oklahoma, and Texas and was forced to retreat. Between 1805 and 1807 Lieutenant Zebulon Pike explored the upper Mississippi Valley and the Colorado region. (He discovered but failed to scale the peak south of Denver that bears his name.) Pike eventually made his way to Santa Fe and the upper reaches of the Rio Grande, but he was not nearly so careful and acute an observer as Lewis and Clark were and consequently brought back much less information. By 1808 fur traders based at St. Louis were beginning to invade the Rockies, and by 1812 there were 75,000 people in the southern section of the new territory, which was admitted to the Union that year as the state of Louisiana. The northern region lay almost untouched until much later.

► *text continues on page 182*

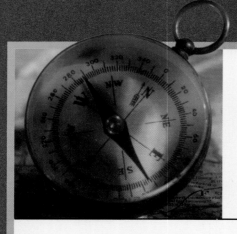

Mapping the Past

A Water Route to the Pacific?

Jefferson's Dream

In the fall of 1802, President Thomas Jefferson asked the Spanish minister whether his government would take offense if a small group of Americans explored the sources of the Missouri River. The expedition, Jefferson assured the Spaniard, would have no purpose other than "the advancement of geography." The minister coolly replied that such an adventure "could not fail to give umbrage to our government." After the meeting, the diplomat promptly alerted his superiors in Madrid that Jefferson was "a lover of glory." The American president's goal, he wrote, was to find a water route to the Pacific, thus facilitating American settlement of the region.

The Spaniard was exactly right. Several months after his meeting with the Spanish minister, Jefferson sent a secret message to Congress. In it he requested an appropriation of $2500 for an expedition to determine whether the Missouri River connected, "possibly with a single portage," to the Western (Pacific) Ocean. Congress approved the resolution. Jefferson chose Meriwether Lewis, his private secretary, and William Clark, an army officer, to head the expedition.

Jefferson's belief in a water route to the Pacific via the Missouri was based on several sources. The first was a book published in 1763 by Simon le Page du Pratz, a French traveler. Du Pratz wrote that an Indian, Moncacht-Apé, followed the Missouri to its source, dragged a canoe over a short portage, and then paddled upon a "Beautiful River" (Belle Rivière) that emptied into a western ocean. A rendering of du Pratz's map appears below, left.

In 1784 Peter Pond, an employee of the North West Company, prepared a map based on similar reports by the company's fur traders (see map far right). They told him that the Missouri River originated within the

Le Page du Pratz, 1758

"Stony (Rocky) Mountains." Beyond them lay the Naberkistagen River, which emptied into the South Sea (presumably the Pacific Ocean). Inspired by such reports, Alexander Mackenzie, a Scotsman in the fur trade, crossed the Continental Divide further north and, after an easy portage, came to the Fraser River, which flowed into the Pacific. Although the raging Fraser was unsuited for commercial navigation, Mackenzie believed that a satisfactory route to the Pacific could be found. In 1801 he published a book advancing this hypothesis and urged Great Britain to develop the route that would ultimately join the Atlantic and the Pacific.

Jefferson, alarmed by British interest in the Northwest, immediately ordered a copy of Mackenzie's book. It arrived at Monticello in the summer of 1802. Jefferson and Lewis poured over the maps. They compared Mackenzie's account with du Pratz's map, and also with a map compiled by Jedidiah Morse. Morse's map, too, suggested that the source of the Missouri nearly connected with the River of the West (see map right). Lewis's mission was to find the easiest route to the Pacific.

Lewis And Clark's Expedition

In the spring of 1804 Lewis and Clark started out with a group of 48 men up the Missouri. By late fall they had reached what is now North Dakota, where they built a small station, Fort Mandan, and spent the winter. In April 1805, they continued their westward journey on small boats and canoes. Among their party was Sacajawea, a 16-year-old Shoshone, then six months pregnant. In June they arrived at the Great Falls of the Missouri. It took them a month to make the portage—hardly the easy trip Moncacht-Apé had related. Nor did the jagged mountains in the distance bear much resemblance to the Appalachians.

Yet Lewis, seemingly oblivious to the boulder-strewn streams and deep ravines that impeded his portage, remained optimistic. On August 10 he wrote that if the Columbia River beyond the mountains was like what he had so far encountered, "a communication across the continent by water will be practicable and safe." A week later, they came to the Shoshone settlement, where Sacajawea was reunited with some of her family. Then Lewis's party began the long climb into the Bitterroot Mountains, eventually coming to the Continental Divide near the Lemhi Pass. Beyond the summit, Lewis saw an endless range of "unknown formidable snow clad Mountains." A navigable water route through the Rockies did not exist.

Morse, 1797

Peter Pond, 1784

Lewis and Clark, 1804–1806

← Lewis and Clark

← Lewis

← Clark

← Ordway and Gass

support camps

encounter with Indians

battle

JEFFERSONIAN DEMOCRACY

With the purchase of Louisiana, Jefferson completed the construction of the political institution known as the Republican party and the philosophy of government known as Jeffersonian democracy. From what sort of materials had he built his juggernaut? In part his success was a matter of personality; in the march of American democracy he stood halfway, temperamentally, between Washington and Andrew Jackson, perfectly in tune with the thinking of his times. The colonial American had practiced democracy without really believing in it; hence, for example, the maintenance of property qualifications for voting in regions where nearly everyone owned property. Stimulated by the libertarian ideas of the Revolution, Americans were rapidly adjusting their beliefs to conform with their practices. However, it took Jefferson, a man of large estates, possessed of the general prejudice in favor of the old-fashioned citizen rooted in the soil, yet deeply committed to majority rule, to oversee the transition.

Jefferson's marvelous talents as a writer help explain his success. He expounded his ideas in language that few people could resist. He had a remarkable facility for discovering practical arguments to justify his beliefs—as when he suggested that by letting everyone vote, elections would be made more honest because with large numbers going to the polls, bribery would become prohibitively expensive.

Jefferson prepared the country for democracy by proving that a democrat could establish and maintain a stable regime. The Federalist tyranny of 1798 was compounded of selfishness and stupidity, but it was also based in part on honest fears that an egalitarian regime would not protect the fabric of society from hotheads and crackpots. The impact of the French Revolution on conservative thinking in the mid-1790s cannot be overestimated. America had fought a seven-year revolution without executing a single Tory, yet during the few months that the Reign of Terror ravaged France, nearly 17,000 persons were officially put to death for political "crimes" and many thousands more were killed in civil disturbances. Worse, in the opinion of many, the French extremists had attempted to destroy Christianity, substituting for it a "cult of reason." They confiscated property, imposed price controls, and abolished slavery in the French colonies. Little wonder that many Americans feared that the Jeffersonians, lovers of France and of *liberté, égalité, fraternité* would try to remodel American society in a similar way.

Jefferson calmed these fears. "Pell-mell" might scandalize the British and Spanish ministers and a few locals, but it was scarcely revolutionary. The most partisan Federalist was hard put to see a Robespierre, leader during the Reign of Terror in France, in the amiable president scratching out state papers at his desk or chatting with a Kentucky congressman at a "republican" dinner party. Furthermore, Jefferson accepted Federalist ideas on public finance, even learning to live with Hamilton's bank. As a good democrat, he drew a nice distinction between his own opinions and the wishes of the majority, which he felt must always take priority. Even in his first inaugural he admitted that manufacturing and commerce were, along with agriculture, the "pillars of our prosperity," and while believing that these activities would thrive best when "left most free to individual enterprise," he accepted the principle that the government should protect them when necessary from "casual embarrassments." Eventually he gave his backing to modest proposals for spending federal money on roads, canals, and other projects that, according to his political philosophy, ought to have been left to the states and private individuals.

During his term the country grew and prospered, the commercial classes sharing in the bounty along with the farmers so close to Jefferson's heart. Blithely he set out to win the support of all who could vote. "It is material to the safety of Republicanism," he wrote in 1803, "to detach the mercantile interests from its enemies and incorporate them into the body of its friends."

Thus Jefferson undermined the Federalists all along the line. They had said that the country must pay a stiff price for prosperity and orderly government, and they demanded prompt payment in full, both in cash (taxes) and in the form of limitations on human liberty. Under Jefferson these much-desired goals had been achieved cheaply and without sacrificing freedom. A land whose riches could only be guessed at had been obtained without firing a shot and without burdening the people with new taxes. "What farmer, what mechanic, what laborer, ever sees a taxgatherer of the United States?" the president could ask in 1805, without a single Federalist rising to challenge him. Order without discipline, security without a large military establishment, prosperity without regulatory legislation, freedom without license—truly the Sage of Monticello appeared to have led his fellow Americans into a golden age.

THE BURR CONSPIRACY

Republican virtue seemed to have triumphed, both at home and abroad. But Jefferson soon found himself in trouble at home and abroad.

In part his difficulties arose from the extent of the Republican victory. In 1805 his Federalist opponents had no useful ideas, no intelligent leadership, no effective numbers. They held only a quarter of the seats

▲ This engraving by J. Stoner, *American Stage Wagon,* depicts the common mode of transportation along federal roads during the Jefferson administration.

in Congress. As often happens in such situations, lack of opposition weakened party discipline and encouraged factionalism among the Republicans.

The Republican who caused Jefferson the most trouble was Aaron Burr, and the president was partly to blame for the difficulty. After their contest for the presidency in 1801, Jefferson pursued Burr vindictively, depriving him of federal patronage in New York and replacing him as the 1804 Republican vice presidential candidate with Governor George Clinton, Burr's chief rival in the state.

While still vice president, Burr began to flirt with treason. He approached Anthony Merry, the British minister in Washington, and offered to "effect a separation of the Western part of the United States." His price was £110,000 and the support of a British fleet off the mouth of the Mississippi. The British did not fall in with his scheme, but Burr went ahead nonetheless. Exactly what he had in mind has long been in dispute. Certainly he dreamed of acquiring a western empire for himself; whether he intended to wrest it from the United States or from Spanish territories beyond Louisiana is unclear. He joined forces with General James Wilkinson, whom Jefferson had appointed governor of the Louisiana Territory, who was secretly in the pay of Spain.

The opening of the Ohio and Mississippi valleys had not totally satisfied land-hungry Westerners. In 1806 Burr and Wilkinson had no difficulty raising a small force at a place called Blennerhassett Island, in the Ohio River. Some six dozen men began to move downriver toward New Orleans under Burr's command. Whether the objective was New Orleans or some part of Mexico, the scheme was clearly illegal. For some reason, however—possibly because he was incapable of loyalty to anyone[2]—Wilkinson betrayed Burr to Jefferson at the last moment. Burr tried to escape to Spanish Florida but was captured in February 1807, brought to Richmond, Virginia, under guard, and charged with high treason.

Any president will deal summarily with traitors, but Jefferson's attitude during Burr's trial reveals the depth of his hatred. He "made himself a party to the prosecution," personally sending evidence to the United States attorney who was handling the case and offering blanket pardons to associates of Burr who would agree to turn state's evidence. In stark contrast, Chief Justice Marshall, presiding at the trial in his capacity as judge of the circuit court, repeatedly showed favoritism to the prisoner.

In this contest between two great men at their worst, Jefferson as a vindictive executive and Marshall

---

[2]John Randolph said of him: "Wilkinson is the only man that I ever saw who was from the bark to the very core a villain."

▲ John Randolph, a Congressman from Roanoke, Virginia, was the most prominent of the Republican critics of Jefferson. He made a fetish of preserving states' rights against invasion by the central government. "Asking one of the States to surrender part of her sovereignty is like asking a lady to surrender part of her chastity," he remarked in one of his typical epigrams.

as a prejudiced judge, the victory went to the judge. Organizing "a military assemblage," Marshall declared on his charge to the jury, "was not a levying of war." To "advise or procure treason" was not in itself treason. Unless two independent witnesses testified to an overt act of treason as thus defined, the accused should be declared innocent. The jury, deliberating only 25 minutes, found Burr not guilty.

Throughout the trial, Burr never lost his self-possession. He seemed to view the proceedings with amiable cynicism. Then, since he was wanted either for murder or for treason in six states, he went into exile in Europe. Some years later he returned to New York, where he spent an unregenerate old age, fathering two illegitimate children in his seventies and being divorced by his second wife on grounds of adultery at 80.

The Burr affair was a blow to Jefferson's prestige; it left him more embittered against Marshall and the federal judiciary, and it added nothing to his reputation as a statesman.

NAPOLEON AND THE BRITISH

Jefferson's difficulties with Burr may be traced at least in part to the purchase of Louisiana, which, empty and unknown, excited the greed of men like Burr and Wilkinson. But problems infinitely more serious were also related to Louisiana.

Napoleon had jettisoned Louisiana to clear the decks before resuming the battle for control of Europe. This war had the effect of stimulating the American economy, for the warring powers needed American goods and American vessels. Shipbuilding boomed; foreign trade, which had quintupled since 1793, nearly doubled again between 1803 and 1805. By the summer of 1807, however, the situation had changed: a most unusual stalemate had developed in the war.

In October 1805 Britain's Horatio Nelson demolished the combined Spanish and French fleets in the Battle of Trafalgar, off the coast of Spain. Napoleon, now at the summit of his powers, quickly redressed the balance, smashing army after army thrown against him by Great Britain's continental allies. By 1807 he was master of Europe, while the British controlled the seas around the Continent. Neither nation could strike directly at the other.

They therefore resorted to commercial warfare, striving to disrupt each other's economy. Napoleon struck first with his Berlin Decree (November 1806), which made "all commerce and correspondence" with Great Britain illegal. The British retaliated with a series of edicts called Orders in Council, blockading most continental ports and barring from them all foreign vessels unless they first stopped at a British port and paid customs duties. Napoleon then issued his Milan Decree (December 1807), declaring any vessel that submitted to the British rules "to have become English property" and thus subject to seizure.

The blockades and counterblockades seemed designed to stop commerce completely, yet this was not the case. Napoleon's "Continental System" was supposed to make Europe self-sufficient and isolate Great Britain, yet he was willing to sell European products to the British (if the price was right); his chief objective was to deprive them of their continental markets. The British were ready to sell anything on the Continent, and to allow others to do so too, provided they first paid a toll. The Continental System was, in John Quincy Adams's pithy phrase, "little more than extortion wearing the mask of prohibition," and British policy was equally immoral—a kind of piracy practiced with impunity because the Royal Navy controlled the seas.

When war first broke out between Britain and France in 1792, the colonial trade of both sides had fallen largely into American hands because the danger of capture drove many belligerent merchant vessels from the seas. This commerce had engaged Americans in some devious practices. Under the Rule of War of 1756, the British denied neutrals the right in time of war to engage in trade from which they were barred by mercantilist regulations in time of peace. If an American ship carried sugar from the French colony of Martinique to France, for example, the British claimed the right to capture it because such traffic was normally confined to French ships by French law.

To avoid this risk, American merchants brought the sugar first to the United States, a legal peacetime voyage under French mercantilism. Then they reshipped it to France as American sugar. Since the United States was a neutral nation and sugar was not contraband of war, the Americans expected the British to let their ships pass with impunity. Continental products likewise reached the French West Indies by way of United States ports, and the American government encouraged the traffic in both directions by refunding customs duties on foreign products reshipped within a year. Between 1803 and 1806 the annual value of foreign products reexported from the United States jumped from $13 million to $60 million! In 1806 the United States exported 47 million pounds of coffee—none, of course, of local origin. An example of this type of trade is offered by Samuel Eliot Morison in his *Maritime History of Massachusetts*:

> The brig *Eliza Hardy* of Plymouth enters her home port from Bordeaux, on May 20, 1806, with a cargo of claret wine. Part of it is immediately reexported to Martinique in the schooner *Pilgrim* which also carries a consignment of brandy that came from Alicante in the brig *Commerce* and another of gin that came from Rotterdam in the barque *Hannah* of Plymouth. The rest of the *Eliza Hardy*'s claret is taken to Philadelphia by coasters, and thence reexported in seven different vessels to Havana, Santiago de Cuba, St. Thomas, and Batavia.

This underhanded commerce irritated the British. In the cases of the *Essex* and the *William* (1805–1806), a British judge, Sir William Grant, decreed that American ships could no longer rely on "mere voluntary *ceremonies*" to circumvent the Rule of 1756. Thus just when Britain and France were cracking down on direct trade by neutrals, Britain determined to halt the American reexport trade, thereby gravely threatening American prosperity.

THE IMPRESSMENT CONTROVERSY

More dismaying were the cruel indignities being visited on American seamen by the British practice of impressment. Under British law any able-bodied subject could be drafted for service in the Royal Navy in an emergency. Normally, when the commander of a warship found himself shorthanded, he put into a British port and sent a "press gang" ashore to round up the necessary men in harborside pubs. When far from home waters, he might hail any passing British merchant ship and commandeer the necessary men, though this practice was understandably unpopular in British maritime circles. He might also stop a *neutral* merchant vessel on the high seas and remove any British subject. Since the United States owned by far the largest merchant fleet among the neutrals, its vessels bore the brunt of this practice.

Impressment had been a cause of Anglo-American conflict for many years; American pride suffered every time a vessel carrying the flag was forced to back topsails and heave to at the command of a British man-of-war. Still more galling was the contemptuous behavior of British officers when they boarded American ships. In 1796 an American captain named Figsby was stopped twice by British warships while carrying a cargo of poultry and other livestock to Guadeloupe. First a privateer, the *Sea Nymph*, impressed two of his crew, confiscated most of his chickens, "abused" him, and stole his ship's flag. Two days later HMS *Unicorn* took another of Figsby's men, the rest of his poultry, four sheep, and three hogs.

Many British captains made little effort to be sure they were impressing British subjects; any likely looking lad might be taken when the need was great. Furthermore, there were legal questions in dispute. When did an English immigrant become an American? When he was naturalized, the United States claimed. Never, the British retorted; "once an Englishman, always an Englishman."

America's lax immigration laws compounded the problem. A foreigner could become a citizen with ridiculous ease; those too impatient to wait the required five years could purchase false naturalization papers for as little as a dollar. Because working conditions in the American merchant marine were superior to those of the British, at least 10,000 British-born sailors were serving on American ships. Some became American citizens legally; others obtained false papers; some admitted to being British subjects; some were deserters from the Royal Navy. From the British point of view, all were liable to impressment.

The Jefferson administration conceded the right of the British to impress their own subjects from American merchant ships. When naturalized Americans were impressed, however, the administration was irritated, and when native-born Americans were taken, it became incensed. Impressment, Secretary of State Madison said in 1807, was "anomalous in principle . . . grievous in practice, and . . . abominable in

▲ Completed in 1797, the 44-gun *Constitution*, one of the largest ships in the U.S. Navy, was no match for the largest British warships, which had twice as many cannon. The *Constitution*'s subsequent success (and the reason that it was preserved) was largely due to the skill of American captains and sailors.

abuse." Between 1803 and 1812 at least 5000 sailors were snatched from the decks of United States vessels and forced to serve in the Royal Navy. Most of them—estimates run as high as three out of every four—were Americans.

The British did not claim the right to impress native-born Americans, and when it could be proved that boarding officers had done so, the men in question were released by higher authority. During the course of the controversy, the British authorities freed 3800 impressed Americans, which suggests that many more were seized. However, the British refused to abandon impressment. "The Pretension advanced by Mr. Madison that the American Flag should protect every Individual sailing under it," one British foreign secretary explained, "is too extravagant to require any serious Refutation."

The combination of impressment, British interference with the reexport trade, and the general harassment of neutral commerce instituted by both Great Britain and France would have perplexed the most informed and hardheaded of leaders, and in dealing with these problems Jefferson was neither informed nor hardheaded. He believed it much wiser to stand up for one's rights than to compromise, yet he hated the very thought of war. Perhaps, being a Southerner, he was less sensitive than he might have been to the needs of New England commercial interests. While the American merchant fleet passed 600,000 tons and continued to grow at an annual rate of over 10 percent, Jefferson kept only a skeleton navy on active service, despite the fact that the great powers were fighting a worldwide, no-holds-barred

war. Instead of building a navy that other nations would have to respect, he relied on a tiny fleet of frigates and a swarm of gunboats that were useless against the Royal Navy—" a macabre monument," in the words of one historian, "to his hasty, ill-digested ideas" about defense.[3]

THE EMBARGO ACT

The frailty of Jefferson's policy became obvious once the warring powers began to attack neutral shipping in earnest. Between 1803 and 1807 the British seized more than 500 American ships, Napoleon more than 200 more. The United States could do nothing.

The ultimate in frustration came on June 22, 1807, off Norfolk, Virginia. The American 46-gun frigate *Chesapeake* had just left port for patrol duty in the Mediterranean. Among its crew were a British sailor who had deserted from HMS *Halifax* and three Americans who had been illegally impressed by the captain of HMS *Melampus* and had later escaped. The *Chesapeake* was barely out of sight of land when HMS *Leopard* (56 guns) approached and signaled it to heave to. Thinking that *Leopard* wanted to make some routine communication, Captain James Barron did so. A British officer came aboard and demanded that the four "deserters" be handed over to him. Barron refused, whereupon as soon as the officer was back on board, *Leopard* opened fire on the unsuspecting American ship, killing three sailors. Barron had to surrender. The "deserters" were seized, and then the crippled *Chesapeake* was allowed to limp back to port.

The attack was in violation of international law, for no nation claimed the right to impress sailors from warships. The British government admitted this, though it delayed making restitution for years. The American press clamored for war, but the country had nothing to fight with. Jefferson contented himself with ordering British warships out of American territorial waters. However, he was determined to put a stop to the indignities being heaped on the flag by Great Britain and France. The result was the Embargo Act.

---

[3]The gunboats had performed effectively against the Barbary pirates, but Jefferson was enamored of them mainly because they were cheap. A gunboat cost about $10,000 to build, a frigate well over $300,000.

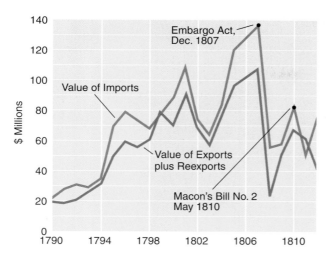

▲ American Foreign Trade, 1790–1812
The embargo's effects are shown graphically here. The space between the upper (import) and the lower (export) line indicates a persistent foreign-trade deficit.

The Embargo Act prohibited all exports. American vessels could not clear for any foreign port, and foreign vessels could do so only if empty. Importing was not forbidden, but few foreign ships would come to the United States if they had to return without a cargo. Although the law was sure to injure the American economy, Jefferson hoped that it would work in two ways to benefit the nation. By keeping U.S. merchant ships off the seas, it would end all chance of injury to them and to the national honor. By cutting off American goods and markets, it would put great economic pressure on Britain and France to moderate policies toward American shipping. The fact that boycotts had repeatedly wrested concessions from the British during the crises preceding the Revolution was certainly in Jefferson's mind when he devised the embargo.

Seldom has a law been so bitterly resented and resisted by a large segment of the public. It demanded of the maritime interests far greater sacrifices than they could reasonably be expected to make. Massachusetts-owned ships alone were earning over $15 million a year in freight charges by 1807, and Bay State merchants w0ere making far larger gains from the buying and selling of goods. Foreign commerce was the most expansive force in the economy,

the chief reason for the nation's prosperity. As John Randolph remarked in a typical sally, the administration was trying "to cure the corns by cutting off the toes."

The Embargo Act had catastrophic effects. Exports fell from $108 million in 1807 to $22 million in 1808, imports from $138 million to less than $57 million. Prices of farm products and manufactured goods reacted violently; seamen were thrown out of work; merchants found their businesses disrupted.

How many Americans violated the law is difficult to determine, but they were ingenious at discovering ways to do so. The most obvious way was to smuggle goods back and forth between Canada and the northeastern states. As James Madison recalled in later years, the political boundary lost all significance. People on both sides made the region "a world of itself," treating the Embargo Act as though the laws of Congress did not apply to them.

As for ocean commerce, American ships made hastily for blue water before the machinery of enforcement could be put into operation, not to return until the law was repealed. Shipping between American ports had not been outlawed, and coasting vessels were allowed to put into foreign ports when in distress. Suddenly, mysterious storms began to drive experienced skippers leagues off their courses, some as far as Europe. The brig *Commerce* en route from Massachusetts to New Orleans, was "forced" by a shortage of water to make for Havana. Having replenished its casks, the brig exchanged its cargo for sugar.

▲ The Ograbme ("embargo" spelled backward), a unique snapping turtle created by cartoonist Alexander Anderson, effectively frustrates an American tobacco smuggler.

▲ The East India Wharf in Salem, Massachusetts in 1806. One of the richest cities in the nation, Salem had a fleet of 200 ships and thirty wharves. Its wealth was chiefly derived from a trade in tea and textiles with India.

The law permitted merchants with property abroad to send ships to fetch it. About 800 ships went off on such errands. Lawbreakers were difficult to punish. In the seaport towns juries were no more willing to convict anyone of violating the Embargo Act than their fathers had been to convict those charged with violating the Townshend Acts. A mob at Gloucester, Massachusetts, destroyed a revenue cutter in the same spirit that Rhode Islanders exhibited in 1772 when they burned the *Gaspee*.

Surely the embargo was a mistake. The United States ought either to have suffered the indignities heaped on its vessels for the sake of profits or, by constructing a powerful navy, made it dangerous for the belligerents to treat its merchant ships so roughly. Jefferson was too proud to choose the former alternative, too parsimonious to choose the latter. Instead he applied harsher and harsher regulations in a futile effort

to accomplish his purpose. Militiamen patrolled the Canadian border; revenuers searched out smuggled goods without proper warrants. The illegal trade continued, and in his last months as president Jefferson simply gave up. Even then he would not admit that the embargo was a fiasco and urge its repeal. Only in Jefferson's last week in office did a leaderless Congress finally abolish it, substituting the Non-Intercourse Act, which forbade trade only with Great Britain and France and authorized the president to end the boycott against either power by proclamation when and if it stopped violating the rights of Americans.

Thus Jefferson's political career ended on a sour note. Several weeks after he had left office and returned to Monticello, he privately advised his successor, James Madison, to trust his own judgment to govern because the people readily succumbed to "the floating lies of the day."

MILESTONES

1800	Jefferson is elected president (Revolution of 1800)	**1804–1806**	Lewis and Clark explore West
1801	Judiciary Act of 1801 allows Adams to appoint many Federalist judges	**1806**	Aaron Burr schemes to take land in West during Burr Conspiracy
1801–1805	U.S. wages war against Barbary pirates in North Africa	**1806–1807**	Napoleon issues Berlin and Milan decrees in order to disrupt British shipping and economy
1803	Supreme Court declares part of Judiciary Act of 1789 unconstitutional (*Marbury* v. *Madison*)	**1807**	HMS *Leopard* attacks USS *Chesapeake*
	Jefferson negotiates Louisiana Purchase with France		Embargo Act prohibits all exports
1804	Aaron Burr kills Alexander Hamilton in duel	**1809**	Non-Intercourse Act forbids trade with Great Britain and France
	Jefferson is reelected		

SUPPLEMENTARY READING

No student interested in Jefferson's political and social philosophy should miss sampling his writings. A useful compilation is Merrill D. Peterson, ed., *Thomas Jefferson* (1984). Lance Banning, *The Jeffersonian Persuasion* (1978), is valuable, as are the books on Jefferson mentioned in Debating the Past (p. 171).

For the election of 1800, see Bernard A. Weisberger, *America Afire* (2000). Arnold Rogow, *Fatal Friendship* (1998), describes the relationship of Hamilton and Burr; see also Joanne B. Freeman, *Affairs of Honor* (2001) on politics and dueling more generally.

For a general treatment of the Jeffersonian era, consult Marshall Smelser, *The Democratic Republic* (1968). On the parties of the era, see James Roger Sharp, *American Politics in the Early Republic* (1993) and N. E. Cunningham, Jr., *The Jeffersonian Republicans in Power* (1963); a useful monograph is Anthony F. C. Wallace, *Jefferson and the Indians* (1999).

Jefferson's battle with the judges can be followed in R. E. Ellis, *The Jeffersonian Crisis* (1971). For *Marbury* v. *Madison*, see J. A. Garraty, ed., *Quarrels That Have Shaped the Constitution* (1964), and D. O. Dewey's more detailed *Marshall Versus Jefferson* (1970) as well as R. Kent Newmeyer, *John Marshall and the Heroic Age of the Supreme Court* (2001).

Thomas Fleming, *The Louisiana Purchase* (2003) is a brief, clear account; Jon Kukla, *A Wilderness So Immense: The Louisiana Purchase and the Destiny of America* (2003) argues that the region was acquired chiefly as a place for resettling Indians.

An excellent general treatment of western exploration is contained in R. A. Billington, *Westward Expansion* (1967). On Lewis and Clark, see Stephen E. Ambrose, *Undaunted Courage* (1996). Thomas P. Slaughter, *Exploring Lewis and Clark* (2003) is a scholarly examination of the explorers' writings.

The best account of the neutral rights question is Bradford Perkins, *Prologue to War* (1961).

SUGGESTED WEBSITES

Thomas Jefferson

http://www.pbs.org/jefferson/

This site, the companion to the PBS series on Jefferson, includes material on how people understand Jefferson today.

Lewis and Clark—The PBS Website

http://www.pbs.org/lewisandclark

This is a companion site to Ken Burns's film, containing a timeline of the expedition, a collection of related links, a bibliography, and more than 800 minutes of unedited, full-length Real Player interviews with seven experts featured in the film.

Thomas Jefferson Resources Online

http://etext.virginia.edu/jefferson/

"Mr. Jefferson's University," The University of Virginia, provides resources about Jefferson and his times.

The Jefferson Home

http://www.monticello.org/

This site explores Jefferson's gifted mind through an examination of Monticello, Jefferson's unique home.

▼ "Hail, Bright Aurora" (c.1815), by an unknown artist. Aurora, the goddess of dawn, represents the ascent of the American nation. The metaphor may have come from the poem, "An Hymn to the Morning," by Phyllis Wheatley, a black slave: "Aurora hail, and all the thousand dies/ Which deck thy progress through the vaulted skies."

CHAPTER CONTENTS

MADISON IN POWER

It is a measure of Jefferson's popularity and of the political ineptitude of the Federalists that the Republicans won the election of 1808 handily despite the embargo. James Madison got 122 of the 173 electoral votes for the presidency, and the party carried both houses of Congress, although by reduced majorities.

In his inaugural address, Madison observed that the "present situation" of the United States was "full of difficulties" and that war continued to rage among European powers. Yet he assumed the presidency, he said, "with no other discouragement than what springs from my own inadequacy." The content of the speech was as modest as its delivery; virtually no one could hear it.

Madison, First
Inaugural
Address

Madison was a small, neat, rather precise person, narrower in his interests than Jefferson but in many ways a deeper thinker. He was more conscientious in the performance of his duties and more consistent in adhering to his principles. Ideologically, however, they were as close as two active and intelligent people could be. Madison had no better solution to offer for the problem of the hour than had Jefferson. The Non-Intercourse Act proved difficult to enforce—once an American ship left port, there was no way to prevent the skipper from steering for England or France—and it exerted little economic pressure on the British, who continued to seize American vessels.

Late in 1809, at the urging of Secretary of the Treasury Gallatin, who was concerned because the government was operating at a deficit, Representative Nathaniel Macon of North Carolina introduced a bill permitting American ships to go anywhere but closing United States ports to the ships of Britain and France. After protracted bickering in Congress, this measure was replaced by another, known as Macon's Bill No. 2, which removed all restrictions on commerce with France and Britain, although French and British warships were still barred from American waters. The bill authorized the president to reapply the principle of nonintercourse to either of the major powers if the other should "cease to violate the neutral commerce of the United States." This bill became law in May 1810.

The volume of United States commerce with the British Isles swiftly zoomed to pre-embargo levels. Trade with France remained much more limited because of the British fleet. Napoleon therefore announced that the Berlin and Milan decrees would be revoked in November with the understanding that Great Britain would abandon its own restrictive policies. Treating this ambiguous proposal as a statement of French policy (which it decidedly was not), and hoping to win concessions from the British, Madison reapplied the nonintercourse policy to Great Britain. Napoleon, having thus tricked Madison into closing American ports to British ships and goods, continued to seize American ships and cargoes whenever it suited him to do so.

The British grimly refused to modify the Orders in Council unless it could be shown that the French had actually repealed the Berlin and Milan decrees—and this despite mounting complaints from their own businessmen that the new American nonimportation policy was cutting off a major market for their manufactures. Madison, on the other hand, could not afford either to admit that Napoleon had deceived him or to reverse American policy still another time. Reluctantly he came to the conclusion that unless Britain repealed the Orders, the United States must declare war.

TECUMSEH AND INDIAN RESISTANCE

There were other reasons for fighting besides British violations of neutral rights. The Indians were again restive, and western farmers believed that the British in Canada were egging them on. This had been true in the past but was no longer the case in 1811 and 1812. American domination of the southern Great Lakes region was no longer in question. Canadian officials had no desire to force a showdown between the Indians and the Americans, for that could have but one result. Aware of their own vulnerability, the Canadians wanted to preserve Indian strength in case war should break out between Great Britain and the United States.

Pennsylvania
Gazette, "Indian
hostilities"

American political leaders tended to believe that Indians should be encouraged to become farmers and to copy the "civilized" ways of whites. However, no government had been able to control the frontiersmen, who by bribery, trickery, and force were driving the tribes back year after year from the rich lands of the Ohio Valley. General William Henry Harrison, governor of the Indiana Territory, a tough, relentless soldier, kept constant pressure on them. He wrested land from one tribe by promising it aid against a traditional enemy, from another as a penalty for having murdered a white man, from others by corrupting a few chiefs. Harrison justified his sordid behavior by citing the end in view—that "one of the fairest portions of the globe" be secured as "the seat of civilization, of science, and of true religion." The "wretched savages" should not be allowed to stand in the path of this worthy objective. As early as 1805 it was clear that unless something drastic was done, Harrison's aggressiveness, together with the corroding effects of white civilization, would soon obliterate the tribes.

At this point the Shawnee chief, Tecumseh, made a bold and imaginative effort to reverse the trend by binding all the tribes east of the Mississippi into a great confederation. Traveling from the Wisconsin country to the Floridas, he persuaded tribe after tribe to join him. "Let the white race perish," Tecumseh declared. "They seize your land; they corrupt your women. . . . Back whence they came, upon a trail of blood, they must be driven!"

To Tecumseh's political movement his brother Tenskwatawa, known as "The Prophet," added the force of a moral crusade. Instead of aping white customs, the Prophet said, Indians must give up white ways, white clothes, and white liquor and reinvigorate their own culture. Ceding lands to the whites must stop because the Great Spirit intended that the land be used in common by all.

▲ As a young man Tecumseh *(left)* was a superb hunter and warrior; his younger brother, Tenskwatawa *(right)* was awkward and inept with weapons; he accidentally gouged out his right eye with an arrow. In 1805 he had a religious vision, became known as "The Prophet," and inspired Tecumseh's warriors.

The Prophet was a fanatic who saw visions and claimed to be able to control the movement of heavenly bodies. Tecumseh, however, possessed true genius. A powerful orator and a great organizer, he had deep insight into the needs of his people. Harrison himself said of Tecumseh: "He is one of those uncommon geniuses which spring up occasionally to produce revolutions and overturn the established order of things." The two brothers made a formidable team. By 1811 thousands of Indians were organizing to drive the whites off their lands. Alarms swept through the West.

With about a thousand soldiers, General Harrison marched boldly against the brothers' camp at Prophetstown, where Tippecanoe Creek joins the Wabash, in Indiana. Tecumseh was away recruiting men, and the Prophet recklessly ordered an assault on Harrison's camp outside the village on November 7, 1811. When the white soldiers held their ground despite the Prophet's magic, the Indians lost confidence and fell back. Harrison then destroyed Prophetstown.

While the Battle of Tippecanoe was pretty much a draw, it disillusioned the Indians and shattered their confederation. Frontier warfare continued, but in the disorganized manner of former times. Like all such fighting it was brutal and bloody.

Unwilling as usual to admit that their own excesses were the chief cause of the trouble, the settlers directed their resentment at the British in Canada. "This combination headed by the Shawanese prophet is a British scheme," a resolution adopted by the citizens of Vincennes, Indiana, proclaimed. As a result, the cry for war with Great Britain rang along the frontier.

DEPRESSION AND LAND HUNGER

Some Westerners pressed for war because they were suffering an agricultural depression. The prices they received for their wheat, tobacco, and other products in the markets of New Orleans were falling, and they attributed the decline to the loss of foreign markets and the depredations of the British. American commercial restrictions had more to do with the western depression than the British, and in any case the slow and cumbersome transportation and distribution system that western farmers were saddled with was the major cause of their difficulties. But the farmers were no more inclined to accept these explanations than they were to absolve the British from responsibility for the Indian difficulties. If only the seas were free,

DEBATING THE PAST

How did Indians and settlers interact? Two Indians *(above)* gaze at a frontier settlement. In 1893 historian Frederick Jackson Turner, the most important historian of his era, credited frontier conditions for creating the stalwart individualists that made the United States distinctive. In his view, the frontier had not been a particular zone or region, but "the outer edge of the wave—the meeting point between savagery and civilization." The nature of the interaction between Indians and settlers was one-sided: the Indians fell back. But in recent decades, historians have challenged this concept not only because it disparaged Indian societies and cultures, but also because it ignored the many ways in which Indians and settlers interacted. Abandoning the concept of an Indian-settler frontier, Richard White (1991) described a "middle ground" and James Merrell (1999) the "edge of the woods," a region where Indians and settlers resolved disputes, traded goods, and exchanged ideas. The concept of a "middle ground" put Indians and settlers on equal footing. But that also may be its chief difficulty. Daniel K. Richter (2001) and Jane T. Merritt (2003) showed that while Indians preferred to co-exist with the settlers rather than fight them, by the eighteenth century raw power prevailed—as did, usually, the settlers.

Frederick Jackson Turner, "The Significance of the Frontier in American History" (1893), Patricka Nelson Limerick, *The Legacy of Conquest* (1987), Richard White, *The Middle Ground* (1991), James Merrell, *Into the Woods* (1999), Daniel K. Richter, *Facing East from Indian Country* (2001), Gregory H. Nobles, *American Frontiers* (1997), Jane T. Merritt, *At the Crossroads* (2003).

they reasoned, costs would go down, prices would rise, and prosperity would return.

To some extent western expansionism also heightened the war fever. The West contained immense tracts of virgin land, but Westerners wanted more. Canada would surely fall to American arms in the event of war, the frontiersmen believed. So, apparently, would Florida, for Spain was now Britain's ally. Florida in itself provided no cause for a war, for it was sure to fall into American hands before long. In 1810

Madison had snapped up the extreme western section without eliciting any effective response from Spain.

So it was primarily because of Canada, nearby and presumably vulnerable, that Westerners wanted war. President Madison probably regarded an attack on Canada as a way to force the British to respect neutral rights. Still more important in Madison's mind, if the United States conquered Canada, Britain's hope of obtaining food in Canada for its West Indian sugar islands would be shattered. Then it would have to end its hateful assaults and restrictions on American merchant ships or the islands' economy would collapse.

But Westerners, and many Easterners too, were more patriots than imperialists or merchants in 1811 and 1812. When the "War Hawks" (their young leaders in Congress) called for war against Great Britain, they did so because they saw no other way to defend the national honor and force repeal of the Orders in Council. The choice seemed to lie between war and surrender of true independence. As Madison put it, to bow to British policy would be to "recolonize" American foreign commerce.

OPPONENTS OF WAR

Large numbers of people, however, thought that a war against Great Britain would be a national calamity. Some Federalists would have resisted anything the administration proposed; Congressman Josiah Quincy of Massachusetts declared that he "could not be kicked" into the war, which he considered a cowardly, futile, and unconstitutional business designed primarily to ensure the reelection of Madison. (Quincy saw no inconsistency between this opinion and his conviction that Madison was a pacifist.) According to Quincy the War Hawks were "backwoodsmen" willing to wage a "cruel, wanton, senseless and wicked" war in order to swallow up Canada.

But other people based their objections on economics and a healthy realism. No shipowner could view with equanimity the idea of taking on the largest navy in the world. Such persons complained sincerely enough about impressment and the Orders in Council, but war seemed worse to them by far. Self-interest led them to urge patience.

Such a policy would have been wise, for Great Britain did not represent a real threat to the United States. British naval officers were high-handed, officials in London complacent, British diplomats in Washington second-rate and obtuse. Yet language, culture, and strong economic ties bound the two countries. Napoleon, on the other hand, represented a tremendous potential danger. He had offhandedly turned over Louisiana, but even Jefferson, the chief beneficiary of his largess, hated everything he stood for. Jefferson called Napoleon "an unprincipled tyrant who is deluging the continent of Europe with blood."

No one understood the Napoleonic danger to America more clearly than the British; part of the stubbornness and arrogance of their maritime policy grew out of their conviction that Napoleon was a threat to all free nations. The *Times* of London declared: "The Alps and the Apennines of America are the British Navy. If ever that should be removed, a short time will suffice to establish the headquarters of a [French] Duke-Marshal at Washington." Yet by going to war with Britain, the United States was aiding Napoleon.

What made the situation even more unfortunate was the fact that by 1812 conditions had changed in England in a way that made a softening of British maritime policy likely. A depression caused chiefly by the increasing effectiveness of Napoleon's Continental System was plaguing the country. Manufacturers, blaming the slump on the loss of American markets, were urging repeal of the Orders in Council. Gradually, though with exasperating slowness, the government prepared to yield. On June 23, after a change of ministries, the new foreign secretary, Lord Castlereagh, suspended the Orders. Five days earlier, alas, the United States had declared war.

THE WAR OF 1812

The illogic of the War Hawks in pressing for a fight was exceeded only by their ineffectiveness in planning and managing the struggle. By what possible strategy could the ostensible objective of the war be achieved? To construct a navy capable of challenging the British fleet would have been the work of many years and a more expensive proposition than the War Hawks were willing to consider. So hopeless was that prospect that Congress failed to undertake any new construction in the first year of the conflict. Several hundred merchant ships lashed a few cannon to their decks and sailed off as privateers to attack British commerce. The navy's seven modern frigates, built during the war scare after the XYZ affair, put to sea. But these forces could make no pretense of disputing Britain's mastery of the Atlantic.

For a brief moment the American frigates held center stage, for they were faster, tougher, larger, and more powerfully armed than their British counterparts. Barely two months after the declaration of war, Captain Isaac Hull in USS *Constitution* chanced upon HMS *Guerrière* in mid-Atlantic, outmaneuvered *Guerrière* brilliantly, brought down its mizzenmast with his first volley, and then gunned it into submission, a hopeless wreck. In October USS *United States,* captained by Stephen Decatur, hero of the war against the Barbary pirates, caught HMS *Macedonian* off the Madeiras, pounded it unmercifully at long range, and forced the British ship to surrender. *Macedonian* was taken into New London as a prize; over a third of the 300-man crew were casualties, while American losses were but a dozen. Then, in December, *Constitution*, now under Captain William Bainbridge, took on the British frigate *Java* off Brazil. "Old Ironsides" shot away *Java's* mainmast and reduced it to a hulk too battered for salvage.

Dec. 14: American Gunboats Destroyed

Dec. 13: British Fleet Arrives, Troops Sent to Sieze Outlying Islands and Forts

Nov. 11: Jackson Returns from Pensacola Operation, Leaving for New Orleans Nov. 22, Almost All of His Troops Are Left in Mobile Under Winchester's Command

Lake Pontchartrain

New Orleans

Jackson's Final Position

Pearl River

Mobile

Dec. 24: Night Battle

Lake of the Quatches

Lake Borgne

Dec. 23: British Land, Jan. 27: British Withdraw Troops

L o u i s i a n a

Mobile Bay

North Chandeleur Is.

FORT ST PHILLIP

Jan. 8–18: Secondary Attack Fails

Breton Is.

M e x i c o

South Chandeleur Is.

Gulf

British New Orleans Campaign, November 22, 1814– February 11, 1815

→ British Advance
→ Jackson's Night Attack
--→ British Withdrawal

▦ Fort
⚓ Fortification

0   15 km
0   15 miles

Nova Scotia

UPPER CANADA

Maine

Lake Champlain

Plattsburg

Vermont   N. H.

→ U.S. and British Movements, 1812
→ U.S. and British Movements, 1813
→ U.S. and British Movements, 1814–1815
⛵ British Blockade
✕ Battle

Indiana Territory

Fort Mackinac

Lake Huron

Oswego

Lake Ontario

Albany

Massachusetts

Battle of the Thames

Fort Niagara

Buffalo

Conn.

R.I.

Michigan Territory

Detroit

Lake Erie

Erie

New York

New York

Lake Michigan

Cleveland

Pennsylvania

Philadelphia

Fort Dearborn

Ohio

Baltimore

New Jersey

Maryland

Delaware

Indiana Territory

Washington

45°

Cincinnati

Virginia

Norfolk

Kentucky

Tennessee

North Carolina

Missouri Territory

South Carolina

Huntsville

ATLANTIC OCEAN

Charleston

Mississippi Territory

Georgia

Vicksburg

Savannah

Louisiana

Mobile

Pensacola

St. Augustine

New Orleans

Florida (Spain.)

30°

Gulf of Mexico

0   300 Kilometers
0   300 Miles

90°

80°

▲ **The War of 1812**

These victories had little influence on the outcome of the war. The Royal Navy had 34 frigates, 7 more powerful ships of the line, and dozens of smaller vessels. As soon as these forces could concentrate against them, the American frigates were immobilized, forced to spend the war gathering barnacles at their moorings while powerful British squadrons ranged offshore. The privateering merchantmen were more effective because they were so numerous; they captured more than 1300 British vessels during the war. The best of them—vessels like *America* and *True-Blooded Yankee*—were redesigned, given more sail to increase their speed, and formidably armed. *America* captured 26 prizes valued at more than a million dollars. *True-Blooded Yankee* took 27 vessels and destroyed 7 more in a Scottish harbor.

Great Britain's one weak spot seemed to be Canada. The colony had but half a million inhabitants to oppose 7.5 million Americans. Only 2257 British regulars guarded the long border from Montréal to Detroit. The Canadian militia was feeble, and many of its members, being American-born, sympathized with the "invaders." According to the War Hawk congressman Henry Clay of Kentucky, the West was one solid horde of ferocious frontiersmen, armed to the teeth and thirsting for Canadian blood. Yet such talk was mostly brag and bluster; when Congress authorized increasing the army by 25,000 men, Kentucky produced 400 enlistments.

American military leadership proved extremely disappointing. Madison showed poor judgment by relying on officers who had served with distinction in the Revolution. In most cases, as one biographer suggested, their abilities "appeared to have evaporated with age and long disuse." Instead of a concentrated strike against Canada's St. Lawrence River lifeline, which would have isolated Upper Canada, the generals planned a complicated three-pronged attack. It failed dismally. In July 1812 General William Hull, veteran of the battles of Trenton, Saratoga, and Monmouth and now governor of the Michigan Territory, marched forth with 2200 men against the Canadian positions facing Detroit. Hoping that the Canadian militia would desert, he delayed his assault, only to find his communications threatened by hostile Indians led by Tecumseh. Hastily he retreated to Detroit, and when the Canadians, under General Isaac Brock, pursued him, he surrendered the fort without firing a shot! In October another force attempted to invade Canada from Fort Niagara. After an initial success it was crushed by superior numbers, while a large contingent of New York militiamen watched from the east bank of the Niagara River, unwilling to fight outside their own state.

▲ With a few exceptions, American forces in the War of 1812 were ill-trained and ill-led, and poor strategy resulted in several disgraceful defeats. Here, a resplendently dressed militia officer consults a map.

The third arm of the American "attack" was equally unsuccessful. Major General Henry Dearborn, who had fought honorably in the Revolution from Bunker Hill to Yorktown, but who had now grown so fat that he needed a specially designed cart to get from place to place, set out from Plattsburgh, New York, at the head of an army of militiamen. Their objective was Montréal, but when they reached the border, the troops refused to cross. Dearborn meekly marched them back to Plattsburgh.

Meanwhile, the British had captured Fort Michilimackinac in northern Michigan, and the Indians had taken Fort Dearborn (now Chicago), massacring 85 captives. Instead of sweeping triumphantly through Canada, the Americans found themselves trying desperately to keep the Canadians out of Ohio.

Stirred by these disasters, Westerners rallied somewhat in 1813. General Harrison, the victor of

▲ In the heat of the Battle of Lake Erie, Perry had to abandon his flagship, the *Lawrence,* which had been shot to pieces by enemy fire. (Over three-fourths of the ship's crew were killed or wounded.) He was rowed to the *Niagara,* from which he directed the rest of the engagement.

Tippecanoe, headed an army of Kentuckians in a series of inconclusive battles against British troops and Indians led by Tecumseh. He found it impossible to recapture Detroit because a British squadron controlling Lake Erie threatened his communications. President Madison therefore assigned Captain Oliver Hazard Perry to the task of building a fleet to challenge this force. In September 1813, at Put-in-Bay near the western end of the lake, Perry destroyed the British vessels in a bloody battle in which 85 of the 103 men on Perry's flagship were casualties. "We have met the enemy and they are ours," he reported. About a quarter of Perry's 400 men were blacks, which led him to remark that "the color of a man's skin" was no more an indication of his worth than "the cut and trimmings" of his coat. With the Americans in control of Lake Erie, Detroit became untenable for the British, and when they fell back, Harrison gave chase and defeated them at the Thames River, some 60 miles northeast of Detroit. Although little more than a skirmish, this battle had large repercussions. Tecumseh

was among the dead (an eccentric American colonel, Richard Mentor Johnson, was to base a long and successful political career, culminating in his election as vice president of the United States in 1836, on his claim of having personally done in the great chief), and without him the Indians lost heart. But American attempts to win control of Lake Ontario and to invade Canada in the Niagara region were again thrown back. Late in 1813 the British captured Fort Niagara and burned the town of Buffalo. The conquest of Canada was as far from realization as ever.

The British fleet had intensified its blockade of American ports, extending its operations to New England waters previously spared to encourage the antiwar sentiments of local maritime interests. All along the coast, patrolling cruisers, contemptuous of Jefferson's puny gunboats, captured small craft, raided shore points to commandeer provisions, and collected ransom from port towns by threatening to bombard them. One captain even sent a detail ashore to dig potatoes for his ship's mess.

BRITAIN ASSUMES THE OFFENSIVE

Until 1814 the British put relatively little effort into the American war, being concerned primarily with the struggle against Napoleon. However, in 1812 Napoleon had invaded Russia and been thrown back; thereafter, one by one, his European satellites rose against him. Gradually he relinquished his conquests; the Allies—his enemies—marched into France, Paris fell, and in April 1814 the emperor abdicated. Then the British, free to strike hard at the United States, dispatched some 14,000 veterans to Canada.

By the spring of 1814 British strategists had devised a master plan for crushing the United States. One army, 11,000 strong, was to march from Montréal, tracing the route that General Burgoyne had followed to disaster in the Revolution. A smaller amphibious force was to make a feint at the Chesapeake Bay area, destroying coastal towns and threatening Washington and Baltimore. A third army was to assemble at Jamaica and sail to attack New Orleans and bottle up the West.

It is necessary, in considering the War of 1812, to remind oneself repeatedly that in the course of the conflict many brave young men lost their lives. Without this sobering reflection it would be easy to dismiss the conflict as a great farce compounded of stupidity, incompetence, and brag. The British, despite their years of experience against Napoleon, were scarcely more effective than the Americans when they assumed the offensive. They achieved significant success only in the diversionary attack in the Chesapeake Bay area.

While the main British army was assembling in Canada, some 4000 veterans under General Robert Ross sailed from Bermuda for the Chesapeake. After making a rendezvous with a fleet commanded by Vice Admiral Sir Alexander Cochrane and Rear Admiral Sir George Cockburn, which had been terrorizing the coast, they landed in Maryland at the mouth of the Patuxent River, southeast of Washington. A squadron of gunboats "protecting" the capital promptly withdrew upstream; when the British pursued, their commander ordered them blown up to keep them from being captured.

DOCUMENT

Dolley Payne Madison to Lucy Payne Todd

The British troops marched rapidly toward Washington. At Bladensburg, on the outskirts of the city, they came upon an army twice their number, commanded by General William H. Winder, a Baltimore lawyer who had already been captured and released by the British in the Canadian fighting. While President Madison and other officials watched, the British charged—and Winder's army turned tail almost without firing a shot. The British swarmed into the capital and put most public buildings to the torch. Before personally setting fire to the White House, Admiral Cockburn took one of the president's hats and a cushion from Dolley Madison's chair as souvenirs, and, finding the table set for dinner, derisively drank a toast to "Jemmy's health," adding, an observer coyly recalled, "pleasantries too vulgar for me to repeat."

This was the sum of the British success. When they attempted to take Baltimore, they were stopped by a formidable line of defenses devised by General Samuel Smith, a militia officer. General Ross fell in the attack. The fleet then moved up the Patapsco River and pounded Fort McHenry with its cannon, raining 1800 shells upon it in a 25-hour bombardment on September 13 and 14.

"THE STAR SPANGLED BANNER"

While this attack was in progress, an American civilian, Francis Scott Key, who had been temporarily detained on one of the British ships, watched anxiously through the night. Key had boarded the vessel before the attack in an effort to obtain the release of an American doctor who had been taken into custody in Washington. As twilight faded, Key had seen the Stars and Stripes flying proudly over the battered fort. During the night the glare of rockets and bursting of bombs gave proof that the defenders were holding out. Then, by the first light of the new day, Key saw again the flag, still waving over Fort McHenry. Drawing an old letter from his pocket, he dashed off the words to "The Star Spangled Banner," which, when set to music, was to become the national anthem of the United States.

To Key that dawn seemed a turning point in the war. He was roughly correct, for in those last weeks of the summer of 1814 the struggle began to move toward resolution. Unable to crack the defenses of Baltimore, the British withdrew to their ships; shortly after, they sailed to Jamaica to join the forces preparing to attack New Orleans.

The destruction of Washington had been a profound shock. Thousands came forward to enlist in the army. The new determination and spirit were strengthened by news from the northern front, where General Sir George Prevost had been leading the main British invasion force south from Montréal. At Plattsburgh, on the western shore of Lake Champlain, his 1000 Redcoats came up against a well-designed defense line manned by 3300 Americans under General Alexander Macomb. Prevost called up his supporting fleet of four ships and a dozen gunboats. An American fleet of roughly similar strength under Captain Thomas Macdonough, a youthful officer who had served with Decatur against the Barbary pirates, came forward to oppose the British. On September 11, in a

▲ *The Bombardment of Fort McHenry* by John Bower, with the Stars and Stripes flying over the fort *(center)*. The British fleet fired 1800 bombs and red-glaring incendiary rockets. The fort did not return fire because the British ships were beyond the range of its cannon. Although "The Star Spangled Banner" celebrates the "home of the brave," the defenders of Fort McHenry sensibly fled the ramparts and took cover below during the bombardment; they sustained only 30 casualties.

brutal battle at point-blank range, Macdonough destroyed the British ships and drove off the gunboats. With the Americans now threatening his flank, Prevost lost heart and retreated to Canada.

THE TREATY OF GHENT

The war might as well have ended with the battles of Plattsburgh, Washington, and Baltimore, for later military developments had no effect on the outcome. Earlier in 1814 both sides had agreed to discuss peace terms. Commissioners were appointed and negotiations begun during the summer at Ghent, in Belgium. The American delegation consisted of former secretary of the treasury Albert Gallatin; Speaker Henry Clay of the House of Representatives; James A. Bayard, a former senator; and two veteran diplomats, Jonathan Russell, minister to Sweden, and John Quincy Adams, minister to Russia. Adams was chairman. The British commissioners were lesser men by far, partly because they could refer important questions to the Foreign Office in nearby London

for decision and partly because Britain's topflight diplomats were engaged in settling the future of Europe at the Congress of Vienna.

The talks at Ghent were drawn out and frustrating. The British were in no hurry to sign a treaty, believing that their three-pronged offensive in 1814 would swing the balance in their favor. They demanded at first that the United States abandon practically all the Northwest Territory to the Indians and cede other points along the northern border to Canada. On the issues of impressment and neutral rights, they would make no concessions at all. The Americans would yield no territory, for public opinion at home would have been outraged if they had. Old John Adams, for example, told President Madison at this time, "I would continue this war forever rather than surrender an acre. . . ."

Fortunately, the British came to realize that by pressing this point they would only spur the Americans to fight on. News of the defeat at Plattsburgh modified their ambitions, and when the Duke of Wellington advised that from a military point of view they had no

DOCUMENT

The Treaty of Ghent

case for territorial concessions so long as the United States controlled the Great Lakes, they agreed to settle for *status quo ante bellum,* to leave things as they were before the war. The other issues, everyone suddenly realized, had simply evaporated. The mighty war triggered by the French Revolution seemed finally over. The seas were free to all ships, and the Royal Navy no longer had need to snatch sailors from the vessels of the United States or of any other power. On Christmas Eve 1814 the treaty, which merely ended the state of hostilities, was signed. Although, like other members of his family, he was not noted for tact, John Quincy Adams rose to the spirit of the occasion. "I hope," he said, "it will be the last treaty of peace between Great Britain and the United States." And so it was.

THE HARTFORD CONVENTION

Before news of the treaty could cross the Atlantic, two events took place that had important effects but that would not have occurred had the news reached America more rapidly. The first was the Hartford Convention, a meeting of New England Federalists held in December 1814 and January 1815 to protest the war and to plan for a convention of the states to revise the Constitution.

Sentiment in New England had opposed the war from the beginning. The governor of Massachusetts titled his annual address in 1813 "On the Present Unhappy War," and the General Court went on record calling the conflict "impolitic, improper, and unjust." The Federalist party had been quick to employ the discontent to revive its fortunes. Federalist-controlled state administrations refused to provide militia to aid in the fight and discouraged individuals and banks from lending money to the hard-pressed national government. Trade with the enemy flourished as long as the British fleet did not crack down on New England ports, and goods flowed across the Canadian line in as great or greater volume as during Jefferson's embargo.

Their attitude toward the war made the Federalists even more unpopular with the rest of the country, and this in turn encouraged extremists to talk of seceding from the Union. After Massachusetts summoned the meeting of the Hartford Convention, the fear was widespread that the delegates would propose a New England Confederacy, thereby striking at the Union in a moment of great trial.

Luckily for the country, moderate Federalists controlled the convention. They approved a statement that in case of "deliberate, dangerous and palpable infractions of the Constitution" a state has the right "to interpose its authority" to protect itself. This concept, similar to that expressed in the Kentucky and Virginia resolutions by the Republicans when they were in the minority, was accompanied by a list of proposed constitutional amendments designed to make the national government conform more closely to the New England ideal. These would have (1) repealed the Three-fifths Compromise on representation and direct taxes, which favored the slaveholding states; (2) required a two-thirds vote of Congress for the admission of new states and for declaring war; (3) reduced Congress's power to restrict trade by measures such as an embargo; (4) limited presidents to a single term; and (5) made it illegal for naturalized citizens to hold national office.

Nothing formally proposed at Hartford was treasonable, but the proceedings were kept secret, and rumors of impending secession were rife. In this atmosphere came the news from Ghent of an honorable peace. The Federalists had been denouncing the war and predicting a British triumph; now they were discredited.

THE BATTLE OF NEW ORLEANS

Still more discrediting to Federalists was the second event that would not have happened had communications been more rapid: the Battle of New Orleans. During the fall of 1814 the British had gathered an army at Negril Bay in Jamaica, commanded by Major General Sir Edward Pakenham, brother-in-law of the Duke of Wellington. Late in November an armada of 60 ships set out for New Orleans with 11,000 soldiers. Instead of sailing directly up from the mouth of the Mississippi as the Americans expected, Pakenham approached the city by way of Lake Borgne, to the east. Proceeding through a maze of swamps and bayous, he advanced close to the city's gates before being detected. Early on the afternoon of December 23, three mud-spattered local planters burst into the headquarters of General Andrew Jackson, commanding the defenses of New Orleans, with the news.

For once in this war of error and incompetence the United States had the right man in the right place at the right time. After his Revolutionary War experiences, Jackson had studied law, then moved West, settling in Nashville, Tennessee. He served briefly in both houses of Congress and was active in Tennessee affairs. Jackson was a hard man and fierce-tempered, frequently involved in brawls and duels, but honest and, by western standards, a good public servant. When the war broke out, he was named major general of volunteers. Almost alone among nonprofessional troops during the conflict, his men won impressive victories, savagely crushing the Creek Indians in a series of battles in Alabama.

Jackson's success was due to his toughness and determination. Discipline based on fear, respect, and their awareness of his genuine concern for their well-being made his individualistic frontier militiamen into an army. His men called Jackson Old Hickory; the Indians called him Sharp Knife.

Following these victories, Jackson was assigned the job of defending the Gulf Coast against the expected British strike. Although he had misjudged Pakenham's destination, he was ready when the news of the British arrival reached him. "By the Eternal," he vowed, "they shall not sleep on our soil." "Gentlemen," he told his staff officers, "the British are below, we must fight them tonight."

While the British rested and awaited reinforcements, planning to take the city the next morning, Jackson rushed up men and guns. At 7:30 P.M. on December 23 he struck hard, taking the British by surprise. But Pakenham's veterans rallied quickly, and the battle was inconclusive. With Redcoats pouring in from the fleet, Jackson fell back to a point 5 miles below New Orleans and dug in.

He chose his position wisely. On his right was the Mississippi, on his left an impenetrable swamp, to the front an open field. On the day before Christmas (while the commissioners in Ghent were signing the peace treaty), Jackson's army, which included a segregated unit of free black militiamen, erected an earthen parapet about 10 yards behind a dry canal bed. Here the Americans would make their stand.

For two weeks Pakenham probed the American line. Jackson strengthened his defenses daily. At night, patrols of silent Tennesseans slipped out with knife and tomahawk to stalk British sentries. They called this grim business "going hunting." On January 8, 1815, Pakenham ordered an all-out frontal assault. The American position was formidable, but these were men who had defeated Napoleon. At dawn, through the lowland mists, the Redcoats moved forward with fixed bayonets. Pakenham assumed that the undisciplined Americans—about 4500 strong—would run at the sight of bare steel.

The Americans did not run. Perhaps they feared the wrath of their commander more than enemy bayonets. Artillery raked the advancing British, and when the range closed to about 150 yards, the riflemen opened up. Jackson had formed his men in three ranks behind the parapet. One rank fired, then stepped down as another took its place. By the time the third had loosed its volley, the first had reloaded and was ready to fire again. Nothing could stand against this rain of lead. General Pakenham was wounded twice, then killed by a shell fragment while

calling up his last reserves. During the battle a single brave British officer reached the top of the parapet. When retreat was finally sounded, the British had suffered almost 2100 casualties, including nearly 300 killed. Thirteen Americans lost their lives, and 58 more were wounded or missing.

VICTORY WEAKENS THE FEDERALISTS

Word of Jackson's magnificent triumph reached Washington almost simultaneously with the good news from Ghent. People found it easy to confuse the chronology and consider the war a victory won on the battlefield below New Orleans instead of the standoff it had been. Jackson became the "Hero of New Orleans"; his proud fellow citizens rated his military abilities superior to those of the Duke of Wellington. The nation rejoiced. One sour Republican complained that the Federalists of Massachusetts had fired off more powder and wounded more men celebrating the victory than they had during the whole course of the conflict. The Senate ratified the peace treaty unanimously, and the frustrations and failures of the past few years were forgotten. Moreover, American success in holding off Great Britain despite internal frictions went a long way toward convincing European nations that both the United States and its republican form of government were here to stay. The powers might accept these truths with less pleasure than the Americans, but accept them they did.

The nation had suffered relatively few casualties and little economic loss, except to the shipping interests. The Indians were the main losers in the contest. When Jackson defeated the Creeks, for example, he forced them to surrender 23 million acres, constituting three-fifths of what is now Alabama and one-fifth of Georgia.

The war completed the destruction of the Federalist party. The success of the Jeffersonians' political techniques had inspired younger Federalists in many parts of the country to adopt the rhetoric of democracy and (more important) to perfect local organizations. In 1812 the party made significant gains in the Northeast, electing numbers of congressmen and winning many state and local offices. They did not run a candidate for president, but their support enabled the dissident New York Republican DeWitt Clinton to obtain 89 electoral votes to Madison's 128.

Their private correspondence reveals that these Federalists were no more enchanted by the virtues of mass democracy than were their elders, but by mouthing democratic slogans they revived the party

▲ In warfare, Indians adopted some of the weapons and strategy of white soldiers. Here Indians congregate in a massed formation, armed with guns and tomahawks, to defend their village; one downed Indian is holding a gun and wearing boots. The federal officers are mounted on horses.

in many districts. Now the results of the war undermined their efforts. They had not supported the war effort; they had argued that the British could not be defeated; they had dealt clandestinely with the enemy; they had even threatened to break up the Union. So long as the issue remained in doubt, these policies won considerable support, but New Orleans made the party an object of ridicule and scorn. It soon disappeared even in New England, swamped beneath a wave of patriotism that flooded the land.

The chief reason for the happy results of the war had little to do with American events. After 1815 Europe settled down to what was to be a century of relative peace. With peace came an end to serious foreign threats to America and a revival of commerce. European emigration to the United States, long held back by the troubled times, spurred ahead, providing the expanding country with its most valuable asset—strong, willing hands to do the work of developing the land. The mood of Jefferson's first term, when democracy had reigned amid peace and plenty, returned with a rush. And the nation, having had its fill of international complications, turned in on itself as Jefferson had wished. The politicians, ever sensitive to public attitudes, had learned what seemed at the time

a valuable lesson. Foreign affairs were a potent cause of domestic conflict. The volatile character of sectional politics was thus another reason why America should escape from involvement in European affairs.

ANGLO-AMERICAN RAPPROCHEMENT

There remained a few matters to straighten out with Great Britain, Spain, and Europe generally. Since no territory had changed hands at Ghent, neither signatory had reason to harbor a grudge. There was no sudden flowering of Anglo-American friendship. Yet for years no serious trouble marred Anglo-American relations. The war had taught the British to respect Americans, if not to love them.

In this atmosphere the two countries worked out peaceful solutions to a number of old problems. American trade was becoming ever more important to the British, that of the sugar islands less so. In July 1815 they therefore signed a commercial convention ending discriminatory duties and making other adjustments favorable to trade. Boundary difficulties also moved toward resolution. At Ghent the diplomats had created several joint commissions to settle the disputed boundary between the United States and Canada. Many years were to pass before the line was finally drawn, but establishing the principle of defining the border by negotiation was important. In time, a line extending over 3000 miles was agreed to without the firing of a single shot.

Immediately after the war the British reinforced their garrisons in Canada and began to rebuild their shattered Great Lakes fleet. The United States took similar steps. But both nations found the cost of rearming more than they cared to bear. When the United States suggested demilitarizing the lakes, the British agreed. The Rush-Bagot Agreement of 1817 limited each country to one 100-ton vessel armed with a single 18-pounder on Lake Champlain and another on Lake Ontario. They were to have two each for all the other Great Lakes.

Gradually, as an outgrowth of this decision, the entire border was demilitarized, a remarkable achievement. In the Convention of 1818 the two countries agreed to the 49th parallel as the northern boundary of the Louisiana Territory between the Lake of the Woods and the Rockies, and to the joint control of the Oregon country for ten years. The question of the rights of Americans in the Labrador and Newfoundland fisheries, which had been much disputed during the Ghent negotiations, was settled amicably.

THE TRANSCONTINENTAL TREATY

The acquisition of Spanish Florida and the settlement of the western boundary of Louisiana were also accomplished as an aftermath of the War of 1812, but in a far different spirit. Spain's control of the Floridas was feeble. West Florida had passed into American hands by 1813, and frontiersmen in Georgia were eyeing East Florida greedily. Indians struck frequently into American territory from Florida, then fled to sanctuary across the line. American slaves who escaped across the border could not be recovered. In 1818 James Monroe, who had been elected president in 1816, ordered General Andrew Jackson to clear raiding Seminole Indians from American soil and to pursue them into Florida if necessary. Seizing on these instructions, Jackson marched into Florida and easily captured two Spanish forts.

Although Jackson eventually withdrew from Florida, the impotence of the Spanish government made it obvious even in Madrid that if nothing were done, the United States would soon fill the power vacuum by seizing the territory. The Spanish also feared for the future of their tottering Latin American empire, especially the northern provinces of Mexico, which stood in the path of American westward expansion.

Spain and the United States had never determined where the Louisiana Territory ended and Spanish Mexico began. In return for American acceptance of a boundary as far east of the Rio Grande as possible, Spain was ready to surrender Florida.

For these reasons the Spanish minister in Washington, Luis de Onís, undertook in December 1817 to negotiate a treaty with John Quincy Adams, Monroe's secretary of state. Adams pressed the minister mercilessly on the question of the western boundary, driving a bargain that would have done credit to the most tightfisted of his Yankee ancestors. Onís opened their talks by proposing a line in the middle of what is now Louisiana, and when Adams countered by demanding a boundary running through present-day Texas, Onís professed to be shocked. Abstract right, not power, should determine the settlement, he said. "Truth is of all times, and reason and justice are founded upon immutable principles." To this Adams replied: "That truth is of all times and that reason and justice are founded upon immutable principles has never been contested by the United States, but neither truth, reason, nor justice consists in stubbornness of assertion, nor in the multiplied repetition of error."

In the end Onís could only yield. He saved Texas for his monarch but accepted a boundary to the Louisiana Territory that followed the Sabine, Red, and Arkansas Rivers to the Continental Divide and the 42nd parallel to the Pacific, thus abandoning Spain's claim to a huge area beyond the Rockies that had no connection at all with the Louisiana Purchase. Adams even compelled him to agree that when the boundary followed rivers, United States territory was to extend to the farthest bank, not merely to midstream. The United States obtained Florida in return for a mere $5 million, and that paid not to Spain but to Americans who held claims against the Spanish government.

This "Transcontinental Treaty" was signed in 1819, although ratification was delayed until 1821. Most Americans at the time thought the acquisition of Florida the most important part of the treaty, but Adams, whose vision of America's future was truly continental, knew better. "The acquisition of a definite line of boundary to the [Pacific] forms a great epoch in our history," he recorded in his diary.

THE MONROE DOCTRINE

Concern with defining the boundaries of the United States did not reflect a desire to limit expansion; rather, the feeling was that there should be no more quibbling and quarreling with foreign powers that might distract the people from the great task of national development. The classic enunciation of this

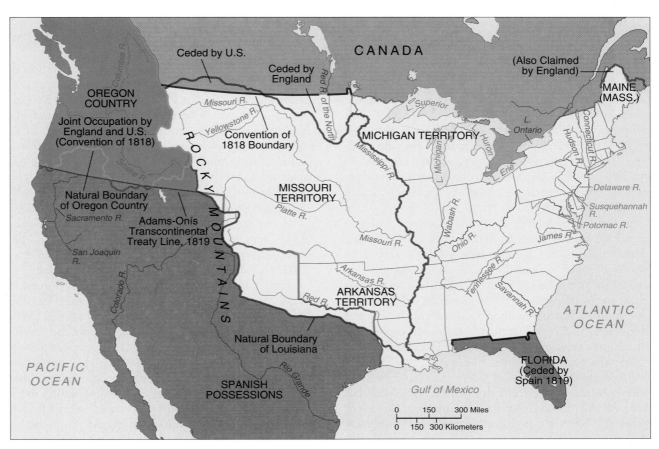

▲ The United States, 1819

point of view, the completion of America's withdrawal from Europe, was the Monroe Doctrine.

Two separate strands met in this pronouncement. The first led from Moscow to Alaska and down the Pacific Coast to the Oregon country. Beginning with the explorations of Vitus Bering in 1741, the Russians had maintained an interest in fishing and fur trading along the northwest coast of North America. In 1821 the czar extended his claim south to the 51st parallel and forbade the ships of other powers to enter coastal waters north of that point. This announcement was disturbing.

The second strand ran from the courts of the European monarchs to Latin America. Between 1817 and 1822 practically all of the region from the Rio Grande to the Strait of Magellan had won its independence. Spain, former master of all the area except Brazil, was too weak to win it back by force, but Austria, Prussia, France, and Russia decided at the Congress of Verona in 1822 to try to regain the area for Spain in the interests of "legitimacy." There was talk of sending a large French army to South America. This possibility also caused grave concern in Washington.

To the Russian threat, Monroe and Secretary of State Adams responded with a terse warning: "The American continents are no longer subjects for any new European colonial establishments." This statement did not impress the Russians, but they had no intention of colonizing the region. In 1824 they signed a treaty with the United States abandoning all claims below the present southern limit of Alaska (54° 40′ north latitude) and removing their restrictions on foreign shipping.

The Latin American problem was more complex. The United States was not alone in its alarm at the prospect of a revival of French or Spanish power in that region. Great Britain, having profited greatly from the breakup of the mercantilist Spanish empire by developing a thriving commerce with the new republics, had no intention of permitting a restoration of the old order. But the British monarchy preferred not to recognize the new revolutionary South American republics, for England itself was only beginning to recover from a period of social upheaval as violent as any in its history. Bad times and high food prices had combined to cause riots, conspiracies, and angry demands for parliamentary reform.

In 1823 the British foreign minister, George Canning, suggested to the American minister in London that the United States and Britain issue a joint statement opposing any French interference in South America, pledging that they themselves would never annex any part of Spain's old empire, and saying nothing about recognition of the new republics. This proposal of joint action with the British was flattering to the United States but scarcely in its best interests. The United States had already recognized the new republics, and it had no desire to help Great Britain retain its South American trade. As Secretary Adams pointed out, to agree to the proposal would be to abandon the possibility of someday adding Cuba or any other part of Latin America to the United States. America should act independently, Adams urged. "It would be more candid, as well as more dignified, to avow our principles explicitly . . . than to come in as a cockboat in the wake of the British man-of-war."

Monroe heartily endorsed Adams's argument and decided to include a statement of American policy in his annual message to Congress in December 1823. "The American continents," he wrote, "by the free and independent condition which they have assumed and maintain, are henceforth not to be considered as subjects for future colonization by any European powers." Europe's political system was "essentially different" from that developing in the New World, and the two should not be mixed. The United States would not interfere with existing European colonies in North or South America and would avoid involvement in strictly European affairs, but any attempt to extend European control to countries in the hemisphere that had already won their independence would be considered, Monroe warned, "the manifestation of an unfriendly disposition toward the United States" and consequently a threat to the nation's "peace and safety."

DOCUMENT
Monroe Doctrine

This policy statement—it was not dignified with the title Monroe Doctrine until decades later—attracted little notice in Europe or Latin America and not much more at home. Obviously the United States, whose own capital had been overrun by a mere raiding party less than ten years before, could not police the entire Western Hemisphere. European statesmen dismissed Monroe's message as "arrogant" and "blustering," worthy only of "the most profound contempt." Latin Americans, while appreciating the intent behind it, knew better than to count on American aid in case of attack.

Nevertheless, the principles laid down by President Monroe so perfectly expressed the wishes of the people of the United States that when the country grew powerful enough to enforce them, there was little need to alter or embellish his pronouncement. However understood at the time, the doctrine may be seen as the final stage in the evolution of American independence.

From this perspective, the famous Declaration of 1776 merely began a process of separation and self-determination. The peace treaty ending the Revolutionary War was a further step, and Washington's Declaration of Neutrality in 1793 was another, demonstrating as it did the capacity of the United States to determine its own best interests despite the treaty of alliance with France. The removal of British troops from the northwest forts, achieved by the otherwise ignominious Jay Treaty, marked the next stage. Then the Louisiana Purchase made a further advance toward true independence by ensuring that the Mississippi River could not be closed to the commerce so vital to the development of the western territories.

The standoff War of 1812 ended any lingering British hope of regaining control of America, the Latin American revolutions further weakened colonialism in the Western Hemisphere, and the Transcontinental Treaty pushed the last European power from the path of westward expansion. Monroe's "doctrine" was a kind of public announcement that the sovereign United States had completed its independence and wanted nothing better than to be left alone to concentrate on its own development. Better yet if Europe could be made to allow the entire hemisphere to follow its own path.

THE ERA OF GOOD FEELINGS

The person who gave his name to the so-called doctrine was an unusually lucky man. James Monroe lived a long life in good health and saw close up most of the great events in the history of the young republic. At the age of 18 he shed his blood for liberty at the Battle of Trenton. He was twice governor of Virginia, a United States senator, and a Cabinet member. He was at various times the nation's representative in Paris, Madrid, and London. Elected president in 1816, his good fortune continued. The world was finally at peace, the country united and prosperous. A person of good feeling who would keep a steady hand on the helm and hold to the present course seemed called for, and Monroe possessed exactly the qualities that the times required. "He is a man whose soul might be turned wrongside outwards, without discovering a blemish," Jefferson said, and John Quincy Adams, a harsh critic of public figures, praised Monroe's courtesy, sincerity, and sound judgment.

Courtesy and purity of soul do not always suffice to make a good president. In more troubled times Monroe might well have brought disaster, for he was

▲ **Population Density, 1790**

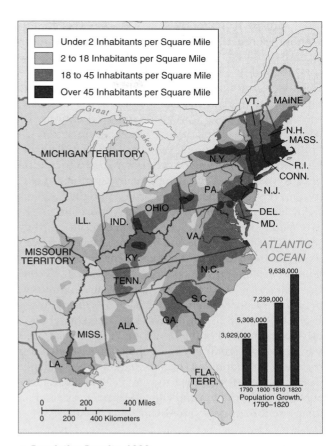

▲ **Population Density, 1820**
The 30 years from 1790 to 1820 saw a sizable increase in population. The growth was especially great in the decade from 1810 to 1820, with a 33.1 percent increase.

neither a person of outstanding intellect nor a forceful leader. He blazed few paths, organized no personal machine. The Monroe Doctrine, by far the most significant achievement of his administration, was as much the work of Secretary of State Adams as his own. No one ever claimed that Monroe was much better than second-rate, yet when his first term ended, he was reelected without organized opposition.

By 1817 the divisive issues of earlier days had vanished. Monroe dramatized their disappearance by beginning his first term with a goodwill tour of New England, heartland of the opposition. The tour was a triumph. Everywhere the president was greeted with tremendous enthusiasm. After he visited Boston, once the headquarters and now the graveyard of Federalism, a Federalist newspaper, the *Columbian Centinel*, gave the age its name. Pointing out that the celebrations attending Monroe's visit had brought together in friendly intercourse many persons "whom party politics had long severed," it dubbed the times the "Era of Good Feelings."

It has often been said that the harmony of Monroe's administrations was superficial, that beneath the calm lay potentially disruptive issues that had not yet begun to influence national politics. The dramatic change from the unanimity of Monroe's second election to the fragmentation of four years later, when four candidates divided the vote and the House of Representatives had to choose the president, supports the point.

Nevertheless, the people of the period had good reasons for thinking it extraordinarily harmonious. Peace, prosperity, liberty, and progress all flourished in 1817 in the United States. The heirs of Jefferson had accepted, with a mixture of resignation and enthusiasm, most of the economic policies advocated by the Hamiltonians.

The Jeffersonian balance between individual liberty and responsible government, having survived both bad management and war, had justified itself to the opposition. The new unity was symbolized by the restored friendship of Jefferson and John Adams. In

1801 Adams had slipped sulkily out of Washington without waiting to attend his successor's inauguration, but after ten years of icy silence, the two old collaborators, abetted by Dr. Benjamin Rush, effected a reconciliation. Although they continued to disagree vigorously about matters of philosophy and government, the bitterness between them disappeared entirely. By Monroe's day, Jefferson was writing long letters to "my dear friend," ranging over such subjects as theology, the proper reading of the classics, and agricultural improvements, and receiving equally warm and voluminous replies. "Whether you or I were right," Adams wrote amiably to Jefferson, "Posterity must judge."

When political divisions appeared again, as they soon did, it was not because the old balance had been shaky. Few of the new controversies challenged Republican principles or revived old issues. Instead, these controversies were children of the present and the future, products of the continuing growth of the country. From 1790 to 1820, the area of the United States doubled, but very little of the Louisiana Purchase had been settled. More significant, the population of the nation had more than doubled, from 4 million to 9.6 million. The pace of the westward movement had also quickened; by 1820 the moving edge of the frontier ran in a long, irregular curve from Michigan to Arkansas.

New Sectional Issues

Sectional tensions led to many disputes over banking, the tariff, federal land policy, and internal improvements. Overshadowing all of these was the debate over slavery.

The War of 1812 and the depression that struck the country in 1819 had shaped many of the controversies. The tariff question was affected by both. Before the War of 1812 the level of duties averaged about 12.5 percent of the value of dutiable products, but to meet the added expenses occasioned by the conflict, Congress doubled all tariffs. In 1816, when the revenue was no longer needed, a new act kept duties close to wartime levels. Infant industries that had grown up during the years of embargo, nonintercourse, and war were able to exert considerable pressure. The act especially favored textiles because the British were dumping cloth in America at bargain prices in their attempt to regain lost markets. Unemployed workers and many farmers became convinced that prosperity would return only if American industry were shielded against foreign competition.

There was backing for high duties in every section. Except for New England, where the shipping interests favored free trade and where the booming textile mills were not seriously injured by foreign competition, the North favored protection. A few Southerners hoped that textile mills would spring up in their region; more supported protection on the ground that national self-sufficiency was necessary in case of war. In the West small manufacturers in the towns added their support, and so did farmers, who were counting on workers in the new eastern factories to consume much of their wheat and corn and hogs. But with the passage of time the South rejected protection almost completely. Industry failed to develop, and since Southerners exported most of their cotton and tobacco, they soon concluded that besides increasing the cost of nearly everything they bought, high duties on imports would limit the foreign market for southern staples by inhibiting international exchange. As this fact became clear, the West tended to divide on the tariff question: the Northwest and much of Kentucky, which had a special interest in protecting its considerable hemp production, favored high duties; the Southwest, where cotton was the major crop, favored low duties.

National banking policy was another important political issue affected by the war and the depression. Presidents Jefferson and Madison had managed to live with the Bank of the United States despite its dubious constitutionality, but its charter was not renewed when it expired in 1811. Aside from the constitutional question, the major opposition to recharter came from state banks eager to take over the business of the Bank for themselves. The fact that English investors owned most of the Bank's stock was also used as an argument against recharter.

Many more state banks were created after 1811, and most extended credit recklessly. When the British raid on Washington and Baltimore in 1814 sent panicky depositors scurrying to convert their deposits into gold or silver, the overextended financiers could not oblige them. All banks outside New England suspended specie payments; that is, they stopped exchanging their bank notes for hard money on demand. Paper money immediately fell in value; a paper dollar was soon worth only 85 cents in coin in Philadelphia, less in Baltimore. Government business also suffered from the absence of a national bank. In October 1814 Secretary of the Treasury Alexander J. Dallas submitted a plan for a second Bank of the United States, and after considerable wrangling over its precise form, the institution was authorized in April 1816.

The new Bank was much larger than its predecessor, being capitalized at $35 million. However, unlike Hamilton's creation, it was badly managed at the start. Its first president, William Jones, a former secretary of the treasury, allowed his institution to join in the irresponsible creation of credit. By the summer of

▲ The Bank of Philadelphia (1801), designed by Benjamin Latrobe, combined the Ionic columns of an ancient Athenian temple and the circular dome of ancient Rome. By appropriating the grandeur of antiquity, Americans were seeking to liberate themselves from modern Europe.

1818 the Bank's 18 branches had issued notes in excess of ten times their specie reserves, far more than was prudent, considering the Bank's responsibilities. When depression struck the country in 1819, the Bank of the United States was as hard pressed as many of the state banks. Jones resigned.

The new president, Langdon Cheves of South Carolina, was as rigid as Jones had been permissive. During the bad times, when easy credit was needed, he pursued a policy of stern curtailment. The Bank thus regained a sound position at the expense of hardship to borrowers. "The Bank was saved," the contemporary economist William Gouge wrote somewhat hyperbolically, "and the people were ruined." Indeed, the bank reached a low point in public favor. Irresponsible state banks resented it, as did the advocates of hard money.

Regional lines were less sharply drawn on the Bank issue than on the tariff. Northern congressmen voted against the Bank 53 to 44 in 1816—many of them because they objected to the particular proposal, not because they were against any national bank. Those from other sections favored it, 58 to 30. The collapse occasioned by the Panic of 1819 produced further opposition to the institution in the West.

Land policy in the West also caused sectional controversy. No one wished to eliminate the system of survey and sale, but there was continuous pressure to reduce the price of public land and the minimum unit offered for sale. The Land Act of 1800 set $2 an acre

as the minimum price and 320 acres (a half section) as the smallest unit. In 1804 the minimum was cut to 160 acres, which could be had for about $80 down, roughly a quarter of what the average artisan could earn in a year.

Since banks were pursuing an easy-credit policy, land sales boomed. In 1818 the government sold nearly 3.5 million acres. Thereafter, continuing expansion and the rapid shrinkage of the foreign market as European farmers resumed production after the Napoleonic Wars led to disaster. Prices fell, the panic struck, and western debtors were forced to the wall by the hundreds.

Sectional attitudes toward the public lands were fairly straightforward. The West wanted cheap land; the North and South tended to look on the national domain as an asset that should be converted into as much cash as possible. Northern manufacturers feared that cheap land in the West would drain off surplus labor and force wages up, while Southern planters were concerned about the competition that would develop when the virgin lands of the Southwest were put to the plow to make cotton. The West, however, was ready to fight to the last line of defense over land policy, while the other regions would usually compromise on the issue to gain support for their own vital interests.

Sectional alignments on the question of internal improvements were similar to those on land policy, but this issue, soon to become very important, had

▲ A slave family is broken up in this mordant painting titled, *After the Sale: Slaves Going Home from Richmond (1853)*, by Eyre Crowe (British). The man at the lower right, holding a whip, is taking money; an American flag flies from the auctioneer's carriage. The moral was obvious.

not greatly agitated national affairs before 1820. As we have seen, the only significant federal internal improvement project undertaken before that date was the National Road.

The most divisive sectional issue was slavery. After the compromises affecting the "peculiar institution" made at the Constitutional Convention, it caused remarkably little conflict in national politics before 1819. Although the importation of blacks rose in the 1790s, Congress abolished the African slave trade in 1808 without major incident. As the nation expanded, free and slave states were added to the Union in equal numbers, Ohio, Indiana, and Illinois being balanced by Louisiana, Mississippi, and Alabama. In 1819 there were 22 states, 11 slave and 11 free. The expansion of slavery occasioned by the cotton boom led Southerners to support it more aggressively, which tended to irritate many Northerners, but most persons considered slavery mainly a local issue.

To the extent that it was a national question, the North opposed it and the South defended it ardently. The West leaned toward the southern point of view, for in addition to the southwestern slave states, the Northwest was sympathetic, partly because much of its produce was sold on southern plantations and partly because at least half of its early settlers came from Virginia, Kentucky, and other slave states.

NORTHERN LEADERS

By 1824 the giants of the Revolutionary generation had completed their work. Washington, Hamilton, Franklin, Samuel Adams, Patrick Henry, and most of their peers were dead. John Adams (88), Thomas Jefferson (81), and James Madison (73) were passing their declining years quietly on their ancestral acres, full of memories and sage advice, but no longer active in national affairs. In every section new leaders had come forward, men shaped by the past but chiefly concerned with the present. Quite suddenly, between the war and the panic, they had inherited power. They would shape the future of the United States.

John Quincy Adams was the best-known political leader of the North in the early 1820s. Just completing his brilliant work as secretary of state under Monroe, highlighted by his negotiation of the Transcontinental Treaty and his design of the Monroe Doctrine, he had behind him a record of public service dating to the Confederation period. At age 11 he was giving English lessons to the French minister to the Continental Congress and his secretary. ("He shows us no mercy and makes us no compliments," the minister remarked.) While in his teens he served as secretary of legation in Russia and Great Britain. Later he was American minister to the Netherlands and to Prussia, and a Federalist United States senator from Massachusetts. Then he gradually switched to the Republican point of view, supporting the Louisiana Purchase and even the Embargo Act.

Adams was farsighted, imaginative, hardworking, and extremely intelligent, but he was inept in personal relations. He had all the virtues and most of the defects of the puritan, being suspicious both of others and of himself. He suffered in two ways from being his father's child: As the son of a president he was under severe pressure to live up to the Adams name, and his father expected a great deal of him. When the boy was only 7, John Adams wrote his wife: "Train [the children] to virtue. Habituate them to industry, activity, and spirit. Make them consider vice as shameful and unmanly. Fire them with ambition to be useful."

Such training made John Quincy an indefatigable worker. Even in winter he normally rose at 5 A.M., and he could never convince himself that most of his associates were not lazy dolts. He set a standard no one could meet and consequently was continually dissatisfied with himself. As one of his grandsons remarked, "He was disappointed because he was not supernatural."

Like his father, John Quincy Adams was a strong nationalist. While New England was still antiprotectionist, he was at least open-minded on the subject of high tariffs. Unlike most Easterners, he believed that the federal government should spend freely on roads and canals in the West. To slavery he was, like most New Englanders, personally opposed. As Monroe's second term drew toward its close, Adams seemed one of the most likely candidates to succeed him, and at this period his ambition to be president was his great failing. It led him to make certain compromises with his principles, which in turn plagued his oversensitive conscience and had a corrosive effect on his peace of mind.

Daniel Webster was recognized as one of the coming leaders of New England. Born in New Hampshire in 1782, he graduated from Dartmouth College in 1801, and by the time of the War of 1812 he had made a local reputation as a lawyer and orator. After serving two terms in Congress during the conflict, he moved to Boston to concentrate on his legal practice. He soon became one of the leading constitutional lawyers of the country. In 1823 he was again elected to Congress.

Webster owed much of his reputation to his formidable presence and his oratorical skill. Dark, broad-chested, large-headed, craggy of brow, with deep-set, brooding eyes and a firm mouth, he projected a remarkable appearance of heroic power and moral strength. His thunderous voice, his resourceful vocabulary, his manner—all backed by the mastery of every oratorical trick—made him unique.

Webster had a first-rate mind, powerful and logical. His faults were largely those of temperament. He was too fond of money, good food, and fine broadcloth, of alcohol and adulation. Generally he bestirred himself only with great effort and then usually to advance his

▲ Eyes like "anthracite furnaces," the English historian Thomas Carlyle remarked of Daniel Webster; this is the "Black Dan" portrait by Francis Alexander (1835).

own cause. He borrowed large sums from his well-to-do admirers but rarely paid them back. Webster could have been a lighthouse in the night, guiding his fellow citizens to safe harbor. More often he was a weather vane, shifting to accommodate the strongest breeze.

Unlike the independent-minded Adams, Webster nearly always reflected the beliefs of the dominant business interests of New England. His opposition to the embargo and the War of 1812 got him into Congress, where he faithfully supported the views of New England merchants. He opposed the high tariff of 1816 because the merchants favored free trade, and he voted against establishing the Bank chiefly on partisan grounds. (His view changed when the Bank hired him as its lawyer.) He was against cheap land and federal construction of internal improvements, but basically he was a nationalist, as was seen in his arguments before the Supreme Court. Ahead of him lay fame, considerable constructive service, but also bitter frustration.

New York's man of the future was a sandy-haired politico named Martin Van Buren. The Red Fox, as he was called, was one of the most talented politicians ever to play a part in American affairs. He was clever and hardworking, but his mind and his energy were always devoted to some political purpose. From 1812 to 1820 he served in the state legislature; in 1820 he was elected United States senator.

Van Buren had great charm and immense tact. By nature affable, he never allowed partisanship to mar his personal relationships with other leaders. The members of his political machine, known as the Albany Regency, were almost fanatically loyal to him, but even his enemies could seldom dislike him as a person.

Somehow Van Buren could reconcile deviousness with honesty. He "rowed to his objective with muffled oars," said Randolph of Roanoke, yet Van Buren was neither crooked nor venal. Politics for him was like a game or a complex puzzle: The object was victory, but one must play by the rules or lose all sense of achievement. Only a fool will cheat at solitaire, and despite his gregariousness Van Buren was at heart a solitary operator.

His positions on the issues of the 1820s are hard to determine because he never took a position if he could avoid doing so. In part this was his politician's desire to straddle every fence; it also reflected his quixotic belief that issues were means rather than ends in the world of politics. No one could say with assurance what he thought about the tariff, and since slavery did not arouse much interest in New York, it is safe to suppose that at this time he had no opinion at all about the institution. Any intelligent observer in the 1820s would have predicted that "the Little Magician" would go far. How far, and in what direction, no one could have guessed.

SOUTHERN LEADERS

The most prominent southern leader was William H. Crawford, Monroe's secretary of the treasury. Following service in the Georgia legislature, where he spoke for the large planters against the interests of yeomen farmers, in 1807 he was elected to the United States Senate. Crawford was direct and friendly, a marvelous storyteller, and one of the few persons in Washington who could teach the fledgling senator Martin Van Buren anything about politics. Crawford was one of the first politicians to try to build a national machine. "Crawford's Act" of 1820, limiting the term of minor federal appointees to four years, was passed, as the name suggests, largely through his efforts, for he realized before nearly anyone else that a handful of petty offices, properly distributed, could win the allegiance of thousands of voters.

Crawford was controversial. Many of his contemporaries considered him no more than a cynical spoilsman, although his administration of the Treasury department was first-rate. Yet he had many friends. His ambition was vast, his power great. Fate, however, was about to strike Crawford a crippling blow.

▲ This striking portrait of John C. Calhoun was painted sometime between 1818 and 1825, probably by Charles Bird King. Calhoun was in his thirties.

John C. Calhoun, the other outstanding southern leader, was born in South Carolina in 1782 and graduated from Yale in 1804. After serving in the South Carolina legislature, he was elected to Congress in 1811. In Congress he took a strong nationalist position on all the issues of the day. In 1817 Monroe made him secretary of war.

Calhoun, a well-to-do planter, was devoted to the South and its institutions, but he took the broadest possible view of political affairs. "Our true system is to look to the country," he said in 1820, "and to support such measures and such men, without regard to sections, as are best calculated to advance the general interest." John Quincy Adams, seldom charitable in his private opinions of colleagues (he called Crawford "a worm" and Henry Clay a "gamester" with an "undigested system of ethics"), praised Calhoun's "enlarged philosophic views" and considered him "above all sectional and factional prejudices."

Calhoun was intelligent, bookish, and given to the study of abstractions. Legend has it that he once tried to write a poem but after putting down the word "Whereas" gave it up as beyond his powers. Some obscure failing made it impossible for him to grasp the essence of the human condition. An English observer once said that Calhoun had "an imperfect acquaintance with human nature." Few contemporaries could maintain themselves in debate against his powerful intelligence, yet that mind—so sharp, so penetrating—was the blind bondsman of his ambition.

WESTERN LEADERS

The outstanding western leader of the 1820s was Henry Clay of Kentucky, one of the most charming and colorful of American statesmen. Clay was the kind of person who made men cheer and women swoon. On the platform he ranked with Webster; behind the political scenes he was the peer of Van Buren. In every environment he was warm and open—what a modern political scientist might call a charismatic personality. Clay loved to drink, swear, tell tales, and play poker. At one sitting he won $40,000 from a friend and then cheerfully told him that a note for $500 would wipe out the obligation. He was a reasonable man, skilled at arranging political compromises, but he possessed a reckless streak: Twice in his career he challenged men to duels for having insulted him. Fortunately, all concerned were poor shots.

Clay was elected to Congress in 1810. He led the War Hawks in 1811 and 1812 and was Speaker of the House from 1811 to 1820 and from 1823 to 1825.

Intellectually the inferior of Adams, Calhoun, and Webster, Clay nevertheless had a perfect temperament

▲ Henry Clay of Kentucky. "Life itself is but a compromise between death and life." He applied this principle to politics.

for politics. He loved power and understood that in the United States it had to be shared to be exercised. His great gift was in seeing national needs from a broad perspective and fashioning a program that could inspire ordinary citizens with something of his vision.

In the early 1820s he was just developing his "American System." In return for eastern support of a policy of federal aid in the construction of roads and canals, the West would back the protective tariff. He justified this deal on the widest national grounds. America has a "great diversity of interests," ranging from agriculture and fishing to manufacturing, shipbuilding, and commerce. "The good of each . . . and of the whole should be carefully consulted. This is the only mode by which we can preserve, in full vigor, the harmony of the whole Union." Stimulating manufacturing, for example, would increase the demand for western raw materials, while western prosperity would lead to greater consumption of eastern manufactured goods.

Although himself a slaveowner, Clay called slavery the "greatest of human evils." He favored freeing the slaves and "colonizing" them in Africa, which could, he said, be accomplished gradually and at relatively minor cost.

The West had other spokesmen in the 1820s. Thomas Hart Benton, elected to the Senate by the new state of Missouri, was an expansionist and a hard-money man of the uncompromising sort, suspicious of paper currency and therefore of all banks. His friends called him "Old Bullion"; his detractors, "Big Bully Bottom." Benton championed the small western farmer, favoring free homesteads for pioneers and an extensive federal internal improvements program. Another western leader was General William Henry Harrison. Although he sat in the Ohio legislature and in both houses of Congress between 1816 and 1828, Harrison was primarily a soldier. He did not identify himself closely with any policy other than the extermination of Indians. He had little to do with the newly developing political alignments of the 1820s.

Much like Harrison was Andrew Jackson, the "Hero of New Orleans," whose popularity greatly exceeded Harrison's. He had many friends, shrewd in the ways of politics, who were working devotedly, if not entirely unselfishly, to make him president. No one knew his views on most questions, but few cared. His chief assets as a presidential candidate were his military reputation and his forceful personality, but both, and especially the latter, were likely to get him into political hot water.

The Missouri Compromise

The sectional concerns of the 1820s repeatedly influenced politics. The depression of 1819 to 1822 increased tensions by making people feel more strongly about the issues of the day. For example, manufacturers who wanted high tariffs in 1816 were more vehemently in favor of protection in 1820 when their business fell off. Even when economic conditions improved, geographic alignments on key issues tended to solidify.

One of the first and most critical of the sectional questions concerned the admission of Missouri as a slave state. When Louisiana entered the Union in 1812, the rest of the Louisiana Purchase was organized as the Missouri Territory. Building on a nucleus of Spanish and French inhabitants, the region west and north of St. Louis grew rapidly, and in 1817 the Missourians petitioned for statehood. A large percentage of the settlers—the population exceeded 60,000 by 1818—were Southerners who had moved into the valleys of the Arkansas and Missouri rivers. Since many of them owned slaves, Missouri would become a slave state.

DOCUMENT

Missouri
Enabling Act

The admission of new states had always been a routine matter, in keeping with the admirable pattern established by the Northwest Ordinance. But during the debate on the Missouri Enabling Act in February 1819, Congressman James Tallmadge of New York introduced an amendment prohibiting

"the further introduction of slavery" and providing that all slaves born in Missouri after the territory became a state should be freed at age 25.

While Tallmadge was merely seeking to apply in the territory the pattern of race relations that had developed in the states immediately east of Missouri, his amendment represented, at least in spirit, something of a revolution. The Northwest Ordinance had prohibited slavery in the land between the Mississippi and the Ohio, but that area had only a handful of slaveowners in 1787 and little prospect of attracting more. Elsewhere no effort to restrict the movement of slaves into new territory had been attempted. If one assumed (as whites always had) that the slaves themselves should have no say in the matter, it appeared democratic to let the settlers of Missouri decide the slavery question for themselves. Nevertheless, the Tallmadge amendment passed the House, the vote following sectional lines closely. The Senate, however, resoundingly rejected it. The less populous southern part of Missouri was then organized separately as the Arkansas Territory, and an attempt to bar slavery there was stifled. The Missouri Enabling Act failed to pass before Congress adjourned.

When the next Congress met in December 1819, the Missouri issue came up at once. The vote on Tallmadge's amendment had shown that the rapidly growing North controlled the House of Representatives. It was vital, Southerners felt, to preserve a balance in the Senate. Yet Northerners objected to the fact that Missouri extended hundreds of miles north of the Ohio River, which they considered slavery's natural boundary. Angry debate raged in Congress for months.

The debate did not turn on the morality of slavery or the rights of blacks. Northerners objected to adding new slave states because under the Three-fifths Compromise these states would be overrepresented in Congress (60 percent of their slaves would be counted in determining the size of the states' delegations in the House of Representatives) and because they did not relish competing with slave labor. Since the question was political influence rather than the rights and wrongs of slavery, a compromise was worked out in 1820. Missouri entered the Union as a slave state and Maine, having been separated from Massachusetts, was admitted as a free state to preserve the balance in the Senate.

To prevent further conflict, Congress adopted the proposal of Senator Jesse B. Thomas of Illinois, which "forever prohibited" slavery in all other parts of the Louisiana Purchase north of 36° 30′ latitude, the westward extension of Missouri's southern boundary. Although this division would keep slavery out of most of the territory, Southerners accepted it cheerfully. The land south of the line, the present states of Arkansas and Oklahoma, seemed ideally suited for the expanded plantation economy, and most persons considered the treeless northern regions little better than

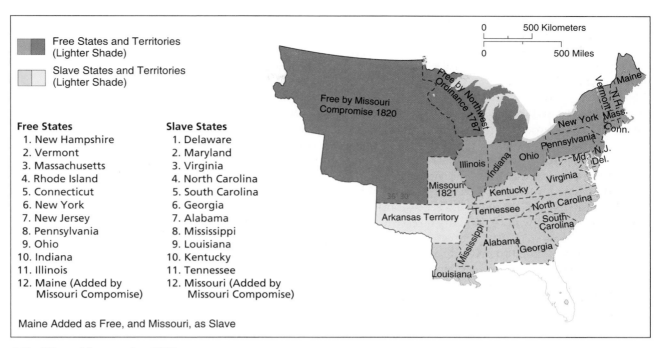

Free States and Territories
(Lighter Shade)

Slave States and Territories
(Lighter Shade)

Free States	Slave States
1. New Hampshire	1. Delaware
2. Vermont	2. Maryland
3. Massachusetts	3. Virginia
4. Rhode Island	4. North Carolina
5. Connecticut	5. South Carolina
6. New York	6. Georgia
7. New Jersey	7. Alabama
8. Pennsylvania	8. Mississippi
9. Ohio	9. Louisiana
10. Indiana	10. Kentucky
11. Illinois	11. Tennessee
12. Maine (Added by Missouri Compomise)	12. Missouri (Added by Missouri Compomise)

Maine Added as Free, and Missouri, as Slave

▲ **The Missouri Compromise, 1820**
The Missouri Compromise temporarily put aside the congressional debate over slavery, with the slave states (12) and free states (12) being in perfect balance. This meant, of course, that the Senate was evenly divided as well. But what would happen when other parts of the Missouri Territory sought admission to the Union as states?

a desert. One northern senator, decrying the division, contemptuously described the land north and west of Missouri, today one of the world's richest agricultural regions, as "a prairie without food or water."

The Missouri Compromise did not end the crisis. When Missouri submitted its constitution for approval by Congress (the final step in the admission process), the document, besides authorizing slavery and prohibiting the emancipation of any slave without the consent of the owner, required the state legislature to pass a law barring free blacks and mulattos from entering the state "under any pretext whatever." This provision plainly violated Article IV, Section 2, of the United States Constitution: "The Citizens of each State shall be entitled to all Privileges and Immunities of Citizens in the several States." It did not, however, represent any more of a break with established racial patterns, North or South, than the Tallmadge amendment; many states east of Missouri barred free blacks without regard for the Constitution.

Nevertheless, northern congressmen hypocritically refused to accept the Missouri constitution. Once more the debate raged. Again, since few Northerners cared to defend the rights of blacks, the issue was compromised. In March 1821 Henry Clay found a face-saving formula: Out of respect for the "supreme law of the land," Congress accepted the Missouri constitution with the demurrer that no law

passed in conformity to it should be construed as contravening Article IV, Section 2.

Every thinking person recognized the political dynamite inherent in the Missouri controversy. The sectional lineup had been terrifyingly compact. What meant the Union if so trivial a matter as one new state could so divide the people? Moreover, despite the timidity and hypocrisy of the North, everyone realized that the rights and wrongs of slavery lay at the heart of the conflict. "We have the wolf by the ears, and we can neither safely hold him, nor safely let him go," Jefferson wrote a month after Missouri became a state. The dispute, he said, "like a fire bell in the night, awakened and filled me with terror." Jefferson knew that the compromise had not quenched the flames ignited by the Missouri debates. "This is a reprieve only," he said. John Quincy Adams called it the "title page to a great tragic volume." Yet one could still hope that the fire bell was only a false alarm, that Adams's tragic volume would remain unread.

THE ELECTION OF 1824

Other controversies that aroused strong feelings did not seem to divide the country so deeply. The question of federal internal improvements caused endless debate that split the country on geographical lines. In 1816 the nationalist-minded Calhoun had pressed a plan to set up a $1.5 million fund for roads and canals. Congress approved this despite strong opposition in New England and a divided South. In 1822 a bill providing money for the upkeep of the National Road caused another sectional split. Both measures were vetoed, but in 1824 Monroe approved a differently worded internal improvement act. Such proposals excited intense reactions. John Randolph, opposing the 1824 bill with his usual ferocity, threatened to employ "every . . . means short of actual insurrection" to defeat it. Yet no one—not even Randolph, it will be noted—threatened the Union on this issue.

The tariff continued to divide the country. When a new, still higher tariff was enacted in 1824, the slave states voted almost unanimously against it, the North and Northwest in favor, and New England remained of two minds. Webster (after conducting a poll of business leaders before deciding how to vote) made a powerful speech against the act, but the measure passed without creating a major storm.

These divisions were not severely disruptive, in part because the major politicians, competing for the presidency, did not dare risk alienating any section by taking too extreme a position. Calhoun, for example, had changed his mind about protective tariffs by 1824, but he avoided declaring himself because of his presidential ambitions. Another reason was that the old party system had broken down; the Federalists had disappeared as a national party and the Jeffersonians, lacking an organized opposition, had become less aggressive and more troubled by factional disputes.

The presidential fight was therefore waged on personal grounds, although the heat generated by the contest began the process of reenergizing party politics. Besides Calhoun the candidates were Jackson, Crawford, Adams, and Clay. The maneuvering among them was complex, the infighting savage. In March 1824, Calhoun, who was young enough to wait for the White House, withdrew and declared for the vice presidency, which he won easily. Crawford, who had the support of many congressional leaders, seemed the likely winner, but he suffered a series of paralytic strokes that gravely injured his chances.

Despite the bitterness of the contest, it attracted relatively little public interest; barely a quarter of those eligible took the trouble to vote. In the Electoral College Jackson led with 99, Adams had 84, Crawford 41, and Clay 37. Since no one had a majority, the contest was thrown into the House of Representatives, which, under the Constitution, had to choose from among the three leaders, each state delegation having one vote. By employing his great influence in the House, Clay swung the balance. Not wishing to advance the fortunes of a rival Westerner like Jackson and feeling, with reason, that Crawford's health made him unavailable, Clay gave his support to Adams, who was thereupon elected.

John Quincy Adams as President

Adams, who took a Hamiltonian view of the future of the country, hoped to use the national authority to foster all sorts of useful projects. He asked Congress for a federal program of internal improvements so vast that even Clay boggled when he realized its scope. He came out for aid to manufacturing and agriculture, for a national university,

DOCUMENT

John Quincy Adams, Inaugural Address

▲ This cartoon for the 1824 election shows Adams's "low pressure" ship sailing toward the victory dock, while Jackson's "high pressure" ship explodes before reaching the dock and the victory prize of the White House. Although Jackson won a plurality of both the popular and electoral votes in the election, he failed to win the necessary majority, and the House of Representatives had to choose the winner from among the top three candidates. When Henry Clay's supporters in the House gave their votes—and the victory— to John Quincy Adams, the Jacksonians complained of having been cheated by a "corrupt bargain."

and even for a government astronomical observatory. For a nationalist of unchallengeable Jeffersonian origins like Clay or Calhoun to have pressed for so extensive a program would have been politically risky. For the son of John Adams to do so was disastrous; every doubter remembered his Federalist background and decided that he was trying to overturn the glorious "Revolution of 1800."

Adams proved to be his own worst enemy, for he was as inept a politician as ever lived. Although capable on occasion of turning a phrase—in his first annual message to Congress he described astronomical observatories as "light-houses of the skies"—his general style of public utterance was bumbling and cumbersome. Knowing that many citizens considered things like observatories impractical extravagances, he urged Congress not to be "palsied by the will of our constituents." To persuade Americans, who were almost pathological on the subject of monarchy, to support his road building program, he cited with approval the work being done abroad by "the nations of Europe and . . . their rulers," which revived fears that all Adamses were royalists at heart. He was insensitive to the ebb and flow of public feeling; even when he wanted to move with the tide, he seldom managed to dramatize and publicize his stand effectively. There was wide support in the country for a federal bankruptcy law, but instead of describing himself in plain language as a friend of poor debtors, Adams called for the "amelioration" of the "often oppressive codes relating to insolvency" and buried the recommendation at the tail end of a dull state paper.

One of Adams's worst political failings was his refusal to use his power of appointment to win support. "I will not dismiss . . . able and faithful political opponents to provide for my own partisans," he said. The attitude was traditional at the time, but Adams carried it to extremes—in four years he removed only 12 men from office. Nevertheless, by appointing Henry Clay secretary of state, he laid himself open to the charge that he had won the presidency by a "corrupt bargain." Thus, despite his politically suicidal attitude toward federal jobs, he was subject to the annoyance of a congressional investigation of his appointments, out of which came no less than six bills designed "to reduce the patronage of the executive."

Calhoun's Exposition and Protest

The tariff question added to the president's troubles. High duties, increasingly more repulsive to the export-conscious South, attracted more and more favor in the North and West. Besides manufacturers, lead

miners in Missouri, hemp raisers in Kentucky, wool growers in New York, and many other interests demanded protection against foreign competition. The absence of party discipline provided an ideal climate for "logrolling" in Congress. Legislators found themselves under pressure from their constituents to raise the duties on products of local importance; to satisfy these demands, they traded votes with other congressmen similarly situated. In this way massive "support" for protection was generated.

In 1828 a new tariff was hammered into shape by the House Committee on Manufactures. Northern and western agricultural interests were in command; they wrote into the bill extremely high duties on raw wool, hemp, flax, fur, and liquor. New England manufacturers protested vociferously, for although their products were protected, the proposed law would increase the cost of their raw materials. This gave Southerners, now hopelessly in the minority on the tariff question, a chance to block the bill. When the New Englanders proposed amendments lowering the duties on raw materials, the Southerners voted nay, hoping to force them to reject the measure on the final vote. This desperate strategy failed. New England had by this time committed its future to manufacturing, a change signaled by the somersault of Webster, who, ever responsive to local pressures, now voted for protection. After winning some minor concessions in the Senate, largely through the intervention of Van Buren, enough New Englanders accepted the so-called Tariff of Abominations to ensure its passage.

Vice President Calhoun, who had watched the debate from the vantage point of his post as president of the Senate, now came to a great turning point in his career. He had thrown in his lot with Jackson, whose running mate he was to be in the coming election, and had been assured that the Jacksonians would oppose the bill. Yet northern Jacksonians had been responsible for drafting and passing it. The new tariff would impoverish the South, he believed. He warned Jackson that relief must soon be provided or the Union would be shaken to its foundations. Then he returned to his South Carolina plantation and wrote an essay, *The South Carolina Exposition and Protest*, repudiating the nationalist philosophy he had previously championed.

The South Carolina legislature released this document to the country in December 1828, along with eight resolutions denouncing the protective tariff as unfair and unconstitutional. The theorist Calhoun, however, was not content with outlining the case against the tariff. His *Exposition* provided an ingenious defense of the right of the people of a state to reject a

► *text continues on page 220*

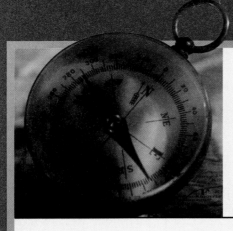

Mapping
the Past

North–South Sectionalism Intensifies

Origins of the "Tariff of Abominations"

After the Napoleonic wars, the "infant industries" of the United States sought and received "protection" against foreign competition in the form of high tariffs on imports. By raising the prices of imported goods, American producers would enjoy a competitive advantage.

A protective tariff was enacted in 1816 without serious controversy. But manufacturers in Massachusetts, New York, and Pennsylvania wanted still higher tariffs. In 1827

Daniel Webster of Massachusetts proposed a law to add an 83-cent tax to every dollar's worth of imported woolen cloth. This would ensure that American woolen manufacturers, many of them located in Massachusetts, would dominate the market; it would also raise the price of woolen cloth to American consumers. The measure was tied in the Senate; Vice President Calhoun cast the deciding vote against the woolen tariff.

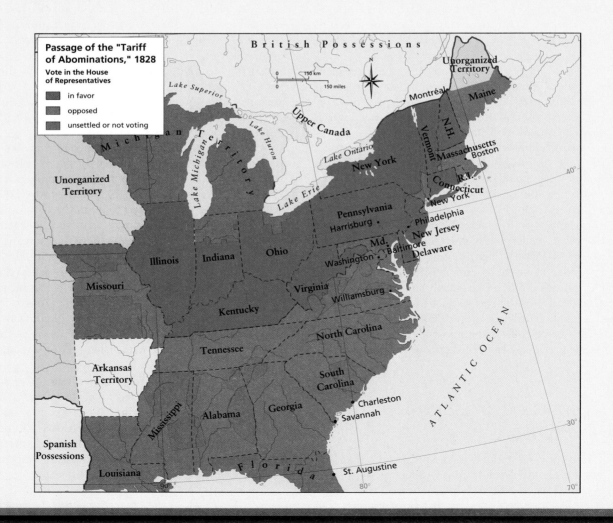

Passage of the "Tariff of Abominations," 1828

Vote in the House of Representatives

- in favor
- opposed
- unsettled or not voting

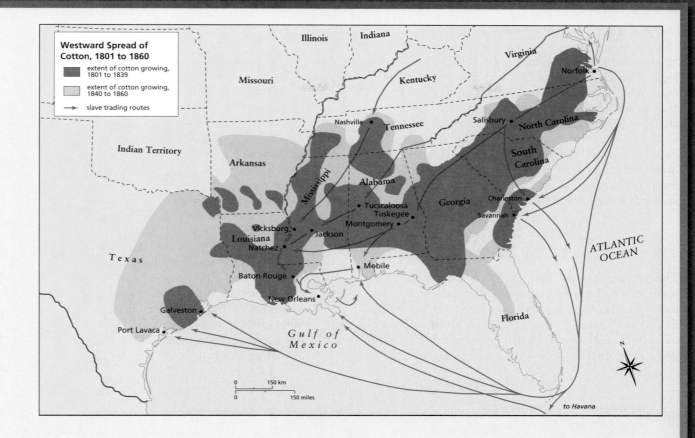

Westward Spread of Cotton, 1801 to 1860

- extent of cotton growing, 1801 to 1839
- extent of cotton growing, 1840 to 1860
- slave trading routes

Redoubling their efforts, the manufacturers convened at Harrisburg, Pennsylvania. They called for far higher duties on woolens and many other products. Their duties would double the price of most woolen goods. Should that happen, a Southerner declared, South Carolina would within a year become "an independent State and her ports will be free ports." But once Congress got hold of the bill, it was transformed. Southerners, to ensure its defeat, attempted to drive a wedge between western farmers and northeastern manufacturers. The Southerners added high taxes on imports of raw materials, such as wool, hemp, and molasses; such measures pleased the sheep farmers and hemp growers of the Mid-Atlantic states and the Midwest, but harmed woolen manufacturers in New England as well as those engaged in shipping. When the final vote came, congressmen in eastern Massachusetts, Rhode Island, and the New York City region voted against the "Tariff of Abominations"; nearly all other northeastern congressmen voted for it, as did nearly every congressman in the West. The vote reflected a profound shift in the nation's political geography. Early in the national period, the most prominent division was often between the more prosperous peoples along the east coast—tidewater planters and urban merchants—and the rough frontiersmen in the western hinterlands. But the vote on the "Tariff of Abominations" of 1828 was an early indication of the emerging political geography reflecting the South's isolation.

Cotton Belt, 1801–1860

Most of the opposition to the "Tariff of Abominations" came from cotton-growing regions—and thus, those dependent on slavery. Slavery had long existed in North America, but by the time of the Revolution the growth of the "peculiar institution" appeared to have been checked. But in 1793 Eli Whitney, a young graduate of Yale College, invented the cotton gin, a simple, hand-operated machine that revitalized cotton cultivation—and slavery. In 1793 only 3000 bales of cotton were produced in the United States. In 1800 output reached 100,000 bales, roughly 500 million pounds; then, there were fewer than a million slaves in the United States, and by the 1820s annual production was averaging more than 400,000 bales. This was only the beginning. Output exceeded 1 million bales in the mid-1830s and nearly 4 million by 1860.

This growth required a huge expansion of the area where cotton was grown. First, cotton took over the fertile Appalachian Piedmont in a band running from southern Virginia into Georgia. Then it spread westward across central Alabama and Mississippi and into the rich alluvial soil of the banks of the Mississippi River, in a broad band from Tennessee and Arkansas to southern Louisiana. Finally, in the 1840s and 1850s, the crop spread into the eastern sections of Texas.

The westward expansion of cotton cultivation served to exacerbate an inherently bad institution. Planters in the Upper South increasingly sold their "surplus" slaves to the more fertile lands in the Mississippi delta, Alabama, and East Texas.

law of Congress. Starting with John Locke's revered concept of government as a contractual relationship, he argued that since the states had created the Union, logic dictated that they be the final arbiters of the meaning of the Constitution, which was its framework. If a special state convention, representing the sovereignty of the people, decided that an act of Congress violated the Constitution, it could interpose its authority and "nullify" the law within its boundaries. Calhoun did not seek to implement this theory in 1828, for he hoped that the next administration would lower the tariff and make nullification unnecessary.

THE MEANING OF SECTIONALISM

The sectional issues that occupied the energies of politicians and strained the ties between the people of the different regions were produced by powerful forces that actually bound the sections together. Growth caused differences that sometimes led to conflict, but growth itself was the product of prosperity.

People were drawn to the West by the expectation that life would be better there, as more often than not it was, at least in the long run. Henry Clay based his American System on the idea that sectional economic differences could be mutually beneficial. He argued plausibly that western farmers would profit by selling their crops to eastern city dwellers and that spending public money on building roads and other internal improvements would make transportation and communication less expensive and thus benefit everyone.

Another force unifying the nation was patriotism; the increasing size and prosperity of the nation made people proud to be part of a growing, dynamic society. Still another was the uniqueness of the American system of government and the people's knowledge that their immediate ancestors had created it. John Adams and Thomas Jefferson died on the same day, July 4, 1826, the fiftieth anniversary of the signing of the Declaration of Independence. People took this not as a remarkable coincidence, but as a sign from the heavens, an indication that God looked with favor on the American experiment.

MILESTONES

1808	James Madison is elected president	**1816**	James Monroe is elected president
1810	Macon's Bill No. 2 removes all restrictions on commerce with Britain and France	**1817**	Rush-Bagot Agreement limits American and British forces on Lake Champlain and Great Lakes
1811	Battle of Tippecanoe shatters Indian confederation	**1819**	United States signs Transcontinental Treaty with Spain
1812	James Madison is reelected president	**1819–1822**	United States experiences economic depression
	Congress declares war on Great Britain	**1820**	James Monroe is reelected president
	USS *Constitution* and *United States* win naval victories	**1820–1821**	Missouri Compromise closes Missouri Territory to slavery, but opens Arkansas Territory to slavery
1813	Captain Oliver Hazard Perry destroys British fleet in Battle of Lake Erie	**1820–1850**	Cities and manufacturing grow rapidly
	General William Henry Harrison defeats British in Battle of the Thames	**1823**	Monroe Doctrine says U.S. will consider future European colonization in western hemisphere a threat to American peace and safety
	Tecumseh dies at Battle of the Thames		
1814	British burn Washington, D.C.		
	Francis Scott Key writes "The Star Spangled Banner" during bombardment of Fort McHenry	**1824–1825**	House of Representatives decides election of 1824 in favor of John Quincy Adams, leading to claims of "corrupt bargain" with Henry Clay
	New England Federalists meet at Hartford Convention		
	Treaty of Ghent officially ends war of 1812	**1828**	Congress passes Tariff of Abominations, leading to nullification debate
1815	General Andrew Jackson defeats British at Battle of New Orleans		

SUPPLEMENTARY READING

On Madison, see Lance Banning, *Sacred Fire of Liberty* (1995), and Jack N. Rakove, *James Madison and the Creation of the American Republic* (1999). The best modern account of the causes and course of the War of 1812 is J. C. A. Stagg, *Mr. Madison's War* (1983). Irving Brant, *James Madison: Commander-in-Chief* (1961), vigorously defends Madison's handling of the war. Jackson's part in the conflict is described in R. V. Remini, *Andrew Jackson and the Course of American Empire* (1977). Richard Barbuto, *Niagara 1814: America Invades Canada* (2000), and David Curtis Skaggs and Larry L. Nelson, *The Sixty Years' War for the Great Lakes* (2001), provide accounts of the war in the North.

On the Treaty of Ghent, see F. L. Engelman, *The Peace of Christmas Eve* (1962), and Bradford Perkins, *Castlereagh and Adams* (1964). For the decline of the Federalist party and the Hartford Convention, consult D. H. Fischer, *The Revolution of American Conservatism* (1965), and J. M. Banner, *To the Hartford Convention* (1981).

For the postwar diplomatic settlements and the Era of Good Feelings, see James Lewis, *The American Union and the Problem of Neighborhood: The United States and the Collapse of the Spanish Empire, 1783–1829* (1998), George Dangerfield, *The Era of Good Feelings* (1952), and Harry Ammon, *James Monroe: The Quest for National Identity* (1971), and on his famous doctrine, Ernest May, *The Making of the Monroe Doctrine* (1976).

Merrill D. Peterson, *The Great Triumvirate* (1987), is an interesting study of Clay, Calhoun, and Webster. Other biographies of statesmen of the period include Paul C. Nagel, *John Quincy Adams* (1997), Robert Remini, *Daniel Webster* (1997), Irving Bartlett, *John C. Calhoun* (1993), Maurice Baxter, *Henry Clay and the American System* (1995), and C. C. Mooney, *William H. Crawford* (1974). On the Missouri Compromise, see Glover Moore, *The Missouri Controversy* (1953). See also P. C. Nagel, *One Nation Indivisible* (1965).

On Indians, in addition to the works cited in Debating the Past (p. 194) see John Sugden, *Tecumseh* (1998), R. David Edmonds, *The Potawatomis* (1978), and Michael N. McConnell, *A Country Between: The Upper Ohio Valley and Its Peoples* (1992).

SUGGESTED WEBSITES

Documents from the War of 1812
http://www.yale.edu/lawweb/avalon/diplomacy/britian/brtreaty.htm
This site includes the important documents from the War of 1812.

The War of 1812
http://members.tripod.com/~war1812/index.html
This site provides in-depth information about the War of 1812.

The Monroe Doctrine
http://www.yale.edu/lawweb/avalon/monroe.htm
Read the Monroe Doctrine, an important early articulation of U.S. foreign policy, online.

The Seminole Indians of Florida
http://www.seminoletribe.com/
Before becoming president, Andrew Jackson began a war against the Seminole Indians.

Toward a National Economy

CHAPTER CONTENTS

DEBATING THE PAST **Was early nineteenth-century America transformed by a "market revolution"?**

MAPPING THE PAST **The Making of the Working Class**

▼ St. Louis during the 1830s, by George Catlin, a lawyer turned painter. Twenty-five years earlier, Catlin's wife had complained of "this wild Country." But by 1830s St. Louis had over 5000 people and regular steamboat service.

Politicians might attribute the growth of the country and the preservation of the Union to their own patriotism and ingenuity, but without the economic and technological developments of the period, neither of these much-to-be-desired objectives could have been attained. The country was still overwhelmingly agricultural in 1820, but the nation was on the brink of a major economic readjustment. Certain obscure seeds planted in the early years of the republic had taken root. Almost unnoticed, new attitudes toward material goods, along with new ways of producing them, were beginning to take hold. The industrial revolution was coming to America with a rush.

GENTILITY AND THE CONSUMER REVOLUTION

The democratic revolution was accompanied by widespread emulation of aristocratic behavior. Sometimes the most ardent American democrats proved the most susceptible to the blandishments of European gentility. Thus young John Adams, while lampooning "the late Refinements in modern manners," nevertheless advised his future wife, Abigail, to be more attentive to posture: "You very often hang your Head like a Bulrush, and you sit with your legs crossed to the ruin of the figure." On his trip to Paris in 1778 on behalf of the Continental Congress, he denounced the splendor of the houses, furniture, and clothing. "I cannot help suspecting that the more

▲ Americans enshrined the simple life and a homespun equality; yet they coveted the cultural markers of aristocracy, such as imported porcelain tea services. This one, made in France, was given to Alexander Hamilton. Gentility spread, historian Richard Bushman writes, "because people longed to be associated with the 'best society.'"

Elegance, the less Virtue," he concluded. Yet despite the exigencies of war, Adams purchased a lavish carriage. On returning to America, he bought a three-story mansion and furnished it with Louis XV chairs and, among other extravagances, an ornate wine cooler from Vincennes.

Among aristocratic circles in Europe, gentility was the product of ancestry and cultivated style; but in America it was largely defined by possession of material goods. Houses with parlors, dining rooms, and hallways bulged with countless articles of consumption: porcelain plates, silver tea services, woolen carpets, walnut tables. By the mid-eighteenth century the "refinement of America" had touched the homes of some Southern planters and urban merchants; but a half century later porcelain plates made by English craftsman Josiah Wedgwood and mahogany washstands by Thomas Chippendale were appearing even in frontier communities. Americans were demanding more goods than such craftsmen could turn out. Everywhere producers sought to expand their workshops, hire and train more artisans, and acquire large stocks of materials and labor-saving machines.

But first they had to locate the requisite capital, find ways to supervise large numbers of workers, and discover how to get raw materials to factories and products to customers. The solutions to these problems, taken together, constituted the "market revolution" of the early nineteenth century. The "industrial revolution" came on its heels.

BIRTH OF THE FACTORY

By the 1770s British manufacturers, especially those in textiles, had made astonishing progress in mechanizing their operations, bringing workers together in buildings called factories where waterpower, and later steam, supplied the force to run new spinning and weaving devices that increased productivity and reduced labor costs.

Because machine-spun cotton was cheaper and of better quality than that spun by hand, producers in other countries were eager to adopt British methods. Americans had depended on Great Britain for such products until the Revolution cut off supplies; then the new spirit of nationalism gave impetus to the development of local industry. A number of state legislatures offered bounties to anyone who would introduce the new machinery. The British, however, guarded their secrets vigilantly. It was illegal to export any of the new machines or to send their plans abroad. Workers skilled in their construction and use were forbidden to leave the country. These restrictions were effective for a time; the principles on which the new machines were based were simple enough, but to construct workable models without plans was another matter. Although a number of persons tried to do so, it was not until Samuel Slater installed his machines in Pawtucket, Rhode Island, that a successful factory was constructed.

Slater, born in England, was more than a skilled mechanic. Attracted by stories of the rewards offered in the United States, he slipped out of England in 1789. Not daring to carry any plans, he depended on his memory and his mechanical sense for the complicated specifications of the necessary machines. Moses Brown brought Slater to Rhode Island to help run his textile-manufacturing operation. Slater insisted on scrapping the crude machinery Brown's company had assembled. Then, working in secrecy with a carpenter who was "under bond not to steal the patterns nor disclose the nature of the work," Slater built and installed his machinery. In December 1790 the first American factory began production.

It was a humble beginning indeed. Slater's machines made only cotton thread, which Brown's company sold in its Providence store and "put out"

▲ A view of Samuel Slater's cotton textile mill at Pawtucket Falls; the fast-running water turned the wheels that powered the machinery.

to individual artisans, who, working for wages, wove it into cloth in their homes. The machines were tended by a labor force of nine children, for the work was simple and the pace slow. The young operatives' pay ranged from 33 to 67 cents a week, about what a youngster could earn in other occupations.[1]

The factory was profitable from the start. Slater soon branched out on his own, and others trained by him opened their own establishments. By 1800 seven mills possessing 2000 spindles were in operation; by 1815, after production had been stimulated by the War of 1812, there were 130,000 spindles turning in 213 factories. Many of the new factories were inefficient, but the well-managed ones earned large profits. Slater began with almost nothing. When he died in 1835 he owned mill properties in Rhode Island, Massachusetts, Connecticut, and New Hampshire in addition to other interests. By the standards of the day he was a rich man.

Before long the Boston Associates, a group of merchants headed by Francis Cabot Lowell, added a new dimension to factory production. Beginning at Waltham, Massachusetts, where the Charles River provided the necessary waterpower, between 1813 and 1850 they revolutionized textile production. Some early factory owners had set up hand looms in their plants, but the weavers could not keep pace with the whirring spinning jennies. Lowell, after an extensive study of British mills, smuggled the plans for an efficient power loom into America. His Boston Manufacturing Company at Waltham, capitalized at $300,000, combined machine production, large-scale operation, efficient management, and centralized marketing procedures. It concentrated on the mass production of a standardized product.

Lowell's cloth, though plain and rather coarse, was durable and cheap. His profits averaged almost 20 percent a year during the Era of Good Feelings. In 1823 the Boston Associates began to harness the power of the Merrimack River, setting up a new $600,000 corporation at the sleepy village of East Chelmsford, Massachusetts (population 300), where there was a fall of 32 feet in the river. Within three years the town, appropriately renamed Lowell, had 2000 inhabitants.

---

[1]This labor pattern persisted for several decades. In 1813 a cotton manufacturer placed the following advertisement in the *Utica* (N.Y.) *Patriot:* "A few sober and industrious families of at least five children each, over the age of eight years are wanted at the Cotton Factory. Widows with large families would do well to attend this notice."

▶ *text continues on page 228*

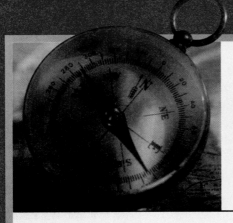

Mapping the Past

The Making of the Working Class

Increasing Physical Separation of Masters and Workers

During the 1700s boys in their teens learned a skill by serving as apprentices to master workmen. After five to seven years of training, apprentices usually became wage-earning journeymen. The master's workshop commonly functioned as both a tiny factory and small store. One journeyman shoemaker in Rochester, New York explained

> It was customary for the boss, with the younger apprentices, to occupy the room in front where, with bared arms and leather aprons, they performed their work and met their customers. A shop in the rear or above would be occupied by the tramping journeyman and the older apprentice. . . . The shops were low rooms in which from fifteen to twenty men worked . . .

Because they lived and worked under the same roof, masters commonly treated apprentices almost as their children. Journeymen usually lived in boardinghouses near the masters'

workshops; if they proved industrious, talented, and frugal, they became master workers, opened a shop of their own, and hired apprentices.

But economic growth during the 1820s and 1830s eroded the ties between masters and workers. Historian Paul Johnson described how this process worked in Rochester, New York. In 1823, the Erie Canal had been completed as far as that city, enabling grain from the Genesee Valley to be loaded onto canal boats and taken to markets in New York City. During the next ten years Rochester became the fastest growing city in the nation. Master workers in Rochester enlarged their shops, hired more workers, and focused more keenly on profits rather than their traditional obligations to workers. They increasingly moved manufacturing processes out of their shops, which now became shoe stores. Journeymen, with paid assistants, performed the work of shoemaking in separate locations.

Class formation: journeymen and master shoemakers in Rochester, New York take separate residences, 1827–1834

● residences of journeymen shoemakers   🏠 masters' households

This physical separation of masters and journeymen is reflected in the maps on page 226. In 1827, for example, most journeymen lived near their masters' shops. But by 1834 journeymen were scattered throughout Rochester. A similar separation of journeymen and masters was found among skilled workers in the building trades. In Johnson's words, the journeymen and apprentices "worked for men they seldom saw." Often such men were becoming estranged from those who paid their wages.

Johnson found the same shift, from apprentice and journeyman to wage earner, and from master to merchant capitalist, in many other trades.

The Journey to Work, Philadelphia, 1850

During the next two decades, the expanding scale of manufacturing operations made the craft-dominated workshop nearly an anachronism. Larger operations required more work space, and the need to locate near suppliers, customers, or a source of waterpower meant that the owner's home could no longer serve as a workplace. By about 1850, Boston, New York, Philadelphia, and other cities had sorted themselves into commercial and residential districts; the residential districts further separated into working-class and employer-class neighborhoods.

Nowadays the term *inner city* often connotes poverty, and *suburbs*, prosperity. But the relationship was reversed in the mid-nineteenth-century city, as historian Sam Bass Warner has shown in his study of Philadelphia. In 1850 affluent Philadelphians resided in the core of the city while factory workers lived in shanties and boardinghouses along its outskirts. The map *(left)*, based on census data for 1850, shows that fewer factory workers lived in downtown Philadelphia than were employed by the factories there. Each day, thousands of factory workers from Penn Township and the eastern section of Passyunk Township walked into town to work in downtown factories.

Philadelphia, 1850: workers' daily journey to factory

- in-migration wards
- out-migration wards
- no net migration
- → migration trend

AN INDUSTRIAL PROLETARIAT?

As machines displaced skilled labor, the ability of laborers to influence working conditions declined. If skilled, they either became employers and developed entrepreneurial and managerial skills, or they descended into the mass of wage earners. Simultaneously, the changing structure of production widened the gap between owners and workers and blurred the distinction between skilled and unskilled labor.

These trends might have been expected to generate hostility between workers and employers. To some extent they did. There were strikes for higher wages and to protest work speedups throughout the 1830s and again in the 1850s. Efforts to found unions and to create political organizations dedicated to advancing the interests of workers were also undertaken. But well into the 1850s Americans displayed few signs of the class solidarity common among European workers.

Why America did not produce a self-conscious working class is a question that has long intrigued historians. As with most such large questions, no single answer has been forthcoming. Some historians argue that the existence of the frontier siphoned off displaced and dissatisfied workers. The number of urban laborers who went West could not have been large, but the fact that the expanding economy created many opportunities for laborers to rise out of the working class was surely another reason why so few of them developed strong class feelings.

Other historians believe that ethnic and racial differences kept workers from seeing themselves as a distinct class with common needs and common enemies. The influx of needy immigrants willing to accept almost any wage was certainly resented by native-born workers. The growing number of free blacks in northern cities—between 1800 and 1830 the number tripled in Philadelphia and quadrupled in New York—also inhibited the development of a self-identified working class.

These answers help explain the relative absence of class conflict during the early stages of the industrial revolution in America, but so does the fact that conditions in the early shops and factories represented an improvement for the people who worked in them. This was the case with nearly all European immigrants, though less so for urban free blacks, since in the South many found work in the skilled trades.

Most workers in the early textile factories were drawn from outside the regular labor market. Relatively few artisan spinners and weavers became factory workers; indeed, some of them continued to work as they had, for it was many years before the factories could even begin to satisfy the ever-increasing demand for cloth. Nor did immigrants attend the new machines. Instead, the mill owners relied chiefly on women and children. They did so because machines lessened the need for skill and strength and because the labor shortage made it necessary to tap unexploited sources. By the early 1820s about half the cotton textile workers in the factories were under 16 years of age.

Most people of that generation considered this a good thing. They reasoned that the work was easy and that it kept youngsters busy at useful tasks while providing their families with extra income. Roxanna Foote, whose daughter, Harriet Beecher Stowe, wrote *Uncle Tom's Cabin*, came from a solid middle-class family in Guilford, Connecticut. Nevertheless, she worked full-time before her marriage in her grandfather's small spinning mill. "This spinning-mill was a favorite spot," a relative recalled many years later. "Here the girls often received visitors, or read or chatted while they spun." Roxanna explained her daily regimen as a mill girl matter-of-factly: "I generally rise with the sun, and, after breakfast, take my wheel, which is my daily companion, and the evening is generally devoted to reading, writing, and knitting."

This seems a somewhat idealized picture, or perhaps working for one's grandfather made a difference. Another young girl, Emily Chubbock, later a well-known writer, had a less pleasant recollection of her experience as an 11-year-old factory hand earning $1.25 a week. "My principal recollections . . . are of noise and filth, bleeding hands and aching feet, and a very sad heart." In any case, a society accustomed to seeing the children of fairly well-to-do farmers working full-time in the fields was not shocked by the sight of children working all day in mills. In factories where laborers were hired in family units, no member earned very much, but with a couple of adolescent daughters and perhaps a son of 9 or 10 helping out, a family could take home enough to live decently. For most working Americans, then as now, that was success enough.

LOWELL'S WALTHAM SYSTEM: WOMEN AS FACTORY WORKERS

Instead of hiring children, the Boston Associates developed the "Waltham System" of employing young, unmarried women in their new textile mills. For a

▲ The first mill operations performed only the task of spinning wool, cotton, and other fibers into thread; soon weaving was also mechanized, so that fabric ready to be cut and sewn was manufactured. Note that the workers are all women, supervised by a male foreman.

DOCUMENT

The Harbinger,
"Female Workers
at Lowell"

generation after the opening of the Merri-mack Manufacturing Company in 1823, the thriving factory towns of Lowell, Chicopee, and Manchester provided the background for a remarkable industrial idyll. Young women came from farms all over New England to work for a year or two in the mills. They were lodged in company boardinghouses, which, like college dormitories, became centers of social life and not merely places to eat and sleep. Unlike modern college dormitories, the boardinghouses were strictly supervised; strait-laced New Englanders did not hesitate to permit their daughters to live in them. The regulations laid down by one company, for example, required that all employees "show that they are penetrated by a laudable love of temperance and virtue." "Ardent spirits" were banished from company property, "games of hazard and cards" prohibited. A 10 P.M. curfew was strictly enforced.

The women earned between $2.50 and $3.25 a week, about half of which went for room and board. Some of the remainder they sent home, the rest (what there was of it) they could spend as they wished.

Most of these young women did not have to support themselves. They worked to save for a trousseau, to help educate a younger brother, or simply for the experience and excitement of meeting new people and escaping the confining environment of the farm. "The feeling that at this new

work, the few hours they had of every-day leisure was entirely their own was a satisfaction to them," one Lowell worker recalled. Anything but an industrial proletariat, they filled the windows of the factories with flowering plants, organized sewing circles, edited their own literary periodicals, and attended lectures on edifying subjects. That such activity was possible on top of a 70-hour work week is a commentary on both the resiliency of youth and the leisurely pace of these early factories. The English novelist Charles Dickens, though scarcely enchanted by other American ways, was impressed by his visit to Lowell, which he compared most favorably to "those great haunts of misery," the English manufacturing towns. "They were all well dressed," he wrote of the workers. "They were healthy in appearance, many of them remarkably so, and had the manners and deportment of young women. . . . The rooms in which they worked were as well ordered as themselves."

Life in the mills was not all it might have been. Although they made up 85 percent of the workforce, women were kept out of supervisory positions. In 1834 workers in several mills "turned out" to protest cuts in their wages and a hike in what they paid for board. This work stoppage did not force a reversal of management policy. Another strike two years later in response to a work speedup was somewhat more successful. But when a drop in prices in

DOCUMENT

Regarding Life
in the Mills

the 1840s led the owners to introduce new rules designed to increase production, workers lacked the organizational strength to block them. By then young women of the kind that had flocked to the mills in the 1820s and 1830s were beginning to find work as schoolteachers and clerks. Mill owners turned increasingly to Irish immigrants to operate their machines.

Irish and German Immigrants

Between 1790 and 1820 the population of the United States had more than doubled to 9.6 million. The most remarkable feature of this growth was that it resulted almost entirely from natural increase. The birthrate in the early nineteenth century exceeded 50 per 1000 population, a rate as high as that of any country in the world today. Fewer than 250,000 immigrants entered the United States between 1790 and 1820. European wars, the ending of the slave trade, and doubts about the viability of the new republic slowed the flow of humanity across the Atlantic to a trickle.

But soon after the final defeat of Napoleon in 1815, immigration began to pick up. In the 1820s, some 150,000 European immigrants arrived; in the 1830s, 600,000; in the 1840s, 1.7 million. The 1850 census, the first to make the distinction, estimated that of the nation's population of 23 million, more than 10 percent were foreign-born. In the Northeast the proportion exceeded 15 percent.

Most of this human tide came from Germany and Ireland, but substantial numbers also came from Great Britain and the Scandinavian countries. As with earlier immigrants, most were drawn to America by what are called "pull" factors: the prospect of abundant land, good wages, and economic opportunity generally, or by the promise of political and religious freedom. But many came because of "push" factors: to stay where they were meant to face starvation. This was particularly true of those from Ireland, where a potato blight triggered the flight of tens of thousands. This Irish exodus continued; by the end of the century there were more people of Irish origin in America than in Ireland.

Once ashore in New York, Boston, or Philadelphia, most relatively prosperous immigrants pushed directly westward. Others found work in the new factory towns along the route of the Erie Canal, in the lower Delaware Valley southeast of Philadelphia, or along the Merrimack River north of Boston. But most of the Irish immigrants, "the poorest and most wretched population that can be found in the world," one of their priests called them, lacked the means to go West. Aside from the cost of transportation, starting a farm required far more capital than they could raise. Like it or not, they had to settle in the eastern cities.

Viewed in historical perspective, this massive wave of immigration stimulated the American economy. In the short run, the influx of the 1830s and 1840s depressed living standards and strained the social fabric. For the first time the nation had acquired a culturally distinctive, citybound, and propertyless class. The poor Irish immigrants had to accept whatever wages employers offered them. By doing so they caused resentment among native workers, resentment exacerbated by the unfamiliarity of the Irish with city ways and by their Roman Catholic faith, which the Protestant majority associated with European authoritarianism and corruption.

The Persistence of the Household System

Since technology affected American industry unevenly, contemporaries found the changes difficult to evaluate. Interchangeable firing pins for rifles did not lead at once even to matching pairs of shoes. More than 15 years passed after John Fitch built and launched the world's first regularly scheduled steamboat in 1790 before it was widely accepted. Few people in the 1820s appreciated how profound the impact of the factory system would be. The city of Lowell seemed remarkable and important but not necessarily a herald of future trends.

Yet in nearly every field apparently minor changes were being made. Beginning around 1815, small improvements in the design of waterwheels, such as the use of leather transmission belts and metal gears, made possible larger and more efficient machinery in mills and factories. The woolen industry gradually became as mechanized as the cotton. Iron production advanced beyond the stage of the blacksmith's forge and the small foundry only slowly; nevertheless, by 1810 machines were stamping out nails at a third of the cost of the hand-forged type, and a few years later sheet iron, formerly hammered out laboriously by hand, was being produced in efficient rolling mills. At about this time the puddling process for refining pig iron made it possible to use coal for fuel instead of expensive charcoal.

Key improvements were made soon after the War of 1812 in the manufacture of paper, glass, and pottery. The commercial canning of sterilized foods

▲ The West Point Foundry in Cold Spring, New York, by Robert Weir Ferguson. This painting conveys how the machines of the industrial revolution are dominating workers' lives.

in airtight containers began about 1820. The invention in that year of a machine for cutting ice, which reduced the cost by over 50 percent, had equally important effects on urban eating habits.

RISE OF CORPORATIONS

Mechanization required substantial capital investment, and capital was chronically in short supply. The modern method of organizing large enterprises, the corporation, was slow to develop. Between 1781 and 1801 only 326 corporations were chartered by the states, and only a few of them were engaged in manufacturing.

The general opinion was that only quasi-public projects, such as roads and waterworks, were entitled to the privilege of incorporation. Anyone interested in organizing a corporation had to obtain a special act

of a state legislature. And even among businessmen there was a tendency to associate corporations with monopoly, with corruption, and with the undermining of individual enterprise. In 1820 the economist Daniel Raymond wrote: "The very object . . . of the act of incorporation is to produce inequality, either in rights, or in the division of property. Prima facie, therefore all money corporations are detrimental to national wealth. They are always created for the benefit of the rich. . . ." Such feelings help explain why as late as the 1860s most manufacturing was being done by unincorporated companies.

While the growth of industry did not suddenly revolutionize American life, it reshaped society in various ways. For a time it lessened the importance of foreign commerce. Some relative decline from the lush years immediately preceding Jefferson's embargo was no doubt inevitable, especially in the fabulously profitable reexport trade. But American industrial growth reduced the need for foreign products and thus the business of merchants. Only in the 1850s, when the wealth and population of the United States were more than three times what they had been in the first years of the century, did the value of American exports climb back to the levels of 1807. As the country moved closer to self-sufficiency (a point it never reached), nationalistic and isolationist sentiments were subtly augmented. During the embargo and the War of 1812 a great deal of capital had been transferred from commerce to industry; afterward new capital continued to prefer industry, attracted by the high profits and growing prestige of manufacturing. The rise of manufacturing affected farmers too, for as cities grew in size and number, the need to feed the populace caused commercial agriculture to flourish. Dairy farming, truck gardening, and fruit growing began to thrive around every manufacturing center.

▲ Eli Whitney's cotton gin was based on a simple concept: the cotton, embedded with seeds, moved through interlocking combs, moving in opposite directions. In the above rendering, the cotton is fed from above; the combed cotton came out lower left, and the seeds, lower right.

COTTON REVOLUTIONIZES THE SOUTH

By far the most important indirect effect of industrialization occurred in the South, which soon began to produce cotton to supply the new textile factories of Great Britain and New England. The possibility of growing large amounts of this crop in America had not been seriously considered in colonial times, but by the 1780s the demand for raw cotton to feed the voracious British mills was causing many American farmers to experiment with the crop. Most of the world's cotton at this time came from Egypt, India, and the East Indies. The plant was considered tropical, most varieties being unable to survive the slightest frost. Hamilton, who missed nothing that related to the economic growth of the country, reported: "It has been observed . . . that the nearer the place of growth to the equator, the better the quality of the cotton."

Beginning in 1786, "sea-island" cotton was grown successfully in the mild, humid lowlands and offshore islands along the coasts of Georgia and South Carolina. This was a high-quality cotton, silky and long-fibered like the Egyptian. But its susceptibility to frost severely limited the area of its cultivation. Elsewhere in the South, "green-seed," or upland, cotton flourished, but this plant had little commercial value because the seeds could not be easily separated from the lint. When sea-island cotton was passed between two rollers, its shiny black seeds simply popped out; with upland cotton the seeds were pulled through with the lint and crushed, the oils and broken bits destroying the value of the fiber. To remove the seeds by hand was laborious; a slave working all day could clean scarcely a pound of the white fluff. This made it an uneconomical crop. In 1791 the usually sanguine Hamilton admitted in his *Report on Manufactures* that "the extensive cultivation of cotton can, perhaps, hardly be expected."

Early American cotton manufacturers used the sea-island variety or imported the foreign fiber, in the latter case paying a duty of 3 cents a pound. However, the planters of South Carolina and Georgia, suffering from hard times after the Revolution, needed a new cash crop. Rice production was not expanding, and indigo, the other staple of the area, had ceased to be profitable when it was no longer possible to claim the British bounty. Cotton seemed an obvious answer. Farmers were experimenting hopefully with varieties of the plant and mulling the problem of how upland cotton could be more easily deseeded.

This was the situation in the spring of 1793, when Eli Whitney was a guest at Mulberry Grove, the plantation of Catherine Greene, widow of General Nathanael Greene, some dozen miles from Savannah.[2] Whitney had accepted a position as private

---

[2]The property, formerly owned by a prominent Georgia Tory, had been given to Greene by the state in gratitude for his having driven out the British during the Revolution.

tutor at 100 guineas a year with a nearby family and had stopped to visit a friend, Phineas Miller, who was overseer of the Greene plantation. While at Mulberry Grove, Whitney, who had never seen a cotton plant before, met a number of the local landowners.

> I heard [he wrote his father] much of the extreme difficulty of ginning Cotton, that is, separating it from its seed. There were a number of very respectable Gentlemen at Mrs. Greene's who all agreed that if a machine could be invented that would clean the Cotton with expedition, it would be a great thing both to the Country and to the inventor.

Whitney thought about the problem for a few days and then "struck out a plan of a machine." He described it to Miller, who enthusiastically offered to finance the invention. Since Whitney had just learned that his job as tutor would pay only 50 guineas, he accepted Miller's proposal.

Within ten days he had solved the problem that had baffled the planters. His gin (engine) consisted of a cylinder covered with rows of wire teeth rotating in a box filled with cotton. As the cylinder turned, the teeth passed through narrow slits in a metal grating. Cotton fibers were caught by the teeth and pulled through the slits. The seeds, too thick to pass through the openings, were left behind. A second cylinder, with brushes rotating in the opposite direction to sweep the cotton from the wires, prevented matting and clogging.

This "absurdly simple contrivance" almost instantly transformed southern agriculture. With a gin a slave could clean 50 times as much cotton as by hand; soon larger models driven by mules and horses were available. The machines were so easy to construct (once the basic idea was understood) that Whitney and Miller were never able to enforce their patent rights effectively. Rival manufacturers shamelessly pirated their work, and countless farmers built gins of their own. Cotton production increased from 3000 bales in 1790 to well over 400,000 bales a year in the early 1820s.

Despite this avalanche, the price of cotton remained high. During the 1790s it ranged between 26 and 44 cents a pound, a veritable bonanza. In the next decade the price was lower (15 to 19 cents), but it still provided high profits even for inefficient planters. The price rose again after 1815, and only once before 1826 did the price fall below 14 cents. With prices at these levels, profits of $50 an acre were not unusual, and the South boomed.

Upland cotton would grow wherever there were 200 consecutive days without frost and 24 inches of rain. The crop engulfed Georgia and South Carolina and spread north into parts of Virginia. After Andrew Jackson smashed the southwestern Indians during the War of 1812, the rich "Black Belt" area of central Alabama and northern

▲ **Cotton Production and Slave Population, 1800–1860**

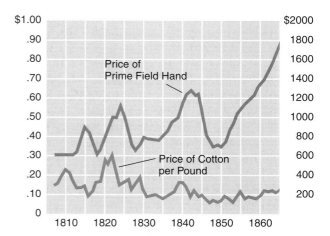

▲ **Prices for Cotton and for Slaves, 1802–1860**
The vertical axis on the left shows cents, and the curve for the price of cotton should be read against it; the right vertical axis shows dollars, and the price of slaves should be read against it. These prices are from New Orleans records. The rising trend of slave prices (and a growing slave population) shows the continuing profitability and viability of slavery up to 1860.

Mississippi and the delta region along the lower Mississippi River were rapidly taken over by the fluffy white staple. In 1821 Alabama alone raised 40,000 bales. Central Tennessee also became important cotton country.

Cotton stimulated the economy of the rest of the nation as well. Most of it was exported, the sale paying for much-needed European products. The transportation, insurance, and final disposition of the crop fell largely into the hands of northern merchants, who profited accordingly. And the surplus corn and hogs of western farmers helped feed the slaves of the new cotton plantations. Cotton was the major force in the economy for a generation, beginning about 1815.

REVIVAL OF SLAVERY

Amid the national rejoicing over this prosperity, one aspect both sad and ominous was easily overlooked. Slavery, a declining or at worst stagnant institution in the decade of the Revolution, was revitalized in the following years.

Libertarian beliefs inspired by the Revolution ran into the roadblock of race prejudice as soon as some of the practical aspects of freedom for blacks became apparent. As disciples of John Locke, the Revolutionary generation had a deep respect for property rights; in the last analysis most white Americans placed these rights ahead of the personal liberty of black Americans in their constellation of values. Forced abolition of slavery therefore attracted few recruits. Moreover, the rhetoric of the Revolution had raised the aspirations of blacks. Increasing signs of rebelliousness appeared among them, especially after the slave uprising in Saint Domingue, which culminated, after a great bloodbath, in the establishment of the black Republic of Haiti in 1804. This example of a successful slave revolt filled white Americans with apprehension. Their fears were irrational (Haitian blacks outnumbered whites and mulattos combined by seven to one) but nonetheless real. And fear led to repression; the exposure in 1801 of a plot to revolt in Virginia, led by the slave Gabriel, resulted in some three dozen executions even though no actual uprising had occurred.

The mood of the Revolutionary decade had led a substantial number of masters to free their slaves. Unfortunately this led many other whites to have second thoughts about ending slavery. "If the blacks see all of their color slaves, it will seem to them a disposition of Providence, and they will be content," a

Virginia legislator, apparently something of an amateur psychologist, claimed. "But if they see others like themselves free . . . they will repine." As the number of free blacks rose, restrictions on them were everywhere tightened.

In the 1780s many opponents of slavery began to think of solving the "Negro problem" by colonizing freed slaves in some distant region—in the western districts or perhaps in Africa. The colonization movement had two aspects. One, a manifestation of an embryonic black nationalism, reflected the disgust of black Americans with local racial attitudes and their interest in African civilization. Paul Cuffe, a Massachusetts Quaker, managed to finance the emigration of 38 of his fellow blacks to British Sierra Leone in 1815, but few others followed. Most influential northern blacks, the most conspicuous among them the Reverend Richard Allen, bishop of the African Methodist Church, opposed the idea vigorously.

The other colonization movement, led by whites, was paternalistic. Some white colonizationists genuinely abhorred slavery. Others could not stomach living with free blacks; to them colonization was merely a polite word for deportation. Most white colonizationists were conservatives who considered themselves realists. Whether they thought African Americans degenerate by nature or the victims of their surroundings, they were sure that American conditions gave them no chance to better their lot and that both races would profit from separation.

The colonization idea became popular in Virginia in the 1790s, but nothing was achieved until after the founding of the American Colonization Society in 1817. The society purchased African land and established the Republic of Liberia. However, despite the cooperation of a handful of black nationalists and the patronage of many important white Southerners, including Presidents Madison and Monroe and Chief Justice Marshall, it accomplished little. Although some white colonizationists expected exslaves to go to Africa as enthusiastic Christian missionaries who would convert and "civilize" the natives, few blacks in fact wished to migrate to a land as alien to their own experience as to their masters'. Only about 12,000 went to Liberia, and the toll taken among them by tropical diseases was large. As late as 1850 the black American population of Liberia was only 6000.

The cotton boom of the early nineteenth century acted as a brake on the colonization movement. As cotton production expanded, the need for labor in the South grew apace. The price of slaves doubled between 1795 and 1804. As it rose, the inclination of even the most kindhearted masters to free their slaves began to falter. Although the importation of slaves from abroad had been outlawed by all the states, perhaps 25,000 were smuggled into the country in the 1790s. In 1804 South Carolina reopened the trade, and between that date and 1808, when the constitutional prohibition of importation became effective, some 40,000 were brought in. Thereafter the miserable traffic in human beings continued clandestinely, though on a small scale.

The cotton boom triggered an internal trade in slaves that frequently wreaked havoc among them. While it had always been legal for owners to transport their own slaves to a new state if they were settling there, many states forbade, or at least severely restricted, interstate commercial transactions in human flesh. A Virginia law of 1778, for example, prohibited the importation of slaves for purposes of sale, and persons entering the state with slaves had to swear that they did not intend to sell them. Once cotton became important, these laws were either repealed or systematically evaded. There was a surplus of slaves in one part of the United States and an acute shortage in another. A migration from the upper South to the cotton lands quickly sprang up. Slaves from "free" New York and New Jersey and even from New England began to appear on the auction blocks of Savannah and Charleston. Early in the Era of Good Feelings, newspapers in New Orleans were carrying reports such as: "Jersey negroes appear to be particularly adapted to this market. . . . We have the right to calculate on large importations in the future, from the success which hitherto attended the sale."

By about 1820 the letter of the law began to be changed. Soon the slave trade became an organized business, cruel and shameful, frowned on by the "best" people of the South, managed by the depraved and the greedy, yet patronized by nearly anyone who needed labor. "The native land of Washington, Jefferson, and Madison," one disgusted Virginian told a French visitor, "[has] become the Guinea of the United States."

The lot of African Americans in the northern states was almost as bad as that of southern free blacks. Except in New England, where there were few blacks to begin with, most were denied the vote, either directly or by extralegal pressures. They could not testify in court, intermarry with whites, obtain decent jobs or housing, or get even a rudimentary education. Most states segregated blacks in theaters, hospitals, and churches and on public transportation facilities. They were barred from hotels and restaurants patronized by whites.

Northern blacks could at least protest and try to convince the white majority of the injustice of their treatment. These rights were denied their southern brethren. They could and did publish newspapers and pamphlets, organize for political action, petition legislatures and the Congress for redress of grievance—in short, they applied methods of peaceful persuasion in an effort to improve their position in society.

ROADS TO MARKET

Inventions and technological improvements were extremely important in the settlement of the West. On superficial examination, this may not seem to have been the case, for the hordes of settlers who struggled across the mountains immediately after the War of 1812 were no better equipped than their ancestors who had pushed up the eastern slopes in previous generations. Many plodded on foot over hundreds of miles, dragging crude carts laden with their meager possessions. More fortunate pioneers traveled on horseback or in heavy, cumbersome wagons, the best known being the hearselike, canvas-topped Conestoga "covered wagons," pulled by horses or oxen.

Expanding America and Internal Improvements

In many cases the pioneers followed trails and roads no better than those of colonial days—quagmires in wet weather, rutted and pitted with potholes a good part of the year. When they settled down, their way of life was no more advanced than that of the Pilgrims. At first they were creatures of the forest, feeding on its abundance, building their homes and simple furniture with its wood, clothing themselves in the furs of forest animals. They usually planted the first crop in a natural glade; thereafter, year by year, they pushed back the trees with ax and saw and fire until the land was cleared. Any source of power more complicated than an ox was beyond their ken. Until the population of the territory had grown large enough to support town life, settlers were as dependent on crude household manufacturers as any earlier pioneer.

The spread of settlement into the Mississippi Valley created challenges that required technological advances if they were to be met. In the social climate of that age in the United States, these advances were not slow in coming. Most were related to transportation, the major problem for Westerners. Without economical means of getting their produce to market, they were condemned to lives of crude self-sufficiency. Everyone recognized that an efficient

▲ This stage, having just passed over a solid road of made of tree trunks, must now make its way across an all-dirt road. Already its wheels have sunk several inches into the mud.

transportation network would increase land values, stimulate domestic and foreign trade, and strengthen the entire economy.

The Mississippi River and its tributaries provided a natural highway for western commerce and communication, but it was one that had grave disadvantages. Farm products could be floated down to New Orleans on rafts and flatboats, but the descent along the Ohio River from Pittsburgh to the Mississippi took at least a month. Transportation upstream was out of the question for anything but the lightest and most valuable products, and even for them it was extremely expensive. In any case, the natural flow of trade was between East and West. That is why, from early in the westward movement, much attention was given to building roads linking the Mississippi Valley to the eastern seaboard.

Constructing decent roads over the rugged Appalachians was a formidable task. The steepest grades had to be reduced by cutting through hills

and filling in low places, all without modern blasting and earth-moving equipment. Streams had to be bridged. Drainage ditches were essential if the roads were not to be washed out by the first rains, and a firm foundation of stones, topped with a well-crowned gravel dressing, had to be provided if they were to stand up under the pounding of heavy wagons. The skills required for building roads of this quality had been developed in Great Britain and France, and the earliest American examples, constructed in the 1790s, were similar to good European highways. The first such road, connecting Philadelphia and Lancaster, Pennsylvania, opened to traffic in 1794.

In heavily populated sections the volume of traffic made good roads worth their cost, which ran to as much as $13,000 a mile where the terrain was difficult, though the average was perhaps half that figure. In some cases good roads ran into fairly remote areas. In New York, always a leading state in the movement for improved transportation, an excellent road had been built all the way from Albany to Lake Erie by the time of the War of 1812, and by 1821 the state had some 4000 miles of good roads.

TRANSPORTATION AND THE GOVERNMENT

Most of the improved highways and many bridges were built as business ventures by private interests. Promoters charged tolls, the rates being set by the states. Tolls were collected at gates along the way; hinged poles suspended across the road were turned back by a guard after receipt of the toll. Hence these thoroughfares were known as turnpikes, or simply pikes.

The profits earned by a few early turnpikes, such as the one between Philadelphia and Lancaster, caused the boom in private road building, but even the most fortunate of the turnpike companies did not make much money. Maintenance was expensive, traffic spotty. (Ordinary public roads paralleling turnpikes were sometimes called "shunpikes" because penny-pinching travelers used them to avoid the tolls.) Some states bought stock to bolster weak companies, and others built and operated turnpikes as public enterprises. Local governments everywhere provided considerable support, for every town was eager to develop efficient communication with its neighbors.

Despite much talk about individual self-reliance and free enterprise, local, state, and national governments contributed heavily to the development of what in the jargon of the day were called "internal improvements." They served as "primary entrepreneurs," supplying capital for risky but socially desirable enterprises, with the result that a fascinating mixture of private and public energy went into the building of these institutions. At the federal level even the parsimonious Jeffersonians became deeply involved. In 1808 Secretary of the Treasury Albert Gallatin drafted a comprehensive plan for constructing much-needed roads at a cost of $16 million. This proposal was not adopted, but the government poured money in an erratic and unending stream into turnpike companies and other organizations created to improve transportation.

Logically, the major highways, especially those over the mountains, should have been built by the national government. Strategic military requirements alone would have justified such a program. One major artery, the Old National Road, running from Cumberland, Maryland, to Wheeling, in western Virginia, was constructed by the United States between 1811 and 1818. In time it was extended as far west as Vandalia, Illinois. However, further federal road building was hampered by political squabbles in Congress, usually phrased in constitutional terms but in fact based on sectional rivalries and other economic conflicts. Thus no comprehensive highway program was undertaken in the nineteenth century.

While the National Road, the New York Pike, and other, rougher trails such as the Wilderness Road into the Kentucky country were adequate for the movement of settlers, they did not begin to answer the West's need for cheap and efficient transportation. Wagon freight rates averaged at least 30 cents a ton-mile around 1815. At such rates, to transport a ton of oats from Buffalo to New York would have cost 12 times the value of the oats! To put the problem another way, four horses could haul a ton and a half of oats about 18 or 20 miles a day over a good road. If they could obtain half their feed by grazing, the horses would still consume about 50 pounds of oats a day. It requires little mathematics to figure out how much oats would be left in the wagon when it reached New York City, almost 400 miles away.

Turnpikes made it possible to transport such goods as clothing, hardware, coffee and books across the Appalachians, but the expense was considerable. It cost more to ship a ton of freight 300 miles over the mountains from Philadelphia to Pittsburgh than from Pittsburgh to Philadelphia by way of New Orleans, more than ten times as far. Until the coming of the railroad, which was just being introduced in England in 1825, the cost of shipping bulky goods by land over the great distances common in America was prohibitive. Businessmen and inventors concentrated instead on improving water transport, first by designing better boats and then by developing artificial waterways.

DEVELOPMENT OF STEAMBOATS

Rafts and flatboats were adequate for downstream travel, but the only practical solution to upstream travel was the steamboat. After John Fitch's work around 1790, a number of others made important contributions to the development of steam navigation. One early enthusiast was John Stevens, a wealthy New Jerseyite, who designed an improved steam boiler for which he received one of the first patents issued by the United States. Stevens got his brother-in-law, Robert R. Livingston, interested in

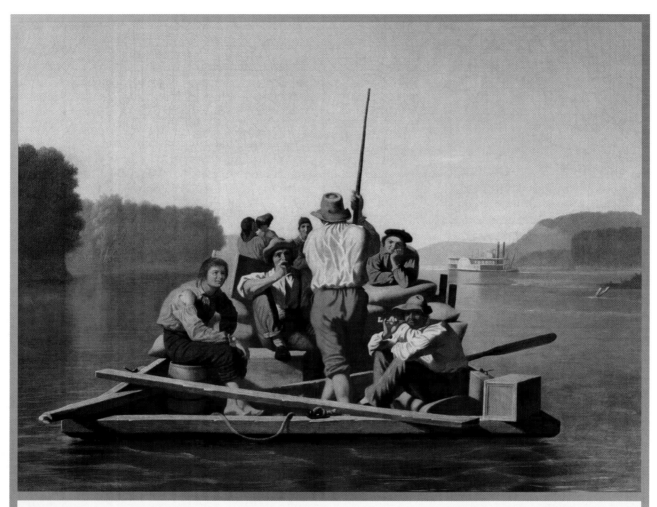

DEBATING THE PAST

Was early nineteenth-century America transformed by a "market revolution"? In this 1847 painting by George Caleb Bingham, a steamboat in the distance has run aground; the men in the flatboat are considering, perhaps, whether to help lighten its load. Their faces brim with satisfaction. *They* are not soot-begrimed wage slaves who shovel coal into smoke-belching machines. *They* work when and where they wish, moved only by the pull of the current and the sweat of their muscles. And yet the viewer senses that their satisfaction will be fleeting. The steamboat will get going again. George Rogers Taylor (1951) proposed that the key factor in the transformation of the economy during the early nineteenth century was a "transportation revolution," the development of a system of canals, steamboats, and railroads. But in the 1990s some suggested that the "transportation revolution" was merely a component of a larger and more powerful process: a "market revolution." The thesis was proposed by Charles Sellers (1991), Harry Watson (1990), and others. They argued that early in the nineteenth century some well-connected entrepreneurs used public funds to establish banks and corporations and to construct the nation's transportation infrastructure. This transformed craftsmen into factory workers and subsistence farmers into petty capitalists. In the frenzy to make money, such people turned their backs on family and community. The "market revolution" thesis has provoked many debates, not the least of which is whether it was a good thing. Sellers had no doubts. "Capitalism commodifies and exploits all life," he declared. But the only judgment that matters was that of the people such as those depicted above. If the steamboat captain were to offer them higher wages and steady work, would they accept?

George Rogers Taylor, *The Transportation Revolution* (1951), Charles Sellers, *The Market Revolution* (1991), Harry Watson, *Liberty and Power* (1990).

▲ On August 17, 1807 thousands of New Yorkers gathered along the Hudson River. Many had come to ridicule the noisy, spark-spuming contraption built by Robert Fulton—a steam-powered boat. But as the paddle wheels began to churn and the boat moved, the jeers turned to cheers. The boat made the 150-mile trip to Albany in eight hours.

the problem, and the latter used his political influence to obtain an exclusive charter to operate steamboats on New York waters. In 1802, while in France trying to buy New Orleans from Napoleon, Livingston got to know Robert Fulton, a young American artist and engineer who was experimenting with steam navigation, and agreed to finance his work. In 1807, after returning to New York, Fulton constructed the *North River Steam Boat,* famous to history as the *Clermont.*

The *Clermont* was 142 feet long, 18 feet abeam, and drew 7 feet of water. With its towering stack belching black smoke, its side wheels could push it along at a steady 5 miles an hour. Nothing about it was radically new, but Fulton brought the essentials—engine, boiler, paddle wheels, and hull—into proper balance and thereby produced an efficient vessel.

No one could patent a steamboat; soon the new vessels were plying the waters of every navigable river from the Mississippi east. After 1815 steamers were making the run from New Orleans as far as Ohio. By 1820 at least 60 vessels were operating between New Orleans and Louisville, and by the end of the decade there were more than 200 steamers on the Mississippi.

The day of the steamboat had dawned, and although the following generation would experience its high noon, even in the 1820s its major effects were clear. The great Mississippi Valley, in the full tide of its development, was immensely enriched. Produce poured down to New Orleans, which soon ranked with New York and Liverpool among the world's great ports. Only 80,000 tons of freight reached New Orleans from the interior in 1816 and 1817, more than 542,000 tons in 1840 and 1841. Upriver traffic was affected even more spectacularly. Freight charges plummeted, in some cases to a tenth of what they had been after the War of 1812. Around 1818 coffee cost 16 cents a pound more in Cincinnati than in New Orleans, a decade later less than 3 cents more. The Northwest emerged from self-sufficiency with a rush and became part of the national market.

Steamboats were far more comfortable than any contemporary form of land transportation, and competition soon led builders to make them positively luxurious. The *General Pike,* launched in 1819, set the fashion. Marble columns, thick carpets, mirrors, and crimson curtains adorned its cabins and public rooms. Soon the finest steamers were floating palaces where passengers could dine, drink, dance, and gamble in luxury as they sped smoothly to their destinations. Yet raft and flatboat traffic increased. Farmers, lumbermen, and others with goods from upriver floated down in the slack winter season and returned in comfort by steamer after selling their produce—and their rafts as well, for lumber was in great demand in New Orleans. Every January and February New Orleans teemed with Westerners and Yankee sailors, their pockets jingling, bent on a fling before going back to work. The shops displayed everything from the latest Paris fashions to teething rings made of alligator teeth mounted in silver. During the carnival season the city became one great festival, where every human pleasure could be tasted, every vice indulged.

THE CANAL BOOM

While the steamboat was conquering western rivers, canals were being constructed that further improved the transportation network. Since the midwestern rivers all emptied into the Gulf of Mexico, they did not provide a direct link with the eastern seaboard. If an artificial waterway could be cut between the great central valley and some navigable stream flowing into the Atlantic, all sections would profit immensely.

Canals were more expensive than roads, but so long as the motive power used in overland transportation was the humble horse, they offered enormous economic advantages to shippers. Because there is less friction to overcome, a team plodding along a towpath could pull a canal barge with a 100-ton load and make better time over long distances than it could pulling a single ton in a wagon on the finest road.

Although canals were as old as Egypt, only about 100 miles of them existed in the United States as late as 1816. Construction costs aside, in a rough and mountainous country canals presented formidable engineering problems. To link the Mississippi Valley and the Atlantic meant somehow circumventing the Appalachian Mountains. Most people thought this impossible.

Mayor DeWitt Clinton of New York believed that such a project was feasible in New York State. In 1810, while serving as state canal commissioner, he traveled across central New York and convinced himself that it would be practicable to dig a canal from Buffalo, on Lake Erie, to the Hudson River. The Mohawk Valley cuts through the Appalachian chain just north of Albany, and at no point along the route to Buffalo does the land rise more than 570 feet above the level of the Hudson. Marshaling a mass of technical, financial, and commercial information and using his political influence cannily, Clinton placed his proposal before the New York legislature. In its defense he was eloquent and farsighted:

> As an organ of communication between the Hudson, the Mississippi, the St. Lawrence, the great lakes of the north and west, and their tributary rivers, [the canal] will create the greatest inland trade ever witnessed. The most fertile and extensive regions of America will avail themselves of its facilities for a market. All their surplus . . . will concentrate in the city of New York. . . . That city will, in the course of time, become the granary of the world, the emporium of commerce, the seat of manufactures, the focus of great moneyed operations. . . . And before the revolution of a century, the whole island of Manhattan, covered with habitations and replenished with a dense population, will constitute one vast city.

The legislators were convinced, and in 1817 the state began construction along a route 363 miles long, most of it across densely forested wilderness. At the time the longest canal in the United States ran less than 28 miles!

AUDIO

The Erie Canal

▲ **Canals and Roads, 1820–1850**

DOCUMENT

Erie Canal 1819

The construction of the Erie Canal, as it was called, was a remarkable accomplishment. The chief engineer, Benjamin Wright, a surveyor-politician from Rome, New York, had had almost no experience with canal building. One of his chief associates, James Geddes, possessed only an elementary school education and knew virtually nothing about surveying. Both learned rapidly by trial and error. Fortunately, Wright proved to be a good organizer and a fine judge of engineering talent. He quickly spotted young men of ability among the workers and pushed them forward. One of his finds, Canvass White, was sent to study British canals. White became an expert on the design of locks; he also discovered an American limestone that could be made into waterproof cement, a vital product in canal construction that had previously been imported at a substantial price from England. Another of Wright's protégés, John B. Jervis, began as an axman, rose in two years to

▲ *Junction of Erie and Northern Canals* by John Hill, c. 1835. Freight rates from Buffalo to New York City had been $100 a ton by wagon; by canal, the cost was only $10.

resident engineer in charge of a section of the project, and went on to become perhaps the outstanding American civil engineer of his time. Workers who learned the business digging the "Big Ditch" supervised the construction of dozens of canals throughout the country in later years.

The Erie, completed in 1825, was an immediate financial success. Together with the companion Champlain Canal, which linked Lake Champlain and the Hudson, it brought in over half a million dollars in tolls in its first year. Soon its entire $7 million cost had been recovered, and it was earning profits of about $3 million a year. The effect of this prosperity on New York State was enormous. Buffalo, Rochester, Syracuse, and half a dozen lesser towns along the canal flourished.

NEW YORK CITY: EMPORIUM OF THE WESTERN WORLD

New York City had already become the largest city in the nation, thanks chiefly to its merchants, who had established a reputation for their rapid and or-

derly way of doing business. In 1818 the Black Ball Line opened the first regularly scheduled freight and passenger service between New York and England. Previously shipments might languish in port for weeks while a skipper waited for additional cargo. Now merchants on both sides of the Atlantic could count on the Black Ball packets to move their goods between Liverpool and New York on schedule whether or not the transporting vessel had a full cargo. This improvement brought much new business to the port. In the same year New York enacted an auction law requiring that imported goods placed on the block could not be withdrawn if a bid satisfactory to the seller was not forthcoming. This, too, was a boon to businessmen, who could be assured that if they outbid the competition, the goods would be theirs.

Now the canal cemented New York's position as the national metropolis. Most European-manufactured goods destined for the Mississippi Valley entered the country at New York and passed on to the West over the canal. The success of the Erie also sparked a nationwide canal-building boom. Most canals were constructed either by the states, as in the case of the Erie, or as "mixed enterprises" that combined public and private energies.

▲ A view of New York's Broadway in 1835. The broad avenue was home to many of the large, modern stores that helped make New York City the commercial center of the nation.

No state profited as much from this construction as New York, for none possessed New York's geographic advantages. The rocky hills of New England discouraged all but fanatics. Canals were built connecting Worcester and Northampton, Massachusetts, with the coast, but they were financial failures. The Delaware and Hudson Canal, running from northeastern Pennsylvania across northern New Jersey and lower New York to the Hudson, was completed by private interests in 1828. It managed to earn respectable dividends by barging coal to the eastern seaboard, but it made no attempt to compete with the Erie for the western trade. Pennsylvania, desperate to keep up with New York, engaged in an orgy of construction. In 1834 it completed a complicated system, part canal and part railroad, over the mountains to Pittsburgh. This Mainline Canal cost a staggering sum for that day. With its 177 locks and cumbersome "inclined-plane railroad" it was slow and expensive to operate and never competed effectively with the Erie. Efforts of Maryland to link Baltimore with the West by water failed utterly.

Beyond the mountains there was even greater zeal for canal construction in the 1820s and still more in the 1830s. Once the Erie opened the way across New York, farmers in the Ohio country demanded that links be built between the Ohio River and the Great Lakes so that they could ship their produce by water directly to the East. Local feeder canals seemed equally necessary; with corn worth 20 cents a bushel at Columbus selling for 50 cents at Marietta, on the Ohio, the value of cheap transportation became obvious to Ohio farmers.

Even before the completion of the Erie, Ohio had begun construction of the Ohio and Erie Canal running from the Ohio River to Cleveland. Another, from Toledo to Cincinnati, was begun in 1832. Meanwhile, Indiana had undertaken the 450-mile Wabash and Erie Canal. These canals were well conceived, but the western states overextended themselves building dozens of feeder lines, trying, it sometimes seemed, to supply all farmers west of the Appalachians with water connections from their barns to the New York docks. Politics made such programs almost inevitable, for in order to win support for their pet projects, legislators had to back the schemes of their fellows. The result was frequently financial disaster. There was not enough traffic to pay for all the waterways that were dug. By 1844, $60 million in state "improvement" bonds were in default. Nevertheless, the canals benefited both western farmers and the national economy.

The Marshall Court

Martin v. Hunter's Lessee

The most important legal advantages bestowed on business in the period were the gift of Chief Justice John Marshall. Historians have tended to forget that Chief Justice John Marshall had six colleagues on the Supreme Court, and that is easy to understand. Marshall's particular combination of charm, logic, and forcefulness made the Court during his long reign, if not a rubber stamp, remarkably submissive to his view of the Constitution. Marshall's belief in a powerful central government explains his tendency to hand down decisions favorable to manufacturing and business interests. He also thought that "the business community was the agent of order and progress" and tended to interpret the Constitution in a way that would advance its interests.

Many important cases came before the Court between 1819 and 1824, and in each one Marshall's decision was applauded by most of the business community. The cases involved two major principles: the "sanctity" of contracts and the supremacy of federal legislation over the laws of the states. Marshall shared the conviction of the Revolutionary generation that property had to be protected against arbitrary seizure if liberty was to be preserved. Contracts between private individuals and between individuals and the government must be strictly enforced, he believed, or chaos would result. He therefore gave the widest possible application to the constitutional provision that no state could pass any law "impairing the Obligation of Contracts."

In *Dartmouth College* v. *Woodward* (1819), which involved an attempt by New Hampshire to alter the charter granted to Dartmouth by King George III in 1769, Marshall held that such a charter was a contract and might not be canceled or altered without the consent of both parties. The state had sought not to destroy the college but to change it from a private to a public institution, yet Marshall held that to do so would violate the contract clause.

McCulloch v. Maryland

Marshall's decisions concerning the division of power between the federal government and the states were even more important. The question of the constitutionality of a national bank, first debated by Hamilton and Jefferson, had not been submitted to the courts during the life of the first Bank of the United States. By the time of the second Bank there were many state banks, and some of them felt that their interests were threatened by the national institution. Responding to pressure from local banks, the Maryland legislature placed an annual tax of

▲ The artist Chester Harding painted John Marshall in 1828, during the Chief Justice's twenty-seventh year on the Supreme Court. "The unpretentious dignity [and] the sober factualism" of Harding's style (as art historian Oliver Larkin describes it) was well suited to Marshall's character.

$15,000 on "foreign" banks, including the Bank of the United States! The Maryland branch of the Bank of the United States refused to pay, whereupon the state brought suit against its cashier, John W. McCulloch. *McCulloch* v. *Maryland* was crucial to the Bank, for five other states had levied taxes on its branches, and others would surely follow suit if the Maryland law were upheld.

Marshall extinguished the threat. The Bank of the United States was constitutional, he announced in phrases taken almost verbatim from Hamilton's 1791 memorandum to Washington on the subject; its legality was implied in many of the powers specifically granted to Congress. Full "discretion" must be allowed Congress in deciding exactly how its powers "are to be carried into execution." Since the Bank was legal, the Maryland tax was unconstitutional. Marshall found a "plain repugnance" in the thought of "conferring on one government a power to control the constitutional measures of another." He put this idea in the simplest possible language: "The power to tax involves the power to destroy . . . the power to destroy may defeat and render useless the power to create." The long-range significance of the decision lay in its strengthening of the implied powers of Congress and its confirmation of the Hamiltonian or "loose" interpretation of the Constitution. By establishing the legality of the Bank, it also aided the growth of the economy.

In 1824 Marshall handed down an important decision involving the regulation of interstate commerce. This was the "steamboat case," *Gibbons* v. *Ogden.* In 1815 Aaron Ogden, former United States senator and governor of New Jersey, had purchased the right to operate a ferry between Elizabeth Point, New Jersey, and New York City from Robert Fulton's backer, Robert R. Livingston, who held a New York monopoly of steamboat navigation on the Hudson. When Thomas Gibbons, who held a federal coasting license, set up a competing line, Ogden sued him. Ogden argued in effect that Gibbons could operate his boat (whose captain was Cornelius Vanderbilt, later a famous railroad magnate) on the New Jersey side of the Hudson but had no right to cross into New York waters. After complicated litigation in the lower courts, the case reached the Supreme Court on appeal. Marshall decided in favor of Gibbons, effectively destroying the New York monopoly. A state can regulate commerce which begins and ends in its own territory but not when the transaction involves crossing a state line; then the national authority takes precedence. "The act of Congress," he said, "is supreme; and the law of the state . . . must yield to it."

This decision threw open the interstate steamboat business to all comers, and since an adequate 100-ton vessel could be built for as little as $7000, dozens of small operators were soon engaged in it. Their competition tended to keep rates low and service efficient, to the great advantage of the country. More important in the long run was the fact that in order to include the ferry business within the federal government's power to regulate interstate commerce, Marshall had given the word the widest possible meaning. "Commerce, undoubtedly, is traffic, but it is something more,—it is intercourse." By construing the "commerce" clause so broadly, he

made it easy for future generations of judges to extend its coverage to include the control of interstate electric power lines and even radio and television transmission.

Many of Marshall's decisions aided the economic development of the country in specific ways, but his chief contribution lay in his broadly national view of economic affairs. When he tried consciously to favor business by making contracts inviolable, his influence was important but limited—and, as it worked out, impermanent. In the steamboat case and in *McCulloch* v. *Maryland,* where he was really deciding between rival property interests, his work was more truly judicial in spirit and far more lasting. In such matters his nationalism enabled him to add form and substance to Hamilton's vision of the economic future of the United States.

Marshall and his colleagues firmly established the principle of judicial limitation on the power of legislatures and made the Supreme Court a vital part of the American system of government. In an age plagued by narrow sectional jealousies, Marshall's contribution was of immense influence and significance, and on it rests his claim to greatness.

John Marshall died in 1835. Two years later, in the *Charles River Bridge* case, the court handed down another decision that aided economic development. The state of Massachusetts had built a bridge across the Charles River between Boston and Cambridge that drew traffic from an older, privately owned toll bridge nearby. Since no tolls were collected from users of the state bridge after construction costs were recovered, owners of the older bridge sued for damages on the ground that the free bridge made the stock in their company worthless. They argued that in building the bridge, Massachusetts had violated the contract clause of the Constitution.

The Court, however, now speaking through the new Chief Justice, Roger B. Taney, decided otherwise. The state had a right to place "the comfort and convenience" of the whole community over that of a particular company, Taney declared. "Improvements" that add to public "wealth and property" take precedence. How John Marshall would have voted in this case, in which he would have had to choose between his Dartmouth College and steamboat case arguments, will never be known. But like most of the decisions of the Court that were made while Marshall was Chief Justice, the Charles River Bridge case advanced the interests of those who favored economic development. Whether they were pursuing political advantage or economic, the Americans of the early nineteenth century seemed committed to a policy of compromise and accommodation.

MILESTONES

1790	Samuel Slater sets up first American factory
1793	Eli Whitney invents cotton gin
1794	Philadelphia–Lancaster turnpike is built
1807	Robert Fulton constructs *North River Steam Boat (Clermont)*
1808	Constitutional prohibition of importation of slaves goes into effect
1813	Boston Manufacturing Company opens in Waltham, Massachusetts
1816	Second Bank of the United States is created
1817	American Colonization Society is founded in order to establish republic of Liberia for freed slaves
1819	Chief Justice John Marshall asserts "sanctity" of contracts in *Dartmouth College* v. *Woodward* Chief Justice Marshall strengthens implied powers of Congress in *McCulloch* v. *Maryland* (Bank of United States)
1824	Chief Justice Marshall defends supremacy of federal government over states in *Gibbons* v. *Ogden* (steamboat case)
1825	Erie Canal is completed
1837	Chief Justice Roger B. Taney rules in favor of the whole community over a particular company in *Charles River Bridge* v. *Warren Bridge*

SUPPLEMENTARY READING

On the consumer revolution, see especially Richard Bushman, *The Refinement of America* (1992). In addition to the works cited in Debating the Past (p. 238) on the market revolution, see Melvyn Stokes and Stephen Conway, eds., *The Market Revolution in America* (1996), and Christopher Clark, *The Roots of Rural Capitalism: Western Massachusetts, 1780–1860* (1991). See also Laurel Thatcher Ulrich, *The Age of Homespun* (2001).

On the industrial revolution in America, see A. D. Chandler, Jr., *The Visible Hand: The Managerial Revolution in American Business* (1977). On the role of inventors, see Carroll Pursell, *The Machine in America* (1995), and B. M. Tucker, *Samuel Slater and the Origins of the American Textile Industry* (1984).

The growth of cities in the Jacksonian era can be traced in Richard C. Wade, *The Urban Frontier* (1957), and Howard Chudacoff, *The Evolution of American Urban Society* (1981). Allen F. Davis and Mark Halle, eds., *The Peoples of Philadelphia* (1973), Oscar Handlin, *Boston's Immigrants* (1968 ed.), and P. R. Knights, *The Plain People of Boston* (1971), deal with individual cities.

On immigration and ethnicity, see P. T. Knoble, *Paddy and the Republic* (1986), J. P. Dolan, *Immigrant Church: New York's Irish and German Catholics* (1982), and, generally, Philip Taylor, *The Distant Mirror: European Migration to the United States* (1971), and Stephan Thernstrom, ed., *Harvard Encyclopedia of American Ethnic Groups* (1980).

On changes in the nature of work, consult Paul Johnson, *A Shopkeeper's Millennium* (1978), Sean Wilentz, *Chants Democratic* (1984), Bruce Laurie, *Artisans into Workers* (1989), Norman Ware, *The Industrial Worker* (1990), and Anthony F. C. Wallace, *Rockdale* (1978); on women in the early factories, see Mary Blewett, *Men, Women, and Work* (1988), and Thomas Dublin, *Women at Work* (1979). On the lengthening commute to work, see Sam Bass Warner, *The Private City: Philadelphia in Three Periods of Its Growth* (1968).

Evan Cornog describes the origins and impact of the Erie Canal in *The Birth of Empire* (1998). On canal building, consult R. E. Shaw, *Canals for a Nation* (1990). Two works by Carter Goodrich, *Government Promotion of American Canals and Railroads* (1960) and *Canals and American Economic Development* (1961), describe the role of government aid in canal construction authoritatively. John Lauritz Larson, *Internal Improvement: National Public Works and the Promise of Popular Government in the Early United States* (2001), blames Andrew Jackson for the abandonment of public support for transportation infrastructure.

R. Kent Newmyer, *John Marshall and the Heroic Age of the Supreme Court* (2001) is strongly supportive of Marshall's actions; see also G. Edward White, *The Marshall Court and Cultural Change* (1991), as well as the sources cited in previous chapters.

SUGGESTED WEBSITES

The Marshall Cases

http://odur.let.rug.nl/~usa/D/1801-1825/
marshallcases/marxx.htm

John Marshall, and the cases he heard, shaped the form and function of the judicial system in the United States.

Whole Cloth: Discovering Science and Technology Through American Textile History

http://www.si.edu/lemelson/centerpieces/whole_cloth/

The Jerome and Dorothy Lemelson Center for the Study of Invention and Innovation/Society for the History of Technology put together this site, which includes activities and sources about early-American manufacturing and industry.

Erie Canal Online

http://www.syracuse.com/features/eriecanal

This site, built around the diary of a 14-year-old girl who traveled from Amsterdam to Syracuse, New York, in the early nineteenth century, explores the construction and importance of the Erie Canal.

The Era of the Mountain Men

http://www.xmission.com/~drudy/amm.html

Private letters help students learn about the concerns and environment of the writers and recipients. This site has correspondence from early settlers west of the Mississippi River.

Jacksonian Democracy

▼ Critics lampooned the raucous behavior of "King Mob" at the White House following the inauguration of Andrew Jackson; but public gatherings taught Americans to think of themselves as partisans in a national political system.

CHAPTER CONTENTS

At 11 A.M. on March 4, 1829, a bright sunny day, Andrew Jackson, hatless and dressed severely in black, left his quarters at Gadsby's Hotel. Accompanied by a few close associates, he walked up Pennsylvania Avenue to the Capitol. At a few minutes after noon he emerged on the East Portico with the justices of the Supreme Court and other dignitaries. Before a throng of more than 15,000 people he delivered an almost inaudible and thoroughly commonplace inaugural address and then took the presidential oath. The first man to congratulate him was Chief Justice Marshall, who had administered the oath. The second was "Honest George" Kremer, a Pennsylvania congressman best known for the leopardskin coat that he affected, who led the cheering crowd that brushed past the barricade and scrambled up the Capitol steps to wring the new president's hand.

Jackson shouldered his way through the crush, mounted a splendid white horse, and rode off to the White House. A reception had been announced, to which "the officially and socially eligible as defined by precedent" had been invited. The day was unseasonably warm after a hard winter, and the streets of Washington were muddy. As Jackson rode down Pennsylvania Avenue, the crowds that had turned out to see the Hero of New Orleans followed—on horseback, in rickety wagons, and on foot. Nothing could keep them out of the executive mansion, and the result was chaos. Long tables laden with cakes, ice cream, and orange punch had been set up in the East Room, but these scarcely deflected the well-wishers. Jackson was pressed back helplessly as men tracked mud across valuable rugs and clambered up on delicate chairs to catch a glimpse of him. The White House shook with their shouts. Glassware splintered, furniture was overturned, women fainted.

Jackson was a thin old man despite his toughness, and soon he was in danger. Fortunately, friends formed a cordon and managed to extricate him through a rear door. The new president spent his first night in office at Gadsby's hotel.

Only a generation earlier Jefferson had felt obliged to introduce pell-mell to encourage informality in the White House (see p. 173). Now a man whom John Quincy Adams called "a barbarian" held Jefferson's office, and, as one Supreme Court justice complained, "The reign of King 'Mob' seemed triumphant."

"DEMOCRATIZING" POLITICS

Jackson's inauguration, and especially this celebration in the White House, symbolized the triumph of "democracy," the achievement of place and station by "the common man." Having been taught by Jefferson that all men are created equal, the Americans of Jackson's day (conveniently ignoring males with black skins, to say nothing of women, regardless of color) found it easy to believe that every person was as competent and as politically important as his neighbor.

The difference between Jeffersonian democracy and the Jackson variety was more one of attitude than of practice. Jefferson had believed that ordinary citizens could be educated to determine what was right. Jackson insisted that they knew what was right by instinct. Jefferson's pell-mell encouraged the average citizen to hold up his head; by the time of Jackson, the "common man" gloried in ordinariness and made mediocrity a virtue. The slightest hint of distinctiveness or servility became suspect. That President Washington required his footmen to wear uniforms was taken as a matter of course in the 1790s, but the British minister in Jackson's day found it next to impossible to find Americans willing to don his splendid livery. While most middle-class families could still hire people to do their cooking and housework, the word *servant* itself fell out of fashion, replaced by the egalitarian *help*.

The Founders had not foreseen all the implications of political democracy for a society like the one that existed in the United States. They believed that the ordinary man should have political power in order to protect himself against the superior man, but they assumed that the latter would always lead. The people would naturally choose the best men to manage public affairs. In Washington's day and even in Jefferson's this was

generally the case, but the inexorable logic of democracy gradually produced a change. The new western states, unfettered by systems created in a less democratic age, drew up constitutions that eliminated property qualifications for voting and holding office. Many more public offices were made elective rather than appointive. The eastern states revised their own frames of government to accomplish the same purposes.

Even the presidency, designed to be removed from direct public control by the Electoral College, felt the impact of the new thinking. By Jackson's time only two states, Delaware and South Carolina, still provided for the choice of presidential electors by the legislature; in all others they were selected by popular vote. The system of permitting the congressional caucus to name the candidates for the presidency came to an end before 1828. Jackson and Adams were put forward by state legislatures, and soon thereafter the still more democratic system of nomination by national party conventions was adopted.

Certain social changes reflected a new way of looking at political affairs. The final disestablishment of churches further reveals the dislike of special privilege. The beginnings of the free-school movement, the earliest glimmerings of interest in adult education, and the slow spread of secondary education all bespeak a concern for improving the knowledge and judgment of the ordinary citizen. The rapid increase in the number of newspapers, their declining prices, and their ever-greater concentration on political affairs indicate an effort to bring political news to the common man's attention.

All these changes emphasized the idea that every citizen was equally important and the conviction that all should participate in government. Officeholders began to stress the fact that they were *representatives* as well as leaders and to appeal more openly and much more intensively for votes. The public responded. At each succeeding presidential election, more people went to the polls. Roughly 300,000 ballots were cast in 1824, 1.1 million four years later, and 2.4 million in 1840.

As voting became more important, so did competition among candidates, and this led to changes in the role and structure of political parties. Running campaigns and getting out the vote required money, people, and organized effort. Party managers, often holders of relatively minor offices, held rallies, staged parades, dreamed up catchy slogans, and printed broadsides, party newspapers, and ballots containing the names of the party's nominees for distribution to their supporters. Parties became powerful institutions that instilled loyalty among adherents.

The parties first formed at the state level. The 1828 election stimulated party formation because instead of several sectional candidates, each dominant in his own region, competing for the presidency, it pitted two nationally known men against each other. This compelled local leaders to make a choice and then to organize their forces in order to convince local voters to accept their judgment. This was especially true in states where neither Adams nor Jackson had a preponderance of backers. Thus the new system established itself much faster in New York and Pennsylvania than in New England, where Adams was strong, or Tennessee, where the native son Jackson had overwhelming support.

Like most institutions, the new parties created bureaucracies to keep them running smoothly. Devoted party workers were rewarded with political office when their efforts were successful. "To the victors belong the spoils," said the New York politician William L. Marcy, and the image, drawn from war and piracy, was appropriate. Although the vigorous wooing of voters constituted recognition of their importance and commitment to keeping them informed, campaigning—another military term—frequently degenerated into demagoguery. The most effective way to attract the average voter, politicians soon decided, was by flattery.

1828: THE NEW PARTY SYSTEM IN EMBRYO

The new system could scarcely have been imagined in 1825 while John Quincy Adams ruled over the White House; Adams was not well equipped either to lead King Mob or to hold it in check. Indeed, it was the battle to succeed Adams that caused the system to develop. The campaign began almost on the day of his selection by the House of Representatives. Jackson felt that he, the man who had received the largest number of votes, had been cheated of the presidency in 1824 by "the corrupt bargain" that he believed Adams had made with Henry Clay, and he sought vindication.

Relying heavily on his military reputation and on Adams's talent for making enemies, Jackson avoided taking a stand on issues and on questions where his views might displease one or another faction. The political situation thus became chaotic, one side unable to marshal support for its policies, the other unwilling to adopt policies for fear of losing support.

The campaign was disgraced by character assassination and lies of the worst sort. Administration supporters denounced Jackson as a bloodthirsty military tyrant, a drunkard, and a gambler. His wife Rachel, ailing and shy, was dragged into the campaign, her

▲ Rachel Jackson, wife of Andrew Jackson. At 17 she had married Lewis Robards, but theirs was a tempestuous marriage. After two years she returned to her family in Natchez, Mississippi. Robards sued for divorce in Virginia on grounds of desertion. Several months later she married Jackson in Mississippi. But, unbeknownst to Jackson, Robards would not finalize the divorce until a year after Rachel's marriage to Jackson. In defending Rachel's honor from a charge of bigamy, Jackson killed a man in a duel. During the 1824 and 1828 presidential campaigns, critics denounced their marriage as immoral.

good name heartlessly besmirched. Previously married to a cruel, unbalanced man named Lewis Robards, she had begun living with Jackson before her divorce from Robards had been legally completed. When this fact came to light, she and Jackson had to remarry. Seizing on this incident, an Adams pamphleteer wrote: "Ought a convicted adulteress and her paramour husband be placed in the highest offices of this free and christian land?"

Furious, the Jacksonians (now calling themselves Democrats) replied in kind. They charged that while American minister to Russia, Adams had supplied a beautiful American virgin for the delectation of the czar. Discovering that while president Adams had purchased a chess set and a billiard table for the White House, they accused him of squandering public money on gambling devices. They translated his long and distinguished public service into the statistic that he had received over the years a sum equal to $16 for every day of his life in government pay. The great questions of the day were largely ignored.

All this was inexcusable, and both sides must share the blame. But as the politicians noticed when the votes were counted, their efforts had certainly brought out the electorate. *Each* candidate received far more votes than all four candidates had received in the preceding presidential election.

When inauguration day arrived, Adams refused to attend the ceremonies because Jackson had failed to pay the traditional preinaugural courtesy call on him at the White House, but the Old Puritan may have been equally, if unconsciously, motivated by shame at tactics he had countenanced during the campaign. Jackson felt vindication, not shame, but in any case, deep personal feelings were uppermost in everyone's mind at the formal changing of the guard. The real issues, however, remained. Andrew Jackson would now have to deal with them.

THE JACKSONIAN APPEAL

Although Jackson's supporters liked to cast him as the political heir of Jefferson, he was in many ways like the conservative Washington: a soldier first, an inveterate speculator in western lands, the owner of a fine plantation and of many slaves, a man with few intellectual interests and only sketchily educated.

Nor was Jackson quite the rough-hewn frontier character he sometimes seemed. True, he could not spell (again, like Washington), he possessed the unsavory habits of the tobacco chewer, and he had a violent temper. But his manners and lifestyle were those of a southern planter. "I have always felt that he was a perfect savage," Grace Fletcher Webster, wife of Senator Daniel Webster, explained. "But," she added, "his manners are very mild and gentlemanly." Jackson's judgment was intuitive yet usually sound; his frequent rages were often feigned, designed to accomplish some carefully thought-out purpose. Once, after scattering a delegation of protesters with an exhibition of wrath, he turned to an observer and said impishly: "They thought I was mad."

Whatever his personal convictions, Jackson stood as the symbol for a movement supported by a new, democratically oriented generation. That he was both a great hero and in many ways a most extraordinary person helps explain his mass appeal. He had defeated a mighty British army and killed hosts of Indians, but he acted on hunches and not always consistently, shouted and pounded his fist when angry, put loyalty to old comrades above efficiency when making appointments,

▲ This painting of Jackson is by Ralph E. W. Earl (1833), whose father, a soldier, had been assigned to do accurate paintings of the battles of Lexington and Concord. The son married a niece of Andrew Jackson and completed this imposing portrait.

distrusted "aristocrats" and all special privilege. Perhaps he was rich, perhaps conservative, but he was a man of the people, born in a frontier cabin, familiar with the problems of the average citizen.

Jackson epitomized many American ideals. He was intensely patriotic, generous to a fault, natural and democratic in manner (at home alike in the forest and in the ballroom of a fine mansion). He admired good horseflesh and beautiful women, yet no sterner moralist ever lived; he was a fighter, a relentless foe, but a gentleman in the best American sense. That some special providence watched over him (as over the United States) appeared beyond argument to those who had followed his career. He seemed, in short, both an average and an ideal American, one the people could identify with and still revere.

For these reasons Jackson drew support from every section and every social class: western farmers and southern planters, urban workers and bankers and merchants. In this sense he was profoundly democratic—and in the sense, too, that whatever his position on public issues, he believed in equality of opportunity, distrusted entrenched status of every sort, and rejected no free American because of humble origins or inadequate education.

THE SPOILS SYSTEM

DOCUMENT

Jackson, First Annual Message to Congress

Jackson took office with the firm intention of punishing the "vile wretches" who had attacked him so viciously during the campaign. (Rachel Jackson died shortly after the election, and her devoted husband was convinced that the indignities heaped on her by Adams partisans had hastened her decline.) The new concept of political office as a reward for victory seemed to justify a housecleaning in Washington. Henry Clay captured the fears of anti-Jackson government workers. "Among the official corps here there is the greatest solicitude and apprehension," he said. "The members of it feel something like the inhabitants of Cairo when the plague breaks out; no one knows who is next to encounter the stroke of death."

Eager for the "spoils," an army of politicians invaded Washington. There was nothing especially innovative about this invasion, for the principle of filling offices with one's partisans was almost as old as the republic. However, the long lapse of time since the last real political shift, and the recent untypical example of John Quincy Adams, who rarely removed or appointed anyone for political reasons, made Jackson's policy appear revolutionary. His removals were not entirely unjustified, for many government workers had grown senile and others corrupt. A number of officials were found to be short in their accounts; a few were hopeless drunks. Jackson was determined to root out the thieves. Even Adams admitted that some of those Jackson dismissed deserved their fate.

Aside from going along with the spoils system and eliminating crooks and incompetents, Jackson advanced another reason for turning experienced government employees out of their jobs: the principle of rotation. "No man has any more intrinsic right to official station than another," he said. Those who hold government jobs for a long time "are apt to acquire a habit of looking with indifference upon the public interests and of tolerating conduct from which an unpracticed man would revolt." By "rotating" jobholders periodically, more citizens could participate in the tasks of government, and the danger of creating an entrenched bureaucracy would be eliminated. The problem was that the constant replacing of trained workers by novices was not likely to increase the efficiency of the government. Jackson's response to this argument was typical: "The duties of all public officers are . . . so plain and simple that men of intelligence may readily qualify themselves for their performance."

Contempt for expert knowledge and the belief that ordinary Americans can do anything they set their minds to became fundamental tenets of Jacksonian democracy. To apply them to present-day government would be to court disaster, but in the early nineteenth century it was not so preposterous, because the role that government played in American life was simple and nontechnical.

Furthermore, Jackson did not practice what he preached. By and large his top appointees were anything but common men. A majority came from the same social and intellectual elite as those they replaced. He did not try to rotate civil servants in the War and Navy departments, where to do so might have been harmful. In general, he left pretty much alone what a modern administrator would call middle management, the backbone of every organization.

Nevertheless, the spoilsmen roamed the capital in force during the spring of 1829, seeking, as the forthright Jackson said, "a tit to suck the treasury pap." Their philosophy was well summarized by a New Yorker: "No d——d rascal who made use of his office . . . for the purpose of keeping Mr. Adams in, and Genl. Jackson out of power is entitled to the least lenity or mercy. . . . Whether or not I shall get anything in the general scramble for plunder, remains to be proven, but I rather guess I shall."

PRESIDENT OF ALL THE PEOPLE

President Jackson was not cynical about the spoils system. As a strong man who intuitively sought to increase his authority, the idea of making government workers dependent on him made excellent sense. His opponents had pictured him as a simple soldier fronting for a rapacious band of politicians, but he soon proved he would exercise his authority directly. Except for Martin Van Buren, the secretary of state, his Cabinet was not distinguished, and he did not rely on it for advice. He turned instead to an informal "Kitchen Cabinet," which consisted of the influential Van Buren and a few close friends. But these men were advisers, not directors; Jackson was clearly master of his own administration.

More than any earlier president, he conceived of himself as the direct representative of all the people and therefore the embodiment of national power. From Washington to John Quincy Adams, his predecessors together had vetoed only nine bills, all on the ground that they believed the measures unconstitutional. Jackson vetoed a dozen, some simply because he thought the legislation inexpedient. Yet he had no ambition to expand the scope of federal authority at the expense of the states. Basically he was a Jeffersonian; he favored a "frugal," constitutionally limited national government. Furthermore, he was a poor administrator, given to penny-pinching and lacking in imagination. His strong prejudices and his contempt for expert advice, even in fields such as banking where his ignorance was almost total, did him no credit and the country considerable harm.

Jackson's great success (not merely his popularity) was primarily the result of his personality. A shrewd French observer, Michel Chevalier, after commenting on "his chivalric character, his lofty integrity, and his ardent patriotism," pointed out what was probably the central element in Jackson's appeal. "His tactic in politics, as well as in war," Chevalier wrote in 1824, "is to throw himself forward with the cry of *Comrades, follow me!*" Sometimes he might be wrong, but always he was a leader.

SECTIONAL TENSIONS REVIVED

In office Jackson had to say something about western lands, the tariff, and other issues. He tried to steer a moderate course, urging a slight reduction of the tariff and "constitutional" internal improvements. He suggested that once the rapidly disappearing federal debt had been paid off, the surplus revenues of the government might be "distributed" among the states.

Even these cautious proposals caused conflict, so complex were the interrelations of sectional disputes. If the federal government turned its expected surplus over to the states, it could not afford to reduce the price of public land without going into the red. This disturbed Westerners, notably Senator Thomas Hart Benton of Missouri, and western concern suggested to southern opponents of the protective tariff an alliance of South and West. The Southerners argued that a tariff levied only to raise revenue would increase the cost of foreign imports, bring more money into the treasury, and thus make it possible to reduce the price of public land.

The question came up in the Senate in December 1829, when Senator Samuel A. Foot of Connecticut suggested restricting the sale of government land. Benton promptly denounced the proposal. On January 19, 1830, Senator Robert Y. Hayne of South Carolina, a spokesman for Vice President Calhoun, supported Benton vigorously, suggesting an alliance of South and West based on cheap land and low tariffs. Daniel Webster then rose to the defense of northeastern interests, cleverly goading Hayne by accusing South Carolina of advocating disunionist policies. Responding to this attack, the South Carolinian, a glib speaker but a rather imprecise thinker,

launched into an impassioned exposition of the states' rights doctrine.

Webster then took the floor again and for two days, before galleries packed with the elite of Washington society, cut Hayne's argument to shreds. The Constitution was a compact of the American people, not merely of the states, he insisted, the Union perpetual and indissoluble. Webster made the states' rights position appear close to treason; his "second reply to Hayne" effectively prevented the formation of a West-South alliance and made Webster a presidential candidate.

JACKSON: "THE BANK . . . I WILL KILL IT!"

In the fall of 1832 Jackson was reelected president, handily defeating Henry Clay. The main issue in this election, aside from Jackson's personal popularity, was the president's determination to destroy the second Bank of the United States. In this "Bank war," Jackson won a complete victory, yet the effects of his triumph were anything but beneficial to the country.

After *McCulloch* v. *Maryland* had presumably established its legality and the conservative Langdon Cheves had gotten it on a sound footing, the Bank of the United States had flourished. In 1823 Cheves was replaced as president by Nicholas Biddle, who managed it brilliantly. A talented Philadelphian, only 37 when he took over the Bank, Biddle was experienced in literature, the law, and diplomacy as well as in finance. Almost alone in the United States, Biddle realized that his institution could act as a rudimentary central bank, regulating the availability of credit throughout the nation by controlling the lending policies of the state banks. Small banks, possessing limited amounts of gold and silver, sometimes overextended themselves in making large amounts of bank notes available to borrowers in order to earn interest. All this paper money was legally convertible into hard cash on demand, but in the ordinary run of business people seldom bothered to convert their notes so long as they thought the issuing bank was sound.

Bank notes passed freely from hand to hand and from bank to bank in every section of the country. Eventually much of the paper money of the local banks came across the counter of one or another of the 22 branches of the Bank of the United States. By collecting these notes and presenting them for conversion into coin, Biddle could compel the local banks to maintain adequate reserves of gold and silver—in other words, make them hold their lending policies within bounds. "The Bank of the United States," he explained, "has succeeded in keeping in

▲ Although the American dollar was the unit of currency in the young nation, the paper currency itself mostly consisted of bank notes, such as this $10 note. The bearer of this note could redeem it in Philadelphia for $10 in gold or silver, unless the bank had issued too many such notes and lacked sufficient specie.

check many institutions which might otherwise have been tempted into extravagant and ruinous excesses."

Biddle's policies in the 1820s were good for the Bank of the United States, which earned substantial profits, for the state banks, and probably for the country. Pressures on local bankers to make loans were enormous. The nation had an insatiable need for capital, and the general mood of the people was optimistic. Everyone wanted to borrow, and everyone expected values to rise, as in general they did. But by making liberal loans to produce merchants, for example, rural bankers indirectly stimulated farmers to expand their output beyond current demand, which eventually led to a decline in prices and an agricultural depression. In every field of economic activity, reckless lending caused inflation and greatly exaggerated the ups and downs of the business cycle. It can be argued, however, that by restricting the lending of state banks, Biddle was slowing the rate of economic growth and that in a predominantly agricultural society an occasional slump was not a large price to pay for rapid economic development.

Biddle's policies acted to stabilize the economy, and many interests, including a substantial percentage of state bankers, supported them. They also provoked a great deal of opposition. In part the opposition originated in pure ignorance: Distrust of paper money did not disappear, and people who disliked all paper saw the Bank as merely the largest (and thus the worst) of many bad institutions. At the other extreme, some bankers chafed under Biddle's restraints because by discouraging them from lending freely, he was limiting their profits. Few financiers realized what

Biddle was trying to accomplish. The historian Bray Hammond estimated that in this period no more than one banker in four understood what was happening when he made a loan. What was "sound" banking practice? Honest people disagreed, and many turned against the ideas of Nicholas Biddle.

Bankers who did understand what Biddle was doing also resisted him. New York bankers resented the fact that a Philadelphia institution could wield so much power over their affairs. New York was the nation's largest importing center; huge amounts of tariff revenue were collected there. Yet since this money was deposited to the credit of the Bank of the United States, Biddle controlled it from Philadelphia.

Finally, some people objected to the Bank because it was a monopoly. Distrust of chartered corporations as agents of special privilege tended to focus on the Bank, which had a monopoly of public funds but was managed by a private citizen and controlled by a handful of rich men. Biddle's wealth and social position intensified this feeling. Like many brilliant people, he sometimes appeared arrogant. He was unused to criticism and disdainful of ignorant and stupid attacks, failing to see that they were sometimes the most dangerous.

JACKSON'S BANK VETO

This formidable opposition to the Bank was diffuse and unorganized until Andrew Jackson brought it together. When he did, the Bank was quickly destroyed. Jackson can be included among the ignorant enemies of the institution, a hard-money man suspicious of all commercial banking. "I think it right to be perfectly frank with you," he told Biddle in 1829. "I do not dislike your Bank any more than all banks. But ever since I read the history of the South Sea Bubble I have been afraid of banks."

Jackson's attitude dismayed Biddle. It also mystified him, since the Bank was the country's best defense against a speculative mania like the eighteenth-century South Sea Bubble, in which hundreds of naive British investors had been fleeced. Almost against his will, Biddle found himself gravitating toward Clay and the new National Republican party, offering advantageous loans and retainers to politicians and newspaper editors in order to build up a following. Thereafter, events moved inevitably toward a showdown, for the president's combative instincts were easily aroused. "The Bank," he told Van Buren, "is trying to kill me, *but I will kill it!*"

Henry Clay, Daniel Webster, and other prominent National Republicans hoped to use the Bank controversy against Jackson. They reasoned that the institution was so important to the country that Jackson's opposition to it would undermine his popularity. They therefore urged Biddle to ask Congress to renew the Bank's charter. The charter would not expire until 1836, but by pressing the issue before the 1832 presidential election, they could force Jackson either to approve the recharter bill or to veto it (which would give candidate Clay a lively issue in the campaign). The banker yielded to this strategy and a recharter bill passed Congress early in July 1832. Jackson promptly vetoed it.

DOCUMENT

Jackson, Veto of the Bank Bill

Jackson's message explaining why he had rejected the bill was immensely popular, but it adds nothing to his reputation as a statesman. Being a good Jeffersonian—and no friend of John Marshall—he insisted that the Bank was unconstitutional. (*McCulloch v. Maryland* he brushed aside, saying that as president he had sworn to uphold the Constitution as *he* understood it.) The Bank was inexpedient, he argued. A dangerous private monopoly that allowed a handful of rich men to accumulate "many millions" of dollars, the Bank was making "the rich richer and the potent more powerful." Furthermore, many of its stockholders were foreigners: "If we must have a bank . . . it should be *purely American.*" Little that he said made any more sense than this absurdity.[1]

The most unfortunate aspect of Jackson's veto was that he could have reformed the Bank instead of

▲ "King Andrew the First," standing atop the United States Constitution—a scepter in one hand, and a veto in another. Compare this drawing to the one of Queen Elizabeth on page 29.

destroying it. The central banking function was too important to be left in private hands. Biddle once boasted that he could put nearly any bank in the United States out of business simply by forcing it to exchange specie for its bank notes. He thought he was demonstrating his forbearance, but in fact he was revealing a dangerous flaw in the system. When the Jacksonians called him Czar Nicholas, they were not far from the mark. Moreover, private bankers were making profits that in justice belonged to the people, for the government received no interest from the large sums it kept on deposit in the Bank. Jackson would not consider reforms. He set out to smash the Bank of the United States without any real idea of what might be put in its place—a foolhardy act.

Biddle considered Jackson's veto "a manifesto of anarchy," its tone like "the fury of a chained panther biting the bars of his cage." A large majority of the voters, however, approved of Jackson's hard-hitting attack.

---

[1]The country needed all the foreign capital it could attract. Foreigners owned only $8 million of the $35 million stock, and in any case they could not vote their shares.

Buttressed by his election triumph, Jackson acted swiftly. "Until I can strangle this hydra of corruption, the Bank, I will not shrink from my duty," he said. Shortly after the start of his second term, he decided to withdraw the government funds deposited in its vaults. Under the law only the secretary of the treasury could remove the deposits. When Secretary Louis McLane refused to do so, believing that the alternative depositories, the state banks, were less safe, Jackson promptly "promoted" him to secretary of state and appointed William J. Duane, a Pennsylvania lawyer, to the treasury post. Foolishly, he failed to ask Duane his views on the issue before appointing him. Too late he discovered that the new secretary agreed with McLane! It would not be "prudent" to entrust the government's money to "local and irresponsible" banks, Duane said.

Believing that Cabinet officers should obey the president as automatically as a colonel obeys a general, Jackson dismissed Duane, replacing him with Attorney General Roger B. Taney, who had been advising him closely on Bank affairs. Taney carried out the order by depositing new federal receipts in seven state banks in eastern cities while continuing to meet government expenses with drafts on the Bank of the United States.

The situation was confused and slightly unethical. Set on winning the Bank war, Jackson lost sight of his fear of unsound paper money. Taney, however, knew exactly what he was doing. One of the state banks receiving federal funds was the Union Bank of Baltimore. Taney owned stock in this institution, and its president was his close friend. Little wonder that Jackson's enemies were soon calling the favored state banks "pet" banks. This charge was not entirely fair because Taney took pains to see that the deposits were placed in financially sound institutions. Furthermore, by 1836 the government's funds had been spread out reasonably equitably in about 90 banks. But neither was the charge entirely unfair; the administration certainly favored institutions whose directors were politically sympathetic to it.

When Taney began to remove the deposits, the government had $9,868,000 to its credit in the Bank of the United States; within three months the figure fell to about $4 million. Faced with the withdrawal of so much cash, Biddle had to contract his operations. He decided to exaggerate the contraction, pressing the state banks hard by presenting all their notes and checks that came across his counter for conversion into specie and drastically limiting his own bank's business loans. He hoped that the resulting shortage of credit would be blamed on Jackson and that it would force the president to return the deposits. "Nothing but the evidence of suffering . . . will produce any effect," he reasoned.

For a time the strategy appeared to be working. Paper money became scarce, specie almost unobtainable. A serious panic threatened. New York banks were soon refusing to make any loans at all. "Nobody buys; nobody can sell," a French visitor to the city observed. Memorials and petitions poured in on Congress. Worried and indignant delegations of businessmen began trooping to Washington seeking "relief." Clay, Webster, and John C. Calhoun thundered against Jackson in the Senate.

The president would not budge. "I am fixed in my course as firm as the Rockey Mountain," he wrote Vice President Van Buren. No "frail mortals" who worshiped "the golden calf" could change his mind. To others he swore he would sooner cut off his right arm and "undergo the torture of ten Spanish inquisitions" than restore the deposits. When delegations came to him, he roared: "Go to Nicholas Biddle. . . . Biddle has all the money!" And in the end—because he was right—business leaders began to take the old general's advice. Pressure on Biddle mounted swiftly, and in July 1834 he suddenly reversed his policy and began to lend money freely. The artificial crisis ended.

JACKSON VERSUS CALHOUN

The Webster-Hayne debate had revived discussion of Calhoun's argument about nullification. Although southern-born, Jackson had devoted too much of his life to fighting for the entire United States to countenance disunion. Therefore, in April 1830, when the states' rights faction invited him to a dinner to celebrate the anniversary of Jefferson's birth, he came prepared. The evening reverberated with speeches and toasts of a states' rights tenor, but when the president was called on to volunteer a toast, he raised his glass, fixed his eyes on John C. Calhoun, and said: "Our *Federal* Union: It must be preserved!" Calhoun took up the challenge at once. "The Union," he retorted, "next to our liberty, most dear!"

It is difficult to measure the importance of the animosity between Jackson and Calhoun in the crisis to which this clash was a prelude. Calhoun wanted very much to be president. He had failed to inherit the office from John Quincy Adams and had accepted the vice presidency again under Jackson in the hope of succeeding him at the end of one term, if not sooner, for Jackson's health was known to be frail. Yet Old Hickory showed no sign of passing on or retiring. Jackson also seemed to place special confidence in the shrewd Van Buren, who, as secretary of state, also had claim to the succession.

A silly social fracas in which Calhoun's wife appeared to take the lead in the systematic snubbing of

Peggy Eaton, wife of the secretary of war, had estranged Jackson and Calhoun. (Peggy was supposed to have had an affair with Eaton while she was still married to another man, and Jackson, undoubtedly sympathetic because of the attacks he and Rachel had endured, stoutly defended her good name.) Then, shortly after the Jefferson Day dinner, Jackson discovered that in 1818, when he had invaded Florida, Calhoun, then secretary of war, had recommended to President Monroe that Jackson be summoned before a court of inquiry and charged with disobeying orders. Since Calhoun had repeatedly led Jackson to believe that he had supported him at the time, the revelation convinced the president that Calhoun was not a man of honor.

The personal difficulties are worth stressing because Jackson and Calhoun were not far apart ideologically except on the ultimate issue of the right of a state to overrule federal authority. Jackson was a strong president, but he did not believe that the area of national power was large or that it should be expanded. His interests in government economy, in the distribution of federal surpluses to the states, and in interpreting the powers of Congress narrowly were all similar to Calhoun's. Like most Westerners, he favored internal improvements, but he preferred that local projects be left to the states. In 1830 he vetoed a bill providing aid for the construction of the Maysville Road because the route was wholly within Kentucky. There were political reasons for this veto, which was a slap at Kentucky's hero, Henry Clay, but it could not fail to please Calhoun.

INDIAN REMOVALS

The president also took a states' rights position in the controversy that arose between the Cherokee Indians and Georgia. Jackson subscribed to the theory, advanced by Jefferson, that Indians were "savage" because they roamed wild in a trackless wilderness. The "original inhabitants of our forests" were "incapable of self-government," Jackson claimed, ignoring the fact that the Cherokee lived settled lives and had governed themselves without trouble before the whites arrived.

The Cherokee inhabited a region coveted by whites because it was suitable for growing cotton. Since most Indians preferred to maintain their tribal ways, Jackson pursued a policy of removing them from the path of white settlement. This policy seems heartless to modern critics, but since few Indians were willing to adopt the white way of life, most contemporary whites considered removal the only humane solution if the nation was to continue to expand. Jackson insisted that the Indians receive fair prices for their lands and that the government bear

▲ When a Sac chief signed a treaty abandoning lands east of the Mississippi River and moved the tribe to Iowa, Black Hawk decided to go to war. In 1832, the year of this painting, he led several hundred warriors back across the Mississippi. Although they repeatedly drew U.S. soldiers into ambushes, Black Hawk and his warriors were driven back. He was captured in 1833 and imprisoned in St. Louis. Later, he was introduced to President Andrew Jackson and was returned to a reservation in Iowa, where he died.

the expense of resettling them. He believed that moving them beyond the Mississippi would protect them from the "degradation and destruction to which they were rapidly hastening . . . in the States."

Many tribes resigned themselves to removal without argument. Between 1831 and 1833, some 15,000 Choctaw migrated from their lands in Mississippi to the region west of the Arkansas Territory.

Native American Removal

In *Democracy in America*, the Frenchman Alexis de Tocqueville described "the frightful sufferings that attend these forced migrations," and he added sadly that the migrants "have no longer a country, and

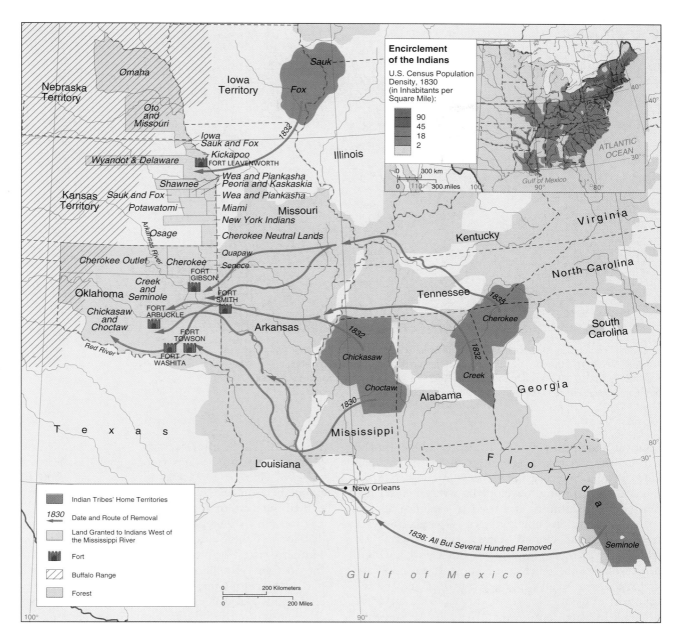

Encirclement
of the Indians

U.S. Census Population
Density, 1830
(in Inhabitants per
Square Mile):

90
45
18
2

▲ **Indian Removals**

soon will not be a people." He vividly described a group of Choctaw crossing the Mississippi River at Memphis in the dead of winter:

> The cold was unusually severe; the snow had frozen hard upon the ground, and the river was drifting huge masses of ice. The Indians had their families with them, and they brought in their train the wounded and the sick, with children newly born and old men upon the verge of death. They possessed neither tents nor wagons, but only their arms and some provisions. I saw them embark to pass the

mighty river, and never will that solemn spectacle fade from my remembrance. No cry, no sob, was heard among the assembled crowd; all were silent.

Tocqueville was particularly moved by the sight of an old woman whom he described in a letter to his mother. She was "naked save for a covering which left visible, at a thousand places, the most emaciated figure imaginable. . . . To leave one's country at that age to seek one's fortune in a foreign land, what misery!"

A few tribes, such as Black Hawk's Sac and Fox in Illinois and Osceola's Seminole in Florida, resisted

▲ Several hundred Seminole Indians in Florida refused to abandon their tribal lands and move west. Although their leader, Osceola, was treacherously captured in 1837 and soon died in prison, other Seminole fought on until forced to surrender in 1842; the warriors in this picture are attacking a federal fort. Some Seminole hid in the swamps and never surrendered.

removal and were subdued by troops. One Indian nation, the Cherokee, sought to hold on to their lands by adjusting to white ways. They took up farming and cattle raising, developed a written language, drafted a constitution, and tried to establish a state within a state in northwestern Georgia. Several treaties with the United States seemed to establish the legality of their government. But Georgia would not recognize the Cherokee Nation. It passed a law in 1828 declaring all Cherokee laws void and the region part of Georgia.

The Indians challenged this law in the Supreme Court. In *Cherokee Nation* v. *Georgia* (1831), Chief Justice John Marshall had ruled that the Cherokee were "not a foreign state, in the sense of the Constitution" and therefore could not sue in a United States court. However, in *Worcester* v. *Georgia* (1832), a case involving two missionaries to the Cherokee who had not procured licenses required by Georgia law, he ruled that the state could not control the Cherokee or their territory. Later, when a Cherokee named Corn Tassel, convicted in a Georgia court of the murder of another Indian, appealed on the ground that the crime had taken place in Cherokee territory, Marshall agreed and declared the Georgia action unconstitutional.

Jackson backed Georgia's position. No independent nation could exist within the United States, he insisted. Georgia thereupon hanged Corn Tassel. In 1838, after Jackson had left the White House, the United States forced 15,000 Cherokee to leave Georgia for Oklahoma. At least 4000 of them died on the way; the route has been aptly named the Trail of Tears.

Jackson's willingness to allow Georgia to ignore decisions of the Supreme Court persuaded extreme southern states' righters that he would not oppose the doctrine of nullification should it be formally applied to a law of Congress. They deceived themselves egregiously. Jackson did not challenge Georgia because he approved of the state's position. He spoke of "the poor deluded . . . Cherokees" and called William Wirt, the distinguished lawyer who defended their cause, a "truly wicked" man. Jackson was not one to worry about being inconsistent. When South Carolina revived the talk of nullification in 1832, he acted in quite a different manner.

THE NULLIFICATION CRISIS

The proposed alliance of South and West to reduce the tariff and the price of land had not materialized, partly because Webster had discredited the South in the eyes of western patriots and partly because the planters of South Carolina and Georgia, fearing the competition of fertile new cotton lands in Alabama and Mississippi, opposed the rapid exploitation of the West almost as vociferously as northern manufacturers did. When a new tariff law was passed in 1832, it lowered duties much less than the Southerners desired. At once talk of nullifying it began to be heard in South Carolina.

In addition to the economic woes of the upcountry cotton planters, the great planter-aristocrats of the rice-growing Tidewater, though relatively prosperous, were troubled by northern criticisms of slavery. In the rice region, blacks outnumbered whites two to one; it was the densest concentration of blacks in the United States. Thousands of these slaves were African-born, brought in during the burst of importations before Congress outlawed the trade in 1808. Controlled usually by overseers of the worst sort, the slaves seemed to their masters like savage beasts straining to rise up against their oppressors. In 1822 the exposure in Charleston of a planned revolt organized by Denmark Vesey, who had bought his freedom with money won in a lottery, had alarmed many whites. News of a far more serious uprising in Virginia led by the slave Nat Turner in 1831, just as the tariff controversy was coming to a head, added to popular concern. Radical South Carolinians saw protective tariffs and agitation against slavery as the two sides of one coin; against both aspects of what appeared to them the tyranny of the majority, nullification seemed the logical defense. Yield on the tariff, editor Henry L. Pinckney of the influential *Charleston Mercury* warned, and "abolition will become the order of the day."

Endless discussions of Calhoun's doctrine after the publication of his *Exposition and Protest* in 1828 had produced much interesting theorizing without clarifying the issue. Admirers of Calhoun praised his "power of analysis & profound philosophical reasonings," but his idea was ingenious rather than profound. Plausible at first glance, it was based on false assumptions: that the Constitution was subject to definitive interpretation; that one party could be permitted to interpret a compact unilaterally without destroying it; that a minority of the nation could reassume its sovereign independence but that a minority of a state could not.

President Jackson was in this respect Calhoun's exact opposite. The South Carolinian's mental gymnastics he brushed aside; intuitively he realized the central reality: If a state could nullify a law of Congress, the Union could not exist. "Tell . . . the Nullifiers from me that they can talk and write resolutions and print threats to their hearts' content," he warned a South Carolina representative when Congress adjourned in July 1832. "But if one drop of blood be shed there in defiance of the laws of the United States, I will hang the first man of them I can get my hands on to the first tree I can find."

The warning was not taken seriously in South Carolina. In October the state legislature provided for the election of a special convention, which, when it met, contained a solid majority of nullifiers. On November 24, 1832, the convention passed an ordinance of nullification prohibiting the collection of tariff duties in the state after February 1, 1833. The legislature then authorized the raising of an army and appropriated money to supply it with weapons.

Jackson quickly began military preparations of his own, telling friends that he would have 50,000 men ready to move in a little over a month. He also made a statesmanlike effort to end the crisis peaceably. First he suggested to Congress that it lower the tariff further. On December 10 he delivered a "Proclamation to the People of South Carolina." Nullification could only lead to the destruction of the Union, he said. "The laws of the United States must be executed. I have no discretionary power on the subject. . . . Those who told you that you might peaceably prevent their execution deceived you." Old Hickory added sternly: "Disunion by armed force is *treason*. Are you really ready to incur its guilt?" Jackson's reasoning profoundly shocked even opponents of nullification. If South Carolina did not back down, the president's threat to use force would mean civil war and possibly the destruction of the Union he claimed to be defending.

Calhoun sought desperately to control the crisis. By prearrangement with Senator Hayne, he resigned as vice president and was appointed to replace Hayne in the Senate, where he led the search for a peaceful solution. Having been defeated in his campaign for the presidency, Clay was a willing ally. In addition, many who admired Jackson nonetheless, as Van Buren later wrote, "distrusted his prudence," fearing that he would "commit some rash act." They believed in dealing with the controversy by discussion and compromise.

DOCUMENT

South Carolina's Ordinance of Nullification

As a result, administration leaders introduced both a new tariff bill and a Force Bill granting the president additional authority to execute the revenue laws. Jackson was perfectly willing to see the tariff reduced but insisted that he was determined to enforce the law. As the February 1 deadline approached, he claimed that he could raise 200,000 men if needed to suppress resistance. "Union men, fear not," he said. "*The Union will be preserved.*"

Jackson's determination sobered the South Carolina radicals. Their appeal for the support of other southern states fell on deaf ears: All rejected the idea of nullification. The unionist minority in South

▲ A South Carolina belle sewing—albeit languorously—a palmetto (a stylized palm leaf) onto a "nullification hat."

Carolina added to the radicals' difficulties by threatening civil war if federal authority were defied. Calhoun, though a brave man, was alarmed for his own safety, for Jackson had threatened to "hang him as high as Haman" if nullification were attempted. Observers described him as "excessively uneasy." He was suddenly eager to avoid a showdown.

Ten days before the deadline, South Carolina postponed nullification pending the outcome of the tariff debate. Then, in March 1833, Calhoun and Clay pushed a compromise tariff through Congress. As part of the agreement Congress also passed the Force Bill, mostly as a face-saving device for the president.

The compromise reflected the willingness of the North and West to make concessions in the interest of national harmony. Senator Silas Wright of New York, closely affiliated with Van Buren, explained the situation: "People will neither cut throats nor dismember the Union for protection. There is more patriotism and love of country than that left yet. The People will never balance this happy government against ten cents a pound upon a pound of wool."

And so the Union weathered the storm. Having stepped to the brink of civil war, the nation had drawn hastily back. The South Carolina legislature professed to be satisfied with the new tariff (in fact it made few immediate reductions, providing for a gradual lowering of rates over a ten-year period) and repealed the Nullification Ordinance, saving face by nullifying the Force Act, which was now a dead letter. But the radical South Carolina planters were becoming convinced that only secession would protect slavery. The nullification fiasco had proved that they could not succeed without the support of other slave states. Thereafter they devoted themselves ceaselessly to obtaining it.

BOOM AND BUST

During 1833 and 1834 Secretary of the Treasury Taney insisted that the pet banks maintain large reserves. But other state banks began to offer credit on easy terms, aided by a large increase in their reserves of gold and silver resulting from causes unconnected with the policies of either the government or Biddle's Bank. A decline in the Chinese demand for Mexican silver led to increased exports of the metal to the United States, and the rise of American interest rates attracted English capital into the country. Heavy English purchases of American cotton at high prices also increased the flow of specie into American banks. These developments caused bank notes in circulation to jump from $82 million in January 1835 to $120 million in December 1836. Bank deposits rose even more rapidly.

Much of the new money flowed into speculation in land; a mania to invest in property swept the country. The increased volume of currency caused prices to soar 15 percent in six months, buoying investors' spirits and making them ever more optimistic about the future. By the summer of 1835 one observer estimated that in New York City, which had about 250,000 residents, enough house lots had been laid out and sold to support a population of 2 million. Chicago at this time had only 2000 to 3000 inhabitants, yet most of the land for 25 miles around had been sold and resold in small lots by speculators anticipating the growth of the area. Throughout the West farmers borrowed money from local banks by mortgaging their land, used the money to buy more land from the government, and then borrowed still more money from the banks on the strength of their new deeds.

So long as prices rose, the process could be repeated endlessly. In 1832, while the Bank of the United States still regulated the money supply, federal income from the sale of land was $2.6 million. In 1834 it was $4.9 million; in 1835, $14.8 million. In 1836 it rose to $24.9 million, and the government found itself totally free of debt and with a surplus of $20 million!

Finally Jackson became alarmed by the speculative mania. In the summer of 1836 he issued the Specie Circular, which provided that purchasers must henceforth pay for public land in gold or silver. At once the rush to buy land came to a halt. As demand slackened, prices sagged. Speculators, unable to dispose of lands mortgaged to the banks, had to abandon them to the banks, but the banks could not realize enough on the foreclosed property to recover their loans. Suddenly the public mood changed. Commodity prices tumbled 30 percent between February and May. Hordes of depositors sought to withdraw their money in the form of specie, and soon the banks exhausted their supplies. Panic swept the country in the spring of 1837 as every bank in the nation was forced to suspend specie payments. The boom was over.

Major swings in the business cycle can never be attributed to the actions of a single person, however powerful, but there is no doubt that Jackson's war against the Bank exaggerated the swings of the economic pendulum, not so much by its direct effects as by the impact of the president's ill-considered policies on popular thinking. His Specie Circular did not prevent speculators from buying land—at most it caused purchasers to pay a premium for gold or silver. But it convinced potential buyers that the boom was going to end and led them to make decisions that in fact ended it. Old Hickory's combination of impetuousness, combativeness, arrogance, and ignorance rendered the nation he loved so dearly a serious disservice.

JACKSONIANISM ABROAD

Jackson's emotional and dogmatic side also influenced his handling of foreign affairs. His patriotism was often so extravagant as to be ludicrous; in less peaceful times he might well have embroiled the country in far bloodier battles than his war with Nicholas Biddle produced. By pushing relentlessly for the solution of minor problems, he won a number of diplomatic successes. Several advantageous reciprocal trade agreements were negotiated, including one with Great Britain that finally opened British West Indian ports to American ships. American claims dating from the Napoleonic Wars were pressed vigorously. The most important result of this policy came in 1831, when France agreed to pay about $5 million to compensate for damages to American property during that long conflict.

This settlement, however, led to trouble because the French Chamber of Deputies refused to appropriate the necessary funds. When the United States submitted a bill for the first installment in 1833, it was unable to collect. Jackson at once adopted a belligerent stance, his ire further aroused by a bill for $170,041.18 submitted by Nicholas Biddle for the services of the Bank of the United States in attempting to collect the money. When France ignored the second installment, Jackson sent a blistering message to Congress, full of such phrases as "not to be tolerated" and "take redress into our own hands." He asked for a law "authorizing reprisals upon French property" if the money was not paid.

Jackson's case was ironclad, yet it did not merit such vigorous prosecution. Congress wisely took no action. Jackson suspended diplomatic relations with France and ordered the navy readied. The French—in part, no doubt, because they were clearly in the wrong—were insulted by Jackson's manner. Irresponsible talk of war was heard in both countries. Fortunately the French Chamber finally appropriated the money, Jackson moderated his public pronouncements, and the issue subsided.

Similarly, when a snag delayed the negotiation of the West Indian treaty, Jackson had suggested forcing Great Britain to make concessions by imposing a boycott on trade with Canada. In both cases he showed poor judgment, being ready to take monumental risks to win petty victories. His behavior reinforced the impression held by foreigners that the United States was a rash young country with a chip on its shoulder, pathologically mistrustful of the good faith of European powers.

THE JACKSONIANS

Jackson's personality had a large impact on the shape and tone of American politics and thus with the development of the second party system. When he came to office, nearly everyone professed to be a follower of Jefferson. By 1836 being a Jeffersonian no longer meant much; what mattered was how one felt about Andrew Jackson. He had ridden to power at the head of a diverse political army, but he left behind him an organization with a fairly cohesive, if not necessarily consistent, body of ideas. This Democratic party contained rich citizens and poor, Easterners and Westerners, abolitionists as well as slaveholders. It was not yet a close-knit national organization, but—always allowing for individual exceptions—the Jacksonians agreed on certain underlying principles. These included suspicion of special privilege and large business corporations, both typified by the Bank of the United States; freedom of economic opportunity, unfettered by private or governmental

DEBATING THE PAST

For whom did Jackson fight? In 1837, his last year as president, Jackson here distributes hunks of a 1400-pound cheese, a gift from New York farmers. They thought it the best present the "farming class" could give to someone who so forcefully had represented "their interest." In 1855 historian George Bancroft maintained that Jackson *was all* America, for he "shared and possessed all the creative ideas of his country and his time." (This is the sort of twaddle that gives nineteenth-century historians a bad name.) In 1945 Arthur M. Schlesinger, Jr.—son of the progressive historian—praised Jackson for battling on behalf of farmers and workers against big business. Jackson approached politics in terms of class rather than geography, and in that sense anticipated Franklin Delano Roosevelt. In both eras, Schlesinger observed, "the business community" had brought "national affairs to a state of crisis." Richard Hofstadter (1948) conceded that Jackson's fight against business had "many superficial points in common" with Roosevelt's. But Jackson had been no friend of the "common man," for he had consistently promoted the interests of well-to-do farmers and local entrepreneurs. This point received some confirmation from Edward Pessen's (1969) study of wealth accumulation during the Jacksonian era: the rich grew richer and the poor, poorer. Robert Remini (1984), on the other hand, argued that Jackson adhered to republican ideals: he did what was good for the nation as a whole. Whatever the reality, many different people *believed* that Jackson represented them. Note that at the public reception above, some wore formal attire and others, work clothes. But all got cheese.

George Bancroft, *Literary and Historical Miscellanies* (1855), Arthur M. Schlesinger, Jr., *Age of Jackson* (1945), Richard Hofstadter, *The American Political Tradition*, Edward Pessen, *Jacksonian America* (1969), Lee Benson, *The Concept of Jacksonian Democracy* (1961), Robert Remini, *Andrew Jackson and the Course of American Democracy* (1984).

restrictions; absolute political freedom, at least for white males; and the conviction that any ordinary man is capable of performing the duties of most public offices.

Jackson's ability to reconcile his belief in the supremacy of the Union with his conviction that national authority should be held within narrow limits tended to make the Democrats the party of those who believed that the powers of the states should not be diminished. Tocqueville caught this aspect of Jackson's philosophy perfectly: "Far from wishing to extend Federal power," he wrote, "the president belongs to the party that wishes to limit that power."

Although the radical Locofoco[2] wing of the party championed the idea, nearly all Jacksonians, like their leader, favored giving the small man his chance—by supporting public education, for example, and by refusing to place much weight on a person's origin, dress, or manners. "One individual is as good as another" (for accuracy we must insert the adjective *white*) was their axiom. This attitude helps explain why immigrants, Catholics, and other minority groups usually voted Democratic. However, the Jacksonians showed no tendency either to penalize the wealthy or to intervene in economic affairs to aid the underprivileged. The motto "That government is best which governs least" graced the masthead of the chief Jacksonian newspaper, the *Washington Globe,* throughout the era.

RISE OF THE WHIGS

The opposition to Jackson was far less cohesive. Henry Clay's National Republican party provided a nucleus, but Clay never dominated that party as Jackson dominated the Democrats. Its orientation was basically anti-Jackson. It was as though the American people were a great block of granite from which some sculptor had just fashioned a statue of Jackson, the chips scattered about the floor of the studio representing the opposition.

While Jackson was president, the impact of his personality delayed the formation of a true two-party system, but as soon as he surrendered power, the opposition, taking heart, began to coalesce. Many Democrats could not accept the odd logic of Jacksonian finance. As early as 1834 they, together with the Clay element, the extreme states' righters who followed Calhoun, and other dissident groups, were calling

themselves Whigs. The name harkened back to the Revolution. It implied patriotic distaste for too-powerful executives, expressed specifically as resistance to the tyranny of "King Andrew."

This coalition possessed great resources of wealth and talent. Anyone who understood banking was almost obliged to become a Whig unless he was connected with one of Jackson's "pets." Those spiritual descendants of Hamilton who rejected the administration's refusal to approach economic problems from a broadly national perspective also joined in large numbers. Those who found the coarseness and "pushiness" of the Jacksonians offensive were another element in the new party. The anti-intellectual and antiscientific bias of the administration (Jackson rejected proposals for a national university, an observatory, and a scientific and literary institute) drove many ministers, lawyers, doctors, and other well-educated people into the Whig fold.

The philosopher Ralph Waldo Emerson was no doubt thinking of these types when he described the Whigs as "the enterprizing, intelligent, well-meaning & wealthy part of the people," but Whig arguments also appealed to ordinary voters who were predisposed to favor strong governments that would check the "excesses" of unrestricted individualism.

The Whigs were slow to develop effective party organization. They had too many generals and not enough troops. It was hard for them to agree on any issue more complicated than opposition to Jackson. Furthermore, they stood in conflict with the major trend of the age: the glorification of the common man.

Lacking a dominant leader in 1836, the Whigs relied on "favorite sons," hoping to throw the presidential election into the House of Representatives. Daniel Webster ran in New England. For the West and South, Hugh Lawson White of Tennessee, a former friend who had broken with Jackson, was counted on to carry the fight. General William Henry Harrison was supposed to win in the Northwest and to draw support everywhere from those who liked to vote for military heroes. This sorry strategy failed; Jackson's handpicked candidate, Martin Van Buren, won a majority of both the popular and the electoral votes.

MARTIN VAN BUREN: JACKSONIANISM WITHOUT JACKSON

Van Buren's brilliance as a political manipulator— the Red Fox, the Little Magician—has tended to obscure his statesmanlike qualities and his engaging

---

[2]A locofoco was a type of friction match. The name was first applied in politics when a group of New York Jacksonians used these matches to light candles when a conservative faction tried to break up their meeting by turning off the gaslights.

personality. He made a powerful argument, for example, that political parties were a force for unity, not for partisan bickering. In addition, high office sobered him, and improved his judgment. He fought the Bank of the United States as a monopoly, but he also opposed irresponsible state banks. New York's Safety Fund System, requiring all banks to contribute to a fund, supervised by the state, to be used to redeem the notes of any member bank that failed, was established largely through his efforts. Van Buren believed in public construction of internal improvements, but he favored state rather than national programs, and he urged a rational approach: Each project must stand on its own as a useful and profitable public utility.

He continued to equivocate spectacularly on the tariff—in his *Autobiography* he described two of his supporters walking home after listening to him talk on the tariff, each convinced that it had been a brilliant speech, but neither having obtained the slightest idea as to where Van Buren stood on the subject—but he was never in the pocket of any special interest group or tariff lobbyist. He accounted himself a good Jeffersonian, tending to prefer state action to federal, but he was by no means doctrinaire. Basically he approached most questions rationally and pragmatically.

Van Buren

Van Buren had outmaneuvered Calhoun easily in the struggle to succeed Jackson, winning the old hero's confidence and serving him well. In 1832 he was elected vice president and thereafter was conceded to be the "heir apparent." In 1835 the Democratic National Convention unanimously nominated him for president.

Van Buren took office just as the Panic of 1837 struck the country. Its effects were frightening but short-lived. When the banks stopped converting paper money into gold and silver, they outraged conservatives but in effect eased the pressure on the money market: Interest rates declined and business loans again became relatively easy to obtain. In 1836, at the height of the boom in land sales, Congress had voted to "distribute" the new treasury surplus to the states, and this flow of money, which the states promptly spent, also stimulated the revival. Late in 1838 the banks resumed specie payments.

But in 1839 a bumper crop caused a sharp decline in the price of cotton. Then a number of state governments that had overextended themselves in road- and canal-building projects were forced to default on their debts. This discouraged investors, particularly foreigners. A general economic depression ensued that lasted until 1843.

Van Buren was not responsible for the panic or the depression, but his manner of dealing with economic issues was scarcely helpful. He saw his role as being concerned only with problems plaguing the government, ignoring the economy as a whole. "The less government interferes with private pursuits the better for the general prosperity," he pontificated. As Daniel Webster scornfully pointed out, Van Buren was following a policy of "leaving the people to shift for themselves," one that many Whigs rejected.

Such a hands-off approach to the depression seems foolish by modern standards. Van Buren's refusal to assume any responsibility for the general welfare appears to explode the theory that the Jacksonians were deeply concerned with the fate of ordinary citizens. In *The Concept of Jacksonian Democracy*, Lee Benson argues that the Whigs, rather than the Democrats, were the "positive liberals" of the era. Benson cites many statements by Whigs about applying "the means of the state boldly and liberally to aid . . . public works."

This approach helps correct past oversimplifications, but it judges the period by the standards of a later age. The country in the 1830s was still mainly agricultural, and for most farmers the depression, though serious, did not spell disaster. Moreover, many Jacksonians were perfectly willing to see the states act to stimulate economic growth in bad times—as indeed most states did.

Van Buren's chief goal was finding a substitute for the state banks as a place to keep federal funds. The depression and the suspension of specie payments embarrassed the government along with private depositors. He soon settled on the idea of "divorcing" the government from all banking activities. His independent treasury bill called for the construction of government owned vaults where federal revenues could be stored until needed. To ensure absolute safety, all payments to the government were to be made in hard cash. After a battle that lasted until the summer of 1840, the Independent Treasury Act passed both the House and the Senate.

Opposition to the Independent Treasury Act had been bitter, and not all of it was partisan. Bankers and businessmen objected to the government's withholding so much specie from the banks, which needed all the hard money they could get to support loans that were the lifeblood of economic growth. It seemed irresponsible for the federal government to turn its back on the banks, which so obviously performed a semipublic function. These criticisms made good sense, but through a lucky combination of circumstances, the system worked reasonably well for many years.

By creating suspicion in the public mind, officially stated distrust of banks acted as a damper on their tendency to overexpand. No acute shortage of specie developed because heavy agricultural exports and the investment of much European capital in American railroads beginning in the mid-1840s brought in large amounts of new gold and silver. After 1849 the discovery of gold in California added another important source of specie. The supply of money and bank credit kept pace roughly with the growth of the economy, but through no fault of the government. "Wildcat" banks proliferated. Fraud and counterfeiting were common, and the operation of everyday business affairs was inconvenienced in countless ways. The disordered state of the currency remained a grave problem until corrected by Civil War banking legislation.

THE LOG CABIN CAMPAIGN

It was not his financial policy that led to Van Buren's defeat in 1840. The depression naturally hurt the Democrats, and the Whigs were far better organized than in 1836. The Whigs also adopted a different strategy. The Jacksonians had come to power on the coattails of a popular general whose views on public questions they concealed or ignored. They had maintained themselves by shouting the praises of the common man. Now the Whigs seized on these techniques and carried them to their logical—or illogical—conclusion. Not even bothering to draft a program, and passing over Clay and Webster, whose views were known and therefore controversial, they nominated General William Henry Harrison for president. The "Hero of Tippecanoe" was counted on to conquer the party created in the image of the Hero of New Orleans. To "balance" the ticket, the Whigs chose a former Democrat, John Tyler of Virginia, an ardent supporter of states' rights, as their vice presidential candidate.

The Whig argument was specious but effective: General Harrison is a plain man of the people who lives in a log cabin (where the latchstring is always out). Contrast him with the suave Van Buren, luxuriating amid "the Regal Splendor of the President's Palace." Harrison drinks ordinary hard cider and eats hog meat and grits, while Van Buren drinks expensive foreign wines and fattens on fancy concoctions prepared by a French chef. The general's furniture is plain and sturdy; the president dines off gold plates and treads on Royal Wilton carpets that cost the people $5

▲ The 1840 presidential campaign was the first to use circus hoopla and the techniques of mass appeal that came to characterize political contests in the United States. This photograph is of a log cabin with a "hard cider" keg that was carried on a pole at rallies for William Henry Harrison.

a yard. In a country where all are equal, the people will reject an aristocrat like "Martin Van Ruin" and put their trust in General Harrison, a simple, brave, honest, public-spirited common man.

Harrison came from a distinguished family, being the son of Benjamin Harrison, a signer of the Declaration of Independence and a former governor of Virginia. He was well educated and in at least comfortable financial circumstances, and he certainly did not live in a log cabin. The Whigs ignored these facts. The log cabin and the cider barrel became their symbols, which every political meeting saw reproduced in a dozen forms. The leading Whig campaign newspaper, edited by a vigorous New Englander named Horace Greeley, was called the *Log Cabin*. Cartoons, doggerel, slogans, and souvenirs were everywhere substituted for argument.

The Democrats used the same methods as the Whigs and were equally well organized, but they had little heart for the fight. The best they could come up with was the fact that their vice presidential candidate,

► *text continues on page 270*

Horace Greeley

Zaccheus ("Zack") Greeley, a farmer in Amherst, New Hampshire, was the son and grandson of men who bore that name,
but for some unexplained reason when his first son was born
in 1811 he named him Horace. Zack Greeley owned 40 acres
of stony land on which he grew corn, oats, and rye, along with
hops, a key ingredient in the making of beer. The local soil
tended to become hard packed. Every few years it had to be
"broken up" by plowing it with four pairs of oxen, led by a
horse. To "ride horse to plough" was one of Horace's tasks by
the time he was 5. "I was early made acquainted with labor,"
Horace recalled many years later. His other jobs included
keeping the oxen out of the corn on frosty autumn mornings
while the harvesters had their breakfast, and digging out
worms and grubs around the corn hills.

The hard times following the Panic of 1819, combined with
ill health and a poor head for business, caused Zack Greeley
to lose his farm in 1820. Indeed, to avoid debtors' prison, he
had to leave his family and hurry across the state line into
Vermont. But after working as a day laborer for a few months
he was able to rent a house in Westhaven, Vermont, and send
for his family. There the Greeleys experienced what Horace
called "genuine poverty,—not beggary, nor dependence, but
the manly American sort." During the winter Zack chopped
wood for 50 cents a day. In the spring he contracted to clear
50 acres of wild land. For the next two years Zack and his two
sons, aged 10 and 8 in 1821, cleared the 50 acres at a rate
of $7 an acre, plus half the usable wood they had cut. They
chopped down trees, sawed the wood into manageable
lengths, and uprooted and burned rotting stumps and brush.
Horace described the work as "rugged and grimy, but
healthy." The next year the Greeleys moved to a nearby small
farm called Flea Knoll. That spring was too wet, the summer
too dry, the fields thick with thistles. Farming, Horace had by
this time decided, was "a mindless, monotonous drudgery."
He was determined to seek a different vocation.

Fortunately he was a bright boy and his parents apparently
noticed his talent early. Before he was 3 they sent him to
school in the winter months in a one-room schoolhouse near
his grandfather's farm. He proved particularly adept at mastering Webster's *Spelling-Book* and soon outdistanced much

older pupils in the school's weekly spelling bees. Reading
proved equally easy for him, and by the time he was 5, with a
little help from his mother, he had made his way through the
entire Bible. Word of his talent spread throughout the community, and when he was 9 a group of "leading men" offered to
send him to Phillips Academy in Exeter, New Hampshire. His
parents, however, politely declined the offer, saying "they
would give their children the best education they could afford,
and then stop."

After the family moved to Vermont, young Greeley continued to go to school in the winter months when his labor was
not needed on the farm. But he was not exposed to any of the
sciences or to any math as far advanced as algebra. Despite
his lack of much formal education, however, he hoped to
become a newspaper man. In 1826 he learned of an opening
for an apprentice on the *Northern Spectator* in the town of
East Poultney, Vermont. He was 15.

He was offered the post and with his father's approval he
signed on to work until the age of 20 for room and board
and $40 a year for clothing. East Poultney, he recalled many
years later, was an excellent place to learn a trade—there
were, he explained, perhaps with tongue in cheek, "few villages wherein the incitements to dissipation and vice are
fewer." The paper was loosely run, editors and printers came
and went frequently. Thus "every one had perfect liberty to
learn whatever he could." Greeley worked at his job very hard
but also found time to scour the shelves of the East Poultney
Public Library.

When his apprenticeship ended, Greeley paid a brief visit
to his family, which had settled in Erie County, Pennsylvania.
Then he found a couple of jobs on papers in Chautauqua
County, New York, before accepting a post as a journeyman
on the Erie [Pennsylvania] *Gazette* for $15 a month. After five
months, however, he was let go. Finding that "the West
seemed to be laboring under a surfeit of printers," he paid a
final visit to his parents and, as he later explained, "with $25
in my pocket, and very little extra clothing in my bundle, I set
my face toward New York." He arrived in the city by Hudson
River steamer on August 17, 1831. He was five months short
of 21 years old.

▲ Greeley reading his newspaper, the *New York Tribune*.

After buying a new suit for $5, Greeley had only $10 to his name. For a year and a half he lived hand-to-mouth, working for a series of printers as a journeyman. Then he managed to set himself up on his own and in 1834 began publishing the *New-Yorker,* a literary magazine. He became heavily involved in Whig politics and on April 10, 1841, launched the newspaper that became his life work, the *New York Tribune.*

Greeley is best known for the line "Go West, young man, go West," advice many mid-nineteenth-century young people of both sexes eagerly accepted. Greeley used, though he did not invent, that expression, but his own career was typical of a far different pattern, the movement of ambitious men and women from farm to city.

Richard Mentor Johnson, had killed Tecumseh, not merely defeated him. Van Buren tried to focus public attention on issues, but his voice could not be heard above the huzzahs of the Whigs. When the Whigs chanted "Tippecanoe and Tyler too!" and "Van, Van, is a used-up man" and rolled out another barrel of hard cider, the best the Democrats could come up with was:

Rumpsey, Dumpsey,
Colonel Johnson
Killed Tecumseh.

A huge turnout (four-fifths of the eligible voters) carried Harrison to victory by a margin of almost 150,000. The electoral vote was 234 to 60.

The Democrats had been blown up by their own bomb. In 1828 they had portrayed John Quincy Adams as a bloated aristocrat and Jackson as a simple farmer. The lurid talk of Van Buren dining off golden plates was no different from the stories that made Adams out to be a passionate gambler. If Van Buren was a lesser man than Adams, Harrison was a pale imitation indeed of Andrew Jackson.

The Whigs continued to repeat history by rushing to gather the spoils of victory. Washington was again flooded by office seekers, the political confusion was monumental. Harrison had no ambition to be an aggressive leader. He believed that Jackson had misused the veto and professed to put as much emphasis as had Washington on the principle of the separation of legislative and executive powers. This delighted the Whig leaders in Congress, who had had their fill of the "executive usurpation" of Jackson. Either Clay or Webster seemed destined to be the real ruler of the new administration, and soon the two were squabbling over their old general like sparrows over a crust.

At the height of their squabble, less than a month after his inauguration, Harrison fell gravely ill. Pneumonia developed, and on April 4 he died. John Tyler of Virginia, honest and conscientious but doctrinaire, became president of the United States. The political climate of the country was changed dramatically. Events began to march in a new direction.

MILESTONES

1828	Andrew Jackson is elected president	**1833**	Treasury Secretary Roger B. Taney orders Treasury funds removed from Bank of the United States
1829	Crowds cause chaos at Jackson's White House inaugural reception		
	Jackson relies on his "Kitchen Cabinet"		Calhoun and Clay push through Compromise Tariff
1830	Daniel Webster, in his "Second Reply to Hayne," calls Union perpetual and indissoluble	**1836**	Jackson issues Specie Circular to control speculation
	Jackson vetoes the Maysville Road Bill		Martin Van Buren is elected president
1831	Nat Turner leads slave rebellion in Virginia	**1837–1838**	Panic sweeps nation, ending boom
	Chief Justice Marshall denies Cherokee rights in *Cherokee Nation v. Georgia*	**1838**	4000 Cherokee die on Trail of Tears to Oklahoma
1831–1838	Southern Indians are removed to Oklahoma	**1840**	Independent Treasury Act divorces federal government from all banking activities
1832	South Carolina defends states' rights in Ordinance of Nullification		"Log Cabin" Campaign is first to use "hoopla"
	Force Bill grants president authority to execute revenue laws		William Henry Harrison is elected president
	Jackson vetoes Bank Recharter Bill	**1841**	Harrison dies one month after inauguration; John Tyler becomes president
	Chief Justice Marshall rules in Cherokees' favor in *Worcester v. Georgia*		
	Jackson is reelected president		

SUPPLEMENTARY READING

The nature of Jacksonian democracy was analyzed brilliantly by Alexis de Tocqueville, *Democracy in America* (1835–1840). Other commentaries by foreigners throw much light on Jacksonian democracy. See especially, in addition to Tocqueville, Frances Trollope, *Domestic Manners of the Americans* (1832), Michel Chevalier, *Society, Manners and Politics in the United States* (1961), Harriet Martineau, *Retrospect of Western Travel* (1838) and *Society in America* (1837), and F. J. Grund, *Aristocracy in America* (1859).

In addition to the works on Jackson cited in Debating the Past (p. 264), see Bray Hammond, *Banks and Politics in America from the Revolution to the Civil War* (1957), and J. M. McFaul, *The Politics of Jacksonian Finance* (1972). Peter Temin, *The Jacksonian Economy* (1969), minimizes the effects of Jackson's policies on economic conditions. Jill Norgren, *The Cherokee Cases* (1996) is critical of Jackson's policies toward Indians; Robert Remini is more supportive in *Andrew Jackson and His Indian Wars* (2001).

On the transformation of political parties, see Richard P. McCormick, *The Second American Party System* (1966), and Michael Holt, *The Rise and Fall of the American Whig Party* (1999), which focuses on variations at the state level. Gerald Leonard, *The Invention of Party Politics* (2002) provides a detailed study of Illinois.

On the nullification controversy, see R. E. Ellis, *The Union at Risk* (1987), and William W. Freehling, *The Road to Disunion* (1990), which stresses the close relationship between the nullifiers and the slavery issue.

For the Van Buren administration, see John Niven, *Martin Van Buren* (1983), and M. L. Wilson, *The Presidency of Martin Van Buren* (1984). The election of 1840 is treated in R. G. Gunderson, *The Log-Cabin Campaign* (1957).

Louis Masur's *1831, Year of Eclipse* (2001), provides an interesting perspective on that pivotal year.

SUGGESTED WEBSITES

Indian Affairs: Laws and Treaties, Compiled and Edited by Charles J. Kappler (1904)
http://digital.library.okstate.edu/kappler/
This digitized text at Oklahoma State University includes preremoval treaties with the Five Civilized Tribes and other tribes.

Andrew Jackson and Indian Removal
http://www.iwchildren.org/genocide/murderer1.htm
This site offers a critical appraisal of Jackson's Indian removal policy.

The Second Bank of the United States, 1816–1836
http://odur.let.rug.nl/~usa/E/usbank/bank04.htm
The political fighting surrounding the Second Bank of the United States occupied the United States during the Jackson era, and led to the rise of the Whig party.

Daniel Webster
http://www.dartmouth.edu/~dwebster
Background information and selected writings from one of the nineteenth century's most noted orators.

The American Whig Party, 1834–1856
http://odur.let.rug.nl/~usa/E/uswhig/whigsxx.htm
This site treats the rise and fall of an important nineteenth-century political movement.

National Museum of the American Indian
http://www.si.edu/nmai
The Smithsonian Institution maintains this site, providing information about the museum that is dedicated to everything about Native Americans.

The Making of Middle-Class America

▼ *Joseph Moore and His Family* (1839), by Erastus Salisbury Field, reflects the emerging middle-class family. Although the painting is named after the father, the mother is carefully placed in a precisely equivalent position; each child has a space of his or her own.

On May 12, 1831, two French aristocrats, Alexis de Tocqueville and Gustave de Beaumont, arrived in New York City from Le Havre on the packet *President*. Their official purpose was to make a study of American prisons for the French government. But they really came, as Tocqueville explained, "to see what a great republic is like."

Tocqueville and Beaumont were only the most insightful of dozens of Europeans who visited the United States during the first half of the nineteenth century in order to study the "natives." Their visit, for example, overlapped with that of Frances Trollope, whose *Domestic Manners of Americans* (1834) advised English readers that Americans were just as uncouth as they had imagined. A decade later, Charles Dickens made what by then had become for foreigners an almost obligatory pass through this crude outpost of civilization, before publishing his report on his "sharp dealing" cousins in *American Notes* (1842). A little later, in a novel, Dickens described the United States as a "Republic . . . full of sores and ulcers."

TOCQUEVILLE AND BEAUMONT IN AMERICA

Unlike Trollope, Dickens, and other uncharitable foreign visitors, Tocqueville and Beaumont believed that Europe was passing from its aristocratic past into a democratic future. How better to prepare for the change, they believed, than by studying the United States, where democracy was already the "enduring and normal state" of the land. In the nine months they spent in America, they traveled from New York to Boston, then back through New York in order to inspect the state prison at Auburn, then on to Ohio. ("No one has been born there; no one wants to stay there," Tocqueville later said.) They examined conditions on the frontier in the Michigan Territory, then sailed down the Mississippi River to New Orleans, where they heard an opera good enough to make them imagine they were back in France, and attended a "Quadroon ball," where, according to Tocqueville, "all the men [were] white, all the women coloured."

From New Orleans they went on to "semi-barbarous" Alabama before turning north to Washington, a city that Beaumont declared to be "very ugly." Finally back to New York, whence they sailed for France on February 20, 1832. All told, they had met and interviewed some 250 individuals, ranking from President Jackson—Beaumont insisted on referring to Old Hickory as "Monsieur"—to a number of Chippewa Indians.

▲ *The Dinner Party* (c. 1825) was perhaps Henry Sargent's most successful painting. It was taken on tour to New York, Boston, Philadelphia, and Salem, with viewers paying 25 cents apiece to see it. It helped establish a genteel standard in interior decoration: ornamented moldings, sideboards, thick carpeting, and tasteful paintings.

It had indeed been a "useful" trip for the two Frenchmen. It resulted in their prison report and in *Marie, ou l'Esclavage aux Etats Unis* (1835), Beaumont's account of American race problems, cast in the form of a novel. But above all else, the visit provided the material for Tocqueville's classic *De la Démocratie en Amérique,* published in France in 1835 and a year later in an English translation. *Democracy in America* has been the starting point for virtually all subsequent writers who have tried to describe what Tocqueville called "the creative elements" of American institutions.

TOCQUEVILLE IN JUDGMENT

The gist of *Democracy in America* is contained in the book's first sentence: "No novelty in the United States struck me more vividly during my stay there than the equality of conditions." Tocqueville meant not that Americans lived in a state of total equality, but that the inequalities that did exist among white Americans were not enforced by institutions or supported by public opinion. Moreover, the inequalities paled when compared with those of Europe. "In America," he concluded, "men are nearer equality than in any other country in the world." The circumstances of one's birth meant little, one's education less, and one's intelligence scarcely anything. Economic differences, while real and certainly "paraded" by those who enjoyed "a pre-eminence of wealth," were transitory. "Such wealth," Tocqueville assured his readers, "is within reach of all."

These sweeping generalizations, however comforting to Americans then and since, are simplifications. Few modern students of Jacksonian America would accept them without qualification. In the 1830s and 1840s a wide and growing gap existed between the rich and poor in the eastern cities. According to one study, the wealthiest 4 percent of the population of New York controlled about half the city's wealth in 1828, about two-thirds in 1845. The number of New Yorkers worth $100,000 or more tripled in that period. A similar concentration of wealth was occurring in Philadelphia and Boston.

Moreover, Tocqueville failed to observe the many poor people in Jacksonian America. Particularly in the cities, bad times forced many unskilled laborers and their families into dire poverty. Tocqueville took little notice of such inequalities, in part because he was so captivated by the theme of American equality. He also had little interest in how industrialization and urbanization were affecting society. When he did take notice of working conditions, he remarked that wages were higher in America than in Europe and the cost of living was lower, facts obvious to the most obtuse European visitor. Furthermore, as with most foreign visitors, nearly all his contacts were with members of the upper crust. "We hardly see anyone," he acknowledged, "except people of distinction."

Despite his blind spots, Tocqueville realized that America was undergoing some fundamental social changes. These changes, he wrote, were being made by "an innumerable crowd who are . . . not exactly rich nor yet quite poor [and who] have enough property to want order and not enough to excite envy." In his notes he put it even more succinctly: "The whole society seems to have turned into one middle class."

A RESTLESS PEOPLE

"In America, men never stay still," Tocqueville noted. "Something is almost always provisional about their lives." Other European observers came away equally struck by the restlessness of Americans, without necessarily agreeing that democratic institutions made them so. Frances Trollope thought their "incessant bustling" similar to their eating too fast and spitting too often. It stemmed from their "universal pursuit of money," she claimed.

One reason Americans seemed continually on the move was that every year there were more of them. The first federal census in 1790 recorded that there were 3.9 million people in the country. In the early 1850s there were six times as many. The population was doubling every 22 years—just about what Franklin had predicted in 1751! The growth can be measured geographically by the admission of new states in the 1830s and 1840s: Arkansas in 1836, Michigan in 1837, Florida in 1845, Texas in 1846, and Wisconsin in 1848.

Yet by contemporary European standards, even the settled parts of the United States were sparsely populated in the 1830s and 1840s. But for people accustomed to the wide open spaces, the presence of more than a handful of neighbors was reason enough for moving on. Abraham Lincoln's father Thomas (1778–1851) was typical: He grew up in Kentucky, pioneered in Indiana, and died in Illinois.

The urge to move had an urban dimension as well. For every "young man" who took the advice of the New York newspaperman Horace Greeley to "go west," several young men and women went instead to town. By the tens of thousands they exchanged the rigors of farming for the uncertain risks and

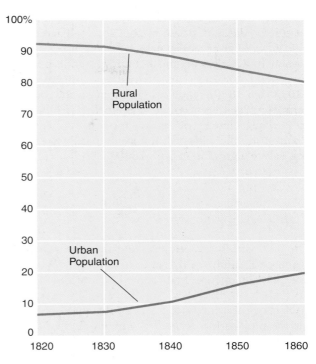

▲ **Rural Versus Urban Population, 1820–1860**
As the balance of rural and urban population began to shift during the years from 1820 to 1860, the number of cities with populations over 100,000 grew from one in 1820—New York—to nine in 1870, including southern and western cities like New Orleans and San Francisco.

rewards of city life. Boston, New York, and Philadelphia had a combined population of 50,000 at the time of the Revolution. Each expanded rapidly during the first half of the next century. Boston had 40,000 residents in 1820, nearly 140,000 in 1850. Philadelphia grew even more rapidly, from just under 100,000 in 1820 to almost 400,000 in 1850. New York, which had forged ahead of Philadelphia around 1810, grew from 125,000 in 1820 to more than 500,000 in 1850.

However spectacular the growth of the largest cities, the emergence of new towns was more significant. In 1820 the Northeast contained 5 cities with populations above 25,000 and 13 with populations above 10,000. Thirty years later, 26 cities had more than 25,000 residents and 62 had more than 10,000.

Even though the Old Northwest remained primarily agricultural, its towns grew as fast as its farms. Pittsburgh, St. Louis, Cincinnati, Louisville, and Lexington attracted settlers in such numbers that by 1850 all but Lexington had populations of over 35,000. Cincinnati, "the Emporium of the West," with a population of 100,000, ranked seventh in the country.

The trek to town that was transforming the Northeast did not occur in the South. There were four cities of respectable size in the region—Mobile, Savannah, Charleston, and Baltimore—and one large city, New Orleans, which had a population of 120,000 in 1850. Yet all were located on the region's perimeter. Neither Virginia nor North Carolina had an urban center of even modest dimensions. Charleston, the oldest and most typically southern city, scarcely grew at all after 1830.

THE FAMILY RECAST

The growth of cities undermined the importance of home and family as the unit of economic production. This happened first in the cities of the Northeast, then in the West, and eventually wherever nonagricultural jobs occupied a substantial percentage of the workforce. More and more people did their work in shops, in offices, or on factory floors. Whether a job was skilled or unskilled, white-collar or blue-collar, or strictly professional, it took the family breadwinner out of the house during working hours six days a week. This did not mean that the family necessarily ceased to be an economic unit. But the labor of the father and any children with jobs came home in the form of cash, thus at least initially in the custody of the individual earners. The social consequences of this change were enormous for the traditional "head of the family" and for his wife and children.

Carey, Rules for Husbands and Wives

Because he was away so much the husband had to surrender to his wife some of the power in the family that he had formerly exercised, if for no other reason than that she was always there. The situation bore a superficial resemblance to the relationship of the king of England to the colonies in the seventeenth century: Whatever the king's power under the law, his authority was limited by his lack of close contact with his colonial "offspring." Perhaps this is what Noah Webster had in mind when he used a similar comparison in describing the ideal father's authority as "like the mild dominion of a limited monarch, and not the iron rule of an austere tyrant." It certainly explains why Tocqueville concluded that "a sort of equality reigns around the domestic hearth" in America. It also explains why American men began to place women on a pedestal, presuming them to be by nature almost saintly, pure of mind and body, selflessly devoted to the care of others.

The new power and prestige that wives and mothers enjoyed were not obtained without cost. Since they were exercising day-to-day control over household affairs, they were expected to tend only to those affairs. Expanding their interest to other fields of human endeavor was frowned on. Where the typical wife had formerly been a partner in a family enterprise, she now left earning a living entirely to her husband. She was certainly not encouraged to have an independent career as, say, a lawyer or doctor. Time spent away from home or devoted to matters unrelated to the care of husband and family was, according to the new doctrine of "separate spheres," time misappropriated.

This trend widened the gap between the middle and lower classes. For a middle-class wife and mother to take a job or, still worse, to devote herself to any "frivolous" activity outside the home was considered a dereliction of duty. Such an attitude could not possibly develop in lower-class families where everyone had to work simply to keep food on the table.

Some women objected to making a cult out of "womanhood": by placing an ideal on so high a pedestal, all real women would fall short. Others escaped its more suffocating aspects by forming close friendships with other women. But most women, including such forceful proponents of women's rights as the educator Catharine Beecher and Sarah Hale, the editor of *Godey's Ladies Book*, subscribed to the view that a woman's place was in the home. "The formation of the moral and intellectual character of the young is committed mainly to the female hand," Beecher wrote in *A Treatise on Domestic Economy for the Use of Young Ladies* (1841). "The mother forms the character of the future man."

Beecher, from *A Treatise on Domestic Economy*

Another reason for the switch in power and influence from husbands to wives was that women began to have fewer children. Here again, the change happened earliest and was most pronounced among families in the rapidly urbanizing Northeast. But the birthrate gradually declined all over the country. People married later than in earlier periods. Long courtships and broken engagements were common, probably because prospective marriage partners were becoming more selective. On average, women began having their children two or three years later than their mothers had, and they stopped two or three years sooner. Apparently many middle-class couples made a conscious effort to limit family size, even when doing so required sexual abstinence.

Having fewer children led parents to value children more highly, or so it would seem from the

▲ Middle-class parents practiced sexual abstinence and even simple forms of contraception to limit family size. By having fewer children, they could lavish more attention and economic resources on each one. Middle-class fathers occupied themselves with business; mothers, with child rearing. Such people often sought to persuade others to similarly control their desires.

additional time and affection they lavished on them. Here again, the mother provided most of both. Child rearing fell within her "sphere" and occupied the time that earlier generations of mothers had devoted to such tasks as weaving, sewing, and farm chores. Not least of these new responsibilities was overseeing the children's education, both secular and religious.

DOCUMENT

Mother's Magazine

As families became smaller, relations within them became more caring. Parents ceased to think of their children mostly as future workers. The earlier tendency even among loving parents to keep their children at arm's length, yet within reach of the strap, gave way to more intimate relationships. Gone was the puritan notion that children possessed "a perverse will, a love of what's forbid," and with it the belief that parents were responsible for crushing all juvenile resistance to their authority. In its place arose the view described by Lydia Maria Child in *The Mother's Book* (1831) that children "come to us from heaven, with their little souls full of innocence and peace." Mothers "should not

interfere with the influence of angels," Child advised her readers.

Bronson Alcott, another proponent of gentle child-rearing practices, went still further. Children, he insisted, were the moral superiors of their parents. Alcott banished "the rod and all its appendages" from his own household, wherein four daughters (one, Louisa May, later the author of *Little Women* and other novels) were raised, and urged other parents to follow his example. "Childhood hath saved me!" he wrote. The English poet William Wordsworth's "Ode on Intimations of Immortality," in which babies entered the world "trailing clouds of glory," served some American parents as a child-rearing manual.

THE SECOND GREAT AWAKENING

Belief in the innate goodness of children was of course in direct conflict with the Calvinist doctrine of infant damnation, to which most American Protes-

▲ Religious revivals stirred passions, as this rendering of an 1839 camp meeting suggests: people are gesticulating, swooning, and writhing on the ground. Finney endorsed such "excitements" as essential for conversion. But some doubted the wisdom of eliciting passions so as to persuade people to exercise more restraint and sin less often.

tant churches formally subscribed. "Of all the impious doctrines which the dark imagination of man ever conceived," Bronson Alcott wrote in his journal, "the worst [is] the belief in original and certain depravity of infant nature." Alcott was far from alone in thinking infant damnation a "debased doctrine," despite its standing as one of the central tenets of orthodox Calvinism.

The inclination to set aside other Calvinist tenets, such as predestination, became more pronounced as a new wave of revivalism took shape in the 1790s. This Second Great Awakening began as a counteroffensive to the deistic thinking and other forms of "infidelity" that New England Congregationalists and southern Methodists alike identified with the French Revolution. Prominent New England ministers, who considered themselves traditionalists but also revivalists,

men such as Yale's president, Timothy Dwight, and Dwight's student, the Reverend Lyman Beecher, placed less stress in their sermons on God's arbitrary power over mortals, more on the promise of the salvation of sinners because of God's mercy and "disinterested benevolence." When another of Dwight's students, Horace Bushnell, declared in a sermon on "Christian nurture" in 1844 that Christian parents should prepare their children "for the skies," he meant that parents could contribute to their children's salvation.

Calvinism came under more direct assault from Charles Grandison Finney, probably the most effective of a number of charismatic evangelists who brought the Second Great Awakening to its crest. In 1821 Finney abandoned a promising career as a

DOCUMENT

Finney, "What a Revival of Religion Is"

lawyer and became an itinerant preacher. His most spectacular successes occurred during a series of revivals conducted in towns along the Erie Canal, a region Finney called "the burned-over district" because it had been the site of so many revivals before his own. From Utica, where his revival began in 1826, to Rochester, where it climaxed in 1831, he exhorted his listeners to take their salvation into their own hands. He insisted that people could control their own fate. He dismissed Calvinism as a "theological fiction." Salvation was available to anyone. But the day of judgment was just around the corner; there was little time to waste.

During and after Finney's efforts in Utica, declared conversions increased sharply. In Rochester, church membership doubled in six months. Elsewhere in the country, churches capitalized on the efforts of other evangelists to fill their pews. In 1831 alone, church membership grew by 100,000, an increase, according to a New England minister, "unparalleled in the history of the church." The success of the evangelists of the Second Great Awakening stemmed from the timeliness of their assault on Calvinist doctrine and even more from their methods. Finney, for example, consciously set out to be entertaining as well as edifying. The singing of hymns and the solicitation of personal testimonies provided his meetings with emotional release and human interest. Prominent among his innovations was the "anxious bench," where leading members of the community awaited the final prompting from within before coming forward to declare themselves saved.

But the economic changes of the times and the impact of these changes on family life had as important effects on the Second Awakening as even the most accomplished of the evangelists. The growth of industry and commerce that followed the completion of the Erie Canal in 1825, along with the disappearance of undeveloped farmland, led hundreds of young men to leave family farms to seek their fortunes in Utica and other towns along the canal. There, uprooted, uncertain, buffeted between ambition, hope, and anxiety, they found it hard to resist the comfort promised by the revivalists to those who were saved.

Women, and especially the wives of the business leaders of the community, felt particularly responsible for the Christian education of their children, which fell within their separate sphere. Many women had servants and thus had time and energy to devote to their own and their offsprings' salvation.

Paradoxically, this caused many of them to venture out of that sphere and in doing so they moved further out of the shadow of their husbands. They founded the Oneida County Female Missionary Society, an association that did most of the organizing and a good deal of the financing of the climactic years of the Second Awakening. The Female Missionary Society raised more than $1000 a year (no small sum at that time) to support the revival in Utica, in its environs, and throughout the burned-over district. Apparently without consciously intending to do so, women challenged the authority of the paternalistic, authoritarian churches they so fervently embraced. Then, by mixtures of exhortation, example, and affection, they set out to save the souls of their loved ones, first their children and ultimately their husbands too.

THE ERA OF ASSOCIATIONS

Alongside the recast family and the "almost revolutionized" church, a third pillar of the emerging American middle class was the voluntary association. Unlike the other two, it had neither colonial precedents nor contemporary European equivalents. The voluntary association of early nineteenth-century America was unique. "In France," Tocqueville wrote of this phenomenon, "if you want to proclaim a truth or propagate some feeling . . . you would find the government or in England some territorial magnate." In America, however, "you are sure to find an association."

The leaders of these associations tended to be ministers, lawyers, or merchants, but the rank and file consisted of tradesmen, foremen, clerks, and their wives. Some of these associations were formed around a local cause that some townspeople wished to advance, such as the provision of religious instruction for orphaned children; others were affiliated with associations elsewhere for the purposes of combating some national evil, such as drunkenness. Some, such as the American Board of Commissioners of Foreign Missions, founded in Boston in 1810, quickly became large and complex enterprises. (By 1860 the board had sent 1250 missionaries into the "heathen world" and raised $8 million to support them.) Others lasted only as long as it took to accomplish a specific good work, such as the construction of a school or a library.

In a sense the associations were assuming functions previously performed in the family, such as caring for old people and providing moral guidance to the young, but without the paternalistic discipline of the old way. They constituted a "benevolent empire," eager to make society over into their members' idea of how God wanted it to be.

BACKWOODS UTOPIAS

Americans frequently belonged to several associations at the same time and more than a few made reform their life's work. The most adventuresome tested their reform theories by withdrawing from workaday American society and establishing experimental communities. The communitarian point of view aimed at "commencing a wholesale social reorganization by first establishing and demonstrating its principles completely on a small scale." The first communitarians were religious reformers. In a sense the Pilgrims fall into this category, along with a number of other groups in colonial times, but only in the nineteenth century did the idea flourish.

One of the most influential of the earlier communities were the Shakers, founded by an Englishwoman, Ann Lee, who came to America in 1774. Mother Ann, as she was called, saw visions that convinced her that Christ would come to earth again as a woman and that she was that woman. With a handful of followers she founded a community near Albany, New York. The group grew rapidly, and after Ann Lee's death in 1784 her movement continued to expand. By the 1830s her followers had established about 20 successful communities.

The Shakers practiced celibacy; believing that the millennium was imminent, they saw no reason for perpetuating the human race. Each group lived in a large Family House, the sexes strictly segregated. Property was held in common but controlled by a ruling hierarchy. So much stress was placed on equality of labor and reward and on voluntary acceptance of the rules, however, that the system does not seem to have been oppressive.

The Shaker religion, joyful and fervent, was marked by much group singing and dancing, which provided the members with emotional release from their tightly controlled regimen. An industrious, skillful people, they made a special virtue of simplicity; some of their designs for buildings and, especially, furniture achieved a classic beauty seldom equaled among untutored artisans. Despite their odd customs, the Shakers were universally tolerated and even admired.

▲ The Shakers segregated the sexes and enforced celibacy. Pent-up sexual tensions were released in religious ecstasy expressed through church dances, as the lines of men and women approached each other—but never touched.

▲ Persecution forced the Mormons to move from New York to Ohio to Missouri, before settling for a time in Nauvoo, Illinois. There, in 1844 Joseph Smith, the Mormon leader, announced his candidacy for presidency of the United States. Smith and his brother Hyrum were arrested by local authorities and murdered in their jail cell by a hostile mob.

Utopian
Communities
before the
Civil War

There were many other religious colonies, such as the Amana Community, which flourished in New York and Iowa in the 1840s and 1850s, and John Humphrey Noyes's Oneida Community, where the members practiced "complex" marriage—a form of promiscuity based on the principle that every man in the group was married to every woman. They prospered by developing a number of manufacturing skills.

The most important of the religious communitarians were the Mormons. A remarkable Vermont farm boy, Joseph Smith, founded the religion in western New York in the 1820s. Smith saw visions; he claimed to have discovered and translated an ancient text, the Book of Mormon, written in hieroglyphics on plates of gold, which described the adventures of a tribe of Israelites that had populated America from biblical times until their destruction in a great war in 400 C.E. With a small band of followers, Smith established a community in Ohio in 1831. The Mormons' dedication and economic efficiency attracted large numbers of converts, but their unorthodox religious views and their exclusivism, a product of their sense of being a chosen people, caused resentment among unbelievers. The Mormons were forced to move first to Missouri and then back to Illinois, where in 1839 they founded the town of Nauvoo.

Nauvoo flourished—by 1844 it was the largest city in the state, with a population of 15,000—but once again the Mormons ran into local trouble. They quarreled among themselves, especially after Smith secretly authorized polygamy (he called it "celestial marriage") and a number of other unusual rites for members of the "Holy Order," the top leaders of the church.[1] They created a paramilitary organization, the Nauvoo Legion, headed by Smith, envisaging themselves as a semi-independent state within the Union. Smith announced that he was a candidate for president of the United States. Rumors circulated that the Mormons intended to take over the entire Northwest for their "empire." Once again local "gentiles" rose against them. Smith was arrested, then murdered by a mob.

Under a new leader, Brigham Young, the Mormons sought a haven beyond the frontier. In 1847

---

[1]One justification of polygamy, paradoxically, was that marriage was a sacred, eternal state. If a man remarried after his wife's death, eventually he would have two wives in Heaven. Therefore why not on earth?

they marched westward, pressing through the mountains until they reached the desolate wilderness on the shores of the Great Salt Lake. There, at last, they established their Zion and began to make their truly significant impact on American history. Irrigation made the desert flourish, precious water wisely being treated as a community asset. Hard, cooperative, intelligently directed effort spelled growth and prosperity; more than 11,000 people were living in the area when it became part of the Utah Territory in 1850. In time the communal Mormon settlement broke down, but the religion has remained—known as the Church of Latter-Day Saints, a major force in the shaping of the West. The Mormon Church is still by far the most powerful single influence in Utah and is a thriving organization in many other parts of the United States and in Europe.

Despite their many common characteristics, the religious communities varied enormously; subordination of the individual to the group did not destroy group individualism. Their sexual practices, for example, ranged from the "complex marriage" of the Oneidans through Mormon polygamy and ordinary monogamy to the reluctant acceptance of sexual intercourse by the Amana Community and the celibacy of the Shakers. The communities are more significant as reflections of the urgent reform spirit of the age than they are for their accomplishments.

The communities had some influence on reformers who wished to experiment with social organization. When Robert Owen, a British utopian socialist who believed in economic as well as political equality and who considered competition debasing, decided to create an ideal community in America, he purchased the Rappite settlement at New Harmony, Indiana. Owen's advocacy of free love and "enlightened atheism" did not add to the stability of his group or to its popularity among outsiders. The colony was a costly failure.

The American followers of Charles Fourier, a French utopian socialist who proposed that society should be organized in cooperative units called phalanxes, fared better. Fourierism did not seek to tamper with sexual and religious mores. Its advocates included important journalists, such as Horace Greeley of the *New York Tribune* and Parke Godwin of the *New York Evening Post*. In the 1840s several dozen Fourierist colonies were established in the northern and western states. Members worked at whatever tasks they wished and only as much as they wished. Wages were paid according to the "repulsiveness" of the tasks performed; the person who "chose" to clean out a cesspool would receive more than someone hoeing corn or mending a fence or

engaging in some task requiring complex skills. As might be expected, none of the communities lasted very long.

THE AGE OF REFORM

The communitarians were the most colorful of the reformers, their proposals the most spectacular. More effective, however, were the many individuals who took on themselves responsibility for caring for the physically and mentally disabled and for the rehabilitation of criminals. The work of Thomas Gallaudet in developing methods for educating deaf people reflects the spirit of the times. Gallaudet's school in Hartford, Connecticut, opened its doors in 1817; by 1851 similar schools for the deaf had been established in 14 states.

Dr. Samuel Gridley Howe did similar work with the blind, devising means for making books with raised letters (Louis Braille's system of raised dots was not introduced until later in the century) that the blind could "read" with their fingers. Howe headed a school for the blind in Boston, the pioneering Perkins Institution, which opened in 1832. Of all that Charles Dickens observed in America, nothing so favorably impressed him as Howe's success in educating 12-year-old Laura Bridgman, who was deaf, mute, and blind. Howe was also interested in trying to educate the mentally defective and in other causes, including antislavery. "Every creature in human shape should command our respect," he insisted. "The strong should help the weak, so that the whole should advance as a band of brethren."

One of the most striking aspects of the reform movement was the emphasis reformers placed on establishing special institutions for dealing with social problems. In the colonial period, orphans, indigent persons, the insane, and the feebleminded were usually cared for by members of their own families or boarded in a neighboring household. They remained part of the community. Even criminals were seldom "locked away" for extended jail terms; punishment commonly consisted of whipping, being placed in stocks in the town square, or (for serious crimes) execution. But once persuaded that people were primarily shaped by their surroundings, reformers demanded that deviant and dependent members of the community be taken from their present corrupting circumstances and placed in specialized institutions where they could be trained or rehabilitated. Almshouses, orphanages, reformatories, prisons, and lunatic asylums sprang up throughout the United States like mushrooms in a forest after a summer rain.

DEBATING THE PAST

Did the antebellum reform movement improve society? The Eastern State Penitentiary in Philadelphia was built in the 1820s. The picture at left was done by Samuel Cowperthwaite, Convict # 2954. Eastern State consisted of seven rows of cells radiating out from the central tower. The design ensured continuous supervision and isolation. The reformers who conceived of the prison thought it would teach an inmate to "listen to the reproaches of his conscience." The dessert plate *(right)* commemorating the jail is proof that some people believed in its mission. After visiting the prison, however, Charles Dickens described its system of confinement as "rigid, strict and hopeless." In *Madness and Civilization* (1961) and *Discipline and Punish* (1975), the French philosopher Michel Foucault similarly regarded such institutions as part of the process whereby modern societies squelched individuality. Those who refused to accept the discipline of teachers, employers, and government officials were labeled "deviants" and sent to institutions that would "reform" them through the imposition of order, a thesis that David J. Rothman (1971) applied to antebellum penitentiaries and asylums. Before Foucault, most scholars had endorsed antebellum reforms. Now these reforms were reassessed more critically. Michael B. Katz (1968) and Stanley K. Schultz (1973) argued that the public schools were means for preparing the young for industrial labor by instilling discipline and regimentation. Movements to promote temperance and suppress prostitution, similarly, were increasingly viewed as unwarranted intrusions on private matters. But in the 1980s women's historians altered this debate. Mary Ryan (1981) and others showed that women dominated nearly all antebellum reform movements, and for good reason. The child who could not attend a school was often subjected to the ceaseless drudgery of farm or factory. The exuberant individualist who tarried at the tavern sometimes beat his wife on returning home. The Eastern State Penitentiary and the antebellum insane asylums were fearsome places, but would their inmates have been better off on the streets? Excessive discipline erodes individuality; excessive individuality erodes social cohesion.

Michel Foucault, *Madness and Civilization* (1961), Michael B. Katz, *The Irony of Early School Reform* (1968), Stanley K. Schultz, *The Culture Factory* (1973), David J. Rothman, *The Discovery of the Asylum* (1971), Carl F. Kaestle, *Pillars of the Republic* (1983), Mary Ryan, *Cradle of the Middle Class* (1981).

The rationale for this movement was scientific; elaborate statistical reports attested to the benefits that such institutions would bring to both inmates and society as a whole. The motivating spirit of the founders of these asylums was humane, although many of the institutions seem anything but humane to the modern eye. The highly regarded Philadelphia prison system was based on strict solitary confinement, which was supposed to lead culprits to reflect on their sins and then reform their ways. The prison was literally a penitentiary, a place to repent. In fact, the system drove some inmates mad, and soon a rival Auburn system was introduced in New York State, which allowed for some social contact among prisoners and for work in shops and stone quarries. Absolute silence was required at all times. The prisoners were herded about in lock step and punished by flogging for the slightest infraction of the rules. Regular "moral and religious instruction" was provided, which the authorities believed would lead inmates to reform their lives. Tocqueville and Beaumont, in their report on American prisons, concluded that the

Philadelphia system produced "the deepest impression on the soul of the convict," while the Auburn system made the convict "more conformable to the habits of man in society."

The hospitals for mental patients were intended to cure inmates, not merely to confine them. The emphasis was on isolating them from the pressures of society; on order, quiet, routine; on control but not on punishment. The unfortunates were seen as *de*ranged; the task was to *ar*range their lives in a rational manner. In practice, shortages of trained personnel, niggardly legislative appropriations, and the inherent difficulty of managing violent and irrational patients often produced deplorable conditions in the asylums.

This situation led Dorothea Dix, a woman of almost saintlike selflessness, to devote 30 years of her life to a campaign to improve the care of the insane. She traveled to every state in the Union, and as far afield as Turkey and Japan, inspecting asylums and poorhouses. Insane persons in Massachusetts, she wrote in a memorial intended to shock state legislators into action, were being kept in cages and closets, "*chained, naked, beaten with rods, and lashed into obedience!*" Her reports led to some improvement in conditions in Massachusetts and other states, but in the long run the bright hopes of the reformers were never realized. Institutions founded to uplift the deviant and dependent all too soon became places where society's "misfits" might safely be kept out of sight.

"DEMON RUM"

DOCUMENT

Beecher, "Six Sermons on Intemperance"

Reformers must of necessity interfere with the affairs of others; thus there is often something of the busybody and arrogant meddler about them. How they are regarded usually turns on the observer's own attitude toward their objectives. What is to some an unjustified infringement on a person's private affairs is to others a necessary intervention for that person's own good and for the good of society. Consider the temperance movement, the most widely supported and successful reform of the Age of Reform.

Americans in the 1820s consumed prodigious amounts of alcohol, more than ever before or since. Not that the colonists had been teetotalers. Liquor, mostly in the form of rum or hard apple cider, was cheap and everywhere available; taverns were an integral part of colonial society. There were alcoholics in colonial America, but because neither political nor religious leaders considered drinking dangerous, there was no alcohol "problem." Most doctors recommended the regular consumption of alcohol as healthy. John Adams, certainly the soul of propriety, drank a tankard of hard cider every day for breakfast. Dr. Benjamin Rush's *Inquiry into the Effects of Ardent Spirits* (1784), which questioned the medicinal benefits of alcohol, fell on deaf ears.

However, alcohol consumption increased markedly in the early years of the new republic, thanks primarily to the availability of cheap corn and rye whiskey distilled in the new states of Kentucky and Tennessee. In the 1820s the per capita consumption of hard liquor reached 5 gallons, well over twice what it is today. Since small children and many grown people did not drink that much, others obviously drank a great deal more. Many women drank, if mostly at home; and reports of carousing among 14-year-old college freshmen show that youngsters did too. But the bulk of the heavy drinking occurred when men got together, at taverns or grogshops and at work. Many prominent politicians, including Clay and Webster, were heavy consumers. Webster is said to have kept several thousand bottles of wine, whiskey, and other alcoholic beverages in his cellar.

Artisans and common laborers regarded their twice-daily "dram" of whiskey as part of their wages. In workshops, masters were expected to halt production periodically to drink with their apprentices and journeymen. Trips to the neighborhood grogshop also figured into the workaday routine. In 1829 Secretary of War John Eaton estimated that three-quarters of the nation's laborers drank at least 4 ounces of distilled spirits a day.

The foundation of the American Temperance Union in 1826 signaled the start of a national crusade against drunkenness. Employing lectures, pamphlets, rallies, essay contests, and other techniques, the union set out to persuade people to "sign the pledge" not to drink liquor. Primitive sociological studies of the effects of drunkenness (reformers were able to show a high statistical correlation between alcohol consumption and crime) added to the effectiveness of the campaign.

In 1840 an organization of reformed drunkards, the Washingtonians, set out to reclaim alcoholics. One of the most effective Washingtonians was John B. Gough, rescued by the organization after seven years in the gutter. "Crawl from the slimy ooze, ye drowned drunkards," Gough would shout, "and with suffocation's blue and livid lips speak out against the drink!"

Revivalist ministers like Charles Grandison Finney argued that alcohol was one of the great barriers to conversion, which helps explain why Utica, a town of fewer than 13,000 residents in 1840, supported four separate temperance societies in that year. Employers all over the country also signed on, declaring their businesses henceforward to be "cold-water" enterprises. Soon the temperance movement claimed a million members. Although women did much of the work at the local level in all antebellum reforms, they were especially active in the temperance movement.

The temperance people aroused bitter opposition, particularly after they moved beyond calls for restraint to demands for prohibition of all alcohol. German and Irish immigrants, for the most part Catholics, and also members of Protestant sects that used wine in their religious services, objected to being told by reformers that their drinking would have to stop. But by the early 1840s the reformers had secured legislation in many states that imposed strict licensing systems and heavy liquor taxes. Local option laws permitted towns and counties to ban the sale of alcohol altogether.

In 1851 Maine passed the first effective law prohibiting the manufacture and sale of alcoholic beverages. The leader of the campaign was Mayor Neal Dow of Portland, a businessman who became a prohibitionist after seeing the damage done by drunkenness among workers in his tannery. By 1855 a dozen other states had passed laws based on the Maine statute, and the nation's per capita consumption of alcohol had plummeted to 2 gallons a year.

THE ABOLITIONIST CRUSADE

No reform movement of this era was more significant, more ambiguous, or more provocative of later historical investigation than the drive to abolish slavery. That slavery should have been a cause of indignation to reform-minded Americans was inevitable. Humanitarians were outraged by the master's whip and by the practice of disrupting families. Democrats protested the denial of political and civil rights to slaves. Perfectionists of all stripes deplored the fact that slaves had no chance to improve themselves. However, well into the 1820s, the abolitionist cause attracted few followers because there seemed to be no way of getting rid of slavery short of revolution. While a few theorists argued that the Fifth Amendment, which provides that no one may be "deprived of life, liberty, or property, without due process of law," could be interpreted to mean

▲ William Lloyd Garrison founded *The Liberator* and edited it for 35 years; the newspaper was one of the nation's leading antislavery publications.

that the Constitution outlawed slavery, the great majority believed that the institution was not subject to federal control.

Particularly in the wake of the Missouri Compromise, antislavery Northerners neatly compartmentalized their thinking. Slavery was wrong; they would not tolerate it in their own communities. But since the Constitution obliged them to tolerate it in states where it existed, they felt no responsibility to fight it. The issue was explosive enough even when limited to the question of the expansion of slavery into the territories. People who advocated any kind of forced abolition in states where it was legal were judged irresponsible in the extreme. In 1820 presidential hopeful John Quincy Adams called slavery "the great and foul stain upon the North American Union." "If the Union must be dissolved," he added, "slavery is precisely the question upon which it ought to break." But Adams expressed these opinions in the privacy of his diary, not in a public speech. Most critics of slavery therefore confined themselves to urging

▶ *text continues on page 288*

American Lives

Sojourner Truth

Isabella was the youngest of ten, or perhaps twelve, children; she was born in 1797, or perhaps 1799. Most details of her early life are unknown. No one bothered to record them because she was a slave. We do know that she was born in Ulster County, New York, and that her owner was Colonel Ardinburgh, a Dutch farmer. He grew tobacco, corn, and flax. Because the rocky hills west of the Hudson River could not sustain large farms, he could make use of only a handful of slaves. He therefore sold most of the slave children, including Isabella's siblings, when they were young.

Isabella's mother used to tell her of the time when Ardinburgh had gathered up her five-year-old brother and three-year-old sister to take them for a sleigh ride. They were initially delighted, but when he tried to lock them into a box, the boy broke free, ran into the house and hid under a bed. He was found and both children were dragged away, never to be seen by their parents again. Isabella lived in terror of being similarly torn from her parents.

In 1807 Ardinburgh died. His heirs sold his "slaves, horses, and other cattle" at auction. A local farmer bought Isabella for $100. Her parents, too old and decrepit to be of value, were given their freedom. Destitute and virtually homeless, they died shortly afterward.

Isabella, who spoke only Dutch, found herself at odds with her new master and his family. Sometimes she did not understand what they wanted her to do. "If they sent me for a frying pan, not knowing what they meant, perhaps I carried them the pot hooks," she recalled. "Then, oh! How angry mistress would be with me." Once, for an order that she did not understand, the master whipped her with a bundle of rods. The lacerations permanently scarred her back.

In 1810 she was sold to John Dumont, a farmer. She remained with him for nearly eighteen years. Though she came to regard him "as a God," she claimed that his wife subjected her to cruel and "unnatural" treatment. What exactly transpired, she refused "from motives of delicacy" to say. Historian Nell I. Painter contends that the mistress likely abused her sexually.

In 1815 Dumont arranged for Isabella to marry another of his slaves. (Slave marriages were recognized by law in most northern states, but not in the South.) Isabella had no say in the choice of a husband, who had previously been mated to at least two other slaves. She had five children by him.

Isabella labored in the fields, sowing and harvesting crops. She also cooked and cleaned the house. In recognition of her diligence, Dumont promised to set her free on July 4, 1826, exactly one year prior to the date set by the New York State legislature to end slavery. But during that final year Isabella injured her hand and could not work as effectively as before. On the proposed date of liberation, Dumont reneged on his promise to release her. Isabella chafed at his decision but said nothing. She dutifully spun 100 pounds of wool—the amount of labor she thought she owed him—and then, as winter was setting in, she heard the voice of God tell her to leave. She picked up her baby and walked to a neighbor's house. When Dumont came to collect her, the neighbor Isaac Van Wagenen paid him $25 for Isabella and the baby and set them free. In gratitude, Isabella took the surname Van Wagenen.

But Isabella learned that her five-year-old son, Peter, had been sold to a planter in Alabama, where no date had been set for the ending of slavery. She angrily confronted the Dumonts, who scoffed at her concern for "a paltry nigger." "I'll have my child again," Isabella retorted. She consulted with a Quaker lawyer, who assured her that New York law forbade such sales. He filed suit in her behalf and in 1828 the boy was returned.

Now on her own, Isabella went to New York City. During these years New York City, like much of the nation, was awash in religious ferment. Isabella, whose views on religion were a complex amalgam of African folkways, spiritualism, temperance, and dietary asceticism, was attracted to various unorthodox religious leaders. The most curious of these was Robert Matthews, a bearded, thundering tyrant who claimed to be the Old Testament prophet Matthias. He proposed to restore the practices of the ancient patriarchs, especially an insistence that men dominate women. Matthews converted Elijah Pierson, a wealthy New York merchant, and persuaded him to finance a religious commune. Matthews acquired a house in the town of Sing Sing, named it Mount Zion, housed nearly a dozen converts, and ruled it with an iron hand. Isabella was among those who joined the commune.

In 1834, Pierson died. Local authorities, who had heard stories of sexual and other irregularities at Mount Zion, arrested Matthews on charges of poisoning Pierson. This sensational story boosted sales of the city's penny press, then in its infancy. When one published story accused Isabella of the murder, she sued the author for libel and collected a judgment of $125.

Isabella then gravitated to William Miller, a zealot who claimed that the world would end in 1843. When it did not, his movement did.

Although she had nearly always been subject to the authority of powerful men, Isabella had by this time become a preacher. Tall and severe in manner, she jabbed at the air with bony fingers and demanded the obedience she had formerly given to others. Now she changed her name to Sojourner Truth, a journeyer conveying God's true spirit, and embarked on a career of antislavery feminism.

▲ Sojourner Truth

"colonization" or persuading slaveowners to treat their property humanely.

One of the few Americans in the 1820s to go further was the Quaker Benjamin Lundy, editor of the Baltimore-based newspaper *The Genius of Universal Emancipation*. Lundy was no fanatic; he urged the use of persuasion in the South rather than interference by the federal government. He also explored the possibility of colonizing free blacks and slaves in Haiti and Canada. But he refused to mince words, and consequently he was subject to frequent harassment.

DOCUMENT

Garrison, First issue of *The Liberator*

Even more provocative and less accommodating to local sensibilities was Lundy's youthful assistant, William Lloyd Garrison of Massachusetts. Garrison pronounced himself for "immediate" abolition. When his extreme position made continued residence in Baltimore impossible, he returned to Boston, where in 1831 he established his own newspaper, *The Liberator*. "I am in earnest," he announced in the first issue. "I will not equivocate—I will not excuse—I will not retreat a single inch—and I will be heard."

Garrison's position, and that espoused by the New England Anti-Slavery Society, which he organized in 1831, was absolutely unyielding: Slaves must be freed immediately and treated as equals; compensated emancipation was unacceptable, colonization unthinkable. Because the United States government countenanced slavery, Garrison refused to engage in political activity to achieve his ends. Burning a copy of the Constitution—that "agreement with hell"—became a regular feature at Society-sponsored public lectures.

Few white Americans found Garrison's line of argument convincing, and many were outraged by his confrontational tactics. Whenever he spoke in public, he risked being mobbed by what newspaper accounts approvingly described as "gentlemen of property and standing." In 1833 a Garrison meeting in New York City was broken up by colonizationists. Two years later a mob dragged Garrison through the streets of his own Boston. That same day a mob broke up the convention of the New York Anti-Slavery Society in Utica. In 1837 Elijah Lovejoy, a Garrisonian newspaper editor in Alton, Illinois, first saw his press destroyed by fire and then was himself murdered by a mob. When the proprietors of Philadelphia's Pennsylvania Hall booked an abolitionist meeting in 1838, a mob burned the hall to the ground to prevent the meeting from taking place.

In the wake of this violence some of Garrison's backers had second thoughts about his call for an immediate end to slavery. The wealthy New York businessmen Arthur and Lewis Tappan, who had subsidized *The Liberator*, turned instead to Theodore Dwight Weld, a young minister who was part of Charles Grandison Finney's "holy band" of revivalists. Weld and his followers spoke of "immediate" emancipation "gradually" achieved, and they were willing to engage in political activity to achieve that goal.

In 1840 the Tappans and Weld broke with Garrison over the issue of involvement in politics and the participation of female abolitionists as public lecturers. Garrison, ever the radical, supported the women; Weld thought they would needlessly antagonize would-be supporters. The Tappans then organized the Liberty Party, which nominated as its presidential candidate James G. Birney, a Kentucky slaveholder who had been converted to evangelical Christianity and abolitionism by Weld. Running on a platform of universal emancipation to be gradually brought about through legislation, Birney received only 7000 votes.

▲ Frederick Douglass in 1847, having escaped from slavery nine years earlier. He attracted large audiences as an antislavery lecturer, though his white supporters worried that he neither looked nor sounded like a former slave. Lest audiences think him an imposter, William Lloyd Garrison counseled him to not sound too "learned." Another thought it would be better if he had "a little of the plantation in his speech." Douglass rejected such suggestions.

Many blacks were abolitionists long before the white movement began to attract attention. In 1830 some 50 black antislavery societies existed, and thereafter these groups grew in size and importance, being generally associated with the Garrisonian wing. White abolitionists eagerly sought out black speakers, especially runaway slaves, whose heart-rending accounts of their experiences aroused sympathies and who, merely by speaking clearly and with conviction, stood as living proof that blacks were neither animals nor fools.

The first prominent black abolitionist was David Walker, whose powerful *Appeal to the Coloured Citizens of the World* (1829) is now considered one of the roots of the modern black nationalist movement. Walker was born free and had experienced American racism extensively in both the South and the North. He denounced white talk of democracy and freedom as pure hypocrisy and predicted that when God finally brought justice to America white "tyrants will wish they were never born!"

Frederick Douglass, a former slave who had escaped from Maryland, was one of the most remarkable Americans of his generation. While a bondsman he had received a full portion of beatings and other indignities, but he had been allowed to learn to read and write and to master a trade, opportunities denied the vast majority of slaves. Settling in Boston, he became an agent of the Massachusetts Anti-Slavery Society and a featured speaker at its public meetings.

DOCUMENT

Passages from
*The Autobiography
of Frederick
Douglass*

Douglass was a tall, majestically handsome man who radiated determination and indignation. Slavery, he told white audiences, "brands your republicanism as a sham, your humanity as a base pretense, your Christianity as a lie." In 1845 he published his *Narrative of the Life of Frederick Douglass,* one of the most gripping autobiographical accounts of a slave's life ever written. Douglass insisted that freedom for blacks required not merely emancipation but full equality, social and economic as well as political. Not many white Northerners accepted his reasoning, but few who heard him or read his works could afterward maintain the illusion that all blacks were dull-witted or resigned to inferior status.

At first Douglass was, in his own words, "a faithful disciple" of Garrison, prepared to tear up the Constitution and destroy the Union to gain his ends. In the late 1840s, however, he changed his mind, deciding that the Constitution, created to "establish Justice, insure domestic Tranquility . . . and secure the Blessings of Liberty," as its preamble states, "could not well have been designed at the same time to maintain and perpetuate a system of rapine and murder like slavery." Thereafter he fought slavery and race prejudice from within the system, something Garrison was never willing to do.

Garrison's importance cannot be measured by the number of his followers, which was never large. Unlike more moderately inclined enemies of slavery, he recognized that abolitionism was a revolutionary movement, not merely one more middle-class reform. He also understood that achieving racial equality, not merely "freeing" the slaves, was the only way to reach the abolitionists' professed objective: full justice for blacks. And he saw clearly that few whites, even among abolitionists, believed that blacks were their equals.

At the same time, Garrison seemed utterly indifferent to what effect the "immediate" freeing of the slaves would have on the South. He and his followers came close to claiming that all southern whites were villains, all blacks saints. Garrison said he would rather be governed by "the inmates of our penitentiaries" than by southern congressmen, whom he characterized as "desperadoes." The life of the slaveowner, he wrote, is "one of unbridled lust, of filthy amalgamation, of swaggering braggadocio, of haughty domination, of cowardly ruffianism, of boundless dissipation, of matchless insolence, of infinite self-conceit, of unequaled oppression, of more than savage cruelty." His followers were no less fanatical in their judgments. "Slavery and cruelty cannot be disjoined," one wrote. "Consequently every slaveholder must be inhuman."

Both Garrison's insights into the limits of northern racial egalitarianism and his blind contempt for southern whites led him to the conclusion that American society was rotten to the core. Hence his refusal to make any concession to the existing establishment, religious or secular. He was hated in the North as much for his explicit denial of the idea that a constitution that supported slavery merited respect as for his implicit denial of the idea that a professed Christian who tolerated slavery for even an instant could hope for salvation. He was, in short, a perfectionist, a trafficker in moral absolutes who wanted his Kingdom of Heaven in the here and now. By contrast, most other American reformers were willing to settle for perfection on the installment plan.

WOMEN'S RIGHTS

The question of slavery was related to another major reform movement of the era, the crusade for women's rights. The relationship was personal and

▲ Anna Elizabeth Klumpke's portrait of Elizabeth Cady Stanton (1887). In 1848 Stanton helped draft the Declaration of Sentiments, spelling out the injustices of man to woman. The conclusion: "He has endeavored, in every way he could, to destroy her confidence in her own powers, to lessen her self-respect, and to make her willing to lead a dependent and abject life."

ideological, direct and indirect, simple and profound. Superficially, the connection can be explained in this way: Women were as likely as men to find slavery offensive and to protest against it. When they did so, they ran into even more adamant resistance, the prejudices of those who objected to abolitionists being reinforced by their feelings that women should not speak in public or participate in political affairs. Thus female abolitionists, driven by the urgencies of conscience, were almost forced to become advocates of women's rights. "We have good cause to be grateful to the slave," the feminist Abby Kelley wrote. "In striving to strike his irons off, we found most surely, that we were manacled ourselves."

At a more profound level, the reference that abolitionists made to the Declaration of Independence to justify their attack on slavery radicalized women with regard to their own place in society. Were only all men created equal and endowed by God with unalienable rights? For many women the question was a consciousness-raising experience; they began to believe that, like blacks, they were imprisoned from birth in a caste system, legally subordinated and assigned menial social and economic roles that prevented them from developing their full potentialities. Such women considered themselves in a sense worse off than blacks, who had at least the psychological advantage of confronting an openly hostile and repressive society rather than one concealed behind the cloying rhetoric of romantic love.

With the major exception of Margaret Fuller, whose book *Women in the Nineteenth Century* (1844) made a frontal assault on all forms of sexual discrimination, the leading advocates of equal rights for women began their public careers in the abolitionist movement. Among the first were Sarah and Angelina Grimké, South Carolinians who abandoned their native state and the domestic sphere to devote themselves to speaking out against slavery. (In 1841 Angelina married Theodore Dwight Weld.) Male objections to the Grimkés' activities soon made them advocates of women's rights. Similarly, the refusal of delegates to the World Anti-Slavery Convention held in London in 1840 to let women participate in their debates precipitated the decision of two American abolitionists, Lucretia Mott and Elizabeth Cady Stanton, to turn their attention to the women's rights movement.

Slavery aside, there were other aspects of feminist consciousness-raising. Some women rejected the idea that they should confine themselves to a sphere of activity consisting mostly of child rearing and housekeeping. The very effort to enforce this kind of specialization made women aware of their second-class citizenship and thus more likely to be dissatisfied. They lacked not merely the right to vote, of which they did not make a major issue, but if married, the right to own property or to make a will. Lydia Maria Child, a popular novelist, found this last restriction particularly offensive. It excited her "towering indignation" that her husband had to sign her will. David Child was not what today would be called a chauvinist, but, as she explained, "I was indignant for womankind made chattels personal from the beginning of time."

As Lydia Child noted, the subordination of women was as old as civilization. The attack on it came not because of any new discrimination but for the same reasons that motivated reformers against other forms of injustice: belief in progress, a sense of personal responsibility, the conviction that institutions could be changed and that the time for changing them was limited.

When women sought to involve themselves in reform, they became aware of perhaps the most serious handicap that society imposed on them—the conflict between their roles as wives and mothers and their urge to participate in the affairs of the larger world. Elizabeth Cady Stanton has left a striking description of this dilemma. She lived in the 1840s in Seneca Falls, a small town in central New York. Her husband was frequently away on business; she had a brood of growing children and little domestic help. When, stimulated by her interest in abolition and women's rights, she sought to become active in the movements, her family responsibilities made it almost impossible even to read about them.

"I now fully understood the practical difficulties most women had to contend with," she recalled in her autobiography, *Eighty Years and More* (1898):

> The general discontent I felt with woman's portion as wife, mother, housekeeper, physician, and spiritual guide, the chaotic condition into which everything fell without her constant supervision, and the wearied, anxious look of the majority of women, impressed me with the strong feeling that some active measures should be taken.

DOCUMENT

Stanton, Declaration of Sentiments

Active measures she took. Together with Lucretia Mott and a few others of like mind, she organized a meeting, the Seneca Falls Convention (July 1848), and drafted a Declaration of Sentiments patterned on the Declaration of Independence. "We hold these truths to be self-evident: that all men and women are created equal," it stated, and it went on to list the "injuries and usurpations" of men, just as Jefferson had outlined those of George III.

From this seed the movement grew. During the 1850s a series of national conventions was held, and more and more reformers, including William Lloyd Garrison, joined the cause. Of the recruits, Susan B. Anthony was the most influential, for she was the first to see the need for thorough organization if effective pressure was to be brought to bear on male-dominated society. Her first campaign, mounted in 1854 and 1855 in behalf of a petition to the New York legislature calling for reform of the property and divorce laws, accumulated 6000 signatures. But the petition did not persuade the legislature to act. Indeed, the feminists achieved very few practical results during the Age of Reform. Their leaders, however, were persevering types, most of them extraordinarily long-lived. Their major efforts lay in the future.

Despite the aggressiveness of many reformers and the extremity of some of their proposals, little social conflict blighted these years. Most citizens readily accepted the need for improving society and showed a healthy tolerance for even the most harebrained

schemes for doing so. When Sylvester Graham, inventor of the graham cracker, traveled up and down the land praising the virtues of hard mattresses, cold showers, and homemade bread, he was mobbed by professional bakers, but otherwise, as his biographer says, "he was the subject of jokes, lampoons, and caustic editorials" rather than violence. Americans argued about everything from prison reform to vegetarianism, from women's rights to phrenology (a pseudoscience much occupied with developing the diagnostic possibilities of measuring the bumps on people's heads). But they seldom came to blows. Even the abolitionist movement might not have caused serious social strife if the territorial expansion of the late 1840s had not dragged the slavery issue back into politics. When that happened, politics again assumed center stage, public discourse grew embittered, and the first great Age of Reform came to an end.

▲ Phrenology sought to determine aptitude and character from the size and shape of a person's head. In the nineteenth century, many regarded it as a science. Bumps in certain parts of the skull suggested an innate penchant for love, while protuberances elsewhere for destructiveness or acquisitiveness.

MILESTONES

1774	Mother Ann Lee founds first Shaker community
1784	Dr. Benjamin Rush's *Inquiry into the Effects of Ardent Spirits* questions alcohol's benefits
1826	American Temperance Union begins campaign against drunkenness
1829	Black abolitionist David Walker publishes *Appeal to the Coloured Citizens of the World*
1830s	Second Great Awakening stresses promise of salvation
	Prison reformers debate Auburn versus Philadelphia system
1830–1850	Utopian communities flourish
1830	Joseph Smith shares his "vision" in *Book of Mormon*
1831	Abolitionist William Lloyd Garrison founds *The Liberator* and New England Anti-Slavery Society
1831–1832	Alexis de Tocqueville and Gustave de Beaumont tour America
1832	Perkins Institution for the Blind opens in Boston
1837	Illinois abolitionist Elijah Lovejoy is murdered
1843	Dorothea Dix exposes treatment of the insane in *Memorial to the Legislature of Massachusetts*
1844	Margaret Fuller condemns sexual discrimination in *Women in the Nineteenth Century*
	Nauvoo mob murders Joseph Smith
1845	Frederick Douglass describes slave life in *Narrative of the Life of Frederick Douglass*
1847	Brigham Young leads Mormon migration to Great Salt Lake
1848	Elizabeth Cady Stanton and Lucretia Mott organize Seneca Falls Convention and draft Declaration of Sentiments
1851	Maine bans alcoholic beverages
1854–1855	Susan B. Anthony leads petition campaign against New York property and divorce laws

SUPPLEMENTARY READING

On Tocqueville and his views of America, see Alexis de Tocqueville, *Democracy in America,* J. P. Mayer, ed. (1966 edition); also Andre Jardin, *Alexis de Tocqueville* (1988). For an analysis of the middle class, see Stuart M. Blumin, *The Emergence of the Middle Class* (1989).

On the changing place of the family and the changes within it, see Mary P. Ryan, *Cradle of the Middle Class: The Family in Oneida, New York* (1981), Catherine E. Kelly, *In the New England Fashion: Reshaping Women's Lives in the Nineteenth Century* (1999), Nancy Cott, *The Bonds of Womanhood* (1977), and Carl Degler, *At Odds: Women and Family in America from the Revolution to the Present* (1980).

The Second Great Awakening has been examined both as a religious and as a social phenomenon. Still useful is Whitney Cross, *The Burned-Over District* (1950), but see also Paul E. Johnson, *A Shopkeeper's Millennium* (1978). Mark A. Noll, *America's God: From Jonathan Edwards to Abraham Lincoln* (2002) provides a broader study of the religious dimension of reform movements. For the Shakers, see Stephen J. Stein, *The Shaker Experience in America* (1992). Richard Bushman, *Joseph Smith and the Beginnings*

of Mormonism (1984), provides a good introduction to the subject. For a broader study see Leonard J. Arrington, *The Mormon Experience* (1992).

For the origins of feminism, see Nancy Cott, *The Grounding of Modern Feminism* (1987), Ellen C. DuBois, *Feminism and Suffrage: The Emergence of an Independent Women's Movement in America, 1848–1869* (1978), and Linda K. Kerber, *No Constitutional Right to Be Ladies* (1998). Bruce Dorsey, *Reforming Men and Women* (2002) shows how men often initiated reforms but women took control of them.

On utopianism generally, see Ronald G. Walters, *American Reformers, 1815–1860* (1978). Accounts of the temperance movement include Barbara L. Epstein, *The Politics of Domesticity* (1981), and W. J. Rorabaugh, *The Alcoholic Republic* (1979).

For a general study of the context of abolitionism, see Richard S. Newman, *The Transformation of American Abolitionism* (2002). For sharply contrasting views of the abolitionist movement, see Stanley Elkins, *Slavery* (1975), and Lewis Perry and Michael Fellman, eds., *Anti-Slavery*

Reconsidered (1979). Women's role in the movement is discussed in Julie Roy Jeffrey, *The Great Silent Army of Abolitionism* (1998). The persistence of slavery in the North, a topic that is often overlooked, is examined in Joanne P. Melish, *Disowning Slavery* (1998). Biographical accounts include John L. Thomas, *The Liberator: William Lloyd Garrison* (1963), Gerda Lerner, *The Grimké Sisters from South Carolina* (1967), and Nathan Huggins, *Slave and Citizen: The Life of Frederick Douglass* (1980).

Carolyn L. Karcher, *The First Woman in the Republic: A Cultural Biography of Lydia Maria Child* (1994), Charles Capper, *Margaret Fuller* (1992), Elizabeth Griffith, *In Her Own Rights: The Life of Elizabeth Cady Stanton* (1984), and Kathryn K. Sklar, *Catharine Beecher* (1973), are solid biographies of important women in the era.

On Sojourner Truth, see Nell Irvin Painter, *Sojourner Truth* (1996) and, for her time with Mathias, Paul F. Johnson and Sean Wilentz, *Kingdom of Mathias* (1994).

SUGGESTED WEBSITES

The Alexis de Tocqueville Tour: Exploring Democracy in America

http://www.tocqueville.org/

Text, images, and teaching suggestions are all part of this companion site to C-SPAN's recent programming on de Tocqueville.

Votes for Women: Selections from the National Women Suffrage Association Collection, 1848–1921

http://memory.loc.gov/ammem/naw/nawshome.html

This Library of Congress site contains books, pamphlets, and other artifacts that document the suffrage campaign.

By Popular Demand: "Votes for Women" Suffrage Pictures, 1850–1922

http://memory.loc.gov/ammem/vfwhtml/
vfwhome.html

Portraits, suffrage parades, picketing suffragists, an anti-suffrage display, and cartoons commenting on the movement are all part of this Library of Congress site.

Important Black Abolitionists

http://www.loc.gov/exhibits/african/afam006.html

An exhibit from the Library of Congress, with pictures and text, that discuss some of the key African American abolitionists and their efforts to end slavery.

Pioneering the Upper Midwest: Books from Michigan, Minnesota, and Wisconsin, ca. 1820–1910

http://memory.loc.gov/ammem/umhtml/
umhome.html

This Library of Congress site looks at first-person accounts, biographies, promotional literature, ethnographic and antiquarian texts, colonial archival documents, and other works from the seventeenth to early twentieth century. It covers many topics and issues that affected Americans in the settlement and development of the upper Midwest.

History of the Suffrage Movement

http://www.rochester.edu/SBA

This site includes a chronology, important texts relating to women's suffrage, and bibliographical information about Susan B. Anthony and Elizabeth Cady Stanton.

An American Culture

▼ Frederic Edwin Church conveyed the romantic sensibility in *Twilight in the Wilderness* (1860). The clouds glow with religious portent, and their reflected light pervades Nature.

As the United States grew larger, richer, and more centralized, it began to evolve a more distinctive culture. Still the child of Europe, by mid-century it was clearly the offspring rather than an imitation of the parent society. Jefferson had drawn most of his ideas from classical authors and seventeenth-century English thinkers. He gave an American cast to these doctrines, as when he stressed the separation of church and state or the pursuit of happiness instead of property in describing the "unalienable rights" of men. But Ralph Waldo Emerson, whose views were roughly similar to Jefferson's and who was also influenced by European thinkers, was an American philosopher. He and his generation of writers, painters, and architects drew quite self-consciously on native sources and inspirations. Some worshiped the pristine beauty of Nature while others celebrated the ebullient energies of a democratic people. Collectively they described convincingly the emergence of a distinctly American culture.

IN SEARCH OF NATIVE GROUNDS

Early nineteenth-century literary groups such as Boston's Anthology Club and the Friendly Club in New York consciously set out to "foster American genius" and to encourage the production of a distinctively American literature. But of the novelists before 1830, only James Fenimore Cooper made successful use of the national heritage. Beginning with *The Spy* (1821), *The Pioneers* (1823), and *The Last of the Mohicans* (1826), he wrote a long series of tales of Indians and settlers that

▲ Part of the mid-nineteenth-century literary renaissance, James Fenimore Cooper was the first American novelist to explore native themes, settings, and characters.

presented a vivid, if romanticized, picture of frontier life. (Cooper's Indians, Mark Twain quipped, belonged to "an extinct tribe that never existed.") Cooper's work marked a shift from the classicism of the eighteenth century, which emphasized reason and orderliness in writing, to the romanticism of the early nineteenth century, with its stress on highly subjective emotional values and its concern for the beauties of nature and the freedom of the individual.

The novel developed along with its readership, which was composed, increasingly, of middle-class women. In novels such as *A New England Tale* (1822) and *Redwood* (1824), Catharine M. Sedgwick painstakingly chronicled the simple virtues of the home and family.

Most of the early novelists slavishly imitated British writers. Some looked to the sentimental novels of Samuel Richardson and Susanna Rowson (Rowson's *Charlotte Temple* went through 150 American editions). Others copied the style of satirical writers like Daniel Defoe and Tobias Smollett. Most popular were historical romances done in the manner of the Waverley novels of Sir Walter Scott. None approached the level of the best British writers, and as a result American novelists were badly outdistanced in their

own country by the British, both in prestige and popularity. Since foreign copyrights were not recognized in the United States, British books were shamelessly pirated and sold cheaply. Half a million volumes of Scott were sold in America before 1823. American readers benefited but not American writers.

New York City was the literary capital of the country. Its leading light was Washington Irving, whose comical *Diedrich Knickerbocker's History of New York* (1809) made its young author famous on both sides of the Atlantic. Yet Irving soon abandoned the United States for Europe. *The Sketch Book* (1819), which included "Rip Van Winkle" and other well-known tales and legends of the Dutch in the Hudson Valley, was written while the author was residing in Birmingham and London. Outside New York there was much less literary activity. New England was only on the verge of its great literary flowering.

American painting in this period reached a level comparable to that of contemporary European work, but the best artists received most of their training in Europe. Benjamin West, the first and in his day the most highly regarded, went to Europe before the Revolution and never returned; he can scarcely be considered an American. John Singleton Copley, whose stern, straight-forward portraits display a more distinctly American character than the work of any of his contemporaries, was a Bostonian. No one so well captured the vigor and integrity of the Revolutionary generation. Charles Willson Peale, after studying under West in London, settled in Philadelphia, where he established a museum containing fossils, stuffed animals, and various natural curiosities as well as paintings. Peale helped found the Pennsylvania Academy of the Fine Arts, and he did much to encourage American painting. Not the least of his achievements was the production of a large brood of artistic children to whom he gave such names as Rembrandt, Titian, and Rubens. The most talented of Peale's children was (appropriately) Rembrandt, whose portrait of Jefferson, executed in 1800, is one of the finest likenesses of the Sage of Monticello.

Another outstanding artist of this generation was Gilbert Stuart, who is best known for his many studies of George Washington. Stuart studied in England with Benjamin West, and his brush was much in demand in London. He was probably the most technically accomplished of the early American portrait painters. He was fond of painting his subjects with ruddy complexions (produced by means of a judicious mixture of vermilion, purple, and white pigment), which made many of his elderly sitters appear positively cherubic. He once remarked that the pallid flesh tones used by a rival looked "like putrid veal a little blown with green flies."

▲ In *The Course of Empire, Destruction* (1836), painter Thomas Cole shows an ancient civilization, evocative of Rome, in apocalyptic decline. Man should not overestimate the permanence or the value of "civilization," Cole suggested, a sentiment that fit with a new American sensibility that enshrined nature and feelings.

In general, the painting of the period was less obviously imitative of European models than the national literature. Wealthy merchants, manufacturers, and planters wished their likenesses preserved, and the demand for portraits of the nation's Revolutionary heroes seemed insatiable. Since paintings could not be reproduced as books could be, American artists did a flourishing business. Yet they remained unmistakably in the European tradition.

THE ROMANTIC VIEW OF LIFE

In the Western world the romantic movement was a revolt against the bloodless logic of the Age of Reason. It was a noticeable if unnamed point of view in Germany, France, and England as early as the 1780s and in America a generation later; by the second quarter of the nineteenth century, few intellectuals were unmarked by it. "Romantics" believed that change and growth were the essence of life, for individuals and for institutions. They valued feeling and intuition over pure thought, and they stressed the dif-

ferences between individuals and societies rather than the similarities. Ardent love of country characterized the movement; individualism, optimism, ingenuousness, and emotion were its bywords. Whereas the puritans, believing that nearly everyone was destined to endure the tortures of Hell for all eternity, contemplated death with dread, romantics, assuming that good people would go to Heaven, professed to look forward to death.

Romanticism perfectly fitted the mood of nineteenth-century America. Interest in raw nature and in primitive peoples, worship of the individual, praise of folk culture, the subordination of intellect to feeling—were these primarily romantic ideas or American ideas? Jacksonian democracy with its self-confidence, careless prodigality, contempt for learning, glorification of the ordinary—was it a product of the American experience or a reflection of a wider world view?

The romantic way of thinking found its greatest American expression in the transcendentalist movement. Transcendentalism, a New England creation, is difficult to describe because it emphasized the indefinable and the unknowable. It was a mystical, intuitive way of looking at life that subordinated facts to feelings. Its literal meaning was "to go beyond the world of the senses," by which the transcendentalists meant the material and observable world. To the transcendentalists, human beings were truly divine because they were part of nature, itself the essence of divinity. Their intellectual capacities did not define their capabilities, for they could "transcend" reason by having faith in themselves and in the fundamental benevolence of the universe. Transcendentalists were complete individualists, seeing the social whole as no more than the sum of its parts. Organized religion, indeed all institutions were unimportant if not counterproductive; what mattered was the single person and that people aspire, stretch *beyond* their known capabilities. Failure resulted only from lack of effort. The expression "Hitch your wagon to a star" is of transcendentalist origin.

EMERSON AND THOREAU

The leading transcendentalist thinker was Ralph Waldo Emerson. Born in 1803 and educated at Harvard, Emerson became a minister, but in 1832 he gave up his pulpit, deciding that "the profession is antiquated." After traveling in Europe, where he met many romantic writers, including Samuel Taylor Coleridge, William Wordsworth, and (especially important) the historian Thomas Carlyle, he settled in Concord, Massachusetts, where he had a long career as an essayist, lecturer, and sage.

DOCUMENT

Emerson, *The Concord Hymn*

Emerson managed to restore to what he called "corpse-cold" Unitarianism the fervor and purposefulness characteristic of seventeenth-century puritanism. His philosophy was at once buoyantly optimistic and rigorously intellectual, self-confident, and conscientious. In "The American Scholar," a notable address he delivered at Harvard in 1837, he urged Americans to put aside their devotion to things European and seek inspiration in their immediate surroundings. Emerson saw himself as pitting "spiritual powers" against "the mechanical powers and the mechanical philosophy of this time." The new industrial society of New England disturbed him profoundly.

Emerson favored change and believed in progress. It was America's destiny to fulfill "the postponed expectations of the world." Temperamentally, however, he was too serene and too much his own man to fight for the causes other reformers espoused, and he was too idealistic to accept the compromises that most reformers make to achieve their ends. To abolitionist friends who sought his aid he said: "God must govern his own world. . . . I have quite other slaves to face than those Negroes, to wit, imprisoned thoughts . . . which have no watchman or lover or defender but me."

Because he put so much emphasis on self-reliance, Emerson disliked powerful governments. "The less government we have the better," he said. In a sense he was the prototype of some modern alienated intellectuals, so repelled by the world as it was that he would not actively try to change it. Nevertheless he thought strong leadership essential, perhaps being influenced in this direction by his friend Carlyle's glorification of the role of great men in history. Emerson also had a strong practical streak. He made his living by lecturing, tracking tirelessly across the country, talking before every type of audience for fees ranging from $50 to several hundreds.

Closely identified with Emerson was his Concord neighbor Henry David Thoreau. After graduating

▲ In 1838 Ralph Waldo Emerson told a bookish audience in Boston that man was "almost smothered under his own institutions." Amongst the stifling encumbrances he enumerated were law, property, church, customs—and books.

▲ Walden Pond, as seen today, where Henry David Thoreau lived from 1845 to 1847: "I went to the woods because I wished to live deliberately, to front only the essential facts of life, and see if I could not learn what it had to teach, and not, when I came to die, to discover that I had not lived."

from Harvard in 1837, Thoreau taught school for a time and helped out in a small pencil-making business run by his family. He was a strange man, gentle, a dreamer, content to absorb the beauties of nature almost intuitively, yet stubborn and individualistic to the point of selfishness. "He is the most unmalleable fellow alive," one acquaintance wrote. The hectic scramble for wealth that Thoreau saw all about him he found disgusting—and alarming, for he believed it was destroying both the natural and the human resources of the country.

Like Emerson, Thoreau objected to many of society's restrictions on the individual. "That government is best which governs not at all," he said, going both Emerson and the Jeffersonians one better. He was perfectly prepared to see himself as a majority of one. Emerson reduced him to a phrase when he called him "a born protestant." "When were the good and the brave ever in a majority?" Thoreau asked. "If a man does not keep pace with his companions," he wrote on another occasion, "perhaps it is because he hears a different drummer."

In 1845 Thoreau decided to put to the test his theory that a person need not depend on society for a satisfying existence. He built a cabin at Walden Pond on some property owned by Emerson and lived there alone for two years. He did not try to be entirely self-sufficient: He was not above returning to his family or to Emerson's for a square meal on occasion, and he generally purchased the building materials and other manufactured articles that he needed. Instead he set out, by experimenting, to prove that *if necessary,* an individual could get along without the products of civilization. He used manufactured plaster in building his Walden cabin, but he also gathered a bushel of clamshells and made a small quantity of lime himself, to prove that it could be done.

At Walden, Thoreau wrote *A Week on the Concord and Merrimack Rivers* (1849), which used an account of a trip he had taken with his brother as a vehicle for a discussion of his ideas about life and literature. He spent much time observing the quiet world around the pond, thinking, and writing in his journal. The best fruit of this period was that extraordinary book *Walden* (1854). Superficially, *Walden* is the story of Thoreau's experiment, movingly and beautifully written. It is also an acid indictment of the social behavior of the average American, an attack on unthinking conformity, on subordinating one's own judgment to that of the herd.

The most graphic illustration of Thoreau's confidence in his own values occurred while he was living at Walden. At that time the Mexican War was raging. Thoreau considered the war immoral because it advanced the cause of slavery. To protest, he refused to pay his Massachusetts poll tax. For this he was arrested and lodged in jail, although only for one night because an aunt promptly paid the tax for him. His essay "Civil Disobedience," explaining his view of the proper relation between the individual and the state, resulted from this experience. Like Emerson, however, Thoreau refused to participate in practical reform movements. "I love Henry," one of his friends said, "but I cannot like him; and as for taking his arm, I should as soon think of taking the arm of an elm tree."

EDGAR ALLAN POE

The work of all the imaginative writers of the period reveals romantic influences, and it is possibly an indication of the affinity of the romantic approach to American conditions that a number of excellent writers of poetry and fiction first appeared in the 1830s and 1840s. Edgar Allan Poe, one of the most remarkable, seems almost a caricature of the romantic image of the tortured genius. Poe was born in Boston in 1809, the son of poor actors who died before he was three years old. He was raised by a wealthy Virginian, John Allan.

Few persons as neurotic as Poe have been able to produce first-rate work. In college he ran up debts of $2500 in less than a year and had to withdraw. He won an appointment to West Point but was discharged after a few months for disobedience and "gross neglect of duty." He was a lifelong alcoholic and an occasional taker of drugs. He married a child of 13.

▲ In 1845 Edgar Allan Poe, impoverished and an alcoholic, was living in the "greatest wretchedness." His young wife was dying of tuberculosis. That same year he wrote "The Raven," a poem about an ill-omened bird that intrudes on a young man's grief over the death of his beloved. "Take thy beak from out of my heart" the man screams. Quoth the raven—famously—"Nevermore."

Poe was obsessed with death. Once he attempted to poison himself; repeatedly he was down and out, even to the verge of starvation. He was haunted by melancholia and hallucinations. Yet he was an excellent magazine editor, a penetrating critic, a poet of unique if somewhat narrow talents, and a fine short story writer. Although he died at age 40, he turned out a large volume of serious, highly original work.

Poe responded strongly to the lure of romanticism. His works abound with examples of wild imagination and fascination with mystery, fright, and the occult. If he did not invent the detective story, he perfected it; his tales "The Murders in the Rue Morgue" and "The Purloined Letter" stressed the thought processes of a clever detective in solving a mystery by reasoning from evidence. Poe was also one of the earliest writers to deal with what are today called science fiction themes, and "The Pit and the Pendulum" and "The Cask of Amontillado" show that he was a master of the horror tale.

Although dissolute in his personal life, when Poe touched pen to paper, he became a disciplined craftsman. The most fantastic passages in his works are the result of careful, reasoned selection; not a word, he believed, could be removed without damage to the whole. And despite his rejection of most of the values prized by middle-class America, Poe was widely read in his own day. His poem "The Raven" won instantaneous popularity when it was published in 1845. Had he been a little more stable, he might have made a good living with his pen—but in that case he might not have written as he did.

NATHANIEL HAWTHORNE

Another product of the prevailing romanticism was Nathaniel Hawthorne of Salem, Massachusetts. Hawthorne was born in 1804. When he was a small child, his father died and his grief-stricken mother became a recluse. Left largely to his own devices, he grew to be a lonely, introspective person. Wandering about New England by himself in summertime, he soaked up local lore, which he drew on in writing short stories. For a time he lived in Concord, where he came to know most of the leading transcendentalists. However, he disliked the egoism of the transcendental point of view and rejected its bland optimism outright. He called Emerson an "everlasting rejector of all that is," a "seeker for he knows not what."

Hawthorne was fascinated by the past, particularly by the puritan heritage of New England and its

▲ "The House of the Seven Gables" in Salem, Massachusetts, on which Nathaniel Hawthorne's novel was based. The house symbolized the past's stranglehold on the present. "If each generation were allowed and expected to build its own houses, that single change . . . would imply almost every reform which society is now suffering for." Love, Hawthorne suggested, was a means to break free of the fetters of the past.

continuing influence on his own generation. He scorned "minute fidelity" to the real world in his fiction, seeking "a severer truth . . . the truth of the human heart." But he was active in politics and an admirer of Andrew Jackson. Three Democratic presidents—Martin Van Buren, James K. Polk, and Franklin Pierce—appointed him to minor political offices.

Hawthorne's early stories, originally published in magazines, were brought together in *Twice-Told Tales* (1837). They made excellent use of New England culture and history for background but were concerned chiefly with the struggles of individuals with sin, guilt, and especially the pride and isolation that often afflict those who place too much reliance on their own judgment. His greatest works were two novels written after the Whigs turned him out of his government job in 1849. *The Scarlet Letter* (1850), a grim yet sympathetic analysis of adultery, condemned not the woman, Hester Prynne, but the people who presumed to judge her. *The House of the Seven Gables* (1851) was a gripping account of the decay of an old New England family brought on by the guilt feelings of the current owners of the

house, caused by the way their ancestors had cheated the original owners of the property.

Like Poe, Hawthorne was appreciated in his own day and widely read; unlike Poe, he made a modest amount of money from his work. Yet he was never very comfortable in the society he inhabited. He had no patience with the second-rate. And despite his success in creating word pictures of a somber, mysterious world, he considered America too prosaic a country to inspire good literature. "There is no shadow, no antiquity, no mystery, no picturesque and gloomy wrong, nor anything but a commonplace prosperity," he complained.

HERMAN MELVILLE

In 1850, while writing *The House of the Seven Gables,* Hawthorne's publisher introduced him to another writer who was in the midst of a novel. The writer was Herman Melville; the book, *Moby Dick.* Hawthorne and Melville became good friends at once, for despite their dissimilar backgrounds, they had a great deal in common. Melville was a New Yorker, born in 1819, one of eight children of a merchant of distinguished lineage. His father, however, lost all his money and died when the boy was 12. Herman left school at 15, worked briefly as a bank clerk, and in 1837 went to sea. For 18 months, in 1841 and 1842, he was crewman on the whaler *Acushnet*. Then he jumped ship in the South Seas. For a time he lived among a tribe of cannibals in the Marquesas; later he made his way to Tahiti, where he idled away nearly a year. After another year at sea he returned to America in the fall of 1844.

Although he had never before attempted serious writing, in 1846 he published *Typee*, an account of his life in the Marquesas. The book was a great success, for Melville had visited a part of the world almost unknown to Americans, and his descriptions of his bizarre experiences suited the taste of a romantic age. Success inspired him to write a sequel, *Omoo* (1847); other books followed quickly.

As he wrote Melville became conscious of deeper powers. In 1849 he began a systematic study of Shakespeare, pondering the bard's intuitive grasp of human nature. Like Hawthorne, Melville could not accept the prevailing optimism of his generation. Unlike his friend, he admired Emerson, seconding the Emersonian demand that Americans reject European ties and develop their own literature. "Believe me," he wrote, "men not very much inferior to Shakespeare are this day being born on the banks of the Ohio." Yet he considered Emerson's vague talk about striving and the inherent goodness of mankind complacent nonsense.

Experience made Melville too aware of the evil in the world to be a transcendentalist. His novel *Redburn* (1849), based on his adventures on a Liverpool packet, was, as the critic F. O. Matthiessen put it, "a study in disillusion, of innocence confronted with the world, of ideals shattered by facts." Yet Melville was no cynic; he expressed deep sympathy for the Indians and for immigrants, crowded like animals into the holds of transatlantic vessels. He denounced the brutality of discipline in the United States Navy in *White-Jacket* (1850). His essay "The Tartarus of Maids," a moving if somewhat overdrawn description of young women working in a paper factory, protested the subordination of human beings to machines.

Hawthorne, whose dark view of human nature coincided with Melville's, encouraged him to press ahead with *Moby Dick* (1851). This book, Melville said, was "broiled in hellfire." Against the background of a whaling voyage (no better account of whaling has ever been written), he dealt subtly and symbolically with the problems of good and evil, of

courage and cowardice, of faith, stubbornness, pride. In Captain Ahab, driven relentlessly to hunt down the huge white whale Moby Dick, which had destroyed his leg, Melville created one of the great figures of literature; in the book as a whole, he produced one of the finest novels written by an American, comparable to the best in any language.

As Melville's work became more profound, it lost its appeal to the average reader, and its originality and symbolic meaning escaped most of the critics. *Moby Dick*, his masterpiece, received little attention and most of that unfavorable. He kept on writing until his death in 1891 but was virtually ignored. Only in the 1920s did the critics rediscover him and give him his merited place in the history of American literature. His "Billy Budd, Foretopman," now considered one of his best stories, was not published until 1924.

WALT WHITMAN

Walt Whitman, whose *Leaves of Grass* (1855) was the last of the great literary works of this brief outpouring of genius, was the most romantic and by far the most

▲ Some scholars regard Walt Whitman as the poet of nature, and others, of the body—a reference to erotic lines such as: "Without shame the man I like knows and avows the deliciousness of his sex, /Without shame the woman I like knows and avows hers." Whitman's *Leaves of Grass* had every leaf in nature, complained critic E. P. Whipple, except the fig leaf.

distinctly American writer of his age. He was born on Long Island, outside New York City, in 1819. At 13 he left school and worked for a printer; thereafter he held a succession of newspaper jobs in the metropolitan area. He was an ardent Jacksonian and later a Free Soiler, which got him into hot water with a number of the publishers for whom he worked.

Although genuinely a "common man," thoroughly at home among tradesmen and laborers, he was surely not an ordinary man. Deeply introspective, he read omnivorously, if in a rather disorganized fashion, while working out a new, intensely personal mode of expression. During the early 1850s, while employed as a carpenter and composing the poems that made up *Leaves of Grass*, he regularly carried a book of Emerson in his lunch box. "I was simmering, simmering, simmering," he later recalled. "Emerson brought me to a boil." The transcendental idea that inspiration and aspiration are at the heart of all achievement captivated him. A poet could best express himself, he believed, by relying uncritically on his natural inclinations without regard for rigid metrical forms.

Leaves of Grass consisted of a preface, in which Whitman made the extraordinary statement that Americans had "probably the fullest poetical nature" of any people in history, and 12 poems in free verse: rambling, uneven, appearing to most readers shocking both in the commonplace nature of the subject matter and the coarseness of the language. Emerson, Thoreau, and a few others saw a fresh talent in these poems, but most

DOCUMENT

Whitman, *Preface to Leaves of Grass*

DEBATING THE PAST

Was there an "American Renaissance"? With the exception of Hawthorne's *The Scarlet Letter* (1850), the extraordinary literary achievements at mid-century went mostly unnoticed. Melville's *Moby Dick* and Thoreau's *Walden* (1854) each sold only a few thousand copies, and Walt Whitman's *Leaves of Grass* (1955) far fewer. A half century later critic Van Wyck Brooks identified these works as distinctly American, but he was unimpressed with what he called *America's Coming of Age* (1915). Transcendentalism he dismissed as "one shining deluge

of righteousness, purity, and practical mysticism." Ever since publication of Emerson's "American Scholar," he added, "the whole of American literature has had the semblance of one vast, all embracing baccalaureate address." Critic F. O. Matthiessen (1941) took a sharply different view. He identified the mid-nineteenth century as an "American Renaissance," a period when American writers ceased to be overshadowed by Europeans. Emerson, Thoreau, and Whitman drew from the energy and optimism of the people of the American nation, and Hawthorne and Melville from its soul. The relationship between American nationalism and letters was overdrawn, Leo Marx (1964) suggested. The great writers of the nineteenth century were reacting against urbanization and industrialization, moving symbolically "away from sophistication toward simplicity, away from the city toward the country." The social upheavals of the 1960s precipitated a backlash against the "elitist" focus on high-brow writers. Ann Douglas (1977) claimed that the "split between elite and mass culture" had occurred precisely during the mid-nineteenth century, when most readers ignored Melville and Whitman and devoured sentimental novels by Harriet Beecher Stowe, Susan Warner, and others, many of which were serialized in *Godey's Ladys' Book*, edited by Sarah Hale. Douglas, however, sided with the elitists, denouncing such novels for their "debased religiosity, their sentimental peddling of Christian belief for its nostalgic value." Nevertheless, one suspects that the girl pictured here in *Godey's Ladys' Book* (1855) was not reading *Moby Dick*.

Van Wyck Brooks, *America's Coming of Age* (1915), F. O. Matthiessen, *The American Renaissance* (1941), Leo Marx, *The Machine in the Garden* (1964), Ann Douglas, *The Feminization of American Culture* (1977), David S. Reynolds, *Beneath the American Renaissance* (1988).

readers and reviewers found them offensive. Indeed, the work was so undisciplined and so much of it had no obvious meaning that it was easy to miss the many passages of great beauty and originality.

Part of Whitman's difficulty arose because there was much of the charlatan in his makeup; often his writing did not ring true. He loved to use foreign words and phrases, and since he had no more than a smattering of any foreign language, he sounded pretentious and sometimes downright foolish when he did so. In reality a sensitive, gentle person, he tried to pose as a great, rough character. (Later in his career he bragged of fathering no less than six illegitimate children, which was assuredly untrue.) He never married, and his work suggests that his strongest emotional ties were with men. Thomas Carlyle once remarked shrewdly that Whitman thought he was a big man because he lived in a big country.

Whitman's work was more authentically American than that of any contemporary. His egoism—he titled one of his finest poems "Song of Myself"—was tempered by his belief that he was typical of all humanity:

> *I celebrate myself and sing myself*
> *And what I assume you shall assume,*
> *For every atom belonging to me as good belongs to you.*

He had a remarkable ear for rendering common speech poetically, for employing slang, for catching the breezy informality of Americans and their faith in themselves:

> *Earth! you seem to look for something at my hands,*
> *Say, old top-knot, what do you want?*
> *I bequeath myself to the dirt to grow from the grass I love,*
> *If you want me again look for me under your boot-soles.*

Because of these qualities and because in his later work, especially during the Civil War, he occasionally struck a popular chord, Whitman was never as neglected as Melville. When he died in 1892, he was, if not entirely understood, at least widely appreciated.

THE WIDER LITERARY RENAISSANCE

Emerson, Thoreau, Poe, Hawthorne, Melville, and Whitman were the great figures of American literature before the Civil War. A number of others, if they lacked genius, were leading literary lights in their own day and are still worth reading. One was Henry Wadsworth Longfellow. In 1835, while still in his twenties, Longfellow became professor of modern languages at Harvard. Although he published a fine translation of Dante's *Divine Comedy* and was expert

in many languages, his fame came from his poems: "The Village Blacksmith"; "Paul Revere's Ride"; *The Courtship of Miles Standish,* a sentimental tale of Pilgrim days; and *The Song of Hiawatha,* the romantic retelling of an Indian legend. These brought him excellent critical notices and considerable fortune; his work was widely translated and reprinted.

Although musical, polished, and full of vivid images, Longfellow's poetry, like the man, lacked profundity, originality, and force. But it was neither cheap nor trivial. When Longfellow wrote "Life is real! life is earnest! / And the grave is not its goal," he expressed the heartfelt belief of most of his generation. In this sense he captured the spirit of his times better than any of his great contemporaries, better even than Whitman.

Longfellow was the most talented of a group of minor New England writers who collectively gave that region great intellectual vitality. John Greenleaf Whittier, a poet nearly as popular as Longfellow, believed ardently in the abolition of slavery. A few of his poems can still be read with pleasure, among them "The Barefoot Boy," dealing with his rural childhood. Somewhat more weighty was the achievement of James Russell Lowell, the first editor of the *Atlantic Monthly,* founded in Boston in 1857. Lowell's humorous stories written in the New England dialect made an original and influential contribution to the national literature. Dr. Oliver Wendell Holmes, professor of medicine at Harvard, was widely known as a poet and essayist. A few of his poems, such as "The Chambered Nautilus" and "Old Ironsides," are interesting examples of American romantic verse.

Collectively these minor writers had a beneficial effect on American culture, for if rather smug and narrow, they were serious and industrious. They fixed their gaze upward and encouraged their readers to do likewise.

So did the important historians of the period, all of them New Englanders. George Bancroft, one of the first Americans to study in Germany, began in 1834 to publish a ten-volume *History of the United States,* based on thorough research. William Hickling Prescott, though nearly blind, wrote extensively on the history of Spain and Spain's American empire, his *Conquest of Mexico* (1843) and *Conquest of Peru* (1847) being his most important works. John Lothrop Motley, another German-trained historian, published his *Rise of the Dutch Republic* in 1856, and Francis Parkman began his great account of the struggle between France and Great Britain for the control of North America with *Conspiracy of Pontiac* in 1851.

Southern literature was even more markedly romantic than that of New England. John Pendleton

Kennedy of Baltimore wrote several novels with regional historical themes, much in the manner of Sir Walter Scott. Kennedy was also a Whig politician of some importance who served several terms in Congress; in 1852 he became secretary of the navy in the Fillmore Cabinet. The more versatile and influential William Gilmore Simms of South Carolina wrote nearly two dozen novels, several volumes of poetry, and a number of biographies. At his peak in the 1830s he earned as much as $6000 a year with his pen. *The Partisan* (1835), one of a series of novels dealing with the Revolution, and *The Yemassee* (1835), the story of an early eighteenth-century Indian war, seem too melodramatic for modern tastes. His portraits of the planter class are too bloodless and reverential to be convincing. His female characters are nearly all pallid and fragile. Only when Simms wrote of frontier life and its people did his work possess much power.

DOMESTIC TASTES

Architecture flourished in the northern cities chiefly as a result of the work of Charles Bulfinch and some of his disciples. Bulfinch was influenced by British architects, but he developed a manner all his own. His

▲ How, in a democracy, could women assent to the authority of husbands? Catharine Beecher, a popular writer, responded that women could promote "intellectual and moral elevation" by transforming their home into a "glorious temple." Women, as homemakers, were to spearhead the nation's religious and moral regeneration.

"Federal" style gave parts of Boston a dignity and charm equal to the finest sections of London. The State House, numerous other public buildings, and, best of all, many of Bulfinch's private houses—austere yet elegant, solid yet airy and graceful—gave the town a distinction it had lacked before the Revolution.

In the 1830s and 1840s new techniques made it possible to weave colored patterns into cloth by machine, to manufacture wallpaper printed with complicated designs, and to produce rugs and hangings that looked like tapestries. Combined with the use of machine methods in the furniture business, these inventions had a powerful impact on public taste. That impact, at least in the short run, was aesthetically unfortunate. In these years the parlor evolved as a room whose chief purpose was to display a piano, stuffed chairs and sofas with flowered prints, wallpaper with vertical stripes, heavy drapes with frilled edges, and all manner of bibelots. "Though your parlor may be crowded," one decorator advised, "it is crowded only with love."

Wood-turning machinery added to the popularity of the elaborately decorated "Gothic" style of architecture. The irregularity and uniqueness of Gothic buildings suited the prevailing romanticism, their aspiring towers, steeples, and arches and their flexibility (a new wing or extension could always be added without spoiling the effect) made them especially attractive to a people enamored of progress. The huge pile of pink masonry of the Smithsonian Institution Building in Washington, with its nine distinct types of towers, represents American Gothic at its most giddy and lugubrious stage. The building, which was designed in 1846 by James Renwick, confounded generations of architects, but with the passage of time it came to seem the perfect setting for the vast collection of mementos that fill "the nation's attic." "Greek" and "Italian" styles also flourished in this period, the former particularly in the South; elsewhere the Gothic was by all odds the most popular.

Increasingly, Americans of the period were purchasing native art. George Catlin, who painted hundreds of pictures of Indians and their surroundings, all rich in authentic detail, displayed his work before admiring crowds in many cities. Genre painters (artists whose canvases told stories, usually drawn from everyday life) were wildly popular. The best were William Sidney Mount of New York and George Caleb Bingham of Missouri. Rumor had it that Mount received $1000 for his first important canvas; Bingham's paintings commanded excellent prices; and the public bought engravings of the work of both men in enormous numbers.

The more academic artists of the period were popular as well. The "luminists" and members of the

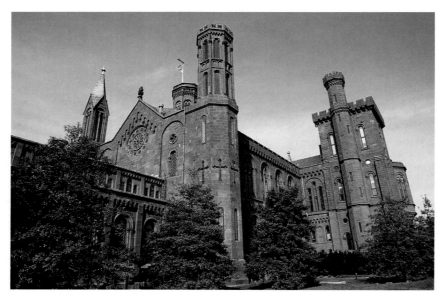

▲ The Smithsonian Institution Building, made of red sandstone, is popularly known as "The Castle" because of its crenellated towers. Its architect, James Renwick, Jr., also designed New York's Grace Church and St. Patrick's Cathedral in the popular Gothic Revival style.

petent American works of art into middle-class homes.

Beginning in the late 1850s, the prints of the firm of Currier and Ives brought a crude but charming kind of art to a still wider audience. Currier and Ives lithographs portrayed horse racing, trains, rural landscapes, and "every tender domestic moment, every sign of national progress, every regional oddity, every private or public disaster from a cut finger to a forest fire." They were issued in very large editions and sold for as little as 15 cents.

romantic Hudson River School specialized in grandiose pictures of wild landscapes. In the 1840s Thomas Doughty regularly collected $500 each for his paintings. The works of Asher B. Durand, John Kensett, and Thomas Cole were in demand. The collector Luman Reed commissioned five large Cole canvases for an allegorical series, *The Course of Empire,* and crowds flocked to see another of Cole's series, *The Voyage of Life,* when it was exhibited in New York.

In 1839 the American Art-Union was formed in New York to encourage native art. The Art-Union hit on the ingenious device of selling what were in effect lottery tickets and using the proceeds to purchase paintings, which became the prizes in the lottery. Annual "memberships" sold for $5; 814 people subscribed in 1839, nearly 19,000 ten years later. Soon the Art-Union was giving every member an engraving of one of its principal prizes. The organization had to disband after a New York court outlawed the lottery in 1851, but in 1854 a new Cosmopolitan Art-Union was established in Ohio. In the years before the Civil War it boomed, reaching a peak of 38,000 members and paying as much as $6000 for an individual work—the sculptor Hiram Powers's boneless female nude, *The Greek Slave.* It also distributed an art magazine and each year gave a young artist a gold medal and $2000 for foreign study.

The art unions made little effort to encourage innovators, but they were a boon to many artists. The American Art-Union paid out as much as $40,000 for its prizes in a single year. By distributing thousands of engravings and colored prints, they introduced com-

EDUCATION FOR DEMOCRACY

Except on the edge of the frontier and in the South, most youngsters between the ages of five and ten attended a school for at least a couple of months of the year. These schools, however, were privately run and charged fees. Attendance was not required and fell off sharply once children learned to read and do their sums well enough to get along in day-to-day life. The teachers were usually young men waiting for something better to turn up.

All this changed with the rise of the common school movement. At the heart of the movement was the belief, widely expressed in the first days of the republic, that a government based on democratic rule must provide the means, as Jefferson put it, to "diffuse knowledge throughout the mass of the people." This meant free tax-supported schools, which all children were expected to attend. It also came to mean that such an educational system should be administered on a statewide basis and that teaching should become a profession that required formal training.

DOCUMENT

Mann, Report of the Massachusetts Board of Ed.

The two most effective leaders of the common school movement were Henry Barnard and Horace Mann. Both were New Englanders, Whigs, trained in the law, and in other ways conservative types. They shared an unquenchable faith in the improvability of the human race through education. Barnard served in educational posts in Connecticut, Rhode Island, and New York in the 1840s and 1850s and as editor of the *American Journal of Education* from 1855 until 1882. Mann drafted the 1837 Massachusetts law creating a state school board and then became its first secretary. Over the next decade Mann's annual reports carried the case for common schools to every

▲ James J. Audubon was perhaps the nation's foremost chronicler of nature in antebellum America. The "Roseate Spoonbill" is from his *The Birds of America* (1827–1838). "I am not a scholar," Audubon wrote in 1830. "But no man living knows better than I do the habits of our birds."

corner of the land. Seldom given to understatement, Mann called common schools "the greatest discovery ever made by man." In his reports he criticized wealthy parents who sent their children to private academies rather than bring them into contact with their poorer neighbors in the local school. He encouraged young women to become teachers while commending them to school boards by claiming that they could get along on lower salaries than men.

By the 1850s every state outside the South provided free elementary schools and supported institutions for training teachers. Many extended public education to include high schools, and Michigan and Iowa even established publicly supported colleges.

Historians differ in explaining the success of the common school movement. Some stress the arguments Mann used to win support from employers by appealing to their need for trained and well-disciplined workers. Others see the schools as designed to "Americanize" the increasing numbers of non-English and non-Protestant immigrants who were flooding into the country. (Supporting this argument is the fact that Catholic bishops in New York and elsewhere opposed laws requiring Catholic children to attend these "Protestant" schools and set up their own private, parochial schools.)

Still other scholars argue that middle-class reformers favored public elementary schools on the theory that they would instill the values of hard work, punctuality, and submissiveness to authority in children of the laboring classes. (See Debating the Past, "Did the antebellum reform movement improve society?" in Chapter 10 [p. 283]).

All these reasons played a part in advancing the cause of the common schools. Yet it remains the case that the most compelling argument for common schools was cultural; more effectively than any other institution, they brought Americans of different economic circumstances and ethnic backgrounds into early and mutually beneficial contact with one another. They served the two roles that Mann assigned to them: "the balance wheel of the social machinery" and "the great equalizer."

READING AND THE DISSEMINATION OF CULTURE

As the population grew and became more concentrated, and as society, especially in the North, was permeated by a middle-class point of view, popular concern for "culture" in the formal sense increased. A

▲ Artist Henry Inman's *Dismissal of School on an October Afternoon* celebrated the one-room schoolhouse, but suggested that life's greater lessons could be learned out-of-doors, amidst the beauty of nature.

largely literate people, committed to the idea of education but not generally well educated, set their hearts on being "refined" and "cultivated." Industrialization made it easier to satisfy this new demand for culture, though the new machines also tended to make the artifacts of culture more stereotyped.

Improved printing techniques reduced the cost of books, magazines, and newspapers. In the 1850s one publisher sold a 50-volume set of Sir Walter Scott for $37.50. The first penny newspaper was the *New York Sun* (1833), but James Gordon Bennett's *New York Herald,* founded in 1835, brought the cheap new journalism to perfection. The *Boston Daily Times* and the *Philadelphia Public Ledger* soon followed. The penny newspapers depended on sensation, crime stories, and society gossip to attract readers, but they covered important national and international news too.

In the 1850s the moralistic and sentimental "domestic" novel entered its prime. The most successful writers in this genre were women, which prompted Hawthorne to complain bitterly that "a

d——d mob of scribbling women" was taking over American literature. Typical were Susan Warner, whose *The Wide, Wide World* (1850) was the sad tale of a pious, submissive girl who cried "more readily and more steadily" than any other tormented child in a novel at the time, and Maria Cummins, author of *The Lamplighter* (1854), the story of little Gerty, an orphan rescued by a kindly lamplighter, appropriately named Trumena Flint. *The Lamplighter* sold 70,000 copies within a year of publication. During these years arboreal pseudonyms were in vogue, among them Fanny Fern and Grace Greenwood. Although some scholars scorn the novels of such writers as sentimental drivel, the nineteenth-century equivalent of television soaps, others regard their books (and perhaps the soaps) as a means of creating imaginative "feminine" communities.

Besides reading countless volumes of sentimental romances (the books of another novelist, Mary Jane Holmes, sold over a million copies in these years), Americans consumed reams of religious literature. In 1840 the American Tract Society distributed 3 million copies of its publications; in 1855, more than 12 million. The society had hundreds of missionary-salesmen, called colporteurs, who fanned out across the country preaching the gospel and selling or giving away religious pamphlets and books. These publications played down denominational differences in favor of a generalized brand of evangelical Christianity. They bore titles such as *Quench Not the Spirit* (over 900,000 copies distributed by 1850) and *The Way to Heaven*. The American Bible Society issued hundreds of thousands of copies of the Old and New Testaments each year. Americans also devoured books on self-improvement, some aimed at uplifting the reader's character; others, which would today be called "how-to" books, at teaching everything from raising chickens to carving tombstones.

Philanthropists contributed large sums to charity and other good causes: Stephen Girard left $6 million for "educating poor white orphan boys" in his adopted Philadelphia; John Jacob Astor of New York and George Peabody of Massachusetts endowed libraries; John Lowell, son of the pioneer cotton manufacturer, left $500,000 to establish the Lowell Institute in Boston to sponsor free public lectures. In the late 1850s the industrialist Peter Cooper founded the Cooper Institute in New York City, where workers could take free courses in practical subjects. Mechanics' libraries sprang up in every industrial center and attracted so many readers that pressure was soon applied to grant them state funds. In 1848 Massachusetts led the way by authorizing the use of public money to back the Boston Public Library, and soon several states were encouraging local communities to found tax-supported libraries.

The desire for knowledge and culture in America is well illustrated by the success of the mutual improvement societies known as lyceums. The movement began in Great Britain; in the United States its prime mover was Josiah Holbrook, an itinerant lecturer and sometime schoolmaster from Connecticut. Holbrook founded the first lyceum in 1826 at Millbury, Massachusetts; within five years there were over a thousand scattered across the country. The lyceums conducted discussions, established libraries, and lobbied for better schools. Soon they began to sponsor lecture series on topics of every sort. Many of the nation's political and intellectual leaders, such as Webster, Emerson, Melville, and Lowell, regularly graced their platforms. So did other less famous lecturers who in the name of culture pronounced on subjects ranging from "Chemistry Applied to the Mechanic Arts" to a description of the tombs of the Egyptian pharaohs.

THE STATE OF THE COLLEGES

Unlike common schools, with their democratic overtones, private colleges had at best a precarious place in Jacksonian America. For one thing, there were too many of them. Any town with pretensions of becoming a regional center felt it had to have a college. Ohio had 25 in the 1850s, Tennessee 16. Many of these institutions were short-lived. Of the 14 colleges founded in Kentucky between 1800 and 1850, only half were still operating in 1860.

The problem of supply was compounded by a demand problem—too few students. Enrollment at the largest, Yale, never topped 400 until the mid-1840s. On the eve of the Civil War the largest state university, North Carolina, had fewer than 500. Higher education was beyond the means of the average family. Although most colleges charged less than half the $55 tuition required by Harvard, that was still too much for most families, wages being what they were. So desperate was the shortage that colleges accepted applicants as young as 11 and 12 and as old as 30.

Once enrolled, students had little worry about making the grade, not least because grades were not given. Since students were hard to come by and classwork was considered relatively unimportant, discipline was lax. Official authority was frequently challenged, and rioting was known to break out over such weighty matters as the quality of meals. A father who visited his son's college dormitory in 1818 found it inhabited by "half a dozen loungers in a state of oriental lethargy, each stretched out upon two or three chairs, with scarce any indication of life in them [other] than the feeble effort to keep up the fire of their cigars."

The typical college curriculum, dominated by the study of Latin and Greek, had almost no practical relevance except for future clergymen. The Yale faculty, most of them ministers, defended the classics as admirably providing for both "the discipline and the furniture of the mind," but these subjects commended themselves to college officials chiefly because they did not require costly equipment or a faculty that knew anything else. Professors spent most of their time in and out of the classroom trying to maintain a semblance of order, "to the exclusion of any great literary undertakings to which their choice might lead them," one explained. "Our country is yet too young for old professors," a Bostonian informed a foreign visitor in the 1830s, "and, besides, they are too poorly paid to induce first rate men to

▶ *text continues on page 312*

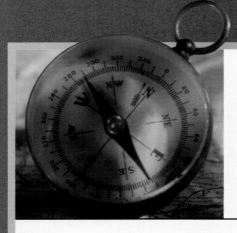

Mapping
the Past

Nature as a Civilizing Force

Thoreau had gone off to Walden Pond to escape the constraints of civilization. "We need the tonic of wildness," he declared. (His wildness, to be sure, was subdued: he was referring to a pasture.) A few years later landscape architect Andrew Jackson Downing similarly conceived of nature as a balm "to soften and humanize" those whose nerves had been rubbed raw by city life. Rather than flee into the woods, Downing proposed to bring nature to every home. Partly this could be accomplished through proper design: houses themselves should blend with nature, and open up to it with broad porches and large windows. Moreover, homes should be *surrounded* by nature. This could be accomplished even in cities by providing for well-landscaped lawns.

Suburban Arcadia

Another solution was to build homes in the suburbs. The first effort in this direction was Llewellyn Park, built in 1856 in West Orange, New Jersey, by Llewellyn S. Haskell, a wealthy New York merchant. Jackson hired Alexander Jackson Davis, author of *Rural Residences* (1837) and a friend of Downing's, to plan the community. Davis conceived of the community as a place for New York City businessmen seeking "accessible, retired, and healthful homes in the country." He cleared expansive vistas and framed the clearing with rocks and trees, constructed seven miles of winding roads with names such as Tulip, Mountain, and Passive, and built a 50-acre pedestrian "Ramble" through adjacent woods *(top right)*.

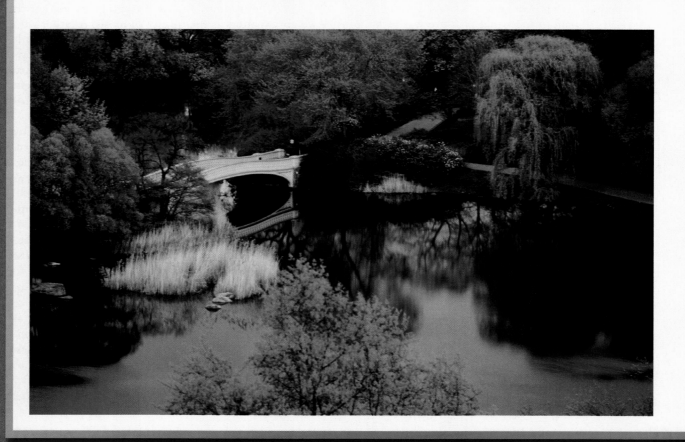

Creation of Central Park

Llewellyn Park was a bucolic idyll for rich business-men. But those who most needed the "softening" and "humanizing" tonic of nature were urban work-ers. Surrounded by machinery or immured in office buildings and counting rooms, they returned "home" to brick and concrete tenements or apartment build-ings. "Nature" could be brought into the city in the form of urban parks. Spirited citizens—or as historian Charles Beard contended in 1926—real estate specu-lators—initiated plans for a park in New York City in the early 1850s.

Frederick Law Olmsted, a landscape architect, travel writer, and editor, and Calvert Vaux, an English land-scape architect who was an associate of Downing, sub-mitted the "Greensward" plan for the design of Central Park. Olmsted and Vaux rejected as models the broad boulevards and symmetrical designs of European parks. They did not want the park to serve as an adorn-ment to the city. Central Park was instead to be a place of refuge from urban life. The roads that would trans-verse the park would be dropped below eye level. Paths would meander around hills and ponds. Clusters of trees would block out the encroaching city. Pastoral vistas would reveal gentle hills and rock outcrop-pings.

Manmade structures, too, would harmonize with nature; bridges would reiterate the nat-ural curves of nature, as illus-trated in the recent picture (left). This idyllic conception of

Central Park was at variance with the wishes of workers who flocked there to play baseball or to listen to band con-certs. "Greensward" became "The People's Playground."

devote themselves to the business of lecturing. . . . We consider professors as secondary men."

Fortunately for the future of higher education, some college officials recognized the need for a drastic overhaul of their institutions. President Francis Wayland of Brown University used his 1842 address, "On the Present Collegiate System," to call for a thorough revamping of the curriculum to make it responsive to the economic realities of American society. This meant more courses in science, economics (where Wayland's own *Elements of Political Economy* might be used), modern history, and applied mathematics; fewer in Hebrew, biblical studies, Greek, and ancient history.

Yale established a separate school of science in 1847, which it hoped would attract serious-minded students and research-minded professors. At Harvard, which also opened a scientific school, students were allowed to choose some of their courses and were compelled to earn grades as a stimulus to study. Colleges in the West and the South began to offer mechanical and agricultural subjects relevant to their regional economies. Oberlin enrolled four female students in 1837, and the first women's college, the Georgia Female College, opened its doors in 1839.

These reforms slowed the downward spiral of colleges; they did not restore them to the honored place they had enjoyed in the Revolutionary era. Of the first six presidents of the United States, only Washington did not graduate from college. Beginning in 1829, seven of the next eleven did not. In this Presidents Jackson, Van Buren, Harrison, Taylor, Fillmore, Lincoln, and Johnson were like 98 of every 100 white males, all blacks and Indians, and all but a handful of white women in mid-nineteenth-century America. Going to college had yet, in Wayland's words, to "commend itself to the good sense and patriotism of the American people."

CIVIC CULTURES

Unlike the capitals of Europe, which were centers of art and culture, Washington was a cultural backwater, and the politicians seemed content to keep it that way. Whether the United States had *any* cultural center, and if so, where it was, is another matter. Boston, Philadelphia, and New York vied for primacy, but many smaller cities, such as Lexington, Kentucky, the self-proclaimed "Athens of the West," set the tone for the surrounding hinterland.

In the cities members of the "learned professions," especially lawyers, were generally accepted as the arbiters of taste in literature and art. "At the bar or the bench the American aristocracy is found," and there too resides "the most intellectual section of society,"

the ever-insightful Tocqueville reported. Lawyers came mostly from the upper reaches of the city's economic order, usually from families long in residence.

Emerson only half mockingly called Boston "the hub of the universe," but this was a case when local pride triumphed over his usual good judgment. Boston was indeed the home of the country's leading literary magazine, the *North American Review,* founded in 1815, but Philadelphia had *Graham's,* the country's first illustrated magazine, and *Godey's Ladies Book,* which reached 150,000 subscribers in the 1850s, an enormous number for that date. By 1825 New York's House of Harper, organized in 1817, was the largest book publisher in the nation. Boston was the home of the nation's leading historians, and Philadelphia, with the Pennsylvania Academy of Fine Arts (1815) and the Philadelphia Academy of Music (1857), was conceded by all but blind Bostonians and tin-eared New Yorkers to predominate in artistic and musical matters.

In the West, Cincinnati could point to its seven weekly and two daily newspapers, a literary monthly, a medical journal, and a magazine for teenagers. The first Beethoven symphony ever heard in America was performed in Cincinnati in 1817. By the 1830s such coups had enabled the "Queen City" to replace the "Athens of the West" as the center of trans-Allegheny culture. Having quickly accomplished so much, its boosters reasoned, Cincinnati would soon assume national leadership in cultural matters, as it already had in the processing of pork bellies.

Even smaller cities like Portland, Providence, Hartford, Albany, and Pittsburgh had literary and natural history societies and were regular stops on the lyceum circuit. All in all, American cities had a vitality and diversity that foreign visitors both celebrated and decried. Life in the towns was by some standards crude; many of the people were pushy, crass, and dedicated to the accumulation of wealth. But on this last count, the English novelist Charles Dickens offered some international perspective. "The golden calf they worship," he wrote of Americans in 1841, "is a pigmy compared with the giant effigies set up in other parts of that vast counting-house which lies beyond the Atlantic; and the almighty dollar sinks into something comparatively insignificant amidst a whole Pantheon of better gods."

AMERICAN HUMOR

The clash between the desire of a few for a "high" culture and the simpler tastes of the majority led James Fenimore Cooper to conclude that Americans would be forever "wanting in most of the high tastes,

Vol. 2.]   "GO AHEAD!!"   [No. 3.

THE CROCKETT ALMANAC
1841.

Tussel with a Bear. See page 9.

Containing Adventures, Exploits, Sprees & Scrapes in the West, & Life and Manners in the Backwoods.

Nashville, Tennessee.   Published by Ben Harding.

▲ *The Crockett Almanacs* were the precursors to modern comic books. These illustrated books included tall-tales of hard-drinking, hard-fighting, and loose-loving heroes. In *Beneath the American Renaissance* (1988), David S. Reynolds argues that the major literary figures of the day derived themes and ideas from such raucous and subversive elements of antebellum culture.

DOCUMENT

James Fenimore Cooper *Notions of America*

and consequently in the high enjoyments." But other writers were not so sure, and some, rather than despair over the cultural incongruities, found in them a rich source of humor.

They were hardly the first to do so. The comic potential in juxtaposing high ideals and low reality had been exploited by the Greek playwright Aristophanes; by Rabelais, the creator of *Gargantua;* and by Cervantes in *The Adventures of Don Quixote*—all, incidentally, works available in mid-century America. William Byrd and Benjamin Franklin had both used the differences between the

pretensions of colonial sophisticates and the ways of common folk to good comic effect. But the possibilities of this kind of humor were greatly enlarged in the Jacksonian era. Where else was there a country theoretically based on equality whose inhabitants were so strikingly varied?

One of the first to exploit the comic aspects of Jackson was Seba Smith, a newspaperman from Portland, Maine. Smith's fictional creation, Major Jack Downing, was a Jackson man from a part of the country suspicious of both the general's politics and intelligence. Smith had Downing accompany the president on his tour of New England, which included, among other adventures, an appearance at Harvard to receive an honorary degree. In the presence of so many learned gentlemen with political views contrary to his own, Downing advised the president "jest to say nothing, but look as knowing as any of them." Which was what Jackson did, even when faced by snickering "sassy students." "The General stood it out like a hero," the major assured readers, "and got through very well."

Life in the Old Southwest provided chroniclers with more than enough violence to capture the attention of their "gentle readers." Violence figures prominently in Augustus Baldwin Longstreet's story "The Fight," in which one Ransy Sniffle, "who, in his earlier days, had fed copiously upon red clay and blackberries," promoted a wrestling match between two toughs, Bill and Bob. After provoking both to do battle, Ransy sat back to enjoy the slaughter. And slaughter it was. Bob, the victor, "entirely lost his left ear and a large piece of his left cheek." As for Bill, he

> presented a hideous spectacle. About a third of his nose, at the lower extremity, was bit off, and his face so swelled and bruised that it was difficult to discover anything of the human visage, much more the fine features which he carried into the fight.

During the 1830s and 1840s, the Davy Crockett Almanacs provided outrageous and ribald tales about frontier life; because they also included humorous pictures, they were akin to modern comic books. An 1837 Crockett story told about a sixteen-year-old girl who on her wedding night "sucked forty rattlesnake eggs, just to give her a sweet breath." Once when she was fighting wildcats, they "scratched her backside so tarnaciously its never itched since." In a new country, it made sense not to take oneself too seriously. While the outcome of the nation's experiment in combining democracy and cultural aspiration remained in doubt, most Americans took their laughs where they could find them.

MILESTONES

1830s–1850s	Hudson River School is first coherent American school of art
1830s–1860s	Machine-made decorations adorn American Gothic architecture
1834	George Bancroft publishes 10-volume *History of the United States*
1834–1836	Thomas Cole paints allegorical *The Course of Empire*
1835	James Gordon Bennett founds *New York Herald*
1836	John Lowell endows Lowell Institute, free public lectures
1837	Ralph Waldo Emerson delivers "The American Scholar" at Harvard
	Oberlin enrolls 4 female students
	Horace Mann and Henry Barnard call for common schools
1839	American Art-Union is formed to encourage native art
1842–1843	Herman Melville lives in Tahiti and other South Pacific islands
1843	Hiram Powers sculpts *The Greek Slave*
1845	Edgar Allan Poe publishes "The Raven"
1845–1846	Henry David Thoreau lives alone at Walden Pond
1846	Smithsonian Institution opens for research
1850	Nathaniel Hawthorne publishes *The Scarlet Letter*
1851	Herman Melville publishes *Moby Dick*
	Francis Parkman publishes *The Conspiracy of Pontiac*
1854	Henry David Thoreau attacks conformity in *Walden*
1855–1892	Walt Whitman publishes *Leaves of Grass* (various editions)
1857	*Atlantic Monthly* is founded
1858	Frederick Law Olmsted and Calvert Vaux win New York Central Park competition
1859	Cooper Institute offers free courses to workers
1850s–1907	Currier & Ives prints reach wide audience

SUPPLEMENTARY READING

Useful surveys of cultural and intellectual currents in this period are Daniel Boorstin, *The Americans: The National Experience* (1967), and Rush Welter, *The Mind of America, 1820–1860* (1975). See also Richard Hofstadter, *Anti-intellectualism in American Life* (1963), and Stow Persons, *The Decline of American Gentility* (1975), for a more critical assessment.

For Emerson and Thoreau, see the biographies by Robert D. Richardson, *Emerson: The Mind on Fire* (1995), and *Henry Thoreau: The Life of the Mind* (1986). For Poe, the biography by Kenneth Silverman (1991) is excellent. David S. Reynold's *Walt Whitman's America* (1995) examines the poet's relation to other trends in American life. See also Hershel Parker, *Herman Melville: 1819–1851* (1996) and *Herman Melville: 1851–1891* (2002).

On the cultural life of the South, see Bertram Wyatt-Brown, *Hearts of Darkness* (2003), and Drew Faust, *A Sacred Circle* (1977).

On education, in addition to works cited in the previous chapter, see Lawrence A. Cremin, *American Education: The National Experience* (1980), and C. F. Kaestle, *Pillars of the Republic* (1983). Jill Lepore, *A Is For American* (2002) is also useful.

Neil Harris, *The Artist in American Society* (1966), puts art in its social setting. See also Barbara Novak, *Nature and Culture: American Landscape Painting* (1980).

Scholars have recently been interested in the proliferation of unconventional popular ideas during these years. See David S. Reynolds, *Beneath the American Renaissance* (1988), and John M. Brooke, *The Refiner's Fire* (1994). In *Carnival on the Page: Popular Print Media in Antebellum America* (2000), Isabelle Lehuu argues that a rowdy and "subversive" popular press was another manifestation of this subversive culture.

SUGGESTED WEBSITES

America's First Look into the Camera: Daguerreotype Portraits and Views, 1839–1862
http://memory.loc.gov/ammem/daghtml/daghome.html
The Library of Congress's daguerreotype collection consists of more than 650 photographs from the 1839–1864 period. Portraits, architectural views, and some street scenes make up most of the collection.

The Era of the Mountain Men
http://www.xmission.com/~drudy/amm.html
Private letters help students of the past learn about the concerns and environment of the writers and recipients. This site has correspondence from early settlers in the area west of the Mississippi River.

Edgar Allan Poe
http://www.eapoe.org/index.html
The Edgar Allan Poe Society of Baltimore provides the original works, history, criticism, images, and more about the writer.

Eastern State Penitentiary Official Homepage
http://www.easternstate.com/index.html
This is the official Website for America's most historic prison; the model for 300 prisons worldwide. Eastern State Penitentiary is now open to the public as an historic site.

CHAPTER 12 Westward Expansion

▼ In *American Progress* (1872), John Gast depicts a feminized (and eroticized!) America moving westward, a school book in one hand and telegraph wire in the other. Confronted with the onslaught of "civilization," the buffalo flee and the Indians cringe.

CHAPTER CONTENTS

John Tyler, who became president after the death of William Henry Harrison, was a thin, rather delicate-appearing man with pale blue eyes and a long nose. Courteous, tactful, soft-spoken, he gave the impression of being weak, an impression reinforced by his professed belief that the president should defer to Congress in the formulation of policy. This was a false impression; John Tyler was stubborn and proud, and these characteristics combined with an almost total lack of imagination to make him worship consistency, as so many second-raters do. He had turned away from Jackson because of the aggressive way the president had used his powers of appointment and the veto, but he also disagreed with Henry Clay and the northern Whigs about the Bank, protection, and federal internal improvements. Being a states' rights Southerner, he considered such measures unconstitutional. Nevertheless, he was prepared to cooperate with Clay as the leader of what he called the "more immediate representatives" of the people, the members of Congress. But he was not prepared to be Clay's puppet. He asked all of Harrison's Cabinet to remain in office.

TYLER'S TROUBLES

Tyler and Clay did not get along, and for this Clay was chiefly to blame. He behaved in an overbearing manner that was out of keeping with his nature, probably because he resented having been passed over by the

▲ John Tyler posed for a daguerreotypist about 1850, after he had retired from public life. Never fully committed to the cause of the party that put him in power, he proved to be an ineffective president.

Whigs in 1840. (When news of Harrison's nomination reached him in Washington, he was half drunk. His face darkened. "I am the most unfortunate man in the history of parties," he said, "always run . . . when sure to be defeated, and now betrayed for a nomination when I, or anyone, would be sure of an election.") He considered himself the real head of the Whig party and intended to exercise his leadership.

In Congress, Clay announced a comprehensive program that ignored Tyler's states' rights view of the Constitution. Most important was his plan to set up a new Bank of the United States. A bill to repeal the Independent Treasury Act caused no difficulty, but when Congress passed a new Bank bill, Tyler vetoed it. The entire Cabinet except Secretary of State Daniel Webster thereupon resigned in protest.

Abandoned by the Whigs, Tyler attempted to build a party of his own. He failed to do so, and for the remainder of his term the political squabbling in Washington was continuous. Clay wanted to distribute the proceeds from land sales to the states, presumably to bolster their sagging finances but actually to reduce federal revenues in order to justify raising the tariff. To win western votes for distribution, he

agreed to support the Preemption Act of 1841 legalizing the right of squatters to occupy unsurveyed land and to buy it later at $1.25 an acre without bidding for it at auction. However, the Southerners insisted on an amendment pledging that distribution would be stopped if the tariff were raised above the 20 percent level, and when the Whigs blithely tried to push a high tariff through Congress without repealing the Distribution Act, Tyler vetoed the bill. Finally, the Distribution Act was repealed and Tyler signed the new Tariff Act of 1842, raising duties to about the levels of 1832.

THE WEBSTER-ASHBURTON TREATY

Webster's decision to remain in the Cabinet was motivated in part by his desire to settle the boundary between Maine and New Brunswick. The intent of the peace treaty of 1783 had been to award the United States all land in the area drained by rivers flowing into the Atlantic rather than into the St. Lawrence, but the wording was obscure and the old maps conflicting. In 1842 the British sent a new minister, Lord Ashburton, to the United States to try to settle all outstanding disputes. Ashburton and Webster easily worked out a compromise boundary. The British needed only a small part of the territory to build a military road connecting Halifax and Quebec. Webster, who thought any settlement desirable simply to eliminate a possible cause of war, willingly agreed.

The problem of placating Maine and Massachusetts, which wanted every acre of the land in dispute, Webster solved in an extraordinary manner. It was known that during the peace negotiations ending the Revolution, Franklin had marked the boundary between Maine and Canada on a map with a heavy red line, but no one could find the Franklin map. Webster obtained an old map of the area and had someone mark off in red a line that followed the British version of the boundary. He showed this document to representatives of Maine and Massachusetts, convincing them that they had better agree to his compromise before the British got wind of it and demanded the whole region! It later came out that the British had a true copy of the Franklin map, which showed that the entire area rightfully belonged to the United States.

Nevertheless, Webster's generosity made excellent sense. Lord Ashburton, gratified by having obtained the strategic territory, made concessions elsewhere along the Canadian and American border. British dependence on foreign foodstuffs was increasing; America's need for British capital was rising. War, or even unsettled affairs, would have injured vital business relations and produced no compensating gains.

THE TEXAS QUESTION

The settlement with Great Britain won support in every section of the United States, but the same could not be said for Tyler's attempt to annex the Republic of Texas, for this involved the question of slavery. In the Transcontinental Treaty of 1819 with Spain, the boundary of the United States had been drawn in such a way as to exclude Texas. This seemed unimportant at the time, yet within months of the treaty's ratification in February 1821, Americans led by Stephen F. Austin had begun to settle in the area. Almost simultaneously Mexico threw off the last vestiges of Spanish rule.

Cotton flourished on the fertile Texas plains, and for a time, the new Mexican authorities offered free land and something approaching local autonomy to groups of settlers from the United States. By 1830 there were some 20,000 white Americans in Texas, about 2000 slaves, and only a few thousand Mexicans.

President John Quincy Adams had offered Mexico $1 million for Texas, and Jackson was willing to pay $5 million, but Mexico would not sell. Nevertheless, by the late 1820s, the flood of American settlers was giving the Mexican authorities second thoughts. The immigrants apparently felt no loyalty to Mexico. Most were Protestants, though Mexican law required that all immigrants be Catholics; few attempted to learn more than a few words of Spanish. When Mexico outlawed slavery in 1829, American settlers evaded the law by "freeing" their slaves and then signing them to lifetime contracts as indentured servants. In 1830 Mexico prohibited further immigration of Americans into Texas, though again the law proved impossible to enforce.

As soon as the Mexican government began to restrict them, the Texans began to seek independence. In 1835 a series of skirmishes escalated into a full-scale rebellion. The Mexican president, Antonio López de Santa Anna, marched north with

▲ *The Fall of the Alamo*, by Robert Onderdonk, commemorating one of the legends of Texan—and American—history. Though valuable for propaganda purposes, the heroic defense of the Alamo was a military debacle. On learning that the entire force had been wiped out, Sam Houston, commander of the Texans, railed against his commanders at the Alamo for allowing their men to be "forted up" and destroyed.

6000 soldiers to subdue the rebels. Late in February 1836 he reached San Antonio.

Travis, *Letter from the Alamo*

A force of 187 men under Colonel William B. Travis held the city. They took refuge behind the stout walls of a former mission called the Alamo. For ten days they beat off Santa Anna's assaults, inflicting terrible casualties on the attackers. Finally, on March 6, the Mexicans breached and scaled the walls. Once inside they killed everyone, even the wounded. Among the dead were the legendary Davy Crockett and Jim Bowie, inventor of the Bowie knife.

After the Alamo and a similar slaughter at another garrison at Goliad, southeast of San Antonio, peaceful settlement of the dispute between Texas and Mexico was impossible. Meanwhile, on March 2, 1836, Texas had declared its independence. Sam Houston, a former congressman and governor of Tennessee and an experienced Indian fighter, was placed in charge of the rebel army. For a time Houston retreated before Santa Anna's troops, who greatly outnumbered his own. At the San Jacinto

▲ This portrait, Davy Crockett's favorite of himself, emphasizes his refinement. It is at odds with the rough-hewn, bawdy frontiersman of Crockett lore, spread especially through dime novels read mostly by middle-class boys.

River he took a stand. On April 21, 1836, shouting "Forward! Charge! Remember the Alamo! Remember Goliad!" his troops routed the Mexican army, which soon retreated across the Rio Grande. In October, Houston was elected president of the Republic of Texas, and a month later a plebiscite revealed that an overwhelming majority favored annexation by the United States.

President Jackson hesitated. To take Texas might lead to war with Mexico. Assuredly it would stir up the slavery controversy. On his last day in office he recognized the republic, but he made no move to accept it into the Union, nor did his successor, Van Buren. Texas thereupon went its own way, which involved developing friendly ties with Great Britain. An independent Texas suited British tastes perfectly, for it could provide an alternative supply of raw cotton and a market for manufactures unfettered by tariffs.

These events caused alarm in the United States, especially among Southerners, who dreaded the possibility that a Texas dominated by Great Britain might abolish slavery. As a Southerner, Tyler shared these feelings; as a beleaguered politician, spurned by the Whigs and held in contempt by most Democrats, he saw in annexation a chance to revive his fortunes. When Webster resigned as secretary of state in 1843, Tyler replaced him with a fellow Virginian, Abel P. Upshur, whom he ordered to seek a treaty of annexation. The South was eager to take Texas, and in the West and even the Northeast the patriotic urge to add such a magnificent new territory to the national domain was great. Counting noses, Upshur convinced himself that the Senate would approve annexation by the necessary two-thirds majority. He negotiated a treaty in February 1844, but before he could sign it he was killed by the accidental explosion of a cannon on USS *Princeton* during a weapons demonstration.

To ensure the winning of Texas, Tyler appointed John C. Calhoun secretary of state. This was a blunder; by then Calhoun was so closely associated with the South and with slavery that his appointment alienated thousands of Northerners who might otherwise have welcomed annexation. Suddenly Texas became a hot political issue. Clay and Van Buren, who seemed assured of the 1844 Whig and Democratic presidential nominations, promptly announced that they opposed annexation, chiefly on the ground that it would probably lead to war with Mexico. With a national election in the offing, northern and western senators refused to vote for annexation, and in June the Senate rejected the treaty, 35 to 16. The Texans were angry and embarrassed, the British eager again to take advantage of the situation.

MANIFEST DESTINY

The Senate, Clay, and Van Buren had all misinterpreted public opinion. John C. Calhoun, whose world was so far removed from that of the average citizen, in this case came much closer to comprehending the mood of the country than any of its other leaders.

For two centuries Americans had been gradually conquering a continent. The first colonists had envisaged a domain extending from the Atlantic to the Pacific, although they had not realized the immensity of the New World. By the time their descendants came to appreciate its size, they had been chastened by the experience of battling the Indians for possession of the land and then laboriously developing it. The Revolution and its aftermath of nationalism greatly stimulated expansion, and then, before the riches of trans-Appalachia had even been inventoried, Jefferson had stunned the country with the purchase of Louisiana, an area so large that the mere thought of it left Americans giddy.

The westward march from the seventeenth century to the 1840s had seemed fraught with peril, the prize golden but attainable only through patient labor and fearful hardships. Wild animals and wild men, mighty forests and mighty foreign powers beset the path. John Adams wrote of "conquering" the West "from the trees and rocks and wild beasts." He was "enflamed" by the possibilities of "that vast scene which is opening in the West," but to win it the United States would have to "march *intrepidly* on."

Quite rapidly (as historians measure time) the atmosphere changed. Each year of national growth increased the power and confidence of the people, and every forward step revealed a wider horizon. Now the West seemed a ripe apple, to be picked almost casually. Where pioneers had once stood in awe before the majesty of the Blue Ridge, then hesitated to venture from the protective shadows of the forest into the open prairies of Illinois, they now shrugged their shoulders at great deserts and began to talk of the Rocky Mountains as "mere molehills" along the road to the Pacific. After 200 years of westward expansion had brought them as far as Missouri and Iowa, Americans perceived their destined goal. *The whole continent was to be theirs!* Theirs to exploit, and theirs to make into one mighty nation, a land of opportunity, a showcase to display the virtues of democratic institutions, living proof that Americans were indeed God's chosen people. A New York journalist, John L. O'Sullivan, captured the new mood in a sentence. Nothing must interfere, he wrote in 1845, with "the fulfillment of our *manifest destiny* to overspread the continent allotted by Providence for the free development of our yearly multiplying millions."

The expansion, stimulated by the natural growth of the population and by a revived flood of immigration, was going on in every section and with little regard for political boundaries. New settlers rolled westward in hordes. Between 1830 and 1835, some 10,000 entered "foreign" Texas, and this was a trickle compared to what the early 1840s were to bring. The politicians did not sense the new mood in 1844; even Calhoun, who saw the acquisition of Texas as part of a broader program, was thinking of balancing sectional interests rather than of national expansion.

LIFE ON THE TRAIL

The romantic myths attached by later generations to this mighty human tide have obscured the adjustments forced on the pioneers and focused attention on the least significant of the dangers they faced and the hardships they endured. For example, Indians could of course be deadly enemies, but pioneers were more likely to complain that the Indians they encountered were dirty, lazy, and pitiably poor than to worry about the danger of Indian attack. Women tended to fear their strangeness, not their actual behavior. One reported that Indian men were commonly "guiltless of clothing."

The greater dangers were accidents on the trail, particularly to children, and also unsanitary conditions and exposure to the elements. "Going west" had always been laborious, but in the 1840s the distances covered were longer by far and the comforts and conveniences of "civilization" that had to be left behind, being more extensive than those available to earlier generations, tended to be more painful to surrender.

Travel on the plains west of the Mississippi was especially taxing for women. Some assumed tasks traditionally performed by men. "I keep close to my gun and dog," a woman from Illinois wrote in her diary. But most found the experience disillusioning. Guidebooks promised them that "regular exercise, in the open air . . . gives additional vigor and strength." But the books did not prepare women for having to collect dried buffalo dung for fuel, for the heat and choking dust of summer, for enduring a week of steady rain, for the monotony, the dirt, the cramped quarters. Caring for an infant or a two-year-old in a wagon could be torture week after week on the trail.

In their letters and journals pioneer women mostly complained of being bone weary. "It is impossible to keep anything clean," one recorded, and it is not hard to envisage the difficulty of doing so while

DOCUMENT

Geer, Oregon Trail Journal

► *text continues on page 324*

Mapping
the Past

Fertility and the Frontier

In 1798 English philosopher Thomas Malthus remarked that the sudden population increase in the United States was "probably without parallel in history." This he attributed to the "extreme cheapness of good land." He reasoned that while the cost of farmland in Europe obliged couples in Europe to marry late and curb sexual desires, frontier couples in the United States, who needed more hands to farm its vast open spaces, married earlier and had many children.

The census of 1800 provided some statistical foundation for Malthus's assertions. It showed that the average white

▲ John Kleeb and his wife are posed with their seven children in Custer County, Nebraska (1880s); all of the children are young; more siblings likely followed. On the frontier, where labor was scarce, even young children could soon earn their keep.

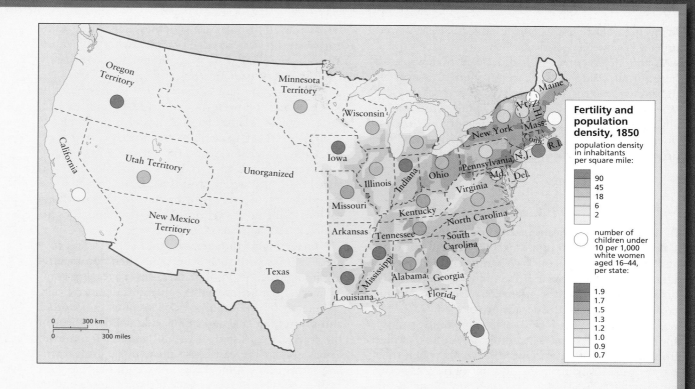

Fertility and population density, 1850

population density in inhabitants per square mile:
- 90
- 45
- 18
- 6
- 2

○ number of children under 10 per 1,000 white women aged 16–44, per state:

- 1.9
- 1.7
- 1.5
- 1.3
- 1.2
- 1.0
- 0.9
- 0.7

woman had many children—on the average, seven. Moreover, census data confirmed that in the frontier regions, where cheap land was most plentiful, women had more children than their counterparts in the more congested East. This geographic gradient—high fertility in the western states, low in New England and the Northeast—persisted during the nineteenth century.

The map "Fertility and Population Density, 1850" *(above)* shows that white women in the most densely populated states, especially New England, had the lowest fertility levels while those in the western states had the highest fertility levels. For example, women between the ages of 16 and 44 in New England had, on the average, fewer than one child under the age of 10; conversely, women in the Oregon Territory, as well as Texas, Louisiana, Arkansas, Iowa, Indiana, Mississippi, Georgia, and Florida had twice as many (2.15) young children as their New England counterparts. (Comparable data are unavailable for African American mothers.)

While this map seems to confirm a direct relationship between frontier life and fertility, a closer examination of the census data suggests the salience of other factors, too. For example, Missouri and Wisconsin were sparsely settled, and yet their fertility rates were lower than Indiana, which was relatively well developed.

Historians have observed that in the late eighteenth and early nineteenth centuries an ideology of domesticity confined women to the home even as it enshrined their role as custodians of the young. Mothers intent on guiding each child's moral development, and fathers intent on saving enough money to establish a foothold in the emerging middle class,

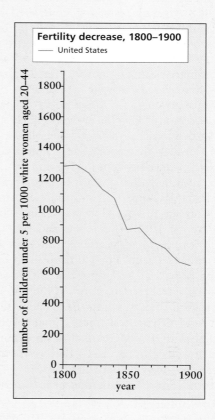

Fertility decrease, 1800–1900

— United States

together decided to limit their families by marrying later, by abstaining from sexual relations for long periods, and perhaps by practicing contraception.

living for weeks on end on the trail. "Felt very tired indeed—went to bed early," was the typical woman's diary entry. "Oh dear," another wrote in her journal, "I do so want to get there, it is now almost four months since we have slept in a house." What sort of a house a pioneer family would actually sleep in when they reached their destination is a question this woman did not record, which was probably fortunate for her peace of mind.

CALIFORNIA AND OREGON

By 1840 many Americans had settled far to the west in California, which was unmistakably Mexican territory, and in the Oregon country, jointly claimed by the United States and Great Britain; and it was to these distant regions that the pioneers were going in increasing numbers as the decade progressed. California was a sparsely settled land of some 7000 Spanish-speaking ranchers and a handful of "Anglo" settlers from the United States. Until the 1830s, when their estates were broken up by the anticlerical Mexican government, 21 Catholic missions, stretching north from San Diego to San Francisco, controlled more than 30,000 Indian converts, who were little better off than slaves. Richard Henry Dana, a Harvard College student, sailed around South America to California as an ordinary seaman on the brig *Pilgrim* in 1834. His account of that voyage in *Two Years Before the Mast* (1840) contains a fine description of what life was like in the region: "There is no working class (the Indians being practically serfs and doing all the hard work) and every rich man looks like a grandee, and every poor scamp like a broken-down gentleman."

Oregon, a vaguely defined area between California and Russian Alaska, proved still more alluring to Americans. Captain Robert Gray had sailed up the Columbia River in 1792, and Lewis and Clark had visited the region on their great expedition. In 1811 John Jacob Astor's Pacific Fur Company had established trading posts on the Columbia. Two decades later Methodist, Presbyterian, and Catholic missionaries began to find their way into the Willamette Valley, a green land of rich soil, mild climate, and tall forests teeming with game. Gradually a small number of settlers followed, until by 1840 there were about 500 Americans in the Willamette area.

In the early 1840s, fired by the spirit of manifest destiny, the country suddenly burned with "Oregon fever." In dozens upon dozens of towns, societies were founded to collect information and organize groups to make the march to the Pacific. Land hunger (stimulated by glowing reports from the scene) drew the new migrants most powerfully, but the patriotic concept of manifest destiny gave the trek

across the 2000 miles of wilderness separating Oregon from the western edge of American settlement in Missouri the character of a crusade. In 1843 nearly 1000 pioneers made the long trip.

The Oregon Trail began at the western border of Missouri and followed the Kansas River and the perverse, muddy Platte ("a mile wide and six inches deep") past Fort Laramie to the Rockies. It crossed the Continental Divide by the relatively easy South Pass, veered south to Fort Bridger, on Mexican soil, and then ran north and west through the valley of the Snake River and eventually, by way of the Columbia, to Fort Vancouver, a British post guarding the entrance to the Willamette Valley.

Over this tortuous path wound the canvas-covered caravans with their scouts and their accompanying herds. Each group became a self-governing community on the march, with regulations democratically agreed on "for the purpose of keeping good order and promoting civil and military discipline." Most of the travelers consisted of young families, some from as far away as the east coast cities, more from towns and farms in the Ohio Valley. Few could be classified as poor because the cost of the trip for a family of four was about $600, no small sum at that time. (The faster and less fatiguing trip by ship around South America cost about $600 per person.)

For large groups Indians posed no great threat (though constant vigilance was necessary), but the five-month trip was full of labor, discomfort, and uncertainty. "It became so monotonous after a while that I would have welcomed an Indian fight if awake," one man wrote. And at the end lay the regular tasks of pioneering. The spirit of the trailblazers is caught in an entry from the diary of James Nesmith:

> Friday, October 27.—Arrived at Oregon City at the falls of the Willamette.
> Saturday, October 28.—Went to work.

Although many women had doubts about their austere new world—"Nothing can atone for the loss of society of friends," one wrote—others took satisfaction. Another homesteader wrote that "any woman who can stand her own company, can see the beauty of the sunset, loves growing things, and is willing to put in as much time at careful labor as she does over the washtub, will certainly succeed, will have independence, plenty to eat all the time, and a home of her own in the end."

Behind the dreams of the Far West as an American Eden lay the commercial importance of the three major west coast harbors: San Diego, San Francisco, and the Strait of Juan de Fuca leading into Puget Sound. Eastern merchants considered these harbors the keys to the trade of the Orient. That San Diego

▲ **Trails West**
The Old Spanish Trail was the earliest of the trails west. Part of it was mapped in 1776 by a Franciscan missionary. The Santa Fe Trail came into use after 1823. The Oregon Trail was pioneered by trappers and missionaries. The Mormon Trail was first traversed in 1847, while the Oxbow Route, developed under a federal mail contract, was used from 1858 to 1861.

and San Francisco were Mexican and the Puget Sound district was claimed by Great Britain only heightened their desire to possess them. As early as 1835, Jackson tried to buy the San Francisco region. Even Calhoun called San Francisco the future New York of the Pacific and proposed buying all of California from Mexico.

THE ELECTION OF 1844

In the spring of 1844 expansion did not seem likely to affect the presidential election. The Whigs nominated Clay unanimously and ignored Texas in their party platform. When the Democrats gathered in convention at Baltimore in May, Van Buren appeared to have the nomination in his pocket. He too wanted to keep

Texas out of the campaign. John C. Calhoun, however, was determined to make Texas a campaign issue.

That a politician of Van Buren's caliber, controlling the party machinery, could be upset at a national convention seemed unthinkable. But upset he was, for the southern delegates rallied round the Calhoun policy of taking Texas to save it for slavery. "I can beat Clay and Van Buren put together on this issue," Calhoun boasted. "They are behind the age." With the aid of a few northern expansionists the Southerners forced through a rule requiring that a candidate must be approved by a two-thirds majority. Van Buren could not muster that much support. After a brief deadlock, a "dark horse," James K. Polk of Tennessee, swept the convention.

Polk was a good Jacksonian; his supporters called him "Young Hickory." He opposed high tariffs and

DEBATING THE PAST

Did the frontier change women's roles? Ada McColl here gathers buffalo chips to be burned for fuel. Women were missing from Frederick Jackson Turner's famous argument (1893) on the centrality of the frontier to American history. Subsequent scholars provided some anecdotal accounts of women on the frontier, but it was not until the 1970s that scholars flocked to the subject. John Mack Faragher (1979) concluded that women on the overland trail had not experienced feminist liberation but had instead been exploited. Women worked ceaselessly—preparing meals, caring for children, cleaning clothes—in nearly impossible conditions. That same year Julie Roy Jeffrey added that husbands still made the "major decisions." Equally important, frontier women themselves endorsed the "cult of true womanhood": They sought to civilize the frontier. Sandra L. Myres (1982), on the other hand, argued that while frontier women accepted traditional women's roles, they also sought to "enlarge the scope of women's place" and in so doing undermined traditions.

Frederick Jackson Turner, "The Significance of the Frontier in American History" (1893), John Mack Faragher, *Women and Men on the Overland Trail* (1979), Julie Roy Jeffrey, *Frontier Women* (1979), Sandra L. Myres, *Westering Women and the Frontier Experience* (1982).

was dead set against establishing another national bank. But he believed in taking Texas, and he favored expansion generally. To mollify Van Buren's supporters, the convention nominated Senator Silas Wright of New York for vice president, but Wright was Van Buren's friend and equally opposed to annexation. When the word was flashed to him in Washington over the new "magnetic telegraph" that Samuel F. B. Morse had just installed between the convention hall in Baltimore and the Capitol, he refused to run. The delegates then picked George M. Dallas of Pennsylvania, who favored annexation of Texas. The Democratic platform demanded that Texas be "reannexed" (implying that it had been part of the Louisiana Purchase) and that all of Oregon be "reoccupied" (suggesting that the joint occupation of the region with Great Britain, which had been agreed to in the Convention of 1818, be abrogated).

Texas was now in the campaign. When Clay sensed the new expansionist sentiment of the voters, he tried to hedge on his opposition to annexation, but by doing so he probably lost as many votes as he gained. The election was extremely close. The campaign followed the pattern established in 1840, with stress on parades, mass meetings, and slogans. Polk carried the country by only 38,000 of 2.7 million votes. In the Electoral College the vote was 170 to 105.

The decisive factor in the contest was the Liberty party, an antislavery splinter group organized in 1840. Only 62,000 voters supported Liberty party candidate James G. Birney, a "reformed" Kentucky slaveholder, but nearly 16,000 of them lived in New York, most in the western part of the state, a Whig stronghold. Since Polk carried New York by barely 5000 votes, the votes cast for Birney probably cost Clay the state. Had Clay won New York's 36 electoral votes, he would have been elected with 141 electoral votes to Polk's 134.

Polk's victory was nevertheless taken as a mandate for expansion. Tyler promptly called on Congress to take Texas by joint resolution, which would avoid the necessity of obtaining a two-thirds majority in the Senate. This was done a few days before Tyler left the White House. Under the resolution, if the new state agreed, as many as four new states might be carved from its territory. Polk accepted this arrangement, and in December 1845 Texas became a state.

POLK AS PRESIDENT

President Polk, a slightly built, erect man with grave, steel-gray eyes, was approaching 50 years of age. His mind was not of the first order, for he was too tense and calculating to allow his intellect free rein, but he was an efficient, hard worker with a strong will and a tough skin, qualities that stood him in good stead in the White House, and he made politics his whole life. It was typical of the man that he developed a special technique of handshaking in order better to cope with the interminable reception lines that every leader has to endure. "When I observed a strong man approaching," he once explained, "I generally took advantage of him by . . . seizing him by the tip of his fingers, giving him a hearty shake, and thus preventing him from getting a full grip upon me." In four years in office he was away from his desk in Washington for a total of only six weeks.

Polk was uncommonly successful in doing what he set out to do as president. He persuaded Congress to lower the tariff of 1842 and to restore the independent treasury. He opposed federal internal improvements and managed to have his way. He made himself the spokesman of American expansion by committing himself to obtaining, in addition to Texas, both Oregon and the great Southwest. Here again, he succeeded.

Oregon was the first order of business. In his inaugural address Polk stated the American claim to the entire region in the plainest terms, but he informed the British minister in Washington, Richard Pakenham, that he would accept a boundary following the 49th parallel to the Pacific. Pakenham rejected this proposal without submitting it to London, and Polk thereupon decided to insist again on the whole area. When Congress met in December 1845, he asked for authority to give the necessary one year's notice for abrogating the 1818 treaty of joint occupation. "The only way to treat John Bull," he told one congressman, "was to look him straight in the eye." Following considerable discussion, Congress complied and in May 1846 Polk notified Great Britain that he intended to terminate the joint occupation.

DOCUMENT

John O'Sullivan, "Annexation"

The British then decided to compromise. Officials of the Hudson's Bay Company had become alarmed by the rapid growth of the American settlement in the Willamette Valley. By 1845 there were some 5000 people there, whereas the country north of the Columbia contained no more than 750 British subjects. A clash between the groups could have but one result. The company decided to shift its base from the Columbia to Vancouver Island. And British experts outside the company reported that the Oregon country could not possibly be defended in case of war. Thus, when Polk accompanied the one-year notice with a hint that he would again consider a compromise, the British foreign secretary, Lord Aberdeen, hastily suggested Polk's earlier proposal, dividing the Oregon territory along the 49th parallel. Polk, abandoning his belligerent attitude, agreed.

▲ "This Is the House That Polk Built" is the title of this 1846 cartoon directed against the president. Polk hatches his eggs and schemes for territorial expansion, reduction of the tariff, and fame—aims the cartoonist saw as flimsy as a house of cards. Contrary to the cartoonist's view, Polk succeeded in his expansion goals.

The treaty followed that line from the Rockies to Puget Sound, but Vancouver Island, which extends below the line, was left entirely to the British, so that both nations retained free use of the Strait of Juan de Fuca. Although some northern Democrats accused Polk of treachery because he had failed to fight for all of Oregon, the treaty so obviously accorded with the national interest that the Senate approved it by a large majority in June 1846. Polk was then free to take up the Texas question in earnest.

WAR WITH MEXICO

One reason for the popularity of the Oregon compromise was that the country was already at war with Mexico and wanted no trouble with Great Britain. The war had broken out in large measure because of the expansionist spirit, and the confidence born of its overwhelming advantages of size and wealth certainly encouraged the United States to bully Mexico. In addition, Mexico had defaulted on debts owed the United States, which caused some people to suggest using force to obtain the money. But Mexican pride was also involved. Texas had been independent for the better part of a decade, and Mexico had made no

► **The War with Mexico, 1846–1848**

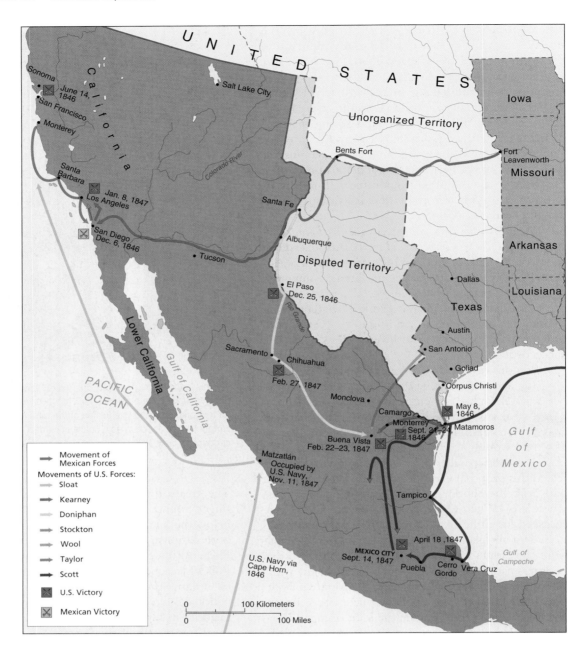

serious effort to reconquer it; nevertheless, Mexico never recognized its independence and promptly broke off diplomatic relations when the United States annexed the republic.

Polk then ordered General Zachary Taylor into Texas to defend the border. However, the location of that border was in dispute. Texas claimed the Rio Grande; Mexico insisted that the boundary was the Nueces River, which emptied into the Gulf of Mexico about 150 miles to the north. Taylor reached the Nueces in July 1845 with about 1500 troops and crossed into the disputed territory. He stopped on the southern bank at Corpus Christi, not wishing

to provoke the Mexicans by marching to the Rio Grande.

In November, Polk sent an envoy, John Slidell, on a secret mission to Mexico to try to obtain the disputed territory by negotiation. He authorized Slidell to cancel the Mexican debt in return for recognition of the annexation of Texas and acceptance of the Rio Grande boundary. The president also empowered Slidell to offer as much as $30 million if Mexico would sell the United States all or part of New Mexico and California.

It would probably have been to Mexico's advantage, at least in the short run, to have made a deal with Slidell. The area Polk wanted, lying in the path of American expansion, was likely to be engulfed as Texas had been, without regard for the actions of the American or Mexican governments. But the Mexican government refused to receive Slidell. Amid a wave of anti-American feeling, a military coup occurred and General Mariano Paredes, the new head of state, promptly reaffirmed his country's claim to all of Texas. Slidell returned to Washington convinced that the Mexicans would not give an inch until they had been "chastised."

Polk had already ordered Taylor to advance to the Rio Grande. By late March 1846 the army, swelled to about 4000, had taken up positions near the Mexican town of Matamoros. The Mexicans crossed the river on April 25 and attacked an American mounted patrol. They were driven back easily, but when news of the fighting reached Washington, Polk asked Congress to declare war. He treated the matter as a *fait accompli*: "War exists," he stated flatly. Congress accepted this reasoning and without actually declaring war voted to raise and supply an additional 50,000 troops.

From the first battle, the outcome of the Mexican War was never in doubt. At Palo Alto, north of the Rio Grande, 2300 Americans scattered a Mexican force more than twice their number. Then, hotly pursuing, 1700 Americans routed 7500 Mexicans at Resaca de la Palma. Fewer than 50 United States soldiers lost their lives in these engagements, while Mexican losses in killed, wounded, and captured exceeded 1000. Within a week of the outbreak of hostilities, the Mexicans had been driven across the Rio Grande and General Taylor had his troops firmly established on the southern bank.

The Mexican army was poorly equipped and, despite a surfeit of high-ranking officers, poorly led. The well-supplied American forces had a hard core of youthful West Pointers eager to make their reputations and regulars trained in Indian warfare to provide the leadership needed to turn volunteer soldiers into first-rate fighting men. Yet Mexico was a large, rugged country with few decent roads; conquering it proved to be a formidable task.

To the Halls of Montezuma

President Polk insisted not only on directing grand strategy (he displayed real ability as a military planner) but on supervising hundreds of petty details, down to the purchase of mules and the promotion of enlisted men. But he allowed party considerations to control his choice of generals. This partisanship caused unnecessary turmoil in army ranks. He wanted, as

Thomas Hart Benton said, "a small war, just large enough to require a treaty of peace, and not large enough to make military reputations dangerous for the presidency."

Unfortunately for Polk, both Taylor and Winfield Scott, the commanding general in Washington, were Whigs. Polk, who tended to suspect the motives of anyone who disagreed with him, feared that one or the other would make political capital of his popularity as a military leader. The examples of his hero, Jackson, and of General Harrison loomed large in Polk's thinking.

Polk's attitude was narrow, almost unpatriotic, but not unrealistic. Zachary Taylor was not a brilliant soldier. He had joined the army in 1808 and made it his whole life. He cared so little for politics that he had never bothered to cast a ballot in an election. Polk believed that he lacked the "grasp of mind" necessary for high command, and General Scott complained of his "comfortable, laborsaving contempt for learning of every kind." But Taylor commanded the love and respect of his men (they called him "Old Rough and Ready" and even "Zack"), and he knew how to deploy them in the field. He had won another victory against a Mexican force three times larger than his own at Buena Vista in February 1847.

The dust had barely settled on the field of Buena Vista when Whig politicians began to pay Taylor court. "Great expectations and great consequences rest upon you," a Kentucky politician explained to him. "People everywhere begin to talk of converting you into a political leader, when the War is done."

Polk's concern was heightened because domestic opposition to the war was growing. Many Northerners feared that the war would lead to the expansion of slavery. Others—among them an obscure Illinois congressman named Abraham Lincoln—felt that Polk

▲ This 1846 daguerreotype is the earliest known American war photograph. U.S. General John E. Wood poses with his staff in Saltillo, Mexico.

▲ The landing of Scott's army near Veracruz on March 9, 1847. Veracruz surrendered within several weeks. Scott then advanced to the interior and encountered the Mexican army, under Santa Anna, dug in along the National Road. Scott seized two hills and outflanked the Mexicans. Mexico City fell to Scott in September.

DOCUMENT

Thomas Corwin, "Against the Mexican War"

had misled Congress about the original outbreak of fighting and that the United States was the aggressor. The farther from the Rio Grande one went in the United States, the less popular "Mr. Polk's war" became; in New England opposition was almost as widespread as it had been to "Mr. Madison's war" in 1812.

Polk's design for prosecuting the war consisted of three parts. First, he would clear the Mexicans from Texas and occupy the northern provinces of Mexico. Second, he would take possession of California and New Mexico. Finally, he would march on Mexico City. Proceeding west from the Rio Grande, Taylor swiftly overran Mexico's northern provinces. In June 1846, American settlers in the Sacramento Valley seized Sonoma and raised the Bear Flag of the Republic of California. Another group, headed by Captain John C. Frémont, leader of an American exploring party that happened to be in the area, clashed with the Mexican authorities around Monterey,

California, and then joined with the Sonoma rebels. A naval squadron under Commodore John D. Sloat captured Monterey and San Francisco in July 1846, and a squadron of cavalry joined the other American units in mopping-up operations around San Diego and Los Angeles. By February 1847 the United States had won control of nearly all of Mexico north of the capital city.

The campaign against Mexico City was the most difficult of the war. Fearful of Taylor's growing popularity and entertaining certain honest misgivings about his ability to oversee a complicated campaign, Polk put Winfield Scott in charge of the offensive. He tried to persuade Congress to make Thomas Hart Benton a lieutenant general so as to have a Democrat in nominal control, but the Senate had the good sense to vote down this absurd proposal.

About Scott's competence no one entertained a doubt. But he seemed even more of a threat to the Democrats than Taylor, because he had political ambitions as well as military ability. In 1840 the Whigs had considered running him for president. Scion of an old Virginia family, Scott was nearly 6½ feet tall; in uniform his presence was commanding. He was intelligent, even-tempered, and cultivated, if somewhat pompous. After a sound but not spectacular record in the War of 1812, he had added to his reputation by helping modernize military administration and strengthen the professional training of officers. The vast difference between the army of 1812 and that of 1846 was chiefly his doing. On the record, and despite the politics of the situation, Polk had little choice but to give him this command.

Scott landed his army south of Veracruz, Mexico, on March 9, 1847, laid siege to the city, and obtained its surrender in less than three weeks with the loss of only a handful of his 10,000 men. Marching westward through hostile country, he maintained effective discipline, avoiding atrocities that might have inflamed the countryside against him. Finding his way blocked by well-placed artillery and a large army at Cerro Gordo, where the National Road rose steeply toward the central highlands, Scott outflanked the Mexican position and then carried it by storm, capturing more than 3000 prisoners and much equipment. By mid-May he had advanced to Puebla, only 80 miles southeast of Mexico City.

After delaying until August for the arrival of reinforcements, he pressed on, won two hard-fought victories at the outskirts of the capital, and on September 14 hammered his way into the city. In every engagement the American troops had been outnumbered, yet they always exacted a far heavier toll from the defenders than they themselves were forced to pay. In the fighting on the edge of Mexico City, for example, Scott's army sustained about 1000 casualties, for the Mexicans defended their capital bravely. But 4000 Mexicans were killed or wounded in the engagements, and 3000 (including eight generals, two of them former presidents of the republic) were taken prisoner. No less an authority than the Duke of Wellington, the conqueror of Napoleon, called Scott's campaign the most brilliant of modern times.

THE TREATY OF GUADALUPE HIDALGO

The Mexicans were thoroughly beaten, but they refused to accept the situation. As soon as the news of the capture of Veracruz reached Washington, Polk sent Nicholas P. Trist, chief clerk of the State Department, to accompany Scott's army and to act as peace commissioner after the fall of Mexico City. Trist possessed impeccable credentials as a Democrat, for he

had married a granddaughter of Thomas Jefferson and had served for a time as secretary to Andrew Jackson. Long residence as United States consul at Havana had given him an excellent command of Spanish.

Trist joined Scott at Veracruz in May. The two men took an instant dislike to each other. Scott considered it a "personal dishonor" to be asked to defer to what he considered a State Department flunky, and his feelings were not salved when Trist sent him an officious 30-page letter discoursing on the nature of his assignment. However, Scott was eager to end the war and realized that a petty quarrel with the president's emissary would not advance that objective. Trist fell ill, and Scott sent him a jar of guava marmalade; after that they became good friends.

Because of the confused state of affairs following the fall of Mexico City, Trist was unable to open negotiations with Mexican peace commissioners until January 1848. Polk, unable to understand the delay, became impatient. Originally he had authorized Trist to pay $30 million for New Mexico, Upper and Lower California, and the right of transit across Mexico's narrow isthmus of Tehuantepec. Now, observing the disorganized state of Mexican affairs, he began to consider demanding more territory and paying less for it. He summoned Trist home.

▲ Winfield Scott, hero of the Mexican War, glares at the observer. Timothy Dwight Johnson, a biographer, wrote that Scott's "ambition fed his arrogance and, in turn, his arrogance fed his ambition." Indisputably, Scott was well fed.

Trist, with Scott's backing, ignored the order. He realized that unless a treaty was arranged soon, the Mexican government might disintegrate, leaving no one in authority to sign a treaty. He dashed off a 65-page letter to the president, in effect refusing to be recalled, and proceeded to negotiate. Early in February the Treaty of Guadalupe Hidalgo was completed. By its terms Mexico accepted the Rio Grande as the boundary of Texas and ceded New Mexico and Upper California to the United States. In return the United States agreed to pay Mexico $15 million and to take on the claims of American citizens against Mexico, which by that time amounted to another $3.25 million.

When he learned that Trist had ignored his orders, the president seethed. Trist was "contemptibly base," he thought, an "impudent and unqualified scoundrel." He ordered Trist placed under arrest and fired from his State Department job.[1] Yet Polk had no choice but to submit the treaty to the Senate, for to have insisted on more territory would have meant more fighting, and the war had become increasingly unpopular. The relatively easy military victory made some people ashamed that their country was crushing a weaker neighbor. Abolitionists, led by William Lloyd Garrison, called it an "invasion . . . waged solely for the detestable and horrible purpose of extending and perpetuating American slavery." The Senate, subject to the same pressures as the president, ratified the agreement by a vote of 38 to 14.

THE FRUITS OF VICTORY: FURTHER ENLARGEMENT OF THE UNITED STATES

United States Territorial Expansion in the 1850s

The Mexican War, won quickly and at relatively small cost in lives and money, brought huge territorial gains. The Pacific coast from south of San Diego to the 49th parallel and all the land between the coast and the Continental Divide had become the property of the American people. Immense amounts of labor and capital would have to be invested before this new territory could be made to yield its bounty, but the country clearly had the capacity to accomplish the job.

In this atmosphere came what seemed a sign from the heavens. In January 1848, while Scott's veterans rested on their victorious arms in Mexico City, a mechanic named James W. Marshall was building a sawmill on the American River in the Sacramento

---

[1]Trist was retired to private life without being paid for his time in Mexico. In 1870, when he was on his deathbed, Congress finally awarded him $14,299.20.

Valley east of San Francisco. One day, while supervising the deepening of the millrace, he noticed a few flecks of yellow in the bed of the stream. These he gathered up and tested. They were pure gold.

Other strikes had been made in California and been treated skeptically or as matters of local curiosity; since the days of Jamestown, too many pioneers had run fruitlessly in search of El Dorado, and too much fool's gold had been passed off as the real thing. Yet this discovery produced an international sensation. The gold was real and plentiful—$200 million of it was extracted in four years—but equally important was the fact that everyone was ready to believe the news. The gold rush reflected the heady confidence inspired by Guadalupe Hidalgo; it seemed the ultimate justification of manifest destiny. Surely an era of continental prosperity and harmony had dawned.

SLAVERY: THE FIRE BELL IN THE NIGHT RINGS AGAIN

Prosperity came in full measure but harmony did not, for once again expansion brought the nation face to face with the divisive question of slavery. This giant chunk of North America, most of it vacant, its future soon to be determined—should it be slave or free? The question, in one sense, seems hardly worth the national crisis it provoked. Slavery appeared to have little future in New Mexico and California, none in Oregon. Why did the South fight so hard for the right to bring slaves into a region that seemed so poorly suited to their exploitation?

Narrow partisanship provides part of the explanation. In districts where slavery was entrenched, a congressman who zealously defended the institution against the most trivial slight usually found himself a popular hero. In the northern states, the representatives who were vigilant in what they might describe as "freedom's cause" seldom regretted it on election day. But slavery raised a moral question. Most Americans tried to avoid confronting this truth; as patriots they assumed that any sectional issue could be solved by compromise. However, while the majority of whites had little respect for blacks, slave or free, few persons, northern or southern, could look upon the ownership of one human being by another as simply an alternative form of economic organization and argue its merits as they would those of the protective tariff or a national bank. Twist the facts as they might, slavery was either right or it was wrong; being on the whole honest and moral, they could not, having faced that truth, stand by unconcerned while the question was debated.

The question could come up in Congress only indirectly, for the Constitution did not give the federal government any control over slavery in the states. But Congress had complete control in the territories. Therefore the fact that slavery had no future in the Mexican cession was unimportant—in fact, for the foes of slavery, it was an advantage. By attacking slavery where it did not and probably never could exist, they could conceal from the slaveholders—and perhaps even from themselves—their hope ultimately to extinguish the institution.

Slavery had complicated the Texas problem from the start, and it beclouded the future of the Southwest even before the Mexican flag had been stripped from the staffs at Santa Fe and Los Angeles. The northern, Van Burenite wing of the Democratic party had become increasingly uneasy about the proslavery cast of Polk's policies, which were unpopular in their part of the country. Once it became likely that the war would bring new territory into the Union, these Northerners felt compelled to try to check the president and to assure their constituents that they would resist the admission of further slave territory. On August 8, 1846, during the debate on a bill appropriating money for the conduct of the war, Democratic Congressman David Wilmot of Pennsylvania introduced an amendment that provided "as an express and fundamental condition to the acquisition of any territory from the Republic of Mexico" that "neither slavery nor involuntary servitude shall ever exist in any part of said territory, except for crime, whereof the party shall first be duly convicted."

Southerners found the Wilmot Proviso particularly insulting. Nevertheless, it passed the House, where northern congressmen outnumbered southern. But it was defeated in the Senate, where Southerners held the balance. To counter the Proviso, Calhoun, once again serving as senator from South Carolina, introduced resolutions in 1846 arguing that Congress had no right to bar slavery from any territory; because territories belonged to all the states, slave and free, all should have equal rights in them. From this position it was only a step (soon taken) to demanding that Congress guarantee the right of slave owners to bring slaves into the territories and establish federal slave codes in the territories. Most Northerners considered this proposal as repulsive as Southerners found the Wilmot Proviso.

Calhoun's resolutions could never pass the House of Representatives, and Wilmot's Proviso had no chance in the Senate. Yet their very existence threatened the Union; as Senator Benton remarked, they were like the blades of a pair of scissors, ineffective separately, an efficient cutting tool taken together.

To resolve the territorial problem, two compromises were offered. One, eventually backed by President Polk, would extend the Missouri Compromise line to the Pacific. The majority of Southerners were willing to go along with this scheme, but most Northerners would no longer agree to the reservation of *any* new territory for slavery. The other possibility, advocated by Senator Lewis Cass of Michigan, called for organizing new territories without mention of slavery, thus leaving it to local settlers, through their territorial legislatures, to determine their own institutions. Cass's "popular sovereignty," known more vulgarly as "squatter sovereignty," had the superficial merit of appearing to be democratic. Its virtue for the members of Congress, however, was that it allowed them to escape the responsibility of deciding the question themselves.

THE ELECTION OF 1848

One test of strength occurred in August, before the 1848 presidential election. After six months of acrimonious debate, Congress passed a bill barring slavery from Oregon. The test, however, proved little. If it required half a year to settle the question for Oregon, how could an answer ever be found for California and New Mexico? Plainly the time had come, in a democracy, to go to the people. The coming presidential election seemed to provide an ideal opportunity.

The opportunity was missed. The politicians of the parties hedged, fearful of losing votes in one section or another. With the issues blurred, voters had no real choice. That the Whigs should behave in such a manner was perhaps to be expected of the party of "Tippecanoe and Tyler Too," but in 1848 they outdid even their 1840 performance, nominating Zachary Taylor for president. They chose the general despite his lack of political sophistication and after he had flatly refused to state his opinion on any current subject. The party offered no platform. Taylor was a brave man and a fine general; the Democrats had mistreated him; he was a common, ordinary fellow, unpretentious and warmhearted. Such was the Whig "argument." Taylor's contribution to the campaign was so naive as to be pathetic. "I am a Whig, *but not an ultra Whig*. . . . If elected . . . I should feel bound to administer the government untrammeled by party schemes."

The Democratic party had little better to offer. All the drive and zeal characteristic of it in the Jackson period had gradually seeped away. Polk's espousal of Texas's annexation had driven many Northerners from its ranks. James Buchanan of Pennsylvania, Polk's secretary of state, and William L. Marcy of New York, his secretary of war, and others like them—cautious, cynical politicians interested chiefly in getting and holding office—now came to the fore in northern Democratic politics.

The Democratic nominee was Lewis Cass, the father of popular sovereignty, but the party did not endorse that or any other solution to the territorial question. Cass was at least an experienced politician, having been governor of the Michigan Territory, secretary of war, minister to France, and senator. Nevertheless, his approach to life was exemplified by an annoying habit he displayed at Washington social functions: A teetotaler, he would circulate among the guests with a glass in hand, raising it to his lips repeatedly but never swallowing a drop.

The Van Buren wing of the Democratic party was known as the Barnburners to call attention to their radicalism—supposedly they would burn down the barn to get rid of the rats. The Barnburners could not stomach Cass, in part because he was willing to countenance the extension of slavery into new territories, in part because he had led the swing to Polk at the 1844 Democratic convention. Combining with the antislavery Liberty party, they formed the Free Soil party and nominated Van Buren.

Van Buren knew he could not be elected, but he believed the time had come to take a stand. "The minds of nearly all mankind have been penetrated by a conviction of the evils of slavery," the onetime "Fox" and "Magician" declared. The Free Soil party polled nearly 300,000 votes, about 10 percent of the total, in a very dull campaign. Offered a choice between the honest ignorance of Taylor and the cynical opportunism of Cass, the voters—by a narrow margin—chose the former, Taylor receiving 1.36 million votes to Cass's 1.22 million. Taylor carried 8 of the 15 slave states and 7 of the 15 free states, proof that the sectional issue had been avoided.

5000 South Americans, and numbers of Europeans joined the rush.

The rough limits of the gold country had been quickly marked out. For 150 miles and more along the western slope of the Sierra stretched the great mother lode. Along the expanse any stream or canyon, any ancient gravel bed might conceal a treasure in nuggets, flakes, or dust. Armed with pickaxes and shovels, with washing pans, even with knives and spoons, eager prospectors hacked and dug and sifted, each accumulating a hoard, some great, some small, of gleaming yellow metal.

The impact on the region was enormous. Between 1849 and 1860 about 200,000 people, nearly all of them males, crossed the Rockies to California and thousands more reached California by ship via Cape Horn. Almost overnight the Spanish American population was reduced to the status of a minority. Disregarding justice and reason alike, the newcomers from the East, as one observer noted, "regarded every man but a native [North] American as an interloper." They referred to people of Latin American origin as "greasers" and sought by law and by violence to keep them from mining for gold. Even the local Californians (now American citizens) were discriminated against. The few free blacks in California and the several thousand more who came in search of gold were treated no better. As for the far larger Indian population, it was almost wiped out. There were about 150,000 Indians in California in the mid-1840s but only 35,000 in 1860.

THE GOLD RUSH

Burrum, from *Six Months in the Gold Mines*

It was now clear that the question of slavery in the territories had to be faced. The discovery of gold had brought an army of prospectors into California. By the summer of 1848 San Francisco had become almost a ghost town, and an estimated two-thirds of the adult males of Oregon had hastened south to the gold fields. After President Polk confirmed the "extraordinary character" of the strike in his annual message of December 1848, there was no containing the gold seekers. During 1849, some 25,000 Americans made their way to California from the East by ship; more than 55,000 others crossed the continent by overland routes. About 8000 Mexicans,

▲ Gold prospectors used a "long Tom" to wash gold from gravel in a stream. The California gold rush brought mostly men—along with a few women—west in search of their fortunes.

The ethnic conflict was only part of the problem. Rough, hard men, separated from women, lusting for gold in a strange wild country where fortunes could be made in a day, gambled away in an hour, or stolen in an instant—the situation demanded the establishment of a territorial government. President Taylor appreciated this, and in his gruff, simple-hearted way he suggested an uncomplicated answer: admit California directly as a state, letting the Californians decide for themselves about slavery. The rest of the Mexican cession could be formed into another state. No need for Congress, with its angry rivalries, to meddle at all, he believed. In this way the nation could avoid the divisive effects of sectional debate.

The Californians reacted favorably to Taylor's proposal. They were overwhelmingly opposed to slavery, though not for humanitarian reasons. On the contrary, they tended to look on blacks as they did Mexicans and feared that if slavery were permitted, white gold seekers would be disadvantaged. "They would be unable," one delegate to the California constitutional convention predicted, "to compete with the bands of negroes who would be set to work under the direction of capitalists. It would become a monopoly." By October 1849 they had drawn up a constitution that outlawed slavery, and by December the new state government was functioning.

Taylor was the owner of a large plantation and more than 100 slaves; Southerners had assumed (without bothering to ask) that he would fight to keep the territories open to slavery. But being a military man, he was above all a nationalist; he disliked the divisiveness that partisan discussion of the issue was producing. Southerners were horrified by the president's reasoning. To admit California would destroy the balance between free and slave states in the Senate; to allow all the new land to become free would doom the South to wither in a corner of the country, surrounded by hostile free states. Should that happen, how long could slavery sustain itself, even in South Carolina? Radicals were already saying that the South would have to choose between secession and surrender. Taylor's plan played into the hands of extremists.

THE COMPROMISE OF 1850

DOCUMENT

Clay, Speech to the U.S. Senate

This was no longer a squabble over territorial governments. With the Union itself at stake, Henry Clay rose to save the day. He had been as angry and frustrated when the Whigs nominated Taylor as he had been when they passed him over for Harrison. Now, well beyond age 70 and in ill health, he put away his ambition and his resentment and for the last time concentrated his remarkable vision on a great, multifaceted national problem. California must be free and soon admitted to the Union, but the South must have some compensation. For that matter, why not seize the opportunity to settle every outstanding sectional conflict related to slavery? Clay wondered long and hard, drew up a plan, then consulted his old Whig rival Webster and obtained his general approval. On January 29, 1850, he laid his proposal, "founded upon mutual forbearance," before the Senate. A few days later he defended it on the floor of the Senate in the last great speech of his life.

California should be brought directly into the Union as a free state, he argued. The rest of the Southwest should be organized as a territory without mention of slavery: The Southerners would retain the right to bring slaves there, while in fact none would do so. "You have got what is worth more than a thousand Wilmot Provisos," Clay pointed out to his northern colleagues. "You have nature on your side." Empty lands in dispute along the Texas border should be assigned to the New Mexico Territory, Clay continued, but in exchange the United States should take over Texas's preannexation debts. The slave trade should be abolished in the District of Columbia (but not slavery itself), and a more effective federal fugitive slave law should be enacted and strictly enforced in the North.

Clay's proposals occasioned one of the most magnificent debates in the history of the Senate. Every important member had his say. Calhoun, perhaps even more than Clay, realized that the future of the nation was at stake and that his own days were numbered (he died four weeks later). He was so feeble that he could not deliver his speech himself. He sat impassive, wrapped in a great cloak, gripping the arms of his chair, while Senator James M. Mason of Virginia read it to the crowded Senate. Calhoun thought his plan would save the Union, but his speech was an argument for secession; he demanded that the North yield completely on every point, ceasing even to discuss the question of slavery. Clay's compromise was unsatisfactory; he himself had no other to offer. If you will not yield, he said to the northern senators, "let the States . . . agree to separate and part in peace. If you are unwilling we should part in peace, tell us so, and we shall know what to do."

Three days later, on March 7, Daniel Webster took the floor. He too had begun to fail. Years of heavy drinking and other forms of self-indulgence had taken their toll. The brilliant volubility and the thunder were gone, and when he spoke his face was bathed in sweat and there were strange pauses in his delivery. But his argument was lucid. Clay's proposals should be adopted. Since the future of all the territories had already been fixed by geographic and economic factors, the Wilmot Proviso was unnecessary. The

DOCUMENT

Webster, Speech to the U.S. Senate

▲ Two leading lights of the day, Clay and Webster, as they looked at about the time they played major roles in the Compromise of 1850. The daguerreotype of Clay *(left)* dates from the late 1840s; that of Webster *(right)* from 1851, a year before his death. Both are by the noted Boston firm of Southworth and Hawes.

North's constitutional obligation to yield fugitive slaves, he said, braving the wrath of New England abolitionists, was "binding in honor and conscience." (A cynic might say that once again Webster was placing property rights above human rights.) The Union, he continued, could not be sundered without bloodshed. At the thought of that dread possibility, the old fire flared: "Peaceable secession!" Webster exclaimed, "Heaven forbid! Where is the flag of the republic to remain? Where is the eagle still to tower?" The debate did not end with the aging giants. Every possible viewpoint was presented, argued, rebutted, rehashed. Senator William H. Seward of New York, a new Whig leader, close to Taylor's ear, caused a stir while arguing against concessions to the slave interests by saying that despite the constitutional obligation to return fugitive slaves, a "higher law" than the Constitution, the law of God, forbade anything that countenanced the evil of slavery.

The majority clearly favored some compromise, but nothing could have been accomplished without the death of President Taylor on July 9, 1850. Obstinate, probably resentful because few people paid him half the heed they paid Clay and other prominent members of Congress, the president had insisted on his own plan to bring both California and New Mexico directly into the Union. When Vice President Millard Fillmore, who was a politician, not an ideologue, succeeded Taylor, the deadlock between the White House and Capitol Hill was broken. Even so, each part of the

compromise had to be voted on separately, for too many stubborn congressmen were willing to overturn the whole plan because they objected to specific parts of it. Senator Benton, for example, announced against Clay's omnibus bill because he objected to the fugitive slave provision and the Texas boundary settlement.

The final congressional maneuvering was managed by another relative newcomer, Senator Stephen A. Douglas of Illinois, who took over when Washington's summer heat prostrated the exhausted Clay. Partisanship and economic interests complicated Douglas's problem. According to rumor, Clay had persuaded an important Virginia newspaper editor to back the compromise by promising him a $100,000 government printing contract. This inflamed many Southerners. New York merchants, fearful of the disruption of their southern business, submitted a petition bearing 25,000 names in favor of compromise, a document that had a favorable effect in the South. The prospect of the federal government's paying the debt of Texas made ardent compromisers of a horde of speculators. Between February and September, Texas bonds rose erratically from 29 to over 60, while men like W. W. Corcoran, whose Washington bank held more than $400,000 of these securities, entertained legislators and supplied lobbyists with large amounts of cash.

In the Senate and then in the House, tangled combinations pushed through the separate measures, one by one. California became the thirty-first state. The rest

▲ **Compromise of 1850**

DOCUMENT

The Fugitive
Slave Act (1850)

of the Mexican cession was divided into two territories, New Mexico and Utah, each to be admitted to the Union when qualified, "with or without slavery as [its] constitution may prescribe." Texas received $10 million to pay off its debt in return for accepting a narrower western boundary. The slave trade in the District of Columbia was abolished as of January 1, 1851. The Fugitive Slave Act of 1793 was amended to provide for the appointment of federal commissioners with authority to issue warrants, summon posses, and compel citizens under pain of fine or imprisonment to assist in the capture of fugitives. Commissioners who decided that an accused person was a runaway received a larger fee than if they declared the person legally free. The accused could not testify in their own defense. They were to be returned to the South without jury trial merely on the submission of an affidavit by their "owner."

Only 4 senators and 28 representatives voted for all these bills. The two sides did not meet somewhere in the middle as is the case with most compromises. Each bill passed because those who preferred it outnumbered those opposed. In general, the Democrats gave more support to the compromise than the Whigs, but party lines never held firmly. In the Senate, for example, 17 Democrats and 15 Whigs voted to admit California as a free state. A large number of congressmen absented themselves when parts of the

settlement unpopular in their home districts came to a vote; 21 senators and 36 representatives failed to commit themselves on the new fugitive slave bill. Senator Jefferson Davis of Mississippi voted for the fugitive slave measure and the bill creating Utah Territory, remained silent on the New Mexico bill, and opposed the other measures. Senator Salmon P. Chase of Ohio, an abolitionist, supported only the admission of California and the abolition of the slave trade.

In this piecemeal fashion the Union was preserved. The credit belongs mostly to Clay, whose original conceptualization of the compromise enabled lesser minds to understand what they must do.

Everywhere sober and conservative citizens sighed with relief. Mass meetings throughout the country "ratified" the result. Hundreds of newspapers gave the compromise editorial approval. In Washington patriotic harmony reigned. "You would suppose that nobody had ever thought of disunion," Webster wrote. "All say they always meant to stand by the Union to the last." When Congress met again in December it seemed that party discord had been buried forever. "I have determined never to make another speech on the slavery question," Senator Douglas told his colleagues. "Let us cease agitating, stop the debate, and drop the subject." If this were done, he predicted, the compromise would be accepted as a "final settlement." With this bit of wishful thinking the year 1850 passed into history.

MILESTONES

1835	Alamo falls to Santa Anna's Mexican army	**1846**	U.S. and Britain settle Oregon boundary dispute
1836	Sam Houston routs Santa Anna at Battle of San Jacinto	**1846–1848**	U.S. wages "Mr. Polk's War" with Mexico
1837	U.S. recognizes Republic of Texas	**1846**	House of Representatives adopts
1840	Richard Henry Dana describes voyage to California in *Two Years Before the Mast*		Wilmot Proviso prohibiting slavery in Mexican cession, but Senate defeats it
	William Henry Harrison is elected president	**1847**	General Winfield Scott captures Mexico City
1841	William Henry Harrison dies; Vice President John Tyler becomes president	**1848**	James W. Marshall discovers gold at Sutter's Mill, California
	Preemption Act grants "squatters' rights" in West		Treaty of Guadalupe Hidalgo brings U.S. huge territorial gains
1842	Webster-Ashburton Treaty determines Maine boundary		Zachary Taylor is elected president
1843	Oregon Trail opens	**1850**	Taylor dies; Vice President Millard Fillmore becomes president
1844	James K. Polk is elected president		Henry Clay's Compromise of 1850 preserves Union
1845	U.S. annexes Texas		
	John L. O'Sullivan coins the expression *manifest destiny*		

SUPPLEMENTARY READING

For John Tyler, perhaps the least examined of the presidents, see Dan Monroe, *The Republican Vision of John Tyler* (2003); on the Whigs more generally, see Michael F. Holt, *The Rise and Fall of the American Whig Party* (1999), and Daniel Walker Howe, *The Political Culture of the American Whigs* (1979).

On diplomatic affairs, see P. A. Varg, *United States Foreign Relations: 1820–1860* (1979), and D. M. Pletcher, *The Diplomacy of Annexation: Texas, Oregon, and the Mexican War* (1973).

The new expansionism is discussed in Frederick Merk, *Manifest Destiny and Mission in American History* (1963) and *The Monroe Doctrine and American Expansionism* (1966). H. N. Smith, *Virgin Land* (1950), is also important for an understanding of this subject. The course of western development is treated in R. A. Billington and Martin Ridge, *The Far Western Frontier* (1982). Important recent studies of the California gold rush include Malcolm J. Rohrbough, *Days of Gold* (1997), and Susan Lee Johnson, *Roaring Camp: The Social World of the California Gold Rush* (2000). On the effects of the settling of the Great Plains, see Elliott West, *The Contested Plains: Indians, Goldseekers and the Rush to Colorado* (1998) and J. D. Unruh, *The Plains Across* (1979). Francis Parkman's classic account, *The Oregon Trail* (1849) is absorbing.

For the election of 1844, see J. C. N. Paul, *Rift in the Democracy* (1961). Two recent, brief biographies of Polk are John Seigenthaler, *James K. Polk* (2004), and Thomas M. Leonard, *James K. Polk: A Clear and Unquestionable Destiny* (2001). The standard biography of Polk is Charles G. Sellers's *James K. Polk* (1957–1966). William Dusinberre, *Slavemaster President: The Double Career of James Polk* (2003) is sharply critical.

On the Mexican War, see Richard Bruce Winders, *Mr. Polk's Army* (1997), R. W. Johannsen, *To the Halls of the Montezumas* (1987), and K. J. Bauer, *The Mexican War* (1974). J. H. Schroeder, *Mr. Polk's War* (1973), discusses American opposition to the conflict. See also Marshall De Bruhl, *Sword of San Jacinto* (1993), a biography of Sam Houston. Randy Roberts and James S. Olson, *A Line in the Sand: The Alamo in Blood and Memory* (2001) is an accessible account.

For the Compromise of 1850, see David M. Potter, *The Impending Crisis, 1848–1861* (1976), and Holman Hamilton, *Prologue to Conflict* (1964). See also Robert Remini, *Daniel Webster: The Man and His Time* (1997), and Irving H. Bartlett, *John C. Calhoun* (1993).

Fertility and the frontier is examined in Yasukichi Yasuba, *Birth Rates of the White Population in the U.S., 1800–1860* (1962), and John Modell, "Family and Fertility on the Indiana Frontier, 1820," in *American Quarterly* (1971). See also Mary Ryan, *The Cradle of the Middle Class* (1981).

SUGGESTED WEBSITES

From Slave to Master

http://moa.umdl.umich.edu/cgi/sgml/
moa-idx?notisid=ABT6752

This site contains an autobiography of a slave who became a master, with strong comments on the place of blacks in pre-Civil War America.

Sam Houston and the Texas Revolution, 1825–1836

http://www.lnstar.com/mall/texasinfo/shouston.htm

This site provides information on the revolution, including the dynamic Sam Houston.

On the Trail in Kansas

http://www.ukans.edu/heritage/owk/128/trails.htm/
#Oregon

This Kansas Collection site provides good primary sources and images relating to the Oregon Trial and America's early movement westward.

"Been Here So Long": Selections from the WPA American Slave Narratives

http://newdeal.feri.org/asn/index.htm

Slave narratives are some of the most interesting primary sources about slavery.

Slave Narratives

http://docsouth.unc.edu/neh/texts.html

This site presents narratives of several slaves housed at the Documents of the American South collection and the University of North Carolina.

The Settlement of African Americans in Liberia

http://www.loc.gov/exhibits/african/afam003.html

This site contains images and text relating to the colonization movement to return African Americans to Africa.

Images of African Americans from the Nineteenth Century

http://digital.nypl.org/schomburg/images_aa19/

The New York Public Library–Schomburg Center for Research in Black Culture site contains numerous visuals of nineteenth-century African Americans.

The Compromise of 1850 and the Fugitive Slave Act

http://www.pbs.org/wgbh/aia/part4

From the series on Africans in America, an analysis of the Compromise of 1850 and the effect of the Fugitive Slave Act on black Americans.

Words and Deeds in American History

http://lcweb2.loc.gov/ammem/mcchtml/
corhome.html

A Library of Congress site containing links to Frederick Douglas, the Compromise of 1850, as well as speeches by John C. Calhoun, Daniel Webster, and Henry Clay; and other topics from the Civil War era.

The Sections Go Their Ways

▼ A railroad engine pierces the darkening wilderness. Man-made light supplants the setting sun, and nature flees before the encroaching machine. The painting is by Andrew W. Melrose.

CHAPTER CONTENTS

Anation growing as rapidly as the United States in the middle decades of the nineteenth century changed continually in hundreds of ways. It was developing a national economy marked by the dependence of each area on all the others, the production of goods in one region for sale in all, the increased specialization of agricultural and industrial producers, and the growth in size of units of production.

Cotton remained the most important southern crop and the major American export. However, manufacturing in the Northeast and the railroads, which revolutionized transportation and communication, became the mainsprings of economic growth. The continuing westward movement of agriculture had significant new effects. American foreign commerce changed radically, and the flood of European immigration had an impact on manufacturing, town life, and farming.

THE SOUTH

The South was less affected than other sections by urbanization, European immigration, the transportation revolution, and industrialization. The region remained predominantly agricultural; cotton was still king, slavery the most distinctive southern institution. But important changes were occurring. Cotton continued to march westward, until by 1859 fully 1.3 million of the 4.3 million bales grown in the United States came from beyond the Mississippi. In the upper South, Virginia held its place as the leading tobacco producer, but states beyond the Appalachians were raising more than half the crop. The introduction of Bright Yellow, a mild variety of tobacco that (miraculously) grew best in poor soil, gave a great stimulus to production. The older sections of Maryland, Virginia, and North Carolina shifted to the kind of diversified farming usually associated with the Northeast. By 1849 the wheat crop of Virginia was worth twice as much as the tobacco crop.

In the time of Washington and Jefferson, progressive Virginia planters had experimented with crop rotation and fertilizers. In the mid-nineteenth century, Edmund Ruffin introduced the use of marl, an earth rich in calcium, to counteract the acidity of worn-out tobacco fields. Ruffin discovered that dressings of marl, combined with the use of fertilizers and with proper drainage and plowing methods, doubled and even tripled the yield of corn and wheat. In the 1840s some Southerners began to import Peruvian guano, a high-nitrogen fertilizer of bird droppings, which increased yields. Others experimented with contour plowing to control erosion and with improved breeds of livestock, new types of plows, and agricultural machinery.

THE ECONOMICS OF SLAVERY

The increased importance of cotton in the South strengthened the hold of slavery on the region. The price of slaves rose until by the 1850s a prime field hand was worth as much as $1800, roughly three times the cost in the 1820s. While the prestige value of owning this kind of property affected prices, the rise chiefly reflected the increasing value of the South's agricultural output. "Crop value per slave" jumped from less than $15 early in the century to more than $125 in 1859.

In the cotton fields of the Deep South slaves brought several hundred dollars per head more than in the older regions; thus the tendency to sell them "down the river" continued. Mississippi took in some 10,000 slaves a year throughout the period; by 1830 the black population of the state exceeded the white. The westward shift of cotton cultivation was accompanied by the forcible transfer of more than a million African American slaves from the seaboard states to the dark, rich soil of regions watered by the Mississippi and Arkansas rivers and their tributaries. This "second great migration" of blacks greatly surpassed the original uprooting of blacks from Africa to the United States.

▲ Price, Birch & Company of Virginia, "dealers in Slaves." Such companies not only sold slaves but also arranged for them to work in nearby shops and factories.

Slave trading became a big business. In the 1850s there were about 50 dealers in Charleston and 200 in New Orleans. The largest traders were Isaac Franklin and John Armfield, who collected slaves from Virginia and Maryland at their "model jail" in Alexandria and shipped them by land and sea to a depot near Natchez. Each of the partners cleared half a million dollars before retiring, and some smaller operators did proportionately well.

The impact of the trade on the slaves was frequently disastrous. Husbands were often separated from wives, parents from children. This was somewhat less likely to happen on large, well-managed plantations than on small farms, but it was common enough everywhere. According to one study, one-third of all slave first "marriages" in the upper South were broken by forced separation and nearly half of all children were separated from at least one parent. Families were torn apart less frequently in the lower South, where far more slaves were bought than sold.

Because the business was so profitable, the prejudice against slave traders abated as the price of slaves rose. Men of high social status became traders, and persons of humble origin who had prospered in the trade had little difficulty in buying land and setting up as respectable planters.

As blacks became more expensive, the ownership of slaves became more concentrated. In 1860

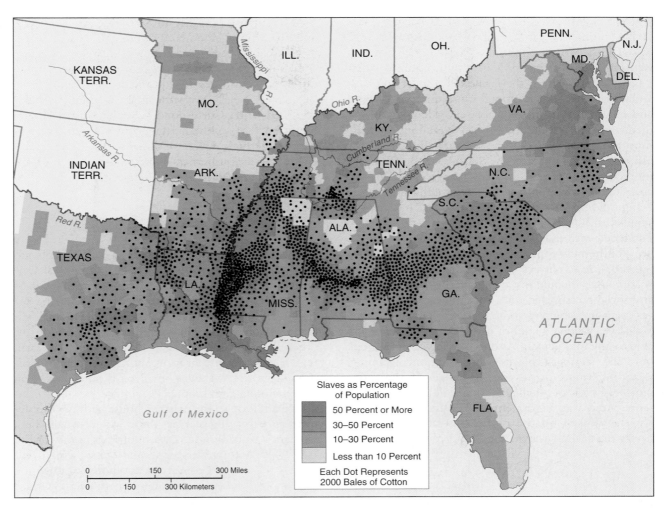

▲ **Cotton and Slaves in the South, 1860**
 Not surprisingly, the areas of greatest cotton production were also the areas with the highest proportion
of slaves in the population. Note the concentrations of both in the Piedmont, the Alabama Black Belt,
and the lower Mississippi Valley, and the relative absence of both in the Appalachian Mountains.

Slavery in the
South

only about 46,000 of the 8 million white residents of the slave states had as many as 20 slaves. When one calculates the cost of 20 slaves and the land to keep them profitably occupied, it is easy to understand why this figure is so small. The most efficient size of a plantation worked by gangs of slaves ranged between 1000 and 2000 acres. In every part of the South the majority of farmers cultivated no more than 200 acres, in many sections fewer than 100 acres. On the eve of the Civil War only one white family in four in the South owned any slaves at all. A few large plantations and many small farms—this was the pattern.

There were few genuine economies of scale in southern agriculture. Small farmers grew the staple crops; and many of them owned a few slaves, often working beside them in the fields. These yeomen farmers were hardworking, self-reliant, and moderately prosperous, quite unlike the "poor white trash" of the pine barrens and the remote valleys of the Appalachians who scratched a meager subsistence from substandard soils and lived in ignorance and squalor.

Well-managed plantations yielded annual profits of 10 percent and more, and, in general, money invested in southern agriculture earned at least a modest return. Considering the way the workforce was exploited, this is hardly surprising. Recent estimates indicate that after allowing for the cost of land and capital, the average plantation slave "earned" cotton worth $78.78 in 1859. It cost masters about $32 a year to feed, clothe, and house a slave. In other words, almost 60 percent of the product of slave labor was expropriated by the masters.

The South failed to develop locally owned marketing and transportation facilities, and for this slavery was at least partly responsible. In 1840 *Hunt's Merchant Magazine* estimated that it cost $2.85 to move a bale of cotton from the farm to a seaport and that additional charges for storage, insurance, port fees, and freight to a European port exceeded $15. Middlemen from outside the South commonly earned most of this money. New York capitalists gradually came to control much of the South's cotton from the moment it was picked, and a large percentage of the crop found its way into New York warehouses before being sold to manufacturers. The same middlemen supplied most of the foreign goods that the planters purchased with their cotton earnings.

Southerners complained about this state of affairs but did little to correct it. Capital tied up in the ownership of labor could not be invested in anything else, and social pressures in the South militated against investment in trade and commerce. Ownership of land and slaves yielded a kind of psychic income not available to any middleman. As one British visitor pointed out, the southern blacks were "a nonconsuming class." Still more depressing, under slavery the enormous reservoir of intelligence and skill that the blacks represented was almost entirely wasted. Many slave artisans worked on the plantations, and a few free blacks made their way in the South remarkably well, but the amount of talent unused, energy misdirected, and imagination smothered can only be guessed.

Foreign observers in New England frequently noted the alertness and industriousness of ordinary laborers and attributed this, justifiably, to the high level of literacy. Nearly everyone in New England could read and write. Correspondingly, the stagnation and inefficiency of southern labor could be attributed in part to the high degree of illiteracy, for over 20 percent of *white* Southerners could not read or write, another tragic squandering of human resources.

ANTEBELLUM PLANTATION LIFE

There was never any such thing as a "typical" plantation, but it is possible to describe, in a general way, what a medium-to-large operation employing 20 or more slaves was like in the two decades preceding the Civil War. Such a plantation was more like a small village than a northern-type agricultural unit, and in another way more like a self-sufficient colonial farm than a nineteenth-century commercial operation, although its major activity involved producing cotton or some other cash crop.

In addition to the master's house with its complement of barns and stables, there would usually be a kitchen, a smokehouse, a washhouse, a home for the overseer should one be employed, perhaps a schoolhouse, a gristmill, a forge, and of course the slave quarters, off at a distance (but not too far) from the center.

Slaveholding families were also quite different from northern families of similar status, in part because they were engaged in agriculture and in part because of their so-called peculiar institution. Husbands and wives did not function in separate spheres to nearly the same extent, although their individual functions were different and gender related.

Although planter families purchased their fine clothes, furniture, and china, as well as other manufactured products such as sewing machines, cooking utensils, books, and musical instruments, plantations were busy centers of household manufacture, turning out most of the clothing of slaves except for shoes and the everyday clothing of their own children, along with bedding and other textiles. Spinning,

▲ This painting of a slave auction highlights an awkward aspect of slavery. The slave woman has light skin, which suggests that her father was likely a slave owner. Those men bidding on her stare with an intensity portending that she will likely share her mother's fate.

weaving, and sewing were women's work, both for whites and blacks. Nearly all the food consumed was raised on the land; only tea and coffee and a few other food items were commonly purchased.

The master was in general charge and his word was law—the system was literally paternalistic. But his wife nearly always had immense responsibilities. Running the household meant supervising the servants (and punishing them when necessary, which often meant wielding a lash), nursing the sick, taking care of the vegetable and flower gardens, planning meals, and seeing to the education of her own children and the training of young slaves. It could also involve running the entire plantation on the frequent occasions when her husband was away on business. At the same time, her role entailed being a "southern lady," refined, graceful, supposedly untroubled by worldly affairs.

Most slaveholding women had to learn all these things by doing; in general, they married while still in their teens and had been given little or no training in the household arts. Unmarried "young ladies" had few responsibilities beyond caring for their own rooms and persons and perhaps such "ladylike" tasks as arranging flowers.

The majority of the slaves of both sexes were field hands who labored on the land from dawn to dusk. Household servants and artisans, indeed any slave other than small children and the aged and infirm, might be called on for such labor when needed. Slave women were expected to cook for their own families and do other chores after working in the fields.

DOCUMENT

Harper, "The Slave Mother"

Children, free and slave, were cared for by slaves, the former by household servants, the latter usually by an elderly woman, perhaps with the help of a girl only a little older than the children. Infants were brought to their mothers in the fields for nursing several times a day, for after a month or two at most, slave mothers were required to go back to work. Slave children were not put to work until they were six or seven years old, and until they were about ten they were given only small tasks such as feeding the chickens or minding a smaller child. Black and white youngsters played together and were often cared for by the same nursemaid.

Slave cabins were simple and crude; most consisted of a single room, dark, with a fireplace for cooking and heat. Usually the flooring was raised above ground level, though some were set on the bare earth. In 1827 Basil Hall, a British naval officer, reported that in a large South Carolina plantation, 140 slaves lived in 28 cottages or huts. These were "uncommonly neat and comfortable, and might have shamed those of many countries I have seen." Yet Hall dismissed the claims of white Southerners that slaves were happier than the peasantry of England. Slavery was, above all, a "humiliation" imposed upon "the whole mass of the labouring population" of the South.

THE SOCIOLOGY OF SLAVERY

It is difficult to generalize about the peculiar institution because so much depended on the individual master's behavior. Although some ex-slaves told of masters who refused to whip them, Bennet Barrow of Louisiana, a harsh master, averaged one whipping a month. "The great secret of our success," another planter recalled years later, "was the great motive power contained in that little instrument." Overseers were commonly instructed to give 20 lashes for ordinary offences, such as shirking work or stealing, and 39 for more serious offenses, such as running away. Sometimes slaves were whipped to death though, by 1821, all southern states had passed laws allowing a master to be charged with murder if he caused a slave's death from excessive punishment. Conviction normally resulted in a fine. In 1840 a South Carolina woman convicted of killing a slave was fined $214.28.

Most owners provided adequate clothing, housing, and food for their slaves. Only a fool or a sadist would fail to take care of such valuable property. However, vital statistics indicate that infant mortality among slaves was twice the white rate, life expectancy at least five years less.

On balance, it is significant that the United States was the only nation in the Western Hemisphere where the slave population grew by natural increase. After the ending of the slave trade in 1808, the black population increased at nearly the same rate as the white. Put differently, during the entire period from the founding of Jamestown to the Civil War, only a little more than half a million slaves were imported into the country, about 5 percent of the number of Africans carried by slavers to the New World. Yet in 1860 there were about 4 million blacks in the United States.

Most owners felt responsibilities toward their slaves, and slaves were dependent on and in some ways imitative of white values. However, powerful fears and resentments, not always recognized, existed on both sides. The plantation environment forced the two races to live in close proximity. From this circumstance could arise every sort of human relationship. One planter, using the appropriate pseudonym Clod Thumper, could write: "Africans are nothing but brutes, and they will love you better for whipping, whether they deserve it or not." Another, describing a slave named Bug, could say: "No one

▲ A slave burial service, painted by John Antrobus in 1860. In an inversion of power relations, a slave preacher leads the mourners while the white overseer and the plantation owners watch uneasily, shunted (literally) to the sides.

knows but myself what feeling I have for him. Black as he is we were raised together." One southern white woman tended a dying servant with "the kindest and most unremitting attention." Another, discovered crying after the death of a slave she had repeatedly abused, is said to have explained her grief by complaining that she "didn't have nobody to whip no more."

Such diametrically conflicting sentiments often existed within the same person. And almost no white Southerners had any difficulty exploiting the labor of slaves for whom they felt genuine affection.

Slaves were without rights; they developed a distinctive way of life by attempting to resist oppression and injustice while accommodating themselves to the system. Their marriages had no legal status, but their partnerships seem to have been as loving and stable as those of their masters. Certainly they were acutely conscious of family relationships and responsibilities.

Slave religion, on the surface an untutored form of Christianity tinctured with some African survivals, seemed to most slave owners a useful instrument for teaching meekness and resignation and for providing

DOCUMENT

A Catechism for Slaves

harmless emotional release, which it sometimes was and did. However, religious meetings, secret and open, provided slaves with the opportunity to organize, which led at times to rebellions and more often to less drastic ways of resisting white domination. Religion also sustained the slaves' sense of their own worth as beings made in the image of God, and it taught them, therefore, that while human beings can be enslaved in body, their spirits cannot be enslaved without their consent.

Observing that slaves often seemed happy and were only rarely overtly rebellious, whites persuaded themselves that most blacks accepted the system without resentment and indeed preferred slavery to the uncertainties of freedom. There was much talk about "loyal and faithful servants." The Civil War, when slaves flocked to the Union lines once assured of freedom and fair treatment, would disabuse them of this illusion.

As the price of slaves rose and as northern opposition to the institution grew more vocal, the system hardened perceptibly. White Southerners made much of the danger of insurrection. When a plot was uncovered or a revolt took place, instant and savage reprisals resulted. In 1822, after the conspiracy of Denmark Vesey was exposed by informers, 37 slaves were executed and another 30-odd deported, although no overt act of rebellion had occurred. After an uprising in Louisiana, 16 blacks were decapitated, their heads left to rot on poles along the Mississippi as a grim warning.

DOCUMENT
Turner, *The Confession of Nat Turner*

The Nat Turner revolt in Virginia in 1831 was the most sensational of the slave uprisings; 57 whites lost their lives before it was suppressed. White Southerners treated runaways almost as brutally as rebels, although they posed no real threat to whites. The authorities tracked down fugitives with bloodhounds and subjected captives to merciless lashings.

After the Nat Turner revolt, interest in doing away with slavery vanished in the white South. The southern states made it increasingly difficult for masters to free their slaves; during 1859 only about 3000 in a slave population of nearly 4 million were given their freedom.

Slavery did not flourish in urban settings, and cities did not flourish in societies where slavery was important. Most southern cities were small, and within them, slaves made up a small fraction of the labor force. The existence of slavery goes a long way toward explaining why the South was so rural and why it had so little industry. Blacks were much harder to supervise and control in urban settings. Individual slaves were successfully employed in southern manufacturing plants, but they made up only an insignificant fraction of the South's small industrial labor supply.

Southern whites considered the existence of free blacks undesirable, no matter where they lived. The mere fact that they could support themselves disproved the notion that blacks were by nature childlike and shiftless, unable to work efficiently without white guidance. From the whites' point of view, free blacks set a bad example for slaves. In a petition calling for the expulsion of free blacks from the state, a group of South Carolinians noted that slaves

continualy have before their eyes, persons of the same color . . . freed from the control of masters, working where they

please, going where they please, and expending their money how they please.

At a minimum, as another Southerner said, the sight of "a vile and lazy free negro lolling in the sunshine" might make slaves envious. Still worse, it might encourage them to try to escape, and worst of all, the free blacks might help them do so.

Many southern states passed laws aimed at forcing free blacks to emigrate, but these laws were not well enforced. There is ample evidence that the white people of, say, Maryland, would have liked to get rid of the state's large free-black population. Free blacks were barred from occupations in which they might cause trouble—no free black could be the captain of a ship, for example—and they were required by law to find a "respectable" white person who would testify as to their "good conduct and character." But whites, who needed slave labor, did not try very hard to expel them.

Some unscrupulous Southerners helped smuggle blacks from Africa. About 54,000 slaves were brought to America illegally after the trade was outlawed in 1808, not a very large number relative to the slave population. British, French, Portuguese, and American naval vessels patrolled the African coast continuously. The American navy alone seized more than 50 suspected slavers in the two decades before 1860. However, the fast, sharklike pirate cruisers were hard to catch, and the anti–slave trade laws were imperfectly worded and unevenly enforced. Many accounts tell of slaves in America long after 1808 with

LIBERTY LINE.
NEW ARRANGEMENT---NIGHT AND DAY.

The improved and splendid Locomotives, Clarkson and Lundy, with their trains fitted up in the best style of accommodation for passengers, will run their regular trips during the present season, between the borders of the Patriarchal Dominion and Libertyville, Upper Canada. Gentlemen and Ladies, who may wish to improve their health or circumstances, by a northern tour, are respectfully invited to give us their patronage.
  SEATS FREE, *irrespective of color.*
  Necessary Clothing furnished gratuitously to such as have *"fallen among thieves."*

"Hide the outcasts—let the oppressed go free."—*Bible.*
☞For seats apply at any of the trap doors, or to the conductor of the train.
        J. CROSS, *Proprietor.*
  N. B. For the special benefit of Pro-Slavery Police Officers, an extra heavy wagon for Texas, will be furnished, whenever it may be necessary, in which they will be forwarded as dead freight, to the "Valley of Rascals," always at the risk of the owners.
  ☞Extra Overcoats provided for such of them as are afflicted with protracted *chilly-phobia.*

▲ An 1844 advertisement from *The Western Citizen* for the "Liberty Line," a tongue-in-cheek reference to the volunteers who helped slaves escape from the South ("the Patriarchal Dominion") to get to Canada ("Libertyville"). Although the ad likened the effort to a railroad speeding hundreds of slaves northward, in fact relatively few slaves ever took this "northern tour."

filed teeth, tattoos, and other signs of African origin, yet no one owning such a person was ever charged with the possession of contraband goods.

PSYCHOLOGICAL EFFECTS OF SLAVERY

The injustice of slavery needs no proof; less obvious is the fact that it had a corrosive effect on the personalities of Southerners, slave and free alike. By "the making of a human being an animal without hope," the system bore heavily on all slaves' sense of their own worth. Some found the condition absolutely unbearable. They became the habitual runaways who collected whip scars like medals, the "loyal" servants who struck out in rage against a master knowing that the result would be certain death, and the leaders of slave revolts.

Denmark Vesey of South Carolina, even after buying his freedom, could not stomach the subservience demanded of slaves by the system. When he saw Charleston slaves step into the gutter to make way for whites, he taunted them: "You deserve to remain slaves!" For years he preached resistance to his fellows, drawing his texts from the Declaration of Independence and the Bible and promising help from black Haiti. So vehemently did he argue that some of his followers claimed they feared Vesey more than their masters, even more than God. He planned his uprising for five years, patiently working out the details, only to see it aborted at the last moment when a few of his recruits lost their nerve and betrayed him. For Denmark Vesey, death was probably preferable to living with such rage as his soul contained.

Yet Veseys were rare. Most slaves appeared, if not contented, at least resigned to their fate. Many seemed even to accept the whites' evaluation of their inherent abilities and place in society. Of course in most instances it is impossible to know whether this apparent subservience was feigned in order to avoid trouble.

Slaves had strong family and group attachments and a complex culture of their own, maintained, so to speak, under the noses of their masters. By a mixture of subterfuge, accommodation, and passive resistance, they erected subtle defenses against exploitation, achieving a sense of community that helped sustain the psychic integrity of individuals. But slavery discouraged, if it did not extinguish, independent judgment and self-reliance. These qualities are difficult enough to develop in human beings under the best of circumstances; when every element in white society encouraged slaves to let others do their thinking for them, to avoid questioning the status quo, to lead a simple life, many did so willingly enough. Was this not slavery's greatest shame?

Whites, too, were harmed by the slave system. Associating working for others with servility discouraged many poor white Southerners from hiring out to earn a stake. Slavery provided the weak, the shiftless, and the unsuccessful with a scapegoat that made their own miserable state easier to bear but harder to escape.

More subtly, the patriarchal nature of the slave system reinforced the already existing tendency toward male dominance over wives and children typical of the larger society. For men of exceptional character, the responsibilities of ownership could be ennobling, but for hotheads, alcoholics, or others with psychological problems, the power could be brutalizing, with terrible effects on the whole plantation community, whites and blacks alike.

Aside from its fundamental immorality, slavery caused basically decent people to commit countless petty cruelties. "I feel badly, got very angry and whipped Lavinia," one Louisiana woman wrote in her diary. "O! for government over my temper." But for slavery, she would surely have had better self-control. The finest white Southerners were often warped by the institution. Even those who abhorred slavery sometimes let it corrupt their thinking: "I consider the labor of a breeding woman as no object, and that a child raised every 2 years is of more profit than the crop of the best laboring man." This cold calculation came from the pen of Thomas Jefferson, author of the Declaration of Independence, a man who, it now seems likely, fathered at least one child by a slave.

MANUFACTURING IN THE SOUTH

Although the temper of southern society discouraged business and commercial activities, considerable manufacturing developed. Small flour and lumber mills flourished. There were important rope-making plants in Kentucky and commercial cotton presses, used to compact cotton into 500-pound bales, in many southern cities. Iron and coal were mined in Virginia, Kentucky, and Tennessee. In the 1850s the Tredegar Iron Works in Richmond did an annual business of about $1 million.

The availability of the raw material and the abundance of waterpower along the Appalachian slopes made it possible to manufacture textiles profitably in the South. By 1825 a thriving factory was functioning at Fayetteville, North Carolina, and soon others sprang up elsewhere in North Carolina and in adjoining states. William Gregg's factory, at Graniteville, South Carolina, established in 1846, was employing about 300 people by 1850. It was a constant moneymaker. An able propagandist as well as a good businessman,

DEBATING THE PAST

Did slaves and masters form emotional bonds?
Slavery, Ulrich Bonnell Phillips (1918) declared, was a benign institution. "Severity was clearly the exception, and kindliness the rule," he remarked. Kenneth Stampp (1956), writing as the civil rights movement of the 1950s was gaining momentum, repudiated Phillips's thesis. Slavery ripped apart families, reduced human beings to chattel, and eroded the slave's sense of self. Stanley Elkins (1959) went further still, comparing southern slavery to the subjugation of inmates in Nazi concentration camps. Slavery was so absolute that the psyche of African Americans was crushed for generations. Two major works in the 1970s challenged this rendering but in different ways. Eugene D. Genovese (1974) argued that masters and slaves were locked in a system of mutual dependence. Slaves were bound to their owners "in an organic relationship so complex and ambivalent that neither could express the simplest human feelings without reference to each other." Their emotional ties, however complicated, were real. Herbert Gutman (1976) insisted that slaves did not bond with their masters. Slave parents, children, and other relatives formed lasting ties that endured. Because it is hard to know what people really felt, the issue resists historical analysis: Did the slave girl in this photograph know for sure how she felt about the child in her arms?

Ulrich Bonnell Phillips, *American Negro Slavery* (1918), Kenneth Stampp, *The Peculiar Institution* (1956), Stanley Elkins, *Slavery* (1959), Eugene D. Genovese, *Roll, Jordan, Roll* (1974), Herbert Gutman, *The Black Family in Slavery and Freedom* (1976).

Gregg saw the textile business not only as a source of profit but also as a device for improving the lot of the South's poor whites. He worked hard to weaken the southern prejudice against manufacturing and made his plant a model of benevolent paternalism similar to that of the early mills of Lowell, Massachusetts. As with every other industry, however, southern textile manufacturing amounted to very little when compared with that of the North. While Gregg was employing 300 textile workers in 1850, the whole state of South Carolina had fewer than 900. Lowell, Massachusetts, had more spindles turning in 1860 than the entire South.

Less than 15 percent of all the goods manufactured in the United States in 1860 came from the South; the region did not really develop an industrial society. Its textile manufacturers depended on the North for machinery, for skilled workers and technicians, for financing, and for insurance. When the English geologist Charles Lyell visited New Orleans in 1846, he was astounded to discover that the thriving city supported not a single book publisher. Even a local guidebook that he purchased bore a New York imprint.

THE NORTHERN INDUSTRIAL JUGGERNAUT

The most obvious change in the North in the decades before the Civil War was the rapid growth of industry. The best estimates suggest that immediately after the War of 1812 the United States was manufacturing less than $200 million worth of goods annually. In 1859 the northeastern states alone produced $1.27 billion of the national total of almost $2 billion.

Manufacturing expanded in so many directions that it is difficult to portray or to summarize its evolution. The factory system made great strides. The development of rich anthracite coal fields in Pennsylvania was particularly important in this connection. The coal could be floated cheaply on canals to convenient sites and used to produce both heat for smelting and metalworking and steam power to drive machinery. Steam permitted greater flexibility in locating factories and in organizing work within them, and since waterpower was already being used to capacity, steam was essential for the expansion of output.

American industry displayed a remarkable receptivity to technological change. The list of inventions and processes developed between 1825 and 1850, included—besides such obviously important items as the sewing machine, the vulcanization of rubber, and the cylinder press—the screw-making machine, the friction match, the lead pencil, and an apparatus for making soda water. A society in flux put a premium on resourcefulness; an environment that offered so much freedom to the individual encouraged experimentation. The expanding market inspired businessmen to use new techniques. With skilled labor always in short supply, the pressure to substitute machines for trained hands was great.

In the 1820s a foreign visitor noted: "Everything new is quickly introduced here, and all the latest inventions. . . . The moment an American hears the word 'invention' he pricks up his ears." Twenty years later a Frenchman wrote: "If they continue to work with the same ardor, they will soon have nothing more to desire or to do. All the mountains will be flattened, the valleys filled, all matter rendered productive." By 1850 the United States led the world in the manufacture of goods that required the use of precision instruments, and in certain industries the country was well on the way toward modern mass production methods. American clocks, pistols, rifles, and locks were outstanding.

The American exhibits at the London Crystal Palace Exhibition of 1851 so impressed the British that they sent two special commissions to the United States to study manufacturing practices. After visiting the Springfield Arsenal, where a worker took apart ten muskets, each made in a different year, mixed up the parts, and then reassembled the guns, each in perfect working order, the British investigators placed a large order for gun-making machinery. They also hired a number of American technicians to help organize what became the Enfield rifle factory. They were amazed by the lock and clock factories of New England and by the plants where screws, files, and similar metal objects were turned out in volume by automatic machinery. Instead of resisting new laborsaving machines, the investigators noted, "the workingmen hail with satisfaction all mechanical improvements."

Invention alone does not account for the industrial advance. Every year new natural resources were discovered and made available by the westward march of settlement, and the expansion of agriculture produced an ever-larger supply of raw materials for the mills and factories. Of the ten leading industries in 1860, eight (flour milling, cotton textiles, lumber, shoes, men's clothing, leather, woolen goods, and liquor) relied on farm products for their raw materials.

In the 1850s the earlier prejudice against the corporation began to break down; by the end of the decade the northern and northwestern states had all passed general incorporation laws. Of course, the corporate device made possible larger accumulations of capital. While the federal government did not charter business corporations, two actions of Congress illustrate the shift in public attitudes. In 1840 a group of scientists sought a federal charter for a National Institution for the Promotion of Science. They were turned down on constitutional grounds; if Congress "went on erecting corporations in this way," one legislator said, "they would come, at last, to have corporations for everything." In 1863, however, the bill creating the National Academy of Science passed both houses without debate.

Industrial growth led to a great increase in the demand for labor. The effects, however, were mixed. Skilled artisans, technicians, and toolmakers earned good wages and found it relatively easy to set themselves up first as independent craftsmen, later as small manufacturers. The expanding frontier drained off much agricultural labor that might otherwise have been attracted to industry, and the thriving new towns of the West absorbed large numbers of eastern artisans of every kind. At the same time, the pay of an unskilled worker was never enough to support a family decently, and the new machines weakened the bargaining power of artisans by making skill less important.

Many other forces acted to stimulate the growth of manufacturing. Immigration increased rapidly in the 1830s and 1840s. An avalanche of strong backs, willing hands, and keen minds descended on the country from Europe. European investors poured large sums into the booming American economy, and the savings of millions of Americans and the great hoard of new California gold added to the supply of capital. Improvements in transportation, population growth, the absence of internal tariff barriers, and the relatively high per capita wealth all meant an ever expanding market for manufactured goods.

DOCUMENT

Morse, "Foreign Immigration"

A NATION OF IMMIGRANTS

Rapid industrialization influenced American life in countless ways, none more significant than its effect on the character of the workforce and consequently on the structure of society. The jobs created by industrial expansion attracted European immigrants by the tens of thousands. It is a truism that America is a nation of immigrants—recall that even the ancestors of the Indians came to the New World from Asia. But only with the development of nationalism, that is, with the establishment of the independent United States, did the word *immigrant,* meaning a foreign-born resident, come into existence.

The "native" population (native in this case meaning those whose ancestors had come from Europe rather than native Americans, the Indians) tended to look down on immigrants, and many of the immigrants, in turn, developed prejudices of their own. The Irish, for example, disliked blacks, with whom they often competed for work. One Irish leader in the old country, Daniel O'Connell, admitted that the American Irish were "among the worst enemies of the colored race." And of course blacks responded with equal bitterness. "Every hour sees us elbowed out of some employment to make room for some newly arrived emigrant from the Emerald Isle, whose hunger and color entitle him to special favor," one of them complained. Antiblack prejudice was less noticeable among other immigrant groups but by no means absent; most immigrants adopted the views of the local majority, which was often unfriendly to African Americans.

Social and racial rivalries aside, unskilled immigrants caused serious disruptions of economic patterns wherever they appeared. Their absorption into the factories of New England speeded the disintegration of the system of hiring young farm women. Already competition and technical advances in the textile industry were increasing the pace of the machines and reducing the number of skilled workers needed to run them. Fewer young farm women were willing to work under these conditions. Recent immigrants, who required less "coddling" and who seemed to provide the mills with a "permanent" working force, replaced the women in large numbers. By 1860 Irish immigrants alone made up more than 50 percent of the labor force in the New England mills.

HOW WAGE EARNERS LIVED

The influx of immigrants does not entirely explain the low standard of living of industrial workers during this period. Low wages and the crowding that resulted from the swift expansion of city populations produced slums that would make the most noisome modern ghetto seem a paradise. A Boston investigation in the late 1840s described one district as "a perfect hive of human beings . . . huddled together like brutes." In New York tens of thousands of the poor lived in dark, rank cellars, those in the waterfront districts often invaded by high tides. Tenement houses like great gloomy prisons rose back to back, each with many windowless rooms and often without heat or running water.

Out of doors, city life for the poor was almost equally squalid. Slum streets were littered with garbage and trash. Recreational facilities were almost nonexistent. Police and fire protection in the cities were pitifully inadequate. "Urban problems" were less critical than a century later only because they affected a smaller part of the population; for those who experienced them, they were, all too often, crushing. In the mid-1850s large numbers of children in New York scrounged a bare existence by begging and scavenging. They took shelter at night in coal bins and empty barrels.

In the early factory towns, most working families maintained small vegetable gardens and a few chickens; low wage rates did not necessarily reflect a low standard of living. But in the new industrial slums even a blade of grass was unusual. In 1851 the editor Horace Greeley's *New York Tribune* published a minimum weekly budget for a family of five. The budget, which allowed nothing for savings, medical bills, recreation, or other amenities (Greeley did include 12 cents a week for newspapers), came to $10.37. Since the weekly pay of a factory hand seldom reached $5, the wives and children of most male factory workers also had to labor in the factories merely to survive. And child labor in the 1850s differed fundamentally from child labor in the 1820s. The pace of the machines had become much faster by then, and the working environment more depressing.

Relatively few workers belonged to unions, but federations of craft unions sprang up in some cities, and during the boom that preceded the Panic of 1837, a National Trades Union representing a few northeastern cities managed to hold conventions. Early in the Jackson era, "workingmen's" political parties enjoyed a brief popularity, occasionally electing a few local officials. These organizations were made up mostly of skilled craftsmen, professional reformers, and even businessmen. They soon expired, destroyed by internal bickering over questions that had little or nothing to do with working conditions.

The depression of the late 1830s led to the demise of most trade unions. Nevertheless, skilled workers improved their lot somewhat in the 1840s and 1850s. The working day declined gradually from about $12\frac{1}{2}$ hours to 10 or 11 hours. Many states passed 10-hour laws and laws regulating child labor, but they were poorly enforced. Most states, however, enacted effective mechanic's lien laws, giving workers first call on the assets of bankrupt and defaulting employers, and the Massachusetts court's decision in the case of *Commonwealth* v. *Hunt* (1842), establishing the legality of labor unions, became a judicial landmark when other state courts followed the precedent.

The flush times of the early 1850s caused the union movement to revive. Many strikes occurred, and a few new national organizations appeared. However, most unions were local institutions, weak and with little control over their membership. The Panic of 1857 dealt the labor movement another body blow. Thus there was no trend toward the general unionization of labor between 1820 and the Civil War.

For this the workers themselves were partly responsible: Craftsmen took little interest in unskilled

▶ *text continues on page 354*

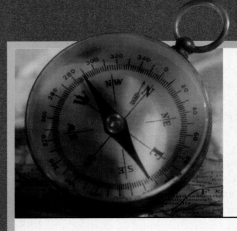

Mapping the Past

Irish and German Immigration

From 1790 to 1820, about 8000 immigrants came into the United States each year. During the next four decades, immigrants flooded into the United States at the rate of about 120,000 annually. By 1860, one in eight of the nation's 32 million people was born in Europe.

The main source of immigrants was rural Ireland, which had been rocked by several economic blows. The first was caused by the end of the Napoleonic Wars in 1815. The return of millions of soldier-peasants to their farms on the European continent caused grain prices in Ireland to fall by nearly 50 percent. Landlords there plowed grain crops under, planted grass for animal fodder, and evicted tenants. Some dispossessed farmers sought work in Dublin, Belfast, or a few other Irish cities; others emigrated to Canada or the United States. But for a time most remained in rural Ireland, hoping to eke out enough food by growing potatoes on small, scrubby plots of land. Thus the population of Ireland, despite the diminishing acreage devoted to cropland, increased from 6.8 million in 1821 to more than 8 million in 1841.

In the fall of 1845, disaster struck when disease devastated the potato crop. Many Irish starved, others braved a winter voyage to the United States, willing to endure, as one said, any misery "save that of remaining in Ireland." The Great Famine persisted for six years. About a million Irish died; another million emigrated to the United States.

Sources of Irish Emigration

The demographic consequences of the Great Famine varied by region. The two maps (above, right) help explain who emigrated and why.

The first map shows that west coast counties of Ireland were the poorest. More than half the residents of Mayo, Galway, Kerry, Clare, and Limerick counties received extended public relief as paupers.

The second map, on population change during the 1840s, shows that tens of thousands of farmers flooded into Dublin, the largest city in Ireland. The prosperous east coast counties—Antrim, Down, Wexford—experienced little decline in population. And the highest population losses were in west and central Ireland. The desperately poor inhabitants of west Ireland—the counties of Mayo, Galway, Clare, and Cork—

lacked the wherewithal to book passage on sailing ships across the Atlantic. Here the population losses were likely a result of starvation. In central Ireland, in counties such as Cavan, Monaghan, Roscommon, and Queens, where poverty was less extreme and people could sell their farms, tools, and furnishings, the high rates of depopulation chiefly resulted from emigration to the United States.

▲ A fisherwoman from Kerry, one of the poorest counties in Ireland. Many were too poor to pay for passage to the United States. Tens of thousands starved.

German and Irish Settlement in the United States

The potato blight spread to the Continent and caused farmers there to emigrate, too. In Germany, the failed democratic revolution of 1848 contributed to the exodus to the United States. In 1854, the peak year of German emigration, some 215,000 made their way to the United States. The map at bottom shows that by 1870 many had settled in rural areas of the Midwest, especially Wisconsin, where they likely resumed farming. But many remained in eastern ports, especially New York, Philadelphia, and Baltimore. Others flocked to the emerging industrial cities of Cincinnati, Chicago, and Milwaukee.

Many Irish immigrants, having sold most of their assets for passage, often lacked the money to move west or buy farms there. Most settled in the port cities along the northeastern seaboard and along the Erie Canal. By 1870 more than a quarter of a million inhabitants of New York City (including Brooklyn) had been born in Ireland. Philadelphia, Jersey City, and Boston had the next largest Irish communities in the nation.

Pauperism in Ireland, 1847–1851

over 50 percent of population pauper for over 1 year by Poor Law union

Population change in Ireland, 1841–1851

percentage of variation per county:
+9
0
–13
–20
–25
–31

German and Irish settlement in the Northeastern U.S., 1870

main area of German settlement (over 5 per sq mile)
main area of Irish settlement (over 5 per sq mile)
main area of German and Irish settlement (over 5 of each per sq mile)
urban settlement in towns of over 25,000 inhabitants:

▲ A strike by 800 women shoemakers in Lynn, Massachusetts, 1860. In 1851 a Lynn shoemaker had adapted a Howe sewing machine so that it could pierce and sew leather, work normally performed by married women in their homes. Because these large machines required women to leave home and children and work at the shoe-stitching factories, few married women would do so; here they are protesting their displacement.

workers except to keep them down. Few common laborers considered themselves part of a permanent working class with different objectives from those of their employers. Although hired labor had existed throughout the colonial period, it was only with the growth of factories and other large enterprises that significant numbers of people worked for wages. To many, wage labor seemed almost un-American, a violation of the republican values of freedom and independence that had triumphed in the Revolution. Jefferson's professed dislike of urban life was based in part on his fear that people who worked for wages would be so beholden to their employers that they could not act independently.

This republican value system, along with the fluidity of society, the influx of job-hungry immigrants, and the widespread employment of women and children in unskilled jobs made labor organization difficult. The assumption was that nearly anyone who was willing to work could eventually escape from the wage-earning class. "If any continue through life in the condition of the hired laborer," Abraham Lincoln

declared in 1859, "it is . . . because of either a dependent nature which prefers it, or improvidence, folly, or singular misfortune."

PROGRESS AND POVERTY

Any investigation of American society before the Civil War reveals a paradox that is obvious but difficult to resolve. The United States was a land of opportunity, a democratic society with a prosperous, expanding economy and few class distinctions. Its people had a high standard of living in comparison with the citizens of European countries. Yet within this rich, confident nation there existed a class of miserably underpaid and depressed unskilled workers, mostly immigrants, who were worse off materially than nearly any southern slave. The literature is full of descriptions of needleworkers earning 12 cents a day, of women driven to prostitution because they could not earn a living decently, of hunger marches and soup kitchens, of disease and crime and people sunk into apathy by hopeless poverty. In 1848 more than 56,000 New Yorkers, about a quarter of the population, were receiving some form of public relief. A police drive in that city in 1860 brought in nearly 500 beggars.

The middle-class majority seemed indifferent to or at best unaware of these conditions. Reformers conducted investigations, published exposés, and labored to help the victims of urbanization and industrialization. They achieved little. Great fires burned in these decades to release the incredible energies of America. The poor were the ashes, sifting down silent and unnoticed beneath the dazzle and the smoke. Industrialization produced poverty and riches (in Marxian terminology, a proletarian class and an aristocracy of capitalists). Tenements sprang up cheek by jowl with the urban palaces of the new rich and the tree-lined streets of the prosperous middle class.

Economic opportunities were great, and taxation was minimal. Little wonder that as the generations passed, the rich got richer. Industrialization accelerated the process and, by stimulating the immigration of masses of poor workers, skewed the social balance still further. Society became more stratified, and differences in wealth and status among citizens grew greater. But the ideology of egalitarian democracy held its own. By the mid-nineteenth century Americans were convinced that all men were equal, and indeed all *white* men had equal political rights. Socially and economically, however, the distances between top and bottom were widening. This situation endured for the rest of the century, and in some respects it still endures.

FOREIGN COMMERCE

Changes in the pattern of foreign commerce were less noticeable than those in manufacturing but were nevertheless significant. After increasing erratically during the 1820s and 1830s, both imports and exports leapt forward in the next 20 years. The nation remained primarily an exporter of raw materials and an importer of manufactured goods, and in most years it imported more than it exported. Cotton continued to be the most valuable export, in 1860 accounting for a record $191 million of total exports of $333 million. Despite America's own thriving industry, textiles still held the lead among imports, with iron products second. As in earlier days, Great Britain was both the best customer of the United States and its leading supplier.

The success of sailing packets, those "square-riggers on schedule," greatly facilitated the movement of passengers and freight. Fifty-two packets were operating between New York and Europe by 1845, and many more plied between New York and other American ports. The packets accelerated the tendency for trade to concentrate in New York and to a lesser extent in Philadelphia, Baltimore, and New Orleans. The commerce of Boston and smaller New England towns like Providence and New Haven, which had flourished in earlier days, now languished.

New Bedford and a few other southern New England towns shrewdly saved their prosperity by concentrating on whaling, which boomed between 1830 and 1860. The supply of whales seemed unlimited—as indeed it was, given the primitive hunting techniques of the age of sail. By the mid-1850s, with sperm oil selling at more than $1.75 a gallon and the country exporting an average of $2.7 million worth of whale oil and whalebone a year, New Bedford boasted a whaling fleet of well over 300 vessels and a population approaching 25,000.

The whalers ranged the oceans of the world; they lived a hard, lonely life punctuated by moments of exhilaration when they sighted the great mammoths of the deep and drove the harpoon home. They also made magnificent profits. To clear 100 percent in a single voyage was merely routine.

The increase in the volume and value of trade and its concentration at larger ports had a marked effect on the construction of ships. By the 1850s the average vessel was three times the size of those built 30 years earlier. Startling improvements in design, culminating in the long, sleek, white-winged clipper ships, made possible speeds previously undreamed of. Appearing just in time to supply the need for fast transportation to the California gold fields, the clippers cut sailing time around Cape Horn to San Francisco from five or six months to three, the record of 89 days being held jointly by *Andrew Jackson* and Donald McKay's famous *Flying Cloud.* Another McKay-designed clipper, *Champion of the Seas,* once logged 465 nautical miles in 24 hours, far in excess of the best efforts of modern yachts. To achieve such speeds, cargo capacity had to be sacrificed, making clippers uneconomical for carrying the bulky produce that was the mainstay of commerce. But for specialty goods, in their brief heyday the clippers were unsurpassed. Hong Kong merchants, never known for extravagance, willingly paid 75 cents a cubic foot to ship tea by clipper to London even though slower vessels charged only 28 cents. In the early 1850s clippers sold for as much as $150,000; with decent luck a ship might earn its full cost in a voyage or two.

STEAM CONQUERS THE ATLANTIC

The reign of the clipper ship was short. Like so many other things, ocean commerce was being mechanized. Steamships conquered the high seas more slowly than the rivers because early models were unsafe in rough

▲ *Giant Steamboats on the Levee at New Orleans* (1853), a painting by Hippolyte Sebron, a Frenchman. A picture of stately elegance, these boats required unusually powerful engines to make way against the strong currents of the Mississippi. Improvements in engine design and iron casting helped boats meet the river's challenge.

waters and uneconomical. A riverboat could take on fuel along its route, whereas an Atlantic steamer had to carry tons of coal across the ocean, thereby reducing its capacity for cargo. However, by the late 1840s, steamships were capturing most of the passenger traffic, mail contracts, and first-class freight. These vessels could not keep up with the clippers in a heavy breeze, but their average speed was far greater, especially on the westward voyage against the prevailing winds. Steamers were soon crossing the Atlantic in less than ten days. Nevertheless, for very long voyages, such as the 15,000-mile haul around South America to California, fast sailing ships held their own for many years.

The steamship, and especially the iron ship, which had greater cargo-carrying capacity and was stronger and less costly to maintain, took away the advantages that American shipbuilders had held since colonial times. American lumber was cheap, but the British excelled in iron technology. Although the United States invested about $14.5 million in subsidies for the shipping industry, the funds were not employed intelligently and did little good. In 1858 government efforts to aid shipping were abandoned.

The combination of competition, government subsidy, and technological advance drove down shipping rates. Between the mid-1820s and the mid-1850s the cost of moving a pound of cotton from New York to Liverpool fell from 1 cent to about a third of a cent. Transatlantic passengers could obtain the best accommodations on the fastest ships for under $200, good accommodations on slower packets for as little as $75.

Rates were especially low for European emigrants willing to travel to America on cargo vessels. By the 1840s at least 4000 ships were engaged in carrying bulky American cotton and Canadian lumber to Europe. On their return trips with manufactured goods they had much unoccupied space, which they converted into rough quarters for passengers. Conditions on these ships were crowded, gloomy, and foul. Frequently epidemics took a fearful toll among steerage passengers. On one crossing of the ship *Lark*, 158 of 440 passengers died of typhus.

Yet without this cheap means of transportation, thousands of poor immigrants would simply have remained at home. Bargain freight rates also help explain the clamor of American manufacturers for high tariffs, for transportation costs added relatively little to the price of European goods.

CANALS AND RAILROADS

Another dramatic change was the shift in the direction of the nation's internal commerce and its immense increase. From the time of the first settlers in the Mississippi Valley, the Great River had controlled the flow of goods from farm to market. The completion of the Erie Canal in 1825 heralded a shift, speeded by the feverish canal construction of the following decade. In 1830 there were 1277 miles of canal in the United States; by 1840 there were 3326 miles.

Each year saw more western produce moving to market through the canals. In 1845 the Erie Canal was still drawing over two-thirds of its west-east traffic from within New York, but by 1847, despite the fact that this local business held steady, more than half of its traffic came from west of Buffalo, and by 1851 more than two-thirds. The volume of western commerce over the Erie Canal in 1851 amounted to more than 20 times what it had been in 1836, while the value of western goods reaching New Orleans in this period increased only two and a half times.

The expanding traffic and New York's enormous share of it caused businessmen in other eastern cities whose canal projects had been unsuccessful to respond promptly when a new means of transport, the railroad, became available. The first railroads were built in England in the 1820s. In 1830 the first American line, the ambitiously named Baltimore and Ohio Railroad, carried 80,000 passengers over a 13-mile stretch of track.

By 1833 Charleston, South Carolina, had a line reaching 136 miles to Hamburg, on the Savannah River. Two years later the cars began rolling on the Boston and Worcester Railroad. The Panic of 1837 slowed construction, but by 1840 the United States had 3328 miles of track, equal to the canal mileage and nearly double the railroad mileage of all Europe.

The first railroads did not compete with the canals for intersectional traffic. The through connections needed to move goods economically over great distances materialized slowly. Of the 6000 miles of track operating in 1848, nearly all lay east of the Appalachians, and little of it had been coordinated into railroad systems. The intention of most early builders had been to monopolize the trade of surrounding districts, not to establish connections with competing centers. Frequently, railroads used tracks of different widths deliberately to prevent other lines from tying into their tracks.

Engineering problems held back growth. Steep grades and sharp curves—unavoidable in many parts of the country if the cost of the roads was not to be prohibitive—required more powerful and flexible engines than yet existed. Sparks from wood-burning locomotives caused fires. Wooden rails topped with strap iron wore out quickly and broke loose under the weight and vibration of heavy cars. In time the iron T rail and the use of crossties set in loose gravel to reduce vibration increased the durability of the tracks and made possible heavier, more efficient equipment. Modifications in the design of locomotives enabled the trains to negotiate sharp curves. Engines that could burn hard coal appeared, thereby eliminating the danger of starting fires along the right-of-way and reducing fuel costs.

▲ *First Railroad Train on the Mohawk and Hudson Road, 1835,* by Edward Lamson Henry (1892). Note how the shape and design of the railroad cars resembled the stagecoach they replaced.

Between 1848 and 1852 railroad mileage nearly doubled. Three years later it had doubled again, and by 1860 the nation had 30,636 miles of track. During this extraordinary burst of activity, four companies drove lines of gleaming iron from the Atlantic seaboard to the great interior valley. In 1851 the Erie Railroad, longest road in the world with 537 miles of track, linked the Hudson River north of New York City with Dunkirk on Lake Erie. Late the next year the Baltimore and Ohio reached the Ohio River at Wheeling, and in 1853 a banker named Erastus Corning consolidated eight short lines connecting Albany and Buffalo to form the New York Central Railroad. Finally, in 1858 the Pennsylvania Railroad completed a line across the mountains from Philadelphia to Pittsburgh.

In the states beyond the Appalachians, building went on at an even more feverish pace. By 1855 passengers could travel from Chicago or St. Louis to the east coast at a cost of $20 to $30, the trip taking, with luck, less than 48 hours. A generation earlier such a trip had required two to three weeks. Construction was slower in the South: Mississippi laid about 800 miles of track, Alabama 600.

Financing the Railroads

Railroad building required immense amounts of labor and capital at a time when many other demands for these resources existed. Immigrants or (in the South) slaves did most of the heavy work. Raising the necessary money proved a more complex task.

Private investors supplied about three-quarters of the money invested in railroads before 1860, more than $800 million in the 1850s alone. Much of this capital came from local merchants and businessmen and from farmers along the proposed rights-of-way. Funds were easy to raise because subscribers seldom had to lay out the full price of their stock at one time; instead they were subject to periodic "calls" for a percentage of their commitment as construction progressed. If the road made money, much of the additional mileage could be paid for out of earnings from the first sections built. The Utica and Schenectady Railroad, one of the lines that became part of the New York Central, was capitalized in 1833 at $2 million (20,000 shares at $100). Only $75 per share was ever called; by 1844 the road had been completed, shares were selling at $129, and shareholders were receiving handsome cash dividends.

The Utica and Schenectady Railroad was a short road in a rich territory; for less favorably situated lines, stocks were hard to sell. Of the lines connecting the seaboard with the Middle West, the New York Central alone needed no public aid, chiefly because it ran through prosperous, well-populated country and across level terrain. The others were all "mixed enterprises," drawing about half their capital from state and local governments, the rest from bonds sold to American and foreign investors.

Public aid took many forms. Towns, counties, and the states themselves lent money to railroads and invested in their stock. Special privileges, such as exemption from taxation and the right to condemn property, were often granted, and in a few cases states built and operated roads as public corporations.

DOCUMENT

Senate Report on the Railroads

As with earlier internal improvement proposals, federal financial aid to railroads was usually blocked in Congress by a combination of eastern and southern votes. But in 1850 a scheme for granting federal lands to the states to build a line from Lake Michigan to the Gulf of Mexico passed both houses. The main beneficiary was the Illinois Central Railroad, which received a 200-foot right-of-way and alternate strips of land along the track 1 mile wide and 6 miles deep, a total of almost 2.6 million acres. By mortgaging this land and by selling portions of it to farmers, the Illinois Central raised nearly all the $23.4 million it spent on construction. The success of this operation led to additional grants of almost 20 million acres in the 1850s, benefiting more than 40 railroads. Far larger federal grants were made after the Civil War, when the transcontinental lines were built.

Frequently, the capitalists who promoted railroads were more concerned with making money out of the construction of the lines than with operating them. The banker Erastus Corning was a good railroad man; his lines were well maintained and efficiently run. Yet he was also mayor of Albany, an important figure in state and national politics, and a manufacturer of iron. He accepted no salary as president of the Utica and Schenectady, "asking only that he have the privilege of supplying all the rails, running gear, tools and other iron and steel articles used." When he could not himself produce rails of the proper quality, he purchased them in England, charging the railroad a commission for his services. Corning's actions led to stockholder complaints, and a committee was appointed to investigate. He managed to control this group easily enough, but it did report that "the practice of buying articles for the use of the Railroad Company from its own officers might in time come to lead to abuses of great magnitude." The prediction proved all too accurate in the generation following the Civil War.

Corning, it must be emphasized, was honest enough; his mistake, if mistake it was, lay in overestimating his own impartiality a little. Others in the business were unashamedly crooked and avidly took advantage of the public passion for railroads. Some officials issued stock to themselves without paying for it and then sold the shares to gullible investors. Others manipulated the books of their corporations and set up special construction companies and paid them exorbitant returns out of railroad assets. These practices did not become widespread until after the Civil War, but all of them first sprang up in the decades preceding the war. At the same time that the country was first developing a truly national economy, it was also producing its first really big-time crooks.

RAILROADS AND THE ECONOMY

The effects of so much railroad construction were profound. Although the main reason that farmers put more land under the plow was an increase in the price of agricultural products, the railroad helped determine just what land was used and how profitably it could be farmed. Much of the fertile prairie through which the Illinois Central ran had been available for settlement for many years before 1850, but development had been slow because it was remote from navigable waters and had no timber. In 1840 the three counties immediately northeast of Springfield had a

population of about 8500. They produced about 59,000 bushels of wheat and 690,000 bushels of corn. In the next decade the region grew slowly by the standards of that day: The three counties had about 14,000 people in 1850 and produced 71,000 bushels of wheat and 2.2 million bushels of corn. Then came the railroad and with it an agricultural revolution. By 1860 the population of the three counties had soared to over 38,000, wheat production had topped 550,000 bushels, and corn 5.7 million bushels. "Land-grant" railroads such as the Illinois Central stimulated agricultural expansion by advertising their lands widely and selling farm sites at low rates on liberal terms.

Access to world markets gave the farmers of the upper Mississippi Valley an incentive to increase output. Land was plentiful and cheap, but farm labor was scarce; consequently agricultural wages rose sharply, especially after 1850. New tools and machines appeared in time to ease the labor shortage. First came the steel plowshare, invented by John Deere, a Vermont-born blacksmith who had moved to Illinois in 1837. The prairie sod was tough and sticky, but Deere's smooth metal plows cut through it easily. In 1839 Deere turned out ten such plows in his little shop in Moline, Illinois. By 1857 he was selling 10,000 a year.

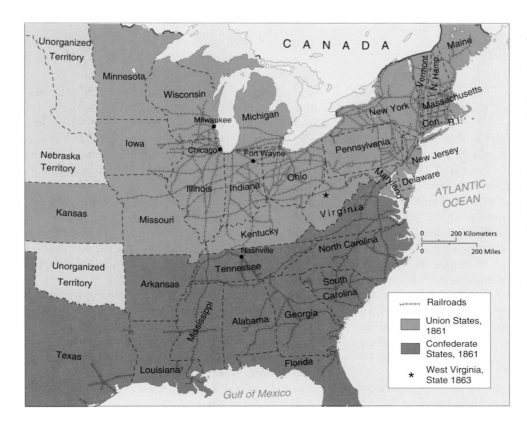

◄ **Railroads, 1860**
This map shows trunk lines (lines carrying through-traffic) in operation in 1860. Certain towns and cities owed their spectacularly rapid growth to the railroad, Chicago being an outstanding example. The map suggests the strong influence of the railroads on the expansion and economic prosperity of smaller cities such as Fort Wayne, Milwaukee, and Nashville. At the outbreak of the Civil War in 1861, the relative lack of railroads in the South was a major disadvantage for the Confederacy.

▶ Agriculture, 1860

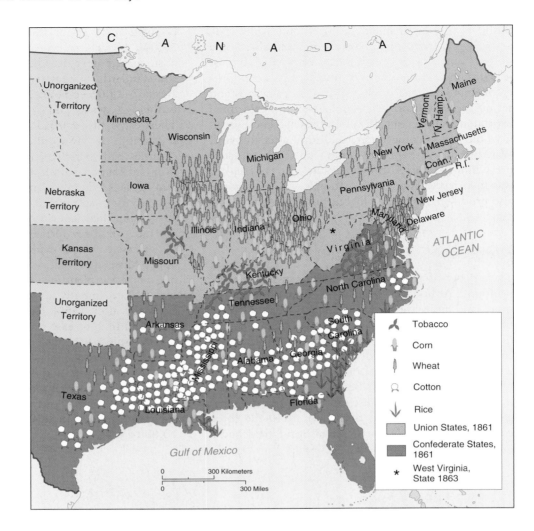

Still more important was the perfection of the mechanical reaper, for wheat production was limited more by the amount that farmers could handle during the brief harvest season than by the acreage they could plant and cultivate. The major figure in the development of the reaper was Cyrus Hall McCormick. McCormick's horse-drawn reaper bent the grain against the cutting knife and then deposited it neatly on a platform, whence it could easily be raked into windrows. With this machine, two workers could cut 14 times as much wheat as with scythes.

McCormick prospered, but despite his patents, he could not keep other manufacturers out of the business. Competition led to continual improvement of the machines and kept prices within the reach of most farmers. Installment selling added to demand. By 1860 nearly 80,000 reapers had been sold; their efficiency helps explain why wheat output rose by nearly 75 percent in the 1850s.

The railroad had an equally powerful impact on American cities. The eastern seaports benefited, and

so did countless intermediate centers, such as Buffalo and Cincinnati. But no city was affected more profoundly by railroads than Chicago. In 1850 not a single line had reached there; five years later it was terminal for 2200 miles of track and controlled the commerce of an imperial domain. By extending half a dozen lines west to the Mississippi, it drained off nearly all the river traffic north of St. Louis. The Illinois Central sucked the expanding output of the prairies into Chicago as well. Most of this freight went eastward over the new railroads or on the Great Lakes and the Erie Canal. Nearly 350,000 tons of shipping plied the lakes by 1855.

The railroads, like the textile industry, stimulated other kinds of economic activity. They transformed agriculture, both real estate values and the buying and selling of land increased whenever the iron horse puffed into a new district. The railroads spurred regional concentration of industry and an increase in the size of business units. Their insatiable need for capital stimulated the growth of investment banking.

The complexity of their operations made them, as the historian Alfred D. Chandler, Jr., writes, "the first modern business enterprises," the first to employ large numbers of salaried managers and to develop "a large internal organizational structure with carefully defined lines of responsibility."

Although they apparently did not have much effect on general manufacturing before the Civil War, the railroads consumed nearly half the nation's output of bar and sheet iron in 1860. Probably more labor and more capital were occupied in economic activities resulting from the development of railroads than in the roads themselves—another way of saying that the railroads were immensely valuable internal improvements.

The proliferation of trunk lines and the competition of the canal system (for many products the slowness of canal transportation was not a serious handicap) led to a sharp decline in freight and passenger rates. Periodically, railroads engaged in "wars" to capture business. At times a person could travel from New York to Buffalo for as little as $4; anthracite was being shipped from the Pennsylvania mines to the coast for $1.50 a ton. The Erie Canal reduced its toll charges by more than two thirds in the face of railroad competition, and the roads in turn cut rates drastically until, on the eve of the Civil War, it cost less than 1 cent per ton-mile to send produce through the canal and only slightly more than 2 cents a mile on the railroads. By that time one could ship a bushel of wheat from Chicago to New York by railroad for less than 35 cents.

Cheap transportation had a revolutionary effect on western agriculture. Farmers in Iowa could now raise grain to feed the factory workers of Lowell and even of Manchester, England. Two-thirds of the meat consumed in New York City was soon arriving by rail from beyond the Appalachians. The center of American wheat production shifted westward to Illinois, Wisconsin, and Indiana. When the Crimean War (1853–1856) and European crop failures increased foreign demand, these regions boomed. Success bred success for farmers and for the railroads. Profits earned from carrying wheat enabled the roads to build feeder lines that opened up still wider areas to commercial agriculture and made it easy to bring in lumber, farm machinery, household furnishings, and the settlers themselves at low cost.

RAILROADS AND THE SECTIONAL CONFLICT

Increased production and cheap transportation boosted the western farmer's income and standard of living. The days of isolation and self-sufficiency, even for the family on the edge of the frontier, rapidly disappeared. Pioneers quickly became operators of businesses and, to a far greater extent than their forebears, consumers, buying all sorts of manufactured articles that their ancestors had made for themselves or done without. These changes had their costs. Like southern planters, they now became dependent on middlemen and lost some of their feeling of self-reliance. Overproduction became a problem. Buying a farm began to require more capital, for as profits increased, so did the price of land. Machinery was an additional expense. The proportion of farm laborers and tenants increased.

The linking of East and West had fateful effects on politics. The increased ease of movement from section to section and the ever more complex social and economic integration of East and West stimulated nationalism and thus became a force for the preservation of the Union. Without the railroads and canals, Illinois and Iowa would scarcely have dared to side against the South in 1861. When the Mississippi ceased to be essential to them, citizens of the upper valley could afford to be more hostile to slavery and especially to its westward extension. Economic ties with the Northeast reinforced cultural connections.

The South might have preserved its influence in the Northwest if it had pressed forward its own railroad-building program. It failed to do so. There were many southern lines but nothing like a southern system. As late as 1856 one could get from Memphis to Richmond or Charleston only by very indirect routes. As late as 1859 the land-grant road extending

▲ John Deere's steel-bladed plow was designed to cut through the tough prairie sod.

the Illinois Central to Mobile, Alabama, was not complete, nor did any economical connection exist between Chicago and New Orleans.

This state of affairs could be accounted for in part by the scattered population of the South, the paucity of passenger traffic, the seasonal nature of much of the freight business, and the absence of large cities. Southerners placed too much reliance on the Mississippi: The fact that traffic on the river continued to be heavy throughout the 1850s blinded them to the precipitous rate at which their relative share of the nation's trade was declining. But the fundamental cause of the South's backwardness in railroad construction was the attitude of its leaders. Southerners of means were no more interested in commerce than in industry; their capital found other outlets.

THE ECONOMY ON THE EVE OF CIVIL WAR

Between the mid-1840s and the mid-1850s the United States experienced one of the most remarkable periods of growth in the history of the world. Every economic indicator surged forward: manufacturing, grain and cotton production, population, railroad mileage, gold production, sales of public land. The building of the railroads stimulated business, and by making transportation cheaper, the completed lines energized the nation's economy. The American System that Henry Clay had dreamed of arrived with a rush just as Clay was passing from the scene.

Inevitably, this growth caused dislocations that were aggravated by the boom psychology that once again infected the popular mind. In 1857 there was a serious collapse. The return of Russian wheat to the world market after the Crimean War caused grain prices to fall. This checked agricultural expansion, which hurt the railroads and cut down on the demand for manufactures. Unemployment increased. Frightened depositors started runs on banks, most of which had to suspend specie payments.

People called this abrupt downturn the Panic of 1857. Yet the vigor of the economy was such that the bad times did not last long. The upper Mississippi Valley suffered most, for so much new land had been opened up that supplies of farm produce greatly exceeded demand. Elsewhere conditions improved rapidly.

The South, somewhat out of the hectic rush to begin with, was affected very little by the collapse of 1857, for cotton prices continued high. This gave planters the false impression that their economy was immune to such violent downturns. Some began to argue that the South would be better off out of the Union.

Before a new national upward swing could become well established, however, the sectional crisis between North and South shook people's confidence in the future. Then the war came, and a new set of forces shaped economic development.

MILESTONES

1808	Congress bans further importation of slaves	1840–1857	Economy surges during boom in manufacturing, railroad construction, and foreign commerce
1822	37 slaves are executed when Denmark Vesey's "conspiracy" is exposed	1842	Massachusetts declares unions legal in *Commonwealth* v. *Hunt*
1825	Erie Canal is completed, connecting East and Middle West	1846	Elias Howe invents sewing machine
1830	Baltimore and Ohio railroad begins operation	1850	Congress grants land to aid construction of Illinois Central Railroad
1831	Nat Turner's slave uprising kills 57 whites	1854	Clipper ship *Flying Cloud* sails from New York to San Francisco in 89 days
1837	Cyrus Hall McCormick invents reaper to harvest wheat	1857	Brief economic depression (Panic of 1857) collapses economy
1839	John Deere begins manufacturing steel plows		

SUPPLEMENTARY READING

Most of the volumes dealing with economic developments mentioned in earlier chapters continue to be useful for this period. On the Panic of 1857, see J. L. Huston, *The Panic of 1857 and the Coming of the Civil War* (1987). For a useful comparative study, see John Majewski, *A House Dividing: Economic Development in Pennsylvania and Virginia before the Civil War* (2000). On the economy of the South, see Gavin Wright, *The Political Economy of the Cotton South* (1978), and Michael Tadman, *Speculators and Slaves* (1989).

On slavery, in addition to the essential works listed in Debating the Past (p. 349), see Brenda Stevenson, *Life in Black and White* (1996), and Walter Johnson, *Soul by Soul: Life Inside the Antebellum Slave Market* (1999), which focuses on New Orleans. Recent evidence of slave resistance is documented in John Hope Franklin and Loren Schweninger, *Runaway Slaves* (1999), David Robertson, *Denmark Vesey* (1999), and Douglas R. Egerton, *Gabriel's Rebellion* (1993). An earlier study is Eugene D. Genovese, *From Rebellion to Revolution* (1979).

Excellent regional studies include Peter Coclanis, *The Shadow of a Dream* (1989), for South Carolina, as well as Charles E. Joyner, *Down by the Riverside: A South Carolina Slave Community* (1984), and Ann Patton Malone, *Sweet Chariot: Slave Family and Household Structure in Nineteenth-Century Louisiana* (1992).

Among specialized volumes, Bertram Wyatt-Brown, *Southern Honor* (1982), and Ira Berlin, *Slaves Without Masters* (1975), are important. Richard C. Wade, *Slavery in the Cities* (1964), contends that urban life eroded slavery, while Robert Starobin, *Industrial Slavery in the Old South* (1970), found that the institution could be adapted to industrial purposes. Most local studies take an intermediate position; see, for example, Midori Takagi, *"Rearing Wolves to Our Own Destruction": Slavery in Richmond, Virginia, 1782-1865* (1999).

Irish emigration is the subject of Tim Pat Coogan's expansive *Wherever Green Is Worn* (2000), and Edward Laxton, *The Famine Ships* (1997), as well as the scholarly collection edited by Arthur Gribben, *The Great Famine and the Irish Diaspora in America* (1999). J. Matthew Gallman, *Receiving Erin's Children* (2000) examines the arrival of Irish famine emigrants in Philadelphia. Although fewer sources on German emigration are available in English, see Marianne Wokeck, *Trade in Strangers* (1999).

On industrial developments, see H. J. Habbakuk, *American and British Technology in the Nineteenth Century* (1962), and Nathan Rosenberg, *Technology and American Economic Growth* (1972). John F. Stover, *American Railroads* (1997), is a good survey. Among the specialized studies of railroad development see Sarah Gordon, *Passage to Union* (1997), which considers the political implications of railroad development, as well as T. C. Cochran, *Railroad Leaders* (1953).

On labor history, many of the books cited in the three previous chapters apply to this one as well. On the New England shoe industry and labor organization, see Mary Blewett, *Men, Women and Work* (1988); for a more general study see her *Constant Turmoil: The Politics of Industrial Life in Nineteenth Century New England* (2000). For workingmen's political activities, Edward Pessen's *Most Uncommon Jacksonians* (1967) remains valuable.

SUGGESTED WEBSITES

"Been Here So Long": Selections from the WPA American Slave Narratives

http://newdeal.feri.org/asn/index.htm

Slave narratives are some of the most interesting primary sources about slavery.

The Settlement of African Americans in Liberia

http://www.loc.gov/exhibits/african/afam003.html

This site contains images and text relating to the colonization movement to return African Americans to Africa.

Images of African Americans from the Nineteenth Century

http://digital.nypl.org/schomburg/images_aa19/

The New York Public Library Schomburg Center for Research in Black Culture site contains numerous visuals of nineteenth-century African Americans.

▼ In *The Ride for Liberty—the Fugitive Slaves* (1863), painter Eastman Johnson foregrounds the slaves' own efforts to escape. In the background, though, the Union Army advances. Few slaves could effect their freedom on their own.

CHAPTER CONTENTS

The political settlement between North and South that Henry Clay designed in 1850 lasted only four years. One specific event wrecked it, but it was probably doomed in any case. Americans continued to migrate westward by the thousands, and as long as slaveholders could carry their human property into federally controlled territories, northern resentment would smolder. Slaves continued to seek freedom in the North, and the federal Fugitive Slave Act of 1850, which imposed fines for hiding or rescuing fugitive slaves, could not guarantee their capture and return. Abolitionists intensified their propaganda.

THE SLAVE POWER COMES NORTH

The new fugitive slave law encouraged more white Southerners to try to recover escaped slaves. Something approaching panic reigned in the black communities of northern cities when slave hunters arrived to seize former slaves. Thousands of blacks, not all of them fugitive slaves, fled to Canada, but many remained, and Northerners frequently refused to stand aside when such people were dragged off in chains.

Shortly after the passage of the act, James Hamlet was seized in New York City, convicted, and returned to slavery in Maryland without even being allowed to communicate with his wife and children. The New York black community was outraged, and with help from white neighbors it swiftly raised $800 to buy his freedom. In 1851 Eu-

KIDNAPPING AGAIN!!

A MAN WAS STOLEN LAST NIGHT BY THE
Fugitive Slave Bill COMMISSIONER!
HE WILL HAVE HIS
MOCK TRIAL
ON SATURDAY, MAY 27, AT 9 O'CLOCK,
In the Kidnapper's 'Court,' before the Hon. Slave Bill Commissioner,
AT THE COURT HOUSE, IN COURT SQUARE.
SHALL BOSTON STEAL ANOTHER MAN?
Thursday, May 26, 1854.

▲ Anthony Burns, the subject of this Boston poster, was the third runaway slave to be seized and returned to the South under the hated Fugitive Slave Act of 1850. The Burns case galvanized public opinion just when Congress was debating the Kansas-Nebraska Act. The passage of that bill further outraged Northerners.

DOCUMENT

Drew, from
Narratives of
Fugitive Slaves
in Canada

phemia Williams, who had lived for years as a free woman in Pennsylvania, was seized, her presumed owner claiming also her six children, all Pennsylvania-born. A federal judge released the Williamses, but the case caused alarm in the North.

Abolitionists often interfered with the enforcement of the law. When two Georgians came to Boston to reclaim William and Ellen Craft, admitted fugitives, a "vigilance committee" hounded them through the streets shouting "slave hunters, slave hunters," and forced them to return home empty-handed. The Crafts prudently—or perhaps in disgust—decided to leave the United States for England. Early in 1851 a Virginia agent captured Frederick "Shadrach" Jenkins, a waiter in a Boston coffeehouse. While Jenkins was being held for deportation, a mob of African Americans broke into the courthouse and hustled him off to Canada. That October a slave named Jerry, who had escaped from Missouri, was arrested in Syracuse, New York. Within minutes the whole town had the news. Crowds surged through the streets, and when night fell, a mob smashed into the building where Jerry was being held and spirited him away to safety in Canada.

Such incidents exacerbated sectional feelings. White Southerners accused the North of reneging on one of the main promises made in the Compromise of 1850, while the sight of harmless human beings being hustled off to a life of slavery disturbed many Northerners who were not abolitionists.

However, most white Northerners were not prepared to interfere with the enforcement of the Fugitive Slave Act themselves. Of the 332 blacks put on trial under the law, about 300 were returned to slavery, most without incident. In March 1854, Sherman M. Ableman, a Wisconsin newspaperman, was charged with having raised a mob to free a runaway. The Wisconsin Supreme Court freed him on the grounds that the Fugitive Slave Act was unconstitutional. However, in *Ableman* v. *Booth* (1859) the United States Supreme Court upheld the act's constitutionality and Booth was jailed. Nevertheless, enforcing the law in the northern states became steadily more difficult.

UNCLE TOM'S CABIN

Tremendously important in increasing sectional tensions and bringing home the evils of slavery to still more people in the North was Harriet Beecher Stowe's novel *Uncle Tom's Cabin* (1852). Stowe was neither a professional writer nor an abolitionist, and she had almost no firsthand knowledge of slavery. But her conscience had been roused by the Fugitive Slave Act. In gathering material for the book, she depended heavily on abolitionist writers, many of whom she knew. She dashed it off quickly; as she later recalled, it seemed to write itself. Nevertheless, *Uncle Tom's Cabin* was an enormous success: 10,000 copies were sold in a week; 300,000 in a year. It was translated into dozens of languages. Dramatized versions were staged in countries throughout the world .

DOCUMENT

Stowe, *Uncle
Tom's Cabin*

Harriet Beecher Stowe was hardly a distinguished writer; it was her approach to the subject that explains the book's success. Her tale of the pious, patient slave Uncle Tom, the saintly white child Eva, and the callous slave driver Simon Legree appealed to an audience far wider than that reached by the abolitionists. She avoided the self-righteous, accusatory tone of most abolitionist tracts and did not seek to convert readers to belief in racial equality. Many of her southern white characters were fine, sensitive people, while the cruel Simon Legree was a transplanted Connecticut Yankee. There were many heart-rending scenes of pain, self-sacrifice, and heroism. The story proved especially effective on the stage: The slave Eliza crossing the frozen Ohio River to freedom, the death of Little Eva, Eva and Tom ascending to Heaven—these scenes left audiences in tears.

Southern critics pointed out, correctly enough, that Stowe's picture of plantation life was distorted, her slaves atypical. They called her a "coarse, ugly, long-tongued woman" and accused her of trying to

▲ A poster advertising *Uncle Tom's Cabin* in 1852, the year of its publication. The following year, Harriet Beecher Stowe published *A Key to Uncle Tom's Cabin,* intended to provide documentary evidence in support of disputed details of her indictment of slavery.

"awaken rancorous hatred and malignant jealousies" that would undermine national unity. Most Northerners, having little basis on which to judge the accuracy of the book, tended to discount southern criticism as biased. In any case, *Uncle Tom's Cabin* raised questions that transcended the issue of accuracy. Did it matter if every slave was not as kindly as Uncle Tom, as determined as George Harris? What if only one white master was as evil as Simon Legree? No earlier white American writer had looked at slaves as people.

Uncle Tom's Cabin touched the hearts of millions. Some became abolitionists; others, still hesitating to step forward, asked themselves as they put the book down: Is slavery just?

DIVERSIONS ABROAD: THE "YOUNG AMERICA" MOVEMENT

Clearly a distraction was needed to help keep the lid on sectional troubles. Some people hoped to find one in foreign affairs. The spirit of manifest destiny explains this in large part; once the United States had reached the Pacific, expansionists began to think of transmitting the dynamic, democratic U.S. spirit to other countries by aiding local revolutionaries, opening new markets, perhaps even annexing foreign lands.

This "Young America" spirit was partly emotional, a mindless confidence that democracy would triumph everywhere, that public opinion was "stronger than the Bayonet." At the time of the European revolutions of 1848, Americans talked freely about helping the liberals in their struggles against autocratic governments. Horace Greeley's *New York Tribune* predicted that Europe would soon become "one great and splendid Republic . . . and we shall all be citizens of the world." When the Austrians crushed a rebellion in Hungary, Secretary of State Daniel Webster addressed an insulting note full of vague threats to the Austrian chargé d'affaires in Washington. Hungarian revolutionary hero Louis Kossuth visited the United States in search of aid in 1851 and 1852; President Fillmore put the USS *Mississippi* at his disposal, and great crowds turned out to cheer him.

The United States had no intention of going to war to win independence for the Hungarians, as Kossuth soon learned to his sorrow. However, the same democratic-expansionist sentiment led to dreams of conquests in the Caribbean area. In 1855 an adventurer named William Walker, backed by an American company engaged in transporting migrants to California across Central America, seized control of Nicaragua and elected himself president. He was ousted two years later but made repeated attempts to regain control until, in 1860, he died before a Honduran firing squad. Another would-be dictator, "General" George W. L. Bickley, claiming that he was disturbed by that "crookedest of all boundary lines, the Rio Grande," tried to organize an expedition to conquer Mexico.

Although many Northerners suspected them of engaging in plots to obtain more territory for slavery, Walker and Bickley were primarily adventurers trying to use the prevailing mood of buoyant expansionism for selfish ends. But there were reasons unrelated to slavery why Central America suddenly seemed important. The rapid development of California created a need for improved communication with the West Coast. A canal across Central America would cut weeks from the sailing time between New York and San Francisco. In 1850 Secretary of State John M. Clayton and the British minister to the United States, Henry Lytton Bulwer, negotiated a treaty providing for the demilitarization and joint Anglo-American control of any canal across the isthmus.

▶ *text continues on page 370*

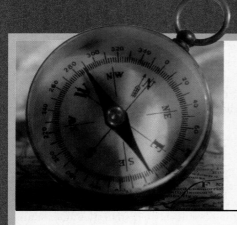

Runaway Slaves: Hard Realities

The Myth of the Underground Railroad

The "Underground Railroad" is a commonplace of American history. The imagery is that of a subway moving masses of slaves out of the South. But the metaphor is deceptive. "The Underground Railroad" was neither as organized nor as extensive as legend suggests, nor did it exist in any slave state.

Each year tens of thousands of slaves fled, often from wrathful masters and overseers, by running into the swamps, hills, woods, or cities of the South. Few had any hope of making it to a free state, much less Canada. Few received help from abolitionists or anyone else. Of the nation's 4 million slaves, probably no more than several thousand a year escaped to a free state. Only a handful of slaves in the Cotton Belt of South Carolina, Georgia, Alabama, and Mississippi made it out of the South. Moreover, runaways in Texas and Louisiana did not go north to Canada, but west to Mexico, where nothing could be done to recover them.

The "Underground Railroad" endangered slavery not by enabling large numbers of slaves to escape, but by posing an explicit challenge to political leaders in the South. They insisted on passage of the Fugitive Slave Act to reaffirm their right to their "property" in slaves.

Actual Slave Escapes

The map "Escape Itineraries" *(right)* underscores the fact that few runaway slaves had much chance of making their way to freedom in the North. The map shows that the greatest concentrations of slaves were in South Carolina, Georgia, Alabama, Mississippi, and Louisiana. Most successful runaways lived near free states, and those who managed to escape possessed exceptional skills, cunning, or luck, and usually a combination of all three. The second map further suggests that escaped slaves generally originated from and fled to places with high proportions of free blacks.

The experience of William and Ellen Craft, slaves in Georgia, is illuminating. William, a cabinet-maker, worked evenings as a waiter and saved some money; his wife, Ellen, a seamstress, made a pair of men's trousers. Exemplary slaves, their master gave them a pass to visit relatives for Christmas and they used this occasion to escape. Ellen, who was light-skinned, put on men's clothing and green eyeglasses; to conceal her inability to write, she put her arm in a sling and, as further disguise, wrapped a bandage around one side of her face. She claimed to be a white gentleman traveling to Philadelphia to see an eye doctor, accompanied by her "servant"— William. With the money he had saved they bought

▲ A print of Ellen Craft, the slave, in the disguise "as a distinguished-looking gentleman" that effected her escape. The deceit was possible, she wrote, because she was "almost white" in appearance.

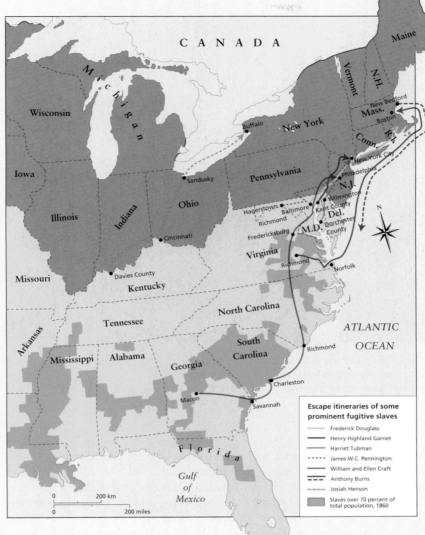

the Ohio River, headed into southern Indiana, and walked northeast to Cincinnati and then to Sandusky, Ohio. From there they sailed to Buffalo. Before the year was out, they passed over to Canada.

James W. C. Pennington escaped from a farm near Hagerstown, Maryland, in 1827. He walked toward Baltimore but was captured near Reisterstown. Then he escaped again, heading northwest into Pennsylvania, where he hid for several months. Then he journeyed northeast through Lancaster County to East Nautmeal in Chester County, Pennsylvania. He settled in New York.

Anthony Burns, who taught himself to read and write, became invaluable as a hired hand who worked at various crafts. While working as a stevedore on the docks in Richmond (see the poster on p. 366), he befriended a sailor who helped him stow away on a ship to Boston. There he was apprehended. Under the terms of the Fugitive Slave Law, he was returned to Richmond. The residents of Boston purchased his freedom in 1855.

Escape itineraries of some prominent fugitive slaves

Frederick Douglass
Henry Highland Garnet
Harriet Tubman
James W.C. Pennington
William and Ellen Craft
Anthony Burns
Josiah Henson

Slaves over 70 percent of total population, 1860

train tickets in Macon and went to Savannah. Then they took several short boat trips: to Charleston and then to Wilmington, North Carolina, and again by train through Virginia and Maryland. They arrived at Philadelphia on Christmas Day, 1848.

Frederick Douglass escaped from Baltimore, Maryland, in 1838, disguised as a sailor, and with borrowed seaman's papers. He traveled by train to Wilmington, Delaware, by boat to Philadelphia, by train to New York City, and by boat to New Bedford, Massachusetts.

Josiah Henson was at a young age made superintendent of a plantation in Maryland. When his master went bankrupt, he was sent to a plantation in Davies County, Kentucky. Fearing he would be sold to the Deep South, in 1830 he escaped on foot with his wife and children. They crossed

Free blacks, c.1860

counties with more than 100 free blacks

concentrations of 2000 or more free blacks

▲ A photograph of Commodore Matthew Perry in 1855 *(left)* juxtaposed with a Japanese portrait of him. When Perry's squadron arrived in Edo Bay (Tokyo), the Japanese ordered him to leave. Japanese writers had long warned of the "barbarians of the west" who with "squinting eyes and limping feet" sought to override the "noble nations" of Asia.

As this area assumed strategic importance to the United States, the desire to obtain Cuba grew stronger. In 1854 President Franklin Pierce instructed his minister to Spain, Pierre Soulé of Louisiana, to offer $130 million for the island. Since Soulé was a hotheaded bungler, the administration arranged for him first to confer in Belgium with the American ministers to Great Britain and France, James Buchanan and John Y. Mason, to work out a plan for persuading Spain to sell. Out of this meeting came the Ostend Manifesto, a confidential dispatch to the State Department suggesting that if Spain refused to sell Cuba, "the great law of self-preservation" might justify "wresting" it from Spain by force.

News of the manifesto leaked out, and it had to be published. Northern opinion was outraged by this "slaveholders' plot." Europeans claimed to be shocked by such "dishonorable" and "clandestine" diplomacy. The government had to disavow the manifesto, and any hope of obtaining Cuba or any other territory in the Caribbean vanished.

The expansionist mood of the moment also explains President Fillmore's dispatching an expedition under Commodore Matthew C. Perry to try for commercial concessions in the isolated kingdom of Japan in 1854. Perry's expedition was a great success. The Japanese, impressed by American naval power, agreed to establish diplomatic relations. In 1858 an American envoy, Townsend Harris, negotiated a commercial treaty that opened to American ships six Japanese ports heretofore closed to foreigners. President Pierce's negotiation of a Canadian reciprocity treaty with Great Britain in 1854 and an unsuccessful attempt, also made under Pierce, to annex the Hawaiian Islands are further demonstrations of the assertive foreign policy of the period.

STEPHEN DOUGLAS: "THE LITTLE GIANT"

The most prominent spokesman of the Young America movement was Stephen A. Douglas. The senator from Illinois was the Henry Clay of his generation. Like Clay at his best, Douglas was able to see the needs of the nation in the broadest perspective. He held a succession of state offices before being elected to Congress in 1842 at the age of 29. After only two terms in the House, he was chosen United States senator.

Douglas succeeded at almost everything he attempted. His law practice was large and prosperous.

He dabbled in Chicago real estate and made a fortune. Politics suited him to perfection. Rarely has a man seemed so closely attuned to his time and place in history. Although very short, he had powerful shoulders, a large head, strong features, and deep-set, piercing eyes. His high forehead was made to appear even bolder by the way he wore his hair, swept back in a pompadour and draped over his collar. His appearance was so imposing that friends called him "the Little Giant." "I live with my constituents," he once boasted, "drink with them, lodge with them, pray with them, laugh, hunt, dance, and work with them. I eat their corn dodgers and fried bacon and sleep two in a bed with them." Yet he was no mere backslapper. He read widely, wrote poetry, financed a number of young American artists, served as a regent of the Smithsonian Institution, and was interested in scientific farming.

The foundations of Douglas's politics were expansion and popular sovereignty. He had been willing to fight for all of Oregon in 1846, and he supported the Mexican War to the hilt, in sharp contrast to his one-term Illinois colleague in Congress, Abraham Lincoln. That local settlers should determine their own institutions was, to his way of thinking, axiomatic. Arguments over the future of slavery in the territories he believed a foolish waste of energy and time since he was convinced that natural conditions would keep the institution out of the West.

The main thing, he insisted, was to get on with the development of the United States. Let the nation build railroads, acquire new territory, expand its trade. He believed slavery "a curse beyond computation" for both blacks and whites, but he refused to admit that

any moral issue was involved. He cared not, he boasted, whether slavery was voted up or voted down. This was not really true, but the question was interfering with the rapid exploitation of the continent. Douglas wanted it settled so that the country could concentrate on more important matters.

Douglas's success in steering the Compromise of 1850 through Congress added to his reputation. In 1851, he set out to win the Democratic presidential nomination, reasoning that since he was the brightest, most imaginative, and hardest-working Democrat around, he had every right to press his claim.

This brash aggressiveness proved his undoing. He expressed open contempt for James Buchanan and said of his other chief rival, Lewis Cass, who had won considerable fame while serving as minister to France, that his "reputation was beyond the C."

At the 1852 Democratic convention Douglas had no chance. Cass and Buchanan killed each other off, and the delegates finally chose a dark horse, Franklin Pierce of New Hampshire. The Whigs, rejecting the colorless Fillmore, nominated General Winfield Scott, who was known as "Old Fuss and Feathers" because of his "punctiliousness in dress and decorum." In the campaign both sides supported the Compromise of 1850. The Democrats won an easy victory, 254 electoral votes to 42.

So handsome a triumph seemed to ensure stability, but in fact it was a prelude to political chaos. The Whig party was crumbling fast. The shifting amalgam of ethnic and cultural issues that held the party together at the local level dissolved as the slavery debate became more heated. The "Cotton" Whigs of the South, alienated by the antislavery sentiments of their northern brethren, were flocking into the Democratic fold. In the North the Whigs, divided between an antislavery wing ("conscience Whigs") and another that was undisturbed by slavery, found themselves more and more at odds with each other. Congress fell overwhelmingly into the hands of proslavery southern Democrats, a development profoundly disturbing to northern Democrats as well as to Whigs.

THE KANSAS-NEBRASKA ACT

Franklin Pierce was a youthful-appearing 48 years old when he took office. He was generally well liked by politicians. His career had included service in both houses of Congress. Alcohol had become a problem for him in Washington, however, and in 1842 he had resigned from the Senate and returned home to try to best the bottle, a struggle in which he was successful. His law practice boomed, and he added to his reputation by serving as a brigadier general during the Mexican War. Although his nomination for president

▲ Stephen A. Douglas, dubbed the "Little Giant" for his height—he was five feet four inches tall—and his pugnacity. John Quincy Adams observed that during a debate Douglas worked himself into "such a heat that if his body had been made of combustible matter it would have burnt out."

▲ Franklin Pierce, a brigadier general during the Mexican War, was thrown from his horse and sustained pelvic and knee injuries. When he attempted to lead his men the next day, he fainted. Another officer, mistaking his unconsciousness, accused him of cowardice. For years, Whigs attacked Pierce's military record. Alluding to his fondness for liquor, they called him "hero of many a bottle."

came as a surprise, once made, it had appeared perfectly reasonable. Great things were expected of his administration, especially after he surrounded himself with men of all factions: To balance his appointment of a radical states' rights Mississippian, Jefferson Davis, as secretary of war, for example, he named a conservative Northerner, William L. Marcy of New York, as secretary of state.

Only a strong leader, however, can manage a ministry of all talents, and that President Pierce was not. The ship of state was soon drifting; Pierce seemed incapable of holding firm the helm.

This was the situation in January 1854 when Senator Douglas, chairman of the Committee on Territories, introduced what looked like a routine bill organizing the land west of Missouri and Iowa as the Nebraska Territory. Since settlers were beginning to trickle into the area, the time had arrived to set up a civil administration. But besides his expansionist motives, Douglas also acted because a territorial government was essential to railroad development. As a director of the Illinois Central line and as a land speculator, he hoped to make Chicago the terminus

of a transcontinental railroad, but construction could not begin until the route was cleared of Indians and brought under some kind of civil control.

Southerners, wishing to bring the transcontinental line to Memphis or New Orleans, pointed out that a right-of-way through organized territory already existed across Texas and the New Mexico Territory. In 1853 the United States minister to Mexico, James Gadsden, a prominent southern railroad executive, had engineered the purchase of more than 29,000 square miles of Mexican territory south of the Gila River, which provided an easy route through the mountains for such a railroad. Douglas, whose vision of the economic potentialities of the nation was Hamiltonian, would have been willing to support the construction of two or even three transcontinental railroads, but he knew that Congress would not go that far. In any case, he believed that the Nebraska region must be organized promptly.

The powerful southern faction in Congress would not go along with Douglas's proposal as it stood. The railroad question aside, Nebraska would presumably become a free state, for it lay north of latitude 36°30′ in a district from which slavery had been excluded by the Missouri Compromise. Under

The Compromise of 1850 and the Kansas-Nebraska Act

pressure from the Southerners, led by Senator David R. Atchison of Missouri, Douglas agreed first to divide the region into two territories, Kansas and Nebraska, and then—a fateful concession—to repeal the part of the Missouri Compromise that excluded slavery from land north of 36°30′. Whether the new territories should become slave or free, he argued, should be left to the decision of the settlers in accordance with the democratic principle of popular sovereignty. The fact that he might advance his presidential ambitions by making concessions to the South must have influenced Douglas too, as must the local political situation in Missouri, where slaveholders feared being "surrounded" on three sides by free states.

Douglas's miscalculation of northern sentiment was monumental. It was one thing to apply popular sovereignty to the new territories in the Southwest, quite another to apply it to a region that had been part of the United States for half a century and free soil for 34 years. Word that the area was to be opened to slavery caused an indignant outcry; many moderate opponents of slavery were radicalized. A group of abolitionist congressmen issued what they called their "Appeal of the Independent Democrats" (actually, all were Free Soilers and Whigs) denouncing the Kansas-Nebraska bill as "a gross violation of a sacred pledge" and calling for a campaign of letter writing, petitions, and public meetings to prevent its passage. The unanimity and force of the northern public's reaction was like nothing in America since the days of the Stamp Act and the Intolerable Acts.

But protests could not defeat the bill. Southerners in both houses backed it regardless of party. Douglas, at his best when under attack, pushed it with all his power. The authors of the "Appeal," he charged, were "the pure unadulterated representatives of Abolitionism, Free Soilism, [and] Niggerism." President Pierce added whatever force the administration could muster. As a result, the northern Democrats split and the bill became law late in May 1854. In this manner the nation took the greatest single step in its march toward the abyss of secession and civil war.

The repeal of the Missouri Compromise struck the North like a slap in the face—at once shameful and challenging. Presumably the question of slavery in the territories had been settled forever; now, seemingly without justification, it had been reopened. On May 24, two days after the Kansas-Nebraska bill passed the House of Representatives, Anthony Burns, a slave who had escaped from Virginia by stowing away on a ship, was arrested in Boston. Massachusetts abolitionists brought suit against Burns's former master, charging false arrest. They also organized a protest meeting at which they inflamed the crowd into attacking the courthouse where Burns was being held. The mob broke into the building and a guard was killed, but federal marshals drove off the attackers.

President Pierce ordered the Boston district attorney to "incur any expense" to enforce the law. He also sent a revenue cutter to Boston to carry Burns back to Virginia. Thus Burns was returned to his master, but it required two companies of soldiers and 1000 police and marines to get him aboard ship. As the grim parade marched past buildings festooned with black crepe, the crowd screamed "Kidnappers! Kidnappers!" at the soldiers. Estimates of the cost of returning this single slave to his owner ran as high as $100,000. A few months later, northern sympathizers bought Burns his freedom—for a few hundred dollars.

In previous cases Boston's conservative leaders, Whig to a man, had tended to hold back; after the Burns incident, they were thoroughly radicalized. "We went to bed one night old fashioned . . . Whigs," one of them explained, "and waked up stark mad Abolitionists."

KNOW-NOTHINGS, REPUBLICANS, AND THE DEMISE OF THE TWO-PARTY SYSTEM

There were 91 free-state Democrats in the House of Representatives when the Kansas-Nebraska Act was passed, only 25 after the next election. With the Whig party already moribund, dissidents flocked to two new parties.

One was the American, or "Know-Nothing," party, so called because it grew out of a secret society whose members used the password "I don't know." The Know-Nothings were primarily nativists—immigration was soaring in the early 1850s, and the influx of poor foreigners was causing genuine social problems. Crime was on the rise in the cities along with drunkenness and other "diseases of poverty."

Several emotion-charged issues related to the fact that a large percentage of the immigrants were Irish and German Catholics also troubled the Know-Nothings. Questions such as public financing of parochial schools, lay control of church policies, the prohibition of alcoholic beverages, and increasing the time before an immigrant could apply for citizenship (the Know-Nothings favored 21 years) were matters of major importance to them. Since these were divisive issues, the established political parties tried to avoid them; hence the development of the new party.

The American party was important in the South as well as in the North, and while most Know-Nothings disliked blacks and considered them inherently inferior beings, they tended to adopt the dominant view of slavery in whichever section they were located. In the North most opposed the Kansas-Nebraska Act.

Operating often in tacit alliance with the antislavery forces (dislike of slavery did not prevent many abolitionists from being prejudiced against Catholics and immigrants), the northern Know-Nothings won a string of local victories in 1854 and elected more than 40 congressmen.

Far more significant in the long run was the formation of the Republican party, which was made up of former Free Soilers, Conscience Whigs, and "Anti-Nebraska" Democrats. The American party was a national organization, but the Republican party was purely sectional. It sprang up spontaneously throughout the Old Northwest and caught on with a rush in New England.

Republicans presented themselves as the party of freedom. They were not abolitionists (though most abolitionists were soon voting Republican), but they insisted that slavery be kept out of the territories. They believed that if America was to remain a land of opportunity, free white labor must have exclusive access to the West. Thus the party appealed not only to voters who disapproved of slavery, but also to those who wished to keep blacks—free or slave—out of their states. In 1854 the Republicans won more than a hundred seats in the House of Representatives and control of many state governments.

The Whig party had almost disappeared in the northern states and the Democratic party had been gravely weakened, but it was unclear how these two new parties would fare. The Know-Nothing party had the superficial advantage of being a nationwide organization, but where slavery was concerned, this was

DEBATING THE PAST

Was the Civil War avoidable? In 1855 Senator William H. Seward, New York's most prominent Whig, declared from the steps of the state capitol in Albany that his party was dead. He advised supporters to join the new Republican Party, which opposed slavery. Three years later Seward, a Republican, declared that conflict between the North and South was "irrepressible." Charles and Mary Beard used the term *irrepressible conflict* as a chapter title in their 1927 history text, arguing that

antithetical economic systems—one based on free labor and the other on slavery—could not coexist. The argument was fleshed out by Arthur Cole in *The Irrepressible Conflict* (1934), who added that slavery was both outmoded and immoral. War had been inevitable, as was the South's defeat. In *The Repressible Conflict* (1939), Avery Craven dismissed Cole's book as a "belated abolitionist tract." War arose, Craven insisted, when northern "fanatics" whipped up sentiment against the South and southern politicians responded with equal vituperation. The "molders of public opinion" divided the nation by creating "the fiction of two distinct peoples." James G. Randall (1942) similarly saw no differences between the North and South of sufficient magnitude to rip the nation apart. The leaders of both sides—he called them a "bungling generation"—should not have allowed overheated passions to ignite a civil war. In the 1970s and 1980s historians who embraced the "new political history," which focused on statistical analyses of voting behavior rather than the rhetoric of politicians, argued that war might have been avoided if the Whig party had not disintegrated. William Gienapp (1987) and Michael Holt (1999) credited the two-party system of the Whigs and Democrats with holding the nation together during difficult times; local coalitions on issues such as temperance and immigration had forestalled the divisive reckoning over slavery. It was the emergence of the Republican Party in these contexts, not the economic tension between the sections, that made war "irrepressible."

Charles and Mary Beard, *The Rise of American Civilization* (1927), Arthur Cole, *The Irrepressible Conflict* (1934), Avery Craven, *The Repressible Conflict* (1939), James G. Randall, *The Coming of the Civil War* (1942), William Gienapp, *The Origins of the Republican Party* (1987), and Michael Holt, *The Rise and Fall of the American Whig Party* (1999).

anything but advantageous. And many Northerners who disliked slavery were troubled by the harsh Know-Nothing policies toward immigrants and Catholics. If the Know-Nothings were in control, said former Whig congressman Abraham Lincoln in 1855, the Declaration of Independence would read "all men are created equal, except negroes, *and foreigners, and catholics.*"

"BLEEDING KANSAS"

The furor over slavery might have died down if settlement of the new territories had proceeded in an orderly manner. Almost none of the settlers who

flocked to Kansas owned slaves and relatively few of them were primarily interested in the slavery question. Most had a low opinion of blacks. ("I kem to Kansas to live in a free state," one Northerner explained. "I don't want niggers a-trampin' over my grave.") Like nearly all frontier settlers, they wanted land and local political office, lucrative government contracts, and other business opportunities.

When Congress opened the gates to settlement in May 1854, none of the land in the territory was available for sale. Treaties extinguishing Indian titles had yet to be ratified, and public lands had not been surveyed. In July Congress authorized squatters to occupy unsurveyed federal lands, but much of this

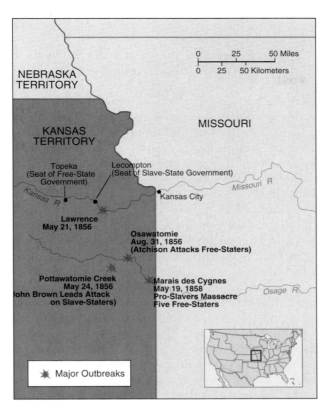

▲ "Bleeding Kansas"

property was far to the west of the frontier and practically inaccessible. The situation led to confusion over property boundaries, to graft and speculation, and to general uncertainty, thereby exacerbating the difficulty of establishing an orderly government.

The legal status of slavery in Kansas became the focus of all these conflicts. Both northern abolitionists and southern defenders of slavery were determined to have Kansas. They made of the territory first a testing ground and then a battlefield, thus exposing the fatal flaw in the Kansas-Nebraska Act and the idea of popular sovereignty. The law said that the people of Kansas were "perfectly free" to decide the slavery question. But the citizens of territories were not entirely free because territories were not sovereign political units. The Act had created a political vacuum, which its vague statement that the settlers must establish their domestic institutions "subject . . . to the Constitution" did not begin to fill. When should the institutions be established? Was it democratic to let a handful of first comers make decisions that would affect the lives of the thousands soon to follow? The virtues of the time-tested system of congressional control established by the Northwest Ordinance became fully apparent only when the system was discarded.

More serious was the fact that outsiders, North and South, refused to permit Kansans to work out their own destiny. The contest for control began at once. The New England Emigrant Aid Society was formed, with grandiose plans for transporting antislavery settlers to the area. The society transported only a handful of New Englanders to Kansas. Yet the New Englanders were very conspicuous, and the society helped many Midwestern antislavery settlers to make the move.

Doing so stirred white Southerners to action. The proslavery forces enjoyed several advantages in this struggle. The first inhabitants in frontier regions nearly always came from lands immediately to the east. In this case they were proslavery Missourians. When word spread that "foreigners" from New England were seeking to "steal" Kansas, many Missourians rushed to protect their "rights." "If we win we carry slavery to the Pacific Ocean," Senator Atchison boasted.

In November 1854 an election was held in Kansas to pick a territorial delegate to Congress. A large band of Missourians crossed over specifically to vote for a proslavery candidate and elected him easily. In March 1855 some 5000 "border ruffians" again descended on Kansas and elected a territorial legislature. A census had recorded 2905 eligible voters, but 6307 votes were cast. The legislature promptly enacted a slave code and laws prohibiting abolitionist agitation. Antislavery settlers refused to recognize this regime and held elections of their own. By January 1856 two governments existed in Kansas, one based on fraud, the other extralegal.

By denouncing the free-state government located at Topeka, President Pierce encouraged the proslavery settlers to assume the offensive. In May, 800 of them sacked the antislavery town of Lawrence. An extremist named John Brown then took the law into his own hands in retaliation. By his reckoning, five Free Soilers had been killed by proslavery forces. In May 1856, together with six companions (four of them his sons), Brown stole into a settlement on Pottawatomie Creek in the dead of night. They dragged five unsuspecting men from their rude cabins and murdered them. This slaughter brought men on both sides to arms by the hundreds. Marauding bands came to blows and terrorized homesteads, first attempting to ascertain the inhabitants' position on slavery.

Brown and his followers escaped capture and were never indicted for the murders, but pressure from federal troops eventually forced him to go into hiding. He finally left Kansas in October 1856. By that time some 200 persons had lost their lives.

A certain amount of violence was normal in any frontier community, but it suited the political interests of the Republicans to make the situation in Kansas seem worse than it was. Exaggerated accounts of "bleeding Kansas" filled the pages of northern newspapers. The

Democrats were also partly to blame, for although residents of nearby states often tried to influence elections in new territories, the actions of the border ruffians made a mockery of the democratic process.

However, the main responsibility for the Kansas tragedy must be borne by the Pierce administration. Under popular sovereignty the national government was supposed to see that elections were orderly and honest. Instead, the president acted as a partisan. When the first governor of the territory objected to the manner in which the proslavery legislature had been elected, Pierce replaced him with a man who backed the southern group without question.

SENATOR SUMNER BECOMES A MARTYR FOR ABOLITIONISM

As counterpoint to the fighting in Kansas there arose an almost continuous clamor in the halls of Congress. Red-faced legislators traded insults and threats. Epithets like "liar" were freely tossed about. Prominent in these angry outbursts was a new senator, Charles Sumner of Massachusetts. Brilliant, learned, and articulate, Sumner had made a name for himself in New England as a reformer interested in the peace movement, prison reform, and the abolition of slavery. He possessed great magnetism and was, according to the tastes of the day, an accomplished orator, but he suffered inner torments of a complex nature that warped his personality. He was egotistical and humorless. His unyielding devotion to his principles was less praiseworthy than it seemed on casual examination, for it resulted from his complete lack of respect for the principles of others. Reform movements evidently provided him with a kind of emotional release; he became combative and totally lacking in objectivity when espousing a cause.

In the Kansas debates Sumner displayed an icy disdain for his foes. Colleagues threatened him with assassination, called him a "filthy reptile" and a "leper." He was impervious to such hostility. In the spring of 1856 he loosed a dreadful blast titled "The Crime Against Kansas." Characterizing administration policy as tyrannical, imbecilic, absurd, and infamous, he demanded that Kansas be admitted to the Union at once as a free state. Then he began a long and intemperate attack on both Douglas and the elderly Senator Andrew P. Butler of South Carolina, who was not present to defend himself.

Sumner described Butler as a "Don Quixote" who had taken "the harlot, slavery" as his mistress, and he spoke scornfully of "the loose expectoration" of Butler's speech. This was an inexcusable reference to the uncontrollable drooling to which the elderly senator was subject. While he was still talking, Douglas, who shrugged off most political name-calling as part of the game, was heard to mutter, "That damn fool will get himself killed by some other damn fool."

Such a "fool" quickly materialized in the person of Congressman Preston S. Brooks of South Carolina, a nephew of Senator Butler. Since Butler was absent from Washington, Brooks, who was probably as mentally unbalanced as Sumner, assumed the responsibility of defending his kinsman's honor. A southern romantic par excellence, he decided that caning Sumner would reflect his contempt more effectively than challenging him to a duel. Two days after the speech, Brooks entered the Senate as it adjourned. Sumner remained at his desk writing. Waiting until a talkative woman in the lobby had left so that she would be spared the sight of violence, Brooks then walked up to Sumner and rained blows on his head with a cane until Sumner fell, unconscious and bloody, to the floor. "I . . . gave him about 30 first-rate stripes," Brooks later boasted. "Towards the last he bellowed like a calf. I wore my cane out completely but saved the head which is gold." The physical damage suffered by Sumner was not life-threatening, but the incident so affected him psychologically that he was unable to return to his seat in Congress until 1859.

▲ Cartoon of Charles Sumner of Massachusetts being caned on the floor of the Senate by Preston Brooks of South Carolina.

Both sides made much of this disgraceful incident. When the House censured him, Brooks resigned, returned to his home district, and was triumphantly reelected. A number of well-wishers sent him souvenir canes. Northerners viewed the affair as illustrating the brutalizing effect of slavery on southern whites and made a hero of Sumner.

BUCHANAN TRIES HIS HAND

Such was the atmosphere surrounding the 1856 presidential election. The Republican party now dominated much of the North. It nominated John C. Frémont, "the Pathfinder," one of the heroes of the conquest of California during the war with Mexico. Frémont fit the Whig tradition of presidential candidates: a popular military man with almost no political experience. Unlike Taylor and Scott, however, he was sound and articulate on the issue of slavery in the territories. Although citizens of diverse interests had joined the party, Republicans expressed their objectives in one simple slogan: "Free soil, free speech, and Frémont."

The Democrats cast aside the ineffectual Pierce, but they did not dare nominate Douglas because he had raised such a storm in the North. They settled on James Buchanan, chiefly because he had been out of the country serving as minister to Great Britain during the long debate over Kansas! The American party nominated former president Millard Fillmore, a choice the remnants of the Whigs endorsed. Walt Whitman had been an ardent Democrat. But the party's stand on slavery in the territories disgusted him. In 1856 he wrote a poem, "The 18th Presidency," denouncing both Buchanan and Fillmore:

> *Two galvanized old men, close on*
> *the summons to depart this life*
> *. . . relics and proofs of the little*
> *political bargains . . .*

In the campaign, the Democrats concentrated on denouncing the Republicans as a sectional party that threatened to destroy the Union. On this issue they carried the day. Buchanan won only a minority of the popular vote, but he had strength in every section. He got 174 electoral votes to Frémont's 114 and Fillmore's 8. The significant contest took place in the populous states just north of slave territory—Pennsylvania, Ohio, Indiana, and Illinois. Of these, Buchanan carried all but Ohio, although by narrow margins.

No one could say that James Buchanan lacked political experience. Elected to the Pennsylvania legislature in 1815 when he was only 24 years old, he served for well over 20 years in Congress and had been minister to Russia, then Polk's secretary of state, then minister to Great Britain under Pierce.

Personally, Buchanan was a bundle of contradictions. Dignified in bearing and by nature cautious, he could consume enormous amounts of liquor without showing the slightest sign of inebriation. A big, heavy man, he was nonetheless remarkably graceful and light on his tiny feet, of which he was inordinately proud. He wore a very high collar to conceal a scarred neck, and because of an eye defect he habitually carried his head to one side and slightly forward, which gave him, as his biographer says, "a perpetual attitude of courteous deference and attentive interest" that sometimes led individuals to believe they had won a greater share of his attention and support than was actually the case. In fact he was extremely stubborn and sometimes vindictive.

Buchanan was said to be popular with women and attracted to them as well, and although he contemplated marriage on more than one occasion, he never took the final step. Over the years many strong men in politics had, like Walt Whitman, held him in contempt. Yet he was patriotic, conscientious, and anything but radical. While Republican extremists called him a "doughface"—they believed he lacked the force of character to stand up against southern extremists—many voters in 1856 thought he had the qualities necessary to steer the nation to calmer waters.

THE DRED SCOTT DECISION

Before Buchanan could fairly take the Kansas problem in hand, an event occurred that drove another deep wedge between North and South. Back in 1834 Dr. John Emerson of St. Louis joined the army as a surgeon and was assigned to duty at Rock Island, Illinois. Later he was transferred to Fort Snelling, in the Wisconsin Territory. In 1838 he returned to Missouri. Accompanying him on these travels was his body servant, Dred Scott, a slave. In 1846, after Emerson's death, Scott and his wife Harriet, whom he had married while in Wisconsin, with the help of a friendly lawyer brought suit in the Missouri courts for their liberty. They claimed that residence in Illinois, where slavery was barred under the Northwest Ordinance, and in the Wisconsin Territory, where the Missouri Compromise outlawed it, had made them free.

The future of Dred and Harriet Scott mattered not at all to the country or the courts; at issue was the question of whether Congress or the local legislatures had the power to outlaw slavery in the territories. After many years of litigation, the case reached the Supreme Court of the United States. On March 6, 1857, two days after Buchanan's inauguration, the high tribunal acted. Free or slave,

DOCUMENT

Opinion of the Supreme Court for *Dred Scott* v. *Sanford*

▲ Dred Scott and his wife, featured on the cover of *Frank Leslie's Illustrated Newspaper*. Historian Joshua Brown in *Beyond the Lines* (2002) argues that this publication was the precursor to today's popular news magazines. Its plentiful pictures were made possible by the new technology of mass-produced wood engraving.

the Court declared, blacks were not citizens; therefore, Scott could not sue in a federal court. This was dubious legal logic because many blacks were accepted as citizens in some states when the Constitution was drafted and ratified, and Article IV, Section 2, says that "the citizens of each state shall be entitled to all privileges and immunities of citizens in the several states." But the decision settled Scott's fate.

However, the Court went further. Since the plaintiff had returned to Missouri, the laws of Illinois no longer applied to him. His residence in the Wisconsin Territory—this was the most controversial part of the decision—did not make him free because the Missouri Compromise was unconstitutional. According to the Bill of Rights (the Fifth Amendment), the federal government cannot deprive any person of life, liberty, or property without due process of law.[1]

Therefore, Chief Justice Roger B. Taney reasoned, "an Act of Congress which deprives a person . . . of his liberty or property merely because he came himself or brought his property into a particular Territory . . . could hardly be dignified with the name of due process of law."

The Dred Scott decision has been widely criticized on legal grounds. Each justice filed his own opinion, and on several important particulars there was no line of argument on which any five of the nine agreed. Some critics have reasoned that the justices should not have gone beyond the minimum of argument necessary to settle the case, and many have made much of the facts that a majority of the justices were Southerners and proslavery Northerners, and that President Buchanan had pressured them to decide the case against the Scotts. It would be going too far, however, to accuse them of plotting to extend slavery. They were trying to settle the vexing question of slavery in the territories once and for all. If this objective could only be accomplished by fuzzy reasoning, it would not be the first or the last time in the history of jurisprudence that an important result rested on shaky logic.

In addition to invalidating the already repealed Missouri Compromise, the decision threatened Douglas's principle of popular sovereignty, for if Congress could not exclude slaves from a territory, how could a mere territorial legislature do so? Until statehood was granted, slavery seemed as inviolate as freedom of religion or speech or any other civil liberty guaranteed by the Constitution. Where formerly freedom (as guaranteed in the Bill of Rights) was a national institution and slavery a local one, now, according to the Court, slavery was nationwide, excluded only where states had specifically abolished it.

The irony of employing the Bill of Rights to keep blacks in chains did not escape northern critics. Now slaves could be brought into the Minnesota Territory, even into Oregon. In his inaugural address Buchanan had sanctimoniously urged the people to accept the forthcoming ruling, "whatever this may be," as a final settlement. Many assumed (indeed, it was true) that he had put pressure on the Court to act as it did and that he knew in advance of his speech what the decision would be. If this "greatest crime in the judicial annals of the Republic" was allowed to stand, Northerners argued, the Republican party would have no reason to exist: Its program had been declared unconstitutional! The Dred Scott decision convinced thousands that the South was engaged in an aggressive attempt to extend the peculiar institution so far that it could no longer be considered peculiar.

---

[1]Some state constitutions had similar provisions, but the slave states obviously did not.

THE LECOMPTON CONSTITUTION

Kansas soon provided a test for northern suspicions. Initially Buchanan handled the problem of Kansas well by appointing Robert J. Walker as governor. Although he was from Mississippi, Walker had no desire to foist slavery on the territory against the will of its inhabitants. He was a small man, only five feet tall, but he had more political stature by far than any previous governor of the territory. A former senator and Cabinet member, he was also courageous, patriotic, and tough-minded, much like Douglas in temperament and belief.

The proslavery leaders in Kansas had managed to convene a constitutional convention at Lecompton, but the Free Soil forces had refused to participate in the election of delegates. When this rump body drafted a proslavery constitution and then refused to submit it to a fair vote of all the settlers, Walker denounced its work and hurried back to Washington to explain the situation to Buchanan.

The president refused to face reality. His prosouthern advisers were clamoring for him to "save" Kansas. Instead of rejecting the Lecompton constitution, he asked Congress to admit Kansas to the Union with this document as its frame of government.

Buchanan's decision brought him head-on against Stephen A. Douglas, and the repercussions of their clash shattered the Democratic party. Principle and self-interest (an irresistible combination) forced Douglas to oppose the leader of his party. If he stood aside while Congress admitted Kansas, he not only would be abandoning popular sovereignty, but he would be committing political suicide as well. He was up for re-election to the Senate in 1858. All but one of the 56 newspapers in Illinois had declared editorially against the Lecompton constitution; if Douglas supported it, his defeat was certain. In a dramatic confrontation at the White House, he and Buchanan argued the question at length, tempers rising. Finally, the president tried to force him into line. "Mr. Douglas," he said, "I desire you to remember that no Democrat ever yet differed from an Administration of his own choice without being crushed." "Mr. President," Douglas replied contemptuously, "I wish you to remember that General Jackson is dead!" And he stalked out of the room.

Buchanan then compounded his error by putting tremendous political pressure on Douglas, cutting off his Illinois patronage on the eve of his reelection campaign. Of course Douglas persisted, openly joining the Republicans in the fight. Congress rejected the Lecompton bill.

Meanwhile, the extent of the fraud perpetrated at Lecompton became clear. In October 1857 a new legislature had been chosen in Kansas, antislavery voters participating in the balloting. It ordered a referendum on the Lecompton constitution in January 1858. The constitution was overwhelmingly rejected; this time the proslavery settlers boycotted the test. When Buchanan persisted in pressing Congress to admit Kansas under the Lecompton constitution, Congress ordered another referendum. To slant the case in favor of approval, the legislators stipulated that if the constitution was voted down, Kansas could not be admitted into the Union until it had a population of 90,000. Nevertheless, the Kansans rejected it by a ratio of six to one.

More than opposition to slavery influenced this vote, for by 1858 most Kansans were totally alienated from the Democratic administration in Washington because of its bungling and corrupt management of the public lands. After delaying sales unconscionably, Buchanan suddenly put 8 million acres up for auction in 1858. Squatters on this land were faced, in the midst of a depression, with finding $200 in cash to cover the minimum price of their quarter sections or losing their improvements. Local protests forced a delay of the sales, but Kansans by the thousands were convinced that Buchanan had thrown the land on the market out of pique at their rejection of the Lecompton constitution.

THE EMERGENCE OF LINCOLN

These were dark days. During the Panic of 1857 Northerners put the blame for the hard times on the southern-dominated Congress, which had just reduced tariff duties to the lowest levels in nearly half a century. As prices plummeted and unemployment rose, they attributed the collapse to foreign competition and accused the South of having sacrificed the prosperity of the rest of the nation for its selfish advantage. The South in turn read in its relative immunity from the depression proof of the superiority of the slave system, which further stimulated the running sectional debate about the relative merits of free and slave labor.

Dissolution threatened the Union. To many Americans, Stephen A. Douglas seemed to offer the best hope of preserving it. For this reason unusual attention was focused on his campaign for reelection to the Senate in 1858. The importance of the contest and Douglas's national prestige put great pressure on the Republicans of Illinois to nominate someone who would make a good showing against him. The man they chose was Abraham Lincoln.

After a towering figure has passed from the stage, it is always difficult to discover what he was like before his rise to prominence. This is especially true of Lincoln, who changed greatly when power, responsibility, and fame came to him. Lincoln was not unknown in 1858, but his public career had not been distinguished. He was born in Kentucky in 1809, and the story of his early life can be condensed, as he once

▲ How Lincoln aged during his term of office is evident in comparing Alexander Hesler's portrait, taken on June 3, 1860, with one by an unnamed photographer taken April 10, 1865.

said himself, into a single line from Gray's *Elegy:* "The short and simple annals of the poor." His illiterate father, Thomas Lincoln, was a typical frontier wanderer. When Abraham was seven years old, the family moved to Indiana. In 1830 they pushed west again into southern Illinois. The boy received almost no formal schooling.

However, Lincoln had a good mind, and he was extremely ambitious.[2] He cut loose from his family, made a trip to New Orleans, and for a time managed a general store in New Salem, Illinois. In 1834, when barely 25, he won a seat in the Illinois legislature as a Whig. Meanwhile, he studied law and was admitted to the bar in 1836.

Lincoln remained in the legislature until 1842, displaying a perfect willingness to adopt the Whig position on all issues. In 1846 he was elected to Congress. While not engaged in politics he worked at the law, maintaining an office in Springfield and following the circuit, taking a variety of cases, few of much importance. He earned a decent but by no means sumptuous living. After one term in Congress, marked by

his partisan opposition to Polk's Mexican policy, his political career petered out. He seemed fated to pass his remaining years as a small-town lawyer.

Even during this period Lincoln's personality was extraordinarily complex. His bawdy sense of humor and his endless fund of stories and tall tales made him a legend first in Illinois and then in Washington. He was admired in Illinois as an expert axman and a champion wrestler. He was thoroughly at home with toughs like the "Clary's Grove Boys" of New Salem and in the convivial atmosphere of a party caucus. But in a society where most men drank heavily, he never touched liquor. And he was subject to periods of melancholy so profound as to appear almost psychopathic. Friends spoke of him as having "cat fits," and he wrote of himself in the early 1840s: "I am now the most miserable man living. If what I felt were equally distributed to the whole human family, there would not be one cheerful face on earth."

In a region swept by repeated waves of religious revivalism, Lincoln managed to be at once a man of calm spirituality and a skeptic without appearing offensive to conventional believers. He was a party wheelhorse, a corporation lawyer, even a railroad lobbyist, yet his reputation for integrity was stainless.

---

[2]His law partner, William Herndon, said that Lincoln's ambition was "a little engine that knows no rest."

The revival of the slavery controversy in 1854 stirred Lincoln deeply. No abolitionist, he had tried to take a "realistic" view of the problem. The Kansas-Nebraska bill led him to see the moral issue more clearly. "If slavery is not wrong, nothing is wrong," he stated with the directness and simplicity of expression for which he later became famous. Compromises made in the past for the sake of sectional harmony had always sought to preserve as much territory as possible for freedom. Yet unlike most Free Soilers, he did not blame the Southerners for slavery. "They are just what we would be in their situation," he confessed.

The moderation of his position combined with its moral force won Lincoln many admirers in the great body of citizens who were trying to reconcile their low opinion of blacks and their patriotic desire to avoid an issue that threatened the Union with their growing conviction that slavery was sinful. Anything that aided slavery was wrong, Lincoln argued. But before casting the first stone, Northerners should look into their own hearts: "If there be a man amongst us who is so impatient of [slavery] as a wrong as to disregard its actual presence among us and the difficulty of getting rid of it suddenly in a satisfactory way . . . that man is misplaced if he is on our platform." And Lincoln confessed:

> If all earthly power were given to me, I should not know what to do as to the existing institution. But . . . [this] furnishes no more excuse for permitting slavery to go into our free territory than it would for reviving the African slave trade.

Thus Lincoln was at once compassionate toward the slave owner and stern toward the institution. "A house divided against itself cannot stand," he warned. "I believe this government cannot endure permanently half slave and half free." Without minimizing the difficulties or urging a hasty or ill-considered solution, Lincoln demanded that the people look toward a day, however remote, when not only Kansas but the entire country would be free.

THE LINCOLN-DOUGLAS DEBATES

As Lincoln developed these ideas his reputation grew. In 1855 he almost won the Whig nomination for senator. He became a Republican shortly thereafter, and in June 1856, at the first Republican National Convention, he received 110 votes for the vice-presidential nomination. He seemed the logical man to pit against Douglas in 1858.

In July, Lincoln challenged Douglas to a series of seven debates. The senator accepted. The debates were well attended and widely reported, for the idea of a direct confrontation between candidates for an important office captured the popular imagination.

The choice of the next senator lay, of course, in the hands of the Illinois legislature. Technically, Douglas and Lincoln were campaigning for candidates for the legislature who were pledged to support them for the Senate seat. They presented a sharp physical contrast that must have helped voters sort out their differing points of view. Douglas was short and stocky, Lincoln long and lean. Douglas gave the impression of irrepressible energy. While speaking, he roamed the platform; he used broad gestures and bold, exaggerated arguments. He did not hesitate to call "Honest Abe" a liar. Lincoln, on his part, was slow and deliberate of speech, his voice curiously high-pitched. He seldom used gestures or oratorical tricks, trying rather to create an impression of utter sincerity to add force to his remarks.

The two employed different political styles, each calculated to project a particular image. Douglas epitomized efficiency and success. He dressed in the latest fashion, favoring flashy vests and the finest broadcloth. He was a glad-hander and a heavy drinker—he apparently died of cirrhosis of the liver. Ordinarily he arrived in town in a private railroad car, to be met by a brass band, then to ride at the head of a parade to the appointed place.

Lincoln appeared before the voters as a man of the people. He wore ill-fitting black suits and a stovepipe hat—repository for letters, bills, scribbled notes, and other scraps—that exaggerated his great height. He presented a worn and rumpled appearance, partly because he traveled from place to place on day coaches, accompanied by only a few advisers. When local supporters came to meet him at the station, he preferred to walk with them through the streets to the scene of the debate.

Lincoln and Douglas maintained a high intellectual level in their speeches, but these were political debates. They were seeking not to influence future historians (who have nonetheless pondered their words endlessly) but to win votes. Both tailored their arguments to appeal to local audiences—more antislavery in the northern counties, more proslavery in the southern. They also tended to exaggerate their differences, which were not in fact enormous. Neither wanted to see slavery in the territories or thought it economically efficient, and neither sought to abolish it by political action or by force. Both believed blacks congenitally inferior to whites, although Douglas took more pleasure in expounding on supposed racial differences than Lincoln did.

Douglas's strategy was to make Lincoln look like an abolitionist. He accused the Republicans of favoring racial equality and refusing to abide by the decision of the Supreme Court in the Dred Scott case. Himself he pictured as a heroic champion of democracy, attacked on one side by the "black" Republicans and on the other by Buchanan supporters, yet ready to fight to his last breath for popular sovereignty.

Lincoln tried to picture Douglas as proslavery and a defender of the Dred Scott decision. "Slavery is an unqualified evil to the negro, to the white man, to the soil, and to the State," he said. "Judge Douglas," he also said, "is blowing out the moral lights around us, when he contends that whoever wants slaves has a right to hold them."

However, Lincoln often weakened the impact of his arguments, being perhaps too eager to demonstrate his conservatism. "All men are created equal," he would say on the authority of the Declaration of Independence, only to add: "I am not, nor ever have been, in favor of bringing about in any way the social and political equality of the white and black races." He opposed allowing blacks to vote, to sit on juries, to marry whites, even to be citizens. He predicted the "ultimate extinction" of slavery, but when pressed he predicted that it would not occur "in less than a hundred years at the least." He took a fence-sitting position on the question of abolition in the District of Columbia and stated flatly that he did not favor repeal of the Fugitive Slave Act.

In the debate at Freeport, a town northwest of Chicago near the Wisconsin line, Lincoln asked Douglas if, considering the Dred Scott decision, the people of a territory could exclude slavery before the territory became a state. Unhesitatingly Douglas replied that they could, simply by not passing the local laws essential for holding blacks in bondage. "It matters not what way the Supreme Court may hereafter decide as to the abstract question," Douglas said. "The people have the lawful means to introduce or exclude it as they please, for the reason that slavery cannot exist . . . unless it is supported by local police regulations."

DOCUMENT

Douglas, Debate at Galesburg, Illinois

This argument saved Douglas in Illinois. The Democrats carried the legislature by a narrow margin, whereas it is almost certain that if Douglas had accepted the Dred Scott decision outright, the balance would have swung to the Republicans. But the so-called Freeport Doctrine cost him heavily two years later when he made his bid for the Democratic presidential nomination. "It matters not what way the Supreme Court may hereafter decide"—southern extremists would not accept a man who suggested that the Dred Scott decision could be circumvented, although in fact Douglas had only stated the obvious.

Probably Lincoln had not thought beyond the senatorial election when he asked the question; he was merely hoping to keep Douglas on the defensive and perhaps injure him in southern Illinois, where considerable proslavery sentiment existed. In any case, defeat did Lincoln no harm politically. He had more than held his own against one of the most formidable debaters in politics, and his distinctive personality and point of view had impressed themselves on thousands of minds. Indeed, the defeat revitalized his political career.

The campaign of 1858 marked Douglas's last triumph, Lincoln's last defeat. Elsewhere the elections in the North went heavily to the Republicans. When the old Congress reconvened in December, northern-sponsored economic measures (a higher tariff, the transcontinental railroad, river and harbor improvements, a free homestead bill) were all blocked by southern votes.

Whether the South could continue to prevent the passage of this legislation in the new Congress was

▲ The Lincoln-Douglas debates began in June 1858 with Lincoln's "House Divided" speech and lasted until October. At rallies such as the one announced in this poster, the tall awkward "Rail Splitter" challenged the "Little Giant" to examine thoroughly the slavery question.

problematical. In early 1859 even many moderate Southerners were uneasy about the future. The radicals, made panicky by Republican victories and their own failure to win in Kansas, spoke openly of secession if a Republican was elected president in 1860. Lincoln's "house divided" speech was quoted out of context, while Douglas's Freeport Doctrine added to southern woes. When Senator William H. Seward of New York spoke of an "irrepressible conflict" between freedom and slavery, white Southerners became still more alarmed.

Naturally they struck back. Led by such self-described "fire-eaters" as William L. Yancey of Alabama and Senators Jefferson Davis of Mississippi, John Slidell of Louisiana, and James H. Hammond of South Carolina, they demanded a federal slave code for the territories and talked of annexing Cuba and reviving the African slave trade.

John Brown's Raid

In October 1859, John Brown, the scourge of Kansas, made his second contribution to the unfolding sectional drama. Gathering a group of 18 followers, white and black, he staged an attack on Harpers Ferry, Virginia, a town on the Potomac River upstream from Washington. Having boned up on guerrilla tactics, he planned to seize the federal arsenal there; arm the slaves, whom he thought would flock to his side; and then establish a black republic in the mountains of Virginia.

Simply by overpowering a few night watchmen, Brown and his men occupied the arsenal and a nearby rifle factory. They captured several hostages, one of them Colonel Lewis Washington, a great-grand-nephew of George Washington. But no slaves came forward to join them. Federal troops commanded by Robert E. Lee soon trapped Brown's men in an engine house of the Baltimore and Ohio Railroad. After a two-day siege in which the attackers picked off ten of his men, Brown was captured.

No incident so well illustrates the role of emotion and irrationality in the sectional crisis as does John Brown's raid. Over the years before his Kansas escapade, Brown had been a drifter, horse thief, and swindler, several times a bankrupt, a failure in everything he attempted. His maternal grandmother, his mother, and five aunts and uncles were certifiably insane, as were 2 of his 20 children and many other relatives. After his ghastly Pottawatomie murders it should have been obvious to anyone that he was both a fanatic and mentally unstable: Some of the victims were hacked to bits with a broadsword. Yet numbers of high-minded Northerners, including Emerson and Thoreau, had supported Brown and his antislavery "work" after 1856. Some—among them Franklin B. Sanborn, a teacher; Thomas Wentworth Higginson, a clergyman; and the merchant George L. Stearns—contributed knowingly to his Harpers Ferry enterprise.

White Southerners reacted to Harpers Ferry with equal irrationality, some with a rage similar to Brown's. Dozens of hapless Northerners in the southern states were arrested, beaten, or driven off. One, falsely suspected of being an accomplice of Brown, was lynched.

Brown's fate lay in the hands of the Virginia authorities. Ignoring his obvious derangement, they charged him with treason, conspiracy, and murder. He was speedily convicted and sentenced to death by hanging.

Yet "Old Brown" had still one more contribution to make to the developing sectional tragedy. Despite the furor he had created, cool heads everywhere called for calm and denounced his attack. Most Republican politicians repudiated him. Even execution would probably not have made a martyr of Brown had he behaved like a madman after his capture. Instead, an enormous dignity descended on him as he lay in his Virginia jail awaiting death. Whatever his faults, he truly believed in racial equality. He addressed blacks who worked for him as "Mister" and arranged for them to eat at his table and sit with his family in church.

This conviction served him well in his last days. "If it is deemed necessary that I should forfeit my life for the furtherance of the ends of justice, and mingle my blood further with the blood of . . . millions in this slave country whose rights are disregarded by wicked, cruel, and unjust enactments," he said before the judge pronounced sentence, "I say, let it be done."

DOCUMENT

John Brown's Address before Sentencing

This John Brown, with his patriarchal beard and sad eyes, so apparently incompatible with the bloody terrorist of Pottawatomie and Harpers Ferry, led thousands in the North to ignore his past and treat him almost as a saint.

And so Brown, hanged on December 2, 1859, became to the North a hero and to the South a symbol of northern ruthlessness. Soon, as the popular song had it, Brown's body lay "a-mouldering in the grave," and the memory of his bloody act did indeed go "marching on."

The Election of 1860

By 1860 the nation was teetering on the brink of disunion. Radicals North and South were heedlessly provoking one another. When a disgruntled North Carolinian, Hinton Rowan Helper, published *The*

▲ After Brown's capture, Emerson called him "a martyr" who would "make the gallows as glorious as the cross." John Brown's principled radicalism found favor during the Depression decade of the 1930s. John Stewart Curry's mural, completed in 1943, depicted the demented John Brown in the pose of Christ on the cross. The image offended the Kansas legislature, which had commissioned Curry to portray Kansas history in a "sane and sensible manner."

Impending Crisis of the South (1857), an attempt to demonstrate statistically that slavery was ruining the South's economy and corrupting its social structure, the Republicans flooded the country with an abridged edition, although they knew that Southerners considered the book an appeal for social revolution. "I have always been a fervid Union man," one Southerner wrote in 1859, "but I confess the [northern] endorsement of the Harpers Ferry outrage and Helper's infernal doctrine has shaken my fidelity."

Extremism was more evident in the South, and to any casual observer that section must have seemed the aggressor in the crisis. Yet even in demanding the reopening of the African slave trade, southern radicals believed that they were defending themselves against attack. They felt surrounded by hostility. The North was growing at a much faster rate; if nothing was done, they feared, a flood of new free states would soon be able to amend the Constitution and emancipate the slaves. John Brown's raid, with its threat of an insurrection like Nat Turner's, reduced them to a state of panic.

When legislatures in state after state in the South cracked down on freedom of expression, made the manumission of slaves illegal, banished free blacks, and took other steps that Northerners considered blatantly provocative, the advocates of these policies believed that they were only defending the status quo. Perhaps, by seceding from the Union, the South

could raise a dike against the tide of abolitionism. Secession also provided an emotional release, a way of dissipating tension by striking back at criticism.

Stephen A. Douglas was probably the last hope of avoiding a rupture between North and South. But when the Democrats met at Charleston, South Carolina, in April 1860 to choose a presidential candidate, the southern delegates would not support him unless he promised not to disturb slavery in the territories. Indeed, they went further in their demands. The North, William L. Yancey of Alabama insisted, must accept the proposition that slavery was not merely tolerable but right. Of course the Northerners would not go so far. "Gentlemen of the South," said Senator George E. Pugh of Ohio in replying to Yancey, "you mistake us—you mistake us! We will not do it!" When southern proposals were voted down, most of the delegates from the deep South walked out and the convention adjourned without naming a candidate.

In June the Democrats reconvened at Baltimore. Again they failed to reach agreement. The two wings then met separately, the Northerners nominating Douglas, the Southerners John C. Breckenridge of Kentucky, Buchanan's vice-president. On the question of slavery in the territories, the Northerners promised to "abide by the decision of the Supreme Court," which meant, in effect, that they stood for Douglas's Freeport Doctrine. The Southerners

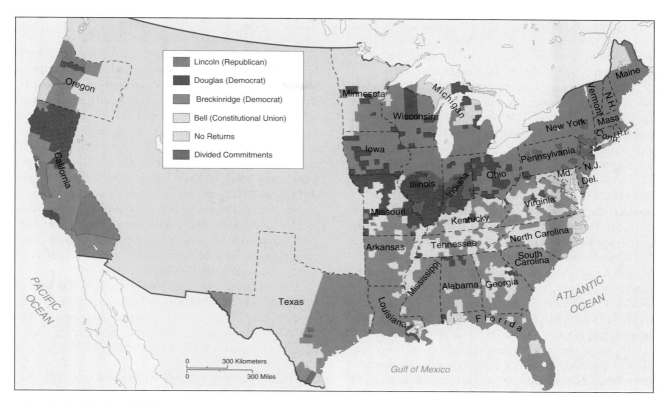

▲ **Presidential Election, 1860**

announced their belief that neither Congress nor any territorial government could prevent citizens from settling "with their property" in any territory.

Meanwhile, the Republicans, who met in Chicago in mid-May, had drafted a platform attractive to all classes and all sections of the northern and western states. For manufacturers they proposed a high tariff, for farmers a homestead law providing free land for settlers. Internal improvements "of a National character," notably a railroad to the Pacific, should receive federal aid. No restrictions should be placed on immigration. As to slavery in the territories, the Republicans did not equivocate: "The normal condition of all the territory of the United States is that of freedom." Neither Congress nor a local legislature could "give legal existence to Slavery in any Territory."

In choosing a presidential candidate the Republicans displayed equally shrewd political judgment. Senator Seward was the front-runner, but he had taken too extreme a stand and appeared unlikely to carry the crucial states of Pennsylvania, Indiana, and Illinois. He led on the first ballot but could not get a majority. Then the delegates began to look closely at Abraham Lincoln. His thoughtful and moderate views on the main issue of the times and his formidable debating skills attracted many, and so did his political personality. "Honest Abe," the "Railsplitter," a man of humble origins (born in a log cabin), self-educated, self-made, a common man but by no means an ordinary man—the combination seemed unbeatable.

It also helped that Lincoln was from a crucial state and had an excellent team of convention managers. Taking advantage of the fact that the convention was meeting in Lincoln's home state, they packed the gallery with leather-lunged Chicago ward heelers who were assigned the task of shouting for their man. They also made a series of deals with the leaders of other state delegations to win additional votes. "I authorize no bargains and will be bound by none," Lincoln telegraphed the convention. "Lincoln ain't here and don't know what we have to meet," one of his managers remarked—and proceeded to trade off two Cabinet posts for the votes of key states.

On the second ballot Lincoln drew shoulder to shoulder with Seward, on the third he was within two votes of victory. Before the roll could be called again, delegates began to switch their votes, and in a landslide, soon made unanimous, Lincoln was nominated.

A few days earlier the remnants of the American and Whig parties had formed the Constitutional Union party and nominated John Bell of Tennessee for president. "It is both the part of patriotism and of duty," they resolved, "to recognize no political principle other than the Constitution of the country, the union of the states, and the enforcement of the laws."

Ostrichlike, the Constitutional Unionists ignored the conflicts rending the nation. Only in the border states, where the consequences of disunion were sure to be most tragic, did they have any following.

With four candidates in the field, no one could win a popular majority, but it soon became clear that Lincoln was going to be elected. Breckenridge had most of the slave states in his pocket and Bell would run strong in the border regions, but the populous northern and western states had a majority of the electoral votes, and there the choice lay between the Republicans and the Douglas Democrats. In such a contest the Republicans, with their attractive economic program and their strong stand against slavery in the territories, were sure to come out on top.

Lincoln avoided campaigning and made no public statements. Douglas, recognizing the certainty of Lincoln's victory, accepted his fate and for the first time in his career rose above ambition. "We must try to save the Union," he said. "I will go South." In the heart of the Cotton Kingdom, he appealed to the voters to stand by the Union regardless of who was elected. He was the only candidate to do so; the others refused to remind the people that their election might result in secession and civil war.

When the votes were counted, Lincoln had 1.866 million, almost a million fewer than the combined total of his three opponents, but he swept the North and West, which gave him 180 electoral votes and the presidency. Douglas received 1.383 million votes, so distributed that he carried only Missouri and part of New Jersey. Breckenridge, with 848,000 popular votes, won most of the South; Bell, with 593,000, carried Virginia, Tennessee, and Kentucky. Lincoln was thus a minority president, but his title to the office was unquestionable. Even if his opponents could have combined their popular votes in each state, Lincoln would have won.

THE SECESSION CRISIS

South Carolina
Declaration of
the Causes of
Secession

Only days after Lincoln's victory, the South Carolina legislature ordered an election of delegates to a convention to decide the state's future course. On December 20 the convention voted unanimously to secede, basing its action on the logic of Calhoun. "The State of South Carolina has resumed her position among the nations of the world," the delegates announced. By February 1, 1861, the six other states of the lower South had followed suit. A week later, at Montgomery, Alabama, a provisional government of the Confederate States of America was established. Virginia, Tennessee, North Carolina, and Arkansas did not leave the Union but announced that

if the federal government attempted to use force against the Confederacy, they too would secede.

Why were white Southerners willing to wreck the Union their forebears had put together with so much love and labor? No simple explanation is possible. The danger that the expanding North would overwhelm them was for neither today nor tomorrow. Lincoln had assured them that he would respect slavery where it existed. The Democrats had retained control of Congress in the election; the Supreme Court was firmly in their hands as well. If the North did try to destroy slavery, secession would perhaps be a logical tactic, but why not wait until the threat materialized? To leave the Union meant abandoning the very objectives for which the South had been contending for over a decade: a share of the federal territories and an enforceable fugitive slave law.

One reason why the South rejected this line of thinking was the tremendous economic energy generated in the North, which seemed to threaten the South's independence. As one Southerner complained at a commercial convention in 1855:

> From the rattle with which the nurse tickles the ear of the child born in the South to the shroud which covers the cold form of the dead, everything comes from the North. We rise from between sheets made in Northern looms, and pillows of Northern feathers, to wash in basins made in the North. . . . We eat from Northern plates and dishes; our rooms are swept with Northern brooms, our gardens dug with Northern spades . . . and the very wood which feeds our fires is cut with Northern axes, helved with hickory brought from Connecticut and New York.

Secession, white Southerners argued, would "liberate" the South and produce the kind of balanced economy that was proving so successful in the North. Moreover, the mere possibility of emancipation was a powerful force for secession. "We must either submit to degradation, and to the loss of property worth four billions," the Mississippi convention declared, "or we must secede."

The years of sectional conflict, the growing northern criticism of slavery, perhaps even an unconscious awareness that this criticism was well founded, had undermined and in many cases destroyed the patriotic feelings of white Southerners. Because of the constant clamor set up by New England antislavery groups, the South tended to identify all Northerners as "Yankee abolitionists" and to resent them with increasing passion. "I look upon the whole New England race as a troublesome unquiet set of meddlers," one Georgian wrote. In addition, a Republican president would not need the consent of Congress to flood the South with unfriendly federal officials—abolitionists and perhaps even blacks. Such a possibility

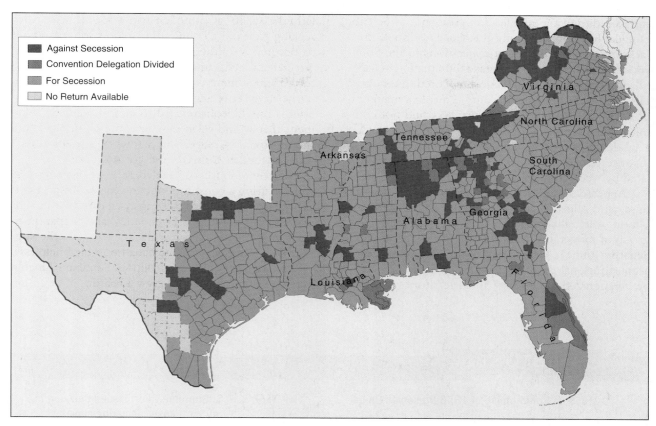

▲ **Secession of the South, 1860–1861**
A comparison of this map with the one on page 343 shows the minimal support for secession in the mainly nonslave mountain areas of the Appalachians. The strong antisecession sentiment in the mountainous areas of Virginia eventually led several counties there to break from Virginia in 1863 and form the new state of West Virginia.

most white Southerners found unsupportable. Fear approaching panic swept the region.

Although states' rights provided the rationale for leaving the Union, and Southerners expounded the strict constructionist interpretation of the Constitution with great ingenuity, the economic and emotional factors were far more basic. The lower South decided to go ahead with secession regardless of the cost. "Let the consequences be what they may," an Atlanta newspaper proclaimed. "Whether the Potomac is crimsoned in human gore, and Pennsylvania Avenue is paved ten fathoms in depth with mangled bodies . . . the South will never submit."

Not every slave owner could contemplate secession with such bloodthirsty equanimity. Some believed that the risks of war and slave insurrection were too great. Others retained a profound loyalty to the United States. Many accepted secession only after the deepest examination of conscience. Lieutenant Colonel Robert E. Lee of Virginia was typical of thousands. "I see only that a fearful calamity is upon us," he wrote during the secession crisis. "There is

no sacrifice I am not ready to make for the preservation of the Union save that of honour. If a disruption takes place, I shall go back in sorrow to my people & share the misery of my native state."

In the North there was a foolish but understandable reluctance to believe that the South really intended to break away. President-elect Lincoln was inclined to write off secession as a bluff designed to win concessions he was determined not to make. He also showed lamentable political caution in refusing to announce his plans or to cooperate with the outgoing Democratic administration before his inauguration.

In the South there was an equally unrealistic expectation that the North would not resist secession forcibly. The "Yankees" were timid materialists who would neither bear the cost nor risk their lives to prevent secession. It was commonly believed that "a lady's thimble will hold all the blood that will be shed." President Buchanan recognized the seriousness of the situation but professed himself powerless. Secession, he said, was illegal, but the federal government had no legal way to prevent it. (This was the same dilemma that had surfaced during the nullification crisis, but as Senator Douglas had reminded him, Buchanan was no Andrew Jackson.) He urged making concessions to the South yet lacked the forcefulness to take the situation in hand.

Of course he faced unprecedented difficulties. His term was about to run out—Lincoln's inauguration day was March 4—and since he could not commit to his successor, his influence was minuscule. Yet a bolder president would have denounced secession in uncompromising terms. Instead Buchanan vacillated between compromise and aimless drift.

Appeasers, well-meaning believers in compromise, and those prepared to fight to preserve the Union were alike incapable of effective action. A group of moderates headed by Henry Clay's disciple, Senator John J. Crittenden of Kentucky, proposed a constitutional amendment in which slavery would be "recognized as existing" in all territories south of latitude 36°30′. Crittenden had a special reason for seeking to avoid a conflict. His oldest son was about to become a southern general, another son a northern general. His amendment also promised that no future amendment would tamper with the institution in the slave states and offered other guarantees to the South. But Lincoln refused to consider any arrangement that would open new territory to slavery. "On the territorial question," he wrote, "I am inflexible." The Crittenden Compromise got nowhere.

The new southern Confederacy set vigorously to work drafting a constitution, choosing Jefferson Davis as provisional president, seizing arsenals and other federal property within its boundaries, and preparing to dispatch diplomatic representatives to enlist the support of foreign powers. Buchanan bumbled helplessly in Washington. And out in Illinois, Abraham Lincoln juggled Cabinet posts and grew a beard.

MILESTONES

Year	Event
1850	Compromise of 1850 preserves Union
	U.S. and Great Britain sign Clayton-Bulwer Treaty on interoceanic canal
1851–1860	Northerners resist enforcement of Fugitive Slave Act
1852	Harriet Beecher Stowe publishes *Uncle Tom's Cabin* depicting slavery
	Franklin Pierce is elected president
1854	U.S. disavows secret Ostend Manifesto on Cuba
	Kansas-Nebraska Act repeals Missouri Compromise
	Commodore Matthew Perry forces Japan to open its ports to U.S. trade
	Senate ratifies Gadsden Purchase of Mexican territory
1855	William Walker seizes power in Nicaragua
1856–1858	Proslavery forces oppose Free Soilers in "Bleeding Kansas" Territory
1856	John Brown and followers murder five proslavery men in Pottawatomie Massacre
	South Carolina's Preston Brooks canes Senator Charles Sumner of Massachusetts on Senate floor
	James Buchanan is elected president
1857	U.S. Supreme Court issues decision in Dred Scott case, declaring slaves are not citizens
	Panic of 1857 collapses economy
1858	Abraham Lincoln loses Senate race to Stephen Douglas after Lincoln-Douglas Debates, but wins national attention
1859	John Brown raids Harpers Ferry, Virginia arsenal
1860	Abraham Lincoln is elected president
	South Carolina secedes from Union
1861	Seven southern states establish Confederate States of America
	Lincoln rejects Crittenden Compromise, last peaceful attempt to save Union

SUPPLEMENTARY READING

On the origins of the Civil War, in addition to the Debating the Past (p. 374), see David M. Potter, *The Impending Crisis* (1976), Don E. Fehrenbacher, *Sectional Crisis and Southern Constitutionalism* (1995), and Marshall De Rosa, *The Politics of Dissolution* (1998). In *States' Rights and the Union* (2000), as in his other works, Forrest McDonald affirms the South's right to secede. William A. Link, *Roots of Secession: Slavery and Politics in Antebellum Virginia* (2003) is a useful state study.

On slave resistance, see especially John Hope Franklin and Loren Schweninger, *Runaway Slaves* (1999), William Dusinberre, *Them Dark Days: Slavery in the American Rice Swamps* (1996), and Steven Weisenburger, *Modern Medea: A Family Story of Slavery and Child-Murder from the Old South* (1998).

On the enforcement of the Fugitive Slave Act, see S. W. Campbell, *The Slave Catchers* (1970), and T. D. Morris, *Free Men All: The Personal Liberty Laws* (1974). Everyone should read Harriet Beecher Stowe's *Uncle Tom's Cabin*. Joan Hedrick's *Harriet Beecher Stowe* (1994) is excellent.

For the foreign policy of the 1850s, see C. H. Brown, *Agents of Manifest Destiny* (1980), and P. B. Wiley and Korogi Ichiro, *Yankees in the Land of the Gods* (1990).

On Stephen A. Douglas, see Robert W. Johannsen, *Stephen A. Douglas* (1973). Sumner's role in the deepening crisis is brilliantly discussed in David H. Donald, *Charles Sumner and the Coming of the Civil War* (1960) and *Charles Sumner and the Rights of Man* (1970); a more recent, brief study is Frederick J. Blue, *Charles Sumner and the Conscience of the North* (1994). Jean Baker, *James Buchanan* (2004) is solid and concise. On Dred Scott, see Paul Finkelman, *Dred Scott v. Sandford* (1997).

For Lincoln's own well-crafted words, see Abraham Lincoln, *Selections* (2 vols., 1989). The best modern biographies of Lincoln are David H. Donald, *Lincoln* (1995), and Mark Neely, *The Last Best Hope on Earth* (1993). Lincoln's early struggles are thoughtfully examined in Douglas L. Wilson, *Honor's Voice: The Transformation of Abraham Lincoln* (1998). W. E. Gienapp, *The Origins of the Republican Party* (1987), and Eric Foner, *Free Soil, Free Labor, Free Men* (1970), are excellent analyses of Republican ideas and policies. Allen Guelzo, *Lincoln's Emancipation Proclamation* (2004) is also useful.

John Stauffer, *Black Hearts of Men* (2001) examines John Brown and other radical abolitionists. See also Stephen B. Oates, *To Purge This Land with Blood* (1984).

SUGGESTED WEBSITES

Secession Era Editorial Project

http://history.furman.edu/~benson/docs/

Furman University is digitizing editorials about the secession crisis and already includes scores of them on this site.

John Brown Trial Links

http://www.law.umkc.edu/faculty/projects/ftrials/Brown.html

For information about the John Brown trial, this site provides a list of excellent links.

Harriett Beecher Stowe and *Uncle Tom's Cabin*

http://xroads.virginia.edu/~HYPER/STOWE/stowe.html

This site provides both text and description of Stowe's important books, as well as information about the author's life.

Abraham Lincoln

http://showcase.netins.net/web/creative/lincoln.html

This site both contains useful information about President Lincoln and links to other web destinations.

Abraham Lincoln Association

http://www.alincolnassoc.com/

This site allows the search of digital versions of Lincoln's papers.

CHAPTER 15 The War to Save the Union

▼ *Prisoners from the Front* (1866) established Winslow Homer's reputation for spare truthfulness. But while the Union officer is depicted as intelligent and upright, the surrendering Confederate soldiers are mere caricatures—a dull-witted fellow, hands in pocket; a beaten patriarch; a defiant cavalier.

CHAPTER CONTENTS

The nomination of Lincoln had succeeded brilliantly for the Republicans, but was his election a good thing for the country? As the inauguration approached, many Americans had doubts. Honest Abe was a clever politician who had spoken well about the central issue of the times, but would he act decisively in this crisis? His behavior as president-elect was not reassuring. He spent much time closeted with politicians. Was he too obtuse to understand the grave threat to the Union posed by secession? People remembered uneasily that he had never held executive office, that his congressional career had been short and undistinguished. When he finally uprooted himself from Springfield in February 1861, his occasional speeches en route to Washington were vague, almost flippant. He kissed babies, shook hands, mouthed platitudes. Some people thought it downright cowardly that he let himself be spirited in the dead of night through Baltimore, where feeling against him ran high.

LINCOLN'S CABINET

Everyone waited tensely to see whether Lincoln would oppose secession with force, but Lincoln seemed concerned only with organizing his Cabinet. The final slate was not ready until the morning of inauguration day, March 4, and shrewd observers found it alarming, for the new president had chosen to construct a "balanced" Cabinet representing a wide range of opinion instead of putting together a group of harmonious advisers who could help him face the crisis.

William H. Seward, the secretary of state, was the ablest and best known of the appointees. Despite his reputation for radicalism, the hawk-nosed, chinless, tousle-haired Seward hoped to conciliate the South and was thus in bad odor with the radical wing of the Republican party. In time Seward proved himself Lincoln's strong right arm, but at the start he underestimated the president and expected to dominate him. Senator Salmon P. Chase, a bald, square-jawed, antislavery leader from Ohio, whom Lincoln named secretary of the treasury, represented the radicals. Chase was humorless and vain but able; he detested Seward. Many of the president's other selections worried thoughtful people.

DOCUMENT

Lincoln, First Inaugural Address

Lincoln's inaugural address was conciliatory but firm. Southern institutions were in no danger from his administration. Secession, however, was illegal, the Union "perpetual." "A husband and wife may be divorced," Lincoln said, employing one of his homely and unconsciously risqué metaphors, "but the different parts of our country cannot. . . . Intercourse, either amicable or hostile, must continue between them." His tone was calm and warm. His concluding words catch the spirit of the inaugural perfectly:

> I am loath to close. We are not enemies, but friends. We must not be enemies. Though passion may have strained, it must not break, our bonds of affection. The mystic chords of memory, stretching from every battlefield and patriot grave to every living heart . . . will yet swell the chorus of the Union when again touched, as surely they will be, by the better angels of our nature.

FORT SUMTER: THE FIRST SHOT

While denying the legality of secession, Lincoln had taken a temporizing position. The Confederates had seized most federal property in the Deep South.

Lincoln admitted frankly that he would not attempt to reclaim this property. However, two strongholds, Fort Sumter, on an island in Charleston harbor, and Fort Pickens, at Pensacola, Florida, were still in loyal Union hands. Most Republicans did not want to surrender them without a show of resistance. To do so, one wrote, would be to convert the American eagle into a "debilitated chicken."

Yet to reinforce the forts might mean bloodshed that would make reconciliation impossible. After weeks of indecision, Lincoln took the moderate step of sending a naval expedition to supply the beleaguered Sumter garrison with food. Unwilling to permit this, the Confederates opened fire on the fort on April 12 before the supply ships arrived. After holding out for 34 hours, Major Robert Anderson and his men surrendered.

The attack precipitated an outburst of patriotic indignation in the North. Lincoln issued a call for 75,000 volunteers; his request prompted Virginia, North Carolina, Arkansas, and Tennessee to secede. After years of crises and compromises, the nation chose to settle the great quarrel between the sections by force of arms.

Southerners considered Lincoln's call for troops an act of naked aggression. When the first Union regiment tried to pass through Baltimore in mid-April, it was attacked by a mob. The prosouthern chief of police telegraphed the Maryland state's attorney: "Streets red with blood. Send . . . for the riflemen to come, without delay. Fresh hordes will be down on us to-morrow." The chief and the mayor of Baltimore then ordered the railroad bridges connecting Baltimore with the northern states destroyed. Order was not restored until Union troops occupied key points in the city.

The Southerners were seeking to exercise what a later generation would call the right of self-determination. How, they asked, could the North square its professed belief in democracy with its refusal to permit the southern states to leave the Union when a majority of their citizens wished to do so?

Lincoln took the position that secession was a rejection of democracy. If the South could refuse to abide by the result of an election in which it had freely participated, then everything that monarchists and other conservatives had said about the instability of republican governments would be proved true. "The central idea of secession is the essence of anarchy," he said. The United States must "demonstrate to the world" that "when ballots have been fairly and constitutionally decided, there can be no successful appeal except to ballots themselves, at succeeding elections."

This was the proper ground to take, both morally and politically. A war against slavery would not have been supported by a majority of Northerners. Slavery was the root cause of secession but not of the North's determination to resist secession, which resulted from the people's commitment to the Union. Although abolition was to be one of the major results of the Civil War, the war was fought for nationalistic reasons, not to destroy slavery. Lincoln made this plain when he wrote in response to an editorial by Horace Greeley urging immediate emancipation: "I would save the Union. . . . If I could save the Union without freeing any slave, I would do it; and if I could save it by freeing all the slaves, I would do it; and if I could do it by freeing some and leaving others alone, I would also do that." He added, however, "I intend no modification of my oft-expressed personal wish that all men, everywhere, could be free."

THE BLUE AND THE GRAY

In any test between the United States and the Confederacy, the former possessed tremendous advantages. There were more than 20 million people in the northern states (excluding Kentucky and Missouri, where opinion was divided) but only 9 million in the South, including 3.5 million slaves whom the whites hesitated to trust with arms. The North's economic capacity to wage war was even more preponderant. It was manufacturing nine times as much as the Confederacy (including 97 percent of the nation's firearms) and had a far larger and more efficient railroad system than the South. Northern control of the merchant marine and the navy made possible a blockade of the Confederacy, a particularly potent threat to a region so dependent on foreign markets.

The Confederates discounted these advantages. Many doubted that public opinion in the North would sustain Lincoln if he attempted to meet secession with force. Northern manufacturers needed southern markets, and merchants depended heavily on southern business. Many western farmers still sent their produce down the Mississippi. War would threaten the prosperity of all these groups, Southerners maintained. Should the North try to cut Europe off from southern cotton, the European powers, particularly Great Britain, would descend on the land in their might, force open southern ports, and provide the Confederacy with the means of defending itself forever. Moreover, the South provided nearly three-fourths of the world's cotton,

essential for most textile mills. "You do not dare to make war on cotton," Senator Hammond of South Carolina had taunted his northern colleagues in 1858. "No power on earth dares to make war upon it. Cotton is king."

The Confederacy also counted on certain military advantages. The new nation need only hold what it had; it could fight a defensive war, less costly in men and material and of great importance in maintaining morale and winning outside sympathy. Southerners would be defending not only their social institutions but also their homes and families.

Luck played a part too; the Confederacy quickly found a great commander, while many of the northern generals in the early stages of the war proved either bungling or indecisive. In battle after battle Union armies were defeated by forces of equal or smaller size.

There was little to distinguish the enlisted men of the two sides. Both, conscious of their forefathers of 1776, fought for liberty, though they interpreted the concept in opposite ways.

Both sides faced massive difficulties in organizing for a war long feared but never properly anticipated. After southern defections, the regular Union army consisted of only 13,000 officers and enlisted men, far too few to absorb the 186,000 who had joined the colors by early summer, much less the additional 450,000 who had volunteered by the end of the year. Recruiting was left to the states, each being assigned a quota; there was little central organization. Natty companies of "Fire Zouaves" and "Garibaldi Guards" in gorgeous uniforms rubbed shoulders with slovenly units composed of toughs and criminals and with regiments of farm boys from

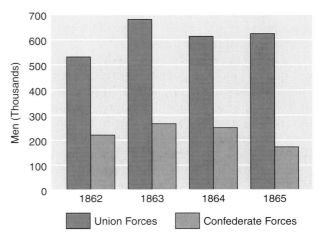

▲ **Men Present for Service in the Civil War**

▲ Young volunteers of the First Virginia Militia, in 1861. Why did they join the Confederate army? "It is better to spend our all in defending our country than to be subjugated and have it taken away from us," one explained, a sentiment that appeared often in the letters of Confederate soldiers. Soldiers on both sides believed that their cause was righteous.

character: He would willingly accept snubs and insults in order to advance the cause. He kept a close check on every aspect of the war effort, but found time for thought too. His young secretary John Nicolay reported seeing him sit sometimes for a whole hour like "a petrified image," lost in contemplation.

Gradually Lincoln's stock rose—first with men like Seward, who saw him close up and experienced both his steel and his gentleness, then with the people at large, who sensed his compassion, his humility, his wisdom. He was only 52 when he became president, and already people were calling him Old Abe. Before long they would call him Father Abraham.

The Confederacy faced far greater problems than the North, for it had to create an entire administration under pressure of war, with the additional handicap of the states' rights philosophy to which it was committed. The Confederate constitution explicitly recognized the sovereignty of the states and contained no broad authorization for laws designed to advance the general welfare. State governments repeatedly defied the central administration, located at Richmond after Virginia seceded, even with regard to military affairs.

Of course, the Confederacy made heavy use of the precedents and administrative machinery taken over from the United States. The government quickly decided that all federal laws would remain in force until specifically repealed, and many former federal officials continued to perform their duties under the new auspices.

The call to arms produced a turnout in the Confederacy perhaps even more impressive than that in the North; by July 1861 about 112,000 men were under arms. As in the North, men of every type enlisted, and morale was high. Some wealthy recruits brought slave servants with them to care for their needs in camp, cavalrymen supplied their own horses, and many men arrived with their own shotguns and hunting rifles. Ordinary militia companies sporting names like Tallapoosa Thrashers, Cherokee Lincoln Killers, and Chickasaw Desperadoes marched in step with troops of "character, blood, and social position"

Iowa, Illinois, and Michigan. Unlike later conflicts in which men from all parts of the country were mixed in each regiment, Civil War units were recruited locally. Men in each company tended to have known one another or had friends in common in civilian life. But few knew even the rudiments of soldiering. The hastily composed high command, headed by the elderly Winfield Scott, debated grand strategy endlessly while regimental commanders lacked decent maps of Virginia.

The Whig prejudice against powerful presidents was part of Lincoln's political heritage; consequently at the start he did not display the firmness of Jackson or Polk in his dealings with Congress and his Cabinet. But his strength lay in his ability to think problems through. When he did, he acted unflinchingly. Anything but a tyrant by nature, he boldly exceeded the conventional limits of presidential power in the emergency, expanding the army without congressional authorization, suspending the writ of habeas corpus, even emancipating the slaves when he thought military necessity demanded that action. Yet he also displayed remarkable patience and depth of

DOCUMENT
Davis, Address to the Provisional Congress

▲ Jefferson Davis sat for this portrait in 1863 in his mansion in Richmond. It is the only wartime portrait from the life of the Confederate president.

bearing names like Richmond Howitzers and Louisiana Zouaves. ("Zouave" mania swept both North and South, prospective soldiers evidently considering broad sashes and baggy breeches the embodiment of military splendor.)

President Jefferson Davis represented the best type of southern planter, noted for his humane treatment of his slaves. In politics he had pursued a somewhat unusual course. While senator from Mississippi, he opposed the Compromise of 1850 and became a leader of the southern radicals. After Pierce made him secretary of war, however, he took a more nationalistic position, one close to that of Douglas. Davis supported the transcontinental railroad idea and spoke in favor of the annexation of Cuba and other Caribbean areas. He rejected Douglas's position during the Kansas controversy but tried to close the breach that Kansas had opened in Democratic ranks. After the 1860 election he supported secession only reluctantly, preferring to give Lincoln a chance to prove that he meant the South no harm.

Davis was courageous, industrious, and intelligent, but he was rather too reserved and opinionated to make either a good politician or a popular leader. As president he devoted too much time to details, failed to delegate authority, and (unlike Lincoln) was impatient with garrulous and dull-witted people, types political leaders frequently have to deal with. Being a graduate of West Point, he fancied himself a military expert, but he was a mediocre military thinker. Unlike Lincoln, he quarreled frequently with his subordinates, held grudges, and allowed personal feelings to distort his judgment. "If anyone disagrees with Mr. Davis," his wife Varina Davis admitted, "he resents it and ascribes the difference to the perversity of his opponent."

THE TEST OF BATTLE: BULL RUN

"Forward to Richmond!" "On to Washington!" Such shouts propelled the armies into battle long before either was properly trained. On July 21 at Manassas Junction, Virginia, some 20 miles below Washington, on a branch of the Potomac called Bull Run, 30,000 Union soldiers under General Irvin McDowell attacked a roughly equal force of Confederates commanded by the "Napoleon of the South," Pierre G. T. Beauregard. McDowell swept back the Confederate left flank. Victory seemed sure. Then a Virginia brigade under Thomas J. Jackson rushed to the field by rail from the Shenandoah Valley in the nick of time, held doggedly to a key hill, and checked the advance. (A South Carolina general, seeking to rally his own men, pointed to the hill and shouted: "Look, there is Jackson with his Virginians, standing like a stone wall against the enemy." Thus "Stonewall" Jackson received his nickname.)

The Southerners then counterattacked, driving the Union soldiers back. As often happens with green troops, retreat quickly turned to rout. McDowell's men fled toward the defenses of Washington, abandoning their weapons, stumbling through lines of supply wagons, trampling foolish sightseers who had come out to watch the battle. Panic engulfed Washington. Richmond exulted. Both sides expected the northern capital to fall within hours.

The inexperienced southern troops were too disorganized to follow up their victory. Casualties on both sides were light, and the battle had little direct effect on anything but morale. Southern confidence soared, while the North began to realize how immense the task of subduing the Confederacy would be.

After Bull Run, Lincoln devised a broader, more systematic strategy for winning the war. The navy would clamp a tight blockade on all southern ports. In the West operations designed to gain control of the Mississippi would be undertaken. (This was part of General Scott's "Anaconda Plan," designed to starve the South into submission.) More important, a new army would be mustered at Washington to invade Virginia. Congress promptly authorized the enlistment of 500,000 three-year volunteers. To lead this army and—after General Scott's retirement in November—to command the Union forces, Lincoln appointed a 34-year-old major general, George B. McClellan.

McClellan was the North's first military hero. Units under his command had driven the Confederates from the pro-Union western counties of Virginia, clearing the way for the admission of West Virginia as a separate state in 1863. The fighting had been on a small scale, but McClellan, an incurable romantic and something of an egomaniac, managed to inflate its importance. "You have annihilated two armies," he proclaimed in a widely publicized message to his troops. Few Northerners noticed that they had "annihilated" only about 250 Confederates.

Despite his penchant for self-glorification, McClellan possessed solid qualifications for command. One was experience. After graduating from West Point second in his class in 1846, he had served in the Mexican War. During the Crimean War he spent a year in the field, talking with British officers and studying fortifications. McClellan had a fine military bearing, a flair for the dramatic, and the ability to inspire troops. He was a talented administrator and organizer. He liked to concoct bold plans and dreamed of striking swiftly at the heart of the Confederacy to capture Richmond, Nashville, even New Orleans. Yet he was sensible enough to insist on massive logistic support, thorough training for the troops, iron discipline, and meticulous staff work before making a move.

PAYING FOR THE WAR

After Bull Run, this policy was exactly right. By the fall of 1861 a real army was taking shape along the Potomac: disciplined, confident, adequately supplied. Northern shops and factories were producing guns, ammunition, wagons, uniforms, shoes, and the countless other supplies needed to fight a great war. Most manufacturers operated on a small scale, but with the armed forces soon wearing out 3 million pairs of shoes and 1.5 million uniforms a year and with men leaving their jobs by the hundreds of thousands to fight, the tendency of industry to mechanize and to increase the size of the average manufacturing unit became ever more pronounced.

At the beginning of the war Secretary of the Treasury Salmon P. Chase underestimated how much it would cost. He learned quickly. In August 1861 Congress passed an income tax law (3 percent on incomes over $800, which effectively exempted ordinary wage earners) and assessed a direct tax on the states. Loans amounting to $140 million were authorized. As the war dragged on and expenses mounted, new excise taxes on every imaginable product and service were passed, and still further borrowing was necessary. In 1863 the banking system was overhauled.

During the war the federal government borrowed a total of $2.2 billion and collected $667 million in taxes, slightly over 20 percent of its total expenditures.

▲ Eighteen-year-olds were the largest age group in the first year of the war in both armies. Soldiers were universally called "the boys"; and officers, even in their thirties, were called "old men." One of the most popular war songs was "Just Before the Battle, Mother."

▲ A family of a soldier in the 31st Philadelphia Infantry, camped near Washington, D.C. Although both armies discouraged women from following soldier-husbands, the practice was fairly common. Women proved indispensable as laundresses and cooks. Although women were initially excluded from army hospitals, the policy quickly changed and camp women often worked as nurses during battles.

These unprecedented large sums proved inadequate. Some obligations were met by printing paper money unredeemable in coin. About $431 million in "greenbacks"—the term distinguished this fiat money from the redeemable yellowback bills—were issued during the conflict. Public confidence in all paper money vacillated with each change in the fortunes of the Union armies, but by the end of the war the cost of living in the North had doubled.

On balance, the heavy emphasis on borrowing and currency inflation was expensive but not irresponsible. In a country still chiefly agricultural, people had relatively low cash incomes and therefore could not easily bear a heavy tax load. Many Americans considered it reasonable to expect future generations to pay part of the dollar cost of saving the Union when theirs was contributing so heavily in labor and blood.

POLITICS AS USUAL

Partisan politics was altered by the war but not suspended. The secession of the southern states left the Republicans with large majorities in both houses of Congress. Most Democrats supported measures necessary for the conduct of the war but objected to the way the Lincoln administration was conducting it. The sharpest conflicts came when slavery and race relations were under discussion. The Democrats adopted a conservative stance, as reflected in the slogan "The Constitution as it is; the Union as it was; the Negroes where they are." The Republicans divided into Moderate and Radical wings. Political divisions on economic issues such as tariffs and land policy tended to cut across party lines and, so far as the Republicans were concerned, to bear little relation to slavery and race. As the war progressed, the Radical faction became increasingly influential.

In 1861 the most prominent Radical senator was Charles Sumner, finally recovered from his caning by Preston Brooks and brimful of hatred for slaveholders. In the House, Thaddeus Stevens of Pennsylvania was the rising power. Sumner and Stevens were uncompromising on all questions relating to slaves; they insisted not merely on abolition but on granting full political and civil rights to blacks. Moderate Republicans objected vehemently to treating blacks as equals and opposed making abolition a war aim, and even many of the so-called Radicals disagreed with Sumner and Stevens on race relations. Senator Benjamin Wade of Ohio, for example, was a lifelong opponent of slavery, yet he had convinced himself that blacks (he habitually called them "niggers") had a distinctive and unpleasant smell. He considered the common white prejudice against blacks perfectly understandable. But prejudice, he maintained, gave no one the right "to do injustice to anybody"; he insisted that blacks were at least as intelligent as whites and were entitled not merely to freedom but to full political equality.

At the other end of the political spectrum stood the so-called Peace Democrats. These "Copperheads" (apparently the reference was not to the poisonous snake but to an earlier time when some hard-money Democrats wore copper pennies around their necks) opposed all measures in support of the war. They hoped to win control of Congress and force a negotiated peace. Few were actually disloyal, but their activities at a time when thousands of men were risking their lives in battle infuriated many Northerners.

Lincoln treated dissenters with a curious mixture of repression and tolerance. He suspended the writ of habeas corpus in critical areas and applied martial law freely. Over 13,000 persons were arrested and held without trial, many, as it later turned out, unjustly. The president argued that the government dared not stand on ceremony in a national emergency. His object, he insisted, was not to punish but to prevent. Arbitrary arrests were rarely, if ever, made for purely political purposes, and free elections were held as scheduled throughout the war.

The federal courts compiled an admirable record in defending civil liberties, although when in conflict with the military, they could not enforce their decrees. In *Ex parte Merryman* (1861), Chief Justice Taney held General George Cadwalader in contempt for failing to produce a prisoner for trial when ordered to do so, but Cadwalader went unpunished and the prisoner continued to languish behind bars. After the war, in *Ex parte Milligan* (1866), the Supreme Court declared illegal the military trials of civilians in areas where the regular courts were functioning, but by that time the question was of only academic interest.

The most notorious domestic foe of the administration was the Peace Democrat Congressman Clement L. Vallandigham of Ohio, who was sent to prison by a military court. There were two rebellions in progress, Vallandigham claimed, "the Secessionist Rebellion" and "the Abolitionist Rebellion." "I am against both," he added. But Lincoln ordered him released and banished to the Confederacy. Once at liberty Vallandigham moved to Canada, from which refuge he ran unsuccessfully for governor of Ohio.

"Perish offices," he once said, "perish life itself, but do the thing that is right." In 1864 he returned to Ohio. Although he campaigned against Lincoln in the presidential election, he was not arrested. Lincoln was no dictator.

Behind Confederate Lines

The South also revised its strategy after Bull Run. Although it might have been wiser to risk everything on a bold invasion of the North, President Davis relied primarily on a strong defense to wear down the Union's will to fight. In 1862 the Confederate Congress passed a conscription act that permitted the hiring of substitutes and exempted many classes of people (including college professors, druggists, and mail carriers) whose work could hardly have been deemed essential. A provision deferring one slave owner or overseer for every plantation of 20 or more slaves led many to grumble about "a rich man's war and a poor man's fight."

Although the Confederacy did not develop a two-party system, there was plenty of internal political strife. Southern devotion to states' rights and individual liberty (for white men) caused endless trouble. Conflicts were continually erupting between Davis and southern governors jealous of their prerogatives as heads of "sovereign" states.

Finance was the Confederacy's most vexing problem. The blockade made it impossible to raise much money through tariffs. The Confederate Congress passed an income tax together with many excise taxes but all told they covered only 2 percent of its needs by taxation. The most effective levy was a tax in kind, amounting to one-tenth of each farmer's production. The South borrowed as much as it could ($712 million), even mortgaging cotton undeliverable because of the blockade, in order to gain European credits. But it relied mainly on printing paper currency; over $1.5 billion poured from the presses during the war. Considering the amount issued, this currency held its value well until late in the war, when the military fortunes of the Confederacy began to decline. Then the bottom fell out, and by early 1865 the Confederate dollar was worth less than 2 cents in gold.

Outfitting the army strained southern resources to the limit. Large supplies of small arms (some 600,000 weapons during the entire war) came from Europe through the blockade, along with other valuable matériel. As the blockade became more efficient, however, it became increasingly difficult to obtain European goods. The Confederates did manage to build a number of munitions plants, and they captured huge amounts of northern arms. No battle was lost because of a lack of guns or other military equipment, although shortages of shoes and uniforms handicapped the Confederate forces on some occasions.

Foreign policy loomed large in Confederate thinking, for the "cotton is king" theory presupposed that the great powers would break any northern blockade to get cotton for their textile mills. Southern expectations were not realized, however. The European nations would have been delighted to see the United States broken up, but none was prepared to support the Confederacy directly. The attitude of Great Britain was decisive. The cutting off of cotton did not hit the British as hard as the South had hoped. They had a large supply on hand when the war broke out, and when that was exhausted, alternative sources in India and Egypt took up part of the slack. Furthermore, British crop failures necessitated the importation of large amounts of northern wheat, providing a powerful reason for not antagonizing the United States. The fact that most ordinary people in Great Britain favored the North also influenced British policy.

Several times the two nations came to the brink of war. In November 1861 the USS *San Jacinto* stopped a British vessel, the *Trent,* on the high seas and forcibly arrested two Confederate envoys, James M. Mason and John Slidell, who were en route to London. This violation of international law would probably have led to war had not Lincoln decided to turn the Southerners loose. In 1862 two powerful cruisers, the *Florida* and the *Alabama,* were built for the Confederates in English shipyards under the most transparent of subterfuges. Despite American protests, they were permitted to put to sea and were soon wreaking havoc among northern merchant ships. When two ironclad "rams" were also built in Britain for the Confederates, the United States made it clear that it would declare war if the ships were delivered. The British government then confiscated the vessels, avoiding a showdown.

Charles Francis Adams, the American minister in London, ably handled the many vexing problems that arose. However, the military situation determined British policy; once the North obtained a clear superiority on the battlefield, the possibility of intervention vanished.

WAR IN THE WEST: SHILOH

After Bull Run no battles were fought until early 1862. Then, while McClellan continued his deliberate preparations to attack Richmond, important fighting occurred far to the west. Most of the Plains Indians sided with the Confederacy, principally because of their resentment of the federal government's policies toward them. White settlers from Colorado to California were mostly Unionists. In March 1862 a Texas army advancing beyond Santa Fe clashed with a Union force in the Battle of Glorieta Pass. The battle was indecisive, but a Union unit destroyed the Texans' supply train. The Texans felt compelled to retreat to the Rio Grande, thus ending the Confederate threat to the Far West.

Meanwhile, far larger Union forces, led by a shabby, cigar-smoking West Pointer named Ulysses S. Grant, had invaded Tennessee from a base at Cairo, Illinois. Making effective use of armored gunboats, Grant captured Fort Henry and Fort Donelson, strongholds on the Tennessee and Cumberland rivers, taking 14,000 prisoners. Next he marched toward Corinth, Mississippi, an important railroad junction.

To check Grant's advance, the Confederates massed 40,000 men under Albert Sidney Johnston. On April 6, while Grant slowly concentrated his forces,

Johnston struck suddenly at Shiloh, 20 miles north of Corinth. Some Union soldiers were caught half-dressed, others in the midst of brewing their morning coffee. A few died in their blankets. "We were more than surprised," one Illinois officer later admitted. "We were astonished." However, Grant's men stood their ground. At the end of a day of ghastly carnage the Confederates held the advantage, but fresh Union troops poured in during the night, and on the second day of battle the tide turned. The Confederates fell back toward Corinth, exhausted and demoralized.

Grant, shaken by the unexpected attack and appalled by his losses, allowed the enemy to escape. This cost him the fine reputation he had won in capturing Fort Henry and Fort Donelson. He was relieved of his command. Although Corinth eventually fell and New Orleans was captured by a naval force under the

▲ **War in the West, 1862**
Although Union forces ultimately took Shiloh in April 1862, the city of Vicksburg, and thus control of the Mississippi, remained in southern hands.

command of Captain David Farragut, Vicksburg, key to control of the Mississippi, remained firmly in Confederate hands. A great opportunity had been lost.

Shiloh had other results. The staggering casualties shook the confidence of both belligerents. More Americans fell there in two days than in all the battles of the Revolution, the War of 1812, and the Mexican War combined. Union losses exceeded 13,000 out of 63,000 engaged; the Confederates lost 10,699, including General Johnston. Technology in the shape of more accurate guns that could be fired far more rapidly than the muskets of earlier times and more powerful artillery were responsible for the carnage. Gradually the generals began to reconsider their tactics and to experiment with field fortifications and other defensive measures. And the people, North and South, stopped thinking of the war as a romantic test of courage and military guile.

McClellan: The Reluctant Warrior

In Virginia, General McClellan, after unaccountable delays, was finally moving against Richmond. Instead of trying to advance across the difficult terrain of northern Virginia, he transported his army by water to the tip of the peninsula formed by the York and James rivers in order to attack Richmond from the southeast. After the famous battle on March 9, 1862, between the USS *Monitor* and the Confederate *Merrimack,* the first fight in history between armored warships, control of these waters was securely in northern hands.

While McClellan's plan alarmed many congressmen because it seemed to leave Washington relatively unprotected, it simplified the problem of keeping the army supplied in hostile country. But McClellan now displayed the weaknesses that eventually ruined his career. His problems were both intellectual and psychological. Basically he approached tactical questions in the manner of a typical eighteenth-century general. He considered war a kind of gentlemanly contest (similar to chess with its castles and knights) in which maneuver, guile, and position determined victory. He saw the Civil War not as a mighty struggle over fundamental beliefs but as a sort of complex game that commanders played at a leisurely pace and for limited stakes. He believed it more important to capture Richmond than to destroy the army protecting it. With their capital in northern hands, surely the Southerners (outwitted and outmaneuvered by a brilliant general) would acknowledge defeat and agree to return to the Union. The idea of crushing the South seemed to him wrongheaded and uncivilized.

Beyond this, McClellan was temperamentally unsuited for a position of so much responsibility. Beneath the swagger he was profoundly insecure. He talked like Napoleon, but he did not like to fight. He called repeatedly for more men; when he got them, he demanded still more. He knew how to get ready, but he was never ready in his own mind. What was said of another Union general would have been better said of McClellan: He was "watching the enemy as fast as he can."

McClellan began the Peninsula campaign in mid-March. Proceeding deliberately, he floated an army of 112,000 men down the Potomac and by May 14 had established a base at White House Landing, less than 25 miles from Richmond. A swift thrust might have ended the war quickly, but McClellan delayed, despite the fact that he had 80,000 men in striking position and large reserves. As he pushed forward slowly, the Confederates caught part of his force separated from the main body by the rain-swollen Chickahominy River and attacked. The Battle of Seven Pines was indecisive yet resulted in more than 10,000 casualties.

At Seven Pines the Confederate commander, General Joseph E. Johnston, was severely wounded; leadership of the Army of Northern Virginia then passed to Robert E. Lee. Although a reluctant supporter of secession, Lee was a superb soldier. During the Mexican War his gallantry under fire inspired General Scott to call him the bravest man in the army; another officer rhapsodized over his "daring reconnaissances pushed up to the cannon's mouth." He also had displayed an almost instinctive mastery of tactics. Admiral Raphael Semmes, who accompanied Scott's army on the march to Mexico City, recalled in 1851 that Lee "seemed to receive impressions intuitively, which it cost other men much labor to acquire."

Lee was McClellan's antithesis. McClellan seemed almost deliberately to avoid understanding his foes, acting as though every southern general was a genius. Lee, a master psychologist on the battlefield, took the measure of each Union general and devised his tactics accordingly. Where McClellan was complex, egotistical, perhaps even unbalanced, Lee was courtly, tactful, and entirely without McClellan's vainglorious belief that he was a man of destiny. Yet on the battlefield Lee's boldness skirted the edge of foolhardiness.

To relieve the pressure on Richmond, Lee sent General "Stonewall" Jackson, soon to be his most trusted lieutenant, on a diversionary raid in the Shenandoah Valley, west of Richmond and Washington. Jackson struck hard and swiftly at scattered Union forces in the region, winning a number of battles and capturing vast stores of equipment. Lincoln dispatched 20,000 reserves to the Shenandoah to check him—to the dismay of McClellan, who wanted

▲ Lee in 1863, by Julian Vannerson. "So great is my confidence in General Lee," Stonewall Jackson remarked, "that I am willing to follow him blind-folded."

the troops to attack Richmond from the north. But after Seven Pines, Lee ordered Jackson back to Richmond. While Union armies streamed toward the valley, Jackson slipped stealthily between them. On June 25 he reached Ashland, directly north of the Confederate capital.

Before that date McClellan had possessed clear numerical superiority yet had only inched ahead; now the advantage lay with Lee, and the very next day he attacked. For seven days the battle raged. Lee's plan was brilliant but too complicated for an army yet untested: The full weight of his force never hit the northern army at any one time. Nevertheless, the shock was formidable. McClellan, who excelled in defense, fell back, his lines intact, exacting a fearful toll. Under difficult conditions he managed to transfer his troops to a new base on the James River at Harrison's Landing, where the guns of the navy could shield his position. Again the loss of life was terrible: Northern casualties totaled 15,800; those of the South nearly 20,000 in the Seven Days' Battle for Richmond.

LEE COUNTERATTACKS: ANTIETAM

McClellan was still within striking distance of Richmond, in an impregnable position with secure supply lines and 86,000 soldiers ready to resume battle. Lee had absorbed heavy losses without winning

any significant advantage. Yet Lincoln was exasperated with McClellan for having surrendered the initiative and, after much deliberation, reduced his authority by placing him under General Henry W. Halleck. Halleck called off the Peninsula campaign and ordered McClellan to move his army from the James to the Potomac, near Washington. He was to join General John Pope, who was gathering a new army between Washington and Richmond.

DOCUMENT

McClellan to Abraham Lincoln (July 7, 1862)

If McClellan had persisted and captured Richmond, the war might have ended and the Union been restored without the abolition of slavery, since at that point the North was still fighting for union, not for freedom for the slaves. By prolonging the war, Lee inadvertently enabled it to destroy slavery along with the Confederacy, though no one at the time looked at the matter this way.

For the president to have lost confidence in McClellan was understandable. Nevertheless, to allow Halleck to pull back the troops was a bad mistake. When they withdrew, Lee seized the initiative. With typical decisiveness and daring, he marched rapidly north. Late in August his Confederates drove General Pope's confused troops from the same ground, Bull Run, where the first major engagement of the war had been fought.

Thirteen months had passed since the first failure at Bull Run, and despite the expenditure of thousands of lives, the Union army stood as far from Richmond as ever. Dismayed by Pope's incompetence, Lincoln turned in desperation back to McClellan. When his secretary protested that McClellan had expressed contempt for the president, Lincoln replied gently: "We must use what tools we have."

While McClellan was regrouping the shaken Union Army, Lee once again took the offensive. He realized that no number of individual southern triumphs could destroy the enormous material advantages of the North. Unless some dramatic blow, delivered on northern soil, persuaded the people of the United States that military victory was impossible, the South would surely be crushed in the long run by the weight of superior resources. Lee therefore marched rapidly northwest around the defenses of Washington.

Acting with even more than his usual boldness, Lee divided his army of 60,000 into a number of units. One, under Stonewall Jackson, descended on weakly defended Harpers Ferry, capturing more than 11,000 prisoners. Another pressed as far north as Hagerstown, Maryland, nearly to the Pennsylvania line. McClellan pursued with his usual deliberation until a captured dispatch revealed to him Lee's dispositions. Then he moved a bit more swiftly, forcing Lee to stand and fight on September 17 at

▲ War in the East, 1861–1862
After the first battle at Bull Run, in July of 1861, there was little action until the following spring, when McClellan launched his Peninsula campaign. The Battle of Antietam was the culmination of the fighting in the summer of 1862.

Sharpsburg, Maryland, between the Potomac and Antietam Creek.[1] On a field that offered Lee no room to maneuver, 70,000 Union soldiers clashed with 40,000 Confederates. When darkness fell, more than 22,000 lay dead or wounded on the bloody field.

Although casualties were evenly divided and the Confederate lines remained intact, Lee's position was perilous. His men were exhausted. McClellan had not yet thrown in his reserves, and new federal units were arriving hourly. A bold northern general would have continued the fight without respite through the night. One of ordinary aggressiveness would have waited for first light and then struck with every soldier who could hold a rifle, for with the Potomac at his back, Lee could not retreat under fire without inviting disaster. McClellan, however, did nothing. For an entire day, while Lee scanned the field in futile search of some weakness in the Union lines, he held his fire. That night the Confederates slipped back across the Potomac into Virginia.

[1]Southerners tended to identify battles by nearby towns, northerners by bodies of water. Thus Manassas and Bull Run, Sharpsburg and Antietam, Murfreesboro and Stone's River, and so on.

Lee's invasion had failed; his army had been badly mauled; the gravest threat to the Union in the war had been checked. But McClellan had let victory slip through his fingers. Soon Lee was back behind the defenses of Richmond, rebuilding his army.

Once again, this time finally, Lincoln dismissed McClellan from his command.

THE EMANCIPATION PROCLAMATION

Antietam, though hardly the victory he had hoped for, gave Lincoln the excuse he needed to take a step that changed the character of the war decisively. When the fighting started, fear of alienating the border states was reason enough for not making emancipation of the slaves a war aim. Lincoln even insisted on enforcing the Fugitive Slave Act for this reason. However, pressures to act against the South's "peculiar institution" mounted steadily. Slavery had divided the nation; now it was driving Northerners to war within themselves. Love of country led them to fight to save the Union, but fighting aroused hatreds and caused many to desire to smash the enemy. Sacrifice, pain, and grief made abolitionists of many who had no love for blacks—they sought to free the slave only to injure the master.

To make abolition an object of the war might encourage the slaves to revolt, but Lincoln disclaimed this objective. Nevertheless, the possibility existed. Already the slaves seemed to be looking to the North for freedom: Whenever Union troops invaded Confederate territory, slaves flocked into their lines.

As the war progressed, the Radical faction in Congress gradually chipped away at slavery. In April 1862 the Radicals pushed through a bill abolishing slavery in the District of Columbia; two months later another measure outlawed it in the territories; in July the Confiscation Act "freed" all slaves owned by persons in rebellion against the United States. In fighting for these measures and in urging general emancipation, some Radicals made statements harshly critical of Lincoln; but while he carefully avoided being identified with them or with any other faction, the president was never very far from their position. He resisted emancipation because he feared it would divide the country and injure the war effort, not because he personally disapproved. Indeed, he frequently cited Radical pressure as an excuse for doing what he wished to do on his own.

Lincoln would have preferred to see slavery done away with by state law, with compensation for slave owners and federal aid for former slaves willing to leave the United States. He tried repeatedly to persuade the loyal slave states to adopt this policy, but without success. By the summer of 1862

DOCUMENT

The Emancipation Proclamation

he was convinced that for military reasons and to win the support of liberal opinion in Europe, the government should make abolition a war aim. "We must free the slaves or be ourselves subdued," he explained to a member of his Cabinet. He delayed temporarily, fearing that a statement in the face of military reverses would be taken as a sign of weakness. The "victory" at Antietam Creek gave him his opportunity, and on September 22 he made public the Emancipation Proclamation. After January 1, 1863, it said, all slaves in areas in rebellion against the United States "shall be then, thenceforward, and forever free."

No single slave was freed directly by Lincoln's announcement, which did not apply to the border states or to those sections of the Confederacy, like New Orleans and Norfolk, Virginia, already controlled by federal troops. The proclamation differed in philosophy, however, from the Confiscation Act in striking at the institution, not at the property of rebels. Henceforth every Union victory would speed the destruction of slavery without regard for the attitudes of individual masters.

Some of the president's advisers thought the proclamation inexpedient, and others considered it illegal. Lincoln justified it as a way to weaken the enemy. The proclamation is full of phrases like "as a fit and necessary war measure" and "warranted by the Constitution upon military necessity."

Southerners considered the Emancipation Proclamation an incitement to slave rebellion—as one of them put it, an "infamous attempt to . . . convert the quiet, ignorant, and dependent black son of toil into a savage incendiary and brutal murderer." Most antislavery groups thought it did not go far enough. Lincoln "is only stopping on the edge of Niagara, to pick up a few chips," one abolitionist declared. "He and they will go over together." Foreign opinion was mixed: Liberals tended to applaud, conservatives to react with alarm or contempt.

As Lincoln anticipated, the proclamation had a subtle but continuing impact in the North. Its immediate effect was to aggravate racial prejudices. Millions of whites disapproved of slavery yet abhorred the idea of equality for blacks. David Wilmot, for example, insisted that his famous proviso was designed to preserve the territories for whites rather than to weaken slavery, and as late as 1857 the people of Iowa rejected black suffrage by a vote of 49,000 to 8000. To some, emancipation seemed to herald an invasion of the North by blacks who would compete for jobs, drive down wages, commit crimes, spread diseases, and eventually destroy the "purity" of the white race. The word *miscegenation* was coined in 1863 by David G. Croly, an editor of the *New York World*, directly as

a result of the Emancipation Proclamation. Its original meaning was "the mingling of the white and black races on the continent *as a consequence of the freedom of the latter.*" Of course, the fact of miscegenation in its current, more general meaning of racial interbreeding long antedated the freeing of any slave.

The Democrats spared no effort to make political capital of these fears and prejudices even before Lincoln's Emancipation Proclamation, and they made large gains in the 1862 election, especially in the Northwest. So strong was antiblack feeling that most of the Republican politicians who defended emancipation did so with racist arguments. Far from encouraging southern blacks to move north, they claimed, the ending of slavery would lead to a mass migration of northern blacks to the South.

When the Emancipation Proclamation began actually to free slaves, the government pursued a policy of "containment," that is, of keeping the former slaves in the South. Panicky fears of an inundation of blacks subsided in the North. Nevertheless, emancipation remained a cause of social discontent. In March 1863, volunteering having fallen off, Congress passed a conscription act. The law applied to all men between ages 20 and 45, but it allowed draftees to hire substitutes and even to buy exemption for $300, provisions that were patently unfair to the poor. During the remainder of the war 46,000 men were actually drafted, whereas 118,000 hired substitutes, and another 161,000 "failed to report." Conscription represented an enormous expansion of national authority, since in effect it gave the government the power of life and death over individual citizens.

THE DRAFT RIOTS

After the passage of the Conscription Act, draft riots erupted in a number of cities. By far the most serious disturbance occurred in New York City in July 1863. Many workers resented conscription in principle and were embittered by the $300 exemption fee (which represented a year's wages). The idea of being forced to risk their lives to free slaves who would then, they believed, compete with them for jobs infuriated them. On July 13 a mob attacked the office where the names of conscripts were being drawn. Most of the rioters were poor Irish Catholic laborers who resented both the blacks and the middle-class Protestant whites who seemed to them responsible for the special attention blacks were suddenly receiving. For four days the city was an inferno. Public buildings, shops, and private residences were put to the torch. What began as a protest against the draft became an assault on blacks and the well-to-do. It took federal troops and the temporary suspension of the draft in the city to put an end to the rioting. By the time order was restored more than a hundred people (most of them rioters) had lost their lives.

The Emancipation Proclamation does not entirely account for the draft riots. The new policy neither reflected nor triggered a revolution in white thinking about the race question. Its significance was subtle but real; both the naive view that Lincoln freed the slaves on January 1, 1863, and the cynical one that his action was a mere propaganda trick are incorrect. Northern hostility to emancipation arose from fear of change more than from hatred of blacks, while liberal disavowals of any intention to treat blacks as equals were in large measure designed to quiet this fear. To a degree the racial backlash that the proclamation inspired reflected the public's awareness that a change, frightening but irreversible, *had occurred*.

Most white Northerners did not surrender their comforting belief in black inferiority, and Lincoln was no exception. Yet Lincoln was evolving. He talked about deporting freed slaves to the tropics, but he did not send any there. And he began to receive black leaders in the White House and to allow black groups to hold meetings on the grounds.

Many other Americans were changing too. The brutality of the New York riots horrified many white citizens. Over $40,000 was swiftly raised to aid the victims, and some conservatives were so appalled by the Irish rioters that they began to talk of giving blacks the vote. The influential *Atlantic Monthly* commented: "It is impossible to name any standard . . . that will give a vote to the Celt [the Irish] and exclude the negro."

THE EMANCIPATED PEOPLE

To blacks, both slave and free, the Emancipation Proclamation served as a beacon. Even if it failed immediately to liberate one slave or to lift the burdens of prejudice from one black back, it stood as a promise of future improvement. "I took the proclamation for a little more than it purported," Frederick Douglass recalled in his autobiography, "and saw in its spirit a life and power far beyond its letter." Lincoln was by modern standards a racist, but

▲ Lithograph of the New York draft riots. Although the main targets of the rioters were blacks, the homes and businesses of prominent Republicans were also attacked. Brooks Brothers was burned. Horace Greeley's newspaper was besieged, as was the *Times*. (Winston Churchill's grandfather manned a Gatling gun on the second floor of the *Times* to drive away the rioters.)

his most militant black contemporaries respected him deeply. The *Anglo-African,* an uncompromising black newspaper (the position of which is revealed in an 1862 editorial that asked: "Poor, chicken-hearted, semi-barbarous Caucasians, when will you learn that 'the earth was made for MAN?'"), referred in 1864 to Lincoln's "many noble acts" and urged his reelection. Douglass said of him: "Lincoln was not . . . either our man or our model. In his interests, in his association, in his habits of thought and in his prejudices, he was a white man." Nevertheless, Douglass described Lincoln as "one whom I could love, honor, and trust without reserve or doubt."

As for the slaves of the South, after January 1, 1863, whenever the "Army of Freedom" approached, they laid down their plows and hoes and flocked to the Union lines in droves. "We-all knows about it," one black confided to a northern clergyman early in 1863. "Only we darsen't let on. We *pretends* not to know." Such behavior came as a shock to the owners. "[The slaves] who loved us best—as we thought—were the first to leave us," one planter mourned. Talk of slave "ingratitude" increased. Instead of referring to their workers as "servants" or "my black family," many owners began to describe them as "slaves" or "niggers."

AFRICAN AMERICAN SOLDIERS

A revolutionary shift occurred in white thinking about using black men as soldiers. Although they had fought in the Revolution and in the Battle of

▶ *text continues on page 408*

▲ The storming of Fort Wagner by the 54th Massachusetts on July 18, 1863. Composed of black volunteers but led by Robert Gould Shaw, a white abolitionist, the 54th Massachusetts breached the ramparts but was eventually thrown back, sustaining heavy losses. Although the focal point of this contemporary painting is the death of Shaw, the broader significance of the battle is shown in the foreground, where two black soldiers are bayoneting their Confederate foes. (See also Re-Viewing the Past: "*Glory,*" pp. 406–407.)

Re-Viewing the Past

Glory

Glory (1989) tells the story of the 54th Massachusetts Volunteer Infantry, a black regiment, from its establishment in the fall of 1862 through its attack on Fort Wagner, South Carolina, on July 18, 1863.

"Historical accuracy," director Edward Zwick declared, was "the goal of everyone involved in the production." Filmmakers of historical subjects commonly make such assertions, but Zwick proved that he had attended to the historical record. For example, he had the peak of Shaw's cap dyed the exact shade of medium green used by officers of the Massachusetts 54th; and when shoes were distributed to the recruits, there were no "lefts" or "rights": shoes were to shape themselves to either foot from wear. Few viewers could be expected to take note of such historical details, but Zwick included them nevertheless.

Zwick's evident commitment to history makes his deviations all the more interesting. Consider the opening scenes. The movie begins with a panoramic shot of rolling hills, dotted with tents. Fog blankets the valley and softens the morning light. The camera moves closer, focusing on Union soldiers around a campfire. Then the quiet is shattered: soldiers hasten to form ranks, trot toward a battlefield, and charge across it, a young officer in the van. (He is Captain Robert Gould Shaw, played by Matthew Broderick). The attackers are decimated. When Shaw turns to rally his troops, he sees that they are fleeing in terror. Then he is hit and loses consciousness.

Shaw is sent home to Boston to convalesce. At a reception, Governor Andrew offers the young officer command of the Massachusetts 54th, a black regiment being raised in Boston. Shaw hesitates for a moment. Then he confers privately with another officer, who is appalled.

"I knew how much you'd like to be a colonel, but a colored regiment?"

"I'm gonna do it," Shaw replies.

"You're not serious."

"Yeah."

These scenes contain truths without being entirely truthful. In fact, Governor Andrew did offer the commission and Shaw accepted it. But at the time Shaw was in Virginia. Andrew, in Boston, conveyed it through Shaw's father and young Shaw initially refused. Zwick has compressed the story chronologically, squeezing weeks into minutes; and he has rearranged it geographically to enable Andrew and young Shaw to meet. Such modifications are common in "reel history," and these do not impair historical understanding.

But *Glory* deviates from the historical record in more significant ways. It suggests, for example, that the Massachusetts 54th was composed mostly of former slaves whose hatred of slavery was based on personal experience. In truth, the Massachusetts 54th was recruited from blacks in northern states, most had been born free.

▼ Matthew Broderick, as Robert Gould Shaw, and Denzel Washington, as former slave recruit Trip, in the movie, *Glory*.

▲ Photographs of Robert Gould Shaw, Commander of the Massachusetts 54th, and private Charles Arnum, a free black volunteer from Springfield, Massachusetts.

The fiction that they had been slaves, however, made it possible for Zwick to examine a larger truth. Of the 178,000 blacks who served in the Union army, fewer than one-fifth were from the North; the great majority *were* former slaves. Nearly 100,000 were recruited from Louisiana, Mississippi, or Tennessee, among the first states occupied by the Union army. *Glory* thus merges the story of the free blacks of the Massachusetts 54th with that of former slaves who were recruited from the Deep South.

Zwick exploited the dramatic potential of the latter groups. How did slaves respond when, having just received their freedom, they were placed under the absolute power of white officers?

Glory develops the question chiefly through the character of Trip (Denzel Washington), a former slave who hates all whites, including Shaw. Shaw illuminates the other side of the question. An inveterate abolitionist, he reluctantly decides that former slaves must be whipped (literally) into shape. When Trip sneaks off one night and is captured for desertion, Shaw orders him flogged. When Trip's back is bared, Shaw sees that it is laced with scars from whippings by slave masters. During the flogging, Trip fixes Shaw with a hateful stare, a powerful scene that underscores the movie's central irony: To end slavery, Shaw has superseded the plantation master while Trip has again become a slave.

Whatever its dramatic merits, the scene is unhistorical. In 1861 Congress had outlawed flogging in the military. Disobedient soldiers were tied in a crouched position, or they were suspended by their thumbs, toes just touching the ground.

Physical punishment was, in fact, one of the chief sources of contention between ex-slave soldiers and white officers. "I am no slave to be driven," one black recruit informed a brutish commander. When an officer of the 38th Colored Infantry tied a black recruit up by the thumbs, his friends cut him down and forced the officers back with bayonets: "No white son of a bitch can tie a man up here," they declared. The blacks were charged with mutiny and several were executed, an incident that shows that former slaves did not willingly submit to army discipline tainted with racism. Though African Americans con-stituted only 8 percent of the Union army, 80 percent of those executed for mutiny were black. Many white officers, as the movie suggests, did assert that former slaves must be treated like slaves. "I no longer wonder why slave drivers were cruel. I am," one white officer confided in a letter to his brother.

Could such soldiers—black recruits and white officers alike—have been good ones? The movie answers the question by recreating the actual attack on Fort Wagner, the first step in the offensive on Charleston. It shows the blacks of the Massachusetts 54th marching to the front of the line, and forming up along a narrow beach. On Shaw's command, they charge forward. Unlike the white troops in the opening scene, the blacks follow him to the ramparts; when he falls, they continue onward until they are wiped out.

Were the soldiers of the Massachusetts 54th as coura-geous as those in the movie? Shortly after the battle, Lieu-tenant Iredell Jones, a Confederate officer, reported: "The negroes fought gallantly, and were headed by as brave a colonel as ever lived." Of the 600 members of the 54th Mass-achusetts, 40 percent were casualties on that day, an extraor-dinarily high ratio. Did ex-slaves fight as courageously as the free blacks of the 54th? The answer to this question came not at Fort Wagner, but at other, less publicized battles. A few weeks earlier, for example, several companies of the Louisiana (Colored) Infantry, composed of former slaves who had been in the army only for several weeks, fought off a furi-ous Confederate assault at Milliken's Bend near Vicksburg. The Confederate general was astonished when whites in the Union army fled but the blacks held their ground despite sus-taining staggering casualties—45 percent—the highest of any single battle in the war.

Thus while *Glory* is a fictional composite—of free black and ex-slave recruits, and of the assault on Fort Wagner and Mil-liken's Bend—it conveys a broader truth about black soldiers. Howell Cobb, a Confederate senator from Georgia, declared: "If the black can make a good soldier, our whole system of government is wrong." *Glory* shows that although white offi-cers and black recruits did not form a harmonious team, they together proved that slavery was doomed.

New Orleans during the War of 1812, a law of 1792 barred blacks from the army. During the early stages of the rebellion, despite the eagerness of thousands of free blacks to enlist, the prohibition remained in force. By 1862, however, the need for manpower was creating pressure for change. In August Secretary of War Edwin M. Stanton authorized the military government of the captured South Carolina sea islands to enlist slaves in the area. After the Emancipation Proclamation specifically authorized the enlistment of blacks, the governor of Massachusetts moved to organize a black regiment, the famous Massachusetts 54th. (See Re-Viewing the Past, *"Glory,"* pp. 406–407.) Swiftly thereafter, other states began to recruit black soldiers, and in May 1863 the federal government established a Bureau of Colored Troops to supervise their enlistment. By the end of the war one soldier in eight in the Union army was black.

DOCUMENT

Letter from a Free Black Volunteer to the *Christian Recorder* (1864)

Enlisting so many black soldiers changed the war from a struggle to save the Union to a kind of revolution. "Let the black man . . . get an eagle on his button and a musket on his shoulder," wrote Frederick Douglass, "and there is no power on earth which can deny that he has won the right to citizenship."

At first black soldiers received only $7 a month, about half what white soldiers were paid. But they soon proved themselves in battle; of the 178,000 who served in the Union army, 37,000 were killed, a rate of loss about 40 percent higher than that among white troops The Congressional Medal of Honor was awarded to 21 blacks.

The higher death rates among black soldiers were partly due to the fury of Confederate soldiers. Many black captives were killed on the spot. After overrunning the garrison of Fort Pillow on the Mississippi River, the Confederates massacred several dozen black soldiers, along with their white commander. Lincoln was tempted to order reprisals, but he and his advisers realized that to do so would have been both morally wrong (two wrongs never make a right) and likely to lead to still more atrocities. "Blood can not restore blood," Lincoln said in his usual direct way.

ANTIETAM TO GETTYSBURG

It was well that Lincoln seized on Antietam to release his proclamation; had he waited for a more impressive victory, he would have waited nearly a year. To

replace McClellan, he chose General Ambrose E. Burnside, best known to history for his magnificent side-whiskers (originally called burnsides, later, at first jokingly, sideburns). Burnside was a good corps commander, but he lacked the self-confidence essential to anyone who takes responsibility for major decisions. He knew his limitations and tried to avoid high command, but patriotism and his sense of duty compelled him, when pressed, to accept leadership of the Army of the Potomac. He prepared to march on Richmond.

The Civil War Part I: 1861–1862

Unlike McClellan, Burnside was aggressive— too aggressive. He planned to ford the Rappahannock River at Fredericksburg. Supply problems and bad weather delayed him until mid-December, giving Lee time to concentrate his army in impregnable positions behind the town. Although he had more than 120,000 men against Lee's 75,000, Burnside should have called off the attack when he saw Lee's advantage; instead he ordered the troops forward. Crossing the river over pontoon bridges, his divisions occupied Fredericksburg. Then, in wave after wave, they charged the Confederate defense line while Lee's artillery riddled them from nearby Marye's Heights. Watching the battle from his command post on the heights, General Lee was deeply moved. Turning to General James Longstreet, he said: "It is well that war is so terrible—we should grow too fond of it!"

On December 14, the day following this futile assault, General Burnside, tears streaming down his cheeks, ordered the evacuation of Fredericksburg. Shortly thereafter General Joseph Hooker replaced him.

Unlike Burnside, "Fighting Joe" Hooker was ill-tempered, vindictive, and devious. In naming him to command the Army of the Potomac, Lincoln sent him a letter that was a measure of his desperation but is now famous for what it reveals of the president's character:

> I think that during Gen. Burnside's command of the Army, you have taken counsel of your ambition, and thwarted him as much as you could, in which you did a great wrong to the country. . . . I have heard, in such a way as to believe it, of you, recently saying that both the Army and the Government need a Dictator. Of course it is not *for* this, but in spite of it, that I have given you the command. Only those generals who gain successes, can set up dictators. What I now ask of you is military success, and I will risk the dictatorship. . . . Beware of rashness, but with energy and sleepless vigilance, go forward, and give us victories.

▲ Gettysburg Campaign, 1863
Gettysburg, in July of 1863, marked the turning point of the war; after it the South never again tried to invade the North.

Hooker proved no better than his predecessor, but his failings were more like McClellan's than Burnside's. By the spring of 1863 he had 125,000 men ready for action. Late in April he forded the Rappahannock and quickly concentrated at Chancellorsville, about 10 miles west of Fredericksburg. His army outnumbered the Confederates by more than two to one; he should have forced a battle at once. Instead he delayed, and while he did, Lee sent Stonewall Jackson's corps of 28,000 men across tangled countryside to a position directly athwart Hooker's unsuspecting flank. At 6 P.M. on May 2, Jackson attacked.

Completely surprised, the Union right crumbled, brigade after brigade overrun before it could wheel to meet Jackson's charge. At the first sound of firing, Lee had struck along the entire front to impede Union troop movements. If the battle had begun earlier in the day, the Confederates might have won a decisive victory; as it happened, nightfall brought a lull, and the next day the Union troops rallied and held their ground. Heavy fighting continued until May 5, when Hooker

abandoned the field and retreated in good order behind the Rappahannock.

Chancellorsville cost the Confederates dearly, for their losses, in excess of 12,000, were almost as heavy as the North's and harder to replace. They also lost Stonewall Jackson, struck down by the bullets of his own men while returning from a reconnaissance. Nevertheless, the Union army had suffered another fearful blow to its morale.

Lee knew that time was still on the side of the North; to defend Richmond was not enough. Already federal troops in the West were closing in on Vicksburg, threatening to cut Confederate communications with Arkansas and Texas. Now was the time to strike, while the morale of the North was at low ebb. With 75,000 soldiers he crossed the Potomac again, a larger Union force dogging his right flank. By late June his army had fanned out across southern Pennsylvania in a 50-mile arc from Chambersburg to the Susquehanna. Gray-clad soldiers ranged 50 miles *northwest* of Baltimore, within 10 miles of Harrisburg, Pennsylvania.

As Union soldiers had been doing in Virginia, Lee's men destroyed property and commandeered food, horses, and clothing wherever they could find them. They even seized a number of blacks and sent them south to be sold as slaves. On July 1 a Confederate division looking for shoes in the town of Gettysburg clashed with two brigades of Union cavalry northwest of the town. Both sides sent out calls for reinforcements. Like iron filings drawn to a magnet, the two armies converged. The Confederates won control of the town, but the Union army, now commanded by General George G. Meade, took a strong position on Cemetery Ridge, a hook-shaped stretch of high ground just to the south. Lee's men occupied Seminary Ridge, a parallel position.

On this field the fate of the Union was probably decided. For two days the Confederates attacked Cemetery Ridge, pounding it with the heaviest artillery barrage ever seen in America and sweeping bravely up its flanks in repeated assaults. During General George E. Pickett's famous charge, a handful of his men actually reached the Union lines, but reserves drove them back. By nightfall on July 3 the Confederate army was spent, the Union lines unbroken.

The following day was the Fourth of July. The two weary forces rested on their arms. Had the Union army attacked in force, the Confederates might have been crushed, but just as McClellan had hesitated after Antietam, Meade let opportunity pass. On July 5 Lee retreated to safety. For the first time he had been clearly bested on the field of battle.

LINCOLN FINDS HIS GENERAL: GRANT AT VICKSBURG

On Independence Day, a day after Gettysburg, federal troops won another great victory far to the west. When General Halleck was called east in July 1862, Ulysses S. Grant resumed command of the Union troops. Grant was one of the most controversial officers in the army. At West Point he had compiled an indifferent record, ranking twenty-first in a class of 39. During the Mexican War he served well, but when he was later assigned to a lonely post in the West, he took to drink and was forced to resign his commission. Thereafter he was by turns a farmer, a real estate agent, and a clerk in a leather goods store. In 1861, approaching age 40, he seemed well into a life of frustration and mediocrity.

The war gave him a second chance. Back in service, however, his reputation as a ne'er-do-well and his unmilitary bearing worked against him, as did the heavy casualties suffered by his troops at Shiloh. Yet the fact that he knew how to manage a large army and win battles did not escape Lincoln. According to

tradition, when a gossip tried to poison the president against Grant by referring to his drinking, Lincoln retorted that if he knew what brand Grant favored, he would send a barrel of it to some of his other generals.[2] Grant never used alcohol as a substitute for courage. "Old Ulysses," one of his soldiers said, "he don't scare worth a damn."

Grant's major aim was to capture Vicksburg, a city of tremendous strategic importance. Together with Port Hudson, a bastion north of Baton Rouge, Louisiana, it guarded a 150-mile stretch of the Mississippi. The river between these points was inaccessible to federal gunboats. So long as Vicksburg remained in southern hands, the trans-Mississippi region could send men and supplies to the rest of the Confederacy.

Vicksburg sits on a bluff overlooking a sharp bend in the river. When it proved unapproachable from either the west or the north, Grant devised an audacious scheme for getting at it from the east. He

---

[2]Lincoln denied having said this, pointing out that it was a version of a remark about General James Wolfe attributed to King George II. When a critic remarked that Wolfe was a madman, the King is said to have replied: "I wish he would bite some of the others."

▲ Grant's bold initiative to seize Vicksburg depended on ferrying his army swiftly across the Mississippi. These Union steamboats brought reinforcements that saved Grant's army. The boats were converted into floating hospitals.

▲ Vicksburg Campaign, 1863
When Vicksburg fell to the Union troops on July 4, 1863, the Mississippi was reopened to the free passage of federal forces.

descended the Mississippi from Memphis to a point a few miles north of the city. Then, leaving part of his force behind to create the impression that he planned to attack from the north, he crossed the west bank and slipped quickly southward. Recrossing the river below Vicksburg, he abandoned his communications and supply lines and struck at Jackson, the capital of Mississippi. In a series of swift engagements his troops captured Jackson, cutting off the army of General John C. Pemberton, defending Vicksburg, from other Confederate units. Turning next on Pemberton, Grant defeated him in two decisive battles, Champion's Hill and Big Black River, and drove him inside the Vicksburg fortifications. By mid-May the city was under siege. Grant applied relentless pressure, and on July 4 Pemberton surrendered. With Vicksburg in Union hands, federal gunboats could range the entire length of the Mississippi.[3] Texas and Arkansas were for all practical purposes lost to the Confederacy.

Lincoln had disliked Grant's plan for capturing Vicksburg. Now he generously confessed his error and placed Grant in command of all federal troops west of the Appalachians. Grant promptly took charge of the fighting around Chattanooga, Tennessee, where Confederate advances, beginning with the Battle of Chickamauga (September 19–20), were

---

[3]Port Hudson, isolated by Vicksburg's fall, surrendered on July 9.

threatening to develop into a major disaster for the North. Shifting corps commanders and bringing up fresh units, he won another decisive victory at Chattanooga in a series of battles ending on November 25, 1863. This cleared the way for an invasion of Georgia. Suddenly this unkempt, stubby little man, who looked more like a tramp than a general, emerged as the military leader the North had been so desperately seeking. In March 1864 Lincoln summoned him to Washington, named him lieutenant general, and gave him supreme command of the armies of the United States.

ECONOMIC AND SOCIAL EFFECTS, NORTH AND SOUTH

Although much blood would yet be spilled, by the end of 1863 the Confederacy was on the road to defeat. Northern military pressure, gradually increasing, was eroding the South's most precious resource: manpower. An ever-tightening naval blockade was reducing its economic strength. Shortages developed that, combined with the flood of currency pouring from the presses, led to drastic inflation. By 1864 an officer's coat cost $2000 in Confederate money, cigars sold for $10 each, butter was $25 a pound, and flour went for $275 a barrel. Wages rose too, but not nearly as rapidly.

The southern railroad network was gradually wearing out, the major lines maintaining operations only by cannibalizing less vital roads. Imported products such as coffee disappeared; even salt became scarce. Efforts to increase manufacturing were only moderately successful because of the shortage of labor, capital, and technical knowledge. In general, southern prejudice against centralized authority prevented the Confederacy from making effective use of its scarce resources. Even blockade running was left in private hands until 1864. Precious cargo space that should have been reserved for medical supplies and arms was often devoted to high-priced luxuries.

In the North, after a brief depression in 1861 caused by the uncertainties of the situation and the loss of southern business, the economy flourished. Government purchases greatly stimulated certain lines of manufacturing, the railroads operated at close to capacity and with increasing efficiency, the farm machinery business boomed because so many farmers left their fields to serve in the army, and bad harvests in Europe boosted agricultural prices.

Congress passed a number of economic measures long desired but held up in the past by southern opposition. The Homestead Act (1862) gave 160 acres to any settler who would farm the land for five years. The Morrill Land Grant Act of the same year provided the states with land at the rate of 30,000 acres for each member of Congress to support state agricultural colleges. Various tariff acts raised the duties on manufactured goods to an average rate of 47 percent in order to protect domestic manufacturers from foreign competition. The Pacific Railway Act (1862) authorized subsidies in land and money for the construction of a transcontinental railroad. And the National Banking Act of 1863 gave the country, at last, a uniform currency.

All these laws stimulated the economy. Whether the overall economic effect of the Civil War on the Union was beneficial is less clear. Since it was fought mostly with rifles, light cannon, horses, and wagons, it had much less effect on heavy industry than later wars would have. Although the economy grew, it did so more slowly during the 1860s than in the decades preceding and following. Prices soared beginning in 1862, averaging about 80 percent over the 1860 level by the end of the war. As in the South, wages did not keep pace. This did not make for a healthy economy; nor did the fact that there were chronic shortages of labor in many fields, shortages aggravated by·a sharp drop in the number of immigrants.

As the war dragged on and the continuing inflation eroded purchasing power, resentment on the part of workers deepened. During the 1850s iron molders, cigar makers, and some other skilled workers had formed national unions. This trend continued through the war years. There were many strikes. Inflation and shortages encouraged speculation and fostered a selfish, materialistic attitude toward life. Many contractors took advantage of wartime confusion to sell the government shoddy goods. By 1864 cotton was worth $1.90 a pound in New England. It could be had for 20 cents a pound in the South. Although it was illegal to traffic in the staple across the lines, unscrupulous operators did so and made huge profits.

Yet the war undoubtedly hastened industrialization and laid the basis for many other aspects of modern civilization. It posed problems of organization and planning, both military and civilian, that challenged the talents of creative persons and thus led to a more complex and efficient economy. The mechanization of production, the growth of large corporations, the creation of a better banking system, and the emergence of business leaders attuned to these conditions would surely have occurred in any case, for industrialization was under way long before the South seceded. Nevertheless, the war greatly speeded all these changes.

Civilian participation in the war effort was far greater than in earlier conflicts. Some churches split over the question of emancipation, but North and South, church leaders took the lead in recruitment drives and in charitable activities aimed at supporting the armed forces. In the North a Christian Commission raised the money and coordinated the personnel needed to provide Union soldiers with half a million Bibles, several million religious tracts, and other books, along with fruit, coffee, and spare clothing.

WOMEN IN WARTIME

Many southern women took over the management of farms and small plantations when their menfolk went off to war. Others became volunteer nurses, and after an initial period of resistance, the Confederate

▲ Women workers filling cartridges at the U.S. arsenal at Watertown, Massachusetts (1861) from an engraving after Winslow Homer.

▲ Women in the South playing croquet during the war, preserving the amenities of plantation life. By 1864 southern leaders were complaining that many southern women had lost their zeal for the Cause. Poor women engaged in bread riots; and well-to-do women held "incessant parties and balls." Through such actions, women registered their discontent with the war—and with the paternalist ethos of southern chivalry, which had manifestly failed to protect and defend southern womanhood.

army began to enlist women in the medical corps. At least two female nurses, Captain Sally Tompkins and Kate Cumming, left records of their experiences that throw much light on how the wounded were treated during the war. Other southern women worked as clerks in newly organized government departments.

Southern "ladyhood" more generally was yet another casualty of the war. The absence or death of husbands or other male relations changed attitudes toward gender roles. When her husband obeyed a military order to abandon Atlanta to the advancing Union armies, Julia Davidson, about to give birth, denounced the "men of Atlanta" for having "run and left Atlanta" and their homes. Such women learned to fend for themselves. "Necessity," Davidson later wrote her husband, would "make a different woman of me."

Large numbers of women also contributed to the northern war effort. As in the South, farm women went out into fields to plant and harvest crops, aided in many instances by new farm machinery. Many others took jobs in textile factories; in establishments making shoes, uniforms, and other supplies for the army; and in government agencies. But as was usually the case, the low wages traditionally paid women acted as a brake on wage increases for their male colleagues.

Besides working in factories and shops and on farms, northern women, again like their southern counterparts, aided the war effort more directly. Elizabeth Blackwell, the first American woman doctor of medicine, had already founded the New York Infirmary for Women and Children. After war broke out she helped set up what became the United States Sanitary Commission, an organization of women similar to the Christian Commission dedicated to improving sanitary conditions at army camps, supplying hospitals with volunteer nurses, and raising money for medical supplies. Many thousands of women volunteers took part in Sanitary Commission and related programs.

DOCUMENT

Barton, Memoirs about Medical Life at the Battlefield

An additional 3000-odd women served as regular army nurses during the conflict. At the start the high command of both armies resisted the efforts of women to help, but necessity and a grudging recognition of the competence of these women gradually brought the generals around. Clara Barton, a school teacher and government clerk, was among the first women to dress wounds at forward stations on the battlefield. After she ran out of bandages at Antietam, she dressed wounds with green corn leaves. The chief surgeon declared her to be "the angel of the battlefield." The "proper sphere" of American woman was expanding, another illustration of the modernizing effect of the war.

GRANT IN THE WILDERNESS

Grant's strategy as supreme commander was simple, logical, and ruthless. He would attack Lee and try to capture Richmond, Virginia. General William

Tecumseh Sherman would drive from Chattanooga toward Atlanta, Georgia. Like a lobster's claw, the two armies could then close to crush all resistance. Early in May 1864 Grant and Sherman commenced operations, each with more than 100,000 men.

Grant marched the Army of the Potomac directly into the tangled wilderness area south of the Rappahannock, where Hooker had been routed a year earlier. Lee, having only 60,000 men, forced the battle in the roughest possible country, where Grant found it difficult to make efficient use of his larger force. For two days (May 5–6) the Battle of the Wilderness raged. When it was over, the North had sustained another 18,000 casualties, far more than the Confederates. But unlike his predecessors, Grant did not fall back after being checked, nor did he expose his army to the kind of devastating counterattack at which Lee was so expert. Instead he shifted his troops to the southeast, attempting to outflank the Confederates. Divining his intent, Lee rushed his divisions southeastward and disposed them behind hastily erected earthworks in well-placed positions around Spotsylvania Court House. Grant attacked. After five more days, at a cost to the Union army of another 12,000 men, the Confederate lines were still intact.

Grant had grasped the fundamental truth that the war could be won only by grinding the South

▲ An 8.5-ton siege gun, mounted on a railroad flatcar, that hurled 200-pound bombs onto Confederate positions at Petersburg. Trench warfare ensued, a chilling harbinger of World War I in early twentieth-century Europe.

down beneath the weight of numbers. His own losses of men and equipment could be replaced; Lee's could not. When critics complained of the cost, he replied doggedly that he intended to fight on in the same manner if it took all summer. Once more he pressed southeastward in an effort to outflank the enemy. At Cold Harbor, 9 miles from Richmond, he found the Confederates once more in strong defenses. He attacked. It was a battle as foolish and nearly as one-sided as General Pakenham's assault on Jackson's line outside New Orleans in 1815. "At Cold Harbor," the forthright Grant confessed in his memoirs, "no advantage whatever was gained to compensate for the heavy losses we sustained."

Sixty thousand casualties in less than a month! The news sent a wave of dismay through the North. There were demands that "Butcher" Grant be removed from command. Lincoln, however, stood firm. Although the price was fearfully high, Grant was gaining his objective. At Cold Harbor, Lee had to fight without a single regiment in general reserve while Grant's army was larger than at the start of the offensive. When Grant next swung around his flank, striking south of the James River toward Petersburg, Lee had to rush his troops to that city to hold him.

As the Confederates dug in, Grant put Petersburg under siege. Soon both armies had constructed complicated lines of breastworks and trenches, running for miles in a great arc south of Petersburg, much like the fortifications that would be used in France in World War I. Methodically the Union forces extended their lines, seeking to weaken the Confederates and cut the rail connections supplying Lee's troops and the city of Richmond. Grant could not overwhelm him, but by late June, Lee was pinned to earth. Moving again would mean having to abandon Richmond—tantamount, in southern eyes, to surrender.

SHERMAN IN GEORGIA

The summer of 1864 saw the North submerged in pessimism. The Army of the Potomac held Lee at bay but appeared powerless to defeat him. In Georgia, General Sherman inched forward methodically against the wily Joseph E. Johnston, but when he tried a direct assault at Kennesaw Mountain on June 27, he was thrown back with heavy casualties. In July Confederate raiders under General Jubal Early dashed suddenly across the Potomac from the

▲ Although Sherman's 100,000 Union soldiers marched to Atlanta, his men were supplied by sixteen railway trains from Chattanooga, Tennessee, each day. After taking Atlanta late in the summer of 1864, Sherman pulled up the railway line and burned the depots. On his march to the sea, he destroyed several hundred miles of railroads.

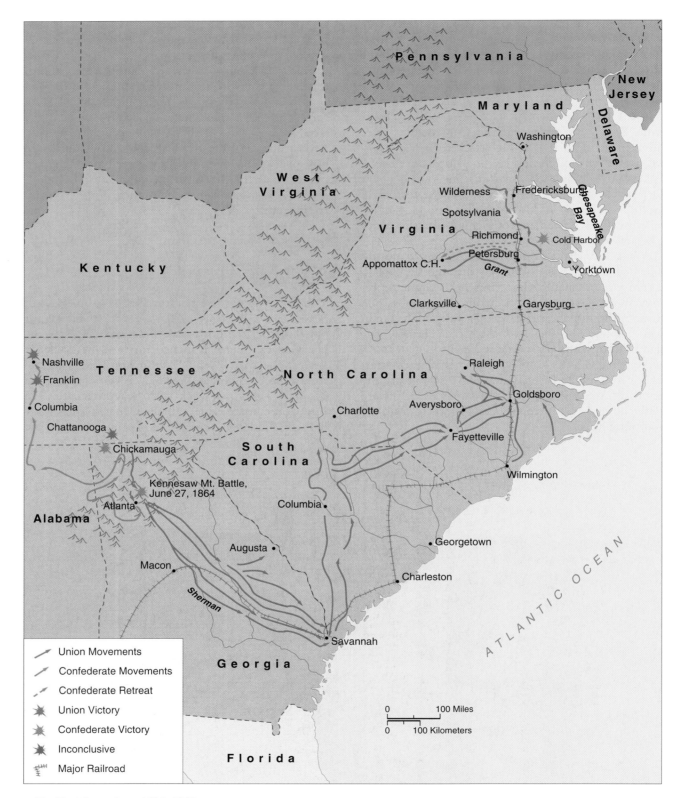

▲ **The Final Campaigns, 1864–1865**
Grant's repeated and costly (60,000 casualties the first month) attempts to outflank Lee are detailed
here. At Five Forks the long siege of Petersburg was broken; Richmond was evacuated. A week later,
Lee surrendered. Sherman's campaign in Georgia and the Carolinas is also depicted.

Shenandoah Valley to within five miles of Washington before being turned back. A draft call for 500,000 additional men did not improve the public temper. Huge losses and the absence of a decisive victory were taxing the northern will to continue the fight.

In June, Lincoln had been renominated on a National Union ticket, with the Tennessee Unionist Andrew Johnson, a former Democrat, as his running mate. He was under attack not only from the Democrats, who nominated General McClellan and came out for a policy that might almost be characterized as peace at any price, but also from the Radical Republicans, many of whom had wished to dump him in favor of Secretary of the Treasury Chase.

Then, almost overnight, the whole atmosphere changed. On September 2, General Sherman's army fought its way into Atlanta. When the Confederates countered with an offensive northward toward Tennessee,[4] Sherman did not follow. Instead he abandoned his communications with Chattanooga and marched unopposed through Georgia, "from Atlanta to the sea."

Sherman was in some ways quite like Grant. He was a West Pointer who resigned his commission only to fare poorly in civilian occupations. Back in the army in 1861, he suffered a brief nervous breakdown. After recovering he fought well under Grant at Shiloh and the two became close friends. "He stood by me when I was crazy," Sherman later recalled, "and I stood by him when he was drunk." Far more completely than most military men of his generation, Sherman believed in total war—in appropriating or destroying everything that might help the enemy continue the fight.

DOCUMENT

Sherman, "The March Through Georgia"

The march through Georgia had many objectives besides conquering territory. One obvious one was economic, the destruction of southern resources. "[We] must make old and young, rich and poor feel the hard hand of war," Sherman said. Before taking Atlanta he wrote his wife: "We have devoured the land. . . . All the people retire before us and desolation is behind. To realize what war is one should follow our tracks."

Another object of Sherman's march was psychological. "If the North can march an army right through the South," he told General Grant, Southerners will take it "as proof positive that the North

can prevail." This was certainly true of Georgia's blacks, who flocked to the invaders by the thousands, women and children as well as men, all cheering mightily when the soldiers put their former masters' homes to the torch. "They pray and shout and mix up my name with Moses," Sherman explained.

Sherman's victories staggered the Confederacy and the anti-Lincoln forces in the North. In November the president was easily reelected, 212 electoral votes to 21. The country was determined to carry on the struggle.

At last the South's will to resist began to crack. Sherman entered Savannah on December 22, having denuded a strip of Georgia 60 miles wide. Early in January 1865 he marched northward, leaving behind "a broad black streak of ruin and desolation— the fences all gone; lonesome smoke-stacks, surrounded by dark heaps of ashes and cinders, marking the spots where human habitations had stood." In February his troops captured Columbia, South Carolina. Soon they were in North Carolina, advancing relentlessly. In Virginia, Grant's vise grew tighter day by day while the Confederate lines became thinner and more ragged.

To Appomattox Court House

On March 4 Lincoln took the presidential oath and delivered his second inaugural address. Photographs taken at about this time show how four years of war had marked him. Somehow he had become both gentle and steel-tough, both haggard and inwardly calm. With victory sure, he spoke for tolerance, mercy, and reconstruction. "Let us judge not," he said after stating again his personal dislike of slavery, "that we be not judged." He urged all Americans to turn without malice to the task of mending the damage and to make a just and lasting peace between the sections.

Now the Confederate troops around Petersburg could no longer withstand the federal pressure. Desperately Lee tried to pull his forces back to the Richmond and Danville Railroad at Lynchburg, but the swift wings of Grant's army enveloped them. Richmond fell on April 3. With fewer than 30,000 men to oppose Grant's 115,000, Lee recognized the futility of further resistance. On April 9 he and Grant met by prearrangement at Appomattox Court House.

MAP

The Civil War Part II: 1863-1865

It was a scene at once pathetic and inspiring. Lee was noble in defeat; Grant, despite his rough-

---

[4]This force was crushed before Nashville in December by a Union army under General George Thomas.

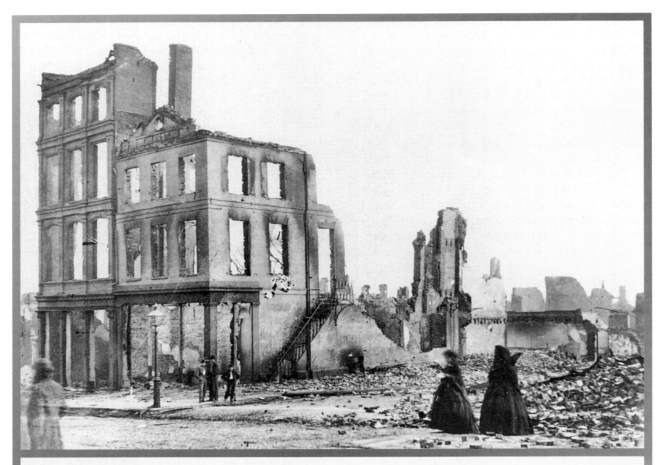

DEBATING THE PAST

Why did the South lose the Civil War? The answer to this question had long been answered with numbers: The South had too few people and factories. But many have rebutted this point by noting that the South nearly *did* win. Moreover, while southern commanders were plagued with shortages, they lost no battles because they ran out of bullets or shells. In a study of industrial output, Emory Thomas (1979) concluded that southern leadership "outdid its northern counterpart in mobilizing for total war." The South's chief deficiency was, surprisingly, in food production. Frank L. Owsley (1925) blamed the South's defeat on "state's rights jealousy and particularism." Confederate states failed to coordinate financing and production and thus made the South's defeat "inevitable." Jeffrey Hummel (1996), however, has advanced the opposite argument: Jefferson Davis's centralization of power strangled the South with bureaucratic inefficiency and deprived it of ideological coherence. Folklore holds that the genius of southern generals, especially Robert E. Lee, overcame all southern deficiencies. But in *Attack and Die* (1982), a book whose thesis is contained in its title, Grady McWhiney and Perry D. Jamieson insisted that Lee's audacity, and that of other southern generals, was ill-suited to the military technology of the day. Rifles were particularly effective at cutting down attacking armies. Detailed statistical analysis, however, has challenged this thesis: the North and South initiated attacks with nearly equal frequency and losses. Edward Channing (1925) proposed that the South was defeated because by 1865 Confederates "lost the will to fight." This is rather like saying that the South stopped fighting because it decided to stop fighting—an instance of circular reasoning. But many historians have found the argument, restated more subtly, to be persuasive. Herman Hattaway and Archer Jones (1986) proposed that while the Confederacy could field and equip an effective army for most of the war, "an insufficient nationalism" failed to "survive the strains imposed by lengthy hostilities." The scene above is of Richmond in April, 1865.

Emory Thomas, *The Confederate Nation* (1979), Frank L. Owsley, *State Rights in the Confederacy* (1925), Grady McWhiney and Perry D. Jamieson, *Attack and Die* (1982), Edward Channing, *History of the United States* (1925), Herman Hattaway and Archer Jones, *How the North Won* (1983), Jeffrey Hummel, *Emancipating Slaves, Enslaving Free Men* (1996).

hewn exterior, sensitive and magnanimous in victory. "I met you once before, General Lee, while we were serving in Mexico," Grant said after they had shaken hands. "I have always remembered your appearance, and I think I should have recognized you anywhere." They talked briefly of that earlier war, and then, acting on Lincoln's instructions, Grant outlined his terms. All that would be required was that the Confederate soldiers lay down their arms. They could return to their homes in peace. When Lee hinted (he was too proud to ask outright for the concession) that his men would profit greatly if allowed to retain possession of their horses, Grant agreed to let them do so.

▲ Casualties of the Civil War
The Union death rate was 23 percent, the Confederate 24 percent. In general, twice as many soldiers were killed by disease as were killed by bullets.

WINNERS, LOSERS, AND THE FUTURE

And so the war ended. It had cost the nation more than 600,000 lives, nearly as many as in all other American wars combined. The story of one of the lost thousands must stand for all, Union and Confederate. Jones Budbury, a tall, 19-year-old red-head, was working in a Pennsylvania textile mill when the war broke out, and he enlisted at once. His regiment first saw action at Bull Run. He took part in McClellan's Peninsula campaign. He fought at Second Bull Run, at Chancellorsville, and at Gettysburg. A few months after Gettysburg he was wounded in the foot and spent some time in an army hospital. By the spring of 1864 he had risen through the ranks to first sergeant and his hair had turned gray. In June he was captured and sent to Andersonville military prison, near Macon, Georgia, but he fell ill and the Confederates released him. In March 1865 he was back with his regiment in the lines besieging Richmond. On April 6, three days before Lee's surrender, Jones Budbury was killed while pursuing Confederate units near Sailor's Creek, Virginia.

The war also caused enormous property losses, especially in the Confederacy. All the human and material destruction explains the eroding hatred and bitterness that the war implanted in millions of hearts. The corruption, the gross materialism, and the selfishness generated by wartime conditions were other disagreeable by-products of the conflict. Such sores fester in any society, but the Civil War bred conditions that inflamed and multiplied them. The war produced many examples of charity, self-sacrifice, and devotion to duty as well, yet if the general moral atmosphere of the postwar generation can be said to have resulted from the experiences of 1861 to 1865, the effect overall was bad.

What had been obtained at this price? Slavery was dead. Paradoxically, while the war had been fought to preserve the Union, after 1865 the people tended to see the United States not as a union of states but as a nation. After Appomattox, secession was almost literally inconceivable. In a strictly political sense, as Lincoln had predicted from the start, the northern victory heartened friends of republican government and democracy throughout the world. A better-integrated society and a more technically advanced and productive economic system also resulted from the war.

The Americans of 1865 estimated the balance between cost and profit according to their individual fortunes and prejudices. Only the wisest realized that no final accounting could be made until the people had decided what to do with the fruits of victory. That the physical damage would be repaired no one could reasonably doubt; that even the loss of human resources would be restored in short order was equally apparent. But would the nation make good use of the opportunities the war had made available? What would the former slaves do with freedom? How would whites, northern and southern, react to emancipation? To what end would the new technology and social efficiency be directed? Would the people be able to forget the recent past and fulfill the hopes for which so many brave soldiers had given their "last full measure of devotion"?

Re-Viewing the Past

Cold Mountain

Cold Mountain (2004), a movie based on Charles Frazier's novel, is a love story set during the Civil War. But this is an unusual love story. The lovers are seldom together; and the hero is a deserter.

Inman (Jude Law), a schoolteacher, and Ada (Nicole Kidman), the well-born daughter of the minister, meet in a town in western North Carolina in the shadows of Cold Mountain. They speak on several occasions, look searchingly at each other, and exchange a single resolute kiss. Then Inman enlists in the Confederate army. They send each other letters, many of which never arrive. They yearn for each other without knowing much about each other. In a world made ugly by war, they need something beautiful to love. They cherish their photographs of the other.

Inman is wounded in the neck during the siege of Petersburg. While convalescing in the hospital, he receives a letter from Ada: "If you are fighting, stop fighting . . . If you are marching, stop marching. Come back to me." He nods grimly and decides to desert. He sneaks out of the hospital and begins his long trek back to Cold Mountain.

The journey is an ordeal. He suffers from cold and hunger. Confederate soldiers chase, capture, and shoot him, leaving him for dead; rogues attack and rob him. If war is hell, leaving it is no picnic, either.

Ada suffers too. Her father dies and she sets the slaves free. A southern lady, she knows nothing about farming and goes hungry. Renée Zellweger, a plucky female farmhand, appears at the farm and sets it aright.

The movie reaches a climax when Inman staggers up Cold Mountain—and into the arms of

▶ Nicole Kidman, as Ada in *Cold Mountain*

Ada. He is closely pursued by ruffians in the Home Guard, a local militia, who shoot him dead.

Can any of this be regarded as history?

There was a man named Inman, the brother of author Frazier's great-great-grandfather. The real Inman had been wounded in the neck at Petersburg, deserted, and was killed in a gunfight with the Home Guard near Cold Mountain. But the known facts of Inman's story, Frazier explained, "could be scrawled on the back of the envelope." Frazier made up everything else, doubtless inspired by Homer's *Odyssey*, another story of a soldier's return home from war.

But if much of the story is the product of Frazier's imagination, it nevertheless illuminates several historically significant themes. *Cold Mountain* examines the psychological effects of the loss of morale in the South, which many historians now regard as the best explanation for its defeat. (See Debating the Past, p. 418.) Official statistics indicate that some 200,000 Union soldiers and 104,000 Confederates deserted. Many more simply walked unarmed into enemy camps and were arrested as "captured." When Robert E. Lee surrendered at Appomattox, his army had dwindled to 28,000 men; another 3800 were reported as deserted and another 14,000 as captured.

The problem of desertion was especially acute in the mountain region of North Carolina, where support for secession had never been strong. In late 1863 and early 1864 the legislature of North Carolina passed laws penalizing sheriffs who failed to assist in capturing deserters and draft dodgers; it also created the Home Guard, local militias composed of men exempt from conscription, and charged them with the task of rounding up deserters. By early 1865, Lee was complaining that

▲ Southern lady with Lookout Mountain, Tennessee, in the background.

entire units were deserting; he especially regretted that "the greatest number of desertions have occurred among the North Carolina troops."

If the movie accurately pinpoints the geography of desertion—North Carolina—was its psychological explanation equally valid? Did southern women, like Ada, encourage their menfolk to desert?

The historical evidence is ambivalent.

On the one hand, the Confederacy made a concerted effort to enlist the support of white women. The South's surprisingly strong economic performance suggests that plenty of women, like Ada, learned how to manage farms and plantations. There is evidence, too, that southern women encouraged their men to fight. In 1862 and again the next year, a letter appeared in many Confederate newspapers in which "The Women of the South" called on their men to enlist and fight. "Never turn your backs on the flag," it advised soldiers, for cowardly behavior would disgrace themselves and their "children's children." When Sergeant Edwin Fay of Louisiana wrote to his wife saying that he wanted to leave "this horrid war," she responded that while she missed him terribly she could not countenance his becoming a deserter.

The Confederacy's appeal to women reflected their increasing importance in public life. Historian Drew Gilpin Faust argues that women's role shifted further as the Confederacy and its menfolk failed to defend white southern "womanhood." "Of necessity," such women assumed a larger role in the management of farms and plantations and they became more assertive in public matters. Some took the lead—as did Ada—in encouraging their men to desert.

"Though the ladies may not be willing to concede the fact," a Confederate official in North Carolina declared, "they are nevertheless responsible for the desertion in the army." James Fowler, a private from North Carolina who had been sentenced to death for desertion, cited his wife's pleas in his appeal for clemency. "I received a letter from my wife stating there [sic] condition and my two children was both at the point of Death and I made evry [sic] effort to get permission to go home honorably."

Cold Mountain is not history. But the movie illuminates the anguish of those who cling to life and love rather than to a war effort that will likely fail.

MILESTONES

1861	Confederates attack Fort Sumter; Lincoln calls for 75,000 volunteers	**1863**	Congress passes Conscription and National Banking acts
	First Battle of Bull Run (Virginia) boosts Confederate morale		Federal troops subdue draft riots in New York City
	Lincoln appoints George B. McClellan Union commander		Union army defeats Confederates at turning point Battle of Gettysburg, Pennsylvania
	Supreme Court rules against Lincoln's suspension of habeas corpus in *Ex parte Merryman*		Union siege and capture of Vicksburg, Mississippi, gives Union control of entire Mississippi River
1862	Confederate Congress passes Conscription Act	**1864**	Grant pushes deep into Virginia in costly Battles of the Wilderness, Spotsylvania Court House, and Cold Harbor
	Battle of Glorieta Pass ends Confederate threat to Far West		Sherman captures Atlanta, Georgia; marches to sea; captures Savannah
	USS *Monitor* defeats Confederate *Merrimack* in first battle between ironclads		
	Battle of Shiloh, Tennessee, leaves 23,000 dead, wounded, or missing	**1864**	Lincoln is reelected president
	Robert E. Lee assumes command of Confederate Army of Northern Virginia	**1864–1865**	Grant takes Petersburg, Virginia, after 10-month siege
	Lee and Stonewall Jackson defeat huge Union army at Seven Days' Battle for Richmond	**1865**	Sherman captures Columbia, South Carolina
	Lee and Jackson defeat Union army at Second Battle of Bull Run	**1865**	Lee surrenders to Grant at Appomattox Court House, Virginia
	Lee's northern advance is stopped at Battle of Antietam; 22,000 die		
	Lincoln's Emancipation Proclamation frees slaves in "areas of rebellion"		
	Congress passes Homestead, Morrill Land Grant, and Pacific Railway acts		

SUPPLEMENTARY READING

The best survey of the Civil War period is James M. McPherson, *Battle Cry of Freedom* (1988), but see also Russell F. Weigley, *A Great Civil War* (2000).

On the precipitating events of the war, see Maury Klein, *Days of Defiance: Sumter, Secession and the Coming of the Civil War* (1997), and Wallace Hettle, *The Peculiar Democracy: Southern Democrats in Peace and Civil War* (2001).

For Lincoln, in addition to books mentioned in previous chapters, see Philip Paludan, *The Presidency of Abraham Lincoln* (1994). Lincoln's dealings with the Radicals have been extensively investigated. H. L. Trefousse, *The Radical Republicans: Lincoln's Vanguard for Racial Justice* (1969), which praises Lincoln's management of the Radicals and minimizes his differences with them, is a good summary, but see also Richard Franklin Bensel, *Yankee*

Leviathan: The Origins of Central State Authority in America (1990). Mark E. Neely, *The Fate of Liberty* (1991) examines Lincoln's position on civil liberties. Frank Klement, *The Limits of Dissent* (1998) focuses on Clement Vallandigham. For the movement to make abolition a war aim and the reaction to it, see Michael Vorenberg, *Final Freedom* (2001).

On economic issues, see Heather Cox Richardson, *The Greatest Nation on Earth: Republican Economy Policies during the Civil War* (1997), and Bray Hammond, *Sovereignty and an Empty Purse: Banks and Politics in the Civil War* (1970).

On African Americans in the Union army, see Joseph T. Glatthaar, *Forged in Battle: The Civil War Alliance of Black Soldiers and White Officers* (1990); Peter Burchard, *One*

Gallant Rush (1965), recounts the story of Robert Gould Shaw and the Massachusetts 54th. See also Martin H. Blatt, *Hope & Glory: Essays on the Legacy of the 54th Massachusetts Regiment* (2001).

For aspects of economic and social history, see Philip S. Paludan, *"A People's Contest": The Union at War* (1988). Edward L. Ayers, *In the Presence of Mine Enemies* (2003) examines the effect of the war on various communities. For women and the war, see Drew Gilpin Faust, *Mothers of Invention* (1997), Judith Ann Giesberg, *Civil War Sisterhood: The U.S. Sanitary Commission and Women's Politics in Transition* (2000), and Laura Edwards, *Scarlett Doesn't Live Here Anymore* (2000). Elizabeth Young considers the literary heritage of women and the war in *Disarming the Nation: Women's Writing and the American Civil War* (1999). See also Iver Bernstein, *The New York City Draft Riots* (1990).

For the Confederacy, see Gary W. Gallagher, *The Confederate War* (1997). See also his edited collection, *Lee the Soldier* (1996). On divisions within the Confederacy, see William W. Freehling, *The South vs. The South: How Anti-Confederate Southerners Shaped the Course of the Civil War* (2001). Important biographies include William Cooper, *Jefferson Davis, American* (2000). See also Mark Grimsley and Brooks D. Simpson, eds., *Collapse of the Confederacy* (2001), and Steven V. Ash, *When the Yankees Came: Conflict and Chaos in the Occupied South* (1995).

Gerald F. Linderman, *Embattled Courage* (1988) argues that the soldiers on both sides grew disillusioned with the fighting; the persistence of the initial ideals is a theme in James McPherson, *What They Fought For, 1861–1865*

(1994), and Reid Mitchell, *The Vacant Chair* (1993). Bertram Wyatt-Brown, *The Shaping of Southern Culture: Honor, Grace and War, 1760s–1880s* (2001) contends that while soldiers on both sides used the same rhetoric to defend their cause, they had different notions of what terms such as "honor" meant.

Among the biographies of Civil War generals, northern and southern, the following are especially noteworthy: Brooks D. Simpson, *Ulysses S. Grant: Triumph over Adversity, 1822–1865* (2000), Jean E. Smith, *Grant* (2001), William S. McFeely, *Grant* (1981), Michael Fellman, *The Making of Robert E. Lee* (2000), Douglass S. Freeman, *R. E. Lee* (1934–1935), James I. Robertson, *Stonewall Jackson* (1997), Stephen W. Sears, *George B. McClellan* (1988), Stanley P. Hirshson, *The White Tecumseh: A Biography of William T. Sherman* (1997), and Chester G. Hearn, *Admiral David Glasgow Farragut* (1998).

The diplomacy of the Civil War period is covered in two works by Howard Jones, *Union in Peril* (1992), on British intervention, and *Abraham Lincoln and a New Birth of Freedom* (1999), on issues of slavery. See also John Taylor, *William Henry Seward* (1991).

John C. Waugh, *Reelecting Lincoln* (1997) considers the election of 1864. The assassination of Lincoln and its aftermath is the subject of Jay Winik, *April 1865: The Month That Saved America* (2001).

The legacy of the Civil War is thoughtfully examined in David W. Blight, *Race and Reunion: The Civil War in American Memory* (2001), and Tony Horwitz, *Confederates in the Attic: Dispatches from the Unfinished Civil War* (1998).

SUGGESTED WEBSITES

The American Civil War Homepage
http://sunsite.utk.edu/civil-war/warweb.html
This site has a great collection of hypertext links to the most useful identified electronic files about the American Civil War.

Abraham Lincoln
http://showcase.netins.net/web/creative/lincoln.html
This site both contains useful information about President Lincoln and links to other web destinations.

Abraham Lincoln Association
http://www.alincolnassoc.com/
This site allows searches of Lincoln's papers.

Assassination of President Abraham Lincoln
http://memory.loc.gov/ammem/alhtml/alrintr.html
Part of the American memory series with introduction, timeline, and gallery.

National Civil War Association
http://www.ncwa.org/
This site documents one of the many Civil War reenactment organizations in the United States.

Selected Civil War Photographs
http://memory.loc.gov/ammem/cwphtml/cwphome.html
Library of Congress site has more than one thousand photographs, many from Matthew Brady.

A Timeline of the Civil War
http://www.historyplace.com/civilwar/index.html
This site offers a comprehensive Civil War timeline that includes photographs.

U.S. Civil War Center
http://www.cwc.lsu.edu/
The mission of this site is to "locate, index and/or make available all appropriate private and public data regarding the Civil War and to promote the study of the Civil War from the perspective of all professional, occupations, and academic disciplines."

Reconstruction and the South

▼ Robert B. Elliott of South Carolina, where blacks outnumbered whites, addressing Congress on civil rights issues in 1874. He had defeated white opponents in 1870 and 1872.

CHAPTER CONTENTS

On April 5, 1865, Abraham Lincoln visited Richmond. The fallen capital lay in ruins, sections blackened by fire, but the president was able to walk the streets unmolested and almost unattended. Everywhere black people crowded around him worshipfully; some fell to their knees as he passed, crying "Glory, Hallelujah," hailing him as a messiah. Even white townspeople seemed to have accepted defeat without resentment.

A few days later, in Washington, Lincoln delivered an important speech on Reconstruction, urging compassion and open-mindedness. On April 14 he held a Cabinet meeting at which postwar readjustment was considered at length. That evening, while Lincoln was watching a performance of the play *Our American Cousin* at Ford's Theater, a half-mad actor, John Wilkes Booth, slipped into his box and shot him in the back of the head with a small pistol. Early the next morning, without having regained consciousness, Lincoln died.

The murder was part of a complicated plot organized by die-hard pro-Southerners. Seldom have fanatics displayed so little understanding of their own interests, for with Lincoln perished the South's best hope for a mild peace. After his body had been taken home to Illinois, the national mood hardened; apparently the awesome drama was still unfolding—retribution and a final humbling of the South were inevitable.

PRESIDENTIAL RECONSTRUCTION

Despite its bloodiness, the Civil War had caused less intersectional hatred than might have been expected. Although civilian property was often seized or destroyed, the invading armies treated the southern population with forbearance, both during the war and after Appomattox. While confederate President Davis was ensconced in Richmond behind Lee's army, Northerners boasted that they would "hang Jeff Davis to a sour apple tree," and when he was captured in Georgia in May 1865, he was at once clapped into irons preparatory to being tried for treason and murder. But feeling against Davis subsided quickly. In 1867 the military turned him over to the civil courts, which released him on bail. He was never brought to trial. A few other Confederate officials spent short periods behind bars, but the only Southerner executed for war crimes was Major Henry Wirz, the commandant of Andersonville military prison.

The legal questions related to bringing the defeated states back into the Union were extremely complex. Since Southerners believed that secession was legal, logic should have compelled them to argue that they were out of the Union and would thus have to be formally readmitted. Northerners should have taken the contrary position, for they had fought to prove that secession was illegal. Yet the people of both sections did just the opposite. Senator Charles Sumner and Congressman Thaddeus Stevens, in 1861 uncompromising expounders of the theory that the Union was indissoluble, now insisted that the Confederate states had "committed suicide" and should be treated like "conquered provinces." Lincoln believed the issue a "pernicious abstraction" and tried to ignore it.

The process of readmission began in 1862, when Lincoln reappointed provisional governors for those parts of the South that had been occupied by federal troops. On December 8, 1863, he issued a proclamation setting forth a general policy. With the exception of high Confederate officials and a few other special groups, all Southerners could reinstate themselves as United States citizens by taking a simple loyalty oath. When, in any state, a number equal to 10 percent of those voting in the 1860 election had taken this oath, they could set up state government. Such governments had to be republican in form, must recognize the "permanent freedom" of the slaves, and must provide for black education. The plan, however, did not require that blacks be given the right to vote.

The "Ten Percent Plan" reflected Lincoln's lack of vindictiveness and his political wisdom. He realized that any government based on such a small minority of the population would be, as he put it, merely "a tangible nucleus which the remainder . . . may rally around as fast as it can," a sort of puppet regime, like the paper government established in those sections of Virginia under federal control.[1] The regimes estab-

lished under this plan in Tennessee, Louisiana, and Arkansas bore, in the president's mind, the same relation to finally reconstructed states that an egg bears to a chicken. "We shall sooner have the fowl by hatching it than by smashing it," he remarked. He knew that eventually representatives of the southern states would again be sitting in Congress, and he wished to lay the groundwork for a strong Republican party in the section. Yet he realized that Congress had no intention of seating representatives from the "10 percent" states at once.

The Radicals in Congress disliked the 10 percent plan, partly because of its moderation and partly because it enabled Lincoln to determine Union policy toward the recaptured regions. In July 1864 they passed the Wade-Davis bill, which provided for constitutional conventions only after a majority of the others in a southern state had taken a loyalty oath. Confederate officials and anyone who had "voluntarily borne arms against the United States" were barred from voting in the election or serving at the convention. Besides prohibiting slavery, the new state constitutions would have to repudiate Confederate debts. Lincoln disposed of the Wade-Davis bill with a pocket veto and there matters stood when Andrew Johnson became president following the assassination.

Lincoln had picked Johnson for a running mate in 1864 because he was a border-state Unionist Democrat and something of a hero as a result of his courageous service as military governor of Tennessee. His political strength came from the poor whites and yeomen farmers of eastern Tennessee, and he was fond of extolling the common man and attacking "stuck-up aristocrats."

Thaddeus Stevens called Johnson a "rank demagogue" and a "damned scoundrel," and it is true that Johnson was a masterful rabble-rouser. But few men of his generation labored so consistently on behalf of small farmers. Free homesteads, public education, absolute social equality—such were his objectives. The father of communism, Karl Marx, a close observer of American affairs at this time, wrote approvingly of Johnson's "deadly hatred of the oligarchy."

Johnson was a Democrat, but because of his record and his reassuring penchant for excoriating southern aristocrats, the Republicans in Congress were ready to cooperate with him. "Johnson, we have faith in you," said Senator Ben Wade, author of the Wade-Davis bill, the day after Lincoln's death. "By the gods, there will be no trouble now in running the government!"

Johnson's reply, "Treason must be made infamous," delighted the Radicals, but the president proved temperamentally unable to work with them. Like Randolph of Roanoke, his antithesis intellectually and socially, opposition was his specialty; he soon alienated every powerful Republican in Washington.

---

[1]By approving the separation of the western counties that had refused to secede, this government provided a legal pretext for the creation of West Virginia.

▲ Andrew Johnson in 1855, from a painting by William Cooper. From origins even more lowly than Lincoln's, Johnson had risen to be congressman, governor of Tennessee, and United States senator. He was able and ambitious but fundamentally unsure of himself, as could be seen in his boastfulness and stubbornness.

Radical Republicans listened to Johnson's diatribes against secessionists and the great planters and assumed that he was anti-southern. Nothing could have been further from the truth. He had great respect for states' rights and he shared most of his poor white Tennessee constituents' contempt of blacks. "Damn the negroes, I am fighting these traitorous aristocrats, their masters," he told a friend during the war. "I wish to God," he said on another occasion, "every head of a family in the United States had one slave to take the drudgery and menial service off his family."

The new president did not want to injure or humiliate all white Southerners. He issued an amnesty proclamation only slightly more rigorous than Lincoln's. It assumed, correctly enough, that with the war over most southern voters would freely take the loyalty oath; thus it contained no 10 percent clause. More classes of Confederates, including those who owned taxable property in excess of $20,000, were excluded from the general pardon. By the time Congress convened in December 1865, all the southern states had organized governments, ratified the Thirteenth Amendment abolishing slavery, and elected senators and representatives. Johnson promptly recommended these new governments to the attention of Congress.

REPUBLICAN RADICALS

Peace found the Republicans in Congress no more united than they had been during the war. A small group of "ultra" Radicals were demanding immediate and absolute civil and political equality for blacks; they should be given, for example, the vote, a plot of land, and access to a decent education. Senator Sumner led this faction. A second group of Radicals, headed by Thaddeus Stevens in the House and Ben Wade in the Senate, agreed with the ultras' objectives but were prepared to accept half a loaf if necessary to win the support of less radical colleagues.

Nearly all Radicals distinguished between the "natural" God-given rights described in the Declaration of Independence, and social equality. "Equality," said Stevens, "does not mean that a negro shall sit in the same seat or eat at the same table with a white man. That is a matter of taste which every man must

▲ Mathew Brady's photograph of the stalwart radical Republican Thaddeus Stevens. Stevens insisted on being buried in a black cemetery. He wrote his own epitaph: "I repose in this quiet and secluded spot, not from any natural preference for solitude, but finding other cemeteries limited as to race, by charter rules, I have chosen this that I might illustrate in my death the principles which I advocated through a long life, equality of man before his Creator."

decide for himself." This did not reflect personal prejudice in Stevens's case. When he died, he was buried in a black cemetery.

The moderate Republicans wanted to protect the former slaves from exploitation and guarantee their basic rights but were unprepared to push for full political equality. A handful of Republicans sided with the Democrats in support of Johnson's approach, but all the rest insisted at least on the minimal demands of the moderates. Thus Johnsonian Reconstruction was doomed.

Johnson's proposal had no chance in Congress for reasons having little to do with black rights. The Thirteenth Amendment had the effect of increasing the representation of the southern states in Congress because it made the Three-fifths Compromise meaningless. Henceforth those who had been slaves would be counted as whole persons in apportioning seats in the House of Representatives. If Congress seated the Southerners, the balance of power might swing to the Democrats. To expect the Republicans to surrender power in such a fashion was unrealistic. Former Copperheads gushing with extravagant praise for Johnson put them instantly on guard.

In addition, the ex-Confederates were not overflowing with goodwill toward their conquerors. A minority would have nothing to do with amnesties and pardons:

> *Oh, I'm a good old rebel,*
> *Now that's just what I am;*
> *For the "fair land of freedom,"*
> *I do not care a dam.*
> *I'm glad I fit against it—*
> *I only wish we'd won*
> *And I don't want no pardon*
> *For anything I done.*

Southern voters had further provoked northern resentment by their choice of congressmen. Georgia elected Alexander H. Stephens, vice president of the Confederacy, to the Senate, although he was still in a federal prison awaiting trial for treason! Several dozen men who had served in the Confederate Congress had been elected to either the House or the Senate, together with four generals and many other high officials. The southern people understandably selected locally respected and experienced leaders, but it was equally reasonable that these choices would sit poorly with Northerners.

Finally, the so-called Black Codes enacted by southern governments to control former slaves alarmed the North. These varied in severity from state to state, but all, as one planter admitted, set out to keep the blacks "as near to a state of bondage as possible."

When seen in historical perspective, even the strictest codes represented some improvement over slavery. Most permitted blacks to sue and to testify in court, at least in cases involving members of their own race. Blacks were allowed to own certain kinds of property; other rights were guaranteed. However, blacks could not bear arms, be employed in occupations other than farming and domestic service, or leave their jobs without forfeiting back pay. The Mississippi code required them to sign labor contracts for the year in January, and, in addition, drunkards, vagrants, beggars, "common night-walkers," and even "mischief makers" and persons who "misspend what they earn" and who could not pay the stiff fines assessed for such misbehavior were to be "hired out . . . at public outcry" to the white persons who would take them for the shortest period in return for paying the fines. Such laws, apparently designed to get around the Thirteenth Amendment, outraged Northerners.

Congress Rejects Johnsonian Reconstruction

For all these reasons the Republicans in Congress rejected Johnsonian Reconstruction. Quickly they created a joint committee on Reconstruction, headed by Senator William P. Fessenden of Maine, a moderate, to study the question of readmitting the southern states.

The committee held public hearings that produced much evidence of the mistreatment of blacks. Colonel George A. Custer, stationed in Texas, testified: "It is of weekly, if not of daily occurrence that Freedmen are murdered." The nurse Clara Barton told a gruesome tale about a pregnant woman who had been brutally whipped. Others described the intimidation of blacks by poor whites. The hearings strengthened the Radicals, who had been claiming all along that the South was perpetuating slavery under another name.

President Johnson's attitude speeded the swing toward the Radical position. While the hearings were in progress, Congress passed a bill expanding and extending the Freedmen's Bureau, which had been established in March 1865 to care for refugees. The bureau, a branch of the War Department, was already exercising considerable coercive and supervisory power in the South. Now Congress sought to add to its authority in order to protect the black population. Although the bill had wide support, Johnson vetoed it, arguing that it was an unconstitutional extension of military authority in peacetime. Congress then passed a Civil Rights Act that, besides declaring specifically that blacks were citizens of the

▲ Agents of the Freedmen's Bureau helped defend former slaves against white attacks and provided them with food, clothing, and medical care. They also set up schools. However, hostility toward the activities of the Freedmen's Bureau was widespread. In 1866, during a race riot in Memphis, mobs killed 46 blacks and burned this Freedmen's schoolhouse.

United States, denied the states the power to restrict their rights to testify in court, to make contracts for their labor, and to hold property. In other words, it put teeth in the Thirteenth Amendment.

Once again the president refused to go along, although his veto was sure to drive more moderates into the arms of the Radicals. On April 9, 1866, Congress repassed the Civil Rights Act by a two-thirds majority, the first time in American history that a major piece of legislation became law over the veto of a president. This event marked a revolution in the history of Reconstruction. Thereafter Congress, not President Johnson, had the upper hand.

In the clash between the president and Congress, Johnson was his own worst enemy. His language was often intemperate, his handling of opponents inept, his analysis of southern conditions incorrect. He had assumed that the small southern farmers who made up the majority in the Confederacy shared his prejudices against the planter class. They did not, as their choices in the postwar elections demonstrated. In fact, Johnson's hatred of the southern aristocracy may have been based more on jealousy than on principle. Under the Reconstruction plan, persons excluded from the blanket amnesty could apply individually for the restoration of their rights. When wealthy and socially prominent southerners flocked to Washington, hat in hand, he found their flattery and humility exhilarating. He issued pardons wholesale. "I did not expect to keep out all who were excluded from the amnesty," he explained. "I intended they should sue for pardon, and so realize the enormity of their crime."

The president misread northern opinion. He believed that Congress had no right to pass laws affecting the South before southern representatives had been readmitted to Congress. However, in the light of the refusal of most southern whites to grant any real power or responsibility to the freedmen (an attitude that Johnson did not condemn), the public would not accept this point of view. Johnson placed his own judgment over that of the overwhelming majority of northern voters, and this was a great error, morally and tactically. By encouraging white Southerners to resist efforts to improve the lot of blacks, Johnson played into the hands of the Radicals.

The Radicals encountered grave problems in fighting for their program. Northerners might object to the Black Codes and to seating "rebels" in Congress, but few believed in racial equality. Between 1865 and 1868, Wisconsin, Minnesota, Connecticut, Nebraska, New Jersey, Ohio, Michigan, and Pennsylvania all rejected bills granting blacks the vote.

The Radicals were in effect demanding not merely equal rights for freedmen but extra rights; not merely the vote but special protection of that right against the pressure that southern whites would surely apply to undermine it. This idea flew in the face of conventional American beliefs in equality before the law and individual self-reliance. Such protection would involve interference by the federal government in local affairs, a concept at variance with American practice. Events were to show that the Radicals were correct—that what amounted to a political revolution in state-federal relations was essential if blacks were to achieve real equality. But in the climate of that day their proposals encountered bitter resistance, and not only from white Southerners.

Thus, while the Radicals sought partisan advantage in their battle with Johnson and sometimes played on war-bred passions in achieving their ends, they were taking large political risks in defense of genuinely held principles. One historian has aptly called them the "moral trustees" of the Civil War.

THE FOURTEENTH AMENDMENT

13th, 14th, and 15th Amendments

In June 1866 Congress submitted to the states a new amendment to the Constitution. The Fourteenth Amendment was, in the context of the times, a truly radical measure. Never before had newly freed slaves been granted significant political rights. For example, in the British Caribbean sugar islands, where slavery had been abolished in the 1830s, stiff property qualifications and poll taxes kept freedmen from voting. The Fourteenth Amendment was also a milestone along the road to the centralization of political power in the United States because it reduced the power of all the states. In this sense it confirmed the great change wrought by the Civil War: the growth of a more complex, more closely integrated social and economic structure requiring closer national supervision. Few people understood this aspect of the amendment at the time.

First the amendment supplied a broad definition of American citizenship: "All persons born or naturalized in the United States, and subject to the jurisdiction thereof, are citizens of the United States and of the State wherein they reside." Obviously this included blacks. Then it struck at discriminatory legislation like the Black Codes: "No State shall make or enforce any law which shall abridge the privileges or immunities of citizens of the United States; nor shall any State deprive any person of life, liberty, or property, without due process of law." The next section attempted to force the southern states to permit blacks to vote. If a state denied the vote to any class of its adult male citizens, its representation was to be reduced proportionately. Under another clause, former federal officials who had served the Confederacy were barred from holding either state or federal office unless specifically pardoned by a two-thirds vote of Congress. Finally, the Confederate debt was repudiated.

Reconstruction

While the amendment did not specifically outlaw segregation or prevent a state from disenfranchising blacks, the southern states would have none of it. Without them the necessary three-fourths majority of the states could not be obtained.

President Johnson vowed to make the choice between the Fourteenth Amendment and his own policy the main issue of the 1866 congressional elections. He embarked on "a swing around the circle" to rally the public to his cause. He failed dismally. Northern women objected to the implication in the amendment that black men were more fitted to vote than white women, but a large majority of northern voters was determined that African Americans must have at least formal legal equality. The Republicans won better

than two-thirds of the seats in both houses, together with control of all the northern state governments. Johnson emerged from the campaign discredited, the Radicals stronger and determined to have their way. The southern states, Congressman James A. Garfield of Ohio said in February 1867, have "flung back into our teeth the magnanimous offer of a generous nation. It is now our turn to act."

THE RECONSTRUCTION ACTS

Had the southern states been willing to accept the Fourteenth Amendment, coercive measures might have been avoided. Their recalcitrance and continuing indications that local authorities were persecuting blacks finally led to the passage, on March 2, 1867, of the First Reconstruction Act. This law divided the former Confederacy—exclusive of Tennessee, which had ratified the Fourteenth Amendment—into five military districts, each controlled by a major general. It gave these officers almost dictatorial power to protect the civil rights of "all persons," maintain order, and supervise the administration of justice. To rid themselves of military rule, the former states were required to adopt new state constitutions guaranteeing blacks the right to vote and disenfranchising broad classes of ex-Confederates. If the new constitutions proved satisfactory to Congress, and if the new governments ratified the Fourteenth Amendment, their representatives would be admitted to Congress and military rule ended. Johnson's veto of the act was easily overridden.

Although drastic, the Reconstruction Act was so vague that it proved unworkable. Military control was easily established. But in deference to moderate Republican views, the law had not spelled out the process by which the new constitutions were to be drawn up. Southern whites preferred the status quo, even under army control, to enfranchising blacks and retiring their own respected leaders. They made no effort to follow the steps laid down in the law. Congress therefore passed a second act, requiring the military authorities to register voters and supervise the election of delegates to constitutional conventions. A third act further clarified procedures.

Still white Southerners resisted. The laws required that the constitutions be approved by a majority of the registered voters. Simply by staying away from the polls, whites prevented ratification in state after state. At last, in March 1868, a full year after the First Reconstruction Act, Congress changed the rules again. The constitutions were to be ratified by a majority of the voters. In June 1868 Arkansas, having fulfilled the requirements, was readmitted to the Union, and by July a sufficient number of states had ratified the Fourteenth Amendment to make it part of the Constitution. But it was not until July 1870 that the last southern state, Georgia, qualified to the satisfaction of Congress.

CONGRESS SUPREME

To carry out this program in the face of determined southern resistance required a degree of single-mindedness over a long period seldom demonstrated by an American legislature. The persistence resulted in part from the suffering and frustrations of the war years. The refusal of the South to accept the spirit of even the mild reconstruction designed by Johnson goaded the North to ever more overbearing efforts to bring the ex-Confederates to heel. President Johnson's stubbornness also influenced the Republicans. They became obsessed with the need to defeat him. The unsettled times and the large Republican majorities, always threatened by the possibility of a Democratic resurgence if "unreconstructed" southern congressmen were readmitted, sustained their determination.

These considerations led Republicans to attempt a kind of grand revision of the federal government, one that almost destroyed the balance between judicial, executive, and legislative power established in 1789. A series of measures passed between 1866 and 1868 increased the authority of Congress over the army, over the process of amending the Constitution, and over Cabinet members and lesser appointive officers. Even the Supreme Court was affected. Its size was reduced and its jurisdiction over civil rights cases limited. Finally, in a showdown caused by emotion more than by practical considerations, the Republicans attempted to remove President Johnson from office.

Johnson was a poor president and out of touch with public opinion, but he had done nothing to merit ejection from office. While he had a low opinion of African Americans, his opinion was so widely shared by whites that it is unhistorical to condemn him as a reactionary on this ground. Johnson believed that he was fighting to preserve constitutional government. He was honest and devoted to duty, and his record easily withstood the most searching examination. When Congress passed laws taking away powers granted him by the Constitution, he refused to submit.

The chief issue was the Tenure of Office Act of 1867, which prohibited the president from removing officials who had been appointed with the consent of the Senate without first obtaining Senate approval. In February 1868 Johnson "violated" this act by dismissing Secretary of War Edwin M. Stanton, who

had been openly in sympathy with the Radicals for some time. The House, acting under the procedure set up in the Constitution for removing the president, promptly impeached him before the bar of the Senate, Chief Justice Salmon P. Chase presiding.

In the trial, Johnson's lawyers easily established that he had removed Stanton only in an effort to prove the Tenure of Office Act unconstitutional. They demonstrated that the act did not protect Stanton to begin with, since it gave Cabinet members tenure "during the term of the President by whom they may have been appointed," and Stanton had been appointed in 1862, during Lincoln's first term!

Nevertheless the Radicals pressed the charges (11 separate articles) relentlessly. To the argument that Johnson had committed no crime, the learned Senator Sumner retorted that the proceedings were "political in character" rather than judicial. Thaddeus Stevens, directing the attack on behalf of the House, warned the senators that although "no corrupt or wicked motive" could be attributed to Johnson, they would "be tortured on the gibbet of everlasting obloquy" if they did not convict him. Tremendous pressure was applied to the handful of Republican senators who were unwilling to disregard the evidence.

Seven of them resisted to the end, and the Senate failed by a single vote to convict Johnson. This was probably fortunate. The trial weakened the presidency, but if Johnson had been forced from office on such flimsy grounds, the independence of the executive might have been permanently undermined. Then the legislative branch would have become supreme.

THE FIFTEENTH AMENDMENT

The failure of the impeachment did not affect the course of Reconstruction. The president was acquitted on May 16, 1868. A few days later, the Republican National Convention nominated General Ulysses S. Grant for the presidency. At the Democratic convention Johnson had considerable support, but the delegates nominated Horatio Seymour, a former governor of New York. In November Grant won an easy victory in the Electoral College, 214 to 80, but the popular vote was close: 3 million to 2.7 million. Although he would probably have carried the Electoral College in any case, Grant's margin in the popular vote was supplied by southern blacks enfranchised under the Reconstruction acts, about 450,000 of whom supported him. A majority of white voters probably preferred

▶ *text continues on page 434*

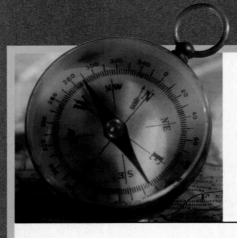

Mapping the Past

The Politics of Reconstruction

The map below, "Imposition of Union military control," summarizes the rise and fall of Reconstruction in the South. The Reconstruction Acts of 1867 divided the Confederacy into five military districts. In 1868 Arkansas was the first state to be readmitted to the Union; Georgia, in July 1870, was the last. The legislative enactments of Congress, led by the Radical Republicans, were enforced by the Union army. Republican electoral success in the South was similarly predicated on the presence of the Union army; but this map also shows that Democrats reestablished their political power in most states prior to the Compromise of 1877: Virginia (1869), Georgia (1872), Texas (1874), Arkansas (1874), and Mississippi (1876) are examples.

Triumph of the Republican Party in the South, 1870

In the late 1860s the rise of the Republican party was due both to the weakness of the southern Democrats and to the enfranchisement of black men. African Americans voted solidly Republican—the party of Lincoln—and they exercised their vote diligently. In many elections, the black voter turnout approached 90 percent. "It is the hardest thing in the world to keep a negro away from the polls," decried a white Alabama politician.

The power of the black vote in 1870 is demonstrated in the map at right, top. Of the 15 congressional districts that encompassed the interior counties from Louisiana through South Carolina, it was in the Cotton Belt, where blacks comprised the majority, that Republican candidates won 14 seats. Throughout the South, Republicans took 31 of the 57 seats in the House of Representatives. In the three states where blacks outnumbered whites—South Carolina, Mississippi, and Louisiana—the Republicans won every House seat.

Five blacks were among the Republican victors. With the exception of Josiah Walls, a former slave who had fought with the Union army and represented Florida, all of the blacks were from areas with a substantial black majority: three from South Carolina, the other from Alabama.

"Carpetbaggers," Republicans from the North, were also strong in the areas where blacks had a majority, especially Louisiana, Mississippi, and Virginia. Except for the two congressional districts in lower Louisiana, no "carpetbaggers" won House seats where blacks did not constitute a majority of the population.

"Scalawags," white Southerners who endorsed the Republican party, did take some seats in areas with white majorities. Usually these victories were in districts that had been Whig strongholds.

Collapse of the Republican Party in the South, 1878

With the Compromise of 1877 and subsequent withdrawal of Union troops, the Republican political power in the South collapsed. Tennessee, excluded from the Union military district, never experienced a period of Republican domination; in Virginia, the Democrats were firmly back in power by 1869.

The map at bottom right shows that by 1878, Democrats, all of them white, recaptured 77 of the 83 House seats in the South. All of the black House representatives had been defeated. No Republican was elected in Texas, Arkansas, Louisiana, Mississippi, Alabama, Georgia, South Carolina, or North Carolina. The South was not exactly "solid"—independent Democrats and Greenback representatives won a handful of seats. But the South would remain a Democratic bastion for over a century.

Imposition of Union military control

—— boundary of military districts established under 1867 Reconstruction acts	*1870* year of readmission to the Union
	(1876) year in which conservative rule was fully restored

1870 (1869)

1866 (1869)

1868 (1874)

1868 (1877)

1870 (1872)

1868 (1877)

1868 (1874)

1870 (1874)

1868 (1877)

1870 (1874)

1868 (1877)

1868 (1877)

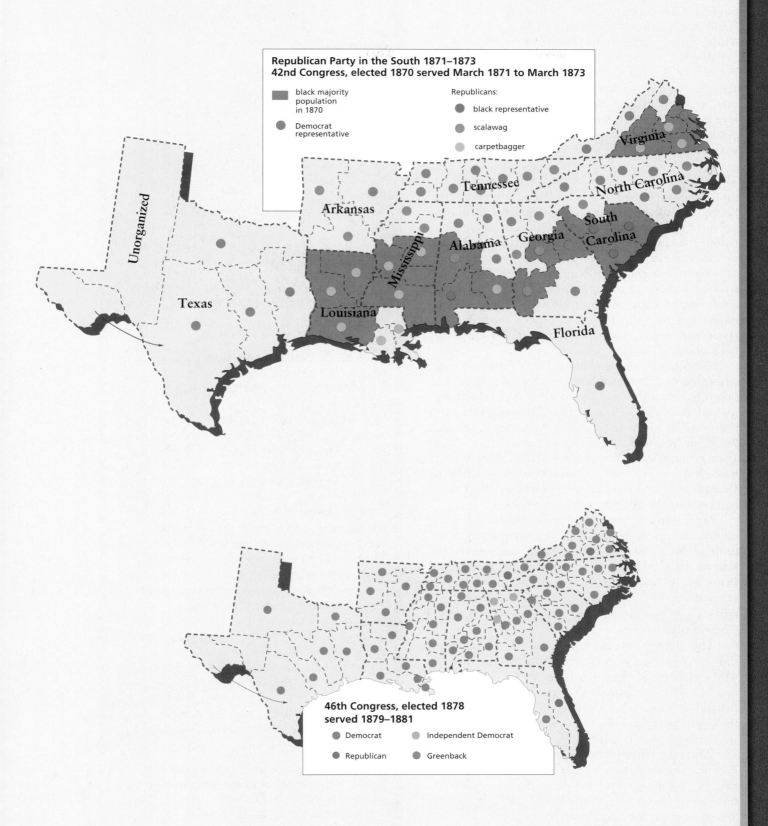

Republican Party in the South 1871–1873
42nd Congress, elected 1870 served March 1871 to March 1873

- black majority population in 1870
- Democrat representative

Republicans:
- black representative
- scalawag
- carpetbagger

Unorganized

Texas

Arkansas

Louisiana

Mississippi

Tennessee

Alabama

Georgia

South Carolina

North Carolina

Virginia

Florida

46th Congress, elected 1878 served 1879–1881

- Democrat
- Republican
- Independent Democrat
- Greenback

Seymour. Since many citizens undoubtedly voted Republican because of personal admiration for General Grant, the election statistics suggest that a substantial white majority opposed the policies of the Radicals.

The Reconstruction acts and the ratification of the Fourteenth Amendment achieved the purpose of enabling black Southerners to vote. The Radicals, however, were not satisfied; despite the unpopularity of the idea in the North, they wished to guarantee the right of blacks to vote in every state. Another amendment seemed the only way to accomplish this objective, but passage of such an amendment appeared impossible. The Republican platform in the 1868 election had smugly distinguished between blacks voting in the South ("demanded by every consideration of public safety, of gratitude, and of justice") and in the North (where the question "properly belongs to the people").

However, after the election had demonstrated how important the black vote could be, Republican strategy shifted. Grant had carried Indiana by fewer than 10,000 votes and lost New York by a similar number. If blacks in these and other closely divided states had voted, Republican strength would have been greatly enhanced.

Suddenly Congress blossomed with suffrage amendments. After considerable bickering over details, the Fifteenth Amendment was sent to the states for ratification in February 1869. It forbade all the states to deny the vote to anyone "on account of race, color, or previous condition of servitude." Once again nothing was said about denial of the vote on the basis of sex, which caused feminists, such as Elizabeth Cady Stanton, to be even more outraged than they had been by the Fourteenth Amendment.

Most southern states, still under federal pressure, ratified the amendment swiftly. The same was true in most of New England and in some western states. Bitter battles were waged in Connecticut, New York, Pennsylvania, and the states immediately north of the Ohio River, but by March 1870 most of them had ratified the amendment and it became part of the Constitution.

The debates occasioned by these conventions show that partisan advantage was not the only reason why voters approved black suffrage at last. The unfairness of a double standard of voting, North and South, the contribution of black soldiers during the war, and the hope that by passing the amendment the strife of Reconstruction could finally be ended all played a part.

When the Fifteenth Amendment went into effect, President Grant called it "the greatest civil change and . . . the most important event that has occurred since the nation came to life." The American Anti-Slavery Society formally dissolved itself, its work apparently completed. "The Fifteenth Amendment confers upon the African race the care of its own destiny,"

DEBATING THE PAST

Were Reconstruction governments corrupt? Racist depictions of Reconstruction were common. This one by Thomas Nast was entitled "Colored Rule in a Reconstructed (?) State" and appeared in *Harper's Weekly* (1874). In 1902 Columbia historian William A. Dunning similarly declared that free slaves were mere children, incapable of holding office. In 1910 W. E. B. Du Bois, an African American scholar, was the first to applaud Reconstruction for broadening educational opportunities and democratizing government, but few historians concurred. In the 1960s, as the civil rights movement was gaining momentum, more scholars came out in support of Reconstruction. In 1965 Kenneth Stampp emphasized the Reconstruction governments' attempts to protect freedmen; that same year, Joel Williamson turned Dunning's thesis on its head and endorsed nearly all aspects of Reconstruction. More recent scholars have generally taken a moderate position: Reconstruction may have failed, but its accomplishments under difficult circumstances of white opposition were substantial; see, for example, Eric Foner (1988). Certain facts are beyond argument. Black officeholders were neither numerous nor inordinately influential. None was ever elected governor of a state; fewer than a dozen and a half during the entire period served in Congress.

William A. Dunning, *Reconstruction and the Constitution* (1902), W. E. B. Du Bois, *Black Reconstruction* in *America* (1935), Kenneth Stampp, *The Peculiar Institution* (1965), Joel Williamson, *After Slavery* (1965), Eric Foner, *Reconstruction* (1988).

Radical Congressman James A. Garfield wrote proudly after the amendment was ratified. "It places their fortunes in their own hands."

Many of the celebrants lived to see the amendment subverted in the South. That it could be evaded by literacy tests and other restrictions was apparent at the time and may even have influenced some persons who voted for it. But a stronger amendment—one, for instance, that positively granted the right to vote to all men and put the supervision of elections under national control—could not have been ratified.

"Black Republican" Reconstruction: Scalawags and Carpetbaggers

The Radicals had at last succeeded in imposing their will on the South. Throughout the region former slaves had real political influence; they voted, held office, and exercised the "privileges" and enjoyed the "immunities" guaranteed them by the Fourteenth Amendment. Almost to a man they voted Republican.

The spectacle of blacks not five years removed from slavery in positions of power and responsibility attracted much attention at the time and has since been examined exhaustively by historians (see Debating the Past, p. 434). But the real rulers of the "black Republican" governments were white: the "scalawags"—Southerners willing to cooperate with the Republicans because they accepted the results of the war and wished to advance their own interests—and the "carpetbaggers"—Northerners who went to the South as idealists to help the freed slaves, as employees of the federal government, or more commonly as settlers hoping to improve themselves.

The scalawags were by far the more numerous. A few were prewar politicians or well-to-do planters, men such as the Mississippi planter John L. Alcorn and Joseph E. Brown, the Confederate governor of Georgia. General James Longstreet, one of Lee's most important lieutenants, was another prominent Southerner who cooperated with the Republicans. But most were people who had supported the Whig party before the secession crisis and who saw the Republicans as the logical successors of the Whigs.

The carpetbaggers were a particularly varied lot. Most had mixed motives for coming south and personal gain was certainly among them. But so were opposition to slavery and the belief that blacks deserved to be treated decently and given a chance to get ahead in the world.

Many northern blacks became carpetbaggers: former Union soldiers, missionaries from northern black churches, and also teachers, lawyers, and other members of the small northern black professional class. Many of these became officeholders, but like southern black politicians their influence was limited.

That blacks should fail to dominate southern governments is certainly understandable. They lacked experience in politics and were mostly poor and uneducated. They were nearly everywhere a minority. Those blacks who held office during Reconstruction tended to be better educated and more prosperous than most southern blacks. A disproportionate number had been free before the war. Of those freed by the Thirteenth Amendment, a large percentage had been house servants or artisans, not field hands. Mulatto politicians were also disproportionately numerous and (as a group) more conservative and economically better off than other black leaders.

In South Carolina and elsewhere, blacks proved in the main able and conscientious public servants: able because the best tended to rise to the top in such a fluid situation and conscientious because most of those who achieved importance sought eagerly to demonstrate the capacity of their race for self-government. Even at the local level, where the quality of officials was usually poor, there was little difference in the degree of competence displayed by white and black officeholders. In power, the blacks were not vindictive; by and large they did not seek to restrict the rights of ex-Confederates.

Not all black legislators and administrators were paragons of virtue. In South Carolina, despite their

▲ During Reconstruction, 14 blacks won election to the House of Representatives and two, Hiram Revels and Blanche K. Bruce, served in the Senate. Revels, at far left, won the Mississippi Senate seat that Jefferson Davis had once held. He later became president of Alcorn University. Congressman R. Brown Elliot, at far right, had been educated at Eton in England.

control of the legislature, they broke up into factions repeatedly and failed to press for laws that would improve the lot of poor black farm workers. In *The Prostrate South* (1874), James S. Pike, a northern newspaperman, wrote: "The rule of South Carolina should not be dignified with the name of government. It is the installation of a huge system of brigandage." Like many northern commentators, Pike exaggerated the immorality and incompetence of the blacks, but waste and corruption were common during Reconstruction governments. Half the budget of Louisiana in some years went for salaries and "mileage" for representatives and their staffs. One Arkansas black took $9000 from the state for repairing a bridge that had cost only $500 to build. A South Carolina legislator was voted an additional $1000 in salary after he lost that sum betting on a horse race.

However, the corruption must be seen in perspective. The big thieves were nearly always white; blacks got mostly crumbs. Furthermore, graft and callous disregard of the public interest characterized government in every section and at every level during the decade after Appomattox. Big-city bosses in the North embezzled sums that dwarfed the most brazen southern frauds. The New York City Tweed Ring probably made off with more money than all the southern thieves, black and white, combined. While the evidence does not justify the southern corruption, it suggests that the unique features of Reconstruction politics—black suffrage, military supervision, carpetbagger and scalawag influence—do not explain it.

The "black Republican" governments displayed qualities that grew directly from the ignorance and political inexperience of the former slaves. There was a tragicomic aspect to the South Carolina legislature during these years, its many black members—some dressed in old frock coats, others in rude farm clothes—rising to points of order and personal privilege without reason, discoursing ponderously on subjects they did not understand. But those who complained about the ignorance and irresponsibility of blacks conveniently forgot that the tendency of nineteenth-century American democracy was away from educational, financial, or any other restrictions on the franchise. Thousands of white Southerners were as illiterate and uncultured as the freedmen, yet no one suggested depriving them of the ballot.

In fact, the Radical southern governments accomplished a great deal. They spent money freely but not entirely wastefully. Tax rates zoomed, but the money financed the repair and expansion of the South's dilapidated railroad network, rebuilt crumbling levees, and expanded social services. Before the Civil War, southern planters possessed a dispropor-

tionate share of political as well as economic power, and they spent relatively little public money on education and public services of all kinds.

During Reconstruction an enormous gap had to be filled, and it took money to fill it. The Freedmen's Bureau made a major contribution. Northern religious and philanthropic organizations also did important work. Eventually, however, the state governments established and supported hospitals, asylums, and systems of free public education that, while segregated, greatly benefited everyone, whites as well as blacks. Much state money was also spent on economic development: land reclamation, repairing and expanding the war-ravaged railroads, maintaining levees.

The former slaves grasped eagerly at the opportunities to learn. Schools and other institutions were supported chiefly by property taxes, and these, of course, hit well-to-do planters hard. Hence much of the complaining about the "extravagance" of Reconstruction governments concealed traditional selfish objections to paying for public projects. Eventually the benefits of expanded government services to the entire population became clear, and when white supremacy was reestablished, most of the new services remained in force, and the corruption and inefficiency inherited from the carpetbagger governments continued.

THE RAVAGED LAND

The South's grave economic problems complicated the rebuilding of its political system. The section had never been as prosperous as the North, and wartime destruction left it desperately poor by any standard. In the long run the abolition of slavery released immeasurable quantities of human energy previously stifled, but the immediate effect was to create confusion. Freedom to move without a pass, to "see the world," was one of the former slaves' most cherished benefits of emancipation. Understandably, many at first equated legal freedom with freedom from having to earn a living, a tendency reinforced for a time by the willingness of the Freedmen's Bureau to provide rations and other forms of relief in war-devastated areas. Most, however, soon accepted the fact that they must earn a living; a small plot of land of their own ("40 acres and a mule") would complete their independence.

This objective was forcefully supported by the relentless Congressman Thaddeus Stevens, whose hatred of the planter class was pathological. "The property of the chief rebels should be seized," he stated. If the lands of the richest "70,000 proud, bloated and defiant rebels" were confiscated, the federal government would obtain 394 million acres. Every adult male ex-slave could easily be supplied with 40 acres.

▲ The Freedmen's Bureau built 4329 schools, attended by some 250,000 former slaves, in the postwar South. Many of the teachers in these schools were abolitionists or missionaries from New England. The schools drew African Americans of all ages, from children to grandparents, who were eager for the advantages offered by education.

The beauty of his scheme, Stevens insisted, was that "nine-tenths of the [southern] people would remain untouched." Dispossessing the great planters would make the South "a safe republic," its lands cultivated by "the free labor of intelligent citizens." If the plan drove the planters into exile, "all the better."

Although Stevens's figures were faulty, many Radicals agreed with him. "We must see that the freedmen are established on the soil," Senator Sumner declared. "The great plantations, which have been so many nurseries of the rebellion, must be broken up, and the freedmen must have the pieces." Stevens, Sumner, and others who wanted to give land to the freedmen weakened their case by associating it with the idea of punishing the former rebels; the average American had too much respect for property rights to support a policy of confiscation.

Aside from its vindictiveness, the extremists' view was simplistic. Land without tools, seed, and other necessities would have done the freedmen little good. Congress did throw open 46 million acres of poor-quality federal land in the South to blacks under the Homestead Act, but few settled on it. Establishing former slaves on small farms with adequate financial aid would have been of incalculable benefit to them. This would have been practicable, but extremely expensive. It was not done.

The former slaves therefore had either to agree to work for their former owners or strike out on their own. White planters, influenced by the precipitous decline of sugar production in Jamaica and other Caribbean islands that had followed the abolition of slavery there, expected freed blacks to be incapable of self-directed effort. If allowed to become independent farmers, they would either starve to death or descend into barbarism. Of course the blacks did neither. True, the output of cotton and other southern staples declined precipitously after slavery was abolished. Observers soon came to the conclusion that a free black produced much less than a slave had produced. "You can't get only about two-thirds as much out of 'em now as you could when they were slaves," an Arkansas planter complained.

However, the decline in productivity was not caused by the inability of free blacks to work independently. They simply chose no longer to work like slaves. They let their children play instead of forcing them into the fields. Mothers devoted more time to childcare and housework, less to farm labor. Elderly blacks worked less.

Noting these changes, white critics spoke scornfully of black laziness and shiftlessness. "You cannot make the negro work without physical compulsion," was the common view. Even General

Oliver O. Howard, head of the Freedmen's Bureau, used the phrase "wholesome compulsion" in describing the policy of forcing blacks to sign exploitive labor contracts. A leading southern magazine complained in 1866 that black women now expected their husbands "to support them in idleness." It would never have made such a comment about white housewives. Moreover, studies show that emancipated blacks earned almost 30 percent more than the value of the subsistence provided by their former masters.

The family life of ex-slaves was changed in other ways. Male authority increased when husbands became true heads of families. (Under slavery the ultimate responsibility for providing for women and children was the master's.) When blacks became citizens, the men acquired rights and powers denied to all women, such as the right to hold public office and serve on juries. Similarly, black women became more like white women, devoting themselves to separate "spheres" where their lives revolved around housekeeping and child rearing.

SHARECROPPING AND THE CROP-LIEN SYSTEM

Before the passage of the Reconstruction acts, plantation owners tried to farm their land with gang labor, the same system as before, only now paying wages to the former slaves. This method did not work well for two entirely different reasons. Money was scarce, and capital, never adequate even before the collapse of the Confederacy, accumulated slowly. Interest rates were extremely high. This situation made it difficult for landowners to pay their laborers in cash. More important, blacks did not like working for wages because it kept them under the direction of whites and thus reminded them of slavery. They wanted to be independent, to manage not merely their free time but their entire lives for themselves. "The colored people of this vicinity are so proud," a white Virginian noted, "that they think it is somewhat a second slavery to hire by the month or year." Since the voluntary withdrawal of so much black labor from the workforce had produced a shortage, the blacks had their way. "I had to yield," another white planter admitted, "or lose my labor."

Quite swiftly, a new agricultural system known as sharecropping emerged. Instead of cultivating the land by gang labor as in antebellum times, planters broke up their estates into small units and established on each a black family. The planter provided housing, agricultural implements, draft animals, seed, and

▲ After the Civil War, most blacks worked as sharecroppers on land owned by whites. In this photograph, black sharecroppers pick cotton, a major cash crop of the South with the owner of the land getting a share of the crop (crop-lien). The crop-lien system injured everyone. Diversified farming would have reduced the farmers' need for cash, preserved the fertility of the soil, and, by placing a premium on imagination and shrewdness, aided the best of them to rise in the world. Because the price for cotton remained low, sharecroppers often fell into debt and were tied to the land almost as tightly as under slavery.

other supplies, and the family provided labor. The crop was divided between them, usually on a fifty-fifty basis. If the landlord supplied only land and housing, the laborer got a larger share. This was called share tenancy.

Sharecropping gave blacks the day-to-day control of their lives that they craved and the hope of earning enough to buy a small farm. Consider the example of Daniel Trotter, a Louisiana black who worked for several years as a farm laborer. He then spent four years as a sharecropper on land owned by a man named Clurman, then two more on the farm of one J. H. C. Cosgrove, with whom he split the crop fifty-fifty. He was then able to rent land from Cosgrove and a series of other white farmers. While renting, his wife earned money by sewing and by raising chickens, whose eggs she sold "one or two dozen at a time." The Trotters also raised a few pigs for the market, and

DOCUMENT

A Sharecrop Contract

Daniel, evidently possessing mechanical skills, made some "cash money" repairing farm machinery, clocks, and guns. After 14 years the Trotters had saved $175 in greenbacks and $33 in silver, enough to buy what Trotter proudly described as a "plantation." But relatively few blacks possessed the Trotters' energy, determination, and good luck. As late as 1880 blacks owned less than 10 percent of the agricultural land in the South, although they made up more than half of the region's farm population. Mississippi actually prohibited the purchase of farmland by blacks.

Many white farmers in the South were also trapped by the sharecropping system and by white efforts to keep blacks in a subordinate position. New fencing laws kept them from grazing livestock on undeveloped land, a practice common before the Civil War. But the main cause of southern rural poverty for whites as well as for blacks was the lack of enough capital to finance the sharecropping system. Like their colonial ancestors, the landowners had to borrow against October's harvest to pay for April's seed. Thus the crop-lien system developed.

Under the crop-lien system, both landowner and sharecropper depended on credit supplied by local bankers, merchants, and storekeepers for everything from seed, tools, and fertilizer to overalls, coffee, and salt. Crossroads stores proliferated, and a new class of small merchants appeared. The prices of goods sold on credit were high, adding to the burden borne by the rural population. The small southern merchants were almost equally victimized by the system, for they also lacked capital, bought goods on credit, and had to pay high interest rates.

Five Generations of a Slave Family

Seen in broad perspective, the situation is not difficult to understand. The South, drained of every resource by the war, was competing for funds with the North and West, both vigorous and expanding and therefore voracious consumers of capital. Reconstruction, in the literal sense of the word, was accomplished chiefly at the expense of the standard of living of the producing classes. The crop-lien system and the small storekeeper were only agents of an economic process dictated by national, perhaps even worldwide, conditions.

Compared with the rest of the country, progress was slow. Just before the Civil War cotton harvests averaged about 4 million bales. During the conflict, output fell to about half a million, and the former Confederate states did not enjoy a 4-million-bale year again until 1870. In contrast, national wheat production in 1859 was 175 million bushels and in 1878, 449 million. About 7000 miles of railroad were built in the South between 1865 and 1879; in the rest of the nation nearly 45,000 miles of track were laid.

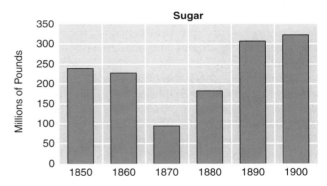

▲ **Southern Agriculture, 1850–1900**
Cotton production recovered to its prewar level by 1880, but tobacco and sugar production lagged. Not until 1900 did tobacco growers have a better year than they had in 1860. The years following 1870 saw a general downward trend in wholesale prices for farm commodities. (Statistics are for the 11 states of the Confederacy.)

But in the late 1870s, cotton production revived. It soon regained, and thereafter long retained, its title as "king" of the southern economy. This was true in large measure because of the crop-lien system.

The South made important gains in manufacturing after the war. The tobacco industry, stimulated by the sudden popularity of the cigarette, expanded rapidly. Virginia and North Carolina tobacco towns like Richmond, Lynchburg, and Durham flourished. The exploitation of the coal and iron deposits of northeastern Alabama in the early 1870s made a boomtown of Birmingham. The manufacture of cotton cloth increased, productive capacity nearly doubling between 1865 and 1880. Yet the mills of Massachusetts alone had eight times the capacity of the entire South in 1880. Despite the increases, the South's share of the national output of manufactured goods declined sharply during the Reconstruction era.

THE WHITE BACKLASH

Radical southern governments could sustain themselves only as long as they had the support of a significant proportion of the white population, for except in South Carolina and Louisiana, the blacks were not numerous enough to win elections alone. The key to survival lay in the hands of the wealthy merchants and planters, mostly former Whigs. People of this sort had nothing to fear from black economic competition. Taking a broad view, they could see that improving the lot of the former slaves would benefit all classes.

Southern white Republicans used the Union League of America, a patriotic club founded during the war, to control the black vote. Employing secret rituals, exotic symbols, and other paraphernalia calculated to impress unsophisticated people, they enrolled the freedmen in droves and marched them to the polls en masse.

Powerless to check the League by open methods, dissident Southerners established a number of secret terrorist societies, bearing such names as the Ku Klux Klan, the Knights of the White Camelia, and the Pale Faces. The most notorious of these organizations was the Klan, which originated in Tennessee in 1866. At first it was purely a social club, but by 1868 it had been taken over by vigilante types dedicated to driving blacks out of politics, and it was spreading rapidly across the South. Sheet-clad nightriders roamed the countryside, frightening the impressionable and chastising the defiant. Klansmen, using a weird mumbo jumbo and claiming to be the ghosts of Confederate soldiers, spread horrendous rumors and published broadsides designed to persuade the freedmen that it was unhealthy for them to participate in politics:

> *Niggers and Leaguers, get out of the way,*
> *We're born of the night and we vanish by day.*
> *No rations have we, but the flesh of man—*
> *And love niggers best—the Ku Klux Klan;*
> *We catch 'em alive and roast 'em whole,*
> *Then hand 'em around with a sharpened pole.*
> *Whole Leagues have been eaten, not leaving a man,*
> *And went away hungry—the Ku Klux Klan. . . .*

When intimidation failed, the Klansmen resorted to force. After being whipped by one group in Ten-

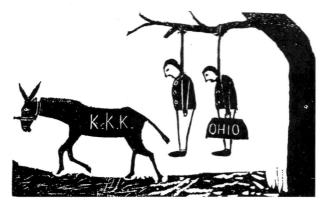

▲ A graphic warning by the Alabama Klan "of the fate in store for" scalawags and carpetbaggers, "those great pests of Southern society," from the *Tuscaloosa Independent Monitor*, September 1, 1868.

nessee, a recently elected justice of the peace reported: "They said they had nothing particular against me . . . but they did not intend any nigger to hold office." In hundreds of cases the KKK murdered their opponents, often in the most gruesome manner.

DOCUMENT

Accounts from Victims of the Ku Klux Klan

Congress struck at the Klan with three Force Acts (1870–1871), which placed elections under federal jurisdiction and imposed fines and prison sentences on persons convicted of interfering with any citizen's exercise of the franchise. Troops were dispatched to areas where the Klan was strong, and by 1872 the federal authorities had arrested enough Klansmen to break up the organization.

Nevertheless the Klan contributed substantially to the destruction of Radical regimes in the South. Its depredations weakened the will of white Republicans (few of whom really believed in racial equality), and it intimidated many blacks, who gave up trying to exercise their rights. The fact that the army had to be called in to suppress it was a glaring illustration of the weakness of the Reconstruction governments.

Gradually it became respectable to intimidate black voters. Beginning in Mississippi in 1874, terrorism spread through the South. Instead of hiding behind masks and operating in the dark, these terrorists donned red shirts, organized into military companies, and paraded openly. Mississippi redshirts seized militant blacks and whipped them publicly. Killings were frequent. When blacks dared to fight back, heavily armed whites put them to rout. In other states similar results followed.

Terrorism fed on fear, fear on terrorism. White violence led to fear of black retaliation and thus to even more brutal attacks. The slightest sign of resistance came to be seen as the beginning of race war, and when the blacks suffered indignities and persecutions in silence, the awareness of how much they must resent the mistreatment made them appear more dangerous still. Thus self-hatred was displaced, guilt suppressed, aggression justified as self-defense, individual conscience submerged in the animality of the mob.

Before long the blacks learned to stay home on election day. One by one, "Conservative" parties—Democratic in national affairs—took over southern state governments. Intimidation was only a partial explanation of this development. The increasing solidarity of whites, northern and southern, was equally significant.

The North had subjected the South to control from Washington while preserving state sovereignty in the North itself. In the long run this discrimination proved unworkable. Many Northerners had supported the Radical policy only out of irritation with President Johnson. After his retirement their enthusiasm waned. The war was fading into the past and with it the worst of the anger it had generated.

Northern voters could still be stirred by references to the sacrifices Republicans had made to save the Union and by reminders that the Democratic party was the organization of rebels, Copperheads, and the Ku Klux Klan. "If the Devil himself were at the helm of the ship of state," wrote the novelist Lydia Maria Child in 1872, "my conscience would not allow me to aid in removing him to make room for the Democratic party." Yet emotional appeals could not convince Northerners that it was still necessary to maintain a large army in the South. In 1869 the occupying forces were down to 11,000 men. After Klan disruption and intimidation had made a farce of the 1874 elections in Mississippi, Governor Ames appealed to Washington for help. President Grant's attorney general, Edwards Pierrepont, refused to act. "The whole public are tired out with these autumnal outbreaks in the South," he told Ames. "Preserve the peace by the forces of your own state."

Nationalism was reasserting itself. Had not Washington and Jefferson been Virginians? Was not Andrew Jackson Carolina-born? Since most Northerners had little real love or respect for blacks, their interest in racial equality flagged once they felt reasonably certain that blacks would not be re-enslaved if left to their own devices in the South.

Another, much subtler force was also at work. The prewar Republican party had stressed the common interest of workers, manufacturers, and farmers in a free and mobile society, a land of equal opportunity where all could work in harmony. Southern whites had insisted that laborers must be disciplined if large enterprises were to be run efficiently. By the 1870s, as large industrial enterprises developed in the northern states, the thinking of business leaders changed—the southern argument began to make sense to them, and they became more sympathetic to the southern demand for more control over "their" labor force.

GRANT AS PRESIDENT

Other matters occupied the attention of northern voters. The expansion of industry and the rapid development of the West, stimulated by a new wave of railroad building, loomed more important to many than the fortunes of the former slaves. Beginning in 1873, when a stock market panic struck at public confidence, economic difficulties plagued the country for nearly a decade. Heated controversies arose over tariff policy, with western agricultural interests seeking to force reductions from the high levels established during the war, and over the handling of the wartime greenback paper money, with debtor groups and many manufacturers favoring further expansion of the supply of dollars and conservative merchants and bankers arguing for retiring the greenbacks in order to return to a "sound" currency.

More damaging to the Republicans was the failure of Ulysses S. Grant to live up to expectations as president. Qualities that had made Grant a fine military leader for a democracy—his dislike of political maneuvering and his simple belief that the popular will could best be observed in the actions of Congress—made him a poor chief executive. When Congress failed to act on his suggestion that the quality of the civil service needed improvement, he announced meekly that if Congress did nothing, he would assume the country did not want anything done. Grant was honest, but his honesty was of the naive type that made him the dupe of unscrupulous friends and schemers.

His most serious weakness as president was his failure to deal effectively with economic and social problems, but the one that injured him and the Republicans most was his inability to cope with government corruption. The worst of the scandals—such as the Whiskey Ring affair, which implicated Grant's private secretary, Orville E. Babcock, and cost the government millions in tax revenue, and the corruption of Secretary of War William W. Belknap in the management of Indian affairs—did not become public knowledge during Grant's first term. However, in 1872 Republican reformers, alarmed by rumors of corruption and disappointed by Grant's failure to press for civil service reform, organized the Liberal Republican party and nominated Horace Greeley, the able but eccentric editor of the *New York Tribune,* for president.

The Liberal Republicans were mostly well-educated, socially prominent types—editors, college presidents, economists, along with a sprinkling of businessmen and politicians. Their liberalism was of

▲ This cartoon—"A Strong Man at the Head of Government"—pokes fun at Grant, whose presidency was weighed down with scandal. Grant did not cause the corruption, nor did he participate in the remotest way in the rush to "fatten at the public trough," as the reformers of the day might have put it. But he did nothing to prevent the scandals that disgraced his administration. Out of a misplaced belief in the sanctity of friendship, he protected some of the worst culprits and allowed calculating tricksters to use his good name and the prestige of his office to advance their own interests at the country's expense. "Mistakes have been made, as all can see and I admit," Grant conceded in his final report to Congress.

the laissez-faire variety; they were for low tariffs and sound money, and against what they called "class legislation," meaning measures benefiting particular groups, whether labor unions or railroad companies or farm organizations. Nearly all had supported Reconstruction at the start, but by the early 1870s most were including southern blacks among the special interests that ought to be left to their own devices. Their observation of urban corruption and of unrestricted immigration led them to disparage universal suffrage, which, one of them said, "can only mean in plain English the government of ignorance and vice."

The Democrats also nominated Greeley in 1872, although he had devoted his political life to flailing the Democratic party in the *Tribune*. That surrender to expediency, together with Greeley's temperamental unsuitability for the presidency, made the campaign a fiasco for the reformers. Grant triumphed easily, with a popular majority of nearly 800,000.

Nevertheless, the defection of the Liberal Republicans hurt the Republican party in Congress. In the 1874 elections, no longer hampered as in the presidential contest by Greeley's notoriety and Grant's fame, the Democrats carried the House of Representatives. It was clear that the days of military rule in the South were ending. By the end of 1875 only three southern states—South Carolina, Florida, and Louisiana—were still under Republican control.

The Republican party in the South was "dead as a doornail," a reporter noted. He reflected the opinion of thousands when he added: "We ought to have a sound sensible republican . . . for the next President as a measure of safety; but only on the condition of absolute noninterference in Southern local affairs, for which there is no further need or excuse."

THE DISPUTED ELECTION OF 1876

Against this background the presidential election of 1876 took place. Since corruption in government was the most widely discussed issue, the Republicans passed over their most attractive political personality, the dynamic James G. Blaine, Speaker of the House of Representatives, who had been connected with some chicanery involving railroad securities. Instead they nominated Governor Rutherford B. Hayes of Ohio, a former general with an untarnished reputation. The Democrats picked Governor Samuel J. Tilden of New York, a wealthy lawyer who had attracted national attention for his part in breaking up the Tweed Ring in New York City.

In November early returns indicated that Tilden had carried New York, New Jersey, Connecticut, Indiana, and all the southern states, including Louisiana, South Carolina, and Florida, where Republican regimes were still in control. This seemed to give him 203 electoral votes to Hayes's 165, and a popular plurality in the neighborhood of 250,000 out of more than 8 million votes cast. However, Republican leaders had anticipated the possible loss of Florida, South Carolina, and Louisiana and were prepared to use their control of the election machinery in those states to throw out sufficient Democratic ballots to alter the results if doing so would change the national outcome. Realizing that the electoral votes of those states were exactly enough to elect their man, they telegraphed their henchmen on the scene, ordering them to go into action. The local Republicans then invalidated Democratic ballots in wholesale lots and filed returns showing Hayes the winner. Naturally the local Democrats protested vigorously and filed their own returns.

The Constitution provides (Article II, Section 1) that presidential electors must meet in their respective states to vote and forward the results to "the Seat of the Government." There, it adds, "the President of the Senate shall, in the Presence of the Senate and House of Representatives, open all the Certificates, and the Votes shall then be counted." But who was to do the counting? The House was Democratic, the Senate Republican; neither would agree to allow the other to do the job. On January 29, 1877, scarcely a month before inauguration day, Congress created an electoral commission to decide the disputed cases. The commission consisted of five senators (three Republicans and two Democrats), five representatives (three Democrats and two Republicans), and five justices of the Supreme Court (two Democrats, two Republicans, and one "independent" judge, David Davis). Since it was a foregone conclusion that the others would vote for their party no matter what the evidence, Davis would presumably swing the balance in the interest of fairness.

But before the commission met, the Illinois legislature elected Davis senator! He had to resign from the Court and the commission. Since independents were rare even on the Supreme Court, no neutral was available to replace him. The vacancy went to Associate Justice Joseph P. Bradley of New Jersey, a Republican.

Evidence presented before the commission revealed a disgraceful picture of election shenanigans. On the one hand, in all three disputed states Democrats had clearly cast a majority of the votes; on the other, it was unquestionable that many blacks had been forcibly prevented from voting.

In truth, both sides were shamefully corrupt. The governor of Louisiana was reported willing to sell his state's electoral votes for $200,000. The Florida election board was supposed to have offered itself to Tilden for the same price. "That seems to be the standard figure," Tilden remarked ruefully.

Most modern authorities take the view that in a fair election the Republicans would have carried South Carolina and Louisiana but that Florida would have gone to Tilden, giving him the election, 188 electoral votes to 181. In the last analysis, this opinion has been arrived at simply by counting white and black noses: Blacks were in the majority in South Carolina and Louisiana. Amid the tension and confusion of early 1877, however, even a Solomon would have been hard-pressed to judge rightly amid the rumors, lies, and contradictory statements, and the electoral commission was not composed of Solomons. The Democrats had some hopes that Justice Bradley would be sympathetic to their case, for he was known to be opposed to harsh

Reconstruction policies. On the eve of the commission's decision in the Florida controversy, he was apparently ready to vote in favor of Tilden. But the Republicans subjected him to tremendous political pressure. When he read his opinion on February 8, it was for Hayes. Thus, by a vote of 8 to 7, the commission awarded Florida's electoral votes to the Republicans.

The rest of the proceedings was routine. The commission assigned all the disputed electoral votes (including one in Oregon where the Democratic governor had seized on a technicality to replace a single Republican elector with a Democrat) to Hayes.

Democratic institutions, shaken by the South's refusal to go along with the majority in 1860 and by the suppression of civil rights during the rebellion, and further weakened by military intervention and the intimidation of blacks in the South during Reconstruction, seemed now a farce. According to Tilden's campaign manager, angry Democrats in 15 states, chiefly war veterans, were readying themselves to march on Washington to force the inauguration of Tilden. Tempers flared in Congress, where some spoke ominously of a filibuster that would prevent the recording of the electoral vote and leave the country, on March 4, with no president at all.

THE COMPROMISE OF 1877

Forces for compromise had been at work behind the scenes in Washington for some time. Although northern Democrats threatened to fight to the last

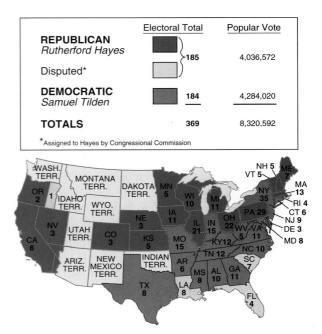

		Electoral Total	Popular Vote
REPUBLICAN *Rutherford Hayes*			4,036,572
Disputed*		185	
DEMOCRATIC *Samuel Tilden*		184	4,284,020
TOTALS		369	8,320,592

*Assigned to Hayes by Congressional Commission

▲ **The Compromise of 1877**

ditch, many southern Democrats were willing to accept Hayes if he would promise to remove the troops and allow the southern states to manage their internal affairs by themselves. Ex-Whig planters and merchants who had reluctantly abandoned the carpetbag governments and who sympathized with Republican economic policies hoped that by supporting Hayes they might contribute to the restoration of the two-party system that had been destroyed in the South during the 1850s. Ohio Congressman James A. Garfield urged Hayes to find "some discreet way" of showing these Southerners that he favored "internal improvements." Hayes replied: "Your views are so nearly the same as mine that I need not say a word."

Tradition has it that a great compromise between the sections was worked out during a dramatic meeting at the Wormley Hotel[2] in Washington on February 26. Actually the negotiations were drawn out and informal, and the Wormley conference was but one of many. With the tacit support of many Democrats, the electoral vote was counted by the president of the Senate on March 2, and Hayes was declared elected, 185 votes to 184.

---

[2]Ironically, the hotel was owned by James Wormley, reputedly the wealthiest black in Washington.

Like all compromises, this agreement was not entirely satisfactory; like most, it was not honored in every detail. Hayes recalled the last troops from South Carolina and Louisiana in April. He appointed a former Confederate general, David M. Key of Tennessee, postmaster general and delegated to him the congenial task of finding Southerners willing to serve their country as officials of a Republican administration. But the alliance of ex-Whigs and northern Republicans did not flourish; the South remained solidly Democratic. The major significance of the compromise, one of the great intersectional political accommodations of American history, was that it ended Reconstruction and inaugurated a new political order in the South. More than the Constitutional amendments and federal statutes, this new regime would shape the destinies of the four million freedmen.

For most, this future was to be bleak. Forgotten in the North, manipulated and then callously rejected by the South, rebuffed by the Supreme Court, voiceless in national affairs, they and their descendants were condemned in the interests of sectional harmony to lives of poverty, indignity, and little hope. Meanwhile, the rest of the United States continued its golden march toward wealth and power.

MILESTONES

1863	Lincoln announces "Ten Percent Plan" for Reconstruction
1865	Federal government sets up Freedmen's Bureau to ease transition from slavery to freedom
	General Lee surrenders at Appomattox Court House
	Abraham Lincoln is assassinated; Andrew Johnson becomes president
	Johnson issues amnesty proclamation
	States ratify Thirteenth Amendment abolishing slavery
1865–1866	Southern states enact Black Codes
1866	Civil Rights Act passes over Johnson's veto
	Johnson campaigns for his Reconstruction policy
1867	First Reconstruction Act puts former Confederacy under military rule
	Tenure of Office Act protects Senate appointees
1868	House of Representatives impeaches Johnson
1868	Fourth Reconstruction Act requires a majority of Southern voters to ratify state constitutions
	Senate acquits Johnson
	States ratify Fourteenth Amendment extending rights to freed slaves
	Ulysses S. Grant is elected president
	Ku Klux Klan uses intimidation and force throughout South
1870	States ratify Fifteenth Amendment granting black suffrage
1870–1871	Force (Ku Klux Klan) Act destroys Klan
1872	Liberal Republican party nominates Horace Greeley for president
	Grant is reelected president
1876	Rutherford B. Hayes runs against Samuel Tilden in disputed presidential election
1877	Electoral Commission awards disputed votes to Rutherford B. Hayes who becomes president
	Hayes agrees to Compromise of 1877 ending Reconstruction

SUPPLEMENTARY READING

Lincoln's ideas about Reconstruction are analyzed in William C. Harris, *With Charity for All* (1997) and in many of the Lincoln volumes mentioned in earlier chapters. Hans Trefousse, *Andrew Johnson: A Biography* (1989) is a balanced account. See also Brooks D. Simpson, *The Reconstruction Presidents* (2001), Eric L. McKitrick, *Andrew Johnson and Reconstruction* (1960), and M. L. Benedict, *The Impeachment and Trial of Andrew Johnson* (1973).

A number of biographies provide information helpful in understanding the Radicals. The most important are Hans Trefousse, *Thaddeus Stevens* (1997), and David Donald, *Charles Sumner and the Rights of Man* (1970). J. M. McPherson, *The Struggle for Equality: Abolitionists and the Negro in the Civil War and Reconstruction* (1964) is also valuable. On the Fourteenth Amendment, see W. E. Nelson, *The Fourteenth Amendment* (1988); on the Fifteenth Amendment, see William Gillette, *The Right to Vote* (1965).

Conditions in the South during Reconstruction are discussed in Edward Ayers, *The Promise of the New South* (1992). The Freedmen's Bureau is examined in Paul Cimbala, *Under the Guardianship of the Nation* (1997). See also R. H. Abbott, *The Republican Party and the South* (1986), Michael Perman, *Reunion Without Compromise* (1973), H. N. Rabinowitz, *Race Relations in the Urban South* (1978), J. L. Roark, *Masters Without Slaves* (1977), and Leon Litwack, *Been in the Storm Too Long* (1979). For recent general studies, see Don E. Fehrenbacher, *The Slaveholding Republic* (2001), and Pamela Brandwein, *Reconstructing Reconstruction* (1999). Daniel Stowell's *Rebuilding Zion* (1998) explores the religious dimensions of Reconstruction.

Of state studies see, for Virginia, Jane E. Dailey, *Before Jim Crow* (2000); for South Carolina, Julie Saville, *The Work of Reconstruction* (1994), W. L. Rose, *Rehearsal for Reconstruction* (1964), Thomas Holt, *Black over White: Negro Political Leadership in South Carolina* (1977); for Texas, Randolph B. Campbell, *Grass-Roots Reconstruction in Texas* (1997). Much recent work on the Ku Klux Klan similarly focuses on particular states: see Lou F. Williams, *The Great South Carolina Ku Klux Klan Trials* (1996), Glenn Feldman, *Politics, Society and the Klan in Alabama* (1999), and Noel Fisher, *War at Every Door* (1997), which examines East Tennessee.

On the economic and social effects of Reconstruction, see G. D. Jaynes, *Branches Without Roots: Genesis of the Black Working Class* (1986), R. L. Ransom and Richard Sutch, *One Kind of Freedom: The Economic Consequences of Emancipation* (1977), Robert Higgs, *Competition and Coercion* (1977), and C. F. Oubre, *Forty Acres and a Mule* (1978). The ambiguities of dependence and independence as they relate to racial and gender issues are explored in Laura F. Edwards, *Gendered Strife and Confusion* (1997), and Amy Dru Stanley, *From Bondage to Contract* (1998).

On Grant's presidency, see Jean Edwards Smith, *Grant* (2001), Geoffrey Perret, *Ulysses S. Grant* (1997), and W. S. McFeely, *Grant* (1981). On the Republican reform movement, see J. G. Sproat, *"The Best Men": Liberal Reformers in the Gilded Age* (1968). For the disputed election of 1876 and the compromise following it, consult C. V. Woodward, *Reunion and Reaction* (1951), and William Gillette, *Retreat from Reconstruction* (1980).

David W. Blight, *Race and Reunion* (2001) considers the Civil War and Reconstruction in a deeper historical perspective.

SUGGESTED WEBSITES

The Impeachment of Andrew Johnson
 http://www.impeach-andrewjohnson.com/
This HarpWeek site about the impeachment includes images and text from the Reconstruction period.

Diary and Letters of Rutherford B. Hayes
 http://www.ohiohistory.org/onlinedoc/hayes/index.cfm
The Rutherford B. Hayes Presidential Center in Fremont, Ohio, maintains this searchable database of Hayes's writings.

Rutherford B. Hayes
 http://www.ipl.org/ref/POTUS/rbhayes.html
This site contains information relating to Hayes and his presidency.

Images of African Americans from the Nineteenth Century
 http://digital.nypl.org/schomburg/images_aa19/
The New York Public Library–Schomburg Center for Research in Black Culture site contains numerous visuals.

Freedman and Southern Society Project (University of Maryland, College Park)
 http://www.inform.umd.edu/ARHU/Depts/History/Freedman/home.html
This site contains a chronology and sample documents from several collections or primary sources about emancipation and freedom in the 1860s.

Appendix

The Declaration of Independence

The Articles of Confederation

The Constitution of the United States of America

Amendments to the Constitution

Presidential Election Maps, 1789–2004

For additional reference material, go to
www.ablongman.com/carnes12e/appendix

The online appendix includes the following:

The Declaration of Independence

The Articles of Confederation

The Constitution of the United States of America

Amendments to the Constitution

Presidential Elections

Vice Presidents and Cabinet Members by Administration

Supreme Court Justices

Presidents, Congresses, and Chief Justices, 1789–2001

Territorial Expansion of the United States (map)

Admission of States of the Union

U.S. Population, 1790–2000

Ten Largest Cities by Population, 1700–1990

Birthrate, 1820–2000 (chart)

Death Rate, 1900–2000 (chart)

Life Expectancy, 1900–2000 (chart)

Urban/Rural Population, 1750–1900 (chart)

Women in the Labor Force, 1890–1990 (chart)

United States Physical Features (map)

United States Native Vegetation (map)

Ancient Native American Communities (map)

Native American Peoples, c. 1500 (map)

Present Day United States (map)

The Declaration of Independence

In Congress, July 4, 1776

The Unanimous Declaration of the Thirteen United States of America,

When, in the course of human events, it becomes necessary for one people to dissolve the political bonds which have connected them with another, and to assume, among the powers of the earth, the separate and equal station to which the laws of nature and of nature's God entitle them, a decent respect to the opinions of mankind requires that they should declare the causes which impel them to the separation.

We hold these truths to be self-evident: That all men are created equal; that they are endowed by their Creator with certain unalienable rights; that among these are life, liberty, and the pursuit of happiness; that, to secure these rights, governments are instituted among men, deriving their just powers from the consent of the governed; that whenever any form of government becomes destructive of these ends, it is the right of the people to alter or to abolish it, and to institute new government, laying its foundation on such principles, and organizing its powers in such form, as to them shall seem most likely to effect their safety and happiness. Prudence, indeed, will dictate that governments long established should not be changed for light and transient causes; and accordingly all experience hath shown that mankind are more disposed to suffer, while evils are sufferable, than to right themselves by abolishing the forms to which they are accustomed. But when a long train of abuses and usurpations, pursuing invariably the same object, evinces a design to reduce them under absolute despotism, it is their right, it is their duty, to throw off such government, and to provide new guards for their future security. Such has been the patient sufferance of these colonies; and such is now the necessity which constrains them to alter their former systems of government. The history of the present King of Great Britain is a history of repeated injuries and usurpations, all having in direct object the establishment of an absolute tyranny over these states. To prove this, let facts be submitted to a candid world.

He has refused his assent to laws, the most wholesome and necessary for the public good.

He has forbidden his governors to pass laws of immediate and pressing importance, unless suspended in their operation till his assent should be obtained; and, when so suspended, he has utterly neglected to attend to them.

He has refused to pass other laws for the accommodation of large districts of people, unless those people would relinquish the right of representation in the legislature, a right inestimable to them, and formidable to tyrants only.

He has called together legislative bodies at places unusual, uncomfortable, and distant from the depository of their public records, for the sole purpose of fatiguing them into compliance with his measures.

He has dissolved representative houses repeatedly, for opposing, with manly firmness, his invasions on the rights of the people.

He has refused for a long time, after such dissolutions, to cause others to be elected; whereby the legislative powers, incapable of annihilation, have returned to the people at large for their exercise; the state remaining, in the mean time, exposed to all the dangers of invasions from without and convulsions within.

He has endeavored to prevent the population of these states; for that purpose obstructing the laws for naturalization of foreigners; refusing to pass others to encourage their migration hither, and raising the conditions of new appropriations of lands.

He has obstructed the administration of justice, by refusing his assent to laws for establishing judiciary powers.

He has made judges dependent on his will alone, for the tenure of their offices, and the amount and payment of their salaries.

He has erected a multitude of new offices, and sent hither swarms of officers to harass our people and eat out their substance.

He has kept among us, in times of peace, standing armies, without the consent of our legislatures.

He has affected to render the military independent of, and superior to, the civil power.

He has combined with others to subject us to a jurisdiction foreign to our constitution, and unacknowledged by our laws, giving his assent to their acts of pretended legislation:

For quartering large bodies of armed troops among us;

For protecting them, by a mock trial, from punishment for any murder which they should commit on the inhabitants of these states;

For cutting off our trade with all parts of the world;

For imposing taxes on us without our consent;

For depriving us, in many cases, of the benefits of trial by jury;

For transporting us beyond seas, to be tried for pretended offenses;

For abolishing the free system of English laws in a neighboring province, establishing therein an arbitrary government, and enlarging its boundaries, so as to render it at once an example and fit instrument for introducing the same absolute rule into these colonies;

For taking away our charters, abolishing our most valuable laws, and altering fundamentally the forms of our governments;

For suspending our own legislatures, and declaring themselves invested with power to legislate for us in all cases whatsoever.

He has abdicated government here, by declaring us out of his protection and waging war against us.

He has plundered our seas, ravaged our coasts, burned our towns, and destroyed the lives of our people.

He is at this time transporting large armies of foreign mercenaries to complete the works of death, desolation, and tyranny already begun with circumstances of cruelty and perfidy scarcely paralleled in the most barbarous ages, and totally unworthy the head of a civilized nation.

He has constrained our fellow-citizens, taken captive on the high seas, to bear arms against their country, to become the executioners of their friends and brethren, or to fall themselves by their hands.

He has excited domestic insurrection among us, and has endeavored to bring on the inhabitants of our frontiers the merciless Indian savages, whose known rule of warfare is an undistinguished destruction of all ages, sexes, and conditions.

In every stage of these oppressions we have petitioned for redress in the most humble terms; our repeated petitions have been answered only by repeated injury. A prince, whose character is thus marked by every act which may define a tyrant, is unfit to be the ruler of a free people.

Nor have we been wanting in our attentions to our British brethren. We have warned them, from time to time, of attempts by their legislature to extend an unwarrantable jurisdiction over us. We have reminded them of the circumstances of our emigration and settlement here. We have appealed to their native justice and magnanimity; and we have conjured them, by the ties of our common kindred, to disavow these usurpations, which would inevitably interrupt our connections and correspondence. They, too, have been deaf to the voice of justice and of consanguinity. We must, therefore, acquiesce in the necessity which denounces our separation, and hold them, as we hold the rest of mankind, enemies in war, in peace friends.

We, therefore, the representatives of the United States of America, in General Congress assembled, appealing to the Supreme Judge of the world for the rectitude of our intentions, do, in the name and by the authority of the good people of these colonies, solemnly publish and declare, that these United Colonies are, and of right ought to be, FREE AND INDEPENDENT STATES; that they are absolved from all allegiance to the British crown, and that all political connection between them and the state of Great Britain is, and ought to be, totally dissolved; and that, as free and independent states, they have full power to levy war, conclude peace, contract alliances, establish commerce, and do all other acts and things which independent states may of right do. And for the support of this declaration, with a firm reliance on the protection of Divine Providence, we mutually pledge to each other our lives, our fortunes, and our sacred honor.

JOHN HANCOCK

New Hampshire
Josiah Bartlett
William Whipple
Matthew Thornton

Massachusetts
John Adams
Samuel Adams
Robert Treat Paine
Elbridge Gerry

New York
William Floyd
Philip Livingston
Francis Lewis
Lewis Morris

Rhode Island
Stephen Hopkins
William Ellery

New Jersey
Richard Stockton
John Witherspoon
Francis Hopkinson
John Hart
Abraham Clark

Pennsylvania
Robert Morris
Benjamin Rush
Benjamin Franklin
John Morton
George Clymer
James Smith
George Taylor
James Wilson
George Ross

Delaware
Caeser Rodney
George Read
Thomas McKean

Maryland
Samuel Chase
William Paca
Thomas Stone
Charles Carroll
of Carrollton

North Carolina
William Hooper
Joseph Hewes
John Penn

Virginia
George Wythe
Richard Henry Lee
Thomas Jefferson
Benjamin Harrison
Thomas Nelson, Jr.
Francis Lightfoot Lee
Carter Braxton

South Carolina
Edward Rutledge
Thomas Heyward, Jr.
Thomas Lynch, Jr.
Arthur Middleton

Connecticut
Roger Sherman
Samuel Huntington
William Williams
Oliver Wolcott

Georgia
Button Gwinnett
Lyman Hall
George Walton

The Articles of Confederation

Between the States of New Hampshire, Massachusetts Bay, Rhode Island and Providence Plantations, Connecticut, New York, New Jersey, Pennsylvania, Delaware, Maryland, Virginia, North Carolina, South Carolina, Georgia

Article 1

The stile of this confederacy shall be "The United States of America."

Article 2

Each State retains its sovereignty, freedom and independence, and every power, jurisdiction, and right, which is not by this confederation expressly delegated to the United States, in Congress assembled.

Article 3

The said states hereby severally enter into a firm league of friendship with each other for their common defence, the security of their liberties and their mutual and general welfare; binding themselves to assist each other against all force offered to, or attacks made upon them, or any of them, on account of religion, sovereignty, trade, or any other pretence whatever.

Article 4

The better to secure and perpetuate mutual friendship and intercourse among the people of the different states in this union, the free inhabitants of each of these states, paupers, vagabonds, and fugitives from justice excepted, shall be entitled to all privileges and immunities of free citizens in the several states; and the people of each State shall have free ingress and regress to and from any other State, and shall enjoy therein all the privileges of trade and commerce, subject to the same duties, impositions, and restrictions, as the inhabitants thereof respectively; provided, that such restrictions shall not extend so far as to prevent the removal of property, imported into any State, to any other State of which the owner is an inhabitant; provided also, that no imposition, duties, or restriction, shall be laid by any State on the property of the United States, or either of them.

If any person guilty of, or charged with treason, felony, or other high misdemeanor in any State, shall flee from justice and be found in any of the United States, he shall, upon demand of the governor or executive power of the State from which he fled, be delivered up and removed to the State having jurisdiction of his offence.

Full faith and credit shall be given in each of these states to the records, acts, and judicial proceedings of the courts and magistrates of every other State.

Article 5

For the more convenient management of the general interests of the United States, delegates shall be annually appointed, in such manner as the legislature of each State shall direct, to meet in Congress, on the 1st Monday in November in every year, with a power reserved to each State to recall its delegates, or any of them, at any time within the year, and to send others in their stead for the remainder of the year.

No State shall be represented in Congress by less than two, nor by more than seven members; and no person shall be capable of being a delegate for more than three years in any term of six years; nor shall any person, being a delegate, be capable of holding any office under the United States, for which he, or any other for his benefit, receives any salary, fees, or emolument of any kind.

Each State shall maintain its own delegates in a meeting of the states, and while they act as members of the committee of the states.

In determining questions in the United States, in Congress assembled, each State shall have one vote.

Freedom of speech and debate in Congress shall not be impeached or questioned in any court or place out of Congress: and the members of Congress shall be protected in their persons from arrests and imprisonments, during the time of their going to and from, and attendance on Congress, except for treason, felony, or breach of the peace.

Article 6

No State, without the consent of the United States, in Congress assembled, shall send any embassy to, or receive any embassy from, or enter into any conference, agreement, alliance, or treaty with any king, prince, or state; nor shall any person, holding any office of profit or trust under the United States, or any of them, accept of any present, emolument, office or title, of any kind whatever, from any king, prince, or foreign state; nor shall the United States, in Congress assembled, or any of them, grant any title of nobility.

No two or more states shall enter into any treaty, confederation, or alliance, whatever, between them, without the consent of the United States, in Congress assembled, specifying accurately the purposes for which the same is to be entered into, and how long it shall continue.

No State shall lay any imposts or duties which may interfere with any stipulations in treaties entered into by the United States, in Congress assembled, with any king, prince, or state, in pursuance of any treaties already proposed by Congress to the courts of France and Spain.

No vessels of war shall be kept up in time of peace by any State, except such number only as shall be deemed necessary by the United States, in Congress assembled, for the defence of such State or its trade; nor shall any body of forces be kept up by any State, in time of peace, except such number only as, in the judgment of the United States, in Congress assembled, shall be deemed requisite to garrison the forts necessary for the defence of such State; but every State shall always keep up a well regulated and disciplined militia, sufficiently armed and accoutred, and shall provide, and constantly have ready for use, in public stores, a due number of field pieces and tents, and a proper quantity of arms, ammunition and camp equipage.

No State shall engage in any war without the consent of the United States, in Congress assembled, unless such State be actually invaded by enemies, or shall have received certain advice of a resolution being formed by some nation of Indians to invade such State, and the danger is so imminent as not to admit of a delay till the United States, in Congress assembled, can be consulted; nor shall any State grant commissions to any ships or vessels of war, nor letters of marque or reprisal, except it be after a declaration of war by the United States, in Congress assembled, and then only against the kingdom or state, and the subjects thereof, against which war has been so declared, and under such regulations as shall be established by the United States, in Congress assembled, unless such States be infested by pirates, in which case vessels of war may be fitted out for that occasion, and kept so long as the danger shall continue, or until the United States, in Congress assembled, shall determine otherwise.

Article 7

When land forces are raised by any State for the common defence, all officers of or under the rank of colonel, shall be appointed by the legislature of each State respectively, by whom such forces shall be raised, or in such manner as such State shall direct; and all vacancies shall be filled up by the State which first made the appointment.

Article 8

All charges of war and all other expences, that shall be incurred for the common defence or general welfare, and allowed by the United States, in Congress assembled, shall be defrayed out of a common treasury, which shall be supplied by the several states, in proportion to the value of all land within each State, granted to or surveyed for any person, as such land and the buildings and improvements thereon shall be estimated according to such mode as the United States, in Congress assembled, shall, from time to time, direct and appoint.

The taxes for paying that proportion shall be laid and levied by the authority and direction of the legislatures of the several states, within the time agreed upon by the United States, in Congress assembled.

Article 9

The United States, in Congress assembled, shall have the sole and exclusive right and power of determining on peace and war, except in the cases mentioned in the 6th article; of sending and receiving ambassadors; entering into treaties and alliances, provided that no treaty of commerce shall be made, whereby the legislative power of the respective states shall be restrained from imposing such imposts and duties on foreigners as their own people are subjected to, or from prohibiting the exportation or importation of any species of goods or commodities whatsoever; of establishing rules for deciding, in all cases, what captures on land or water shall be legal, and in what manner prizes, taken by land or naval forces in the service of the United States, shall be divided or appropriated; of granting letters of marque and reprisal in times of peace; appointing courts for the trial of piracies and felonies committed on the high seas, and establishing courts for receiving and determining, finally, appeals in all cases of captures; provided, that no member of Congress shall be appointed a judge of any of the said courts.

The United States, in Congress assembled, shall also be the last resort on appeal in all disputes and differences now subsisting, or that hereafter may arise between two or more states sconcerning boundary, jurisdiction or any other cause whatever; which authority shall always be exercised in the manner following: whenever the legislative or executive authority, or lawful agent of any State, in controversy with another, shall present a petition to Congress, stating the matter in question, and praying for a hearing, notice thereof shall be given, by order of Congress, to the legislative or executive authority of the other State in controversy, and a day assigned for the appearance of the parties by their lawful agents, who shall then be directed to appoint, by joint consent, commissioners or judges to constitute a court for hearing and determining the matter in question; but, if they cannot agree, Congress shall name three persons out of each of the United States, and from the list of such persons each party shall alternately strike out one, in the petitioners beginning, until the number shall be reduced to thirteen; and from that number not less than seven, nor more than nine names, as Congress shall direct, shall, in the presence of Congress, be drawn out by lot; and the persons whose names shall be drawn, or any five of them, shall be commissioners or judges to hear and finally determine the controversy, so always as a major part of the judges who shall hear the cause shall agree in the determination; and if either party shall neglect to attend at the day appointed, without shewing reasons which Congress shall judge sufficient, or, being present, shall refuse to strike, the Congress shall proceed to nominate three persons out of each State, and the secretary of Congress shall strike in behalf of such party absent or refusing; and the judgment and sentence of the court to be appointed, in the manner before prescribed, shall be final and conclusive; and if any of the parties shall refuse to submit to the authority of such court, or to appear or defend their claim or cause, the court shall nevertheless proceed to pronounce sentence or judgment, which shall, in like manner, be final and decisive, the judgment or sentence and other proceedings being, in either case, transmitted to Congress, and lodged among the acts of Congress for the security of the parties concerned: provided, that every commissioner, before he sits in judgment, shall take an oath, to be administered by one of the judges of the supreme or superior court of the State where the cause shall be tried, "well and truly to hear and determine the matter in question, according to the best of his judgment, without favour, affection, or hope of reward": provided, also, that no State shall be deprived of territory for the benefit of the United States.

All controversies concerning the private right of soil, claimed under different grants of two or more states, whose jurisdictions, as they may respect such lands and the states which passed such grants, are adjusted, the said grants, or either of them, being at the same time claimed to have originated antecedent to such settlement of jurisdiction, shall, on the petition of either party to the Congress of the United States, be finally determined, as near as may be, in the same manner as is before prescribed for deciding disputes respecting territorial jurisdiction between different states.

The United States, in Congress assembled, shall also have the sole and exclusive right and power of regulating the alloy and value of coin struck by their own authority, or by that of the respective states; fixing the standard of weights and measures throughout the United States; regulating the trade and managing all affairs with the Indians not members of any of the states; provided that the legislative right of any State within its own limits be not infringed or violated; establishing and regulating post offices from one State to another throughout all the United States, and exacting such postage on the papers passing through the same as may be requisite to defray the expences of the said office; appointing all officers of the land forces in the service of the United States, excepting regimental officers; appointing all the officers of the naval forces, and commissioning all officers whatever in the service of the United States; making rules for the government and regulation of the said land and naval forces, and directing their operations.

The United States, in Congress assembled, shall have authority to appoint a committee to sit in the recess of Congress, to be denominated "a Committee of the States," and to consist of one delegate from each State, and to appoint such other committees and civil officers as may be necessary for managing the general affairs of the United States, under their direction; to appoint one of their number to preside; provided that no person be allowed to serve in the office of president more than one year in any term of three years; to ascertain the necessary sums of money to be raised for the service of the United States, and to appropriate and apply the same for defraying the public expences; to borrow money or emit bills on the credit of the United States, transmitting, every half year, to the respective states, an account of the sums of money so borrowed or emitted; to build and equip a navy; to agree upon the number of land forces, and to make requisitions from each State for its quota, in proportion to the number of white inhabitants in such State; which requisitions shall be binding; and, thereupon, the legislature of each State shall appoint the regimental officers, raise the men, and cloathe, arm, and equip them in a soldierlike manner, at the expence of the United States; and the officers and men so cloathed, armed, and equipped, shall march to the place appointed and within the time agreed on by the United States, in Congress assembled; but if the United States, in Congress assembled, shall, on consideration of circumstances, judge proper that any State should not raise men, or should raise a smaller number than its quota, and that any other State should raise a greater number of men than the quota thereof, such extra number shall be raised, officered, cloathed, armed, and equipped in the same manner as the quota of such State, unless the legislature of such State shall judge that such extra number cannot be safely spared out of the same, in which case they shall raise, officer, cloathe, arm, and equip as many of such extra number as they judge can be safely spared. And the officers and men so cloathed, armed, and equipped, shall march to the place appointed and within the time agreed on by the United States, in Congress assembled.

The United States, in Congress assembled, shall never engage in a war, nor grant letters of marque and reprisal in time of peace, nor enter into any treaties or alliances, nor coin money, nor regulate the value thereof, nor ascertain the sums and expences necessary for the defence and welfare of the United States, or any of them: nor emit bills, nor borrow money on the credit of the United States, nor appropriate money, nor agree upon the number of vessels of war to be built or purchased, or the number of land or sea forces to be raised, nor appoint a commander in chief of the army or navy, unless nine states assent to the same; nor shall a question on any other point, except for adjourning from day to day, be determined, unless by the votes of a majority of the United States, in Congress assembled.

The Congress of the United States shall have power to adjourn to any time within the year, and to any place within the United States, so that no period of adjournment be for a longer duration than the space of six months, and shall publish the journal of their proceedings monthly, except such parts thereof, relating to treaties, alliances or military operations, as, in their judgment, require secrecy; and the yeas and nays of the delegates of each State on any question shall be entered on the journal, when it is desired by any delegate; and the delegates of a State, or any of them, at his, or their request, shall be furnished with a transcript of the said journal, except such parts as are above excepted, to lay before the legislatures of the several states.

Article 10

The committee of the states, or any nine of them, shall be authorized to execute, in the recess of Congress, such of the powers of Congress as the United States, in Congress assembled, by the consent of nine states, shall, from time to time, think expedient to vest them with; provided, that no power be delegated to the said committee for the exercise of which, by the articles of confederation, the voice of nine states, in the Congress of the United States assembled, is requisite.

Article 11

Canada acceding to this confederation, and joining in the measures of the United States, shall be admitted into and entitled to all the advantages of this union; but no other colony shall be admitted into the same, unless such admission be agreed to by nine states.

Article 12

All bills of credit emitted, monies borrowed and debts contracted by, or under the authority of Congress before the assembling of the United States, in pursuance of the present confederation, shall be deemed and considered as a charge against the United States, for payment and satisfaction whereof the said United States and the public faith are hereby solemnly pledged.

Article 13

Every State shall abide by the determinations of the United States, in Congress assembled, on all questions which, by this confederation, are submitted to them. And the articles of this confederation shall be inviolably observed by every State, and the union shall be perpetual; nor shall any alteration at any time hereafter be made in any of them, unless such alteration be agreed to in a Congress of the United States, and be afterwards confirmed by the legislatures of every State.

These articles shall be proposed to the legislatures of all the United States, to be considered, and if approved of by them, they are advised to authorize their delegates to ratify the same in the Congress of the United States; which being done, the same shall become conclusive.

The Constitution of the United States of America

Preamble

We the People of the United States, in Order to form a more perfect Union, establish Justice, insure domestic Tranquility, provide for the common defence, promote the general Welfare, and secure the Blessings of Liberty to ourselves and our Posterity, do ordain and establish this Constitution for the United States of America.

Article I

Section 1

All legislative Powers herein granted shall be vested in a Congress of the United States, which shall consist of a Senate and House of Representatives.

Section 2

The House of Representatives shall be composed of Members chosen every second Year by the People of the several States, and the Electors in each State shall have the Qualifications requisite for Electors of the most numerous Branch of the State Legislature.

No Person shall be a Representative who shall not have attained to the Age of twenty five Years, and been seven Years a Citizen of the United States, and who shall not, when elected, be an inhabitant of that State in which he shall be chosen.

Representatives and direct Taxes shall be apportioned among the several States which may be included within this Union, according to their respective Numbers, *which shall be determined by adding to the whole Number of free Persons, including those bound to Service for a Term of Years, and excluding Indians not taxed, three fifths of all other Persons.* * The actual Enumeration shall be made within three Years after the first Meeting of the Congress of the United States, and within every subsequent Term of ten Years, in such Manner as they shall by Law direct. The Number of Representatives shall not exceed one for every thirty Thousand, but each State shall have at Least one Representative; *and until such enumeration shall be made, the State of New Hampshire shall be entitled to chuse three, Massachusetts eight, Rhode-Island and Providence Plantations one, Connecticut five, New York six, New Jersey four, Pennsylvania eight, Delaware one, Maryland six, Virginia ten, North Carolina five, South Carolina five, and Georgia three.*

When vacancies happen in the Representation from any State, the Executive Authority thereof shall issue Writs of Election to fill such Vacancies.

The House of Representatives shall chuse their Speaker and other Officers; and shall have the sole Power of Impeachment.

Section 3

The Senate of the United States shall be composed of two Senators from each State, *chosen by the Legislature thereof,* for six Years; and each Senator shall have one Vote.

Immediately after they shall be assembled in Consequence of the first Election, they shall be divided as equally as may be into three Classes. The Seats of the Senators of the first Class shall be vacated at the Expiration of the second Year, of the second Class at the Expiration of the fourth Year, and of the third Class at the Expiration of the sixth Year so that one third may be chosen every second Year; and if Vacancies happen by Resignation, or otherwise, during the Recess of the Legislature of any state, the Executive thereof may make temporary Appointments until the next Meeting of the Legislature, which shall then fill such Vacancies.

No Person shall be a Senator who shall not have attained to the Age of thirty Years, and been nine Years a Citizen of the United States, and who shall not, when elected, be an Inhabitant of that State for which he shall be chosen.

The Vice President of the United States shall be President of the Senate, but shall have no Vote, unless they be equally divided.

The Senate shall chuse their other Officers, and also a President *pro tempore,* in the Absence of the Vice President, or when he shall exercise the Office of President of the United States.

The Senate shall have the sole Power to try all Impeachments. When sitting for that Purpose, they shall be on Oath or Affirmation. When the President of the United States is tried the Chief Justice shall preside: And no Person shall be convicted without the Concurrence of two thirds of the Members present.

Judgment in Cases of Impeachment shall not extend further than to removal from Office, and disqualification to hold and enjoy any Office of honor, Trust or Profit under the United States: but the Party convicted shall nevertheless be liable and subject to Indictment, Trial, Judgment and Punishment, according to Law.

Section 4

The Times, Places and Manner of holding Elections for Senators and Representatives, shall be prescribed in each State by the Legislature thereof; but the Congress may at

---

*Passages no longer in effect are printed in italic type.

any time by Law make or alter such Regulations, except as to the Places of chusing Senators.

The Congress shall assemble at least once in every Year, *and such Meeting shall be on the first Monday in December, unless they shall by Law appoint a different Day.*

Section 5

Each House shall be the Judge of the Elections, Returns and Qualifications of its own Members, and a Majority of each shall constitute a Quorum to do Business; but a smaller Number may adjourn from day to day, and may be authorized to compel the Attendance of absent Members, in such Manner, and under such Penalties as each House may provide.

Each House may determine the Rules of its Proceedings, punish its Members for disorderly Behaviour, and, with the Concurrence of two thirds, expel a Member.

Each House shall keep a Journal of its Proceedings, and from time to time publish the same, excepting such Parts as may in their Judgment require Secrecy; and the Yeas and Nays of the Members of either House on any question shall, at the Desire of one fifth of those Present, be entered on the Journal.

Neither House, during the Session of Congress, shall, without the Consent of the other, adjourn for more than three days, nor to any other Place than that in which the two Houses shall be sitting.

Section 6

The Senators and Representatives shall receive a Compensation for their Services, to be ascertained by Law, and paid out of the Treasury of the United States. They shall in all Cases, except Treason, Felony and Breach of the Peace, be privileged from Arrest during their Attendance at the Session of their respective Houses, and in going to and returning from the same; and for any Speech or Debate in either House, they shall not be questioned in any other Place.

No Senator or Representative shall, during the Time for which he was elected, be appointed to any civil Office under the Authority of the United States, which shall have been created, or the Emoluments whereof shall have been encreased during such time, and no Person holding any Office under the United States, shall be a Member of either House during his Continuance in Office.

Section 7

All Bills for raising Revenue shall originate in the House of Representatives; but the Senate may propose or concur with Amendments as on other Bills.

Every Bill which shall have passed the House of Representatives and the Senate, shall, before it become a Law, be presented to the President of the United States; If he approve he shall sign it, but if not he shall return it, with his Objections to the House in which it shall have originated, who shall enter the Objections at large on their Journal, and proceed to reconsider it. If after such Reconsideration two thirds of that House shall agree to pass the Bill, it shall be sent, together with the Objections, to the other House, by which it shall likewise be reconsidered, and if approved by two thirds of that House, it shall become a Law. But in all such Cases the Votes of both Houses shall be determined by yeas and Nays, and the Names of the Persons voting for and against the Bill shall be entered on the Journal of each House respectively. If any Bill shall not be returned by the President within ten Days (Sundays excepted) after it shall have been presented to him, the Same shall be a Law, in like Manner as if he had signed it, unless the Congress by their Adjournment prevent its Return, in which Case it shall not be a Law.

Every Order, Resolution, or Vote to which the Concurrence of the Senate and House of Representatives may be necessary (except on a question of Adjournment) shall be presented to the President of the United States; and before the Same shall take Effect, shall be approved by him, or being disapproved by him, shall be repassed by two thirds of the Senate and House of Representatives, according to the Rules and Limitations prescribed in the Case of a Bill.

Section 8

The Congress shall have Power To lay and collect Taxes, Duties, Imposts and Excises, to pay the Debts and provide for the common Defence and general Welfare of the United States; but all Duties, Imposts and Excises shall be uniform throughout the United States;

To borrow Money on the credit of the United States;

To regulate Commerce with foreign Nations, and among the several States, and with the Indian Tribes;

To establish an uniform Rule of Naturalization, and uniform Laws on the subject of Bankruptcies throughout the United States;

To coin Money, regulate the Value thereof, and of foreign Coin, and fix the Standard of Weights and Measures;

To provide for the Punishment of counterfeiting the Securities and current Coin of the United States;

To establish Post Offices and post Roads;

To promote the Progress of Science and useful Arts, by securing for limited Times to Authors and Inventors the exclusive Right to their respective Writings and Discoveries;

To constitute Tribunals inferior to the supreme Court;

To define and punish Piracies and Felonies committed on the high Seas, and Offences against the Law of Nations;

To declare War, grant Letters of Marque and Reprisal, and make Rules concerning Captures on Land and Water;

To raise and support Armies, but no Appropriation of Money to that Use shall be for a longer Term than two Years;

To provide and maintain a Navy;

To make Rules for the Government and Regulation of the land and naval Forces;

To provide for calling forth the Militia to execute the Laws of the Union, suppress Insurrections and repel Invasions;

To provide for organizing, arming, and disciplining, the Militia, and for governing such Part of them as may be employed in the Service of the United States, reserving to the States respectively, the Appointment of the Officers, and the Authority of training the Militia according to the discipline prescribed by Congress;

To exercise exclusive Legislation in all Cases whatsoever, over such District (not exceeding ten Miles square) as may, by Cession of particular States, and the Acceptance of Congress, become the Seat of the Government of the United States, and to exercise like Authority over all Places purchased by the Consent of the Legislature of the State in which the Same shall be, for the Erection of Forts, Magazines, Arsenals, dockYards, and other needful Buildings;—And

To make all Laws which shall be necessary and proper for carrying into Execution the foregoing Powers, and all other Powers vested by this Constitution in the Government of the United States, or in any Department of Officer thereof.

Section 9

The Migration or Importation of such Persons as any of the States now existing shall think proper to admit, shall not be prohibited by the Congress prior to the Year one thousand eight hundred and eight, but a Tax or duty may be imposed on such Importation, not exceeding ten dollars for each Person.

The Privilege of the Writ of Habeas Corpus shall not be suspended, unless when in Cases of Rebellion or Invasion the public Safety may require it.

No Bill of Attainder or ex post facto Law shall be passed.

No Capitation, or other direct, Tax shall be laid, unless in Proportion to the Census or Enumeration herein before directed to be taken.

No Tax or Duty shall be laid on Articles exported from any State.

No Preference shall be given by any Regulation of Commerce or Revenue to the Ports of one State over those of another: nor shall Vessels bound to, or from, one State, be obliged to enter, clear, or pay Duties in another.

No Money shall be drawn from the Treasury, but in Consequence of Appropriations made by Law; and a regular Statement and Account of the Receipts and Expenditures of all public Money shall be published from time to time.

No Title of Nobility shall be granted by the United States: And no Person holding any Office of Profit or Trust under them, shall, without the Consent of the Congress, accept of any present, Emolument, Office, or Title, of any kind whatever, from any King, Prince, or foreign State.

Section 10

No State shall enter into any Treaty, Alliance, or Confederation; grant Letters of Marque and Reprisal; coin Money; emit Bills of Credit; make any Thing but gold and silver Coin a Tender in Payment of Debts; pass any Bill of Attainder, ex post facto Law, or Law impairing the obligation of Contracts, or grant any Title of Nobility.

No State shall, without the Consent of the Congress, lay any Imposts or Duties on Imports or Exports, except what may be absolutely necessary for executing its inspection Laws: and the net Produce of all Duties and Imposts, laid by any State on Imports or Exports, shall be for the Use of the Treasury of the United States; and all such Laws shall be subject to the Revision and Controul of the Congress.

No State shall, without the Consent of Congress, lay any Duty of Tonnage, keep Troops, or Ships of War in time of Peace, enter into any Agreement or Compact with another State, or with a foreign Power, or engage in War, unless actually invaded, or in such imminent Danger as will not admit of delay.

Article II

Section 1

The executive Power shall be vested in a President of the United States of America. He shall hold his Office during the Term of four Years, and, together with the Vice President, chosen for the same Term, be elected, as follows:

Each State shall appoint, in such Manner as the Legislature thereof may direct, a Number of Electors, equal to the whole Number of Senators and Representatives to which the State may be entitled in the Congress: but no Senator or Representative, or Person holding an Office of Trust or Profit under the United States, shall be appointed an Elector.

The Electors shall meet in their respective States, and vote by Ballot for two Persons, of whom one at least shall not be an Inhabitant of the same State with themselves. And they shall make a List of all the Persons voted for, and of the Number of Votes for each; which List they shall sign and certify, and transmit sealed to the Seat of the Government of the United States, directed to the President of the Senate. The President of the Senate shall, in the Presence of the Senate and House of Representatives, open all the Certificates, and the Votes shall then be counted. The Person having the greatest Number of Votes shall be the President, if such Number be a Majority of the whole number of Electors appointed; and if there be more than one who have such Majority, and have an equal Number of Votes, then the House of Representatives shall immediately chuse by Ballot one of them for President; and if no Person have a Majority, then from the five highest on the List the said House shall in like Manner chuse the President. But in chusing the President, the Votes shall be taken by States, the Representation from each State having one Vote; A quorum for this Purpose shall consist of a Member or Members from two thirds of the States, and a Majority of all the States shall be necessary to a Choice. In every Case, after the Choice of the President, the Person having the greatest Number of Votes of the Electors shall be the Vice President. But if there should remain two or more who have equal Votes, the Senate shall chuse from them by Ballot the Vice President.

The Congress may determine the time of chusing the Electors, and the Day on which they shall give their Votes; which Day shall be the same throughout the United States.

No person except a natural born Citizen, *or a Citizen of the United States, at the time of the Adoption of this Constitution*, shall be eligible to the Office of President; neither shall any Person be eligible to that Office who shall not have attained to the Age of thirty five Years, and been fourteen Years a Resident within the United States.

In Case of the Removal of the President from Office, or of his Death, Resignation, or Inability to discharge the Powers and Duties of the said Office, the Same shall devolve on the Vice President, and the Congress may by Law provide for the Case of Removal, Death, Resignation or Inability, both of the President and Vice President, declaring what Officer shall then act as President, and such Officer shall act accordingly, until the Disability be removed, or a President shall be elected.

The President shall, at stated Times, receive for his Services, a Compensation, which shall neither be increased nor diminished during the Period for which he shall have been elected, and he shall not receive within that period any other Emolument from the United States, or any of them.

Before he enter on the Execution of his Office, he shall take the following Oath or Affirmation:—"I do solemnly swear (or affirm) that I will faithfully execute the Office of President of the United States, and will to the best of my Ability, preserve, protect and defend the Constitution of the United States."

Section 2

The President shall be Commander in Chief of the Army and Navy of the United States, and of the Militia of the several States, when called into the actual Service of the United States; he may require the Opinion, in writing, of the principal Officer in each of the executive Departments, upon any Subject relating to the Duties of their respective Offices, and he shall have Power to grant Reprieves and Pardons for Offences against the United States, except in Cases of Impeachment.

He shall have Power, by and with the Advice and Consent of the Senate, to make Treaties, provided two thirds of the Senators present concur; and he shall nominate, and by and with the Advice and Consent of the Senate, shall appoint Ambassadors, other public Ministers and Consuls, Judges of the supreme Court, and all other Officers of the United States, whose Appointments are not herein otherwise provided for, and which shall be established by Law: but the Congress may by Law vest the Appointment of such inferior Officers, as they think proper in the President alone, in the Courts of Law, or in the Heads of Departments.

The President shall have Power to fill up all Vacancies that may happen during the Recess of the Senate, by granting Commissions which shall expire at the End of their next Session.

Section 3

He shall from time to time give to the Congress Information of the State of the Union, and recommend to their Consideration such Measures as he shall judge necessary and expedient; he may, on extraordinary Occasions, convene both Houses, or either of them, and in Case of disagreement between them, with Respect to the Time of Adjournment, he may adjourn them to such Time as he shall think proper; he shall receive Ambassadors and other public Ministers; he shall take Care that the Laws be faithfully executed, and shall Commission all the officers of the United States.

Section 4

The President, Vice President and all civil Officers of the United States, shall be removed from Office on Impeachment for, and Conviction of, Treason, Bribery or other high Crimes and Misdemeanors.

Article III

Section 1

The judicial Power of the United States, shall be vested in one supreme Court, and in such inferior Courts as the Congress may from time to time ordain and establish. The Judges, both of the supreme and inferior Courts, shall hold their offices during good Behaviour, and shall, at stated Times, receive for their Services, a Compensation, which shall not be diminished during their Continuance in Office.

Section 2

The judicial Power shall extend to all Cases, in Law and Equity, arising under this Constitution, the Laws of the United States, and Treaties made, or which shall be made, under their Authority;—to all Cases affecting Ambassadors, other public Ministers and Consuls;—to all Cases of admiralty and maritime Jurisdiction;—to Controversies to which the United States shall be a Party;—to Controversies between two or more States;—*between a State and Citizens of another State;*—between Citizens of different States;—between Citizens of the same State claiming Lands under Grants of different States, and between a State, or the Citizens thereof, and foreign States, Citizens or Subjects.

In all Cases affecting Ambassadors, other public Ministers and Consuls, and those in which a State shall be Party, the supreme Court shall have original Jurisdiction. In all the other Cases before mentioned, the supreme Court shall have appellate Jurisdiction, both as to Law and Fact, with such Exceptions, and under such Regulations as the Congress shall make.

The Trial of all Crimes, except in Cases of Impeachment, shall be by Jury; and such Trial shall be held in the State where the said Crimes shall have been committed, but when not committed within any State, the Trial shall be at such Place or Places as the Congress may by Law have directed.

Section 3

Treason against the United States, shall consist only in levying War against them, or in adhering to their Enemies, giving them Aid and Comfort. No person shall be convicted of Treason unless on the Testimony of two Witnesses to the same overt Act, or on Confession in open Court.

The Congress shall have Power to declare the Punishment of Treason, but no Attainder of Treason shall work Corruption of Blood, or Forfeiture except during the Life of the Person attainted.

Article IV

Section 1

Full Faith and Credit shall be given in each State to the public Acts, Records, and judicial Proceedings of every other State. And the Congress may by general Laws prescribe the Manner in which such Acts, Records and Proceedings shall be proved, and the Effect thereof.

Section 2

The Citizens of each State shall be entitled to all Privileges and Immunities of Citizens in the several States.

A Person charged in any State with Treason, Felony, or other Crime, who shall flee from Justice, and be found in another State, shall on Demand of the executive Authority of the State from which he fled, be delivered up, to be removed to the State having Jurisdiction of the Crime.

No Person held to Service or Labour in one State, under the Laws thereof, escaping into another, shall, in Consequence of any Law or Regulation therein, be discharged from such Service or Labour, but shall be delivered up on Claim of the Party to whom such Service or Labour may be due.

Section 3

New States may be admitted by the Congress into this Union; but no new State shall be formed or erected within the Jurisdiction of any other State; nor any State be formed by the Junction of two or more States, or Parts of States, without the Consent of the Legislatures of the States concerned as well as of the Congress.

The Congress shall have Power to dispose of and make all needful Rules and Regulations respecting the Territory or other Property belonging to the United States; and nothing in this Constitution shall be so construed as to Prejudice any Claims of the United States, or of any particular States.

Section 4

The United States shall guarantee to every State in this Union a Republican Form of Government, and shall protect each of them against Invasion; and on Application of the Legislature, or of the Executive (when the Legislature cannot be convened) against domestic violence.

Article V

The Congress, whenever two thirds of both Houses shall deem it necessary, shall propose Amendments to this Constitution, or, on the Application of the Legislatures of two thirds of the several States, shall call a Convention for proposing Amendments, which, in either Case, shall be valid to all Intents and Purposes, as Part of this Constitution, when ratified by the Legislatures of three fourths of the several States, or by Conventions in three fourths thereof, as the one or the other Mode of Ratification may be proposed by the Congress; Provided *that no Amendment which may be made prior to the Year One thousand eight hundred and eight shall in any Manner affect the first and fourth Clauses in the Ninth Section of the first Article;* and that no State, without its Consent, shall be deprived of its equal Suffrage in the Senate.

Article VI

All Debts contracted and Engagements entered into, before the Adoption of this Constitution, shall be as valid against the United States under this Constitution, as under the Confederation.

This Constitution, and Laws of the United States which shall be made in Pursuance thereof; and all Treaties made, or which shall be made, under the Authority of the United States, shall be the supreme Law of the Land; and the Judges in every State shall be bound thereby, any Thing in the Constitution or Laws of any State to the Contrary notwithstanding.

The Senators and Representatives before mentioned, and the Members of the several State Legislatures, and all executive and Judicial Officers, both of the United States and of the several States, shall be bound by Oath or Affirmation, to support this Constitution; but no religious Test shall ever be required as a Qualification to any Office of public Trust under the United States.

Article VII

The Ratification of the Conventions of nine States, shall be sufficient for the Establishment of this Constitution between the States so ratifying the Same.

Done in Convention by the Unanimous Consent of the States present the Seventeenth Day of September in the Year of our Lord one thousand seven hundred and Eighty seven and of the Independence of the United States of America the Twelfth[†] IN WITNESS whereof We have hereunto subscribed our Names,

George Washington
President and Deputy from Virginia

Delaware
George Read
Gunning Bedford, Jr.
John Dickinson
Richard Bassett
Jacob Broom

Maryland
James McHenry
Daniel of St. Thomas Jenifer
Daniel Carroll

Virginia
John Blair
James Madison, Jr.

North Carolina
William Blount
Richard Dobbs Spraight
Hugh Williamson

South Carolina
John Rutledge
Charles Cotesworth Pinckney
Charles Pinckney
Pierce Butler

Georgia
William Paterson
William Few
Abraham Baldwin

New Hampshire
John Langdon
Nicholas Gilman

Massachusetts
Nathaniel Gorham
Rufus King

Connecticut
William Samuel Johnson
Roger Sherman

New York
Alexander Hamilton

New Jersey
William Livingston
David Brearley
Jonathan Dayton

Pennsylvania
Benjamin Franklin
Thomas Mifflin
Robert Morris
George Clymer
Thomas FitzSimons
Jared Ingersoll
James Wilson
Gouverneur Morris

[†]The Constitution was submitted on September 17, 1787, by the Constitutional Convention, was ratified by the Convention of several states at various dates up to May 29, 1790, and became effective on March 4, 1789.

Amendments to the Constitution

Amendment I

Congress shall make no law respecting an establishment of religion, or prohibiting the free exercise thereof; or abridging the freedom of speech, or of the press; or the right of the people peaceably to assemble, and to petition the Government for a redress of grievances.

Amendment II

A well regulated Militia being necessary to the security of a free State, the right of the people to keep and bear Arms, shall not be infringed.

Amendment III

No Soldier shall, in time of peace be quartered in any house, without the consent of the Owner, nor in time of war, but in a manner to be prescribed by law.

Amendment IV

The right of the people to be secure in their persons, houses, papers, and effects, against unreasonable searches and seizures, shall not be violated, and no Warrants shall issue, but upon probable cause, supported by Oath or affirmation, and particularly describing the place to be searched, and the persons or things to be seized.

Amendment V

No person shall be held to answer for a capital, or otherwise infamous crime, unless on a presentment or indictment of a Grand Jury, except in cases arising in the land or naval forces, or in the Militia, when in actual service in time of War or public danger; nor shall any person be subject for the same offense to be twice put in jeopardy of life or limb; nor shall be compelled in any criminal case to be a witness against himself, nor be deprived of life, liberty, or property, without due process of law; nor shall private property be taken for public use, without just compensation.

Amendment VI

In all criminal prosecutions, the accused shall enjoy the right to a speedy and public trial, by an impartial jury of the State and district wherein the crime shall have been committed, which district shall have been previously ascertained by law, and to be informed of the nature and cause of the accusation; to be confronted with the witnesses against him; to have compulsory process for obtaining witnesses in his favor, and to have the Assistance of Counsel for his defence.

Amendment VII

In Suits at common law, where the value in controversy shall exceed twenty dollars, the right of trial by jury shall be preserved, and no fact tried by a jury, shall be otherwise reexamined in any Court of the United States, than according to the rules of the common law.

Amendment VIII

Excessive bail shall not be required, nor excessive fines imposed, nor cruel and unusual punishments inflicted.

Amendment IX

The enumeration in the Constitution, of certain rights, shall not be construed to deny or disparage others retained by the people.

Amendment X*

The powers not delegated to the United States by the Constitution, nor prohibited by it to the States, are reserved to the States respectively, or to the people.

Amendment XI
[Adopted 1798]

The Judicial power of the United States shall not be construed to extend to any suit in law or equity, commenced or prosecuted against one of the United States by Citizens of another State, or by Citizens or Subjects of any Foreign State.

Amendment XII
[Adopted 1804]

The Electors shall meet in their respective states, and vote by ballot for President and Vice President, one of whom,

---

*The first ten amendments (the Bill of Rights) were ratified and their adoption was certified on December 15, 1791.

at least, shall not be an inhabitant of the same state with themselves; they shall name in their ballots the person voted for as President, and in distinct ballots the person voted for as Vice President, and they shall make distinct lists of all persons voted for as President, and of all persons voted for as Vice President, and of the number of votes for each, which lists they shall sign and certify, and transmit sealed to the seat of the government of the United States, directed to the President of the Senate;—The President of the Senate shall, in the presence of the Senate and House of Representatives, open all the certificates and the votes shall then be counted;—The person having the greatest number of votes for President, shall be the President, if such number be a majority of the whole number of Electors appointed; and if no person have such majority, then from the persons having the highest numbers not exceeding three on the list of those voted for as President, the House of Representatives shall choose immediately, by ballot, the President. But in choosing the President, the votes shall be taken by states, the representation from each state having one vote; a quorum for this purpose shall consist of a member or members from two-thirds of the states, and a majority of all the states shall be necessary to a choice. And if the House of Representatives shall not choose a President whenever the right of choice shall devolve upon them, before *the fourth day of March* next following, then the Vice President shall act as President, as in the case of the death or other constitutional disability of the President.—The person having the greatest number of votes as Vice President, shall be the Vice President, if such number be a majority of the whole number of Electors appointed, and if no person have a majority, then from the two highest numbers on the list, the Senate shall choose the Vice President; a quorum for the purpose shall consist of two-thirds of the whole number of Senators, and a majority of the whole number shall be necessary to a choice. But no person constitutionally ineligible to the office of President shall be eligible to that of Vice President of the United States.

Amendment XIII
[Adopted 1865]
Section 1

Neither slavery nor involuntary servitude, except as a punishment for crime whereof the party shall have been duly convicted, shall exist within the United States, or any place subject to their jurisdiction.

Section 2

Congress shall have power to enforce this article by appropriate legislation.

Amendment XIV
[Adopted 1868]
Section 1

All persons born or naturalized in the United States, and subject to the jurisdiction thereof, are citizens of the United States and of the State wherein they reside. No State shall make or enforce any law which shall abridge the privileges or immunities of citizens of the United States; nor shall any State deprive any person of life, liberty, or property, without due process of law; nor deny to any person within its jurisdiction the equal protection of the laws.

Section 2

Representatives shall be apportioned among the several States according to their respective numbers, counting the whole number of persons in each State, excluding Indians not taxed. But when the right to vote at any election for the choice of electors for President and Vice President of the United States, Representatives in Congress, the Executive and Judicial officers of a State, or the members of the Legislature thereof, is denied to any of the male inhabitants of such State, being twenty-one years of age, and citizens of the United States, or in any way abridged, except for participation in rebellion, or other crime, the basis of representation therein shall be reduced in the proportion which the number of such male citizens shall bear to the whole number of male citizens twenty-one years of age in such State.

Section 3

No person shall be a Senator or Representative in Congress, or elector of President and Vice President, or hold any office, civil or military, under the United States, or under any State, who, having previously taken an oath, as a member of Congress, or as an officer of the United States, or as a member of any State legislature, or as an executive or judicial officer of any State, to support the Constitution of the United States, shall have engaged in insurrection or rebellion against the same, or given aid or comfort to the enemies thereof. But Congress may by a vote of two-thirds of each House, remove such disability.

Section 4

The validity of the public debt of the United States, authorized by law, including debts incurred for payment of pensions and bounties for services in suppressing insurrection or rebellion, shall not be questioned. But neither the United States nor any State shall assume or pay any debt or obligation incurred in aid of insurrection or rebellion against the United States, or any claim for the loss or emancipation of any slave; but all such debts, obligations and claims shall be held illegal and void.

Section 5

The Congress shall have power to enforce, by appropriate legislation, the provisions of this article.

Amendment XV
[Adopted 1870]
Section 1

The right of citizens of the United States to vote shall not be denied or abridged by the United States or by any State on account of race, color, or previous condition of servitude.

Section 2

The Congress shall have power to enforce this article by appropriate legislation.

Amendment XVI

[Adopted 1913]

The Congress shall have power to lay and collect taxes on incomes, from whatever source derived, without apportionment among the several States, and without regard to any census or enumeration.

Amendment XVII

[Adopted 1913]

The Senate of the United States shall be composed of two Senators from each State, elected by the people thereof, for six years; and each Senator shall have one vote. The electors in each State shall have the qualifications requisite for electors of the most numerous branch of the State legislatures.

When vacancies happen in the representation of any State in the Senate, the executive authority of such State shall issue writs of election to fill such vacancies: *Provided,* That the legislature of any State may empower the executive thereof to make temporary appointments until the people fill the vacancies by election as the legislature may direct.

This amendment shall not be so construed as to affect the election or term of any Senator chosen before it becomes valid as part of the Constitution.

Amendment XVIII

[Adopted 1919, repealed 1933]

Section 1

After one year from the ratification of this article the manufacture, sale, or transportation of intoxicating liquors within, the importation thereof into, or the exportation thereof from the United States and all territory subject to the jurisdiction thereof for beverage purposes is hereby prohibited.

Section 2

The Congress and the several States shall have concurrent power to enforce this article by appropriate legislation.

Section 3

This article shall be inoperative unless it shall have been ratified as an amendment to the Constitution by the legislatures of the several States, as provided in the Constitution, within seven years from the date of the submission hereof to the States by the Congress.

Amendment XIX

[Adopted 1920]

The right of citizens of the United States to vote shall not be denied or abridged by the United States or by any State on account of sex.

Congress shall have power to enforce this article by appropriate legislation.

Amendment XX

[Adopted 1933]

Section 1

The terms of the President and Vice President shall end at noon on the 20th day of January, and the terms of Senators and Representatives at noon on the 3d day of January, of the years in which such terms would have ended if this article had not been ratified and the terms of their successors shall then begin.

Section 2

The Congress shall assemble at least once in every year, and such meeting shall begin at noon on the 3d day of January, unless they shall by law appoint a different day.

Section 3

If, at the time fixed for the beginning of the term of the President, the President elect shall have died, the Vice President elect shall become President. If a President shall not have been chosen before the time fixed for the beginning of his term, or if the President elect shall have failed to qualify, then the Vice President elect shall act as President until a President shall have qualified; and the Congress may by law provide for the case wherein neither a President elect nor a Vice President elect shall have qualified, declaring who shall then act as President, or the manner in which one who is to act shall be selected, and such person shall act accordingly until a President or Vice President shall have qualified.

Section 4

The Congress may by law provide for the case of the death of any of the persons from whom the House of Representatives may choose a President whenever the right of choice shall have devolved upon them, and for the case of the death of any of the persons from whom the Senate may choose a Vice President whenever the right of choice shall have devolved upon them.

Section 5

Sections 1 and 2 shall take effect on the 15th day of October following the ratification of this article.

Section 6

This article shall be inoperative unless it shall have been ratified as an amendment to the Constitution by the legislatures of three fourths of the several States within seven years from the date of its submission.

Amendment XXI

[Adopted 1933]

Section 1

The eighteenth article of amendment to the Constitution of the United States is hereby repealed.

Section 2

The transportation or importation into any State, Territory, or possession of the United States for delivery or use therein of intoxicating liquors in violation of the laws thereof, is hereby prohibited.

Section 3

This article shall be inoperative unless it shall have been ratified as an amendment to the Constitution by conventions in the several States, as provided in the Constitution, within seven years from the date of the submission hereof to the States by the Congress.

Amendment XXII
[Adopted 1951]
Section 1

No person shall be elected to the office of the President more than twice, and no person who has held the office of President, or acted as President, for more than two years of a term to which some other person was elected President shall be elected to the office of the President more than once. But this Article shall not apply to any person holding the office of President when this Article was proposed by the Congress, and shall not prevent any person who may be holding the office of President, or acting as President, during the term within which this Article becomes operative from holding the office of President or acting as President during the remainder of such term.

Section 2

This article shall be inoperative unless it shall have been ratified as an amendment to the Constitution by the legislatures of three-fourths of the several States within seven years from the date of its submission to the States by the Congress.

Amendment XXIII
[Adopted 1961]
Section 1

The District constituting the seat of Government of the United States shall appoint in such manner as the Congress shall direct:

A number of electors of President and Vice President equal to the whole number of Senators and Representatives in Congress to which the District would be entitled if it were a State, but in no event more than the least populous State; they shall be in addition to those appointed by the States, but they shall be considered, for the purposes of the election of President and Vice President, to be electors appointed by a State; and they shall meet in the District and perform such duties as provided by the twelfth article of amendment.

Section 2

The Congress shall have power to enforce this article by appropriate legislation.

Amendment XXIV
[Adopted 1964]
Section 1

The right of citizens of the United States to vote in any primary or other election for President or Vice President, for electors for President or Vice President, or for Senator or Representative in Congress, shall not be denied or abridged by the United States or any state by reason of failure to pay any poll tax or other tax.

Section 2

The Congress shall have the power to enforce this article by appropriate legislation.

Amendment XXV
[Adopted 1967]
Section 1

In case of the removal of the President from office or his death or resignation, the Vice President shall become President.

Section 2

Whenever there is a vacancy in the office of the Vice President, the President shall nominate a Vice President who shall take the office upon confirmation by a majority vote of both houses of Congress.

Section 3

Whenever the President transmits to the President pro tempore of the Senate and the Speaker of the House of Representatives his written declaration that he is unable to discharge the powers and duties of his office, and until he transmits to them a written declaration to the contrary, such powers and duties shall be discharged by the Vice President as Acting President.

Section 4

Whenever the Vice President and a majority of either the principal officers of the executive departments or of such other body as Congress may by law provide, transmit to the President pro tempore of the Senate and the Speaker of the House of Representatives their written declaration that the President is unable to discharge the powers and duties of his office, the Vice President shall immediately assume the powers and duties of the office as Acting President.

Thereafter, when the President transmits to the President pro tempore of the Senate and the Speaker of the House of Representatives his written declaration that no inability exists, he shall resume the powers and duties of his office unless the Vice President and a majority of either the principal officers of the executive department or of such other body as Congress may by law provide, transmit within four days to the President pro tempore of the Senate and the Speaker of the House of Representatives their written declaration that the President is unable to discharge the powers and duties of his office. Thereupon Congress shall decide the issue, assembling within 48 hours for that purpose if not in session. If the Congress, within 21 days after receipt of the latter written declaration, or, if Congress is not in session, within 21 days after Congress is required to assemble, determines by two-thirds vote of both houses that the President is unable to discharge the powers and duties of his office, the Vice President shall continue to discharge the same as Acting President; otherwise, the President shall resume the powers and duties of his office.

Amendment XXVI
[Adopted 1971]

Section 1

The right of citizens of the United States, who are 18 years of age or older, to vote shall not be denied or abridged by the United States or any state on account of age.

Section 2

The Congress shall have the power to enforce this article by appropriate legislation.

Amendment XXVII
[Adopted 1992]

No law, varying the compensation for the services of the Senators and Representatives shall take effect, until an election of Representatives shall have intervened.

Presidential Election Maps, 1789–2004

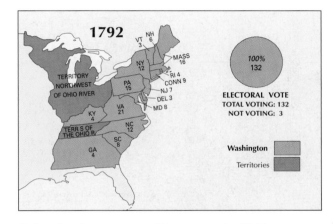

Each voting elector cast one of his two votes for Washington. New York failed to appoint its allotted eight electors in time and cast no electoral votes. North Carolina and Rhode Island did not vote because they had yet ratified the Constitution.

Each voting elector cast one of his two votes for Washington.

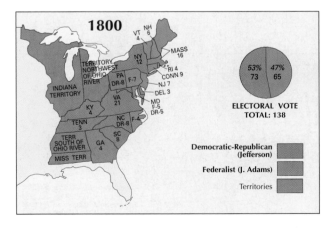

Democratic-Republican candidates Jefferson and Burr each received 73 electoral votes. The election was decided in the House of Representatives, where Jefferson was chosen President.

In the elections prior to 1804, each elector voted for two candidates for President. The candidate who received the largest number of votes, if that number was a majority, was declared President, and the candidate who received the second largest number of votes was declared Vice President.

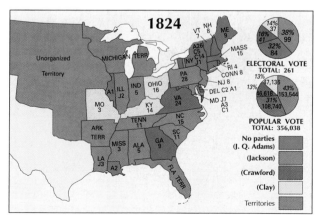

Because none of the candidates had a majority in the electoral college, the election was decided in the House of Representatives, where J.Q. Adams was chosen President.

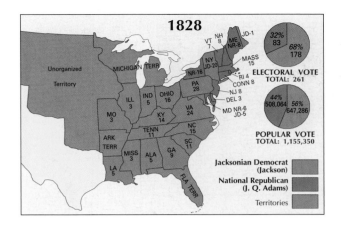

1828

VT 7
NH 8
ME — NR-8, JD-1
MASS 15
NY 16, JD-20
RI 4
CONN 8
NJ 8
DEL 3
MD NR-6, JD-5
PA 28
VA 24
NC 15
SC 11
GA 9
ALA 5
MISS 3
LA 5
TENN 11
KY 14
MO 3
ILL 3
IND 5
OHIO 16
MICHIGAN TERR
ARK TERR
FLA TERR
Unorganized Territory

32% 83 / 68% 178
ELECTORAL VOTE
TOTAL: 261

44% 508,064 / 56% 647,286
POPULAR VOTE
TOTAL: 1,155,350

Jacksonian Democrat (Jackson)
National Republican (J. Q. Adams)
Territories

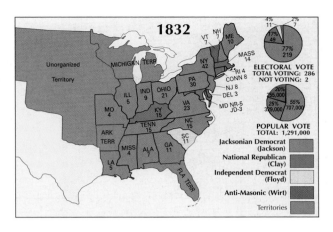

1832

VT 7
NH 7
ME 10
MASS 14
NY 42
RI 4
CONN 8
NJ 8
DEL 3
MD NR-5, JD-3
PA 30
VA 23
NC 15
SC 11
GA 11
ALA 7
MISS 4
LA 5
TENN 15
KY 15
MO 4
ILL 5
IND 9
OHIO 21
MICHIGAN TERR
ARK TERR
FLA TERR
Unorganized Territory

4% 11 / 2% 7
17% 49 / 77% 219
ELECTORAL VOTE
TOTAL VOTING: 286
NOT VOTING: 2

20% 255,000 / 55% 707,000
25% 329,000
POPULAR VOTE
TOTAL: 1,291,000

Jacksonian Democrat (Jackson)
National Republican (Clay)
Independent Democrat (Floyd)
Anti-Masonic (Wirt)
Territories

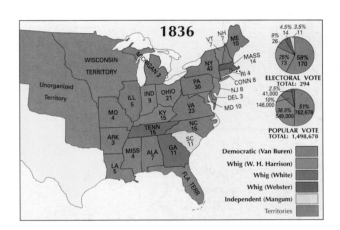

1836

VT 7
NH 7
ME 10
MASS 14
NY 42
RI 4
CONN 8
NJ 8
DEL 3
MD 10
PA 30
VA 23
NC 15
SC 11
GA 11
ALA 7
MISS 4
LA 5
TENN 15
KY 15
MO 4
ILL 5
IND 9
OHIO 21
MICHIGAN 3
WISCONSIN TERRITORY
ARK 3
FLA TERR
Unorganized Territory

4.5% 14 / 3.5% 11
9% 26 / 25% 73 / 58% 170
ELECTORAL VOTE
TOTAL: 294

2.5% 41,000 / 51% 762,678
10% 146,000 / 36.5% 549,000
POPULAR VOTE
TOTAL: 1,498,678

Democratic (Van Buren)
Whig (W. H. Harrison)
Whig (White)
Whig (Webster)
Independent (Mangum)
Territories

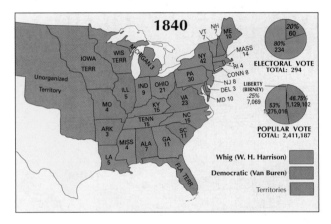

1840

VT 7
NH 7
ME 10
MASS 14
NY 42
RI 4
CONN 8
NJ 8
DEL 3
MD 10
PA 30
VA 23
NC 15
SC 11
GA 11
ALA 7
MISS 4
LA 5
TENN 15
KY 15
MO 4
ILL 5
IND 9
OHIO 21
MICHIGAN 3
WIS TERR
IOWA TERR
ARK 3
FLA TERR
Unorganized Territory

20% 60 / 80% 234
ELECTORAL VOTE
TOTAL: 294

LIBERTY (BIRNEY) .25% 7,069
46.75% 1,129,102 / 53% 1,275,016
POPULAR VOTE
TOTAL: 2,411,187

Whig (W. H. Harrison)
Democratic (Van Buren)
Territories

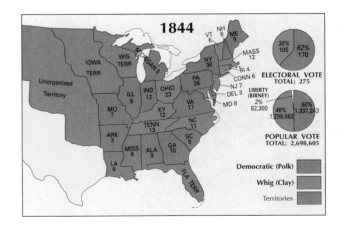

1844

VT 6
NH 6
ME 9
MASS 12
NY 36
RI 4
CONN 6
NJ 7
DEL 3
MD 8
PA 26
VA 17
NC 11
SC 9
GA 10
ALA 9
MISS 6
LA 6
TENN 13
KY 12
MO 7
ILL 9
IND 12
OHIO 23
MICHIGAN 5
WIS TERR
IOWA TERR
ARK 3
FLA TERR
Unorganized Territory

38% 105 / 62% 170
ELECTORAL VOTE
TOTAL: 275

LIBERTY (BIRNEY) 2% 62,300
48% 1,299,062 / 50% 1,337,243
POPULAR VOTE
TOTAL: 2,698,605

Democratic (Polk)
Whig (Clay)
Territories

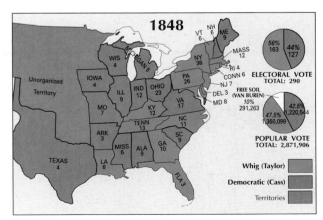

1848

VT 6
NH 6
ME 9
MASS 12
NY 36
RI 4
CONN 6
NJ 7
DEL 3
MD 8
PA 26
VA 17
NC 11
SC 9
GA 10
ALA 9
MISS 6
LA 6
TENN 13
KY 12
MO 7
ILL 9
IND 12
OHIO 23
MICHIGAN 5
WIS 4
IOWA 4
ARK 3
FLA 3
TEXAS 4
Unorganized Territory

56% 163 / 44% 127
ELECTORAL VOTE
TOTAL: 290

FREE SOIL (VAN BUREN) 10% 291,263
42.5% 1,220,544 / 47.5% 1,360,099
POPULAR VOTE
TOTAL: 2,871,906

Whig (Taylor)
Democratic (Cass)
Territories

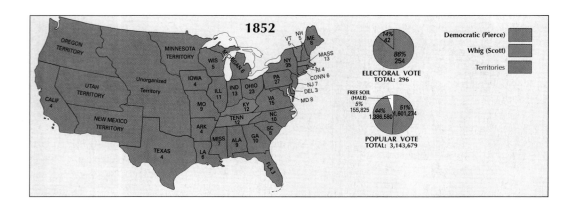

1852

ELECTORAL VOTE
TOTAL: 296

14%
42

86%
254

Democratic (Pierce)
Whig (Scott)
Territories

FREE SOIL
(HALE)
5%
155,825

44%
1,386,580

51%
1,601,274

POPULAR VOTE
TOTAL: 3,143,679

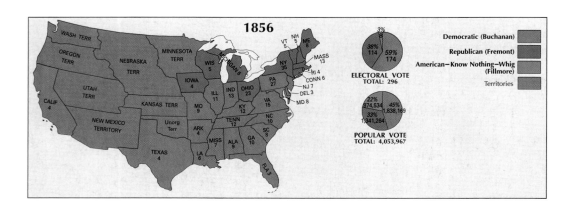

1856

ELECTORAL VOTE
TOTAL: 296

3%
8

38%
114

59%
174

Democratic (Buchanan)
Republican (Fremont)
American–Know Nothing–Whig (Fillmore)
Territories

22%
874,534

45%
1,838,169

33%
1,341,264

POPULAR VOTE
TOTAL: 4,053,967

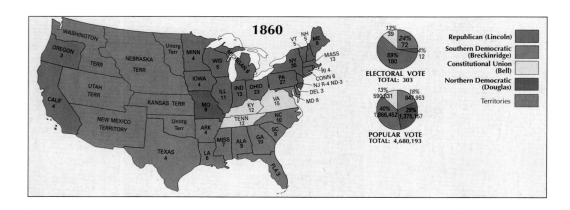

1860

ELECTORAL VOTE
TOTAL: 303

13%
39

24%
72

4%
12

59%
180

Republican (Lincoln)
Southern Democratic (Breckinridge)
Constitutional Union (Bell)
Northern Democratic (Douglas)
Territories

13%
590,631

18%
847,953

40%
1,866,452

29%
1,375,157

POPULAR VOTE
TOTAL: 4,680,193

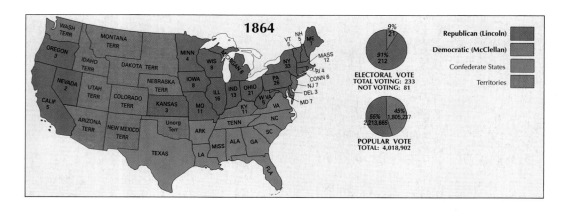

1864

ELECTORAL VOTE
TOTAL VOTING: 233
NOT VOTING: 81

9%
21

91%
212

Republican (Lincoln)
Democratic (McClellan)
Confederate States
Territories

55%
2,213,665

45%
1,805,237

POPULAR VOTE
TOTAL: 4,018,902

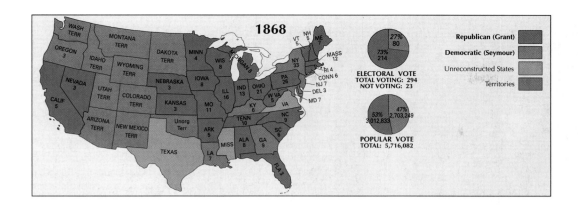

1868

ELECTORAL VOTE
TOTAL VOTING: 294
NOT VOTING: 23

27% 80
73% 214

POPULAR VOTE
TOTAL: 5,716,082

53% 3,012,833
47% 2,703,249

Republican (Grant)
Democratic (Seymour)
Unreconstructed States
Territories

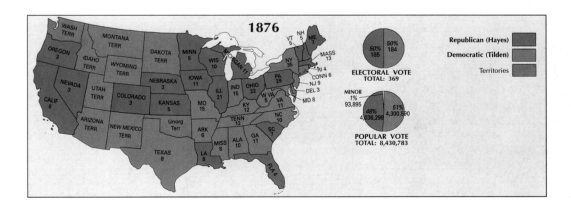

1872

5% 18
1% 3
.5% 2
12% 42
81% 286
.5% 1

ELECTORAL VOTE
TOTAL VOTING: 352
NOT VOTING: 14

MINOR .5% 35,097
55.5% 3,597,132
44% 2,834,125

POPULAR VOTE
TOTAL: 6,466,354

Republican (Grant)
Independent Democratic (Hendricks)
Democratic (Brown)
Democratic (Greeley)
Democratic (Jenkins)
Democratic (Davis)
Territories

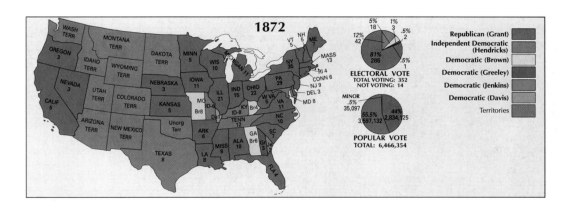

1876

50% 185
50% 184

ELECTORAL VOTE
TOTAL: 369

MINOR 1% 93,895
48% 4,036,298
51% 4,300,590

POPULAR VOTE
TOTAL: 8,430,783

Republican (Hayes)
Democratic (Tilden)
Territories

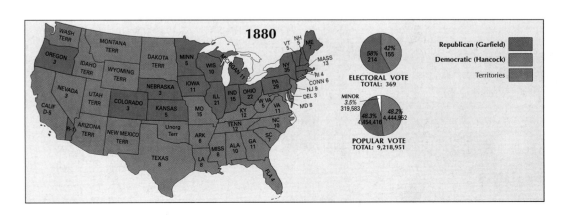

1880

58% 214
42% 155

ELECTORAL VOTE
TOTAL: 369

MINOR 3.5% 319,583
48.3% 4,454,416
48.2% 4,444,952

POPULAR VOTE
TOTAL: 9,218,951

Republican (Garfield)
Democratic (Hancock)
Territories

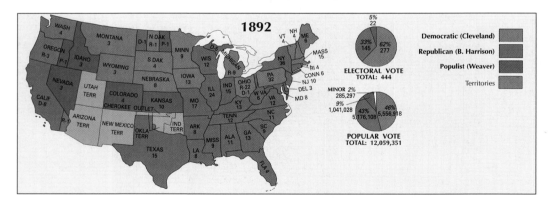

Republican candidate Harrison won the electoral vote but lost the popular vote to Democratic candidate Cleveland. Greer County (Oklahoma) voted as part of Texas.

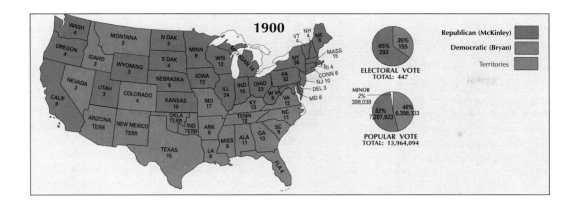

1900

ELECTORAL VOTE
TOTAL: 447

65% 292 — 35% 155

MINOR 2% 398,038
52% 7,207,923 — 46% 6,358,133

POPULAR VOTE
TOTAL: 13,964,094

Republican (McKinley)
Democratic (Bryan)
Territories

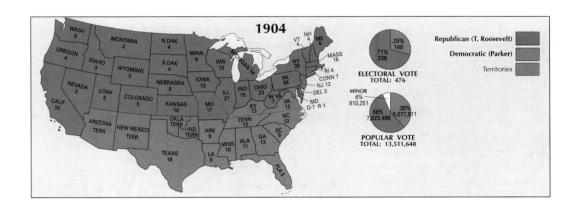

1904

ELECTORAL VOTE
TOTAL: 476

71% 336 — 29% 140

MINOR 6% 810,251
56% 7,623,486 — 38% 5,077,911

POPULAR VOTE
TOTAL: 13,511,648

Republican (T. Roosevelt)
Democratic (Parker)
Territories

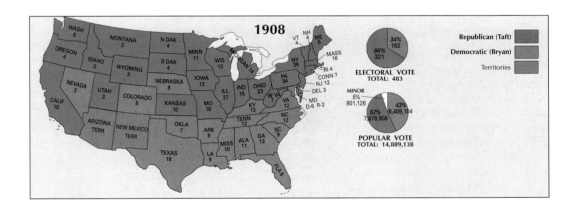

1908

ELECTORAL VOTE
TOTAL: 483

66% 321 — 34% 162

MINOR 5% 801,126
52% 7,678,908 — 43% 6,409,104

POPULAR VOTE
TOTAL: 14,889,138

Republican (Taft)
Democratic (Bryan)
Territories

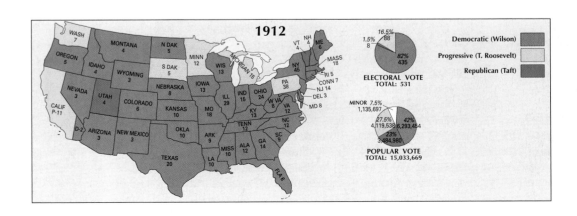

1912

ELECTORAL VOTE
TOTAL: 531

82% 435 — 16.5% 88 — 1.5% 8

MINOR 7.5% 1,135,697
42% 6,293,454 — 27.5% 4,119,538 — 23% 3,484,980

POPULAR VOTE
TOTAL: 15,033,669

Democratic (Wilson)
Progressive (T. Roosevelt)
Republican (Taft)

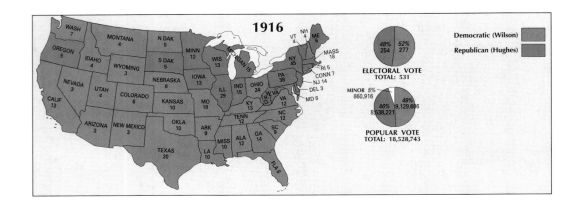

1916

Democratic (Wilson)
Republican (Hughes)

48% 254 | 52% 277
ELECTORAL VOTE
TOTAL: 531

MINOR 5% 860,916 | 49% 9,129,606 | 46% 8,538,221
POPULAR VOTE
TOTAL: 18,528,743

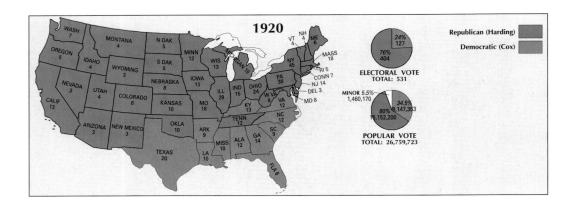

1920

Republican (Harding)
Democratic (Cox)

24% 127 | 76% 404
ELECTORAL VOTE
TOTAL: 531

MINOR 5.5% 1,460,170 | 34.5% 9,147,353 | 60% 16,152,200
POPULAR VOTE
TOTAL: 26,759,723

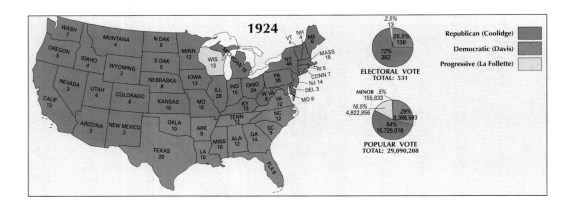

1924

Republican (Coolidge)
Democratic (Davis)
Progressive (La Follette)

2.5% 13 | 25.5% 136 | 72% 382
ELECTORAL VOTE
TOTAL: 531

MINOR .5% 155,833 | 16.5% 4,822,856 | 29% 8,386,503 | 54% 15,725,016
POPULAR VOTE
TOTAL: 29,090,208

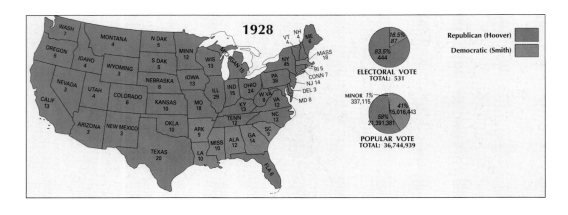

1928

Republican (Hoover)
Democratic (Smith)

16.5% 87 | 83.5% 444
ELECTORAL VOTE
TOTAL: 531

MINOR 1% 337,115 | 41% 15,016,443 | 58% 21,391,381
POPULAR VOTE
TOTAL: 36,744,939

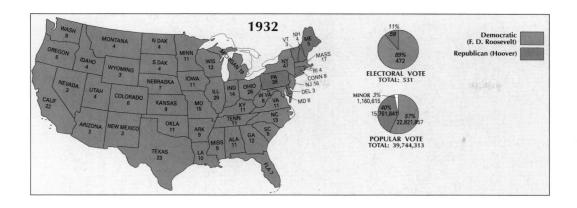

1932

WASH 8 · MONTANA 4 · N DAK 4 · VT 3 · NH 4 · ME 5 · OREGON 5 · IDAHO 4 · WYOMING 3 · S DAK 4 · MINN 11 · WIS 12 · MICHIGAN 19 · MASS 17 · NY 47 · RI 4 · CONN 8 · NEVADA 3 · UTAH 4 · COLORADO 6 · NEBRASKA 7 · IOWA 11 · ILL 29 · IND 14 · OHIO 26 · PA 38 · NJ 16 · DEL 3 · CALIF 22 · KANSAS 9 · MO 15 · KY 11 · W VA 8 · VA 11 · MD 8 · ARIZONA 3 · NEW MEXICO 3 · OKLA 11 · ARK 9 · TENN 11 · NC 13 · SC 8 · TEXAS 23 · LA 10 · MISS 9 · ALA 11 · GA 12 · FLA 7

ELECTORAL VOTE TOTAL: 531
11% 59 — 89% 472

POPULAR VOTE TOTAL: 39,744,313
MINOR 3% 1,160,615 — 40% 15,761,841 — 57% 22,821,857

Democratic (F. D. Roosevelt)
Republican (Hoover)

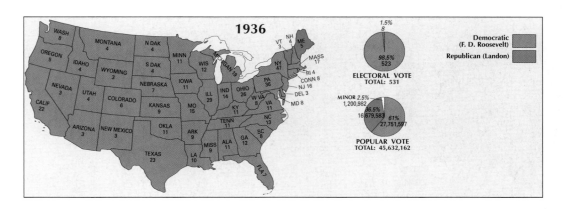

1936

WASH 8 · MONTANA 4 · N DAK 4 · VT 3 · NH 4 · ME 5 · OREGON 5 · IDAHO 4 · WYOMING 3 · S DAK 4 · MINN 11 · WIS 12 · MICHIGAN 19 · MASS 17 · NY 47 · RI 4 · CONN 8 · NEVADA 3 · UTAH 4 · COLORADO 6 · NEBRASKA 7 · IOWA 11 · ILL 29 · IND 14 · OHIO 26 · PA 36 · NJ 16 · DEL 3 · CALIF 22 · KANSAS 9 · MO 15 · KY 11 · W VA 8 · VA 11 · MD 8 · ARIZONA 3 · NEW MEXICO 3 · OKLA 11 · ARK 9 · TENN 11 · NC 13 · SC 8 · TEXAS 23 · LA 10 · MISS 9 · ALA 11 · GA 12 · FLA 7

ELECTORAL VOTE TOTAL: 531
1.5% 8 — 98.5% 523

POPULAR VOTE TOTAL: 45,632,162
MINOR 2.5% 1,200,982 — 36.5% 16,679,583 — 61% 27,751,597

Democratic (F. D. Roosevelt)
Republican (Landon)

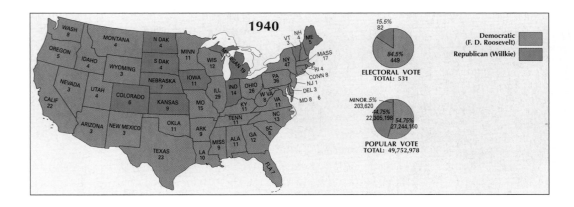

1940

WASH 8 · MONTANA 4 · N DAK 4 · VT 3 · NH 4 · ME 5 · OREGON 5 · IDAHO 4 · WYOMING 3 · S DAK 4 · MINN 11 · WIS 12 · MICHIGAN 19 · MASS 17 · NY 47 · RI 4 · CONN 8 · NEVADA 3 · UTAH 4 · COLORADO 6 · NEBRASKA 7 · IOWA 11 · ILL 29 · IND 14 · OHIO 26 · PA 36 · NJ 1 · DEL 3 · CALIF 22 · KANSAS 9 · MO 15 · KY 11 · W VA 8 · VA 11 · MD 8 · 6 · ARIZONA 3 · NEW MEXICO 3 · OKLA 11 · ARK 9 · TENN 11 · NC 13 · SC 8 · TEXAS 23 · LA 10 · MISS 9 · ALA 11 · GA 12 · FLA 7

ELECTORAL VOTE TOTAL: 531
15.5% 82 — 84.5% 449

POPULAR VOTE TOTAL: 49,752,978
MINOR .5% 203,620 — 44.75% 22,305,198 — 54.75% 27,244,160

Democratic (F. D. Roosevelt)
Republican (Willkie)

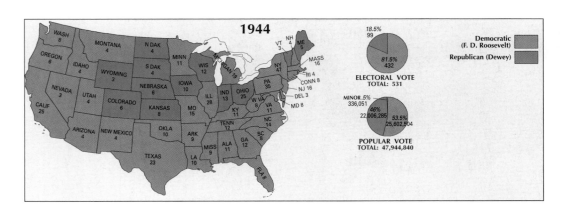

1944

WASH 8 · MONTANA 4 · N DAK 4 · VT 3 · NH 4 · ME 5 · OREGON 6 · IDAHO 4 · WYOMING 3 · S DAK 4 · MINN 11 · WIS 12 · MICHIGAN 19 · MASS 16 · NY 47 · RI 4 · CONN 8 · NEVADA 3 · UTAH 4 · COLORADO 6 · NEBRASKA 6 · IOWA 10 · ILL 28 · IND 13 · OHIO 25 · PA 35 · NJ 16 · DEL 3 · CALIF 25 · KANSAS 8 · MO 15 · KY 11 · W VA 8 · VA 11 · MD 8 · ARIZONA 4 · NEW MEXICO 4 · OKLA 10 · ARK 9 · TENN 14 · NC 14 · SC 8 · TEXAS 23 · LA 10 · MISS 9 · ALA 11 · GA 12 · FLA 8

ELECTORAL VOTE TOTAL: 531
18.5% 99 — 81.5% 432

POPULAR VOTE TOTAL: 47,944,840
MINOR .5% 336,051 — 46% 22,006,285 — 53.5% 25,602,504

Democratic (F. D. Roosevelt)
Republican (Dewey)

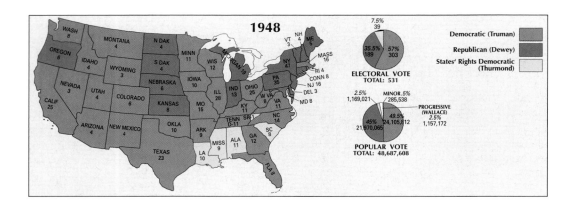

1948

ELECTORAL VOTE
TOTAL: 531

7.5%
39

35.5%
189

57%
303

POPULAR VOTE
TOTAL: 48,687,608

2.5%
1,169,021

MINOR .5%
285,538

PROGRESSIVE
(WALLACE)
2.5%
1,157,172

45%
21,970,065

49.5%
24,105,812

Democratic (Truman)

Republican (Dewey)

States' Rights Democratic
(Thurmond)

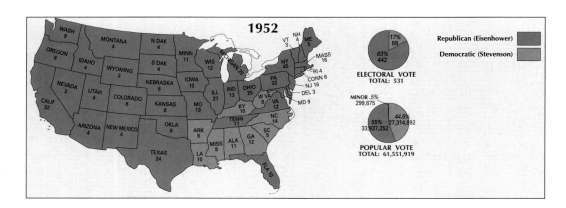

1952

ELECTORAL VOTE
TOTAL: 531

17%
89

83%
442

POPULAR VOTE
TOTAL: 61,551,919

MINOR .5%
299,675

55%
33,937,252

44.5%
27,314,992

Republican (Eisenhower)

Democratic (Stevenson)

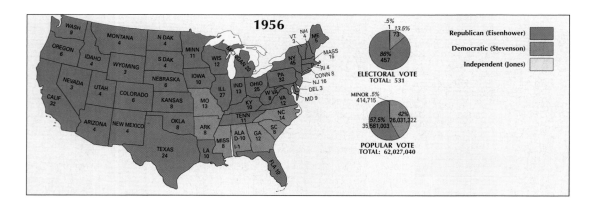

1956

ELECTORAL VOTE
TOTAL: 531

.5%
1

13.5%
73

86%
457

POPULAR VOTE
TOTAL: 62,027,040

MINOR .5%
414,715

57.5%
35,581,003

42%
26,031,322

Republican (Eisenhower)

Democratic (Stevenson)

Independent (Jones)

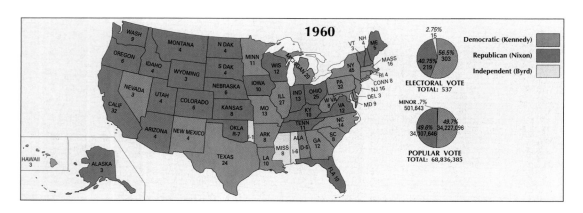

1960

ELECTORAL VOTE
TOTAL: 537

2.75%
15

40.75%
219

56.5%
303

POPULAR VOTE
TOTAL: 68,836,385

MINOR .7%
501,643

49.8%
34,107,646

49.7%
34,227,096

Democratic (Kennedy)

Republican (Nixon)

Independent (Byrd)

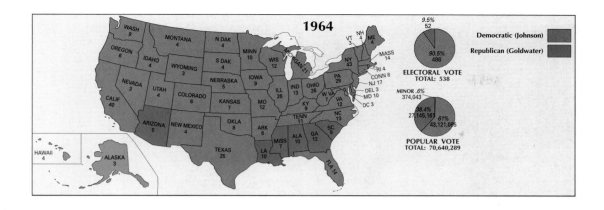

1964

Democratic (Johnson)	
Republican (Goldwater)	

9.5%
52

90.5%
486

ELECTORAL VOTE
TOTAL: 538

MINOR .6%
374,043

38.4%
27,145,161

61%
43,121,085

POPULAR VOTE
TOTAL: 70,640,289

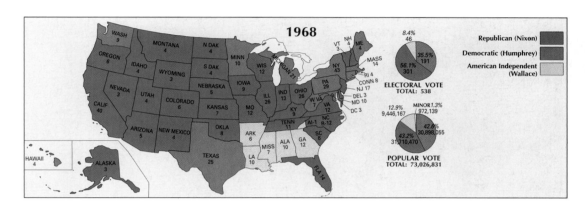

1968

Republican (Nixon)	
Democratic (Humphrey)	
American Independent (Wallace)	

8.4%
46

35.5%
191

56.1%
301

ELECTORAL VOTE
TOTAL: 538

MINOR 1.3%
972,139

12.9%
9,446,167

42.8%
30,898,055

43.2%
31,710,470

POPULAR VOTE
TOTAL: 73,026,831

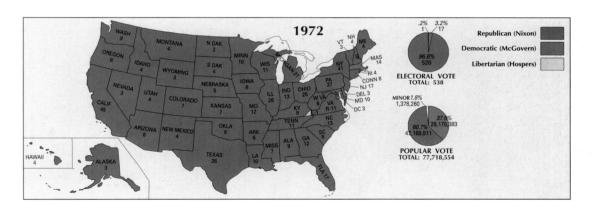

1972

Republican (Nixon)	
Democratic (McGovern)	
Libertarian (Hospers)	

.2%
1

3.2%
17

96.6%
520

ELECTORAL VOTE
TOTAL: 538

MINOR 1.8%
1,378,260

37.5%
29,170,383

60.7%
47,169,911

POPULAR VOTE
TOTAL: 77,718,554

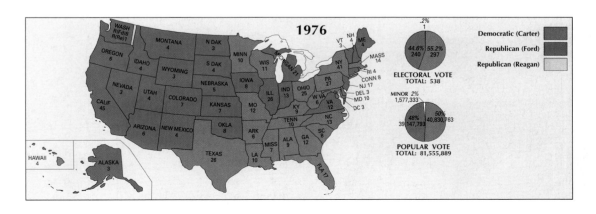

1976

Democratic (Carter)	
Republican (Ford)	
Republican (Reagan)	

.2%
1

44.6%
240

55.2%
297

ELECTORAL VOTE
TOTAL: 538

MINOR 2%
1,577,333

48%
39,147,793

50%
40,830,763

POPULAR VOTE
TOTAL: 81,555,889

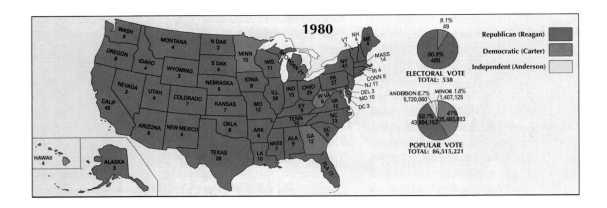

1980

ELECTORAL VOTE
TOTAL: 538

9.1%
49

90.9%
489

Republican (Reagan)
Democratic (Carter)
Independent (Anderson)

ANDERSON 6.7%
5,720,060

MINOR 1.6%
1,407,125

50.7%
43,904,153

41%
35,483,883

POPULAR VOTE
TOTAL: 86,515,221

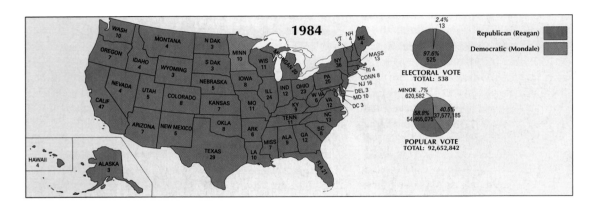

1984

ELECTORAL VOTE
TOTAL: 538

2.4%
13

97.6%
525

Republican (Reagan)
Democratic (Mondale)

MINOR .7%
620,582

58.8%
54,455,075

40.5%
37,577,185

POPULAR VOTE
TOTAL: 92,652,842

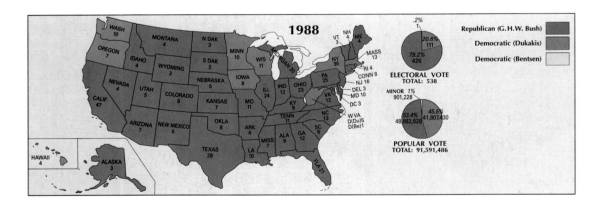

1988

ELECTORAL VOTE
TOTAL: 538

.2%
1

20.6%
111

79.2%
426

Republican (G.H.W. Bush)
Democratic (Dukakis)
Democratic (Bentsen)

MINOR 1%
901,228

53.4%
48,882,828

45.6%
41,807,430

POPULAR VOTE
TOTAL: 91,591,486

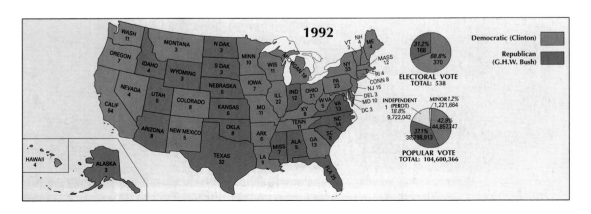

1992

ELECTORAL VOTE
TOTAL: 538

31.2%
168

68.8%
370

Democratic (Clinton)
Republican
(G.H.W. Bush)

INDEPENDENT
(PEROT)
18.8%
9,722,042

MINOR 1.2%
1,221,664

37.1%
38,798,913

42.9%
44,857,147

POPULAR VOTE
TOTAL: 104,600,366

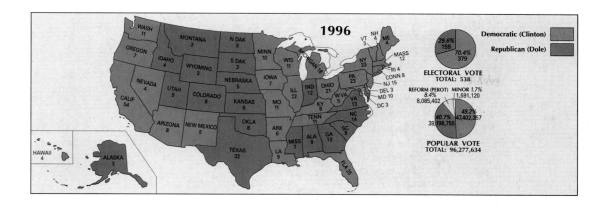

1996

Democratic (Clinton)
Republican (Dole)

29.6%
159
70.4%
379

ELECTORAL VOTE
TOTAL: 538

REFORM (PEROT)   MINOR 1.7%
8.4%   1,591,120
8,085,402

49.2%
40.7%   47,402,357
39,198,755

POPULAR VOTE
TOTAL: 96,277,634

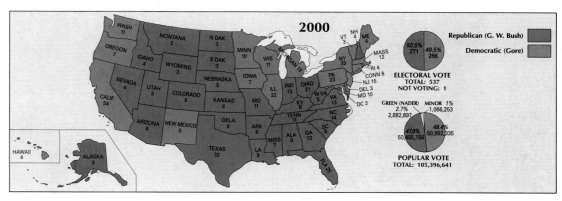

2000

Republican (G. W. Bush)
Democratic (Gore)

50.5%
271   49.5%
       266

ELECTORAL VOTE
TOTAL: 537
NOT VOTING: 1

GREEN (NADER)   MINOR 1%
2.7%   1,066,253
2,882,897

47.9%
50,455,156   48.4%
              50,992,335

POPULAR VOTE
TOTAL: 105,396,641

Republican candidate G. W. Bush won the electoral vote but lost the popular vote to Democratic candidate Gore. One elector from the District of Columbia abstained from voting.

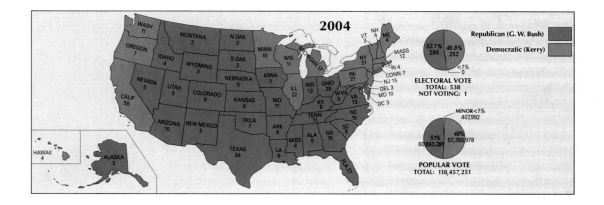

2004

Republican (G. W. Bush)
Democratic (Kerry)

53.1%
286   46.8%
       252

<1%
0

ELECTORAL VOTE
TOTAL: 538
NOT VOTING: 1

MINOR <1%
407,992

51%
60,693,281   48%
              57,355,978

POPULAR VOTE
TOTAL: 118,457,251

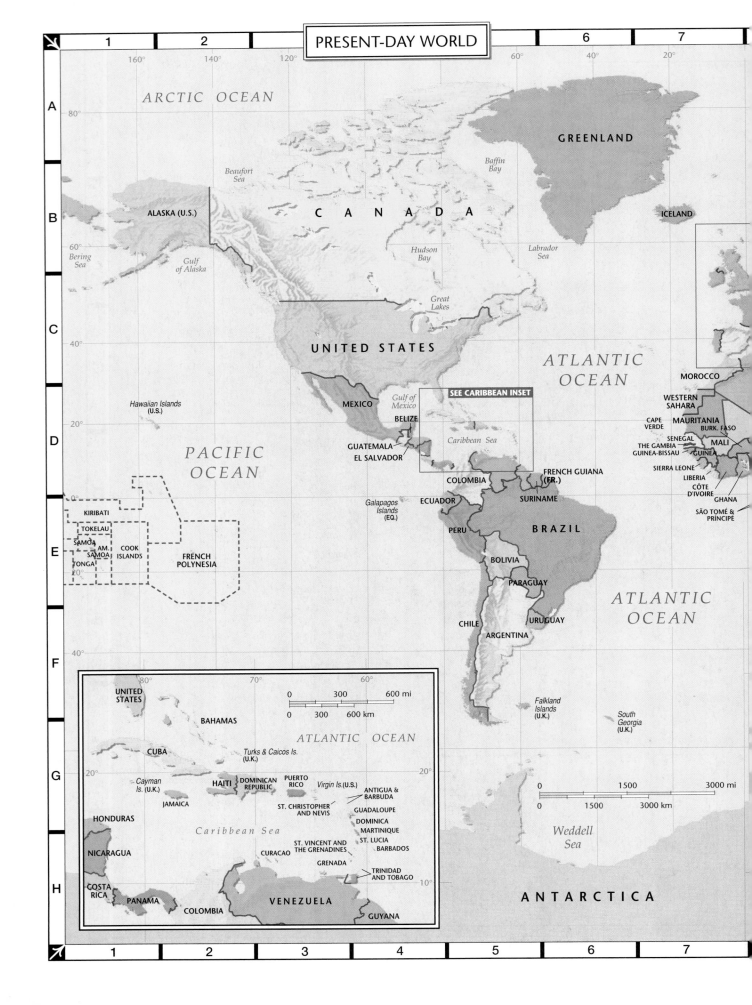

ARCTIC OCEAN

GREENLAND

ICELAND

CANADA

Beaufort
Sea

Baffin
Bay

ALASKA (U.S.)

Bering
Sea

Gulf
of Alaska

Hudson
Bay

Labrador
Sea

Great
Lakes

UNITED STATES

ATLANTIC
OCEAN

MOROCCO

WESTERN
SAHARA

PACIFIC
OCEAN

Hawaiian Islands
(U.S.)

MEXICO

Gulf of
Mexico

SEE CARIBBEAN INSET

BELIZE

GUATEMALA
EL SALVADOR

Caribbean Sea

CAPE
VERDE

MAURITANIA
BURK. FASO

SENEGAL
THE GAMBIA
GUINEA-BISSAU

MALI

GUINEA

COLOMBIA

FRENCH GUIANA
(FR.)

SIERRA LEONE
LIBERIA
CÔTE
D'IVOIRE

GHANA

KIRIBATI

Galapagos
Islands
(EQ.)

ECUADOR

SURINAME

SÃO TOMÉ &
PRÍNCIPE

TOKELAU

PERU

BRAZIL

SAMOA
AM.
SAMOA
TONGA

COOK
ISLANDS

FRENCH
POLYNESIA

BOLIVIA

PARAGUAY

ATLANTIC
OCEAN

CHILE

URUGUAY

ARGENTINA

Falkland
Islands
(U.K.)

South
Georgia
(U.K.)

Weddell
Sea

ANTARCTICA

Caribbean Inset

UNITED
STATES

BAHAMAS

ATLANTIC OCEAN

0   300   600 mi
0   300   600 km

CUBA

Turks & Caicos Is.
(U.K.)

PUERTO
RICO

Virgin Is.(U.S.)

ANTIGUA &
BARBUDA

Cayman
Is. (U.K.)

HAITI

DOMINICAN
REPUBLIC

JAMAICA

ST. CHRISTOPHER
AND NEVIS

GUADALOUPE

DOMINICA
MARTINIQUE
ST. LUCIA
BARBADOS

HONDURAS

Caribbean Sea

ST. VINCENT AND
THE GRENADINES

NICARAGUA

CURACAO

GRENADA

TRINIDAD
AND TOBAGO

COSTA
RICA

PANAMA

COLOMBIA

VENEZUELA

GUYANA

0   1500   3000 mi
0   1500   3000 km

Picture Credits

INDEX

Note: Italicized letters *f*, *m*, and *n* following page numbers indicate figures (photos, illustrations, and graphs), maps, and footnotes, respectively.

Primary Source Documents

How to Analyze Primary Source Documents

Historians study sources to reconstruct the lifestyles and events of previous generations (what actually happened in the past), as well as to understand the past as the people who lived it did—to examine their ideas and thoughts about the world. By using sources, historians actually recreate history. They craft an understanding of the people, events, ideas, trends, and themes of the past based upon interpretation of those sources.

Primary sources are generally firsthand accounts or records. They may have been written or created during the time period under investigation, or perhaps were written by someone who lived then. Most crucially, they have not been interpreted by anyone else, though they may offer interpretations of the events they describe.

The primary source documents presented here give you the opportunity to put your investigative skills to the test by analyzing the sources yourself, rather than by reading others' interpretations.

WHEN ANALYZING A PRIMARY SOURCE, YOU SHOULD ASK SEVEN KEY QUESTIONS

1. **Who is the author?**
   Who wrote or created this? Is there a single or multiple authors? An author's identity sometimes helps you answer the later questions.

2. **What type of source is this?**
   All the sources here are documents, but what type? Is it a biography or a government document? This is a simple but crucial step because you must consider what you can expect to learn from the document.

3. **What is the message of this source?**
   What is the author describing? What is happening in the text? What is the story?

4. **Who is the intended audience?**
   Who is the author addressing? Was the source intended for private or public consumption? Identifying the audience will help you answer the next question.

5. **Why was this source created?**
   Does the author have an agenda, a larger purpose? Is the author trying to persuade the audience? Is the document or source simply a compilation of facts, or does it include opinion, inference, or interpretation?

6. **Is this source credible and accurate?**
   Historians must examine every source with a critical eye. What do you know about the author? Does the document make sense? Do the facts presented by the author or what you know about the time period support the thesis, statement, assertion, or story the author is conveying? Why should you trust, or distrust, this source?

7. **How is this source valuable to me?**
   How does the source relate to other sources from the time period or along the same issue or theme? Does it support or contradict them? Does it repeat information from other sources or add new information? How relevant is the source to your topic of inquiry? Does it extensively cover your topic, or only marginally or not at all? Remember, you should explore enough sources to obtain a variety of viewpoints.

Let's take a look at a portion of the document from Chapter 16 to see how this process works. Reading the full document selection, of course, provides even more clues to understanding this source.

DOCUMENT 16.1
Carl Schurz, *Report on the Condition of the South* (1865)

Carl Schurz was a German immigrant who rose to great political prominence in the United States. He was a leading member of the Republican Party from its founding and was a great supporter of Lincoln. During the Civil War he attained the rank of major general. After the war, Schurz continued to be active in politics, supporting many reform movements. In addition, he was writer and editor for several English- and German-language newspapers, and he wrote several books. In 1865 President Andrew Johnson sent Schurz to tour the South in order to report on its postwar status. An excerpt from Schurz's report appears below. The president was not pleased with the report.

We ought to keep in view, above all, the nature of the problem which is to be solved. As to what is commonly termed "reconstruction," it is not only the political machinery of the States and their constitutional relations to the general government, but the whole organism of southern society that must be reconstructed, or rather constructed anew, so as to bring it in harmony with the rest of American society. The difficulties of this task are not to be considered overcome when the people of the south take the oath of allegiance and elect governors and legislatures and members of Congress, and militia captains. That this would be done had become certain as soon as the surrenders of the southern armies had made further resistance impossible, and nothing in the world was left, even to the most uncompromising rebel, but to submit or to emigrate. It was also natural that they should avail themselves of every chance offered them to resume control of their home affairs and to regain their influence in the Union. But this can hardly be called the first step towards the solution of the true problem, and it is a fair question to ask, whether the hasty gratification of their desire to resume such control would not create new embarrassments.

NOW LET'S LOOK AT WHAT WE CAN LEARN FROM THIS TEXT

1. **Who is the author?**

   From the head note, we know that Carl Schurz was a Republican politician, a Union officer in the Civil War, a German immigrant, and an author.

2. **What type of source is this?**

   This is an official government report commissioned by President Johnson.

3. **What is the message of this source?**

   In this first paragraph, Schurz is describing the potential difficulties of "reconstructing" the South after the Civil War. He is presenting what he perceives to be the goal of Reconstruction (to bring the South "in harmony with the rest of American society") as well as the potential pitfalls of quickly returning the southern states to the control of former Confederates ("creat[ing] new embarrassments").

4. **Who is the intended audience?**

   Schurz's primary audience is President Johnson, who commissioned the tour and report. You should consider, however, that since it was commissioned by a government official, other members of the government may have had access to it as well. The head note does not tell us if it was published for the public at large. Some minimal additional research, however, would confirm that it was published as a U.S. Senate Executive Document for the 1st session of the 39th Congress.

5. **Why was this source created?**

   In the very first sentence, Schurz presents Reconstruction as "the problem which is to be solved." From this statement we can infer that he felt his duty was not only to report on the "condition of the South," as described in the title, but to present his interpretation of the primary problems facing the nation as well as possible solutions.

6. **Is this source credible and accurate?**

   Though this is a government document, we must remember that Schurz likely could not be considered an impartial observer. He was from the North, was a Republican (the head note identifies him as "a great supporter of Lincoln"), and had fought in the Civil War. The overall tone of this paragraph, however, is very matter-of-fact. This may be attributable to Schurz's experience as a writer and editor. But we also know, from answering question 5, that Schurz felt his job was to do more than simply report. He framed his report in the form of problems and solutions. You must decide if these factors affected Schurz's credibility and accuracy as an observer of the conditions of the South in 1865. Here is the opportunity to begin to craft your interpretation of Reconstruction.

7. **How is this source valuable to you?**

   You must place the source within the context of your own research. Here are a few examples.

   This source would be an invaluable central component if you were researching:
   - firsthand accounts of the conditions in the South following the Civil War
   - a biographical paper on Carl Schurz

   It would be an important part of a paper on:
   - the various stages of Reconstruction
   - the disagreements between President Johnson and members of the Republican Party

   It would be crucial background information if you were researching:
   - Andrew Johnson's presidency
   - the return of Democratic rule in the former Confederacy

You now have the basic tools to begin analyzing historical documents yourself. As you apply these skills to the documents contained here, you will likely find that your skill level will rapidly increase. You may even find yourself reading others' interpretations of primary source documents with a more critical eye.

DOCUMENT P.1
Pima Creation Story (Traditional—Ancient)

The Pima lived in the Arizona Desert along the Gila and Salt Rivers, a remote location that helped them resist European influence. They were named "Pima" in the fifteenth century by the Spanish, who later recorded their first narratives. However, no creation stories were transcribed until the early twentieth century when a Pima named Edward H. Wood met J. W. Lloyd at the Pan-American Fair in Buffalo and asked his help in preserving the legends of Wood's grand-uncle, Thin Leather. The Pima creation story takes us to a landscape on the other side of the North American continent, to a people who favored stability, settlement, and peace and whose artistic traditions were long and rich.

In the beginning there was no earth, no water—nothing. There was only a Person, Juh-wert-a-Mah-kai, "The Doctor of the Earth."

He just floated, for there was no place for him to stand upon. There was no sun, no light, and he just floated about in the darkness, which was Darkness itself.

He wandered around in the nowhere till he thought he had wandered enough. Then he rubbed on his breast and rubbed out moah-haht-tack, that is, perspiration, or "greasy earth." This he rubbed out on the palm of his hand and held out. It tipped over three times, but the fourth time it stayed straight in the middle of the air and there it remains now as the world.

The first bush he created was the greasewood bush.

And he made ants, little tiny ants, to live on that bush, on its gum which comes out of its stem.

But these little ants did not do any good, so he created white ants, and these worked and enlarged the earth, and they kept on increasing it, larger and larger until it at last was big enough for himself to rest upon.

Then he created a Person. He made him out of his eye, out of the shadow of his eyes, to assist him, to be like him, and to help him in creating trees and human beings and everything that was to be on the earth.

The name of this being was Noo-ee—the buzzard.

Noo-ee was given all power, but he did not do the work he was created for. He did not care to help Juh-wert-a-Mah-kai, but let him go by himself.

And so The Doctor of the Earth himself created the mountains and everything that has seed and is good to eat. For if he had created human beings first they would have had nothing to live on.

DOCUMENT ANALYSIS

1. How does this creation story differ from the traditions of the Judeo-Christian experience?

_____

_____

_____

2. Does every society have a creation story/tradition? Give some examples.

_____

_____

_____

DOCUMENT P.2
Iroquois Creation Story (Traditional—Ancient)

The original homeland of the Iroquois was in upstate New York between the Adirondack Mountains and Niagara Falls. Through conquest and migration, the Iroquois gained control of most of the northeastern United States and eastern Canada. At its maximum in 1680, their empire extended west from the north shore of Chesapeake Bay through Kentucky to the junction of the Ohio and Mississippi Rivers. The following is an excerpt of the tribe's creation story.

Among the ancients there were two worlds in existence. The lower world was in great darkness—the possession of the great monster—but the upper world was inhabited by mankind; and there was a woman conceived who would have the twins born. When her travail drew near and her situation seemed to produce a great distress on her mind, she was induced by some of her relations to lay herself on a mattress which was prepared so as to gain refreshments for her wearied body. While she was asleep the very place sunk down towards the dark world.

The monsters of the great water were alarmed at her appearance of descending to the lower world. In consequence all the species of the creatures were immediately collected into where it was expected she would fall. When the monsters were assembled they made consultation, and one of them was appointed in haste to search the great deep in order to procure some earth, if it could be obtained. Accordingly the monster descends, succeeds, and returns to the place. Another requisition was presented: who would be capable to secure the woman from the terrors of the great water? None was able to comply until a great turtle came forward and proposed to endure her lasting weight. A small quantity of earth was varnished on the back part of the turtle. The woman alights on the seat prepared, and she receives a satisfaction.

While holding her, the turtle increased every moment and became a considerable island of earth, and apparently covered with great bushes. The woman remained in a state of unlimited darkness, and she was overtaken by her travail. While she was in the limits of distress one of the infants in her womb was moved by an evil opinion and he was determined to pass out under the side of the parent's arm, and the other infant in vain endeavored to prevent his design. The woman was in a painful condition during their disputes and the infants entered the dark world by compulsion, and their parent expired in a few moments. They had the power of sustenance without a nurse, and remained in the dark regions.

After a time the turtle increased to a great island and the infants were grown up, and one of them possessed a gentle disposition and was named Eni-gorio, or "the good mind." The other youth possessed an insolence of character and was named Enigon-ha-het-gea, or "the bad mind." The good mind was not content to remain in a dark situation and he was anxious to create a great light in the dark world; but the bad mind was desirous that the world should remain in a natural state. The good mind took the parent's head, of which he created an orb and established it in the center of the firmament, and it became of a very superior nature to bestow light to the new world—now, the sun. And again, he took the remnant of the body and formed another orb which was inferior to the light—now, the moon.

Whenever the light extended to the dark world the monsters were displeased and immediately concealed themselves in the deep places. The good mind continued the works of creation, and he formed numerous creeks and rivers on the Great Island, and then created numerous species of animals of the smallest and the greatest to inhabit the forests, and fishes of all kinds to inhabit the waters.

DOCUMENT ANALYSIS

1. Which sea animal was crucial to the creation of the world?

_____

_____

_____

2. From where does the sun come in the Iroquois legend?

_____

_____

_____

DOCUMENT 1.1

Captain John Smith, President in Virginia, to the Treasurer and Council of the Virginia Company, from Smith's *The Generall Historie of Virginia* (1624)

Virginia was the first and, for a time, the only English colony in the continental New World. Its boundaries spread as far to the north and west as its early explorers could imagine. In the document reproduced below, Virginia's president, John Smith, reports to the council of the underwriting Virginia Company to clarify some points and plead for a more rational approach to manpower and future shipments of provisions.

Right Honorable, &c.

I received your letter, wherein you write, that our minds are so set upon faction, and idle conceits in dividing the country without your consents, and that we feed you but with ifs and ands, hopes, and some few proofs; as if we would keep the mystery of the business to ourselves: and that we must expressly follow your instructions sent by Captain Newport: the charge of whose voyage amounts to near two thousand pounds, the which if we cannot defray by the ships' return, we are like to remain as banished men. To these particulars I humbly entreat your pardons if I offend you with my rude answer.

For our factions, unless you would have me run away and leave the country, I cannot prevent them: because I do make many stay that would else fly any whither. For the idle letter sent to my Lord of Salisbury, by the President and his confederates, for dividing the country &c. What it was I know not, for you saw no hand of mine to it; nor ever dreamed I of any such matter. That we feed you with hopes, &c. Though I be no scholar, I am past a school-boy; and I desire but to know, what either you, and these here, do know but that I have learned to tell you by the continual hazard of my life. I have not concealed from you anything I know; but I fear some cause you to believe much more than is true. . .

For the charge of this voyage of two or three thousand pounds, we have not received the value of a hundred pounds. And for the quartered boat to be borne by the soldiers over the falls, Newport had 120 of the best men he could choose. If he had burnt her to ashes, one might have carried her in a bag; but as she is, five hundred cannot, to a navigable place above the falls. And for him at that time to find in the South Sea, a mine of gold, or any of them sent by Sir Walter Raleigh; at our consultation I told them was as likely as the rest. But during this great discovery of thirty miles, (which might as well have been done by one man, and much more, for the value of a pound of copper at a seasonable time) they had the pinnace and all the boats with them, but one that remained with me to serve the fort.

In their absence I followed the new begun works of pitch and tar, glass, soap ashes, and clapboard; whereof some small quantities we have sent you. But if you rightly consider, what an infinite toil it is in Russia and Swethland [Sweden], where the woods are proper for naught else, and though there by the help both of man and beast in those ancient commonwealths, which many a hundred years have used it; yet thousands of those poor people can scarce get necessaries to live, but from hand to mouth. And though your factors there can buy as much in a week as will fraught you a ship, or as much as you please; you must not expect from us any such matter, which are but a many of ignorant, miserable souls, that are scarce able to get wherewith to live, and defend ourselves against the inconstant savages: finding but here and there a tree fit for the purpose, and want all things else the Russians have.

. . . From your ship we have not provision in victuals worth twenty pound, and we are more than two hundred to live upon this: the one half sick, the other little better. For the sailors (I confess) they daily make good cheer, but our diet is a little meal and water, and not sufficient of that. Though there be fish in the sea, fowls in the air, and beasts in the woods, their bounds are so large, they so wild, and we so weak and ignorant, we cannot much trouble them. . .

Now that you should know, I have made you as great a discovery as [Captain Newport], for less charge than he spendeth you every meal; I have sent you this map of the bay and rivers, with an annexed relation of the countries and nations that inhabit them, as you may see at large. Also two barrels of stones, and such as I take to be good iron ore at the least; so divided, as by their notes you may see in what places I found them.

. . . When you send again I entreat you rather send but thirty carpenters, husbandsmen, gardners, fishermen, blacksmiths, masons, and diggers up of trees, roots, well provided; than a thousand of such as we have: for except we be able both to lodge them, and feed them, the most will consume with want of necessaries before they can be made good for anything.

Thus if you please to consider this account, and of the unnecessary wages to Captain Newport, or his ships so long lingering and staying here (for notwithstanding his boasting to leave us victuals for 12 months; though we had 89 by this discovery lame and sick, and but a pint of corn a day for a man, we were constrained to give him three hogsheads of that to victual him homeward) or yet to send into Germany or Poland for glassmen and the rest, till we be able to sustain ourselves and relieve them when they come. It were better to give five hundred pound a ton for those gross commodities in Denmark, than send for them hither, till more necessary things be provided. For in over-toiling our weak and unskillful bodies, to satisfy this desire of present profit, we can scarce ever recover ourselves from one supply to another.

And I humbly entreat you hereafter, let us know what we should receive, and not stand to the sailors' courtesy to leave us what they please; else you may charge us with what you will, but we not you with anything.

These are the causes that have kept us in Virginia, from laying such a foundation, that ere this might have given much better content and satisfaction; but as yet you must not look for any profitable returns: so I humbly rest.

DOCUMENT ANALYSIS

1. What was Smith's major complaint?

_____

_____

_____

2. Why were the colonists unable to fish and hunt for provisions?

_____

_____

_____

3. What general misconceptions did the treasury council seem to have concerning conditions in Virginia?

_____

_____

_____

DOCUMENT 1.2
John Winthrop, "A Model of Christian Charity" (1630)

When the first settlers came to Virginia they were faced with numerous hardships that nearly devastated their entire venture. In contrast, when the Puritans settled in Massachusetts in 1630 they experienced few major difficulties and grew into a thriving community. The major difference between these two colonies was in their leadership and organization. Specifically, the strict religious beliefs and firm authority of the Puritans' leader, John Winthrop, and the established order he created before arriving in America enabled the Puritans to meet the challenges of colonization better than the Virginia colonists did.

On board the ship Arabella, *Winthrop delivered the following sermon, entitled "A Model of Christian Charity." Notice how Winthrop portrayed their purpose in America as a divine mandate to serve as an example for the rest of the world.*

God almighty in His most holy and wise providence hath so disposed of the condition of mankind, as in all times some must be rich, some poor, some high and eminent in power and dignity, others mean and in subjection.

Reason: First, to hold conformity with the rest of His works, being delighted to show forth the glory of His wisdom in the variety and difference of the creatures and the glory of His power, in ordering all these differences for the preservation and good of the whole.

Reason: Secondly, that He might have the more occasion to manifest the work of His spirit. First, upon the wicked in moderating and restraining them, so that the rich and mighty should not eat up the poor, nor the poor and despised rise up against their superiors and shake off their yoke. Secondly, in the regenerate in exercising His graces in them, as in the great ones, their love, mercy, gentleness, temperance, etc., in the poor and inferior sort, their faith, patience, obedience, etc.

Reason: Thirdly, that every man might have need of other, and from hence they might all be knit more nearly together in the bond of brotherly affection. From hence it appears plainly that no man is made more honorable than another, or more wealthy, etc., out of any particular and singular respect to himself, but for the glory of his creator and the common good of the creature, man.

Thus stands the cause between God and us. We are entered into covenant with Him for this work, we have taken out a commission, the Lord hath given us leave to draw our own articles, we have professed to enterprise these actions upon these and these ends, we have hereupon besought Him of favor and blessing. Now if the Lord shall please to hear us, and bring us in peace to the place we desire, then hath He ratified this covenant and sealed our commission, [and] will expect a strict performance of the articles contained in it, but if we shall neglect the observations

of these articles which are the ends we have propounded, and dissembling with our God, shall fall to embrace this present world and prosecute our carnal intentions seeking great things for ourselves and our posterity, the Lord will surely break out in wrath against us, be revenged of such a perjured people, and make us know the price of the breach of such a covenant.

Now the only way to avoid this shipwreck and to provide for our posterity is to follow the counsel of Micah, to do justly, to love mercy, to walk humbly with our God. For this end we must be knit together in this work as one man, we must entertain each other in brotherly affection, we must be willing to abridge ourselves of our superfluities for the supply of others' necessities, we must uphold a familiar commerce together in all meekness, gentleness, patience, and liberality, we must delight in each other, make others' conditions our own, rejoice together, mourn together, labor and suffer together, always having before our eyes our commission and community in the work, our community as members of the same body. So shall we keep the unity of the spirit in the bond of peace.

The Lord will be our God and delight in all our ways, so that we shall see much more of His wisdom, power, goodness, and truth than formerly we have been acquainted with. We shall find that the God of Israel is among us, when ten of us shall be able to resist a thousand of our enemies, when He shall make us a praise and glory, that men shall say of succeeding plantations, the Lord make it like that of New England. For we must consider that we shall be as a city upon a hill, the eyes of all people are upon us. So that if we shall deal falsely with our God in this work we have undertaken and so cause Him to withdraw His present help from us, we shall be made a story and byword throughout the world, we shall open the mouths of enemies to speak evil of the ways of God and all professors for God's sake, we shall shame the faces of many of God's worthy servants, and cause their prayers to be turned into curses upon us till we be consumed out of the good land whither we are going.

And to shut up this discourse with that exhortation of Moses, that faithful servant of the Lord in His last farewell to Israel, Deut. 30., Beloved there is now set before us life and good, death and evil, in that we are commanded this day to love the Lord our God, and to love one another, to walk in His ways and to keep His commandments and His ordinance, and His laws, and the articles of our covenant with Him that we may live and be multiplied, and that the Lord our God my bless us in the land whither we go to possess it. But if our hearts shall turn away so that we will not obey, but shall be seduced and worship other Gods, our pleasures, our profits, and serve them, it is propounded unto us this day we shall surely perish out of the good land whither we pass over this vast sea to possess it. Therefore let us choose life, that we, and our seed, may live, and by obeying His voice, and cleaving to Him, for He is our life and our prosperity.

DOCUMENT ANALYSIS

1. To which biblical events did Winthrop compare the Puritan voyage? Why?

_____

_____

_____

2. What did Winthrop mean when he asserted that the new colony should be like a "city on a hill"? What, in his interpretation, was the duty of all the Puritan settlers?

_____

_____

_____

DOCUMENT 2.1
Alexander Falconbridge, The African Slave Trade (1788)

Alexander Falconbridge served as ship's surgeon on slaving ships during the latter half of the eighteenth century. During his voyages across the Atlantic, Falconbridge had occasion to observe the abhorrent treatment of the slaves at the hands of the crews. During one such voyage, Falconbridge wrote this account of the conditions on the ship, including his own views on the practice of slavery.

As soon as the wretched Africans, purchased at the fairs, fall into the hands of the black traders, they experience an earnest of those dreadful sufferings which they are doomed in future to undergo. And there is not the least room to doubt, but that even before they can reach the fairs, great numbers perish from cruel usage, want of food, travelling through inhospitable deserts, etc. They are brought from the places where they are purchased to Bonny, etc. in canoes; at the bottom of which they lie, having their hands tied with a kind of willow twigs, and a strict watch is kept over them. Their usage in other respects, during the time of passage, which generally lasts several days, is equally cruel. Their allowance of food is so scanty, that it is barely sufficient to support nature. They are, besides, much exposed to the violent rains which frequently fall here, being covered only with mats that afford but a slight defense; and as there is usually water at the bottom of the canoes, from their leaking, they are scarcely every dry.

Nor do these unhappying beings, after they become the property of the Europeans (from whom as a more civilized people, more humanity might naturally be expected), find their situation in the least amended. Their treatment is no less rigorous. The men Negroes, on being brought aboard the ship, are immediately fastened together, two and two, by handcuffs on their wrists, and irons riveted on their legs. They are then sent down between the decks, and placed in an apartment partitioned off for that purpose. The women likewise are placed in a separate room, on the same deck, but without being ironed. And an adjoining room, on the same deck is besides appointed for the boys. Thus are they placed in different apartments.

But at the same time, they are frequently stowed so close, as to admit of no other posture than lying on their sides. Neither will the height between decks, unless directly under the grating, permit them the indulgence of an erect posture; especially where there are platforms, which is generally the case. These platforms are a kind of shelf, about eight or nine feet in breadth, extending from the side of the ship towards the centre. They are placed nearly midway between the decks, at the distance of two or three feet from each deck. Upon these the Negroes are stowed in the same manner as they are on the deck underneath.

. . . About eight o'clock in the morning the Negroes are generally brought upon deck. Their irons being examined, a long chain, which is locked to a ring-bolt, fixed in the deck, is run through the rings of the shackles of the men, and then locked to another ring-bolt, fixed also in the deck. By this means fifty or sixty, and sometimes more, are fastened to one chain, in order to prevent them from rising, or endeavoring to escape. If the weather proves favorable, they are permitted to remain in that situation till four or five in the afternoon, when they are disengaged from the chain, and sent down.

. . . Upon the Negroes refusing to take sustenance, I have seen coals of fire, glowing hot, put on a shovel, and placed so near their lips, as to scorch and burn them. And this has been accompanied with threats, of forcing them to swallow the coals, if they any longer persisted in refusing to eat. These means have generally had the desired effect. I have also been credibly informed that a certain captain in the slave trade poured melted lead on such of the Negroes as obstinately refused their food.

Exercise being deemed necessary for the preservation of their health, they are sometimes obligated to dance, when the weather will permit their coming on deck. If they go about it reluctantly, or do not move with agility, they are flogged; a person standing by them all the time with a cat-o'-nine-tails in his hand for that purpose. Their music, upon these occasions, consists of a drum, sometimes with only one head; and when that is worn out, they do not scruple to make use of the bottom of one of the tubs before described. The poor wretches are frequently compelled to sing also; but when they do so, their songs are generally, as may naturally be expected, melancholy lamentations of their exile from their native country.

. . . On board some ships, the common sailors are allowed to have intercourse with such of the black women whose consent they can procure. And some of them have been known to take the inconstancy of their paramours so much to heart, as to leap overboard and drown themselves. The officers are permitted to indulge their passions among them at pleasure, and sometimes are guilty of such brutal excesses as disgrace human nature.

The hardships and inconveniences suffered by the Negroes during the passage are scarcely to be enumerated or conceived. They are far more violently affected by the seasickness than the Europeans. It frequently terminates in death, especially among the women. But the exclusion of the fresh air is among the most intolerable. For the purpose of admitting this needful refreshment, most of the ships in the slave trade are provided, between the decks, with five or six air-ports on each side of the ship, of about six inches in length, and four in breadth; in addition to which, some few ships, but not one in twenty, have what they denominate windsails. But whenever the sea is rough and the rain heavy, it becomes necessary to shut these, and every other conveyance by which the air is admitted. The fresh air being thus excluded, the Negroes' rooms very soon grow intolerably hot. The confined air, rendered noxious by the effluvia exhaled from their bodies, and by being repeatedly breathed, soon produces fevers and fluxes, which generally carries off great numbers of them.

. . . One morning, upon examining the place allotted for the sick Negroes, I perceived that one of them, who was so emaciated as scarcely to be able to walk, was missing, and was convinced that he must have gone overboard in the night, probably to put a more expeditious period to his sufferings. And, to conclude on this subject, I could not help being sensibly affected, on a former voyage, at observing with what apparent eagerness a black woman seized some dirt from off an African yam, and put it into her mouth, seeming to rejoice at the opportunity of possessing some of her native earth.

From these instances I think it may have been clearly deduced that the unhappy Africans are not bereft of the finer feelings, but have a strong attachment to their native country, together with a just sense of the value of liberty. And the situation of the miserable beings above described, more forcibly urges the necessity of abolishing a trade which is the source of such evils, than the most eloquent harangue, or persuasive arguments could do.

DOCUMENT ANALYSIS

1. What information does Falconbridge's account provide us about how Africans were taken into slavery, who participated in the African slave trade, and what role commerce and trade played in the slave trade system?

_____

_____

_____

2. How would Falconbridge's descriptions of the slave trade be of assistance to opponents of slavery?

_____

_____

_____

DOCUMENT 2.2
Gottlieb Mittelberger, On the Misfortune of Indentured Servants (1754)

Gottlieb Mittelberger emigrated to Pennsylvania from Germany in 1750 on a ship filled with poorer immigrants who would become indentured servants in Philadelphia. Mittelberger's own fortunes were not so bleak: he served as a schoolmaster and organist in Philadelphia for three years. He returned to Germany in 1754.

Both in Rotterdam and in Amsterdam the people are packed densely, like herrings so to say, in the large sea-vessels. One person receives a place of scarcely 2 feet width and 6 feet length in the bedstead, while many a ship carries four to six hundred souls; not to mention the innumerable implements, tools, provisions, water-barrels and other things which likewise occupy such space.

On account of contrary winds it takes the ships sometimes 2, 3, and 4 weeks to make the trip from Holland to England. But when the wind is good, they get there in 8 days or even sooner. Everything is examined there and the custom-duties paid, whence it comes that the ships ride there 8, 10 or 14 days and even longer at anchor, till they have taken in their full cargoes. During that time every one is compelled to spend his last remaining money and to consume his little stock of provisions which had been reserved for the sea; so that most passengers, finding themselves on the ocean where they would be in greater need of them, must greatly suffer from hunger and want. Many suffer want already on the water between Holland and Old England.

When the ships have for the last time weighed their anchors near the city of Kaupp [Cowes] in Old England, the real misery begins with the long voyage. For from there the ships, unless they have good wind, must often sail 8, 9, 10 to 12 weeks before they reach Philadelphia. But even with the best wind the voyage lasts 7 weeks.

But during the voyage there is on board these ships terrible misery, stench, fumes, horror, vomiting, many kinds of sea-sickness, fever, dysentery, headache, heat, constipation, boils, scurvy, cancer, mouth rot, and the like, all of which come from old and sharply salted food and meat, also from very bad and foul water, so that many die miserably.

Add to this want of provisions, hunger, thirst, frost, heat, dampness, anxiety, want, afflictions and lamentations, together with other trouble, as the lice abound so frightfully, especially on sick people, that they can be scraped off the body. The misery reaches the climax when a gale rages for 2 or 3 nights and days, so that every one believes that the ship will go to the bottom with all human beings on board. In such a visitation the people cry and pray most piteously.

Children from 1 to 7 years rarely survive the voyage. I witnessed misery in no less than 32 children in our ship, all of whom were thrown into the sea. The parents grieve all the more since their children find no resting-place in the earth, but are devoured by the monsters of the sea.

That most of the people get sick is not surprising, because, in addition to all other trials and hardships, warm food is served only three times a week, the rations being very poor and very little. Such meals can hardly be eaten, on account of being so unclean. The water which is served out of the ships is often very black, thick and full of worms, so that one cannot drink it without loathing, even with the greatest thirst. Toward the end we were compelled to eat the ship's biscuit which had been spoiled long ago; though in a whole biscuit there was scarcely a piece the size of a dollar that had not been full of red worms and spiders' nests.

At length, when, after a long and tedious voyage, the ships come in sight of land, so that the promontories can be seen, which the people were so eager and anxious to see, all creep from below on deck to see the land from afar, and they weep for joy, and pray and sing, thanking and praising God. The sight of the land makes the people on board the ship, especially the sick and the half-dead, alive again, so that their hearts leap within them; they shout and rejoice, and are content to bear their misery in patience, in the hope that they may soon reach the land in safety. But alas!

When the ships have landed at Philadelphia after their long voyage, no one is permitted to leave them except those who pay for their passage or can give good security; the others, who cannot pay, must remain on board the ships till they are purchased, and are released from the ships by their purchasers. The sick always fare the worst, for the healthy are naturally preferred and purchased first; and so the sick and wretched must often remain on board in front of the city for 2 or 3 weeks, and frequently die, whereas many a one, if he could pay his debt and were permitted to leave the ship immediately, might recover and remain alive.

The sale of human beings in the market on board the ship is carried out thus: Every day Englishmen, Dutchmen and High-German people come from the city of Philadelphia and other places, in part from a great distance, say 20, 30, or 40 hours away, and go on board the newly arrived ship that has brought and offers for sale passengers from Europe, and select among the healthy persons such as they deem suitable for their business, and bargain with them how long they will serve for their passage money, which most of them are still in debt for. When they have come to an agreement, it happens that adult persons bind themselves in writing to serve 3, 4, 5 or 6 years for the amount due by them, according to their age and strength. But very young people, from 10 to 15 years, must serve till they are 21 years old.

Many parents must sell and trade away their children like so many head of cattle; for if their children take the debt upon themselves, the parents can leave the ship free and unrestrained; but as the parents often do not know where and to what people their children are going, it often happens that such parents and children, after leaving the ship, do not see each other again for many years, perhaps no more in all their lives.

It often happens that whole families: husband, wife and children, are separated by being sold to different purchasers, especially when they have not paid any part of their passage money.

When a husband or wife has died at sea, when the ship has made more than half of her trip, the survivor must pay or serve not only for himself or herself but also for the deceased.

When both parents have died over half-way at sea, their children, especially when they are young and have nothing to pawn or pay, must stand for their own and their parents' passage, and serve till they are 21 years old. When one has served his or her term, he or she is entitled to a new suit of clothes at parting; and if it has been so stipulated, a man gets in addition a horse, a woman, or a cow. When a serf has an opportunity to marry in this country, he or she must pay for each year which he or she would have yet to serve, 5 or 6 pounds.

DOCUMENT ANALYSIS

1. What was indentured servitude like in the colonies? Was it much different from being a slave?

_____

_____

_____

DOCUMENT 3.1
Boston Gazette, Description of the Boston Massacre (1770)

The Boston Massacre took place on March 5, 1770, and was covered in detail by the Boston Gazette. *British troops had been stationed in the city since late 1768 to protect British customs officers and tensions between the soldiers and citizens of Boston had been building. The resulting clash between a group of citizens and soldiers on March 5 resulted in five civilian deaths, the removal of British troops from Boston, and trials for some of the soldiers involved. The Boston Massacre became a crucial element in anti-British propaganda in the colonies.*

. . . On the evening of Monday, being the fifth current, several soldiers of the 29th Regiment were seen parading the streets with their drawn cutlasses and bayonets, abusing and wounding numbers of the inhabitants.

A few minutes after nine o'clock four youths, named Edward Archbald, William Merchant, Francis Archbald, and John Leech, Jr., came down Cornhill together, and separating at Doctor Loring's corner, the two former were passing the narrow alley leading to Murray's barrack in which was a soldier brandishing a broad sword of an uncommon size against the walls, out of which he struck fire plentifully. A person of mean countenance armed with a large cudgel bore him company. Edward Archbald admonished Mr. Merchant to take care of the sword, on which the soldier turned round and struck Archbald on the arm, then pushed at Merchant and pierced through his clothes inside the arm close to the armpit and grazed the skin. Merchant then struck the soldier with a short stick he had; and the other person ran to the barrack and brought with him two soldiers, one armed with a pair of tongs, the other with a shovel. He with the tongs pursued Archbald back through the alley, collared and laid him over the head with the tongs. The noise brought people together; and John Hicks, a young lad, coming up, knocked the soldier down but let him get up again; and more lads gathering, drove them back to the barrack where the boys stood some time as it were to keep them in. In less than a minute ten or twelve of them came out with drawn cutlasses, clubs, and bayonets and set upon the unarmed boys and young folk who stood them a little while but, finding the inequality of their equipment, dis-

persed. On hearing the noise, one Samuel Atwood came up to see what was the matter; and entering the alley from dock square, heard the latter part of the combat; and when the boys had dispersed he met the ten or twelve soldiers aforesaid rushing down the alley towards the square and asked them if they intended to murder people? They answered "Yes, by God, root and branch!" With that one of them struck Mr. Atwood with a club which was repeated by another; and being unarmed, he turned to go off and received a wound on the left shoulder which reached the bone and gave him much pain. Retreating a few steps, Mr. Atwood met two officers and said, "Gentlemen, what is the matter?" They answered, "You'll see by and by." Immediately after, those heroes appeared in the square, asking "Where were the boogers? Where were the cowards?" But notwithstanding their fierceness to naked men, one of them advanced towards a youth who had a split of a raw stave in his hand and said, "Damn them, here is one of them." But the young man seeing a person near him with a drawn sword and good cane ready to support him, held up his stave in defiance; and they quietly passed by him up the little alley by Mr. Silsby's to King Street where they attacked single and unarmed persons till they raised much clamor, and then turned down Cornhill Street, insulting all they met in like manner and pursuing some to their very doors. Thirty or forty persons, mostly lads, being by this means gathered in King Street, Captain Preston with a party of men with charged bayonets, came from the main guard to the commissioner's house, the soldiers pushing their bayonets, crying, "Make way!" They took place by the custom house and, continuing to push to drive the people off, pricked some in several places, on which they were clamorous and, it is said, threw snowballs. On this, the Captain commanded them to fire; and more snowballs coming, he again said, "Damn you, fire, be the consequence what it will!" One soldier then fired, and a townsman with a cudgel struck him over the hands with such force that he dropped his firelock; and, rushing forward, aimed a blow at the Captain's head which grazed his hat and fell pretty heavy upon his arm. However, the soldiers continued the fire successively till seven or eight or, as some say, eleven guns were discharged.

DOCUMENT ANALYSIS

1. How does the author of this account describe the soldiers and pro-British persons? What adjectives does he use?

_____

_____

_____

2. Who are the "lads" in this account? How are they portrayed? What terms does the author use to describe them?

_____

_____

_____

3. Is the author of this account biased? If so, do his words and descriptions indicate that he is pro-British or anti-British?

_____

_____

_____

Benjamin Franklin was one of America's foremost statesmen and scientists. A philosopher of the Enlightenment period, Franklin advocated the use of practical experimentation and reason in all areas of human existence. Despite this scientific orientation, Franklin found himself quite moved by the sermons of revivalist preacher George Whitefield, especially those that solicited funds for establishing an orphanage in the new colony of Georgia. This selection is excerpted from The Autobiography of Benjamin Franklin (1771).

In 1739 arriv'd among us from England the Rev. Mr. Whitefield, who had made himself remarkable there as an itinerant preacher. . . . The Multitudes of all Sects and Denominations that attended his Sermons were enormous, and it was matter of Speculation to me who was one of the Number, to observe the extraordinary Influence of his Oratory on his Hearers, and how much they admir'd & respected him, notwithstanding his common Abuse of them, by assuring them they were naturally half Beasts and half Devils. It was wonderful to see the Change soon made in the Manners of our Inhabitants; from being thoughtless or indifferent about Religion, it seem'd as if all the World were growing Religious; so that one could not walk thro' the Town in an Evening without Hearing Psalms sung in different Families of every Street. . . .

Mr. Whitefield, in leaving us, went preaching all the Way thro' the Colonies to Georgia. The Settlement of that Province had lately been begun; but instead of being made with hardy industrious Husbandmen accustomed to Labor, the only People fit for such an Enterprise, it was with Families of broken Shopkeepers and other insolvent Debtors, many of indolent & idle habits, taken out of the jails, who being set down in the Woods, unqualified for clearing Land, & unable to endure the Hardships of a new Settlement, perished in Numbers, leaving many helpless Children unprovided for. The Sight of their miserable Situation inspired the benevolent Heart of Mr. Whitefield with the idea of building an Orphan House there. . . .

Returning northward he preached up this Charity, & made large Collections; for his Eloquence had a wonderful Power over the Hearts and Purses of his Hearers, of which I myself was an Instance. I did not disapprove of the Design, but as Georgia was then destitute of Materials & Workmen, and it was propos'd to send them from Philadelphia at a great Expense, I thought it would have been better to have built the House here & Brought the Children to it. This I advis'd, but he was resolute in his first Project, and rejected my Counsel, and I thereupon refus'd to contribute. I happened soon after on one of his Sermons, in the Course of which I perceived he intended to finish with a Collection, & I silently resolved he should get nothing from me. I had in my Pocket a Handful of Copper Money, three or four silver Dollars, and five Pistoles in gold. As he proceeded I began to soften, and concluded to give the Coppers. Another Stroke of his Oratory made me asham'd of that, and determin'd me to give the Silver & he finished so admirably, that I empty'd my Pocket wholly into the Collector's Dish, Gold and all. At this Sermon there was also one of our Club, who being of my Sentiments respecting the Building in Georgia, and suspecting a Collection might be intended, had by Precaution emptied his Pockets before he came from home; towards the Conclusion of the Discourse, however, he felt a strong Desire to give, and apply'd to a Neighbor who stood near him to borrow some Money for the Purpose.

DOCUMENT ANALYSIS

1. How does Franklin explain the great impact that Whitefield's sermons had on him? How does Franklin fit his rational Enlightenment beliefs with Whitefield's evangelical religion of the Great Awakening?

_____

_____

_____

2. What kind of attitude does Franklin betray in his opinions of the new colony of Georgia?

_____

_____

_____

DOCUMENT 4.1
Joseph Warren, "Account of the Battle of Lexington" (1775)

In April 1775, following the battles at Lexington and Concord, Dr. Joseph Warren of Boston, a zealous champion of American liberty and president of the Massachusetts Provincial Congress, wrote an open letter to the British people giving the colonists' view of the events. It had been Warren who dispatched William Dawes and Paul Revere by separate routes to warn John Hancock, Samuel Adams, and other patriot leaders of the impending British march on Lexington.

MASSACHUSETTS.
IN PROVINCIAL CONGRESS
Watertown, April 26, 1775

TO THE INHABITANTS OF GREAT BRITAIN.

Friends and fellow subjects,

Hostilities are at length commenced in this colony, by the troops under command of general Gage; and it being of the greatest importance, that an early, true, and authentic account of this inhuman proceeding should be known to you, the congress of this colony have transmitted the same, and for want of a session of the hon. continental congress, think it proper to address you on this alarming occasion.

By the clearest depositions, relative to this transaction, it will appear, *that*, on the night preceding the 19th of April, instant, a body of the king's troops, under command of colonel Smith, were secretly landed at Cambridge, with an apparent design to take or destroy the military and other stores, provided for the defence of this colony, and deposited at Concord; that some inhabitants of the colony, on the night aforesaid whilst travelling peaceable on the road between Boston and Concord, were seized and greatly abused by armed men, who appeared to be officers of general Gage's army; that the town of Lexington, by these means, was alarmed, and a company of the inhabitants mustered on the occasion; that the regular troops, on their way to Concord, marched into the said town of Lexington, and the said company, on their approach, began to disperse; that notwithstanding this, the regulars rushed on with great violence, and first began hostilities, by firing on the said Lexington company, whereby, they killed eight, and wounded several others; that the regulars continued their fire until those of the said company, who were neither killed nor wounded, had made their escape; that colonel Smith, with the detachment, then marched to Concord, where a number of provincials were again fired on by the troops, two of them killed and several wounded, before any of the provincials fired on them; and that these hostile measures of the troops produced an engagement that lasted through the day, in which many of he provincials, and more of the regular troops, were killed and wounded.

To give a particular account of the ravages of the troops, as they retreated from Concord to Charles Town, would be very difficult, if not impracticable; let it suffice to say, that a great number of the houses on the road were plundered, and rendered unfit for use; several were burnt; women in child-bed were driven by the soldiery naked into the streets; old men, peaceably in their houses, were shot dead, and such scenes exhibited, as would disgrace the annals of the most uncivilized nations.

These, brethren, are marks of ministerial vengeance against this colony, for refusing, with her sister colonies, a submission to slavery; but they have not yet detached us from our royal sovereign, we profess to be his loyal and dutiful subjects; and so hardly dealt with as we have been, are still ready, with our lives and fortunes, to defend his person, family, crown and dignity; nevertheless, to the persecution and tyranny of his cruel ministry, we will not tamely submit; appealing to Heaven for the justice of our cause, "we determine to die, or be free."

We cannot think that the honor, wisdom, and valor of Britons, will suffer them to be longer inactive spectators of *measures*, in which they themselves are so deeply interested; measures pursued in opposition to the solemn protests of many noble lords, and expressed sense of conspicuous commons, whose knowledge and virtue have long characterized them as some of the greatest men in the nation; *measures*, executing, contrary to the interest, petitions, and resolves of many large, respectable counties, cities, and boroughs, in Great Britain; measures highly incompatible with justice, but still pursued with a specious pretence of easing the nation of its burthens; *measures* which, if successful, must end in the ruin and slavery of Britain, as well as the persecuted American colonies.

We sincerely hope, that the Great Sovereign of the Universe, who hath so often appeared for the English nation, will support you in every rational and manly exertion with these colonies, for saving it from ruin, and that, in a constitutional connection with our mother country, we shall soon be altogether a free and happy people.

Signed by order,
JOS. WARREN, president

DOCUMENT ANALYSIS

1. Who are the primary aggressors according to this account? Describe some of the actions detailed in this account as evidence of this aggression.

_____

_____

_____

2. What appeal does Warren make to the people of Britain? What is the goal of this document?

_____

_____

_____

DOCUMENT 4.2
Slave Petition to the General Assembly in Connecticut (1779)

From Gary B. Nash, *Race and Revolution* (Madison, WI: Madison House, 1990), pp. 174–176.

The petition reproduced below was signed by two slaves, Prime and Prince, in Fairfield County, Connecticut, on behalf of all slaves in that county. Combining—as did other slave petitions—references to both the ongoing Revolutionary War and Christianity, their plea is representative of this particular era of U.S. history. The petition was denied, and Connecticut instead opted for a plan of gradual emancipation. In 1774 the legislature had outlawed the importation of slaves. In 1784 and 1797, the legislature passed additional laws that freed children born as slaves at ages 25 and 21, respectively. Slavery was not completely abolished in the state until 1848.

To the Honorable General Assembly of the State of Connecticut to be held at Hartford on the Second Thursday of Instant May [1779]—The Petition of the Negroes in the Towns of Stratford and Fairfield in the County of Fairfield who are held in a State of Slavery humbly showeth—

That many of your Petitioners, were (as they verily believe) most unjustly torn, from the Bosom of their dear Parents, and Friends, and without any Crime, by them committed, doomed, and bound down, to perpetual Slavery; and as if the Perpetrators of this horrid Wickedness, were conscious (that we poor Ignorant Africans, upon the least Glimmering Sight, derived from a Knowledge of the Sense and Practice of civilized Nations) should Convince them of their Sin, they have added another dreadful Evil, that of holding us in gross Ignorance, so as to render Our Subjection more easy and tolerable. May it please your Honors, we are most grievously affected, under the Consideration of the flagrant Injustice; Your Honors who are nobly contending, in the Cause of Liberty, whose Conduct excites the Admiration, and Reverence, of all the great Empires of the World; will not resent, our thus freely animadverting, on this detestable Practice; although our Skins are different in Color, from those whom we serve, Yet Reason & Revelation join to declare, that we are the Creatures of that God, who made of one Blood, and Kindred, all the Nations of the Earth; we perceive by our own Reflection, that we are endowed with the same Faculties with our masters, and there is nothing that leads us to a Belief, or Suspicion, that we are any more obliged to serve them, than they us, and the more we Consider of this matter, the more we are Convinced of our Right (by the Laws of Nature and by the whole Tenor of the Christian Religion, so far as we have been taught) to be free; we have endeavored rightly to understand what is our Right, and what is our Duty, and can never be convinced that we were made to be Slaves. Although God almighty may justly lay this, and more upon us, yet we deserve it not, from the hands of Men, we are impatient under the grievous Yoke, but our Reason teaches us that it is not best for us to use violent measures, to cast it off; we are also convinced, that we are unable to extricate ourselves from our abject State; but we think we may with the greatest Propriety look up to your Honors, (who are the fathers of the People) for Relief. And we not only groan under our own burden, but with concern, & Horror, look forward, & contemplate, the miserable Condition of our Children, who are training up, and kept in Preparation, for a like State of Bondage, and Servitude. We beg leave to submit, to your Honors serious Consideration, whether it is consistent with the present Claims, of the united States, to hold so many Thousands, of the Race of Adam, our Common Father, in perpetual Slavery. Can human Nature endure the Shocking Idea? can your Honors any longer Suffer this great Evil to prevail under your Government: we entreat your Honors, let no considerations of Public Inconvenience deter your Honors from interposing in behalf of your Petitioners; we ask for nothing, but what we are fully persuaded is ours to Claim. We beseech your Honors to weigh this matter in the Scale of Justice, and in your great Wisdom and goodness, apply such Remedy as the Evil does require; and let your Petitioners rejoice with your Honors in the Participation with your Honors of that inestimable Blessing, Freedom and your Humble Petitioners, as in Duty bound shall ever pray &c.

dated in Fairfield the 11th Day of May A D 1779—

Prime—a Negro man

servant to Mr. Vam A. Sturge of Fairfield

his mark

Prince—a Negro man

his mark

servant of Capt. Stephen Jenings of Fairfield—

in Behalf of themselves and the other Petitioners

DOCUMENT ANALYSIS

1. What religious argument did the petitioners offer?

_____

_____

_____

2. What did the petitioners describe as their greatest "horror" when contemplating the slave system?

_____

_____

_____

3. How did the petitioners place their argument within a global perspective? Which of their arguments referenced the Revolutionary War?

_____

_____

_____

DOCUMENT 5.1
George Washington, Sixth Annual Address to Congress (1794)

The Whiskey Rebellion of 1794 took place in western Pennsylvania. The reason for the rebellion was a federal tax on distilled spirits that had been levied in 1791. Producers resisted the tax, claiming that only the state had the right to impose such taxes. In a show of federal strength, President George Washington called up a militia to suppress the insurrection. The event was significant because it was the first challenge to federal authority in the United States and the first time a U.S. president called up state militias to enforce federal law. In this address Washington describes the rebellion and his decision to suppress it.

Fellow Citizens of the Senate and of the House of Representatives: When we call to mind the gracious indulgence of Heaven, by which the American People became a nation; when we survey the general prosperity of our country, and look forward to the riches, power, and happiness, to which it seems destined; with the deepest regret do I announce to you, that during your recess, some of the citizens of the United States have been found capable of an insurrection. It is due, however, to the character of our government, and to its stability, which cannot be shaken by the enemies of order, freely to unfold the course of this event.

During the session of the year one thousand seven hundred and ninety, it was expedient to exercise the legislative power, granted by the constitution of the United States, "to lay and collect excises." In a majority of the States, scarcely an objection was heard to this mode of taxation. In some, indeed, alarms were at first conceived, until they were banished by reason and patriotism. In the four western counties of Pennsylvania, a prejudice, fostered and embittered by the artifice of men, who labored for an ascendancy over the will of others, by the guidance of their passions, produced symptoms of riot and violence. It is well known, that Congress did not hesitate to examine the complaints which were presented, and to relieve them, as far as justice dictated, or general convenience would permit, but the impression, which this moderation made on the discontented, did not correspond, with what it deserved. The arts of delusion were no longer confined to the efforts of designing individuals.

The very forbearance to press prosecutions was misinterpreted into a fear of urging the execution of the laws; and associations of men began to denounce threats against the officers employed. From a belief, that by a more formal concert, their operation might be defeated, certain self-created societies assumed the tone of condemnation. Hence, while the greater part of Pennsylvania itself were conforming themselves to the acts of excise, a few counties were resolved to frustrate them. It was now perceived, that every expectation from the tenderness which had been hitherto pursued, was unavailing, and that further delay could only create an opinion of impotency or irresolution in the government. Legal process was, therefore, delivered to the marshal, against the rioters and delinquent distillers.

No sooner was he understood to be engaged in this duty, than the vengeance of armed men was aimed at his person, and the person and property of the inspector of the revenue. They fired upon the marshal, arrested him, and detained him for some time, as a prisoner. He was obliged, by the jeopardy of his life, to renounce the service of other process, on the west side of the Allegany mountain; and a deputation was afterwards sent to him to demand a surrender of that which he had served. A numerous body repeatedly attacked the house of the inspector, seized his papers of office, and finally destroyed by fire, his buildings, and whatsoever they contained. Both of these officers, from a just regard to their safety, fled to the seat of government; it being avowed, that the motives to such outrages were to compel the resignation of the inspector, to withstand by force of arms the authority of the United States, and thereby to extort a repeal of the laws of excise, and an alteration in the conduct of government.

Upon the testimony of these facts, an associate Justice of the Supreme Court of the United States notified to me, that "in the counties of Washington and Allegany, in Pennsylvania, laws of the United States were opposed, and the execution thereof obstructed by combinations, too powerful to be suppressed by the ordinary course of judicial proceedings, or by the powers vested in the marshal of that district." On this call, mo-

mentous in the extreme, I sought and weighed, what might best subdue the crisis. On the one hand, the judiciary was pronounced to be stripped of its capacity to enforce the laws; crimes, which reached the very existence of social order, were perpetrated without control, the friends of government were insulted, abused, and overawed into silence, or an apparent acquiescence; and the yield to the treasonable fury of so small a portion of the United States, would be to violate the fundamental principle of our constitution, which enjoins that the will of the majority shall prevail. On the other, to array citizen against citizen, to publish the dishonor of such excesses, to encounter the expense, and other embarrassments of so distant an expedition, were steps too delicate, too closely interwoven with many affecting considerations, to be lightly adopted. I postponed, therefore, the summoning of the militia immediately into the field. But I required them to be held in readiness, that if my anxious endeavors to reclaim the deluded, and to convince the malignant of their danger, should be fruitless, military force might be prepared to act, before the season should be too far advanced.

My Proclamation of the 7th of August last was accordingly issued, and accompanied by the appointment of Commissioners, who were charged to repair to the scene of insurrection. They were authorized to confer with any bodies of men, or individuals. They were instructed to be candid and explicit, in stating the sensations, which had been excited in the Executive, and his earnest wish to avoid a resort to coercion. To represent, however, that without submission, coercion must be the resort; but to invite them, at the same time, to return to the demeanor of faithful citizens, by such accommodations as lay within the sphere of the executive power. Pardon, too, was tendered to them by the government of the United States, and that of Pennsylvania, upon no other condition, than a satisfactory assurance of obedience to the laws.

Although the report of the commissioners marks their firmness and abilities, and must unite all virtuous men, by showing, that the means of conciliation have been exhausted, all of those who had committed or abetted the tumults, did not subscribe the mild form, which was proposed, as the atonement; and the indications of a peaceable temper were neither sufficiently general, nor conclusive, to recommend or warrant, a further suspension of the march of the militia.

Thus, the painful alternative could not be discarded. I ordered the militia to march, after once more admonishing the insurgents, in my proclamation of the 25th of September last. It was a task too difficult to ascertain with precision, the lowest degree of force, competent to the quelling of the insurrection. From a respect, indeed, to economy, and the ease of my fellow citizens belonging to the militia, it would have gratified me to accomplish such an estimate. My very reluctance to ascribe too much importance to the opposition, had its extent been accurately seen, would have been a decided inducement to the smallest efficient numbers.

In this uncertainty, therefore, I put in motion fifteen thousand men, as being an army, which according to all human calculation, would be prompt, and adequate in every view; and might perhaps, by rendering resistance desperate, prevent the effusion of blood. Quotas had been assigned to the states of New-Jersey, Pennsylvania, Maryland, and Virginia; the governor of Pennsylvania having declared on this occasion, an opinion which justified a requisition to the other states.

As commander in chief of the militia, when called into the actual service of the United States, I have visited the places of general rendezvous, to obtain more exact information, and to direct a plan for ulterior movements. Had there been room for a persuasion, that the laws were secure from obstruction; that the civil magistrate was able to bring to justice such of the most culpable, as have not embraced the proffered terms of amnesty, and may be deemed fit objects of example; that the friends to peace and good government were not in need of that aid and countenance, which they ought always to receive, and I trust, ever will receive, against the vicious and turbulent; I should have caught with avidity the opportunity of restoring the militia to their families and home. But succeeding intelligence has tended to manifest the necessity of what has been done; it being now confessed by those who were not inclined to exaggerate the ill-conduct of the insurgents, that their malevolence was not pointed merely to a particular law; but that a spirit, inimical to all order, has actuated many of the offenders. If the state of things had afforded reason for the continuance of my presence with the army, it would not have been denied.

But every appearance assuring such an issue, as will redound to the reputation and strength of the United States, I have judged it most proper, to resume my duties at the seat of government, leaving the chief command with the governor of Virginia. Still, however, as it is probable, that in a commotion like the present, whatsoever may be the pretence, the purposes of mischief and revenge may not be laid aside; the stationing of a small force for a certain period in the four western counties of Pennsylvania will be indispensable; whether we contemplate the situation of those, who are connected with the execution of the laws; or of others who may have exposed themselves by an honorable attachment to them. . . .

While there is cause to lament, that occurrences of this nature should have disgraced the name, or interrupted the tranquility of any part of our community, or should have diverted to a new application, any portion of the public resources, there are not wanting real and substantial consolations for the misfortune. It has demonstrated, that our prosperity rests on solid foundations; by furnishing an additional proof, that my fellow citizens understand the true principles of government and liberty: that they feel their inseparable union: that notwithstanding all the devices which have been used to sway them from their interest and duty, they are now as ready to maintain the authority of the laws against licentious invasions, as they were to defend their rights against usurpation. It has been a spectacle, displaying to the highest advantage, the value of Republican Government, to behold the most and least wealthy of our citizens standing in the same ranks as private soldiers; pre-eminently distinguished by being the army of the constitution; undeterred by a march of three hundred miles over rugged mountains, by the approach of an inclement season, or by any other discouragement. Nor ought I to omit to acknowledge the efficacious and patriotic co-operation, which I have experienced from the chief magistrates of the states, to which my requisitions have been addressed.

To every description, indeed, of citizens let praise be given. But let them persevere in their affectionate vigilance over that precious depository of American happiness, the constitution of the United States. Let them cherish it too, for the sake of those, who from every clime are daily seeking a dwelling in our land. And when in the calm moments of reflection, they shall have retraced the origin and progress of the insurrection, let them determine whether it has not been fomented by combinations of men, who, careless of consequences, and disregarding the unerring truth, that those who rouse, cannot always appease a civil convulsion, have disseminated, from an ignorance of perversion of facts, suspicions, jealousies, and accusations of the whole government.

Having thus fulfilled the engagement, which I took, when I entered this office, "to the best of my ability to preserve, protect, and defend the constitution of the United States," on you, Gentlemen, and the people by whom you are deputed, I rely for support. In the arrangements, to which the possibility of a similar contingency will naturally draw your attention, it ought not to be forgotten, that the militia laws have exhibited such striking defects, as could not have been supplied but by the zeal of our citizens. Besides the extraordinary expense and waste, which are not the least of the defects, every appeal to those laws is attended with a doubt of its success. The devising and establishing of a well regulated militia, would be a genuine source of legislative honor, and a perfect title to public gratitude. I, therefore, entertain a hope, that the present session will not pass, without carrying to its full energy the power of organizing, arming, and disciplining the militia; and thus providing, in the language of the constitution, for calling them forth to execute the laws of the union, suppress insurrections, and repel invasions. As auxiliary to the state of our defense, to which Congress can never too frequently recur, they will not omit to enquire whether the fortifications, which have been already licensed by law, be commensurate with our exigencies. . . .

An estimate of the necessary appropriations, including the expenditures into which we have been driven by the insurrection, will be submitted to Congress. Gentlemen of the Senate, and of the House of Representatives: The mint of the United States has entered upon the coinage of the precious metals; and considerable sums of defective coins and bullion have been lodged with the director by individuals. There is a pleasing prospect that the institution will, at no remote day, realize the expectation which was originally formed of its utility.

In subsequent communications, certain circumstances of our intercourse with foreign nations, will be transmitted to Congress. However, it may not be unseasonable to announce that my policy in our foreign transactions has been, to cultivate peace with all the world; to observe treaties with pure and absolute faith; to check every deviation from the line of impartiality; to explain what may have been misapprehended; and having thus acquired the right, to lose no time in acquiring the ability, to insist upon justice being done to ourselves.

Let us unite, therefore, in imploring the Supreme Ruler of nations, to spread his holy protection over these United States: to turn the machinations of the wicked to the confirming of our constitution: to enable us at all times to root out internal sedition, and put invasion to flight: to perpetuate to our country that prosperity, which his goodness has already conferred, and to verify the anticipations of this government being a safe guard to human rights.

DOCUMENT ANALYSIS

1. How did Washington defend his actions? What did he cite as the basis of his power to suppress the rebellion?

_____

_____

_____

2. What did Washington ask Congress to do in this address?

_____

_____

_____

3. How did Washington describe those who participated in the rebellion? In your opinion, was this a fair assessment? Why or why not?

_____

_____

_____

DOCUMENT 6.1
Opinion of the Supreme Court for *Marbury v. Madison* (1803)

Prior to leaving office, President Adams appointed several Federalist judges to the federal courts. Angered by these "midnight" appointments, Jefferson and his administration made several attempts to block the nominations and unseat the judges. The new administration failed to block any of the appointments except for that of William Marbury in the District of Columbia. Angered over the administration's actions, Marbury sued the new secretary of state, James Madison. This case, Marbury v. Madison, *failed to win Marbury his seat, but it officially established the Supreme Court's right to judicial review.*

In the order in which the Court has viewed this subject, the following questions have been considered and decided: 1st. Has the applicant a right to the commission he demands? 2nd. If he has a right, and that right has been violated, do the laws of this country afford him a remedy? 3rd. If they do afford him a remedy, is it a mandamus issuing from this court?. . .

It is . . . the opinion of the Court: 1st. That by signing the commission of Mr. Marbury, the President of the United States appointed him a justice of the peace for the county of Washington, in the District of Columbia; and that the seal of the United States, affixed thereto by the secretary of state, is conclusive testimony of the verity of the signature, and of the completion of the appointment; and that the appointment conferred on him a legal right to the office of the space of five years. 2nd. That, having this legal title to the office, he has a consequent right to the commission; a refusal to deliver which is a plain violation of that right, for which the laws of his country afford him a remedy. 3rd. It remains to be inquired whether he is entitled to the remedy for which he applies?. . .

This . . . is a plain case of a mandamus, either to deliver the commission, or a copy of it from the record; and it only remains to be inquired, whether it can issue from this court?

The act to establish the judicial courts of the United States authorizes the Supreme Court, "to issue writs of mandamus, in cases warranted by the principles and usages of law, to any courts appointed or persons holding office, under the authority of the United States." The secretary of state, being a person holding an office under the authority of the United States, is precisely within the letter of this description; and if this court is not authorized to issue a writ of mandamus to such an office, it must be because the law is unconstitutional. . .

The Constitution vests the whole judicial power of the United States in one Supreme Court, and such inferior courts as Congress shall, from time to time, ordain and establish. . .

In the distribution of this power, it is declared that "the Supreme Court shall have original jurisdiction in all cases affecting ambassadors, other public ministers and consuls, and those in which a state shall be a party. In all other cases, the Supreme Court shall have appellate jurisdiction.". . .

If it had been intended to leave it in the discretion of the legislature to apportion the judicial power between the supreme and inferior courts according to the will of that body, it would certainly have been useless to have proceeded further than to have defined the judicial power, and the tribunals in which it should be vested. The subsequent part of the section is mere surplus, is entirely without meaning,. . .

It cannot be presumed that any clause in the Constitution is intended to be without effect. . .

To enable this court, then, to issue a mandamus, it must be shown to be an exercise of appellate jurisdiction. . .

The authority, therefore, given to the Supreme Court, by the Act establishing the judicial courts of the United States, to issue writs of mandamus to public officers, appears not to be warranted by the Constitution. . .

DOCUMENT ANALYSIS

1. What role does Chief Justice Marshall hope the Supreme Court adopts in regards to the U.S. Constitution?

_____

_____

_____

2. Why was it important that the Chief Justice should be seen as speaking for all the members of the Supreme Court on this issue?

_____

_____

_____

DOCUMENT 6.2
Lewis and Clark Meet the Shoshone, August 17, 1805

Meriwether Lewis and William Clark were chosen by President Thomas Jefferson to survey the area known as Louisiana, purchased from France in 1803. Here, Lewis describes their first meeting with the Shoshone and the reunion of their guide Sacagawea with her people.

This morning I arose very early and dispatched Drewyer and the Indian down to the river. Sent Shields to hunt. I made McNeal cook the remainder of our meat which afforded a slight breakfast for ourselves and the chief. Drewyer had been gone about two hours when an Indian who had straggled some little distance down the river returned and reported that the white men were coming, that he had seen them just below. They all appeared transported with joy, and the chief repeated his fraternal hug. I felt quite as much gratified at this information as the Indians appeared to be. Shortly after Captain Clark arrived with the interpreter Charbono,

and the Indian woman, who proved to be a sister of the Chief Cameahwait. The meeting of those people was really affecting, particularly between Sah-cah-gar-we-ah [Sacagawea] and an Indian woman, who had been taken prisoner at the same time with her and who, had afterwards escaped from the Minnetares and rejoined her nation. At noon the canoes arrived, and we had the satisfaction once more to find ourselves all together, with a flattering prospect of being able to obtain as many horses shortly as would enable us to prosecute our voyage by land should that by water be deemed unadvisable.

We now formed our camp just below the junction of the forks on the larboard side in a level smooth bottom covered with a fine turf of greensward. Here we unloaded our canoes and arranged our baggage on shore; formed a canopy of one of our large sails and planted some willow brush in the ground to form a shade for the Indians to set under while we spoke to them, which we thought it best to do this evening. Accordingly about 4 PM we called them together and through the medium of Labuish, Charbono and Sah-cah-gar-we-ah, we communicated to them fully the objects which had brought us into this distant part of the country, in which we took care to make them a conspicuous object of our own good wishes and the care of our government. We made them sensible of their dependence on the will of our government for every species of merchandise as well for their defense and comfort; and apprised them of the strength of our government and its friendly dispositions towards them. We also gave them as a reason why we wished to penetrate the country as far as the ocean to the west of them was to examine and find out a more direct way to bring merchandise to them. That as no trade could be carried on with them before our return to our homes that it was mutually advantageous to them as well as to ourselves, that they should render us such aids as they had it in their power to furnish in order to hasten our voyage and of course our return home, that such were their horses to transport our baggage without which we could not subsist, and that a pilot to conduct us through the mountains was also necessary if we could not descend the river by water, but that we did not ask either their horses or their services without giving a satisfactory compensation in return, that at present we wished them to collect as many horses as were necessary to transport our baggage to their village on the Columbia where we would then trade with them at our leisure for such horses as they could spare us.

They appeared well pleased with what had been said. The chief thanked us for friendship towards himself and nation and declared his wish to serve us in every respect, that he was sorry to find that it must yet be some time before they could be furnished with firearms but said they could live as they had done heretofore until we brought them as we had promised. He said they had not horses enough with them at present to remove our baggage to their village over the mountain, but that he would return to-morrow and encourage his people to come over with their horses and that he would bring his own and assist us. This was complying with all we wished at present. We next inquired who were chiefs among them. Cameahwait pointed out two others whom he said were chiefs. We gave him a medal of the small size with the likeness of Mr. Jefferson the President of the United States in relief on one side and clasp hands with a pipe and tomahawk on the other, to the other chiefs we gave each a small medal which were struck in the president of George Washington Esq. We also gave small medals of the last description to two young men whom the first chief informed us were good young men and much respected among them. We gave the first chief a uniform coat, shirt, a pair of scarlet leggings, a carrot of tobacco and some small articles. To each of the others we gave a shi[r]t, legging[s], handkerchief, a knife, some tobacco and a few small articles. We also distributed a good quantity paint, moccasins, awles, knives, beads, looking-glasses, &c. among the other Indians and gave them a plentiful meal of lyed corn which was the first they had ever eaten in their lives. They were much pleased with it. Every article about us appeared to excite astonishment in their minds; the appearance of the men, their arms, the canoes, our manner of working them, the black man York, and the sagacity of my dog were equally objects of admiration. I also shot my air-gun which was so perfectly incomprehensible that they immediately denominated it the great medicine. The idea which the Indians mean to convey by this appellation is something that emanates from or acts immediately by the influence or power of the Great Spirit; or that, in which, the power of God is manifest by its incomprehensible power of action. Our hunters killed four deer and an antelope this evening of which we also gave the Indians a good proportion. The ceremony of our council and smoking the pipe was in conformity of the custom of this nation performed barefoot. On those occasions points of etiquette are quite as much attended to by the Indians as among civilized nations. To keep Indians in a good humor you must not fatigue them with too much business at one time. Therefore after the council we gave them to eat and amused them a while by showing them such articles as we thought would be entertaining to them, and then renewed our inquiries with respect to the country. The information we derived was only a repetition of that they had given me before and in which they appeared to be so candid that I could not avoid yielding confidence to what they had said. Captain Clark and myself now concerted measures for our future operations, and it was mutually agreed that he should set out to-morrow morning with eleven men furnished with axes and other necessary tools for making canoes, their arms, accoutrements and as much of their baggage as they could carry; also to take the Indians, Charbono and the Indian woman with him; that on his arrival at the Shoshone camp he was to leave Charbono and the Indian woman to hasten the return of the Indians with their horses to this place, and to proceed himself with the eleven men down the Columbia in order to examine the river and if he found it navigable and could obtain timber to set about making canoes immediately. In the meantime I was to bring on the party and baggage to the Shoshone camp, calculating that by the time I should reach that place that he would have sufficiently informed himself with respect to the state of the river &c. as to determine us whether to prosecute our journey from thence by land or water. In the former case we should want all the horses which we could purchase, and in the latter only to hire the Indians to transport our baggage to the place at which we made the canoes. In order to inform me as early as possible of the state of the river he was to send back one of the men with the necessary information as soon as he should satisfy himself on this subject. This plan being settled we gave orders accordingly and the men prepared for an early march. The nights are very cold and the sun excessively hot in the day. We have no fuel here but a few dry willow brush and from the appearance of the country I am confident we shall not find game here to subsist us many days. These are additional reasons why I conceive it necessary to get under way as soon as possible. This morning Captain Clark had delayed until 7 A.M. before he set out just about which time Drewyer arrived with the Indian; he left the canoes to come on after him, and immediately set out and joined me as has been before mentioned. The spirits of the men were now much elated at the prospect of getting horses.

DOCUMENT ANALYSIS

1. In this excerpt, Lewis asserts that he and Clark "communicated to them fully the objects which had brought us into this distant part of the country." What messages did they attempt to convey to the Shoshone concerning the nature of their mission? How did they portray their country and its government? How do you think the Shoshone received these messages?

_____

_____

_____

2. How would you characterize Lewis's attitude toward the Shoshone?

_____

_____

_____

DOCUMENT 7.1
Pennsylvania Gazette, Letter Extract Concerning "Indian Hostilities" (1812)

Stories of the British inciting Native American groups to attack American settlers abounded in the days immediately preceding the War of 1812. The following excerpt from the Pennsylvania Gazette *blames the British for "Indian hostilities" in the Indiana and Illinois territories.*

The following is an extract of a letter from a gentleman at St. Charles, Louisiana Territory, dated Jan. 10, 1812.

In answer to your enquiry, respecting Indian hostilities in this quarter, I have to inform you, that some of the reports that have found their way into the public prints are much exaggerated, but are generally true. The depredations committed by them have been principally in Indiana and Illinois territories; some horses have been taken in this territory, but I believe no murders have been committed by them for the last ten or twelve months. I had flattered myself that the drubbing given them by the troops under the command of Gov. Harrison would have disposed them to return to order. In this it appears I was mistaken, for this day, by an express from Fort Madison, we are informed of cruel murders committed on some traders, about 100 miles above that Fort, by a party of the Pecant

nation. A Mr. Hunt, son of the late Col. Hunt, of the United States' army, and a Mr. Prior, were trading in that quarter—their houses about 3 miles distance from each other. The party of Indians came to Hunt's house, and appeared friendly until they obtained admittance into the house—they then shot down two men that Mr. Hunt had with him, seized him and a boy, who was his interpreter, tied them, and packed up the goods that were in the house, and carried them off. Mr. Hunt discovered that they believed him to be an Englishman, and on that account saved his life. They told him that they had sent another party to kill Prior, and carry off his goods, and that they intended in a short time to take the Fort—after which they would come on and kill every American they could find. They took Mr. Hunt and his boy with them some distance, but night came on, and proved extremely dark, which fortunately gave them an opportunity of escaping, and they arrived safe at Fort Madison on the sixth day.

The hostilities that have taken place, together with the mysterious conduct of the few Indians that are passing amongst us, lead me to believe they are determined for war, and that they are set on by British agents. If we go to war with England, I calculate on some very warm work in this quarter.

DOCUMENT ANALYSIS

1. What does the author of this letter foresee as the consequences of a war between England and the United States?

_____

_____

_____

2. Which historical event does "the drubbing given them by the troops under the command of Gov. Harrison" refer to?

_____

_____

_____

DOCUMENT 7.2
Letter from Dolley Payne Madison to Lucy Payne Todd (1814)
From Dolley Madison Papers, Library of Congress, Washington, DC.

The War of 1812 between the United States and Britain is often remembered for two particular events. One is the Battle of New Orleans, won by U.S. forces under Andrew Jackson after the Treaty of Ghent had already been signed. The other is the burning of Washington, D.C., including the White House. Dolley Madison, wife of President James Madison, famously saved the Gilbert Stuart portrait of George Washington as well as official state papers when she fled before British troops. The letter below is the document generally cited by historians to illustrate the event, although there is some suspicion that it might actually have been written years later.

Extract from a letter written to my sister published in the sketch of my life written for the "National Portrait Gallery."

Tuesday Augt. 23d. 1814

Dear Sister

My husband left me yesterday morng. to join Gen. Winder. He enquired anxiously whether I had courage, or firmness to remain in the President's house [White House] until his return, on the morrow, or succeeding day, and on my assurance that I had no fear but for him and the success of our army, he left me, beseeching me to take care of myself, and of the cabinet papers, public and private. I have since recd. two despatches

from him, written with a pencil; the last is alarming, because he desires I should be ready at a moment's warning to enter my carriage and leave the city; that the enemy seemed stronger than had been reported and that it might happen that they would reach the city, with intention to destroy it. . . . I am accordingly ready; I have pressed as many cabinet papers into trunks as to fill one carriage; our private property must be sacrificed, as it is impossible to procure wagons for its transportation. I am determined not to go myself until I see Mr. Madison safe, and he can accompany me, as I hear of much hostility towards him, . . . disaffection stalks around us. . . . My friends and acquaintances are all gone; Even Col. C with his hundred men, who were stationed as a guard in the enclosure . . . French John (a faithful domestic,) with his usual activity and resolution, offers to spike the cannon at the gate, and to lay a train of powder which would blow up the British, should they enter the house. To the last proposition I positively object, without being able, however, to make him understand why all advantages in war may not be taken.

Wednesday morng., twelve o'clock. Since sunrise I have been turning my spyglass in every direction and watching with unwearied anxiety, hoping to discern the approach of my dear husband and his friends, but, alas, I can descry only groups of military wandering in all directions, as if there was a lack of arms, or of spirit to fight for their own firesides!

Three O'clock. Will you believe it, my sister? We have had a battle or skirmish near Bladensburg, and I am still here within sound of the cannon! Mr. Madison comes not; may God protect him! Two messengers covered with dust, come to bid me fly; but I wait for him. . . . At this late hour a wagon has been procured, I have had it filled with the plate and most valuable portable articles belonging to the house; whether it will reach its destination; the Bank of Maryland, or fall into the hands of British soldiery, events must determine.

Our kind friend, Mr. Carroll, has come to hasten my departure, and is in a very bad humor with me because I insist on waiting until the large picture of Gen. Washington is secured, and it requires to be unscrewed from the wall. This process was found too tedious for these perilous moments; I have ordered the frame to be broken, and the canvass taken out it is done, and the precious portrait placed in the hands of two gentlemen of New York, for safe keeping. And now, dear sister, I must leave this house, or t[he] retreating army will make me a prisoner in it, by filling up the road I am direc[ted] to take. When I shall again write you, or where I shall be tomorrow, I cannot tell!!

DOCUMENT ANALYSIS

1. What about this letter would make it such a popular historical artifact?

_____

_____

_____

2. If the letter was written at a later date with an eye toward documenting an historical event, would it be any less valuable as a primary source?

_____

_____

_____

DOCUMENT 8.1
Extract from the Albany *Daily Advertiser* (1819)

The Erie Canal was not completed until 1825, but the middle section, which ran from Utica to Rome, was completed in 1819. That opening is recounted in the excerpt below. The impact of the canal was immense. When completed, it traversed New York State and linked New York Harbor to the Great Lakes. It provided commercial transportation, encouraged westward expansion, and was the engineering marvel of its age. Cities and towns along its banks prospered, and New York City became the nation's shipping center.

The last two days have presented in this village, a scene of the liveliest interest; and I consider it among the privileges of my life to have been present to witness it. On Friday afternoon I walked to the head of the grand canal, the eastern extremity of which reaches within a very short distance of the village, and from one of the slight and airy bridges which crossed it, I had a sight that could not but exhilirate and elevate the mind. The waters were rushing in from the westward, and coming down their untried channel towards the sea. Their course, owing to the absorption of the new banks of the canal, and the distance they had to run from where the stream entered it, was much slower than I had anticipated; they continued gradually to steal along from bridge to bridge, and at first only spreading over the bed of the canal, imperceptibly rose and washed its sides with a gentle wave. It was dark before they reached the eastern extremity; but at sunrise next morning, they were on a level, two feet and a half deep throughout the whole distance of thirteen miles. The interest manifested by the whole country, as this new internal river rolled its first waves through the state, cannot be described. You might see the people running across the fields, climbing on trees and fences, and crowding the bank of the canal to gaze upon the welcome sight. A boat had been prepared at Rome, and as the waters came down the canal, you might mark their progress by that of this new Argo, which floated triumphantly along the Hellespont of the west, accompanied by the shouts of the peasantry, and having on her deck a military band. At nine the next morning, the bells began a merry peal, and the commissioners in carriages, proceeded from Bagg's hotel, to the place of embarkation.

The governor, accompanied by Gen. Van Rensselaer, Rev. Mr. Stansbury, of Albany, Rev. Dr. Blatchford, of Lansingburgh, Judge Miller, of Utica, Mr. Holly, Mr. Seymour, Judge Wright, Col. Lansing, Mr. Childs, Mr. Clark, Mr. Bunner, and a large company of their friends, embarked, at a quarter past nine, and were received with the roll of the drum, and the shouts of a large multitude of spectators. The boat, which received them, is built for passengers;—is sixty-one feet in length, and seven and an half feet in width;—having two rising cabins, of fourteen feet each, with a flat deck between them. In forty minutes the company reached Whitesborough, a distance of two miles and three quarters; the boat being drawn by a single horse, which walked on the towing path, attached to a tow rope, of about sixty feet long. The horse travelled, apparently, with the utmost ease. The boat, though literally loaded with passengers, drew but fourteen inches water. A military band played patriotic airs. From bridge to bridge, from village to village, the procession was saluted with cannon, and every bell whose sound could reach the canal, swung, as with instinctive life, as it passed by. At Whitesborough, a number of ladies embarked, and heightened, by their smiles, a scene which wanted but this to make it complete.

DOCUMENT ANALYSIS

1. How far did the boat travel on the canal in 40 minutes? How does this performance compare to modern means of transportation?

_____

_____

_____

2. Why was the canal such an innovation? How had goods and people been transported prior to its opening?

_____

_____

_____

2. Which transportation modes eventually replaced the canal system? Why?

_____

_____

_____

DOCUMENT 8.2
"A Week in the Mill," *The Lowell Offering*, Vol. V (1845): 217–218

The Lowell Offering was a monthly literary magazine published (primarily between 1841 and 1845) by women factory workers in the textile mills of Lowell, Massachusetts. For many of the women and girls who worked in the factories, working at Lowell offered an opportunity to earn the highest wages of any women workers in America. Despite their long work hours, the Lowell workers could devote some of their time to attending evening classes and lectures, accessing Lowell's circulating library, or working on the magazine.

Much has been said of the factory girl and her employment. By some she has been represented as dwelling in a sort of brick-and-mortar paradise, having little to occupy thought save the weaving of gay and romantic fancies, while the spindle or the wheel flies obediently beneath her glance. Others have deemed her a mere servile drudge, chained to her labor by almost as strong a power as that which holds a bondman in his fetters; and, indeed, some have already given her the title of "the white slave of the North." Her real situation approaches neither one nor the other of these extremes. Her occupation is as laborious as that of almost any female who earns her own living, while it has also its sunny spots and its cheerful intervals, which make her hard labor seem comparatively pleasant and easy.

Look at her as she commences her weekly task. The rest of the Sabbath has made her heart and her step light, and she is early at her accustomed place, awaiting the starting of the machinery. Every thing having been cleaned and neatly arranged on the Saturday night, she has less to occupy her on Monday than on other days; and you may see her leaning from the window to watch the glitter of the sunrise on the water, or looking away at the distant forests and fields, while memory wanders to her beloved country home; or, it may be that she is conversing with a sister-laborer near; returning at regular intervals to see that her work is in order.

Soon the breakfast bell rings; in a moment the whirling wheels are stopped, and she hastens to join the throng which is pouring through the open gate. At the table she mingles with a various group. Each dispatches the meal hurriedly, though not often in silence; and if, as is sometimes the case, the rules of politeness are not punctiliously observed by all, the excuse of some lively country girl would be, "They don't give us time for manners."

The short half-hour is soon over; the bell rings again; and now our factory girl feels that she has commenced her day's work in earnest. The time is often apt to drag heavily till the dinner hour arrives. Perhaps some part of the work becomes deranged and stops; the constant friction causes a belt of leather to burst into a flame; a stranger visits the room, and scans the features and dress of its inmates inquiringly; and there is little else to break the monotony. The afternoon passes in much the same manner. Now and then she mingles with a knot of busy talkers who have collected to discuss some new occurrence, or holds pleasant converse with some intelligent and agreeable friend, whose acquaintance she has formed since her factory life commenced; but much of the time she is left to her own thoughts. While at her work, the clattering and rumbling around her prevent any other noise from attracting her attention, and she must think, or her life would be dull indeed.

Thus the day passes on, and evening comes; the time which she feels to be exclusively her own. How much is done in the three short hours from seven to ten o'clock. She has a new dress to finish; a call to make on some distant corporation; a meeting to attend; there is a lecture or a concert at some one of the public halls, and the attendance will be thin if she and her associates are not present; or, if nothing more imperative demands her time, she takes a stroll through the street or to the river with some of her mates, or sits down at home to peruse a new book. At ten o'clock all is still for the night.

The clang of the early bell awakes her to another day, very nearly the counterpart of the one which preceded it. And so the week rolls on, in the same routine, till Saturday comes. Saturday! the welcome sound! She busies herself to remove every particle of cotton and dust from her frame or looms, cheering herself meanwhile with sweet thoughts of the coming Sabbath; and when, at an earlier hour than usual, the mill is stopped, it looks almost beautiful in its neatness.

DOCUMENT ANALYSIS

1. Does this excerpt present an essentially positive or negative portrait of the Lowell factory system? Explain your answer.

_____

_____

_____

2. According to the excerpt, what resting period makes the balance of the working week endurable?

_____

_____

_____

3. Does the lifestyle of Lowell more clearly benefit the workers or the factory owners?

_____

_____

_____

DOCUMENT 9.1
Davy Crockett, Advice to Politicians (1833)

Davy Crockett had a great deal in common with Andrew Jackson. Both men were from Tennessee, both fought in the Indian wars (for a time Crockett even served under Jackson), and both used their military successes to propel their political careers. Crockett's advice to politicians reflects the new political culture that emerged in the so-called "Jacksonian Era." This era, characterized by the emergence of the "common man" in U.S. politics, was the ideal time for Crockett to pursue his career as a congressman.

"Attend all public meetings," says I, "and get some friend to move that you take the chair. If you fail in this attempt, make a push to be appointed secretary. The proceeding of course will be published, and your name is introduced to the public. But should you fail in both undertakings, get two or three acquaintances, over a bottle of whisky, to pass some resolutions, no matter on what subject. Publish them, even if you pay the printer. It will answer the purpose of breaking the ice, which is the main point in these matters.

"Intrigue until you are elected an officer of the militia. This is the second step toward promotion, and can be accomplished with ease, as I know an instance of an election being advertised, and no one attending, the innkeeper at whose house it was to be held, having a military turn, elected himself colonel of his regiment." Says I, "You may not accomplish your ends with as little difficulty, but do not be discouraged—Rome wasn't built in a day.

"If your ambition or circumstances compel you to serve your country and earn three dollars a day, by becoming a member of the legislature, you must first publicly avow that the constitution of the state is a shackle upon free and liberal legislation, and is, therefore, of as little use in the present enlightened age as an old almanac of the year in which the instrument was framed. There is policy in this measure, for by making the constitution a mere dead letter, your headlong proceedings will be attributed to a bold and unshackled mind; whereas, it might otherwise be thought they arose from sheer mulish ignorance. 'The Government' has set the example in his [Jackson's] attack upon the Constitution of the United States, and who should fear to follow where 'the Government' leads?

"When the day of election approaches, visit your constituents far and wide. Treat liberally, and drink freely, in order to rise in their estimation, though you fall in your own. True, you may be called a drunken dog by some of the clean-shirt and silk-stocking gentry, but the real roughnecks will style you a jovial fellow. Their votes are certain, and frequently count double.

"Do all you can to appear to advantage in the eyes of the women. That's easily done. You have but to kiss and slabber [slobber over] their children, wipe their noses, and pat them on the head. This cannot fail to please their mothers, and you may rely on your business being done in that quarter.

"Promise all that is asked," said I, "and more if you can think of anything. Offer to build a bridge or a church, to divide a county, create a batch of new offices, make a turnpike, or anything they like. Promises cost nothing; therefore, deny nobody who has a vote or sufficient influence to obtain one.

"Get up on all occasions, and sometimes on no occasion at all, and make long-winded speeches, though composed of nothing else than wind. Talk of your devotion to your country, your modesty and disinterestedness, or on any such fanciful subject. Rail against taxes of all kinds, officeholders, and bad harvest weather; and wind up with a flourish about the heroes who fought and bled for our liberties in the times that tried men's souls. To be sure, you run the risk of being considered a bladder of wind, or an empty barrel. But never mind that; you will find enough of the same fraternity to keep you in countenance.

"If any charity be going forward, be at the top of it, provided it is to be advertised publicly. If not, it isn't worth your while. None but a fool would place his candle under a bushel on such an occasion.

"These few directions." said I, "if properly attended to, will do your business. And when once elected—why, a fig for the dirty children, the promises, the bridges, the churches, the taxes, the offices, and the subscriptions. For it is absolutely necessary to forget all these before you can become a thoroughgoing politician, and a patriot of the first water."

DOCUMENT ANALYSIS

1. To whom does Crockett suggest a candidate should appeal for support?

_____

_____

_____

2. What does Crockett see as most important issues for politicians to consider?

_____

_____

_____

DOCUMENT 9.2
Black Hawk, Excerpt from "The Life of Black Hawk" (1833)

Sauk warrior Black Hawk led the Sauk and Fox peoples in their resistance against attempts by the U.S. government to take their lands. In 1804 a small group of tribal representatives supposedly conceded a vast amount of territory to the United States, much of it in present-day Illinois. Black Hawk eventually emerged as the leader of the Sauk and Fox peoples who refused to abandon these lands. This dispute culminated in the Black Hawk War of 1832 in which the Indians won a few initial battles but were ultimately defeated and lost their lands. Black Hawk was taken prisoner, and he wrote his autobiography the following year.

We generally paid a visit to St. Louis every summer; but, in consequence of the protracted war in which we had been engaged, I had not been there for some years. Our difficulties having all been settled, I concluded to take a small party, that summer, and go down to see our Spanish father. We went—and on our arrival, put up our lodges where the market-house now stands. After painting and dressing, we called to see our Spanish father, and were well received. He gave us a variety of presents, and plenty of provisions. We danced through the town as usual, and its inhabitants all seemed to be well pleased. They appeared to us like brothers and always gave us good advice.

On my next, and last, visit to my Spanish father, I discovered, on landing, that all was not right: every countenance seemed sad and gloomy! I inquired the cause, and was informed that the Americans were coming to take possession of the town and country! And that we should then lose our Spanish father! This news made myself and band sad—because we had always heard bad accounts of the Americans from Indians who had lived near them!—and we were sorry to lose our Spanish father, who had always treated us with great friendship.

A few days afterwards, the Americans arrived. I took my band, and went to take leave, for the last time, of our father. The Americans came to see him also. Seeing them approach, we passed out at one door, as they entered another—and immediately started, in canoes, for our village on Rock river—not liking the change any more than our friends appeared to, at St. Louis.

On arriving at our village, we gave the news, that strange people had taken St. Louis—and that we should never see our Spanish father again! This information made all our people sorry!

Some time afterwards, a boat came up the river, with a young American chief, and a small party of soldiers. We heard of them, (by runners,) soon after he had passed Salt river. Some of our young braves watched him every day, to see what sort of people he had on board! The boat, at length, arrived at Rock river, and the young chief came on shore with his interpreter, made a speech, and gave us some presents! We, in return, presented him with meat, and such provisions as we could spare.

We were all well pleased with the speech of the young chief. He gave us good advice; said our American father would treat us well. He presented us an American flag, which was hoisted. He then requested us to pull down our British flags—and give him our British medals promising to send us others on his return to St. Louis. This we declined, as we wished to have two Fathers!

When the young chief started, we sent runners to the Fox village, some miles distant, to direct them to treat him well as he passed—which they did. He went to the head of the Mississippi, and then returned to St. Louis. We did not see any Americans again for some time, being supplied with goods by British traders.

We were fortunate in not giving up our medals, for we learned afterwards, from our traders, that the chiefs high up on the Mississippi, who gave theirs, never received any in exchange for them. But the fault was not with the young American chief. He was a good man, and a great brave—and died in his country's service.

Some moons after this young chief descended the Mississippi, one of our people killed an American—and was confined, in the prison at St. Louis, for the offence. We held a council at our village to see what could be done for him,—which determined that Quàsh-quà-me, Pà-she-pa-ho, Oú-che-quà-ka, and Hà-she-quar-hi-qua, should go down to St. Louis, see our American father, and do all they could to have our friend released: by paying for the person killed—thus covering the blood, and satisfying the relations of the man murdered! This being the only means with us of saving a person who had killed another—and we then thought it was the same way with the whites!

The party started with the good wishes of the whole nation—hoping they would accomplish the object of their mission. The relatives of the prisoner blacked their faces, and fasted—hoping the Great Spirit would take pity on them, and return the husband and father to his wife and children.

Quàsh-quà-me and party remained a long time absent. They at length returned, and encamped a short distance below the village—but did not come up that day—nor did any person approach their camp! They appeared to be dressed in fine coats, and had medals! From these circumstances, we were in hopes that they had brought good news. Early the next morning, the Council Lodge was crowded—Quàsh-quà-me and party came up, and gave us the following account of their mission:

"On their arrival at St. Louis, they met their American father, and explained to him their business, and urged the release of their friend. The American chief told them he wanted land—and they had agreed to give him some on the west side of the Mississippi, and some on the Illinois side opposite the Jeffreon. When the business was all arranged, they expected to have their friend released to come home with them. But about the time they were ready to start, their friend was let out of prison, who ran a short distance, and was shot dead! This is all they could recollect of what was said and done. They had been drunk the greater part of the time they were in St. Louis."

This is all myself or nation knew of the treaty of 1804. It has been explained to me since. I find, by that treaty, all our country, east of the Mississippi, and south of the Jeffreon, was ceded to the United States for one thousand dollars a year! I will leave it to the people of the United States to say, whether our nation was properly represented in this treaty? or whether we received a fair compensation for the extent of country ceded by those four individuals? I could say much about this treaty, but I will not, at this time. It has been the origin of all our difficulties.

DOCUMENT ANALYSIS

1. What event did Black Hawk describe as "the origin of all our difficulties"?

_____

_____

_____

2. What were Black Hawk's initial impressions of the first Americans he encountered? Based on this account, could you have predicted his future conflicts with the United States?

_____

_____

_____

DOCUMENT 10.1
National Convention of Colored People, Report on Abolition (1847)

The National Convention of Colored People's Committee on Abolition included many runaway slaves who had become abolitionists, such as Frederick Douglass. Douglass and other African Americans advocated reform both on their own and through participation in organizations led by whites such as William Lloyd Garrison.

The Committee appointed to draft a Report respecting the best means of abolishing Slavery and destroying Caste in the United States, beg leave most respectfully to Report: That they have had the important subjects referred to them, under consideration, and have carefully endeavored to examine all their points and bearings to the best of their ability; and from every view they have been able to take they have arrived at the conclusion that the best means of abolishing slavery is proclamation of truth, and that the best means of destroying caste is the mental, moral and industrial improvement of our people.

First, as respects Slavery, Your Committee find this monstrous crime, this stupendous iniquity, closely interwoven with all the great interests, institutions and organizations of the country; pervading and influencing every class and grade of society, securing their support, obtaining their approbation, and commanding their homage. Availing itself of the advantage which age gives to crime, it has perverted the judgment, blunted the moral sense, blasted the sympathies, and created in the great mass,—the overwhelming majority of the people—a moral sentiment altogether favorable to its own character, and its own continuance. Press and pulpit are alike prostituted and made to serve the end of this infernal institution. The power of the government, and the sanctity of religion, church and state, are joined with the guilty oppressor against the oppressed-and the voice of this great nation is thundering in the ear of our enslaved fellow countrymen the terrible fiat, you shall be slaves or die!

The slave is in the minority, a small minority. The oppressors are an overwhelming majority. The oppressed are three millions, their oppressors are seventeen millions. The one is weak, the other is strong; the one is without arms, without means of concert, and without government; the other possess every advantage in these respects; and the deadly aim of their million of musketry, and loud-mouthed cannon tells the downtrodden slave in unmistakable language, he must be a slave or die.

In these circumstances, your committee are called upon to report as to the best means of abolishing slavery. And without pretending parties and factions, though did time permit, they would gladly do so, they beg at once to state their entire disapprobation of any plan of emancipation involving a resort to bloodshed. With the facts of our condition before us, it is impossible for us to contemplate any appeal to the slave to take vengeance on his guilty master, but with the utmost reprobation. Your Committee regards any counsel of this sort as the perfection of folly, suicidal in the extreme, and abominably wicked. We should utterly frown down and wholly discountenance any attempt to lead our people to confide in brute force as a reformatory instrumentality. All argument put forth in favor of insurrection and bloodshed, however well intended, is either the result of an unpardonable impatience or an atheistic want of faith in the power of truth as a means of regenerating and reforming the world.

Again we repeat, let us set our faces against all such absurd, unavailing, dangerous and mischievous ravings, emanating from what source they may. The voice of God and of common sense, equally point out a more excellent way, and that way is a faithful, earnest, and persevering enforcement of the great principles of justice and morality, religion and humanity. These are the only invincible and infallible means within our reach with which to overthrow this foul system of blood and ruin. Your Committee deem it susceptible of the clearest demonstration, that slavery exists in this country, because the people of this country WILL its existence. And they deem it equally clear, that no system or institution can exist for an hour against the earnestly-expressed WILL of the people. It were quite easy to bring to the support of the foregoing proposition powerful and conclusive illustrations from the history of reform in all ages, and especially in our own. But the palpable truths of the propositions, as well as the familiarity of the facts illustrating them, entirely obviate such a necessity.

Our age is an age of great discoveries; and one of the greatest is that which revealed that this world is to be ruled, shaped and guided by the marvelous might of mind. The human voice must supersede the roar of cannon. Truth alone is the legitimate antidote of falsehood. Liberty is always sufficient to grapple with tyranny. Free speech—free discussion—peaceful agitation, the foolishness of preaching these, under God, will subvert this giant crime, and send it reeling to its grave, as if smitten by a voice from the throne of God. Slavery exists because it is popular. It will cease to exist when it is made unpopular. Whatever therefore tends to make Slavery unpopular tends to its destruction. This every Slaveholder knows full well, and hence his opposition to all discussion of the subject. It is an evidence of intense feeling of alarm, when John C. Calhoun calls upon the North to put down what he is pleased to term "this plundering agitation." Let us give the Slaveholder what he most dislikes.

Let us expose his crimes and his foul abominations. He is reputable and must be made disreputable. He must be regarded as a moral leper—slummed as a loathsome wretch-outlawed from Christian communion, and from social respectability—an enemy of God and man, to be execrated by the community till he shall repent of his foul crimes, and give proof of his sincerity by breaking every chain and letting the oppressed go free. Let us invoke the Press and appeal to the pulpit to deal out the righteous denunciations of heaven against oppression, fraud and wrong, and the desire of our hearts will soon be given us in the triumph of Liberty throughout all the land. . .

DOCUMENT ANALYSIS

1. What are the principal ways the committee believed abolitionists could resist and overcome slavery? What means should be avoided? Why?

_____

_____

_____

2. How successful do you think the committee's strategy to abolish slavery would have been if the Civil War had not intervened?

_____

_____

_____

DOCUMENT 10.2
Mathew Carey, "Rules for Husbands and Wives" (1830)

Irish-born Mathew Carey eventually settled in Philadelphia, where he became a publisher, bookseller, and economist, with a special fondness for universal education. His Miscellaneous Essays *included the excerpt below, which outlined what he believed to be proper behavior between married persons. The United States was changing in the early 1830s, as recorded by Alexis de Tocqueville in* Democracy in America. *This period was marked by economic growth, westward expansion, expanding international and domestic markets, and scientific progress. The antislavery movement was gaining momentum, and from within that movement would emerge the women's rights movement. Carey's essay is an early reconsideration of proper gender roles in American society.*

Having seen various sets of maxims for the conduct of married life, which have appeared to me to contain some very injudicious items, degrading to wives, sinking them below the rank they ought to occupy, and reducing them in some degree to the level of mere housekeepers, and believing them radically erroneous, I annex a set which appear more rational and just than most of those which I have seen:

1. A good husband will always regard his wife as his equal; treat her with kindness, respect and attention; and never address her with an air of authority, as if she were, as some husbands appear to regard their wives, a mere housekeeper.
2. He will never interfere in her domestic concerns, hiring servants, &c.
3. He will always keep her liberally supplied with money for furnishing his table in a style proportioned to his means, and for the purchase of dress suitable to her station in life.
4. He will cheerfully and promptly comply with all her reasonable requests, when it can be done, without loss, or great inconvenience.
5. He will never allow himself to lose his temper towards her, by indifferent cookery, or irregularity in the hours of meals, or any other mismanagement of her servants, knowing the difficulty of making them do their duty.
6. If she have prudence and good sense, he will consult her on all great operations, involving the risk of ruin, or serious injury in case of failure. Many a man has been rescued from destruction by the wise counsels of his wife. Many a foolish husband has most seriously in-jured himself and family by the rejection of the advice of his wife, fearing, lest, if he followed it, he would be regarded as ruled by her! A husband can never procure a counselor more deeply interested in his welfare than his wife.
7. If distressed, or embarrassed in his circumstances, he will communicate his situation to her with candor, that she may bear his difficulties in mind, in her expenditures. Women sometimes, believing their husband's circumstances to be far better than they really are, expend money which cannot well be afforded, and which, if they knew their real situation, they would shrink from expending.

1. A good wife will always receive her husband with smiles,—leave nothing undone to render home agreeable—and gratefully reciprocate his kindness and attention.
2. She will study to discover means to gratify his inclinations, in regard to food and cookery; in the management of her family; in her dress, manners and deportment.
3. She will never attempt to rule, or appear to rule her husband. Such conduct degrades husbands—and wives always partake largely of the degradation of their husbands.
4. She will, in every thing reasonable, comply with his wishes—and, as far as possible, anticipate them.
5. She will avoid all altercations or arguments leading to ill-humor—and more especially before company.
6. She will never attempt to interfere in his business, unless he ask her advice or counsel, and will never attempt to control him in the management of it.

Should differences arise between husband and wife, the contest ought to be, not who will display the most spirit, but who will make the first advances. There is scarcely a more prolific source of unhappiness in the married state, than this "spirit," the legitimate offspring of pride and want of feeling.

Perhaps the whole art of happiness in the married state, might be compressed into these two maxims—"Bear and forbear"—and "let the husband treat his wife, and the wife treat her husband, with as much respect and attention, as he would a strange lady, and she a strange gentleman." And surely this is not an extravagant requisition.

DOCUMENT ANALYSIS

1. Would any aspects of this essay have been considered radical in 1830? If so, then which ones?

_____

_____

_____

2. Why did Carey feel he is qualified to write such an essay? Upon what did he base his authority?

_____

_____

_____

3. In what ways did Carey's maxims challenge traditional gender roles, and in what ways did they reinforce them?

_____

_____

_____

DOCUMENT 11.1
O. A. Brownson, "Brook Farm," *United States Magazine and Democratic Review* 11 (November 1842)

Transcendentalism was a literary and philosophical movement that was popular in New England from the 1830s to the 1860s. It gained a wide audience thanks to works such as Henry David Thoreau's Walden. *Among its founders were some of the nation's most famous intellectuals and writers, including Nathaniel Hawthorne, Charles A. Dana, Ralph Waldo Emerson, Margaret Fuller, and Horace Greeley. Transcendentalism never included a strict religious philosophy, but most of its adherents believed in the divinity of humanity and the natural world and focused on the importance of intuition. Individualism and the satisfaction gained from physical work were central to transcendentalism, and Brook Farm, a utopian community in Massachusetts that existed from 1841 until 1847, attempted to transform those ideas into reality. In its last years Brook Farm was also greatly influenced by Fourierism, a utopian socialist philosophy named for its founder, the French philosopher Charles Fourier. The author of the excerpt below, O. A. Brownson, served as editor of the* United States Magazine and Democratic Review *from 1842 to 1844. Brownson was such an admirer of Brook Farm and its members that he sent his son there and he worked with community members on various publications.*

With respect to the labor, which is the material wealth of the establishment, and the body of its life, they intend to have all trades and occupations which contribute to necessities and healthy elegancies, within their own borders, so as not to buy them from without, which is too expensive; but at present their labor is agriculture, and the simplest housekeeping. . . .

Every one prescribes his own hours of labor, controlled only by his conscience, and the spirit of place, which tends to great industry, and almost to too much exertion. A drone would soon find himself isolated and neglected, and could not live there. The new comers, especially if they come from the city, have to begin gradually, but soon learn to increase the labor of one hour a day in the field, to six or seven hours, and some work all day long; but there can be no drudgery where there is no constraint. As all eat together, they change their dress for their meals; and so after tea they are all ready for grouping, in the parlors of the ladies, or in the library, or in the music-room, or they can go to their private rooms, or into the woods, or anywhere. They visit a good deal; and when they have business out of the community, nothing seems more easy than for them to arrange with others of their own number, to take their work or teaching for the time being; so that while they may work more than people out of the community, none seem such prisoners of their duties. The association of labor makes distribution according to taste and ability easy, and this takes the sting out of fatigue. . . .

For the women, there is, besides many branches of teaching, washing and ironing, housekeeping, sewing for the other sex, and for the children, and conducting all the social life. They have to hire one washerwoman now, but hope, bye and bye, to do all the washing within themselves. By the wide distribution of these labors, no one has any great weight of any one thing. They iron every forenoon but one; but they take turns, and each irons as long as she thinks right. The care of the houses is also distributed among those who are most active, in a way mutually satisfactory. . . .

. . . It is truly a most religious life, and does it not realize in miniature that identity of church and state which you think is the deepest idea of our American government? It seems to me that this community, point by point, corresponds with the great community of the Republic, whose divine lineaments are so much obscured by the rubbish of reported abuses (that, however, only lie on the surface, and may be shaken off, "like dewdrops from the lion's mane";) and whose divine proportions are now lost to our sight by the majestic grandeur with which they tower beyond the apprehension of our time-bound senses. For the theory of our government also proposes education (the freest development of the individual, according to the law of God) as its main end; an equal distribution of the results of labor among the laborers, as its means; and a mutual respect of each man by his neighbor as the basis. Only in America, I think, could such a community have so succeeded as I have described, composed of persons coming by chance, as it were, from all circumstances of life, and united only by a common idea and plan of life. They have succeeded, because they are the children of a government the ideal of which is the same as their own, although, as a mass, we are unconscious of it; so little do we understand our high vocation, and act up to it. But these miniatures of the great original shall educate us to the apprehension and realization of it, as a nation.

DOCUMENT ANALYSIS

1. In the final paragraph, what is the meaning of the phrase "in miniature that identity of church and state which you think is the deepest idea of our American government"?

_____

_____

2. How was labor divided at Brook Farm? What restrictions, if any, were imposed on members of the community?

_____

_____

3. Explain, in your own words, Brownson's reasoning that such a community could succeed only in America.

_____

_____

Ralph Waldo Emerson, "The Concord Hymn" (1837)

The great resurgence of national pride that characterized Jackson's rise to the presidency touched every aspect of American life. One of the most evident manifestations of this national pride came in the form of a renewed interest in commemorating the accomplishments of the nation's forefathers, who liberated the nation and provided for the prosperity at the time. "The Concord Hymn" by Ralph Waldo Emerson is an excellent example of the nationalistic pride felt by many Americans in the early nineteenth century. Emerson describes in great detail the sacrifices made by the men who fought at Concord, a great testament to the strength and will of the American nation.

By the rude bridge that arched the flood,
Their flag to April's breeze unfurled,
Here once the embattled farmers stood,
And fired the shot heard round the world.

The foe long since in silence slept;
Alike the conqueror silent sleeps;
And Time the ruined bridge has swept
Down the dark stream which seaward creeps.

On this green bank, by this soft stream,
We set to-day a votive stone;
That memory may their deed redeem,
When, like our sires, our sons are gone.

Spirit, that made those heroes dare
To die, or leave their children free,
Bid Time and Nature gently spare
The shaft we raise to them and thee.

DOCUMENT ANALYSIS

1. How do you think this poem was received by the American people? Would Americans from every part of the country have appreciated it for the same reasons? Why or why not?

_____

_____

_____

2. Why did Emerson describe the battle of Concord as "the shot heard round the world"?

_____

_____

_____

DOCUMENT 12.1
Richard Henry Dana, Jr., Assesses California in *Two Years Before the Mast* (1840)

Richard Henry Dana, Jr., distinguished himself as a Harvard graduate and an eminent lawyer who argued on behalf of slaves prosecuted under the Fugitive Slave Law and ultimately served in the Lincoln administration as U.S. attorney for Massachusetts. In addition, Dana enjoyed a literary career, based in large part upon the novel Two Years Before the Mast, his account of the time he spent as a sailor aboard the Pilgrim. Dana undertook this adventure after an attack of measles had left his eyesight too poor to pursue his studies. The book was widely hailed in the United States and England as an excellent account of life at sea. Dana's voyage took him to California, and his observations offer a valuable glimpse of the region when it was still a part of Mexico, before the Mexican-American War and the Gold Rush.

The Californians are an idle, thriftless people, and can make nothing for themselves. The country abounds in grapes, yet they buy bad wine made in Boston and brought round by us, at an immense price, and retail it among themselves at a real [a Spanish coin then worth 12 1/2 cents] by the small wine-glass. Their hides, too, which they value at two dollars in money, they give for something which costs seventy-five cents in Boston; and buy shoes (as like as not, made of their own hides, which have been carried twice round Cape Horn) at three and four dollars, and "chicken-skin" boots at fifteen dollars apiece. Things sell, on an average, at an advance of nearly three hundred per cent upon the Boston prices. . . .

Their complexions are various, depending—as well as their dress and manner—upon their rank; or, in other words, upon the amount of Spanish blood they can lay claim to. Those who are of pure Spanish blood, having never intermarried with the aborigines, have clear brunette complexions, and sometimes, even as fair as those of English women. There are but few of these families in California. . . . These form the aristocracy; intermarrying, and keeping up an exclusive system in every respect. They can be told by their complexions, dress, manner, and also by their speech. . . . From this upper class, they go down by regular shades, growing more and more dark and muddy, until you come to the pure Indian, who runs about with nothing upon him but a small piece of cloth, kept up by a wide leather strap drawn round his waist. Generally speaking, each person's caste is decided by the quality of the blood, which shows itself, too plainly to be concealed, at first sight. Yet the least drop of Spanish blood . . . is sufficient to raise them from the rank of slaves, and entitle them to a suit of clothes—boots, hat, cloak, spurs, long knife, and all complete, though coarse and dirty as may be—and to call themselves Espanolos, and to hold property, if they can get any. . . .

Another thing that surprised me was the quantity of silver that was in circulation. . . . The truth is, they have no credit system, no banks, and no way of investing money but in cattle. They have no circulating medium but silver and hides—which the sailors call "California bank notes." . . . Everything that they buy they must pay for in one or the other of these things. The hides they bring down dried and doubled, in clumsy ox-carts, or upon mules' backs, and the money they carry tied up in a handkerchief;—fifty, eighty, or an hundred dollars and half dollars. . . .

No Protestant has any civil rights, nor can he hold any property, or, indeed, remain more than a few weeks on shore, unless he belongs to some vessel. Consequently, the Americans and English who intend to reside here become Catholics, to a man; the current phrase among them being—"A man must leave his conscience at Cape Horn." . . .

The government of the country is an arbitrary democracy; having no common law, and no judiciary. Their only laws are made and unmade at the caprice of the legislature, and are as variable as the legislature itself. . . . Revolutions are matters of constant occurrence in California. They are got up by men who are at the foot of the ladder and in desperate circumstances, just as a new political party is started by such men in our own country. The only object, of course, is the loaves and fishes; and instead of caucusing, paragraphing, libelling, feasting, promising, and lying, as with us, they take muskets and bayonets, seizing upon the presidio and custom-house, divide the spoils, and declare a new dynasty. As for justice, they know no law but will and fear . . . .

Such are the people who inhabit a country embracing four or five hundred miles of sea-coast, with several good harbors; with fine forests in the north; the waters filled with fish, and the plains covered with thousands of herds of cattle; blessed with a climate, than which there can be no better in the world; free from all manner of diseases . . . ; and with a soil which corn yields from seventy to eighty fold. In the hands of an enterprising people, what a country this might be! we are ready to say. Yet how long would a people remain so, in such a country? The Americans (as those from the United States are called) and Englishmen, who are fast filling up the principal towns, and getting the trade into their hands, are indeed more industrious and effective than the Spaniards; yet their children are brought up Spaniards, in every respect, and if the "California fever" (laziness) spares the first generation, it always attacks the second.

DOCUMENT ANALYSIS

1. How does Dana's assessment of California's people compare to his assessment of the physical terrain and resources?

_____

_____

_____

2. Why did residents have to convert to Catholicism?

_____

_____

_____

3. What are Dana's feelings regarding California's political system? Does it compare favorably with the U.S. system, in his opinion?

_____

_____

_____

DOCUMENT 12.2
John C. Calhoun, Proposal to Preserve the Union (1850)

In the antebellum period, Senator John C. Calhoun was an ardent advocate of states' rights. In the great debates of the Jacksonian era, Calhoun combated federal tariff legislation by arguing that the states enjoyed the right to nullify certain pieces of federal legislation. In the ensuing years, Calhoun became increasingly strident in his defense of southern particularity. In this 1850 speech, Calhoun summarized his views on the present condition of the Union and his fears for the future.

I have, Senators, believed from the first that the agitation of the subject of slavery would, if not prevented by some timely and effective measure, end in disunion. . . . The agitation has been permitted to proceed, with almost no attempt to resist it, until it has reached a period when it can no longer be disguised or denied that the Union is in danger. You have thus had forced upon you the greatest and the gravest question that can ever come under your consideration: How can the Union be preserved?

. . . The first question, then, presented for consideration, in the investigation I propose to make, in order to obtain such knowledge, is: What is it that has endangered the Union?

To this question there can be but one answer: That the immediate cause is the almost universal discontent which pervades all the States composing the southern section of the Union. . . .

It is a great mistake to suppose, as is by some, that it originated with demagogues. . . . No; some cause, far deeper and more powerful than the one supposed must exist to account for discontent so wide and deep. The question, then, recurs: What is the cause of this discontent? It will be found in the belief of the people of the southern States, as prevalent as the discontent itself, that they cannot remain, as things now are, consistently with honor and safety, in the Union. The next question to be considered is: What has caused this belief?

One of the causes is, undoubtedly, to be traced to the long-continued agitation of the slave question on the part of the North, and the many aggressions which they have made on the rights of the South during the time. . . .

There is another, lying back of it, with which this is intimately connected, that may be regarded as the great and primary cause. That is to be found in the fact that the equilibrium between the two sections in the Government, as it stood when the Constitution was ratified and the Government put in action has been destroyed. At that time there was nearly a perfect equilibrium between the two, which afforded ample means to each to protect itself against the aggression of the other; but, as it now stands, one section has the exclusive power of controlling the Government, which leaves the other without any adequate means of protecting itself against its encroachment and oppression. . . .

[The] great increase of Senators, added to the great increase of the House of Representatives and the electoral college on the part of the North, which must take place under the next decade, will effectually and irretrievably destroy the equilibrium which existed when the Government commenced. . . .

What was once a constitutional federal republic is now converted, in reality, into one as absolute as that of the Autocrat of Russia, and as despotic in its tendency as any absolute Government that ever existed.

As, then, the North has the absolute control over the Government, it is manifest that on all questions between it and the South, where there is a diversity of interests, the interests of the latter will be sacrificed to the former, however oppressive the effects may be. . . . But if there was no question of vital importance to the South, in reference to which there was a diversity of views between the two sections, this state of things might be endured without the hazard of destruction to the South. But such is not the fact. . . .

I refer to the relation between the two races in the southern section, which constitutes a vital portion of her social organization. Every portion of the North entertains views and feelings more or less hostile to it. . . .

If the agitation goes on, the same force, acting with increased intensity, as has been shown, will finally snap every cord, when nothing will be left to bind the States together except force. . . .

How can the Union be saved? To this I answer, there is but one way by which it can be, and that is by adopting such measures as will satisfy the States belonging to the southern section that they can remain in the Union consistently with their honor and their safety.

DOCUMENT ANALYSIS

1. What presumptions do you think underlay Calhoun's thinking?

_____

_____

_____

2. Judging by this document, was it likely that a peaceful solution could have been found to the nation's sectional crisis in the 1850s, or was war inevitable?

_____

_____

_____

DOCUMENT 13.1
Nat Turner, *The Confession of Nat Turner* (1831)

*In 1831 Nat Turner, a literate slave who had gained a considerable fol-
lowing among the slaves in Virginia, led an insurrection of slaves against
their masters. Fifty-five whites were killed in the revolt, and at least that
many African Americans were killed in immediate and delayed retaliation. The slave owners suspected a much wider conspiracy, however, and
they responded with increasingly restrictive legal codes to prevent another uprising. Turner addressed his confession, which is excerpted below, to his white lawyer, Thomas R. Gray.*

. . . To a mind like mine, restless, inquisitive and observant of every
thing that was passing, it is easy to suppose that religion was the subject to
which it would be directed, and although this subject principally occupied my thoughts—there was nothing that I saw or heard of to which my
attention was not directed—The manner in which I learned to read and
write, not only had great influence on my own mind, as I acquired it with
the most perfect ease, so much so, that I have no recollection whatever of
learning the alphabet—but to the astonishment of the family, one day,
when a book was shewn to me to keep me from crying, I began spelling
the names of different objects—this was a source of wonder to all in the
neighborhood, particularly the blacks—and this learning was constantly
improved at all opportunities—when I got large enough to go to work,
while employed, I was reflecting on many things that would present
themselves to my imagination, and whenever an opportunity occurred of
looking at a book, when the school children were getting their lessons, I
would find many things that the fertility of my own imagination had depicted to me before. . . .

[A]ll my time, not devoted to my master's service, was spent either
in prayer, or in making experiments in casting different things in moulds
made of earth, in attempting to make paper, gun-powder, and many
other experiments, that although I could not perfect, yet convinced me of
its practicability if I had the means.

I was not addicted to stealing in my youth, nor have ever been—Yet
such was the confidence of the negroes in the neighborhood, even at this
early period of my life, in my superior judgment, that they would often
carry me with them when they were going on any roguery, to plan for
them. Growing up among them, with this confidence in my superior
judgment, and when this, in their opinions, was perfected by Divine inspiration, from the circumstances already alluded to in my infancy, and
which belief was ever afterwards zealously inculcated by the austerity of
my life and manners, which became the subject of remark by white and
black.

Having soon discovered to be great, I must appear so, and therefore
studiously avoided mixing in society, and wrapped myself in mystery, devoting my time to fasting and prayer—by this time, having arrived to
man's estate, and hearing the scriptures commented on at meetings, I was
struck with that particular passage which says: "Seek ye the kingdom of
Heaven and all things shall be added unto you." I reflected much on this
passage, and prayed daily for light on this subject—As I was praying one
day at my plough, the spirit spoke to me, saying "Seek ye the kingdom of
Heaven and all things shall be added unto you."

Question—what do you mean by the Spirit? Ans.—The Spirit that
spoke to the prophets in former days—and I was greatly astonished, and
for two years prayed continually, whenever my duty would permit—and
then again I had the same revelation, which fully confirmed me in the impression that I was ordained for some great purpose in the hands of the
Almighty.

Several years rolled round, in which many events occurred to
strengthen me in this my belief. At this time I reverted in my mind to the
remarks made of me in my childhood, and the things that had been
shewn me—and as it had been said of me in my childhood by those by
whom I had been taught to pray, both white and black, and in whom I
had the greatest confidence, that I had too much sense to be raised, and if
I was, I would never be of any use to any one as a slave. Now finding I had
arrived to man's estate, and was a slave, and these revelations being made
known to me, I began to direct my attention to this great object, to fulfill
the purpose for which, by this time, I felt assured I was intended.

Knowing the influence I had obtained over the minds of my fellow
servants (not by the means of conjuring and such like tricks—for to them
I always spoke of such things with contempt) but by the communion of
the Spirit whose revelations I often communicated to them, and they believed and said my wisdom came from God. I now began to prepare them
for my purpose, by telling them something was about to happen that
would terminate in fulfilling the great promise that had been made to
me— . . .

DOCUMENT ANALYSIS

1. Ultimately, what did Nat Turner and his followers lack that was necessary for a successful uprising?

_____

_____

_____

2. Although the rebellion failed, what effect did it have on both slave owners and slaves?

_____

_____

_____

DOCUMENT 13.2
Horace Greeley, "An Overland Journey" (1860)

Horace Greeley was the editor of the New York Tribune *from 1841 to 1872. An outspoken reformer, Greeley championed such causes as temperance, public education, and abolition. Greeley is also associated with the westward migration of the nineteenth century and in this document argues in favor of a railroad connecting the Atlantic and Pacific coasts. The first transcontinental railroad was completed on May 10, 1869.*

The social, moral, and intellectual blessings of a Pacific railroad can hardly be glanced at within the limits of an article. Suffice it for the present that I merely suggest them.

1. Our mails are now carried to and from California by steamships, via Panama, in twenty to thirty days, starting once a fortnight. The average time of transit from writers throughout the Atlantic states to their correspondents on the Pacific exceeds thirty days. With a Pacific railroad, this would be reduced to ten; for the letters written in Illinois or Michigan would reach their destinations in the mining counties of California quicker than letters sent from New York or Philadelphia would reach San Francisco. With a daily mail by railroad from each of our Atlantic cities to and from California, it is hardly possible that the amount of both letters and printed matter transmitted, and consequently of postage, should not be speedily quadrupled.

2. The first need of California today is a large influx of intelligent, capable, virtuous women. With a railroad to the Pacific, avoiding the miseries and perils of six thousand miles of ocean transportation, and making the transit a pleasant and interesting overland journey of ten days, at a reduced cost, the migration of this class would be immensely accelerated and increased. With wages for all kinds of women's work at least thrice as high on the Pacific as in this quarter, and with larger opportunities for honorable and fit settlement in life, I cannot doubt that tens of thousands would annually cross the Plains, to the signal benefit of California and of the whole country, as well as the improvement of their own fortunes and the profit of the railroad.

3. Thousands now staying in California, expecting to "go home" so soon as they shall have somewhat improved their circumstances, would send or come for their families and settle on the Pacific for life, if a railroad were opened. Tens of thousands who have been to California and come back, unwilling either to live away from their families or to expose them to the present hardships of migration thither, would return with all they have, prepared to spend their remaining days in the land of gold, if there were a Pacific railroad.

4. Education is the vital want of California, second to its need of true women. School-books, and all the material of education, are now scarce and dear there. Almost all books sell there twice as high as here, and many of the best are scarcely attainable at any rate. With the Pacific railroad, all this would be changed for the better. The proportion of school-houses to grogshops would rapidly increase. All the elements of moral and religious melioration would be multiplied. Tens of thousands of our best citizens would visit the Pacific coast, receiving novel ideas and impressions, to their own profit and that of the people thus visited. Civilization, intelligence, refinement, on both sides of the mountain—still more, in the Great Basin enclosed by them—would receive a new and immense impulse, and the Union would acquire a greater accession of strength, power, endurance, and true glory, than it would from the acquisition of the whole continent down to Cape Horn.

The only points of view in which a railroad from the Missouri to the Pacific remains to be considered are those of its practicability, cost, location, and the ways and means. Let us look at them:

As to practicability, there is no room for hesitation or doubt. The Massachusetts Western, the Erie, the Pennsylvania, and the Baltimore and Ohio, have each encountered difficulties as formidable as any to be overcome by a Pacific railroad this side of the Sierra Nevada. Were the railroad simply to follow the principal emigrant trail up the Platte and down the Snake and Columbia to Oregon, or south-westwardly from the South Pass to the foot of the Sierra, it would encounter no serious obstacle. . . .

But let that government simply resolve that the Pacific road shall be built—let Congress enact that sealed proposals for its construction shall be invited, and that whichever responsible company or corporation shall offer adequate security for that construction, to be completed within ten years, on the lowest terms, shall have public aid, provided the amount required do not exceed fifty millions of dollars, and the work will be done, certainly for fifty millions' bonus, probably for much less. The government on its part should concede to the company a mile in width, according to the section lines, of the public lands on either side of the road as built, with the right to take timber, stone and earth from any public lands without charge; and should require of said company that it carry a daily through-mail each way at the price paid other roads for conveying mails on first-class routes; and should moreover stipulate for the conveyance at all times of troops, arms, munitions, provisions, etc., for the public service, at the lowest rates, with a right to the exclusive possession and use of the road whenever a national exigency shall seem to require it. The government should leave the choice of route entirely to the company, only stipulating that it shall connect the navigable waters of the Mississippi with those of the Pacific Ocean, and that it shall be constructed wholly through our own territory. . . .

By adopting this plan, the rivalries of routes will be made to work for, instead of working against, the construction of the road. Strenuous efforts will be made by the friends of each to put themselves in position to bid low enough to secure the location; and the lowest rate at which the work can safely be undertaken will unquestionably be bid. The road will be the property of the company constructing it, subject only to the rights of use, stipulated and paid for by the government. And, even were it to cost the latter a bonus of fully fifty millions, I feel certain that every farthing of that large sum will have been reimbursed to the treasury within five years after the completion of the work in the proceeds of land sales, in increased postages, and in duties on goods imported, sold, and consumed because of this railroad—not to speak of the annual saving of millions in the cost of transporting and supplying troops.

Men and brethren! let us resolve to have a railroad to the Pacific—to have it soon. It will add more to the strength and wealth of our country than would the acquisition of a dozen Cubas. It will prove a bond of union not easily broken, and a new spring to our national industry, prosperity and wealth. It will call new manufactures into existence, and increase the demand for the products of those already existing. It will open new vistas to national and to individual aspiration, and crush out filibusterism by giving a new and wholesome direction to the public mind. My long, fatiguing journey was undertaken in the hope that I might do something toward the early construction of the Pacific Railroad; and I trust that it has not been made wholly in vain.

DOCUMENT ANALYSIS

1. What were Greeley's major arguments in support of constructing a Pacific railroad?

_____

_____

2. Greeley asserted that constructing a Pacific railroad would contribute more to the nation's prosperity "than would the acquisition of a dozen Cubas." What is the significance of this observation, especially considering the year in which Greeley composed this piece?

_____

_____

DOCUMENT 14.1
Opinion of the Supreme Court for *Dred Scott v. Sanford* (1857)

Dred Scott was a slave whose master had taken him to Illinois and the Wisconsin Territory, both of which prohibited slavery, before moving to Missouri, a slave state. In Missouri, Scott sued to gain his freedom. He argued that because his master had taken him to free states, he was no longer a slave. Scott fought his case all the way to the U.S. Supreme Court, where he ultimately lost. Beyond Scott's individual fate, the Court's decision had serious consequences for the fate of slaves, free African Americans, and the abolitionist cause in general. Not only the Court's judgment, but also the opinions of each of the justices, damaged the abolitionist cause. Particularly damning was the decision of Chief Justice Roger Taney, excerpted below.

Chief Justice Roger B. Taney: The Question is simply this: Can a negro, whose ancestors were imported into this country, and sold as slaves, become a member of the political community formed and brought into existence by the Constitution of the United States, and as such become entitled to all the rights, and privileges, and immunities, guarantied [sic] by that instrument to the citizen? One of which rights is the privilege of suing in a court of the United States in the cases specified in the constitution.

. . . The only matter in issue before the Court, therefore, is, whether the descendants of such slaves, when they shall be emancipated, or who are born of parents who had become free before their birth, are citizens of a State, in the sense which the word citizen is used in the Constitution.

. . .The words "people of the United States" and "citizens" are synonymous terms. . . . They both describe the political body who, according to our republican institutions, form the sovereignty, and who hold the power and conduct the government through their representatives. . . . The question before us is, whether the class of persons described in the plea in abatement compose a portion of this people, and are constituent members of this sovereignty? We think they are not, under the word "cit-

izens" in the Constitution, and can therefore claim none of the rights and privileges which that instrument provides for and secures to citizens of the United States. On the contrary, they were at that time considered as a subordinate and inferior class of beings, who had been subjugated by the dominant race, and whether emancipated or not, yet remained subject to their authority, and had no rights or privileges but such as those who held the power and the government might choose to grant them. . . .

In discussing the question, we must not confound the rights of citizenship which a State may confer within its own limits, and the rights of citizenship as a member of the Union. It does not by any means follow, because he has all the rights and privileges of a citizen of a State, that he must be a citizen of the United States. . . .

In the opinion of the court, the legislation and histories of the times, and the language used in the Declaration of Independence, show, that neither the class of persons who had been imported as slaves, nor their descendants, whether they had become free or not, were then acknowledged as a part of the people, nor intended to be included in the general words used in that memorable instrument. . . .

They had for more than a century before been regarded as beings of an inferior order, and altogether unfit to associate with the white race, either in social or political relations, and so far inferior, that they had no rights which the white man was bound to respect; and that the negro might justly and lawfully be reduced to slavery for his benefit. . . .

. . . there are two clauses in the constitution which point directly and specifically to the negro race as a separate class of persons, and show clearly that they were not regarded as a portion of the people or citizens of the government then formed.

. . . upon full and careful consideration of the subject, the court is of opinion, that, upon the facts stated. . . , Dred Scott was not a citizen of Missouri within the meaning of the constitution of the United States and not entitled as such to sue in its courts. . . .

DOCUMENT ANALYSIS

1. Why did the language of this case so upset Northerners who were not necessarily in favor of abolishing slavery in the South?

_____

_____

_____

2. What effect did this ruling have on the status of free African Americans? How might this ruling have strengthened the abolitionist cause among Americans who did not consider African Americans their equals?

_____

_____

_____

DOCUMENT 14.2
Levi Coffin, Reminiscences of the Underground Railroad in the 1850s

Levi Coffin and his wife, Catherine, are remembered for their tireless work in assisting slaves to reach the safety of Canada via the Underground Railroad, a series of safe havens between the South and Montreal. Though originally from North Carolina, the Coffins were Quakers who adamantly opposed slavery. After moving to Indiana, they began working with the Underground Railroad in 1826. They continued their efforts after moving to Cincinnati in the 1840s. Eventually they helped more than 3,000 slaves to escape the South. Levi and Catherine were ostensibly the models for the characters Simeon and Rachel Halliday in Harriet Beecher Stowe's classic novel, Uncle Tom's Cabin. *Levi's memoirs were published in 1876.*

I was personally acquainted with all the active and reliable workers on the Underground Railroad in the city, both colored and white. There were a few wise and careful managers among the colored people, but it was not safe to trust all of them with the affairs of our work. Most of them were too careless, and a few were unworthy—they could be bribed by the slave hunters to betray the hiding places of the fugitives. We soon found it to be the best policy to confine our affairs to a few persons and to let the whereabouts of the slaves be known to as few people as possible.

When slave hunters were prowling around the city we found it necessary to use every precaution. We were soon fully initiated into the management of Underground Railroad matters in Cincinnati, and did not lack for work. Our willingness to aid the slaves was soon known, and hardly a fugitive came to the city without applying to us for assistance. There seemed to be a continual increase of runaways, and such was the vigilance of the pursuers that I was obliged to devote a large share of time from my business to making arrangements for their concealment and safe conveyance of the fugitives.

They sometimes came to our door frightened and panting and in a destitute condition, having fled in such haste and fear that they had no time to bring any clothing except what they had on, and that was often very scant. The expense of providing suitable clothing for them when it was necessary for them to go on immediately, or of feeding them when they were obliged to be concealed for days or weeks, was very heavy. . . .

Our house was large and well adapted for secreting fugitives. Very often slaves would lie concealed in upper chambers for weeks without the boarders or frequent visitors at the house knowing anything about it. My wife had a quiet unconcerned way of going about her work as if nothing unusual was on hand, which was calculated to lull every suspicion of those who might be watching, and who would have been at once aroused by any sign of secrecy or mystery. Even the intimate friends of the family did not know when there were slaves hidden in the house. . . .

The fugitives generally arrived in the night and were secreted among the friendly colored people or hidden in the upper room of our house. They came alone or in companies, and in a few instances had a white guide to direct them. . . .

DOCUMENT ANALYSIS

1. According to Coffin, what precautions or tactics did the Coffins employ to conceal fugitive slaves?

_____

_____

_____

2. Why did Coffin feel that he and his wife were successful conductors on the Underground Railroad?

_____

_____

_____

3. How did Coffin describe the plight of the fugitive slaves who fled to Cincinnati?

_____

_____

_____

DOCUMENT 15.1
Letter from H. Ford Douglas to Frederick Douglass's *Monthly* (January 8, 1863)

From: Edwin S. Redkey, ed., *A Grand Army of Black Men* (1992), pp. 24–25.

Edwin S. Redkey's book is a collection of more than 150 letters from African American soldiers to various newspapers and journals. The excerpt below was written just days after the Emancipation Proclamation was issued on January 1, 1863. At that point the Union decided to accept, and in fact encourage, black enlistment in the army and navy. Although enlistment was slow at first, black leaders such as Frederick Douglass openly encouraged enlistment because they believed it would help assure black citizenship when the war was over. By May 1863 the U.S. government had established the Bureau of Colored Troops. Eventually, 179,000 black men served in the army, and another 19,000 in the navy.

My wife sent me this morning the *Monthly* for December containing your appeal to England to "hands off" in this fearful conflict for freedom. It was indeed gratifying to me who have always felt more than a friendly interest in you and yours to read your eloquent and manly words of admonition to the Old Saxon mother States to give no moral or legal countenance to the claims of the impious Confederate States of America in their attempt to set up a Government established upon the idea of the perpetual bondage of the Negro. England has wisely withstood every temptation to do so—Abraham Lincoln has crossed the Rubicon and by one simple act of Justice to the slave links his memory with immortality.

The slaves are free! How can I write these precious words? And yet it is so unless twenty millions of people cradled in Christianity and civilization for a thousand years commit the foulest perjury that ever blackened the pages of history. In anticipation of this result I enlisted six months ago in order to be better prepared to play my part in the great drama of the Negro's redemption. I wanted its drill, its practical details, for mere theory does not make a good soldier. I have learned something of war, for I have seen war in its brightest as well as its bloodiest phase, and yet I have

nothing to regret. For since the stern necessities of this struggle have laid bare the naked issue of freedom on one side and slavery on the other—freedom shall have, in the future of this conflict if necessary, my blood as it has had in the past my earnest and best words. It seems to me that you can have no good reason for withholding from the government your hearty cooperation. This war will educate Mr. Lincoln out of his idea of the deportation of the Negro quite as fast as it has some of his other pro-slavery ideas with respect to employing them as soldiers.

Hitherto they have been socially and politically ignored by this government, but now by the fortunes of war they are cast morally and mentally helpless (so to speak) into the broad sunlight of our Republican civilization there to be educated and lifted to a higher and nobler life. National duties and responsibilities are not to be colonized, they must be heroically met and religiously performed. This mighty waste of manhood resulting from the dehumanizing character of slave institutions of America is now to be given back to the world through the patient toil and self-denial of this proud and haughty race. They must now pay back the negro in Spiritual culture in opportunities for self-improvement what they have taken from him for two hundred years by the constant over-taxing of his physical nature. This law of supply and demand regulates itself. And so this question of the colonization of the negro; it will be settled by laws over which war has no control. Now is the time for you to finish the crowning work of your life. Go to work at once and raise a Regiment and offer your services to the government, and I am confident they will be accepted. They say we will not fight. I want to see it tried on. You are the one to me of all others, to demonstrate this fact.

I belong to company G, 95th Regiment Illinois Volunteers—Captain Eliot N. Bush—a Christian and a gentleman. . . .

DOCUMENT ANALYSIS

1. Why did Douglas enlist in the army? What did he hope to gain from his enlistment?

_____

_____

_____

2. What was his opinion of the idea that African Americans should be colonized?

_____

_____

_____

3. What did he mean by the phrase "Abraham Lincoln has crossed the Rubicon"?

_____

_____

_____

DOCUMENT 15.2
Clara Barton, Memoirs of Medical Life at the Battlefield (1862)

Clara Barton was one of many women who supported the war effort by nursing troops, raising funds, and making clothes and bandages. This selection from her memoirs describes her initial ambivalence about exposing herself to the horrors of combat and the nightmarish conditions she found on the battlefields at Cedar Mountain and Second Manassas (Bull Run) during the summer of 1862.

I was strong and thought I might go to the rescue of the men who fell. . . What could I do but go with them, or work for them and my country? The patriot blood of my father was warm in my veins. The country which he had fought for, I might at least work for. . .

But I struggled long and hard with my sense of propriety—with the appalling fact that I was only a woman whispering in one ear, and thundering in the other the groans of suffering men dying like dogs—unfed and unsheltered, for the life of every institution which had protected and educated me!

I said that I struggled long and hard with my sense of propriety and I say it with humiliation and shame. I am ashamed that I thought of such a thing.

When our armies fought on Cedar Mountain, I broke the shackles and went to the field. . .

Five days and nights with three hours sleep—a narrow escape from capture—and some days of getting the wounded into hospitals at Washington, brought Saturday, August 30. And if you chance to feel, that the positions I occupied were rough and unseemly for a woman—I can only reply that they were rough and unseemly for men. But under all, lay the life of the nation. I had inherited the rich blessing of health and strength of constitution—such as are seldom given to woman—and I felt that some return was due from me and that I ought to be there. . .

. . .Our coaches were not elegant or commodious; they had no seats, no platforms, no steps, a slide door on the side the only entrance, and this higher than my head. For my man attaining my elevated position, I must beg of you to draw on your imaginations and spare me the labor of reproducing the boxes, boards, and rails, which in those days, seemed to help me up and down the world. We did not criticize the unsightly helpers and were thankful that the stiff springs did not quite jostle us out. This need not be limited to this particular trip or train, but will for all that I have known in Army life. This is the kind of conveyance which your tons of generous gifts have reached the field with the freights. These trains through day and night, sunshine and heat and cold, have thundered over heights, across plains, the ravines, and over hastily built army bridges 90 feet across the stream beneath.

At 10 o'clock Sunday (August 31) our train drew up at Fairfax Station. The ground, for acres, was a thinly wooded slope—and among the trees on the leaves and grass, were laid the wounded who pouring in by scores of wagon loads, as picked up on the field the flag of truce. All day they came and the whole hillside was red. Bales of hay were broken open and scattered over the ground littering of cattle, and the sore, famishing men were laid upon it.

And when the night shut in, in the mist and darkness about us, we knew that standing apart from the world of anxious hearts, throbbing over the whole country, we were a little band of almost empty handed workers literally by ourselves in the wild woods of Virginia, with 3,000 suffering men crowded upon the few acres within our reach.

After gathering up every available implement or convenience for our work, our domestic inventory stood 2 water buckets, 5 tin cups, 1 camp kettle, 1 stew pan, 2 lanterns, 4 bread knives, 3 plates, and a 2-quart tin dish, and 3,000 guests to serve.

You will perceive by this, that I had not yet learned to equip myself, for I was no Pallas, ready armed, but grew into my work by hard thinking and sad experience. It may serve to relieve your apprehension for the future of my labors if I assure you that I was never caught so again.

But the most fearful scene was reserved for the night. I have said that the ground was littered with dry hay and that we had only two lanterns, but there were plenty of candles. The wounded were laid so close that it was impossible to move about in the dark. The slightest misstep brought a torrent of groans from some poor mangled fellow in your path.

Consequently here were seen persons of all grades from the careful man of God who walked with a prayer upon his lips to the careless driver hunting for his lost whip—each wandering about among this hay with an open flaming candle in his hands.

The slightest accident, the mere dropping of a light could have enveloped in flames this whole mass of helpless men.

How we watched and pleaded and cautioned as we worked and wept that night! How we put socks and slippers upon their cold feet, wrapped your blankets and quilts about them, and when we no longer these to give, how we covered them in the hay and left them to their rest!. . .

The slight, naked chest of a fair-haired lad caught my eye. Dropping down beside him, I bent low to draw the remnant of his blouse about him, when with a quick cry he threw his left arm across my neck and, burying his face in the folds of my dress, wept like a child at his mother's knee. I took his head in my hands and held it until great burst of grief passed away. "And do you know me?" he asked at length, "I am Charley Hamilton, we used to carry your satchel home from school!" My faithful pupil, poor Charley. That mangled right hand would never carry a satchel again.

About three o'clock in the morning I observed a surgeon with a little flickering candle in hand approaching me with cautious step up in the wood. "Lady," he said as he drew near, "will you go with me? Out on the hills is a poor distressed lad, mortally wounded, and dying. His piteous cries for his sister have touched all our hearts; none of us can relieve him but rather seem to distress him by presence."

By this time I was following him back over the bloody track, with great beseeching eyes of anguish on every side looking up into our faces, saying so plainly "Don't step on us."

DOCUMENT ANALYSIS

1. What conditions did Barton face when she reached the hospital in Fairfax? How did she cope with them?

_____

_____

_____

2. Women traditionally did not serve as nurses at this time period. How did that reality affect Barton's efforts at helping the men? How did the soldiers react to her assistance?

_____

_____

_____

DOCUMENT 16.1
Carl Schurz, *Report on the Condition of the South* (1865)

*Carl Schurz was a German immigrant who rose to great political promi-
nence in the United States. He was a leading member of the Republican
Party and a great supporter of Lincoln. During the Civil War he attained
the rank of major general. After the war, Schurz continued to be active in
politics, supporting many reform movements. He was writer and editor
for several English- and German-language newspapers, and he published
several books. In 1865 President Andrew Johnson sent Schurz to tour the
South and to report on its postwar status. An excerpt from Schurz's report
appears below. The president was not pleased with the report.*

We ought to keep in view, above all, the nature of the problem which
is to be solved. As to what is commonly termed "reconstruction," it is not
only the political machinery of the States and their constitutional relations
to the general government, but the whole organism of southern society
that must be reconstructed, or rather constructed anew, so as to bring it in
harmony with the rest of American society. The difficulties of this task are
not to be considered overcome when the people of the south take the oath
of allegiance and elect governors and legislatures and members of Congress, and militia captains. That this would be done had become certain as
soon as the surrenders of the southern armies had made further resistance
impossible, and nothing in the world was left, even to the most uncompromising rebel, but to submit or to emigrate. It was also natural that they
should avail themselves of every chance offered them to resume control of
their home affairs and to regain their influence in the Union. But this can
hardly be called the first step towards the solution of the true problem,
and it is a fair question to ask, whether the hasty gratification of their desire to resume such control would not create new embarrassments.

The true nature of the difficulties of the situation is this: The general
government of the republic has, by proclaiming the emancipation of the
slaves, commenced a great social revolution in the south, but has, as yet,
not completed it. Only the negative part of it is accomplished. The slaves
are emancipated in point of form, but free labor has not yet been put in
the place of slavery in point of fact. And now, in the midst of this critical
period of transition, the power which originated the revolution is expected to turn over its whole future development to another power which
from the beginning was hostile to it and has never yet entered into its
spirit, leaving the class in whose favor it was made completely without
power to protect itself and to take an influential part in that development.
The history of the world will be searched in vain for a proceeding similar
to this which did not lead either to a rapid and violent reaction, or to the
most serious trouble and civil disorder. It cannot be said that the conduct
of the southern people since the close of the war has exhibited such extraordinary wisdom and self-abnegation as to make them an exception to
the rule. In my dispatches from the south I repeatedly expressed the opinion that the people were not yet in a frame of mind to legislate calmly and
understandingly upon the subject of free negro labor. And this I reported
to be the opinion of some of our most prominent military commanders
and other observing men.

It is, indeed, difficult to imagine circumstances more unfavorable for
the development of a calm and unprejudiced public opinion than those
under which the southern people are at present laboring. The war has not
only defeated their political aspirations, but it has broken up their whole
social organization. When the rebellion was put down they found themselves not only conquered in a political and military sense, but economically ruined. The planters, who represented the wealth of the southern
country, are partly laboring under the severest embarrassments, partly reduced to absolute poverty. Many who are stripped of all available means,
and have nothing but their land, cross their arms in gloomy despondency,
incapable of rising to a manly resolution. Others, who still possess means,
are at a loss how to use them, as their old way of doing things is, by the
abolition of slavery, rendered impracticable, at least where the military
arm of the government has enforced emancipation. Others are still trying
to go on in the old way, and that old way is in fact the only one they understand, and in which they have any confidence. Only a minority is try-

ing to adopt the new order of things. A large number of the plantations,
probably a considerable majority of the more valuable estates, is under
heavy mortgages, and the owners know that, unless they retrieve their fortunes in a comparatively short space of time, their property will pass out
of their hands. Almost all are, to some extent, embarrassed.

The nervous anxiety which such a state of things produces extends
also to those classes of society which, although not composed of planters,
were always in close business connection with the planting interest, and
there was hardly a branch of commerce or industry in the south which
was not directly or indirectly so connected. Besides, the southern soldiers,
when returning from the war, did not, like the northern soldiers, find a
prosperous community which merely waited for their arrival to give them
remunerative employment. They found, many of them, their homesteads
destroyed, their farms devastated, their families in distress; and those that
were less unfortunate found, at all events, an impoverished and exhausted
community which had but little to offer them. Thus a great many have
been thrown upon the world to shift as best they can. They must do
something honest or dishonest, and must do it soon, to make a living,
and their prospects are, at present, not very bright. Thus that nervous
anxiety to hastily repair broken fortunes, and to prevent still greater ruin
and distress, embraces nearly all classes, and imprints upon all the movements of the social body a morbid character. In which direction will these
people be most apt to turn their eyes? Leaving the prejudice of race out of
the question, from early youth they have been acquainted with but one
system of labor, and with that one system they have been in the habit of
identifying all their interests. They know of no way to help themselves but
the one they are accustomed to. Another system of labor is presented to
them, which, however, owing to circumstances which they do not appreciate, appears at first in an unpromising light. To try it they consider an
experiment which they cannot afford to make while their wants are urgent. They have not reasoned calmly enough to convince themselves that
the trial must be made. It is, indeed, not wonderful that, under such circumstances, they should study, not how to introduce and develop free labor, but how to avoid its introduction, and how to return as much and as
quickly as possible to something like the old order of things. Nor is it
wonderful that such studies should find an expression in their attempts at
legislation. But the circumstance that this tendency is natural does not
render it less dangerous and objectionable.

The practical question presents itself: Is the immediate restoration
of the late rebel States to absolute self-control so necessary that it must be
done even at the risk of endangering one of the great results of the war,
and of bringing on in those States insurrection or anarchy, or would it
not be better to postpone that restoration until such dangers are passed?
If, as long as the change from slavery to free labor is known to the southern people only by its destructive results, these people must be expected
to throw obstacles in its way, would it not seem necessary that the movement of social "reconstruction" be kept in the right channel by the hand
of the power which originated the change, until that change can have dis-
closed some of its beneficial effects? It is certain that every success of free
negro labor will augment the number of its friends, and disarm some of
the prejudices and assumptions of its opponents. I am convinced one
good harvest made by unadulterated free labor in the south would have a
far better effect than all the oaths that have been taken, and all the ordi-
nances that have as yet been passed by southern conventions. But how
can such a result be attained?

The facts enumerated in this report, as well as the news we receive
from the south from day to day, must make it evident to every unbiased
observer that unadulterated free labor cannot be had at present, unless
the national government holds its protective and controlling hand over it.
It appears, also, that the more efficient this protection of free labor against
all disturbing and reactionary influences, the sooner may such a satisfactory result be looked for. One reason why the southern people are so slow
in accommodating themselves to the new order of things is, that they
confidently expect soon to be permitted to regulate matters according to